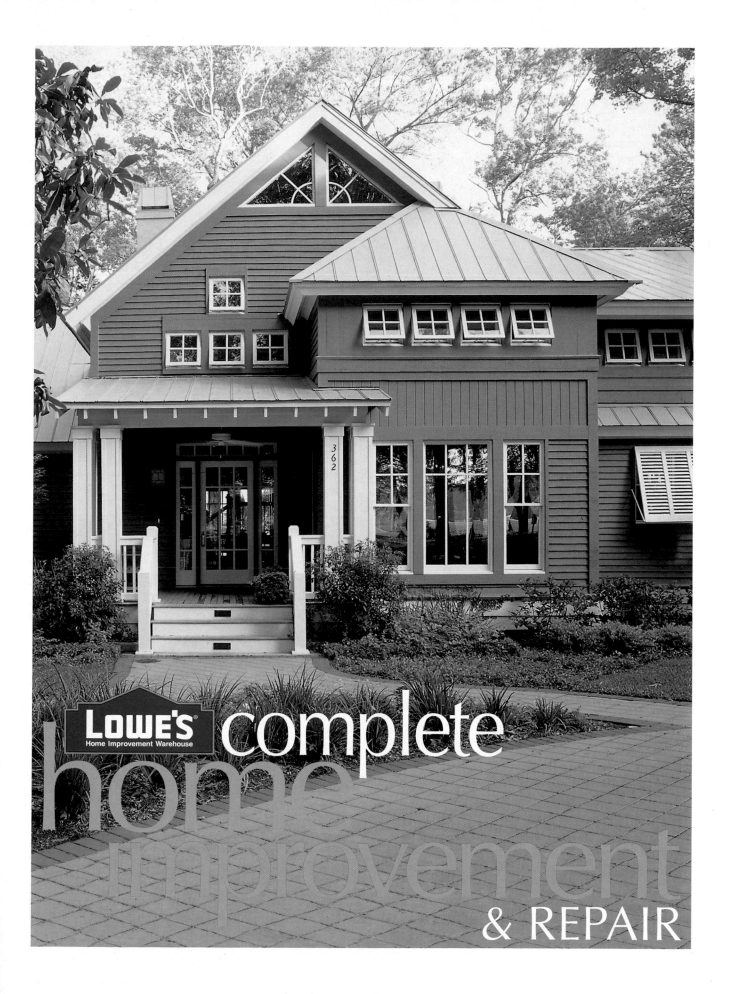

LOWE'S
Home Improvement Warehouse

complete
home
improvement
& REPAIR

LOWE'S SERIES
Project Director **René Klein**
Senior Editor **Sally W. Smith**

**STAFF FOR LOWE'S COMPLETE
HOME IMPROVEMENT & REPAIR**
Editor **Don Vandervort, HomeTips**
Managing Editor **Louise Damberg**
Art Director **Dan Nadeau**
Assistant Editor **Gabriel Vandervort**
Copy Editor **Kristinha Anding**
Contributing Editor **Carol A. Crotta**
Design and Page Makeup Assistant **Libby Ellis**
Prepress Coordinator **Eligio Hernandez**
Editorial Assistant **Emily Lerner**
Photo Assistant **Carrie Dodson Davis**
Production Director **Lory Day**
Digital Production **Mark Hawkins/Leisure Arts**
Production Specialist **Linda M. Bouchard**

On the Cover
Top left: photo by Margot Hartford; Fox Design
Group, Architects. Top right: photo by Corbis.
Bottom left: photo by John Granen; design by
Deena Rauen, D Studio. Bottom right: photo by
Brian Vanden Brink; Smith Alvarez Seinkiewycz
Architects.

Cover design by Vasken Guiragossian.

Whether you are remodeling your
kitchen or seeking to maintain
your home's exterior, you will find all
the information you need in this book.
The table of contents begins on page 4.

welcome home

LOWE'S OPENED ITS FIRST STORE IN 1946, AS THE DO-IT-YOURSELF MOVEMENT was emerging, and quickly earned a reputation for quality products, customer care, and everyday low prices. Today, more than 1,100 Lowe's stores offer homeowners tens of thousands of quality products and a multitude of services.

Lowe's Complete Home Improvement & Repair is an extension of those services. The first edition of this book, published in 2000, was a premier resource for homeowners. This new edition is even better. We have enlarged it to 560 pages and added several hundred more step-by-step photographs along with updated guides for the home products and tools needed to do projects. You'll find great ideas, advice, techniques, and tips for the maintenance, repair, and improvement of every part of your home.

This and the other Lowe's books—*Complete Bathroom, Complete Home Decorating, Complete Kitchen, Complete Landscaping, Decorating With Paint & Color, Complete Patio & Deck, Complete Tile & Flooring*, along with the Lowe's Creative Ideas series that now includes *Outdoor Living, Organizing Your Home*, and *Kids' Spaces*—are part of our commitment to providing all the know-how you need for projects around your home. From the tools and materials stocked in every Lowe's store to the information you'll find online at Lowes.com, from the hands-on expertise of Lowe's sales specialists and in-store clinics to the inspiration and how-to guidance you find in our books, Lowe's has the resources to help you make a success of every home project.

Lowe's has been actively improving home improvement for more than five decades now. As you seek to maintain and improve your home, let Lowe's lend a hand.

LOWE'S COMPANIES, INC.

Robert Niblock
President, CEO, and
Chairman of the Board

Larry D. Stone
Senior Executive VP,
Merchandising and Marketing

Bob Gfeller
Senior VP, Marketing

Mike Menser
Senior VP, General
Merchandise Manager

Melissa S. Birdsong
VP, Trend and Design

Jean Melton
VP, Merchandising

Ann Serafin
Merchandising Director

Peggy Rees
Customer Marketing Manager

Paul B. Lovett
Merchandiser

contents

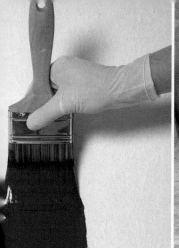

CONTENTS CONTINUES ➡

contents CONTINUED

how to use this book

WHEN ALL OF A HOUSE'S PARTS WORK SMOOTHLY, YOU HARDLY NOTICE THEY EXIST. On the other hand, when something is out of whack, you begin to become keenly aware of that system and its failings. A crisis can occur—a burst pipe or leaking roof. Or you may simply have grown tired of the lack of light, storage, or living space in certain areas. That's where *Lowe's Complete Home Improvement & Repair* steps in.

BELOW: **Throughout the book, illustrations reveal basic construction techniques.**

This book offers an inside look at your home, examining the anatomy of how its components are crafted and providing a compendium of the tools you will need to work on them. It takes you step by step through typical projects, from minor fixes to major improvements. The goal is to give you enough information so that you can tackle projects yourself or make informed decisions about hiring professionals to do the work for you.

Whether you are looking for guidance sorting through available home products, advice on dealing with planning and construction, or do-it-yourself step-by-step instructions for common projects, you've come to the right place.

Finding the information you want in a book as large and comprehensive as *Lowe's*

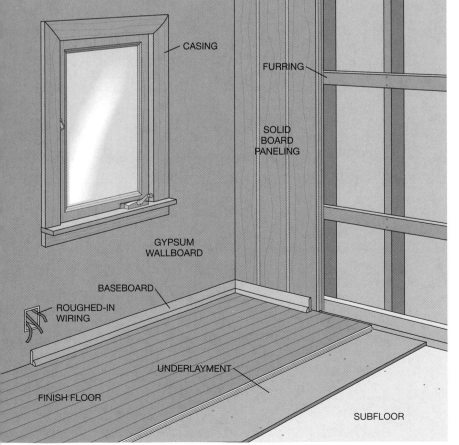

CASING

FURRING

SOLID BOARD PANELING

GYPSUM WALLBOARD

BASEBOARD

ROUGHED-IN WIRING

UNDERLAYMENT

FINISH FLOOR

SUBFLOOR

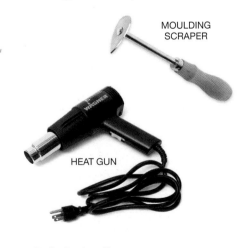

MOULDING SCRAPER

HEAT GUN

ABOVE: **Each chapter offers an overview of the tools needed for improvement projects and repairs.**

Complete Home Improvement & Repair might seem a bit intimidating at first. However, this book has been organized in an intuitive, easy-to-follow format. Below are the most direct routes to locating the information you need:

the planning workbook

If you are looking for general guidance that you can use when planning a project, turn to the Planning Workbook that begins on page 12. This section takes you through the development phase, including discussions about creating a budget; hiring and managing professionals; utilizing Lowe's installation services; handling plans and contracts; dealing with building codes, permits, and zoning; and giving attention to safety issues.

improvements & repairs

When seeking help for a specific type of project, a good place to start is the table of contents. Note that the book begins with chapters on painting (page 24) and wallpapering (page 76). These are, by far, the most common improvements homeowners handle themselves. You will find buying guides for paint and wallpaper, discussions of the tools required, and the step-by-step instructions needed for every aspect of handling your painting and wallpapering projects.

The next few chapters look at the house area by area and piece by piece. The chapters begin inside, focusing on walls and ceilings, flooring, windows and doors, and cabinets and storage. Then the book moves outside and examines siding, roofing, and garages. Each of these chapters offers an overview of typical construction practices, a look at the tools needed for many improvements and repairs, and then complete step-by-step instructions for an assortment of typical projects. The project discussions are organized to begin with improvement projects and end with information on repairs. Throughout, you will find helpful photographs and illustrations to guide you through the techniques.

ABOVE: **Step-by-step photos guide you through an array of do-it-yourself projects.**

Beginning on page 376, you will find chapters on working with the systems embedded in the house: electrical, plumbing, and comfort. Each chapter offers an overview of how the system operates, a look at the tools needed for improvements and repairs, and then specific guidance for improvement and repair projects.

Throughout the book, you will be aided by easy-to-read graphic presentations. In addition to the clear step-by-step instructions, there are cautionary safety messages for do-it-yourselfers. And Lowe's Quick Tips, located in the margins, are loaded with professional advice for streamlining the job.

LOWE'S QUICK TIP
Watch for these helpful tip boxes for practical, hands-on advice from Lowe's specialists.

improving your home

SINCE THE DAWN OF TIME, PEOPLE HAVE SOUGHT COMFORT AND SHELTER WITHIN the walls of one sort of house or another, from primitive huts to modern marvels. But in contemporary life, a house is far more than simple shelter. It is the heart of family life, the place where we spend time that matters—building family memories, enjoying friends, and recharging our batteries.

A house also makes a statement to others about who we are and what's important to us. It can be a point of pride or—if it's in poor repair—a source of embarrassment. For these reasons, and because a house is such an important financial investment, it only makes sense to provide it with tender loving care.

Home improvements accomplish a variety of things. Beyond keeping your home running smoothly, safely, and efficiently, improvements such as wallpapering, tiling a counter, or changing a bathroom fixture can reflect your family's tastes and lifestyle. Change can be wonderful—the prospect of adding a new room or creating the kitchen

Before & After: A wraparound front porch with a built-in pediment clearly marking the front entry unifies the hodgepodge elements of this home's facade. Quality paint, roofing, and detail work give the home value and an air of distinction.

or master suite of your dreams is infinitely exciting. Such improvements can also increase the value of your house.

the value of improving

So how much are home improvements worth? The answer depends on a number of different factors. In the short term, not all improvements will return your total investment, so you need to do your homework if you are thinking of improving for profit. On the other hand, if you are living in your potential dream house and intend to stay there for a at least 10 years or more, improving your home makes sense.

Avoid "overbuilding." If your improvements result in a house of far greater value than others in the neighborhood, you may not be able to recoup your costs when you sell. However, if you intend to stay put, this factor may not matter to you.

Certain improvements—particularly to landscaping, kitchens, and baths—show a strong payoff when it comes time to sell your home. Other improvements—that hot tub, billiard room, or swimming pool, for instance—do not.

New wood floors are among the most popular home improvements because of the dramatic change they can make in any room.

Some improvements can speed up a house sale. For example, the elements of the facade—siding, roofing, doors, and windows—are so prominent that any one of them can determine whether your home looks appealing or appalling. A shipshape facade protects your house from structural damage and gives it an aura of quality. It says that behind the pretty face is a home that's sound, secure, and weatherproof.

Of course, there are home improvement benefits that have nothing to do with financial profit. A major one is getting the house you want without having to move.

Be advised that major improvements often mean major temporary hassles. It can be distressing to have your back wall ripped out, your roof removed, your interior covered with dust, and a slew of workers on your doorstep at 7 a.m. every day (if you are lucky!). If you have extensive improvements, you may need to move out for a time—a factor to work into the budget.

Whether or not to improve is a question that the whole family should consider. The more thought, research, and planning you put into your improvements up front, the more prepared you will be to make important decisions and guide the project to a happy conclusion.

planning workbook

ALTHOUGH SIMPLE REPAIRS ARE OFTEN HANDLED AT THE SPUR OF THE MOMENT, when you contemplate major repairs or improvements, you need to develop a plan of attack. The more carefully researched and considered the plan, the better your chances of accomplishing the project successfully.

A well-mapped plan will serve you whether you opt to do the work yourself or hire a professional to do it for you. Creating a plan takes some organization, phoning, legwork, and quiet study time, but in the end, you and your project will profit from the thoughtful preparation.

First, clearly delineate your goal and define the extent of the work you want to accomplish. Establish a budget. Use this figure as the standard against which you will weigh any bids or cost estimates you receive or independently put together. Also consider your timeline, from project start to finish date. It may be helpful to collect all this data, including prices for materials and services, in a notebook.

Beware of the "while we're at it" syndrome, which can destroy the best intentions for your budget and schedule. Remodeling projects can open the floodgate to many other improvements and repairs. Unless you have unlimited funds, if you are remodeling your bathroom, stick to that goal, and avoid expanding the project to include other areas or improvements. Likewise, think twice before turning a simple roof repair into a complete reroofing, unless that becomes clearly necessary.

Take some time to research your project. This book is designed to facilitate the process. Carefully read through the appropriate sections, making sure you understand each step. Also look for any other materials on the subject, and, by all means, seek the advice of the sales specialists at Lowe's.

should you do it yourself?

ONCE YOU UNDERSTAND WHAT WILL BE INVOLVED IN GETTING THE JOB DONE, give honest thought to your time, your tools, and your talents. Depending on the scale of the project, you may find it calls for more than you're prepared to put into it.

your time

When it comes to home improvements or repairs, most people tend to undervalue their time enormously. You may enjoy hands-on experience and developing new skills, as well as the sense of pride and accomplishment from a job well done. But your time has value, too. Consider carefully whether your investment in time is worth the cost savings. Remember that you probably will be doing the work on nights and weekends, which means it will take longer to complete than if you have a professional do it. Also take into account the time away from family.

your tools

Even if you have the time and talent to do a particular job, do you have all the necessary tools? In each of this book's chapters, you will find information on the tools necessary to complete the various step-by-step improvements and repairs

Carefully conceived plans are critical to every home improvement project. If you have a facility with basic drafting tools, you may be able to draw your own plans for simple projects.

outlined in each section. Certain jobs, such as laying tile, call for many specialized tools that are not commonly needed for other household tasks. Other jobs, particularly carpentry jobs, call for the basic tools that are commonly used by do-it-yourselfers.

If you lack the necessary tools for your project, everything from a hammer to a jackhammer is usually available for rental. If there are tools you think you may need in the future, it is probably worth the investment to buy them. Make a list of the tools you need, and head over to Lowe's, where you know you can get quality tools at the best prices. Whether you decide to buy or rent, factor all of the costs into your budget because they can elevate the price tag significantly. Once you take into account the purchase of new tools, a professional's bid may end up not looking so high after all.

If the tools are unfamiliar to you, be sure to have someone instruct you in their safe use. Spend some time practicing on scrap pieces before you put a tool to use on actual materials. If your results are not what you expected—your mitered corners look like boomerangs, or your tile turns into mosaic when you try to cut it—either practice until you achieve the desired result or reconsider having a professional do the work.

your talent

In addition to the questions of your time and your tools, be realistic about your talent—your experience and skill level—when considering doing the job yourself. Taking on a project you haven't tried before is an exciting challenge and an opportunity for growth. If you have an aptitude for this

type of work, you may be able to step up to the plate easily. Only you can judge whether a project will be a logical next step in your construction education or too big a leap for your abilities.

Also consider how visible and how permanent the results of your work will be. The more visible, or the more lasting, the greater the stakes. Refinishing a hardwood floor, for example, is challenging, and any mistakes caused by problems operating a power sander can be expensive to remedy. Painting a room, on the other hand, is virtually risk-free. If your paint comes out streaky or blotchy, or the absolute worst shade of green, you can simply repaint—and paint is relatively cheap. The more permanent and significant the look of a repair or improvement, the more important it is to consider hiring a professional.

Also think about how strenuous the job may be. Concrete work, or anything that involves digging foundations or lifting weighty beams, is physically demanding. Professionals who deal with these materials and projects every day have built up the necessary strength and stamina. For you—even if you are reasonably fit and in good health—such heavy labor can take a physical toll.

In addition, evaluate the potential hazards of doing a project on your own. You may be capable of patching the roof, but think twice about it if your roof pitch is so steep that scaling it poses a danger.

doing part of the work

Sometimes a project may just seem too intriguing to pass up, but you realize that doing all of it is too time-consuming or beyond your skill level. What can you do yourself and what can you hand off to a professional? You could, for example, install bathroom cabinetry yourself but have a plumber hook up the pipes and drains. An electrician could do the rough wiring, but you could put in the switches and fixtures. Have a carpenter build your new closet while you construct the closet organizer. Just observing a professional

contribute to a job you are working on is a good way to learn some new techniques.

Putting together an effective plan in this manner is the best way to keep control of your project, save on costs, and guarantee a satisfying result.

When it's time to develop your budget or select an improvement loan, you will need to do a little homework.

TIPS FOR DO-IT-YOURSELFERS

If you decide to do a repair project yourself, consider these helpful tips:

- For reference, take some close-up and detailed photographs (digital or instant cameras are ideal) of anything you decide to take apart.
- Label parts, either numerically or alphabetically, in the order of removal, so reassembly will be easy.
- If you know a part is defective, take it with you to your local Lowe's home improvement center so you can buy the correct replacement.

working with pros

EVEN IF YOU HAVE DETERMINED THAT YOU WANT TO HIRE A PROFESSIONAL TO accomplish your project, your work is not over. Now you will need to call upon your delegation skills. Knowing how to choose your professional—someone who is experienced, licensed, and bonded—is key to achieving a solid and safely completed job.

finding the right pro

When it comes to finding reliable professionals—including general contractors and individual specialists such as plumbers, concrete workers, carpenters, electricians, and painters—nothing is better than referrals from people whose opinion you trust. In addition to asking about the quality of the professional's work, ask about the person's responsiveness and punctuality, the accuracy of the cost and time estimates, and about how clean he or she left the work area each day.

A wide variety of installation and remodeling services are available through your Lowe's store, and these will connect you with some of the best subcontractors in your area. For more about this, see "Lowe's Services" on page 18.

As you find qualified contractors and subcontractors to work on your project, take advantage of the opportunity to log their contact numbers. Establishing a relationship with a plumber, an electrician, and other tradespeople can pay dividends when pipes burst or power fails on a Sunday morning.

Depending on the size of the job, you may want to solicit several bids. Have candidates tender their bids in writing, and request a breakdown of time, hourly rates, cost of materials, and start and finish dates. Ask about how much experience they have had with similar projects and how long they have been in the business.

Also ask what type of guarantee they provide for their work—specifically, if a problem occurs within a reasonable time after the construction, will they return without charge to correct it? Educate yourself through this book and other reference materials about your project so you will understand what they propose to do and why. When they arrive for the job, don't be shy about occasionally looking over their shoulders and asking questions, but don't become a pest or hindrance. Respect the skills and expertise of the people you choose unless you find reason to take issue with their work.

hiring contractors

If you are planning a major improvement such as an addition, kitchen remodel, or any other job that requires multiple technical skills, you may want to hire a general contractor. A general contractor negotiates a contract with you and then uses his or her own crew and/or hires subcontractors to get the work done. Considering what's at stake with any major improvement, it's wise to solicit more than three bids, and spend some time interviewing each contractor in person.

Compatibility is important, too, because you will have a close working relationship for your project's duration.

The key facts to find out are:

■ Do they have experience with jobs such as yours, and can they provide you with a list of references?

■ Do they have their own crew for some of the work, or do they rely solely on a stable of subcontractors?

■ How many other jobs will they be working on simultaneously with yours,

LEFT: **Lowe's professionals offer installation, design, and financial services, with complete satisfaction guaranteed.**

how long the bid will be valid—the period should be at least 30 days.

When the bids come in, don't make price your only criterion for selection. Reliability, quality of work, and on-time performance are very valuable. These factors are best determined by interviews with the contractor's references, so do not shortchange this process. Ask to see photographs of some projects. If possible, make a visit to one of the sites; examine the workmanship; and ask questions about the professional's work practices, punctuality, and cleanliness. These may seem minor before the project begins, but they can quickly become major issues when you are in the throes of construction.

and how available will their various subcontractors be?

- Will they be working or supervising? If supervising, how much time will they be on-site each day?

- When are they available to start your project, and how long do they estimate it will take?

- Are they licensed and insured, and what amount of liability insurance do they carry? (Obtain a copy of the insurance policy.)

Be sure to give all of your contractor candidates identical sets of plans. Review the plans with them, and be honest about your expectations. They, in turn, should be honest with you about the realities of budget, time, and potential disruption to your homestead. Encourage each candidate to suggest cost-saving ideas and point out the plans' high-cost elements, such as custom doors or windows and cabinetry. Request a bid broken out by task or technical expertise—such as plumbing, framing, and electrical—and agree on a date for the bid's submission. Find out

CHOOSING THE RIGHT SKILLS

If you are planning a major remodel, consider whether you will need an architect or designer or if a contractor alone will do.

Generally, if you are planning to do structural work that involves building or removing walls, you will want to call an architect. Architects are usually the priciest of the three options, but they can draw plans acceptable to building department officials, solicit bids, help you select a contractor, and supervise the contractor's work to ensure that your plans and time schedule are met. Architects must be licensed, and some even double as contractors.

Designers can do much of the above, but if stress calculations need to be made, designers need to engage state-licensed engineers to design the structure and sign the working drawings. Most states do not require designers to be licensed.

Contractors can also be skilled draftspeople, able to draw working plans acceptable to building department officials. They are limited, however, in the same way that designers are.

Many architects are members of the American Institute of Architects, and many designers belong to the American Institute of Building Designers. Certain home areas, such as kitchens and baths, have their own associations. Each association has a code of ethics and sponsors continuing programs to inform members about the latest building materials and techniques.

Architects and designers may charge for time spent in an exploratory interview, while a contractor may simply charge a fee or percentage of the project. For plans, you will probably be charged on an hourly basis. Architects and designers also often will agree to actively supervise construction, usually for either an hourly or a set fee based on a percentage of the project. Take advantage of this offer. With any of these professionals, make sure they describe the scope of their services in writing before performing any work.

contracts

When Lowe's provides installation services for your project, product quality and satisfactory installation are guaranteed. Your sales associate will help you fill out a simple agreement that outlines the work to be performed.

If you choose to work with independent professionals, you should make sure a number of important points are outlined in a written agreement. This will help prevent misunderstandings and disagreements and will serve as a backup if a dispute should arise.

A contractor may propose a "time and materials" contract instead of a fixed-price contract. "Time and materials" means that the contractor charges in fees that are a percentage of the cost of materials and labor. While this sounds enticing, it can become a budget booby trap. Under this form of contract, the homeowner bears the risk of changing costs in materials such as lumber, drywall, doors, and windows and is playing roulette with the amount of time a particular job will take. If, for example, something unforeseen comes up, such as unusual drainage problems or a large granite slab where the foundation should go, the homeowner bears the cost of the additional time and labor. Generally, a fixed-price contract protects you from these cost increases.

A contract is a legal agreement that obligates the people who sign it to perform specific acts. Note the word "specific." Make sure any contract you sign spells out exactly what you expect from any professional you hire. Here are some elements you should include:

- Start and finish dates. You may want to include the phrase "time is of the essence," which may give you added leverage if a delay leads to a dispute.

- The right to settle disputes by arbitration. In the event of a dispute, arbitration can often be speedier and less costly than a court proceeding.

- A warranty of at least one year on all work and materials. Some states require a contractor to warranty his or her work for at least five years (10 years for hidden problems).

- A payment schedule. When working with Lowe's, you pay for goods and services up front and then rely on Lowe's long-standing reputation of quality workmanship. But when working with an independent contractor, no matter how highly recommended this person has come, it is important to provide continual incentives for completing work—and to protect yourself from a contractor who might disappear with your money—by phasing payments. Check with your state contractors board for recommended practices. If speed is important, you may want to include a late-penalty clause and/or a bonus for early completion.

- Detailed job and materials descriptions. After deciding on materials, spell out

LOWE'S SERVICES

When you shop at Lowe's, you can arrange for installation services while making a purchase. All work is done by licensed professionals and is fully guaranteed by Lowe's. Just tell your sales associate which items you would like to have installed, and pay for the items and the installation services at the same time. An installer will call you to arrange an appointment, and the work will be done efficiently and neatly at a time that is convenient for you. Lowe's guarantees that you will be completely satisfied with the results. Please note that Lowe's installation services do not include plumbing or hardwiring. To find out more about how Lowe's professional installers can help with your project, visit your Lowe's store or call (877) GO-LOWES.

those choices in your contract. If you want flooring made of 3-inch-wide No. 1 maple, put it in writing. Be sure that contractual allowances will cover the cabinets, fixtures, appliances, and materials you want.

■ A waiver of subcontractor liens. In some states, subcontractors can place a lien on your property if the general contractor fails to pay them. To protect yourself from this consequence, specify that final payment will not be made until the contractor gives you an unconditional release of these rights from all subcontractors and suppliers who provided services or materials.

■ If amendments or "change orders" are made along the way, make sure the documents are initialed by both parties before any new materials are purchased or work has begun.

avoiding conflicts

A contract will help you establish productive relationships with the professionals you hire, but it does not guarantee that your project will go smoothly. A piece of paper cannot substitute for basic courtesy and common sense.

Use this book to educate yourself about the fundamentals of your project so you will understand what the professional is proposing and why.

Before you sign a contract, study it to verify that you and the professional have the same understanding of what will be done. Check your research to be sure that contractual price caps will cover the costs of the elements you want.

When professionals arrive at the job site, respect their skills. It's fine to ask questions and keep tabs on the progress of your project, but don't pester the workers or hover around the job site.

Be polite, but do speak up promptly if you have any concerns. The longer you wait, the more difficult it will be to make a change.

HANDLING INDEPENDENT CONTRACTOR PROBLEMS

If you're unhappy with the way your independent contractor is handling your project, your first step should be simply to express your concerns in person. Most contractors will make every effort to ensure that you are satisfied with their work. Should you reach an impasse, an architect, designer, or other professional who knows your project may be able to help broker an agreement. If such personal approaches do not work, you can act upon one or more of the following recommendations, beginning with the least drastic measure:

1. Send a certified letter outlining the contract requirements you consider to be unfulfilled and stipulating a reasonable time frame for compliance. Sometimes this is enough to inspire action.

2. File a complaint with the Better Business Bureau by calling (703) 276-0100 or visiting www.bbb.org. The BBB will forward your complaint to the contractor, who may consider your requests in order to avoid an unfavorable BBB report.

3. Contact the local or state board that licenses contractors, if one exists in your area. Contractors have a strong incentive to maintain a clean record with the licensing board because some of these boards have the power to levy a fine or even revoke a license in cases involving serious negligence or incompetence.

4. If both parties agree, try to resolve the dispute informally with the assistance of a mediator. The BBB and many local organizations offer mediation services to help businesses and consumers work out mutually agreeable solutions.

5. Present your case before an impartial arbitrator. More formal than mediation, but much less costly and time-consuming than litigation, arbitration gives both parties the opportunity to present evidence in a joint hearing. The arbitrator's decision is usually binding. You can arrange for this option through the Better Business Bureau or through the American Arbitration Association (www.adr.org).

6. If you are seeking minimal damages (the amount varies from state to state but is usually no more than a few thousand dollars), bring your case to small claims court. You will not need an attorney, and court costs are usually modest.

7. If you are suing for a large amount of money, you can consider filing a civil suit. This option has definite drawbacks: The case may drag on for months or even years, and your costs can exceed any award you may receive. Remember that if you have fired a contractor who has essentially done the work as agreed, you are the one who will be found to have breached the contract. Make every effort then, when drawing up a contract, to be explicit about the work to be done.

codes & permits

IF YOUR PROJECT INVOLVES MINOR COSMETIC SURGERY, YOU PROBABLY WILL NOT have to worry about building codes and ordinances. If you are making changes to your house's structure, plumbing, or electrical wiring, you will need to obtain permits from your city or county building department before you begin your project. You may also be required to submit detailed drawings of the changes you plan to make. During construction, the building department will send inspectors at several points to verify the work has been done satisfactorily. (Usually, it is up to you to schedule the inspections.)

If you are working with an architect or a general contractor, this professional will handle permits and inspections. Each is familiar with local building codes and can be enormously helpful in getting plans approved, obtaining variances, and passing inspections.

your to-do list

Here's a to-do list if you decide to act as your own general contractor:

- Check with your building department if you are putting on an addition. Local codes usually specify how far from the property line a house must be. If your addition is too close, you may need a variance, or you may be prohibited from building at all.

- Find out whether you will need to submit your plans for approval.

- Ask whether the building department can send you printed information about the ordinances that apply to your remodel and the various types of permits you will need.

- Be aware that only certified electricians or plumbers are legally allowed to install or upgrade wiring and pipes in some regions. Check with your local building department before doing any of this work yourself.

- Prepare for inspections. Read pertinent sections of the building code so you will know exactly what things the inspector will be looking for. If you hire subcontractors, ask them to be present when their work is inspected.

Keep an approved set of your building plans at the job site so building officials can refer to them during inspections.

the purpose of a permit

A permit protects the homeowner and the future occupants of the home. If a professional suggests that you do not need one, check with the building department yourself; you probably do, and it is to your advantage to get one. In fact, this suggestion is usually a red flag that your architect or contractor is trying to cut corners to your detriment. In most cases, you will pay a fee based on the value of the project. (Do not overestimate the value of your work, or you will pay more than necessary.)

A permit ensures oversight of your contractor's work (or yours). The scrutiny of an inspector can guard against mistakes and shoddy workmanship and ensure that the work adheres to building codes. You'll sleep better knowing your project meets safety standards for materials and construction techniques.

A permit will also help you avoid headaches in the future. If building officials discover that you have done work without a permit, you could be required to dismantle your remodel and start over again. If you sell your house, you might be legally obligated to disclose that you have remodeled without a permit, and the buyer could demand that you bring work up to code.

inspections

When you obtain a permit for your remodel, your building department can tell you what inspections you will need and when they should be done. Some tasks require more than one inspection. Electrical work, for example, is inspected when circuits are roughed in; again when changes to the electrical service are completed; and finally when all appliances and devices have been installed, grounded, and energized. Inspectors will look for the following things when they visit your work site:

■ A copy of the building permit, posted where it can be seen easily.

■ A record of all inspections that have been completed, with inspectors' signatures included.

■ Proof that mechanical equipment such as wiring and pipes were installed by certified professionals.

■ Compliance with local codes, including safety and zoning codes. Obtain copies of all relevant ordinances from your local building department.

Altering the roofline, changing the house's structure, and moving or replacing plumbing fixtures or electrical wiring—these are just a few of the jobs that require a building permit and are usually best left to professionals.

WHEN DO YOU NEED A PERMIT?

You probably need a permit if you plan to...
- Change the footprint of your house
- Move a load-bearing wall
- Alter the roofline
- Create a new door or window opening
- Replace an electric stove with a natural-gas model
- Move a sink
- Install new electrical wiring

But not if you plan to...
- Install new floor coverings
- Replace doors or windows without altering the structure
- Change a countertop
- Replace a faucet

working safely

IF YOU INTEND TO TACKLE SOME OR ALL OF YOUR OWN HOME IMPROVEMENTS and repairs, you will need a fairly complete assortment of tools and the know-how to use them properly. Having the right tool, and knowing how to use it correctly, will make a big difference in the relative ease of a task and will often affect the quality of the final result. Here are a few important rules and practices that will help you use tools and materials safely.

safe workplace Work in a well-lit, uncluttered area. Keep all tools and materials organized. Plan your setup carefully before you begin working. Whenever possible, avoid working with a partner in cramped quarters; you can too easily be injured by the swing of another's hammer or by a wrecking bar dropped from above. Clean up as you go to prevent the accumulation of bent nails or wood scraps and to eliminate spills that can cause you to slip and fall.

toxic materials Some materials you encounter when making improvements and repairs can be dangerous to your health. These include wood preservatives; oil-base enamel, varnish, and lacquer (and their solvents); adhesives (especially resorcinol, epoxy, and contact cement); insulation (asbestos fibers and urea formaldehyde); and even sawdust or dust particles from wallboard joint compound. Read all the precautions on product labels, and follow instructions exactly. Ventilate the workplace adequately, and clean the area frequently and thoroughly.

clothing & gear Wear sturdy clothing and appropriate safety gear to avoid contact with dangerous materials. Always wear safety glasses when using power tools or tools that involve striking an object, such as a hammer and chisel.

power-tool safety Although power tools can cause injuries, these tools can be quite safe when you handle them with respect and adopt some basic safety habits. Read the owner's manual carefully before using a tool to understand the product's capabilities and limitations. Be absolutely certain to unplug a tool before servicing or adjusting it and when you have finished using it. Check that any safety devices, such as guards, are in good working order. Follow the manufacturer's specifications carefully to clean and lubricate all of your tools, and make sure all blades and bits are sharp and undamaged.

safety with electricity Unless it is double-insulated, a power tool should be properly grounded. Power tools that are neither grounded nor double-insulated can give a serious—and even fatal—shock. Double-insulated tools are the best defense against a questionable electrical source. These tools contain a built-in second barrier of protective insulation; they are clearly marked and should not be grounded (they will have two-prong plugs only). If you are working in a damp area or outdoors, a ground fault circuit interrupter—either the portable type or one that is built into the outlet—is an essential piece of equipment.

Use the shortest extension cord you can find for the job. A very long cord can overheat, creating a potential fire hazard. Furthermore, the longer the cord, the less amperage it delivers, which translates into less power for the tool's motor. The most important factor to consider is the maximum amp load your extension cord needs to carry. Look for the nameplate on the tool, which contains its amperage requirement. Add up the requirements of all the tools you plan to plug into the cord at the same time, and make sure it has an amp capacity that equals or, better yet, exceeds this sum.

controlling disasters

Even when everything goes smoothly, a project can be trying. And when things go wrong, it can be downright traumatic. You can minimize irritations and inconveniences and prevent calamities by taking a few simple precautions:

■ Plan carefully. It's a grievous and unnecessary inconvenience to live with a hole in an exterior wall while you are waiting for the out-of-stock window you should have ordered earlier.

■ Time the work to avoid inclement weather and major holidays. If you are planning to have Christmas dinner at your house, for example, do not start a major remodel in October; you will want to avoid having to work under such an inflexible deadline. Also, do not expect much work to happen over the holidays.

■ Do not go on vacation. Even if you have a general contractor, you will need to make decisions and keep an eye on the progress of your project.

■ Do arrange to be out of the house for a short time when there will be significant noise, noxious fumes, or any other threats to your health or well-being.

■ Get phone numbers for the key people who will be working on your project, and ask the general contractor for a home number and/or cell phone number. Make sure that every tradesperson knows how to reach you. If you do not have a cell phone, consider getting one unless you are easily reachable during work hours.

Safety glasses, a dust mask, and protective gloves are essential items for many home improvement projects.

■ Establish and post a set of house rules about using phones and bathrooms, keeping pets indoors or outside, and similar issues.

■ Make sure interior doorways are sealed with plastic sheeting and duct tape to keep out dust, especially when drywall is being sanded.

■ Be mindful of home security. Remember that you will have many strangers in your house. Be careful about giving out keys and burglar-alarm combinations. Do not leave valuables unattended.

SAFETY GEAR YOU SHOULD HAVE ON HAND:
Safety glasses Protect your eyes when using power tools or tools that involve striking an object (a hammer and chisel, for example).
Hard hat Wear one if you will be working with a partner in a cramped space or if falling objects could hit you.
Ear protectors Use these when working with noisy machinery.
Dust mask or respirator Be sure that a respirator is approved for filtering the pollutants you will be handling, which can include dust, fibers, and harmful vapors. A dust mask such as the one shown above is helpful when you are working around common dust or insulation.
Gloves Choose leather to protect your hands from scratches and splinters rubber when handling caustic chemicals.

paint

PAINT IS THE ULTIMATE INTERIOR AND EXTERIOR DECORATOR. IT SETS THE MOOD, freshens the look, and even underscores the period of your home outside and in, show-casing architecture and architectural details as well as interior design. There is no faster nor more economical way to transform a house than with paint, especially if colors are well chosen, complementary, and creatively applied.

Once you learn some tricks of using color, you will be amazed at the opportunities paint offers. A well-painted exterior, with an interesting interplay of colors that high-lights architectural strengths and brings the landscaping to life, translates into real property value. Inside, paint choices can warm up or cool down rooms, create drama or soothe, and expand a space visually or imbue it with coziness.

Don't be afraid to experiment with such decorative paint techniques as sponging, ragging, and stenciling (see pages 60, 64, and 66) to bring a new level of texture and interest to a wall's surface. Paint is enor-mously forgiving; if you do not like the result, you can buy a new can and start over again.

On the following pages, you will learn all you need to know about paint and painting techniques. We begin with a primer on choosing paint. We offer advice on preparing and painting interior walls, doors, windows, trim, and cabinetry, as well as instructions for the decorative techniques of sponging, dragging, colorwashing, ragging, and stenciling. Then we take you outside to learn proper methods for preparing and painting your home's siding and trim.

choosing paint

THE MOST COMMON TYPES OF PAINT FOR INTERIOR AND EXTERIOR SURFACES ARE water-base (latex) and oil-base (alkyd). Primers, wood stains, and clear finishes also are generally available in both latex and alkyd formulations. The chief advantage of using high-quality, more expensive products is better "hiding," which means fewer coats, and better washability.

interior paints

Interior-use paints are available in a range of finishes, from flat to gloss. These paint formulations differ slightly among manufacturers, but generally the finish of semigloss paint is halfway between flat and gloss, and eggshell paint is halfway between flat and semigloss.

Higher-gloss finishes are more washable and durable, but they will show more surface imperfections. High-gloss paint generally is reserved for trim. Semigloss is also excellent on trim, as well as on kitchen, bathroom, and other surfaces exposed to grease, moisture, and heavy wear. A flat or eggshell finish is best for surfaces that receive less wear, such as living room and bedroom walls and ceilings.

latex paints Latex accounts for the vast majority of house paints sold today, and for good reason: It cleans up with soap

From traditional to contemporary, a home's decor can be reborn and enhanced with a new coat of paint. When choosing paint, be sure to consider durability and ease of application.

LOWE'S QUICK TIP
To test if existing paint is alkyd or latex, apply nail-polish remover to a small section. Latex paint will dissolve; alkyd paint will not.

and water, dries quickly, is practically odorless, and poses the least threat to the environment. It also has excellent resistance to yellowing with age.

The type of resin used in the formula determines the quality of latex paint. The highest-quality and most durable paints contain 100 percent acrylic resin, which provides excellent adhesion over alkyds. Vinyl acrylic and other blends are next in quality. Paint containing solely vinyl resin is the least durable and lowest-quality of the available latex formulations.

alkyd paints Alkyds, or solvent-base paints, level out better than latexes, drying virtually free of brush marks for a smoother, harder finish. They are a wise choice for glossy surfaces because they offer good adhesion. Alkyds, however, are harder to apply. They also tend to sag more and dry more slowly than latexes. In addition, they require cleanup with paint thinner. When painting large areas with alkyd paint, make sure the room is well ventilated, or wear a respirator.

INTERIOR PAINTS FOR ALL SURFACES

SURFACE	PRIME OR FIRST COAT	FINISH COAT(S)	COMMENTS
New wallboard	Prime with latex sealer, and let it dry at least 4 hours.	Apply two coats of latex or alkyd paint in your chosen finish. Sand lightly between coats of eggshell, semigloss, or gloss alkyd paint.	Don't use alkyd primer—it will raise nap in the paper surface.
New plaster	Prime with latex sealer, and let it dry at least 4 hours.	Apply two coats of latex or alkyd paint in your chosen finish. Sand lightly between coats of eggshell, semigloss, or gloss alkyd paint.	
Existing wallboard or plaster	When painting over existing latex paint, scuff-sand to remove surface imperfections. Wash and rinse the surface thoroughly first.	Apply two coats of latex or alkyd paint in your chosen finish. Sand lightly between coats of eggshell, semigloss, or gloss alkyd paint.	
Bare wood to be painted	Use an alkyd enamel undercoat.	Lightly sand the enamel undercoat before applying two coats of the finish paint.	Use eggshell for minimal sheen. Semigloss is preferable on doors and trim.
Painted wood to be repainted	Remove loose, flaking paint, and sand the area smooth. Spot-prime bare wood with an alkyd enamel undercoat.	Apply a coat of latex or alkyd enamel paint; let it dry thoroughly. Sand lightly, apply a second coat, and allow it to dry overnight.	Use eggshell for minimal sheen. Semigloss is preferable on doors and trim.
Bare wood to be stained	Sand the wood smooth. Apply a single coat of wood conditioner, and allow it to dry overnight.	Apply one coat of water- or oil-base polyurethane stain according to label directions and allow it to dry. Sand the area lightly with steel wool or fine sandpaper. Apply at least one more coat, repeating the drying and sanding. Finish with one or two coats of clear polyurethane.	
Bare wood to be coated with a clear finish	Apply varnish, polyurethane, or another clear wood finish in your desired sheen.	Apply two or three additional coats of clear finish, sanding lightly between coats.	Don't apply polyurethane over shellac or sanding sealers—adhesion problems can result.
Masonry	On new concrete block, use latex block filler. On poured concrete or brick, prime the area with latex masonry primer.	Apply two coats of latex paint.	White powdery residue (efflorescence) is a sign of moisture in masonry. Check exterior walls for drainage problems, and make needed repairs.
Metal	Remove rust with a wire brush. Prime with rust-inhibitive primer.	Apply two coats of finish paint.	Use of flat finish paint is not recommended.

Two ingredients are essential for a superior paint job: quality paint and meticulous craftsmanship.

clear finishes

If you want to display the grain of wood that is bare or has been stained, choose polyurethane, varnish, shellac, or one of several clear, nonyellowing water-base coatings. Most come in a range of finishes, from flat to gloss.

polyurethane Polyurethane is favored for cabinets, wood paneling, and other surfaces where maximum durability is a primary concern.

varnish While durable, varnishes are not as tough as polyurethane. Ask your paint dealer for the best type for your job. Thin and clean up varnish with paint thinner.

shellac Apply shellac, which comes in orange or white, only over bare or stained wood. It is not recommended for areas exposed to moisture because water can cause spotting on the finish. Most brush marks disappear when shellac dries. Thin and clean up with denatured alcohol.

water-base transparent coatings

Some transparent coatings, including nonyellowing types, can be used on bare or stained wood as well as on painted surfaces, specifically to protect decorative finishes (see pages 58–59).

special-use paints The word "enamel" usually refers to high-gloss paints—either alkyd or latex—that dry to a hard finish. These paints are typically used on interior trim. Polyurethane enamel, sometimes called liquid-plastic paint, is used for floors because of its high abrasion resistance. Pigmented (or dye-colored) wiping stain is commonly applied to bare wood. You simply apply the stain, wait, and wipe it off. If the surface feels rough, apply a clear, quick-drying sanding sealer, and then sand it smooth. Milk paint, sold as a powder to be mixed with water, is made from milk protein, clay, natural pigments, and lime. It is mostly used on wood.

HOW PAINT IS CHANGING

Paint contains thinners, or solvents, that release volatile organic compounds as they evaporate. These contribute to smog and can pose health risks. Modern oil-base paints, made with synthetic resins called alkyds, have less thinner and give off fewer odors and toxic fumes than their oil-base predecessors. Still, thinner is an essential component of alkyd paint.

Because the thinner content of latex paint has always been much less than that of alkyd paint, there has been a dramatic shift over the years toward latex. In fact, some oil-base paints are now restricted or illegal in certain areas of the country. The already low solvent content of latex paints (a maximum of 8 percent) has been reduced to zero in some cases. These paints are marked "0 VOC" (short for "zero volatile organic compounds"). While this is good news for the environment, 0 VOC paint can be difficult to work with because it dries very quickly.

primers

You need a primer when the surface to be painted is porous or the paints are incompatible (such as when you apply latex paint over alkyd).

An existing painted surface in good condition and compatible with the finish coat may not need an additional primer. Consult the chart below to determine if a primer is required.

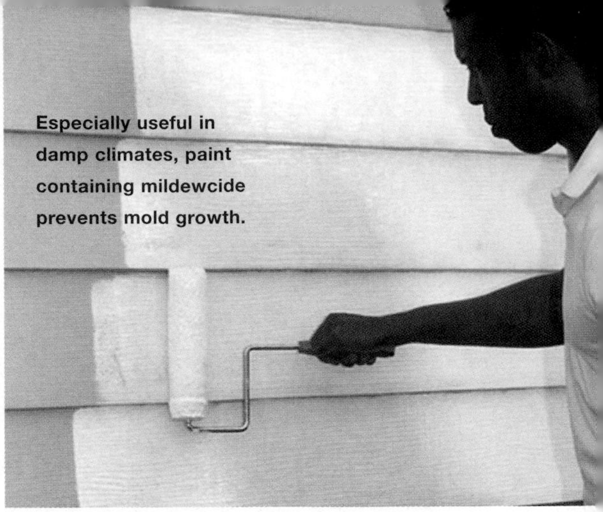

Especially useful in damp climates, paint containing mildewcide prevents mold growth.

exterior paints

One difference between exterior alkyd and latex paints is how they cure. Alkyd paints usually are dry to the touch in 4 to 6 hours and can be recoated in 8 to 12 hours. They continue to harden several months after application, providing an excellent barrier to moisture. Latex paint usually is dry to the touch in 30 minutes and, in warm, dry weather, is resistant to light showers or dew after about 4 hours.

FINISHES FOR EXTERIOR SURFACES

This chart does not recommend the use of primers in all cases: Wood does not need primer if it will be stained or painted with enamel. Vinyl or aluminum siding is sufficiently covered with two coats of acrylic latex. Before applying primer or paint, make sure the surface is clean, smooth, and dry.

SURFACE	PRIMER	FINISH
Wood or plywood siding	Alkyd primer	2 coats alkyd paint, flat/semigloss/gloss
	Latex primer	2 coats latex paint, flat/semigloss/gloss
	None	2 coats latex stain, solid hide
	None	2 coats alkyd stain, solid hide/semitransparent
Hardboard siding	Alkyd primer	2 coats latex paint, semigloss/gloss
Wood trim	Latex primer	2 coats latex paint, semigloss/gloss
	Alkyd primer	2 coats alkyd paint, flat/semigloss/gloss
Wood deck	None	2 coats stain or clear wood preservative
Vinyl or aluminum siding	None	2 coats acrylic latex paint, flat/semigloss/gloss
Brick	Latex masonry primer	2 coats latex paint, flat
Block	Latex block filler	2 coats latex paint, flat
Stucco	Latex masonry primer	2 coats latex paint, flat
Concrete	Latex masonry primer	2 coats latex paint, flat
Ferrous metal	Metal primer	2 coats alkyd paint, gloss
Galvanized metal	Galvanized metal primer	2 coats alkyd paint, gloss

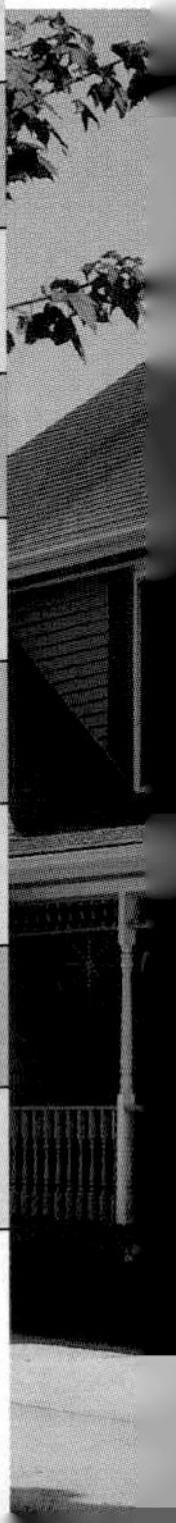

Whether you choose alkyd or latex, flat paint is best on siding for resisting moisture, and semigloss or gloss are best for trim and doors because of their durability.

alkyd paints Alkyd paints are available in enamel and so-called house paint. Enamel paint is typically found in a range of ready-to-mix colors suitable for general use and is a particularly good choice for trim. Alkyd enamel dries to a hard and nonporous finish.

Alkyd house paint is more flexible than enamel, but it is not available in some states because of air-quality regulations. In other states, it is available only in quart cans, making it expensive to use as a coating for exterior siding.

Alkyd paints tend to adhere better than latex to problematic and glossy surfaces. Because they dry more slowly than latex, alkyds give brush and roller marks more time to flow out, leaving a smoother finish on the surface.

latex paints The best exterior latex paint is made with all-acrylic resin. Lower-quality varieties are made with vinyl acrylic and other additives. While all-acrylic paints are more expensive, they offer better adhesion, gloss, and color retention than acrylic mixtures.

Stucco siding calls for a latex-base paint; first apply a primer formulated for stucco.

The water-base formulation of latex paints also makes them easier to clean up, less expensive, and faster drying than alkyds. In addition, latex paint dries to a porous finish, allowing moisture in wood to evaporate through the paint film, which prevents peeling.

stains Stains come in transparent, semitransparent, and solid-hide formulations. Solid-hide stains, the most durable and protective type available, are essentially wood-toned paints. Semitransparent stains are the right choice for areas where you want to show the natural grain of the wood. Transparent formulations are used where you want to display the wood's natural beauty while offering a degree of weather protection.

LEFT: Wood siding can be painted with either alkyd or latex paint; latex is popular because it resists peeling and cracking and is easy to clean up.

Be generous when estimating your paint needs, especially if the room has an irregular shape.

LOWE'S QUICK TIP

If you are doing a job that requires more than one can of paint, it is a good idea to "box"—or mix—your paint to avoid having color discrepancies from one can to the next. To box paint, simply pour two or more cans of the same color into a 5-gallon bucket and stir.

estimating paint needs

To figure out how much paint you will need, you must know the square footage of the area to be painted and the spread rate of the paint. (The spread rate is usually about 400 square feet to the gallon, but check the can to be sure.)

To determine square footage, measure the width of each wall, add the figures together, and multiply the total by the height of the surface. Next, estimate how much of this area will not be painted, taking into account fireplaces, wallpaper, windows, and sections you will paint separately, such as trim. If these surfaces account for 10 percent or more of the room, deduct their square footage from the total.

Finally, divide the total square footage by the spread rate of the paint. Calculate the amount of trim paint separately, or expect that you will use about a quarter as much trim paint as wall paint.

painting safely

Although paint is fairly user-friendly, exercise caution when working with it. Following are some basic guidelines for painting safely:

■ Always work in a well-ventilated area. Open doors and windows, and use exhaust fans. Also keep pets out of freshly painted rooms.

■ If you cannot ventilate the area well enough to get rid of fumes, wear a respirator approved for such use.

■ Wear a dust mask and safety goggles when sanding to keep yourself from breathing in dust particles and to protect your eyes.

■ Wear safety goggles, gloves, and a respirator when you are using chemical strippers, caustic cleaning compounds, or strong solvents.

■ Use canvas drop cloths on the floor. Cloth stays in place and isn't as slippery as plastic.

■ Do not use or store paint products near a flame or heat source. Avoid smoking while painting or using thinner.

■ Inspect ladders for sturdiness. Make sure that all four legs rest squarely on the floor and that both cross braces are locked in place. Never stand on the top step or the utility shelf. Never lean away from a ladder; get off and move it if you cannot reach a spot easily.

■ Clean up promptly after painting, and properly dispose of soiled rags. To eliminate any chance of spontaneous combustion, spread rags soaked with alkyd paint or thinner outdoors and let these dry all day before disposing of them at a toxic-waste dump. Do not leave rags to dry in areas accessible to children or pets.

PAINT FAILURE

Daily exposure to elements takes a toll on painted surfaces. Other factors—including poor surface preparation, incompatible paints, or sloppy application—can hasten decay. Depending on the symptoms, surfaces may need to be stripped bare or may require no more than a light sanding or scraping.

1) Inter-coat peeling Applying latex finish coats over surfaces previously painted with gloss alkyd often results in poor adhesion. To treat, sand off the latex paint, prime the surface with an alkyd primer, and then apply latex finish coats. Some top-of-the-line acrylic paints can be applied over old alkyd paint without the need for priming, but thorough sanding is required first to give the surface "bite."

2) Chalking Chalking is the normal breakdown of a paint finish after long exposure to sunlight. To treat, wash off the loose, powdery material and repaint.

3) Wrinkling Wrinkling results when one coat of paint is applied over another that is not thoroughly dry or when a coat is applied too heavily. To treat, allow the paint to dry thoroughly, sand off the wrinkles, and repaint.

4) Alligatoring Alligatoring can be caused by applying a hard finish coat over a soft primer or by the loss of flexibility that results when thick layers of paint are applied to wood surfaces. To treat, scrape and sand off all the old paint and then repaint the area with a primer and two finish coats.

5) Multiple-coat peeling Structures that have been painted over many times, especially those painted over with oil-base paints, sometimes will show paint failure down to the bare wood. This is caused by the paint layers becoming brittle and then cracking as the wood below expands and contracts with temperature changes. These cracks allow moisture to enter and cause peeling. To treat, strip the surface down to the bare wood and prepare the area as you would prepare new wood before repainting.

6) Blistering Blistering can be caused by moisture invading the subsurface of paint because there is no vapor barrier or because of cracked boards or poor caulking. Blistering also can be caused by applying oil-base paints in hot weather, which can trap solvents. In either case, scrape and sand the blistered paint, and repair any sources of moisture. Then repaint in cool weather.

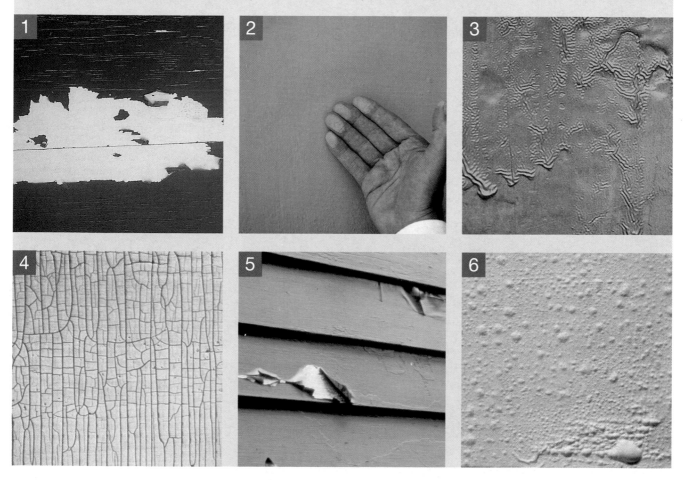

BASIC TOOLS FOR CONVENTIONAL PAINTING

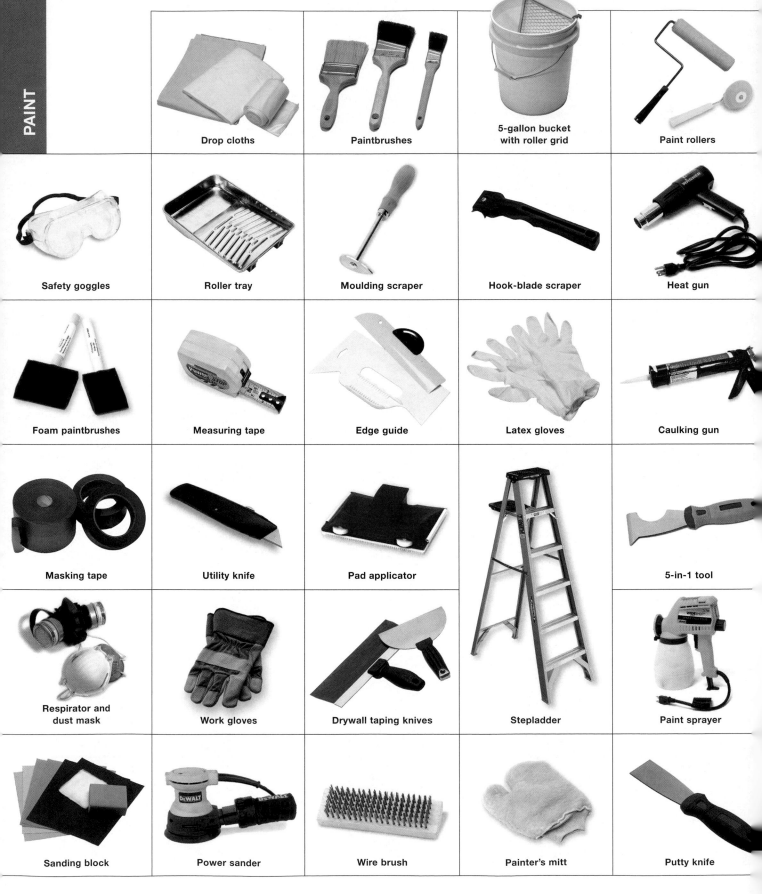

Drop cloths	Paintbrushes	5-gallon bucket with roller grid	Paint rollers
Safety goggles	Roller tray	Moulding scraper	Hook-blade scraper	Heat gun
Foam paintbrushes	Measuring tape	Edge guide	Latex gloves	Caulking gun
Masking tape	Utility knife	Pad applicator		5-in-1 tool
Respirator and dust mask	Work gloves	Drywall taping knives	Stepladder	Paint sprayer
Sanding block	Power sander	Wire brush	Painter's mitt	Putty knife

painting tools

A VARIETY OF TOOLS ARE HELPFUL FOR COMPLETING A SUCCESSFUL PAINT JOB. Some tools are necessary whether you are working on an interior, an exterior, or a decorative painting job. Other tools are specialized for specific tasks. On the next few pages, we'll take a closer look at the primary tools you will want to have on hand before you begin painting. High-quality tools will go a long way toward achieving a professional-looking paint job.

paint removal tools

Scrapers, sanders, heat guns, and related tools are essential for removing loose paint or, when necessary, an entire finish before painting a surface. A disk sander is useful for big sanding jobs, such as for preparing to paint exterior siding.

SANDPAPER AND SANDING BLOCK

WIRE BRUSH

POWER SANDER WITH SANDING DISKS

PUTTY KNIFE

DRYWALL TAPING KNIVES

HOOK-BLADE SCRAPER

HEAT GUN

MOULDING SCRAPER

TOOLS FOR REMOVING PAINT

For removing loose or peeling paint, you may need a sanding block and sandpaper, a wire brush, a couple of different types of scrapers, and drywall taping knives or putty knives for getting under the paint and making repairs. A heat gun and a power sander can make paint removal much easier.

4" PAINTBRUSH

2" TRIM BRUSH

1½" ANGLED SASH BRUSH

PAINTBRUSHES

These three brushes will get you through most conventional paint jobs. Use synthetic bristles for latex paint and natural bristles for alkyd paint.

ROLLER TRAY

PAINT ROLLER

5-GALLON BUCKET WITH ROLLER GRID

BEVELED CORNER ROLLER

ROLLER EQUIPMENT

Though a tray suffices for small jobs, rolling from a grid in a 5-gallon bucket ensures a quicker, neater job. Add an extension pole to your supplies to lengthen your reach and attain more leverage.

paintbrushes

Natural-bristle brushes are traditionally utilized to apply alkyd paint and other finishes that require the use of paint thinner for cleanup. Avoid using these brushes when applying latex paint and other water-base products because the bristles become limp when they soak up water. For latex paint, choose synthetic bristles. Polyester brushes stay stiff in water, humidity, and heat, and also keep their shape for detail work. Nylon is more abrasion-resistant but can lose stiffness on hot days.

For most projects, you can get by nicely with three paintbrushes: a 2-inch trim brush, a 1½-inch sash brush, and a 4-inch straight-edged brush. High-quality brushes perform very differently than cheap ones. A good brush has long, tapered bristles set firmly into a wooden handle with epoxy cement, not glue. The bristles are flagged, or split at the ends, enabling them to hold more paint. Look for multiple lengths of flagged bristles packed tightly through a ¾- to 1-inch thickness for a standard 4-inch brush.

Always test a brush before purchase by holding it as you would during painting (see page 48). It should feel comfortable in your hand, not awkward or heavy. Test it for springiness and make sure that it has little fanning and no bristle gaps.

paint rollers

Look for the type of roller that has a heavy-gauge steel frame and a comfortable handle threaded with a metal sleeve inside to accommodate an extension pole. Nine-inch rollers will handle nearly all jobs, but for some work you may prefer a special roller: a trim roller for trim and window sashes; a beveled corner roller for corners, ceiling borders, and grooves in paneling; and a roller made of grooved foam for acoustical surfaces.

Choose the right nap for the paint you are using. When applying latex, choose a nylon nap. Nylon and wool blend, lambskin, and mohair covers are recommended

PAINT

for alkyd paint. Nap thickness varies from $\frac{1}{16}$ inch to $1\frac{1}{4}$ inches. The smoother the surface that you are painting or the higher the gloss of paint you are applying, the shorter the nap you will need.

A 3- to 4-foot extension pole lets you reach high walls and ceilings, eliminating the need for a ladder in many cases. You can also use an extension pole for painting low areas, eliminating the need to squat or stoop.

For large jobs, rolling from a 5-gallon bucket equipped with a roller grid is faster and neater than using a tray.

other paint applicators

Disposable foam brushes come in handy for small jobs and quick touch-ups. A pad applicator with a replaceable pad is useful for painting corners and edges. As with roller covers, nylon pads are used for

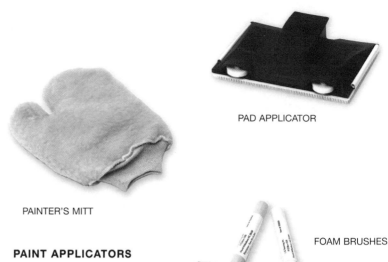

PAD APPLICATOR

PAINTER'S MITT

PAINT APPLICATORS
Disposable foam brushes are convenient for small jobs and apply paint in a very smooth coat. A pad applicator works well for painting corners and edges. If you have metalwork or highly irregular surfaces, use a painter's mitt.

FOAM BRUSHES

CAULKING GUN

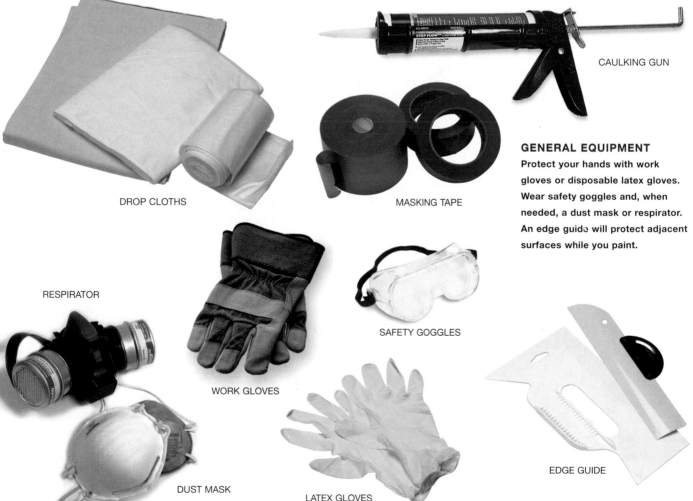

DROP CLOTHS

MASKING TAPE

GENERAL EQUIPMENT
Protect your hands with work gloves or disposable latex gloves. Wear safety goggles and, when needed, a dust mask or respirator. An edge guide will protect adjacent surfaces while you paint.

RESPIRATOR

WORK GLOVES

SAFETY GOGGLES

DUST MASK

LATEX GLOVES

EDGE GUIDE

STEP STOOL
An aluminum step stool, paired with a second step stool, and two 2-by-6 (or wider) planks create a solid low-level scaffold.

ARTICULATED LADDER
Three locking joints allow these ladders to be bent into several positions.

STEPLADDER
A 5- or 6-foot stepladder is convenient for many different tasks, both indoors and outdoors.

EXTENSION LADDER
The upper section of this ladder can be extended from the ground with a pulley system and then locked in place.

latex paints; nylon- and wool-blend, lamb-skin, and mohair pads are recommended for alkyds. Finally, a painter's mitt is an ideal choice for coating irregular, textured, or contoured surfaces, such as pipes, grilles, and radiators.

ladders & scaffolding
Most exterior painting projects require at least one ladder and a scaffolding unit. The stepladder is the standard for most interior jobs and will provide good service for exterior jobs if the walls are not too high.

Aluminum ladders are stronger than wooden ones and are particularly recommended when you require an extension ladder because they are much lighter in weight. There are three grades of aluminum extension ladders, each measured by how much weight it can hold: residential, commercial, and industrial. A commercial-grade ladder provides the perfect balance between strength and lightness of weight. Though they are more costly than residential ladders, if you are painting your house yourself, you should consider buying one for ease of use and safety (for ladder safety tips, see page 341).

With two extension ladders, doubled 2-by-10 wooden planks, and special triangular brackets called ladder jacks locked onto ladder rungs, you can make a simple scaffold. But because these units have no safety rails, only use them if you have experience working at heights and feel confident that you can work safely.

power sprayers

Power sprayers can save you considerable time, particularly on surfaces such as shingle siding. Although there is some disagreement among paint professionals about whether sprayed surfaces are as durable as brushed surfaces, most agree that if the sprayer is used properly, the finish will last just as long as one created with a brush or roller. The most common paint sprayers, known as airless sprayers, come in many sizes.

Sprayers are particularly useful for painting deeply textured, hard-to-reach, or multipiece surfaces with many nooks and crannies, such as eaves, lattices, or even rough stucco. These surfaces will require you to carefully mask the area and put down plenty of drop cloths. Never use a sprayer on windy or even breezy days.

When using a power sprayer, follow these tips:

- Test the sprayer on a large piece of cardboard, adjusting the unit to get a uniform spray pattern with a minimum amount of pressure.

- To achieve a smooth, even coat, keep the gun about 10 inches from the surface and then spray a succession of overlapping strips. Move the sprayer in a smooth motion and at a consistent pace—about 3 inches per second. Release the trigger at the end of each stroke, and then pull it again as you begin to reverse direction.

- Spray straight at the surface, and avoid swinging your arm back and forth.

- Once you have begun to work, do not leave the sprayer idle for more than 20 minutes or the paint will begin to harden.

- When you have finished painting for the day or are taking a break of significant length, be sure to clean the paint from the unit, carefully following the manufacturer's instructions.

- To avoid mishaps or injury, always wear protective clothing and gloves, as well as goggles. Never point the sprayer head at your body. The powerful jet of paint from a sprayer can force paint through your skin. If that happens, get immediate medical attention.

- Before you clean a power sprayer, turn off and unplug the unit. Then pull the spray-gun trigger to release the remaining pressure in the hose.

- Make sure to set the safety lock on the spray gun when you are not spraying.

A handheld power sprayer like this one can be very helpful for small paint jobs. For bigger tasks, buy or rent a larger airless sprayer.

WINDOW SCRAPER

UTILITY KNIFE

CLEANUP TOOLS
A utility knife is useful for removing masking tape around freshly painted window frames, and a scraper is handy for removing paint around muntins.

decorative painting tools

ALTHOUGH THERE ARE NUMEROUS SPECIALTY BRUSHES AND ROLLERS AVAILABLE for decorative painting, you really don't need many of them for the techniques featured in this book. Don't hesitate to work with the inexpensive chip brushes and foam brushes that are frequently specified. When house painter's, specialty, or artist's brushes are called for, however, use the best quality you can afford.

A pale-lime glaze color-washed over the walls adds a patina of age to this contemporary living room—a perfect counter-point to the room's sleek leather sofa and wood coffee table.

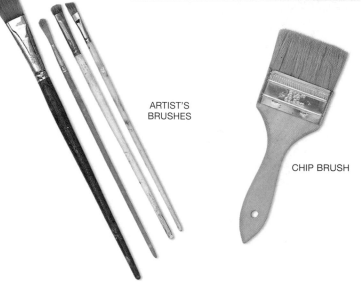

ARTIST'S BRUSHES

CHIP BRUSH

artist's brushes These flat, round, and angled specialty brushes are essential for many faux finishes, as well as for adding details to stenciling (see pages 66–67) and for general touchup. Instead of throwing out worn or inexpensive artist's brushes, save them to mix glazes.

chip brush Inexpensive and versatile, the chip brush is used to apply glaze as well as to soften—and it is much cheaper than the badger-hair softening brush tra-ditionally used in faux finishing. You can also use it to apply glaze to mouldings.

5-IN-1 TOOL

JERSEY RAGS

SEA SPONGE

SOFTENING BRUSHES

STENCIL BRUSHES

STIPPLING BRUSH

5-in-1 tool This handy tool has a crescent blade for scraping excess glaze or paint off a roller. It can also be used for opening paint cans as well as for scraping inside corners.

jersey rags Cotton-knit rags, also called jersey rags, are used to rub glazes. They may be sold in plastic bags or 5-pound boxes. Buy the jersey (smooth-knit) type, not the ribbed variety. Cheesecloth can be substituted for cotton rags. It is packaged in both precut and continuous lengths.

sea sponge The natural sea sponge is used for sponging on and off. The larger the pores and more jagged the edges, the more open the decorative effect will be.

softening brushes Softening brushes are used to mute or soften details or to apply overall effects such as colorwashing (see page 63).

stippling brush This broad brush, made with hog-hair or horsehair bristles, is designed to be pounced rather than brushed over a surface. Several sizes are available.

stencil brushes These blunt-cut, cylindrical brushes made with hog-hair bristles are used to pounce or swirl paint onto a surface through a stencil (for more on this, see pages 66–67). Their handles are usually short, but European stencil brushes are sometimes long-handled.

preparing a room

PROPER PREPARATION MAKES PAINTING EASIER, REDUCES THE POSSIBILITY OF making messes and mistakes that could cost hours of tedious cleanup, and helps ensure a quality, long-lasting job. Here are a few key steps you should take when painting a room:

To prevent cleanup nightmares later, take the time to cover floors, furniture, and other surfaces completely.

clearing the room

Move light furniture and all decorative objects out of the room. Remove everything possible from the walls, including all heating-register covers and electrical faceplates (turn off the power first). Put a piece of masking tape over switches and receptacles. Ideally, remove knobs, handles, and locks from doors and windows (mark them so you can replace them correctly later), or else mask them.

Push heavy furniture into the middle of the room, and cover these items with drop cloths. Cover the floor with plastic sheeting and then with a canvas drop cloth. If you cannot take down a light fixture, tie a plastic garbage bag around it.

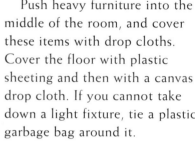

removing wallpaper

Although you can sometimes paint over wallpaper (see page 54), it is usually better to remove it. (For information on removing wallpaper, see page 84.) After all the adhesive is removed, wash the wall with an abrasive cleaner, rinse it well, and let it dry for 24 hours.

scraping or stripping

Chipped or peeling paint must be scraped off before new paint is applied. The trick is to scrape hard enough to remove the paint, but not so hard that you dig into the surface. The best scrapers have edges that can be sharpened with a metal file. A broad knife does a fast job on large areas; a hook-blade scraper is more convenient for small areas. A wire brush is effective for removing any paint that is lightly flaking.

Sometimes the old finish on woodwork is in such bad condition that the paint must be removed entirely. The easiest way to strip old paint from woodwork is with a commercial liquid paint stripper; carefully follow the instructions on the container.

making repairs

Small holes, cracks, and other minor surface blemishes are relatively easy problems to fix on your own. For extensive damage, you may need to call in a professional. Large cracks in a wall or ceiling may indicate uneven settling of the foundation. If you can fit the tip of your little finger into a crack, consider having the foundation inspected.

Use your finger or a putty knife to fill nail holes or very small cracks with joint compound—or wood filler if you are patching wood. Before patching other small holes and cracks, brush them clean and dampen the surface. Using a putty knife, apply a layer of joint compound or wood filler. After patching the area, allow the patch to dry, and then smooth and spot-prime it.

For a small hole larger than a nail hole, cut two lengths of a self-adhesive mesh joint tape that is wider than the hole. Center one piece over the hole, and press it into the wall. Center the other piece over the hole to form an X with the first piece, and press it in place. Then, using a putty knife, cover the mesh with one or more layers of joint compound. When the material is dry, sand and spot-prime the surface area.

ABOVE LEFT: Use a broad knife or putty knife to scrape away old paint layers. ABOVE RIGHT: A wire brush is effective for scratching off small areas of flaking paint.

Mesh tape makes patching small holes fast and easy.

BELOW: Patch nail holes with joint compound.

sanding

One reason to sand a surface is to smooth it. You should sand newly patched areas, bare wood, and areas that have been scraped before beginning to paint. Use fine-grade sandpaper.

Another reason to sand is to rough up glossy surfaces so paint will adhere better. You can use fine-grade sandpaper or, for alkyd paints, liquid deglosser. Trisodium phosphate (TSP) or a phosphate-free substitute will work as a light-duty deglosser. Always wear rubber gloves when using liquid deglosser or TSP. Rinse the wall thoroughly afterward, and allow it to dry for about 24 hours.

cleaning

After vacuuming the room, use a tack cloth to dust all the surfaces that will be painted. Then wash any walls that have a grease film (kitchens) or a soap film (bathrooms) with TSP or a phosphate-free substitute. Wash greasy or mildewed surfaces both before and after you sand. For very greasy spots, sponge on paint thin-ner, blot it dry, and then wash the area with the cleaner. Wearing rubber gloves and safety glasses, scrub mildewed areas with a mixture of 3 ounces TSP or a nonphosphate substitute, 1 ounce dry detergent, 1 quart chlorine bleach, and 3 quarts water. Allow the areas to dry thoroughly (about 24 hours).

masking

If you have a steady hand, you may not need masking tape to protect hardware and surfaces next to those being painted. Most people, however, find tape helpful for keeping surfaces from being splattered and for keeping a crisp edge between two paint types or colors.

If you are using a brush against the tape, use tape with good adhesion rather than all-purpose tape to prevent paint from seeping in. There is a type of low-tack tape (often called painter's tape) that can fasten to delicate surfaces without causing damage when it is pulled away. For more about masking, see below and the facing page.

A sanding block helps you avoid creating dips or low spots in the wood.

LEFT: **Trisodium phosphate will remove mildew from affected areas but should only be applied following safety precautions.** RIGHT: **Apply the sticky edge of the masking or painter's tape adjacent to the area you'll be painting.** BELOW: **To remove tape without pulling off paint, fold it back so it's almost parallel to the wall.**

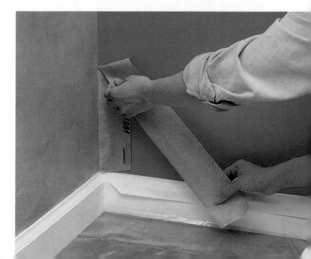

PROTECTING THE AREA

1 Put garbage bags over hanging fixtures, and fasten the bags to the fixtures' cords with twist ties or masking tape. Drape furniture at the center of the room.

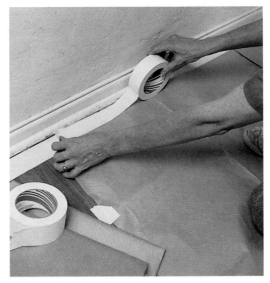

2 To protect the floor, run 2-inch-wide masking or painter's tape along the floor's edge and then secure the drop cloth to the band of tape. A disposable paper drop cloth works fine where you are painting only a wall or trim.

3 To mask adjacent surfaces, run 2-inch painter's tape along the edges of the surface that will not be painted and secure masking strips to it. At the baseboard of a wall, lay the tape along the upper edge to form a ledge to catch paint drips. Cover trim with painter's tape. Tape plastic sheeting to larger wall surfaces, such as wainscoting.

4 Cover hard-to-remove hardware with masking tape. Take off easily removed hardware, put each item and its screws in a separate plastic bag, and note the sequence of the pieces.

5 Mask window glass (unless you have a very steady hand). Press masking tape in place with a putty knife to seal the edges. Remove the tape while the paint is still tacky—about half an hour after painting with latex paint and about 2 hours after applying alkyd paint.

interior painting techniques

ONCE YOUR WALLS, CEILING, AND TRIM ARE SMOOTH, CLEAN, AND BLEMISH-FREE, it is time to prepare for the painting job. By following a well-planned painting sequence, you can avoid making spots on newly painted surfaces or inadvertently touching a just-painted edge. Here are some general rules of thumb.

If you are using stains or clear finishes on woodwork, apply them first. When the finish is completely dry, mask all trim adjacent to the walls and ceilings you will be painting.

Prime any surfaces that need a base coat (see page 30). Your primer should cover the area completely, but it does not have to be as neat as the finish coat. Do the ceiling first and then the walls.

When the primer is dry, paint the ceiling. Then paint the walls, starting from the top and working your way down. If you used a good-quality primer, you can probably cover surfaces in a single coat of premium paint. But if you are painting over a darker color, you may need to apply two coats.

Finally, brush paint on trim as needed. Start with the ceiling moulding, move on to any other horizontal trim, and then finish with the baseboards. You can either

leave the window trim, door trim, and cabinets for last or paint them just before you paint the baseboards.

painting with a brush

Some professionals prefer painting entire walls and ceilings with brushes, which produce a smoother, less porous finish. But brushing is very time-consuming. A faster, more commonly used technique is to use a brush to "cut in" the borders of large areas and to paint trim. Most of each surface can then be painted with a roller. When you paint with a brush, never work directly from a paint can if you can help it. Instead, pour the paint into a large bucket, and stir.

loading the brush Prepare your brush by rolling the bristles between your palms to remove any loose bristles, and then shake the brush vigorously. Dip one-third of the length of the bristles into the container of stirred paint, and then lift and dip the brush again two or three times to saturate the bristles. If this is the first time you are loading the brush, gently stir the paint with it so that the bristles spread slightly; do not do this when reloading. Lift the brush straight up, letting excess paint drip into the bucket. Gently slap both sides of the brush against the inside of the bucket two or three times. Do not wipe the brush against the lip of the bucket; this can cause the bristles to clump, leaving too little paint on the brush.

cutting in with a brush Before you begin painting an entire wall or ceiling with a roller or a brush, cut in the edges

To remove excess paint, slap the brush against the inside of the container rather than scraping the brush against the lip.

with a 2- to 3-inch trim brush. (Use a foam brush for glaze.) If the wall and ceiling will be different colors, you can mask the edge of whichever surface you are not working on or use an edge guide to keep paint from straying.

If you are using flat or eggshell latex paint, you can cut in the entire room before painting the open spaces. For semigloss or gloss latex or for any alkyd

ABOVE: When you cut in, position the brush about two brush lengths from a corner, and paint toward the corner using long, overlapping strokes.
LEFT: The intricate paint job on this fireplace surround requires patience, a steady hand, and correct technique.

BELOW: Always remove receptacle and switch covers before cutting in around outlets or light switches (turn off the power first). Be careful not to paint the switch or outlet itself.

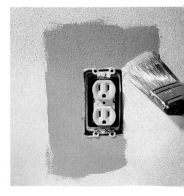

paint, you will get better results if you cut in a small section and then fill it in before moving to the next area. Also, do not let the edge of one section dry before starting on another; this will leave you with a demarcation line.

If you are using the same paint for the ceiling and wall, you can paint several inches out from the ceiling-to-wall connection on both sides. If you are using different colors or types of paint, cut in and paint the ceiling first.

For a ceiling, cut in first where the ceiling meets the wall, working all the way around the room. Then cut in around any hanging fixtures.

For a wall, cut in first along the ceiling. Next move along the vertical edges and above the baseboard, then around the door and window frames, and finally around any light fixtures, outlets, or other fixed items on the wall.

painting whole surfaces with a brush
To paint an entire surface with a brush, first cut in the edges. Then spread paint smoothly and evenly over a 3-foot-square area, holding the paintbrush at a 45-degree angle to the surface and slowly reducing pressure at the end of the stroke.

The grip shown here allows you to hold the brush comfortably and move it efficiently.

PAINTING TIPS & SHORTCUTS

The following tips from professional painters can help you achieve a top-quality job:

- To avoid having to clean your paint tray, line the inside of the tray with aluminum foil or a purchased plastic liner. When the job is done, simply remove the liner.
- To remove bristles that come off as you apply paint, touch them with the tip of your wet brush; the bristles should stick to it. Wipe the stray bristles off the brush with a cloth.
- If insects get trapped in the wet paint, let the paint dry before brushing them off.
- When applying an enamel finish coat, brush paint on generously and use a light touch. Avoid over-brushing when you use enamel—this can produce an irregular finish. Work quickly, and avoid touching up areas that are already painted.
- If you are sensitive to the odor of paint, mix in a few drops of vanilla extract or add a commercial paint fragrance additive. Always wear a respirator if you cannot properly ventilate a room.

Instead of wrapping your hand around the paintbrush handle, hold the brush with your thumb on one side and your four fingers spread on the ferrule. This grip gives you control of the brush and allows you to swivel and angle the brush throughout the brushstroke without moving the rest of your body.

Paint toward a dry area and then back into a wet edge. This helps avoid lap marks. On smooth surfaces, angle the final strokes in one direction, but on rough surfaces, vary the direction. When painting with a semigloss or high-gloss finish, make the final brushstrokes away from the light source in the room. The tiny ridges that a brush leaves will not be as pronounced. On wood, paint parallel to the grain. When the first 3-foot-square area is filled, soften the brush marks by running the brush, unloaded, very lightly over the wet paint. Begin the next area a few inches from the last finished one. When the new section is completed, brush into the previously finished one, blending the overlap.

painting with a roller

Use a brush to cut in the edges of any surface before you use a roller. The process of rolling on paint is essentially the same, whether you are painting a ceiling or a wall. The object is to create a coat that appears seamless.

loading the roller Before you use a new napped roller, you should remove the excess lint. Unroll a length of 3-inch masking tape (regular tape, not painter's). Place the roller cover on a roller frame, and roll the cover back and forth over the tape. This step is not necessary with a foam roller.

Depending on the size of your job, you can paint from either a paint tray or a 5-gallon bucket fitted with a wire mesh grid. If you are using a tray, pour in just enough paint to fill the reservoir. Dip the roller into the reservoir, and then roll up and down on the textured part of the tray to distribute the paint and saturate the nap. For larger jobs, a bucket is more efficient. Pour 1 or 2 gallons of paint into the bucket. Dip the roller in. Run the roller back and forth on the mesh grid to spread the paint evenly, and squeeze out the excess. Whether you use a bucket or a tray, the roller should be saturated with paint, but not dripping, when you start applying it.

rolling the ceiling When painting a ceiling, use an extension pole so you will not have to stand directly under the area you are painting. This minimizes your chances of getting paint drips or splatters on yourself. (Working on a ladder, the other option, forces you to move up and down constantly to change its position.)

Always work across the shorter dimension of the ceiling first, and paint one 3-foot-square section at a time. Start in a corner and paint diagonally in a large M or W shape across the section, and then roll back and forth to distribute the paint evenly over the area. Roll slowly, and reload the roller as needed. When you have completed the whole width of the ceiling, roll the unloaded roller in one long straight stroke along the edge adjacent to the unpainted area. Along the walls, roll as close to the edge of the ceiling as possible to cover any differences in texture between the cut-in brush marks and the roller marks.

BELOW: If you're painting from a 5-gallon bucket, remove excess paint from a roller by running it up and down against a metal grid. BOTTOM: Blot excess paint off the end of a roller with a paper towel or rag.

rolling the walls The most efficient way to cover a wall is to start in one corner and roll the paint onto the surface in a large M- or W-shaped pattern, working in 3-by-4-foot sections.

Load your roller with paint, and off-load the excess. Roll diagonally upward first, keeping a light, even pressure on the roller. Without reloading or lifting, roll down diagonally to form the first point of the letter. Still without reloading or lifting, roll up and down to form the second point of the letter. Avoid spinning the roller as you lift it off the painted surface. Next, roll back and forth to distribute the paint evenly over the area and fill in the letter.

Once you have finished the first section, make the next shape below it. When

PAINTING WALLS

1 Starting at the top of the wall, lay 2-inch masking or painter's tape along the wall that won't be painted, flush with the corner. Working your way down the wall, firmly press the tape in place so paint won't leak beneath it. At the baseboard, lay the tape along the upper edge to form a ledge to catch paint drips. Tape off edges of the floor with 2-inch-wide masking tape, and then secure a drop cloth to the tape.

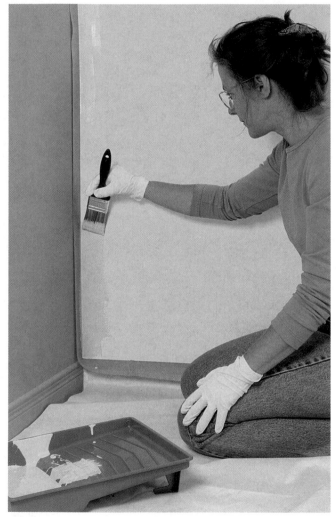

2 Cut in the edges before rolling paint on the wall. Pour some paint into a roller tray, and dip a synthetic-bristle paintbrush into the paint, coating the bottom third of the bristles. Brush off excess paint on the edge of the tray. Cut in first along the ceiling, then follow with the door and window trim, move along adjacent walls, and finish with the baseboard. At an adjacent wall, start about two brush lengths from the ceiling and brush up to the corner. Move down, and brush upward to join the wet edge. Continue until you cut in from the baseboard to the wet edge above it.

you have completed one full length of wall, top to bottom, roll the unloaded roller in one long, straight stroke along the edge adjacent to the unpainted area. Do the same close to the corner of the wall to conceal the differences in texture between the cut-in brush marks and the roller marks. Then repeat the process for the next length of wall.

3 To reach the upper sections of the wall, attach an extension to a roller. Load up the roller in the tray, and roll off the excess paint. Starting a few feet from one top corner of the wall, apply the paint in an M or W shape to a section that is 3 to 4 feet square. Work toward the adjacent wall, overlapping the cut-in edge along the corner.

4 Without recharging the roller with paint, roll back over the same section to fill in unpainted spaces. Still without adding any fresh paint, make a third pass to even out any marks left by the edge of the roller. Apply more pressure for this third pass. Continue rolling paint on the wall in sections until you have covered the wall.

painting woodwork

PAINTING THE WOODWORK OF DOORS, WINDOWS, AND TRIM IS SLIGHTLY MORE exacting than painting ceilings and walls. Be sure to refer to page 28 for more about the appropriate paints for woodwork. Prime bare wood or spackling compound and sanded surfaces. Paint the ceiling, then the walls, and finally the trim.

painting doors

You can paint a door on its hinges if you place a drop cloth beneath it, or you can remove the door from its hinges. To take off the door, slip out the hinge pins, but don't unscrew the hinges. Lean the door against a wall with two small blocks under the bottom edge and a third between the top edge and the wall. You can also lay the door across a pair of sawhorses. If the door is horizontal when you paint, be careful not to apply too much paint, or it may puddle.

Whether you paint a door on or off its hinges, the painting sequence is exactly the same. Work from top to bottom. For flush doors, roll on the paint with a lint-free cover, and then brush in the direction of the grain. For doors with inset panels, follow the sequence shown below left. Match the color of the latch edge to the room the door opens into and the color of the hinge edge to the room the door opens away from.

When painting the door casing, begin with the head casing, and then work down the side casings. If the door opens away from the room, paint the jamb and the two surfaces of the doorstop visible from the room. If the door opens into the room, paint the jamb and the door side of the doorstop. Do not rehang or close the door until all the paint is completely dry.

> **LOWE'S QUICK TIP**
> Use a hammer and nail to puncture the paint can's rim in two or three places so that paint will not pool and spill over.

PAINTING A PANEL DOOR

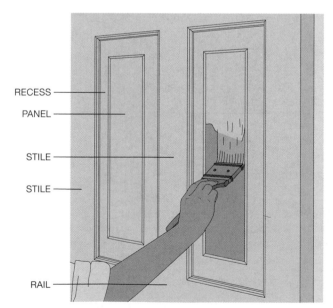

RECESS
PANEL
STILE
STILE
RAIL

1 Paint the parts of a panel door in the following order: recesses, panels, horizontal rails, and vertical stiles.

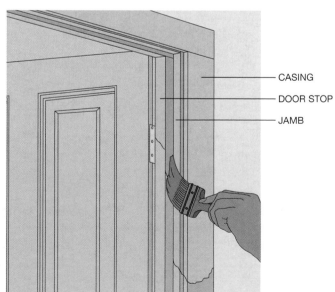

CASING
DOOR STOP
JAMB

2 If the door opens away from the room, paint the jamb and two surfaces of the stop as shown. If the door opens into a room, paint the jamb and then the door side of the stop.

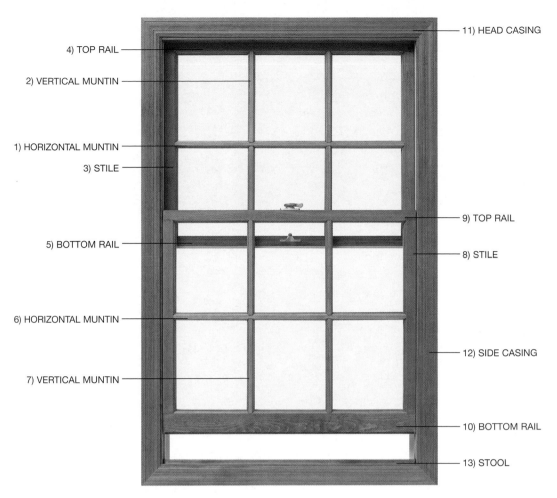

4) TOP RAIL

2) VERTICAL MUNTIN

1) HORIZONTAL MUNTIN

3) STILE

5) BOTTOM RAIL

6) HORIZONTAL MUNTIN

7) VERTICAL MUNTIN

11) HEAD CASING

9) TOP RAIL

8) STILE

12) SIDE CASING

10) BOTTOM RAIL

13) STOOL

Paint the sections of a double-hung window in the order shown. Start with the outer sash, move on to the inner sash, and finish with the frame trim elements.

painting windows

When painting windows, choose an angled sash brush, which will reach into corners. Load the brush lightly.

If you do not have a steady hand, cover the edges of the glass with masking tape (see page 45 for information on masking and page 54 for techniques on removing paint from window panes). But if you feel you can guide a paintbrush in a straight and smooth manner, try painting without masking—and save yourself time and hassle. Use a tapered sash brush, lightly loaded, on the frames. Let the paint lap slightly onto the glass; this will seal the finish to the glass so condensation will not get under the paint and cause it to peel. Then wipe off the excess paint with a rag wrapped around a putty-knife blade.

double-hung windows
If the sashes are removable, lift them out and lay them on a table to paint them. Be prepared to leave the sashes out long enough to dry thoroughly (at least 24 hours). If the sashes are not removable, you will need to raise and lower them as needed to reach all the window parts.

Paint the outer, or upper, sash first. If the window has small glass panes, begin with the horizontal muntins, and then work on the vertical ones. Next, paint the exposed parts of the stiles, the top rail, and the bottom rail, in that order. Then paint the parts of the inner, or lower, sash, starting with the muntins and finishing with the rails.

When painting the trim of a double-hung window, begin with the head casing, and then paint down the sides. Next, paint the stool, and then finish by painting the apron.

casement windows
First paint any vertical muntins and then any horizontal ones. Next, paint the top rails, the bottom

To paint along glass, slowly and steadily draw a lightly loaded tapered sash brush along the window frame; let the paint lap slightly onto the glass.

rails, and the stiles, in that order. Finish the job by painting the casing.

No matter what type of window you have, do not paint the jamb. This may cause the window to stick. After you paint the window, if the jamb is made of wood, wax it with floor wax. This is unnecessary for a metal jamb.

painting trim

New wood trim can be painted ahead of time and then touched up once it has been installed, or it can be painted in place, as with existing trim. If you are painting woodwork in place, always mask adjacent surfaces. When you apply two coats of semigloss or gloss paint to your trim, as is often the case, ensure a good bond by sanding lightly between coats and wiping the dust off with a tack cloth.

Begin with the mouldings closest to the ceiling, and work down. You can paint your door and window trim and frames, as well as any cabinets, either before or after you complete the baseboards.

For the best results, paint narrow trim with a 1½-inch angled sash brush, and use a 2-inch trim brush for wider trim. Begin about 3 inches from a corner, stroke toward the corner, and then brush in the opposite direction to spread the paint evenly. Start the next section several inches beyond where you stopped, and paint back into the wet edge. Paint over any visible caulking.

A flexible edge guide is a handy tool for painting the baseboard below the carpet

After priming—but before painting new trim—run a light bead of latex caulk along all seams, and smooth the caulk with a wet finger.

line. If you have a very tall baseboard that has a wide, flat surface topped with a moulded trim, first paint the moulded edge with an angled sash brush.

PAINTING WALLPAPER OR MASONRY

Because some wallpaper is extremely difficult to remove without damaging the drywall beneath it, painting over wallpaper is sometimes necessary. The surface must be smooth and in good condition, and the seams must be tight. Test a small area before painting the entire room. Scrub the wall with a damp sponge to remove dirt and any residual wallpaper paste. Repair holes or dents with vinyl spackling compound, and allow the substance to dry. Then roll on a tinted shellac-base stain-blocking primer. After this dries, make any final repairs, and then paint.

Brick or concrete walls can be painted, too. Wearing safety goggles and rubber gloves, scrub the surface with a solution of trisodium phosphate or a TSP substitute, and then rinse the area thoroughly to remove residue. Using a roller with a 1-inch nap for brick or a ³⁄₈-inch nap for concrete, roll on a latex primer made for masonry. After the primer dries, roll on latex paint, and touch up the area with a brush.

LOWE'S QUICK TIP

When you need to paint railings or narrow chair spindles, a painter's mitt can do the job more quickly than a paintbrush. Put the thick, soft mitt on your hand, and dip it into a paint tray. Then grasp the railing, and slide the mitt over the surface.

PAINTING BASE MOULDING

1 Begin about 3 inches from a corner (or end) and brush the paint toward the corner. Reverse direction and, going over the applied paint, brush away from the corner. This will help spread the paint evenly. If the paint is still wet, brush lightly over the painted area again to obscure any brushstrokes.

2 Repeat, beginning a few inches from where you stopped and brushing the paint first into the wet edge and then in the opposite direction.

STAINING WOODWORK

When it comes to giving windows, doors, or woodwork a warm, natural appearance, a stained or clear finish is hard to beat. For success, high-quality, defect-free woodwork and craftsmanship are mandatory.

Each wood species has its own color and grain, characteristics that will show through a transparent stain or clear finish. In addition, the wood's density will affect how much stain it will absorb—softwoods absorb stain much faster and, in some cases, less evenly than most hardwoods. You can ensure more even color by applying a wood conditioner (according to label directions) before staining the surface. Be sure to test each finish on a sample, scrap, or back-side of the material you are staining.

A water-base urethane finish is easier to use, quicker to dry, and more environmentally friendly than an oil-base one. Oil-base urethane, however, is more durable and less likely to show brush marks.

Mask off the wall and any glass next to the woodwork with blue painter's tape. Fill any holes or imperfections in the woodwork with matching stainable wood putty. Lightly sand the surface with 180-grit sandpaper, working in line with the wood grain. Vacuum, and then wipe the surface with a clean cloth dampened with alcohol to remove dust.

Wear disposable latex gloves to protect your hands. Apply stain with a brush or a clean rag (such as an old T-shirt) following the label directions. Wipe off excess stain, and allow the surface to dry. Lightly sand the area, and add more stain if necessary. After the stain is dry, apply two coats of clear satin or gloss urethane to seal the finish.

Paint and new cabinet pulls gave these dark, outdated cabinets a new lease on life.

painting cabinets

A FRESH COAT OF PAINT IS A QUICK, INEXPENSIVE WAY TO GIVE YOUR CABINETS a new look. Whether you want to lighten up dark and dingy cabinets or liven up your room with bold colors, paint can provide an instant makeover. Not all cabinets, though, can be painted. Solid-wood or wood-veneer cabinets take paint well, as do metal ones; cabinets and faceframes covered with plastic laminate or thinner melamine plastic cannot be painted because paint will not bond properly to these surfaces.

There are three basic tools you can use to paint cabinetry: a brush, a roller, and a spray gun. Brushing paint on large surfaces will leave brush marks; sprayers are expensive and require an enclosure to contain overspray. Rolling is fast and inexpensive, and it works exceptionally well on large surfaces; a short (4- or 6-inch) foam roller is a good choice because it lets you cover the faceframes with a single stroke and quickly handle the wider doors. As for

paint, satin enamel is an excellent selection—it covers well and is easy to clean.

If you are installing new hinges and pulls, make simple drilling jigs that will allow you to position the hardware accurately. A drilling jig is nothing more than a scrap of ½-inch plywood with holes drilled through it at screw-hole locations and strips of wood glued to two adjacent sides to hold the jig in position (see step 5 on the facing page).

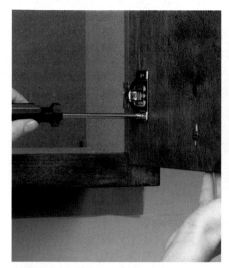

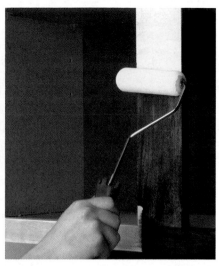

1 Remove all hardware—including screws, hinges, knobs, and pulls—and set aside whichever ones you will be reusing. Empty the drawers, and pull them out. (Although you can try to paint your cabinetry with the doors and drawers in place, it is a lot easier to remove them.) Number the doors, drawers, and hardware to make it easy to replace them when you are done painting.

2 Thoroughly clean all surfaces with trisodium phosphate (TSP). Rinse the surfaces completely with fresh water, and allow them to dry. If you will be installing new hardware, fill all the mounting holes with putty, and allow them to dry. Next, sand all surfaces with 150-grit open-coat sandpaper, and vacuum to remove any dust and sanding grit.

3 Mask off all adjacent surfaces, and position drop cloths to protect countertops and flooring. Begin by painting the faceframes, and then turn your attention to the doors and drawers.

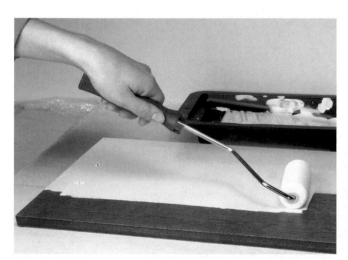

4 Paint the insides of the doors. While the doors dry, paint the drawer fronts. Then paint the fronts of the doors. Depending on the paint you are using, you may or may not need additional coats. If you do need additional coats, allow the first coat to dry overnight, and then sand all surfaces with 220-grit wet/dry sandpaper. Vacuum thoroughly, and apply the next coat.

5 Install the drawers and attach the doors once the painted surfaces are dry. Carefully lay out and drill holes through a jig at the desired hardware location. Position the jig on each door with the strips butted firmly against the door's bottom and side, and drill through the holes in the jig into and through the door. Finally, install the pulls.

LOWE'S QUICK TIP
Often overlooked, the catches that hold your cabinet doors closed will most likely be worn out and will need to be replaced. Magnetic catches are a good choice because they will not wear out.

decorative painting

DECORATIVE FINISHES, FREQUENTLY CALLED FAUX OR FALSE FINISHES, OFTEN FOOL you into thinking that you are looking at wood, marble, or stone. In a larger sense, decorative painting is simply a means to create a colorful, eye-catching finish with depth and vitality. Before undertaking your choice of decorative technique, organize the room, prepare the surfaces, and follow basic painting guidelines as you would for any interior painting project (see pages 42–45).

choosing a technique

Most decorative painting techniques use tinted washes and glazes to achieve textural layers of color. A wash is just latex paint that has been watered down, and a glaze is translucent oil-base or acrylic color that has been thinned.

Techniques fall into two categories: applicative and subtractive. Applicative techniques—sponging, ragging, and colorwashing—involve applying color with the

New walls take on the look of Old World plaster with a buff glaze colorwashed over a lighter buff paint.

appropriate tool, gradually building up layers until the desired effect is achieved. Subtractive techniques—dragging, marbling, and wood graining—first entail applying color and then removing some of it to get the desired effect. In both cases, the background color, or base coat, is intended to be partly visible.

To give walls added dimension and warmth, try colorwashing. To create an abstract pattern, consider sponging or

ragging. If you would like to tie together several decorative elements of a room, a floor-to-ceiling stencil copied from a design on the curtains or rug may be the answer. Marbling is an obvious choice to lend richness and elegance to a fireplace mantel and surround.

Some techniques, such as dragging, look best on a smooth surface because they make flaws more noticeable. Sponging and ragging are the techniques most appropriate for bumpy, irregular walls because these methods serve to camouflage imperfections.

If you do not have much painting experience, try one of the easier techniques, such as sponging, ragging, colorwashing, or stenciling with a precut pattern. More difficult techniques such as sponging off, ragging off, and dragging require a little practice. Marbling and wood graining are the most challenging and may be best left to a professional. Before you take on any of these, do a test on a white piece of cardboard or an area of wall that you

don't mind repainting to see if the colors you have chosen are appealing.

Be aware that if you work with fast-drying latex washes, the edges of the paint will dry quickly, creating lap marks; mixing some commercial glaze into the recipe will lengthen the drying time. Working with a partner also helps. One can apply the base coat while the other does the technique work.

base coat

Examine the base coat on your walls carefully before beginning. If the existing paint is in good shape and the color is compatible with the finish you want, you will not need to repaint. But if the walls are dingy, damaged, or the wrong color, you will need to apply a new base coat.

The water-base mediums—latex washes and acrylic glazes—adhere best to latex base coats with an eggshell, satin, or semigloss finish. They do not stick well to a gloss finish, even if it has been deglossed. Oil glazes adhere well to an eggshell, satin, or semigloss latex or alkyd base. You can even use oil glazes over a high-gloss finish if you sand the surface first. When using applicative techniques, an eggshell base coat is recommended; when using subtractive techniques, a semigloss base coat is best.

transparent coatings

A clear coating protects the painted surface, makes it washable, and can give it a glossy finish. To cover the project with a clear coating, use a nonyellowing water-base product that can be applied over any finish. Most of these coatings are classified as waterborne liquid plastics, varnishes, or urethanes and are available in satin, semigloss, and gloss. Apply these products with a brush because a roller will create air bubbles.

LEFT: Lime wash softens color with a white over-layer. (See page 63 for application methods.)

A red-orange glaze over a brown base gives warm, rich texture to a sitting room.

L'INSTANT TAITTINGER

sponging

SPONGING IS A VERSATILE DECORATIVE PAINTING TECHNIQUE THAT PRODUCES A great variety of effects, depending on the colors you choose and your method of application. Sponging on several colors of glaze can result in a finish with great depth, and sponging off a single glaze color can yield a subtle, dappled look.

Natural sponges were once living creatures with their own shapes, so each sponge imparts its own unique characteristics to the wall. Working with two or three different sponges will avoid a repetitive pattern.

Color choice is one key to success. With the sponge-on technique, imperfections are eye-catching, so it takes a bit of skill to apply contrasting hues attractively. The last color you apply will be the most dominant. An easier approach for a novice is to choose the base coat and glaze from the same color family. With sponging off, on the other hand, the color values of the base coat and glaze must be very different or the effect may not be noticeable at all.

SPONGING ON

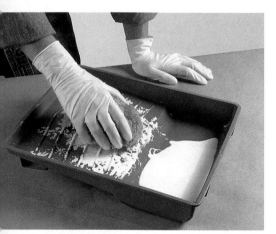

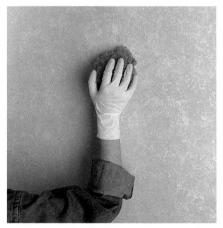

1 Apply the base coat, and let it dry. Tape off any adjacent surfaces you do not wish to paint. Pour some glaze into a paint tray. Dip a sponge into the mixture, and squeeze out any excess glaze. The sponge should be loaded but not clogged. Blot the sponge on the tray, and test it on paper until you can get a neat pattern without smears or blobs.

2 Lightly pounce the surface of a 3-foot-square area with the sponge, rotating the sponge each time you lift it. Space the dabs approximately 3 inches apart in a random pattern. Reload the sponge whenever the impressions begin to lighten. Fill in spaces until the surface is evenly covered; you should not be able to see where one impression stops and another begins. Leave the leading edge of each section irregular so you can blend the sections together smoothly. Repeat this technique section by section until the wall is covered. You can handle corners and edges as you go or wait until the end.

3 Look for gaps and uneven areas once you have completed all the sections. Fill in the gaps and blend in any uneven areas with a sponge that is just barely dampened with glaze. Pounce the areas lightly, and avoid overlapping covered areas.

LOWE'S QUICK TIP
To paint corners and edges, dab a 3-inch piece of sponge loaded with paint into and along these areas.

sponging off

Sponging off—like sponging on—involves the manipulation of a paint-and-glaze mixture using a natural sea sponge. The difference is that the texturing is done by removing the mixture rather than by applying it. Because the mixture is diluted with water, the finished effect of sponging off tends to be subtler than that of sponging on.

Sponging off registers the soft imprints of the sponge. A completed surface appears pebbly and dappled—similar to textured plaster or a sandy beach. Experimenting with contrasting colors can be risky but also can result in surprising and dramatic effects. Sticking to colors from the same family ensures easier-to-live-with effects.

1 Complete the base coat, and allow it to dry for the recommended time: two days for latex paint; two to three days for alkyd paint. Tape off adjacent ceiling, woodwork, and wall surfaces that you do not wish to paint. Combine equal parts of paint, glaze, and water—32 ounces (2 pints) for an average-size room (10 feet by 12 feet)—and pour the mixture into a paint tray. Working top to bottom from one end of the surface to the other, apply the mixture to a 3-foot-square section. Cut in along the edges with a 2-inch paintbrush, and then fill in the area with a 4-inch paint roller, making crisscross passes to avoid creating noticeable edges that would be difficult to blend together.

2 Dip the sponge into a bucket of cold water, and then squeeze it dry. Pounce the surface lightly at varying angles. Leave large spaces between pounces at the outset when the sponge is fresh. Feather edges and even out effect intensities as the sponge becomes saturated with the mixture. The more pouncing you do, the lighter the effect will be. Rinse the sponge and squeeze it dry when it no longer lifts off the mixture—do this two or three times per section. Roll a new section 6 to 12 inches larger or smaller than the first (so the edges of the sections will not be noticeable), and then pounce the new area with the sponge. Continue in this manner.

3 Treat the edges and corners along woodwork and the ceiling as you go or at the end of the project. Tear off a piece of sponge about 3 inches in diameter, and pounce as much as possible along the bottom edge or into the corner. Tear off a smaller piece to pounce spots not reached with the larger piece. Keep the pieces at a uniform dampness to maintain the consistency of the effect.

dragging

DRAGGING GIVES THE IMPRESSION OF AN ELEGANTLY WOVEN FABRIC SUCH AS linen or silk—at a fraction of the cost. The technique has its origins in the 18th century and still imparts classical elegance when paired with traditional mouldings. To create the desired effect, drag a brush straight down through wet glaze to create fine striations. This requires a steady hand, speed, practice, and, ideally, at least one helper—you will get the best results when one person rolls on the glaze and the other drags the brush through it.

In dragging, it is most common to use either base coat and glaze colors with similar tonal qualities or a dark color over a light base. Highly contrasting base and glaze colors, however, can be very striking.

To begin, apply the base coat, and let it dry completely. Tape off any adjacent surfaces that you do not wish to paint. Tape lightweight plumb bobs to the ceiling at 2-foot intervals a few inches in front of the wall you will be painting. Pour some glaze into a paint tray.

Using a foam brush, cut the glaze into the corner where you will begin; also cut in 18 inches along the top and bottom of the wall. Load a roller with glaze, and apply two roller widths of glaze from top to bottom, reloading the roller as often as is needed.

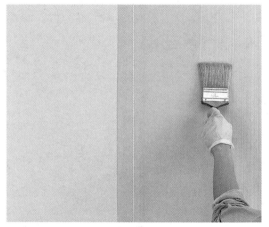

1 Place the tip of a paintbrush on the wall just below the ceiling and against the corner. (The tape on the adjacent wall will allow you to drag right into the corner.) Pressing the body of the brush toward the wall, drag the brush down to the baseboard in one continuous stroke. Use the plumb bobs as guides to keep your lines as straight as possible. Wipe the brush on a rag as you work; when the rag no longer cleans the glaze off the brush, switch to a second brush. Drag a second band adjacent and parallel to the first. Continue to drag the rest of the applied glaze, leaving a 2-inch-wide wet edge. Re-drag the same area, removing as much glaze as needed to create a fine striated pattern.

2 Cut in another 18-inch section along the top and bottom of the wall adjacent to the first section. Apply two roller widths of glaze from top to bottom. Drag the wet glaze, starting with the wet edge of the previous section, as described in Step 3. Repeat the process until the wall is complete. Remove the masking tape, and allow the finish to dry.

LOWE'S QUICK TIP
To create the look of linen, apply a second layer of glaze after the first one has dried and drag it perpendicular to the vertical striations.

colorwashing

COLORWASHING CAN TRANSFORM an otherwise dull room into a lively, airy space. Walls are "washed" with a diluted paint-and-glaze mixture applied in broad crisscross strokes and then passed over with a dry brush. The sweeping texture that results is reminiscent of rustic plaster—it is helpful in disguising small imperfections in a wall—and makes an interesting contrast to painted woodwork.

Color psychology is especially effective with this technique. Pale blues can create the effect of a cool underwater world, and yellows can give a room with little natural light a sunny disposition.

The rich brown tones chosen for this project create a mood of warm intimacy—ideal for a dining room. Colorwash colors are usually kept to the same family, with the glaze a darker shade of the base color; light tones over dark ones tend to look chalky and make the brush strokes obvious.

Start by completing the base coat, and allow it to dry for the recommended time: two days for latex paint; two to three days for alkyd paint. Tape off adjacent ceiling, woodwork, and wall surfaces that you do not wish to paint. Prepare a mixture that is equal parts paint and glaze and two-thirds water—32 ounces (2 pints) for an average-size room (10 feet by 12 feet)—and pour some of the mixture into a paint tray.

1 Apply the mixture with a 4-inch paintbrush to a 3-foot-square section, working top to bottom from one end of the surface to the other. Holding the brush by the base, make sweeping crisscross strokes, moving your wrist to vary the angle. Cover no more than half of the section, and leave large spaces between series of strokes while the brush is fully loaded. Work along the edges and into the corners only when the brush has been partially discharged of mixture.

2 Fill in spaces, and even out effect intensities as the brush becomes less saturated. Continue blending in with the discharged brush, feathering the edges of the strokes.

3 Reload the paintbrush, and begin the next 3-foot-square section at the center, working back to the first section without overlapping the edges. Blend in the section, and then continue in the same way. Vary the starting point of sections both vertically and horizontally to avoid noticeable demarcations.

4 Blend in sections by brushing the spaces between strokes with a partially loaded brush. If you brush directly over previous strokes, you risk intensifying the effect and leaving noticeable demarcations. Continue blending in with the discharged brush, feathering the edges of the strokes.

ragging

SUBTLER THAN SPONGING, RAGGING USES A PAPER TOWEL, RAG, OR PLASTIC SHEET to create a refined finish similar to crushed velvet or soft suede. You can "rag on" using the same technique described on page 60 for sponging on; "rag off," the traditional method shown here; or "rag roll" with a rolled-up cloth (see the facing page).

The results will vary depending on the colors you use, the amount of glaze you remove, and the shape and texture of the material you use to do the ragging. When you rag with plastic, it leaves a bolder texture than ragging with paper or cloth. Rag rolling is much crisper, with a more identifiable pattern.

Whichever material you use, start by applying the base coat and allowing it to dry completely. Tape off any adjacent sur-faces that you do not wish to paint, and pour some glaze into a paint tray.

Using a foam brush, cut the glaze into the corner where you will begin; also cut in for 18 inches along the top and bottom of the wall. Load a roller with glaze, and roll two roller widths of glaze from top to bottom, reloading as needed.

Then follow the techniques below for either ragging off with a paper towel or ragging off with plastic.

RAGGING WITH A PAPER TOWEL

Pounce a paper-towel rag on the wet glaze using quick movements of your wrist (begin in the corner, and work from top to bottom). Bunch the rag as necessary so that it fits into the ceiling and vertical corners. Working in an area approximately 2 feet deep, space the dabs 3 to 6 inches apart; do not work onto the outside edge of the glaze. Continue to dab until you have touched all the open spaces. Vary the pattern by rotating and rearranging the rag. When the rag becomes saturated, switch to a fresh one. After you complete one section, repeat the process, ragging beneath each previously worked area until you reach the baseboard.

RAGGING WITH A PLASTIC SHEET

Beginning at the ceiling, place a piece of plastic over the glaze as close to the corners and edges as you can. Press down lightly in random areas and peel the plastic off. Reposition the plastic below the area just pressed, and repeat. When the plastic becomes saturated, discard it and use a new square. You can reposition the plastic over the same area and then press again to even out the effect. If nec-essary, bunch the plastic to fit into the ceiling and vertical corners.

LOWE'S QUICK TIP
Try ragging with leather scraps, chamois, burlap, or bubble wrap; each material will leave its own unique imprint.

RAG ROLLING

1 Apply the base coat, and let it dry completely. Tape off any adjacent surfaces that you do not wish to paint.

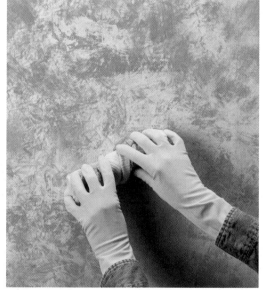

2 Fold a 2-foot-square cotton rag in half and twist it lengthwise. Place it at the top of the wall, aligning one end with the corner. Using your fingertips, roll the rag down the wall, working toward to the baseboard. When the rag stops removing glaze, twist it again to reveal a clean area. When it becomes saturated, switch to a clean rag. Use the end of the cylinder to roll any missed areas in the corners or along edges.

3 Cut in another 18-inch section along the ceiling and baseboard, adjacent to the completed section, with a foam brush. Roll two roller widths of glaze from top to bottom, reloading as needed. Roll your rag from ceiling to floor through the glaze, overlapping the previously rolled section. Repeat this process until all the walls are completed. Remove the masking tape, and allow the finish to dry.

LOWE'S QUICK TIP
Try rolling diagonally instead of vertically to create a fantasy marble effect. Or change hand angles and positions frequently if you want more variety in the pattern.

PAINT

painting with precut stencils

PRECUT STENCILS ARE AVAILABLE IN MYRIAD PATTERNS TO SUIT EVERY ARCHITEC-
tural style—traditional, contemporary, sophisticated, and whimsical. Although some
stencils can be applied wherever you choose—on a cabinet door, on the back of a chair,
or all over the wall—others are designed to create a border. A single-color motif is easiest to apply because there is only one stencil. For a motif using different colors for each
stencil, you must carefully superimpose each stencil over the portion of the design you
have already created after the paint has dried.

If you do not see a design you want to repeat around your room, consider combining
several different ones. Changing colors can transform a simple stencil into one with
unexpected visual appeal. For instance, you can use a stencil of a single rose but alter-
nate pink, yellow, and peach as you work across the wall.

This project involves a two-color motif
with two stencils. When working with
more than one stencil, you use registration marks to position the second (and
any following) stencil precisely. A registration mark may be a small circle or
crossed lines cut in the corners of the
stencil sheets; you apply paint in these
cutouts to make a mark on the wall. Or a
stencil may have a cutout of one element
of the design you have already painted;
you superimpose the new stencil over the
dry paint. If you do not want visible registration marks on the wall, place small
pieces of masking tape on the wall where
the registration marks will hit. Remove
the tape after stenciling.

You can simplify the project by using a
single color—or make the project more
complex by adding a third color freehand
after your stenciling has dried.

**This two-color stencil along
the top of a bathroom wall
is accompanied by stamped
sea creatures in the same
light green and blue.**

66 LOWE'S COMPLETE HOME IMPROVEMENT & REPAIR

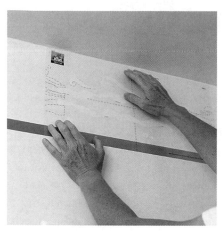

1 Mark points for the bottom of the stenciled border using a carpenter's level. Press masking tape along the line. Use a hobby knife to clear away parts of the stencil pattern that are not cut out completely. Pick a starting point, and plan the stencil spacing. Especially with stencils that do not bend, try to have the design end before the corners; acetate stencils can work around corners (see Step 4). Spray adhesive on the back of the stencil, adjusting the tip so the spray covers the width of the stencil; let the adhesive set until it is tacky. Line up the stencil's lower edge with the tape guideline, and press it into position.

2 Pour the first color into a container. If your stencil does not indicate color, write the name of the shade on a masking-tape label on the side of the stencil that will face you when you paint. Using a circular motion, swirl a stencil brush in the paint. Rub the bristles over a paper towel until the brush is almost dry. Working from the outside of the stencil in, lightly pounce the brush into each cutout. Avoid brushing sideways to keep paint from getting under the stencil. Vary the angle of the brush to achieve texture; let some of the wall color show through. Make the paint as translucent, opaque, or varied as you like.

3 Remove the stencil carefully. Reposition it along the tape guideline, aligning its registration marks with those on the section you have just painted. Apply paint to the cutouts, reposition the stencil, and continue across the wall, cleaning the stencil with a rag or sponge and reapplying adhesive as needed. Complete the full length of the border with the first stencil before working with the second.

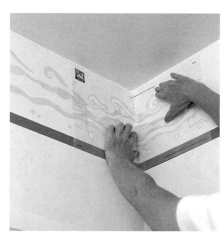

4 To turn a corner with an acetate stencil, match the stencil's registration marks with the pattern you have already painted, and stick that side of the stencil in place. Then gently press the stencil into the corner, bending but not creasing it, and stick the other side in place. Apply paint to the cutouts, working as far into the corner as possible.

5 Pour the second color into a container when you have finished applying the first color and the paint is completely dry. Position the second stencil at the starting point, matching up the registration marks. Repeat Steps 2 through 4, using a clean stencil brush.

6 Correct errors and fill in gaps after completing the entire border. Most stencils have bridges that hold the pattern together; you should fill in the gaps they leave. Use an artist's brush to fill in any gaps or missed cutouts. Work with an almost-dry brush, and pounce the surface lightly.

exterior paint preparation

WHEN PAINTING YOUR HOME'S EXTERIOR WALLS, PREPARATION IS CRITICAL TO a successful and lasting job. In many cases, simply washing the surface to be painted is not enough. Paint that has begun to fail usually must be completely removed to ensure that the new coat will adhere properly. While this is a significant job, the reward is a great-looking, durable finish. Begin by washing the siding (see Step 1 on facing page).

scraping

To scrape small areas of peeling paint, a paint scraper, putty knife, or moulding scraper is sufficient. Use these tools, too, where a sander is needed to remove an entire finish; you will need to scrape areas that the sanding wheel cannot reach, such as corners and other tight spots.

To be sure you loosen as much paint as possible, scrape areas of loose paint from every direction; sometimes old paint that's scraped from left to right seems solid but comes off easily when scraped from the opposite direction. Place two hands on the scraper, and keep it flat to avoid gouging the wood. If you do happen to create gouge marks, sand them down or fill them with a vinyl exterior spackling compound so they will not show through the new paint job. If the paint that remains after scraping has high or rough edges, sand, or "feather," them with coarse sandpaper to make them less noticeable.

power sanding

Power sanders can be used to smooth the edges of scraped areas or to clear an entire surface of paint. For big jobs, a commercial grade 7-inch sander works best. You can buy one or rent one from an equipment rental company.

Sanding is accomplished in two stages: First the paint cover is completely removed with coarse sandpaper—60-grit paper is recommended. This will leave cuts in the wood, so you must smooth the area with medium sandpaper (100-grit).

Sanding is a meticulous process that requires the following precautions:

- Make sure that the sander is running at full speed before touching the wheel to the surface.

- As you bring the sander into contact with the wall, lean on the tool slightly until you hear the motor slow, and keep moving it along the surface so you do not gouge the wood.

- Keep the sanding wheel at a slight angle (5 to 10 degrees) to the wall; otherwise, the wheel will spin out of control across the surface.

- Discard sanding disks as they become clogged with paint; otherwise they will begin to burn the surface.

- Do not use a power sander in the rain.

LOWE'S SAFETY TIP

When using a power sander, protect yourself from flying paint chips, dust, and noise with safety glasses, a dust mask, and ear protectors.

PAINT REMOVAL ALTERNATIVES

Although scraping and sanding are the most commonly used methods for preparing a surface for a new paint job, other options make more sense in certain circumstances.

Liquid paint remover Ornate woodwork can be damaged by scraping and sanding. Liquid paint remover breaks down the bond between the paint and the surface, causing the paint to bubble and soften and allowing it to be removed from the surface with a putty knife or paint scraper. Liquid paint removers are caustic, so use them only in the open air, and always wear protective gloves and safety goggles.

Heat guns To remove especially tenacious areas of paint, a heat gun is an option (see page 35). Heat guns, though, can be dangerous because they function at extremely high temperatures and can easily ignite any surrounding flammable material. Wear protective gloves, and hold the tool several inches from the surface. As the paint begins to bubble, turn off the heat gun and scrape off the paint with a putty knife or paint scraper.

PREPARING SIDING FOR PAINT

1 Begin by hosing down the siding, and then scrub it with a stiff-bristle brush mounted on a broomstick type of pole. Clean the area with a solution of water and trisodium phosphate (TSP) or a nonphosphate substitute, following label directions. Because this solution is caustic, do not use it on bare wood, and wear rubber gloves and safety goggles.

2 Scrape loose paint, and, if necessary, use a power sander to remove large areas of paint or to smooth any roughly scraped surfaces. When using a sander, work in 3-foot sections at a time. Move horizontally across the top of a board, then in a wave-like pattern across the middle, and finally, along the underside of the lip.

3 Fill any holes or deep gouges, using a putty knife to apply vinyl exterior spackling compound. Note: Use a matching wood-toned filler if you intend to apply a semitransparent stain. Allow the spackling compound to dry.

4 Use a sanding block or a palm sander with 100-grit sandpaper to sand each patch until it is smooth. Finally, sweep away any residual dust or scrapings.

preparing trim

When it comes to damage from sun, rain, and wind, one of a house's most susceptible elements is its wood trim—and few things look shabbier on a home's exterior than cracking, peeling paint.

At the very least, preparation involves thoroughly cleaning, lightly sanding, and priming the surface. It may also require scraping, stripping, reglazing, wire brushing, filling, and caulking.

Start by scrubbing off all dirt and chalking paint with a scrub brush and a solution of trisodium phosphate (TSP). Rinse the trim thoroughly, and allow it to dry completely before preparing the surfaces for primer and final coats of paint.

Primer seals the surface and provides a base to which the paint can adhere. Slow-drying alkyd-base primers are your best bet. On partially bare wood, apply two coats of primer. To help the paint cover, have your primer tinted with some of the finish color.

Considering the relatively low-cost yet critical function of paint in protecting your house, it does not make sense to skimp on paint quality. When you buy good paint, not only will your paint job last longer, but the paint will also go on more smoothly. If you have prepared the surfaces carefully, as detailed in this section, an acrylic latex paint is your best choice for a topcoat. A good latex paint will actually hold its color and sheen longer than an alkyd-base paint. And the fact that latex paint is water-base means that cleanup is infinitely easier.

LOWE'S QUICK TIP
If you suspect that old paint may contain lead, have it tested before sanding or stripping it (see page 51 for more about lead in paint).

1 Disc-sand the fascia, graduating from rough- to fine-grit paper. Wear safety goggles and a dust mask.

2 Blister the paint with a heat gun, and then peel it away with a putty knife. Keep a hose nearby for safety.

3 Tap out old window glazing compound that is cracked or brittle.

4 Power-sand the windowsills with a palm sander, graduating from rough- to fine-grit paper.

5 Fill cracks and holes with a vinyl exterior spackling compound, and sand the surface when it is dry.

6 Spread new glazing compound along the window frames at an angle, and let it cure.

painting siding & trim

ONCE YOU HAVE MADE ALL THE NECESSARY REPAIRS AND PREPARED THE SURFACES, it's time to paint—almost. Before you begin any exterior project, you must protect the surrounding area with thick cotton drop cloths. Use 3-inch tape to mask roofing or other surfaces that will not be coated but may become splattered with paint. Carry a scraper with you in case you come across small areas of loose paint that you missed during surface preparation. When everything is ready, use the techniques shown on the following two pages to paint.

Paint in fair (above 50-degree), dry weather; cooler temperatures mean poor adherence. Apply paint after the morning dew dries, and stop at least 2 hours before the evening dampness arrives. Avoid painting in direct sunlight; if possible, follow the sun around the house. Do not apply solvent-thinned paints to cool surfaces that will be heated by the sun in a few hours; this may cause the paint to blister.

For the best possible finish, paint the overhangs and gutters, then the main surfaces from the top down, and then the trim. Finish with the shutters, railings, porch, and foundation.

Most people paint the trim a different color than the siding. If that is your plan, wait until the siding has completely dried before beginning the trim. Then apply masking tape to protect the siding from the trim paint, and remove the tape immediately after finishing.

Paint exterior doors and windows using the sequence outlined for interior surfaces (see pages 52–55). Shutters are easier to paint if you remove them and use a power sprayer (see page 39). If you decide to paint shutters with a brush, begin with the joints where the louvers meet the frame, then paint the louvers, and finally paint the frame. Paint against the grain, and finish by painting with the grain.

Let a wall dry fully before deciding whether touchups are needed. A paint finish often will look patchy or uneven until it has fully dried.

A successful paint job requires excellent preparation, planning, and attention to detail.

PAINTING SIDING & TRIM

1 For best results, first brush on a coat of primer—this is a must for any bare wood. By tinting the primer to a color that is similar to your finish color, you will ensure better results with the finish.

2 Beginning at the top of a wall, apply the finish coat with a high-quality paintbrush (see page 34). Dip the brush no more than 1 inch into the paint. When painting lap siding, start by painting along the bottom edges of horizontal boards. To prevent drips and lap marks, paint all the way across three or four boards.

3 Dip the brush about 2 inches into the paint, and tap it against the side of the bucket to clear paint from one side. Then turn the brush parallel to the ground as you lift it. Quickly press the paint-heavy side of the brush against the surface, spreading the paint in a side-to-side motion on horizontal siding or up and down on vertical siding.

4 When painting windows, draw a lightly loaded tapered sash brush along mullions, allowing a slight bead of paint to lap onto the glass. Before the paint dries, remove it from the glass with a rag wrapped around the end of a putty knife. Holding it at an angle, pull it along the joint between the frame and glass. You can remove dry paint with a razor blade.

5 To ensure good coverage on the face of the trim, begin applying the paint by brushing perpendicular to the direction of the wood grain. When painting the sash of an operable window, open it so that it won't be sealed shut by paint. (For information on freeing a stuck sash, see page 225.)

6 When painting trim that abuts siding, mask the siding with painter's tape. First, paint perpendicular to the wood grain to work paint in. Then, to smooth out the paint and create an even cover, finish painting by brushing in line with the grain. Turn the brush diagonally to the trim if it is wider than the trim. Alternatively, you can apply paint with a short trim roller and then work it in with a brush, painting in line with the grain.

EXTERIOR STAINING

Exterior stain—whether for siding, trim, or a deck—requires no primer and is easier to apply than paint. Stain can be applied to new wood, wood sanded clear of paint, and surfaces previously stained.

A disadvantage of stain is that it fades more quickly than paint and so requires more frequent re-coating. But if you apply two or more coats at one application, you can extend the life of the finish considerably. Another downside is that lap marks are more difficult to eliminate because stain dries more quickly than paint. You can minimize them by applying a second coat, but this may darken the finish, so be sure to test it out first.

As you work, be sure to mix the stain at regular intervals because the pigment settles quite quickly.

cleaning up

AFTER YOU FINISH A PAINTING PROJECT, IT MAY BE TEMPTING TO THROW YOUR tools and materials aside and go take a nap. But the job is not complete until you clean up the work area and equipment, store your tools and paint, and dispose of rags and other waste appropriately.

Cleaning your tools and work area not only keeps your equipment in top shape but also protects the environment from potential safety hazards. It is also much easier to clean up before paint dries.

If you plan to return to the project shortly, you can keep wet brushes and rollers wrapped tightly in plastic bags for several days. Put those tools used with alkyd paint in the freezer and those used with latex paint in the refrigerator.

You can easily wash latex paint off tools with soap and water. Use paint thinner to clean tools used with alkyd paint, and protect your hands by wearing rubber gloves. Because you cannot pour thinner down the drain, it is best to save used thinner in an old paint can, or any other container that will not be dissolved by the chemicals in the thinner, until you accumulate enough to dispose of it properly. Do not pour used thinner back into the original container. Thinner can be reused several times before it develops an unpleasant odor and is no longer effective.

cleaning brushes

Remove excess paint from brushes before washing them instead of letting paint go down the drain. First, brush the paint out on cardboard. Put the paintbrush between sheets of newspaper, and press down as you pull out the brush; or use a special brush comb.

To clean remaining latex paint from a synthetic brush, hold the brush under running water until the water runs clear. Wash the brush with detergent and lukewarm water, forcing water into the bristles and the end of the ferrule. Rinse well.

To clean remaining alkyd paint from a brush, work paint thinner into the bristles, and then use a wire comb or brush to remove more paint. Once the paintbrush is clean, remove excess thinner by blotting the brush with paper towels, shaking the brush vigorously, lightly tapping the handle against a hard edge, or using a brush spinner designed to expel liquid from brushes. Wash the brush with warm water and bar soap; blot again. Clean up thinner with

RIGHT: **Use paint thinner to clean alkyd paint from a brush, and then blot the brush with paper towels. FAR RIGHT: A bristle comb is especially effective for removing paint from the bristles at the ferrule.**

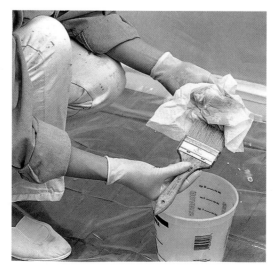

rags or paper towels, and be sure to dispose of them properly.

After cleaning any brush, straighten the bristles with a bristle comb.

cleaning rollers & pad applicators

You may find it easier to dispose of roller covers and pads than to clean them, especially because they are inexpensive. Those with cardboard tubes will not survive the cleaning anyway. (Be sure to dispose of all rollers, applicators, and pads safely and according to local ordinances.) If you want to reuse covers or pads, squeeze out paint by pressing the roller or applicator against the bucket lip or the roller tray, or use a curved painter's tool to scrape the cover or pad dry. Scrape off any caked-on paint with a putty knife. Then remove the cover or pad.

Both covers and pads can be washed in the same way as brushes, using detergent and warm water for latex paint and paint thinner for alkyd paints. Once covers and pads are clean, squeeze out any excess liquid, and blot them lightly with a clean, absorbent cloth. Let the nap or pad dry completely. Wash the frames separately in the appropriate liquid.

cleaning yourself

Wet or dry latex paint readily washes off skin. Latex that has dried, however, does not wash off clothing, so be sure to launder clothes promptly.

To remove alkyd paint, use a mechanic's hand cleaner, which is easier on your skin than paint thinner but just as effective. Use the hand cleaner, not thinner, on fresh alkyd paint on clothing, and then launder the items immediately.

storing brushes & paint

Once your paintbrushes are dry, wrap them in their original covers or in stiff paper. Store the brushes flat or hang them by their handles to maintain the proper bristle shape. Clean roller covers and applicator pads can be stored in plastic

Scrape excess paint off a roller with a curved painter's tool.

bags. Place roller covers on end to allow any water or paint thinner to drain and to prevent the nap from being flattened.

Leftover paint and thinner need to be stored safely. Most paint can be stored in a tightly closed can for several months or more without losing any properties. If less than a quarter of the paint remains in the can, transfer it to a smaller container, where it is less likely to dry out. Before closing the lid, use a paper towel to clean out any paint from the groove. With a paper towel or rag over the lid, firmly hammer it on—without a tight seal, air can pass into the can and cause a skin to form on top of the paint. Even with a tight seal, alkyd paint may still form a film, so place a piece of wax paper directly on top of the paint before you seal the can. Make sure you have labeled each can with the date, type of paint, color, and room where you used it.

Paint should never be stored outdoors or in an uninsulated shed or garage where temperatures go below freezing or above 100 degrees. Cold can cause paint to become lumpy and separate, and extreme heat can cause paint to combust. Store paint thinner and flammable paints in a metal cabinet. Keep all paint products away from children, pets, and sources of flame or heat.

LOWE'S QUICK TIP
When storing paint, place a dot of the paint on the container lid so you can see the color of the contents at a glance.

wallpaper

IF YOU THINK OF WALLPAPER AS CLOTHING FOR YOUR WALLS, YOU WILL BEGIN to get a sense of the possibilities that this versatile decorating material offers. Whatever pattern, color, texture, and period or style you can imagine can be found in wallpaper, in prices ranging from downright cheap to sky's-the-limit expensive. Wallpaper's array of options, including coordinating accent borders and high-quality period reproductions, can be daunting if you are new to the world of decorating. However, you will soon find yourself excited by the sheer variety and multiplicity of effects that are wallpaper's strengths.

Wallpaper originally was created to duplicate the look of hand-painted wall and ceiling treatments at a fraction of the price for a middle-class clientele eager for a touch of luxury. Early wallpapering required the services of skilled paperhangers who had to work quickly and surely to perfect a wall. Happily, most wallpapers today are easier and more forgiving to install—although you still may want to enlist a professional for exceptionally difficult spaces or ultra-expensive papers.

In the following pages, you will learn about calculating amounts and buying wallpaper; preparing surfaces; measuring, marking, cutting, and hanging paper; and such specialized jobs as adding a wallpaper border, wallpapering below a chair rail, and even covering switch plates.

Study the techniques offered explained here, collect some swatches, and be creative!

buying wallpaper

WALLPAPER STORES AND HOME CENTERS HAVE DOZENS OF SAMPLE BOOKS WITH hundreds of colors, patterns, and textures. Before you choose a wallcovering, know where you will hang it and the effect you want to achieve. If possible, take along samples of your upholstery fabric and carpet, as well as a list of textures and colors that are prominent in the room to be papered. Bring along a photo and a scale drawing of the room to help you visualize different wallpapers in the space. Then, before you buy, bring home samples to see how they look in the room—by day and night.

Don't necessarily think in terms of papering an entire room. Perhaps you can get the look you want by papering just one wall or the ceiling. You may decide to use two coordinating papers (if they are both hung on one wall, the darker pattern should be on the bottom) separated by a border. At the ceiling line, a border can accentuate a crown moulding or compensate for the lack of one; chair-rail borders lend a traditional feel to a room.

choosing materials

A wallcovering's material content determines its durability; cost; and ease of installation, cleaning, and removal. Before purchasing any wallpaper, ask about these qualities as well as about guarantees.

The floral border at the top of this Victorian-style wallpaper creates the effect of an elegant crown moulding.

LEFT: The use of two different yet complementary patterns creates the illusion of a room within a room.

vinyl

The most popular wallcoverings are made of a continuous, flexible vinyl film applied to a backing. They are durable and easy to maintain. Backings may be fabric or paper. Fabric-backed vinyl, the sturdier, is washable (often able to be scrubbed), moisture-resistant, and usually strippable (able to be removed from the wall by hand without leaving any residue). Fabric-backed vinyl usually comes unpasted, without any adhesive.

Paper-backed vinyl often comes pre-pasted, so only water is needed to adhere it to the wall. Expanded vinyl, a paper-backed type, produces a three-dimensional effect on the wall and is is also especially well suited to walls that are not perfectly smooth. It frequently comes in styles that mimic the look of such surfaces as rough plaster, granite, textured paint, leather or grass cloth.

Vinyl-coated paper has a vinyl layer so thin that it looks like paper. It lends a finished look to a wall but is best for light-use areas because it stains and tears more easily than papers that have a greater vinyl content.

textiles

These wallcoverings come in many colors and textures, in styles ranging from very casual to formally elegant. They are usually made of either natural fibers, such as cotton or linen, or of polyester bonded to a paper backing. A traditional favorite is grass cloth, which can be hung horizontally, vertically, or in a combination of the two. Hemp, which is similar to grass cloth but with thinner fibers, is easier to install.

hand-screened paper

This vivid, colorful paper is more expensive than most

A border lends a touch of whimsy and a feeling of intimacy to this corner.

solid paper Paper wallcoverings with no vinyl content tear easily and should only be considered for light-use areas.

foils & flocks Foils and flocks (paper resembling damask or cut velvet) can brighten up any small, dark space. They require an absolutely smooth wall surface and can wrinkle easily when applied.

estimating needs

Once you've chosen your wallpaper, be sure to order enough so you will not have to go back for more—you will be much more likely to get all of the rolls from the same lot with little color variance.

the repeat length You will need to determine the repeat length (the distance between one design element on a pattern and the next occurrence of that element) and whether it is a straight-match or drop-match pattern (see illustrations on the facing page). The repeat length is usually printed on the back of the wallpaper sample, but you can measure it, too.

Divide the calculated total square footage of the room (see facing page) by the usable yield of the wallpaper to get the number of rolls needed.

ABOVE: **Flocked papers add a rich, regal look to a room, but their application can be difficult.** RIGHT: **Vinyl wallcoverings are the most popular due to their durability and ease of maintenance.**

machine-printed wallpapers because each color is applied with a separate handmade and hand-placed silk screen. Some new machine-printed papers have the look of hand-screened ones but are less expensive. Hanging these types of papers can be tricky. Patterns may match less evenly than those of many other wallcoverings, and seams often need to be overlapped and then trimmed. Also, because water-soluble dyes are frequently used in the manufacture of such coverings, great care must be taken to ensure that the printed side is kept free of paste and water.

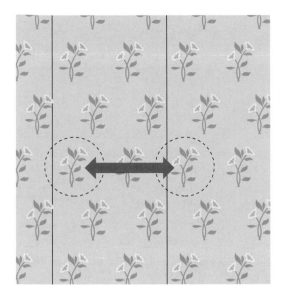

The following estimates will help you determine the wallpaper's usable yield. For a single roll, the usable yield for a repeat length of:

- 0 to 6 inches = 25 square feet

- 7 to 12 inches = 22 square feet

- 13 to 18 inches = 20 square feet

- 19 to 23 inches = 18 square feet

Wallpaper rolls are sold in doubles, so always keep this in mind when estimating.

wall measurements

To calculate the area to be covered, start by measuring the walls from floor to ceiling (excluding baseboards and mouldings). Take your measurements in feet, rounding off to the next highest half or full foot. Then measure the width of the walls, rounding to the next highest half or full foot. Multiply the height by the width to obtain the total square footage. Add 15 percent to this total for wastage. If the wall has several—or large—windows and doors, deduct their total square footage.

multiple papers & borders

When hanging different papers above and below a chair rail, use the same methods to figure out the square footage of the separate spaces. For borders, measure the lengths you will need, and then divide by 3 to get the number of yards—most border material is sold in 5-yard lengths. If you plan to border around doors or windows, add a little extra for mitering the corners (cutting them at 45-degree angles).

ESTIMATING WALLPAPER ROLLS

This chart will help you estimate the number of single rolls you will need for your walls (remember, wallpaper only comes in double rolls, so round up). A rule of thumb is to subtract one-half roll for each standard door or window opening. To allow for cutting and trimming, figure on 25 usable square feet for a single roll if the pattern repeat is less than 4 inches, 22 feet if the repeat is greater.

WALL'S WIDTH (FEET)	WALL'S HEIGHT (FEET)				
	8	9	10	11	12
6	3	3	3	4	5
8	3	4	4	5	6
10	5	5	5	6	7
12	5	5	5	7	8
14	5	5	7	7	8
16	7	7	8	8	9
18	7	8	8	8	10
20	8	8	9	10	11
22	9	9	10	11	12
24	9	9	10	12	13
26	10	10	12	13	14
28	10	12	13	14	16
30	10	12	13	15	16
32	12	13	14	16	18
34	13	14	15	16	18
36	14	14	16	18	20

BASIC TOOLS FOR HANGING WALLPAPER

Drywall taping knives

Natural sponge

Screwdriver

Smoothing brush

Safety goggles

Measuring tape

Water tray

Metal straightedge

Utility knife

Drop cloths

4" paintbrush

Sanding block

Wallpaper-scarifying tool

Wallpaper smoother

5-in-1 tool

Stepladder

Level

Plumb bob

Latex gloves

Roller tray

Putty knife

Seam roller

Wallpaper steamer

Paint roller

Heavy-duty scissors

wallpaper tools

BEFORE YOU START, GATHER TOGETHER THE TOOLS, EQUIPMENT, AND SUPPLIES you will need so everything will be on hand.

You will need a stepladder to reach the tops of the walls and a sander or sanding block and 50-grit sandpaper to smooth the walls. You will also need a bucket; sponges; and trisodium phosphate (TSP), ammonia, or household bleach to clean the walls and kill mildew (wear safety goggles and rubber gloves). In addition, you may need a primer/sealer if the walls are new.

Set up a pasting table—a long table, boards on sawhorses, or a table rented from your wallpaper dealer—and keep a large plastic bag handy for "booking," a technique used to keep pasted strips wet.

Walls, seams, and borders may each require a different adhesive. The type depends on the kind of paper, so check the manufacturer's recommendations. Pre-mixed adhesive is generally easier to work with than dry adhesive. Clay-base products hold to the wall better than cellulose or wheat-base paste, but they are messier and harder to handle. Mix dry paste with distilled water only.

If your wallcovering contains vinyl, buy a tube of vinyl-to-vinyl seam adhesive. To hang borders—even prepasted borders—over vinyl paper, you may need to use vinyl-to-vinyl adhesive in tub form that is formulated specifically for use on vinyl and not on paint.

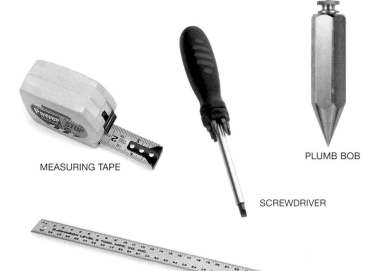

MEASURING TAPE

SCREWDRIVER

PLUMB BOB

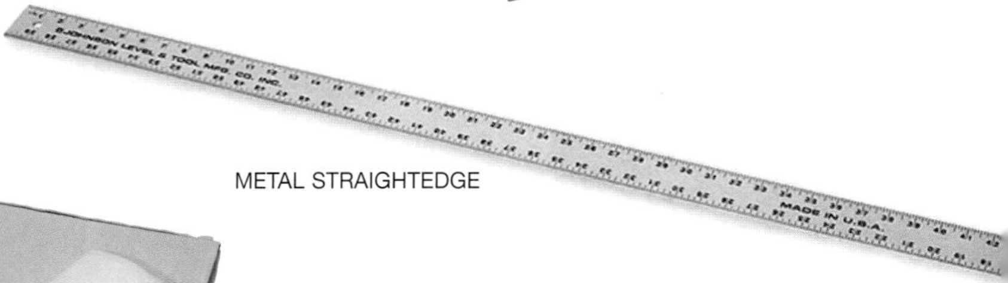

METAL STRAIGHTEDGE

HEAVY-DUTY SCISSORS

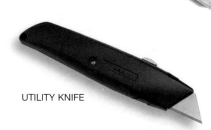

DROP CLOTHS

UTILITY KNIFE

LEVEL

LAYOUT & PREPARATION TOOLS

You will need a measuring tape and, depending on your project, a plumb bob or a long carpenter's level for aligning vertical lines. A short level is handy for use in small spaces and to check the straightness of the paper as you work. You will need a screwdriver for removing electrical covers and a drop cloth to protect the floor.

SANDING BLOCK
AND SANDPAPER

DRYWALL TAPING KNIVES

WALLPAPER REMOVAL TOOLS

To remove old wallpaper, you will need a drywall taping knife, sanding block or wallpaper-scarifying tool, steamer, or product for helping release the old wallpaper. An enzyme-based gel remover goes on with a roller; it is the least messy alternative.

WALLPAPER-SCARIFYING TOOL

WALLPAPER STEAMER

ROLLER TRAY

PASTING TOOLS

For pasting, use a short-napped paint roller with a roller tray (or a pasting brush with a bucket). For prepasted paper, you will need only a water tray.

SHORT-NAPPED PAINT ROLLER

WATER TRAY

WALLPAPER SMOOTHER

NATURAL SPONGE

SMOOTHING TOOLS

For smoothing, work with a wallpaper smoother, a rag, a sponge, and/or a high-quality smoothing brush. The tool you choose should allow you to apply pressure evenly yet feel whether the wallpaper is smooth or uneven. When working with textured or embossed paper, always use a smoothing brush. After paper has dried for about 15 minutes, smooth the wallcovering with a smoother or sponge; using a seam roller (on conventional wallpapers only) flattens seams and makes them unnoticeable.

SEAM ROLLER

SMOOTHING BRUSH

preparing a surface

THE FIRST STEP TOWARD A SUCCESSFUL WALLPAPERING JOB IS MAKING SURE YOUR walls are clean, smooth, and free of surface treatments that could cause adhesion problems. Proper wall preparation also will help make the process quick and easy.

preparing a papered wall

You can hang new wallpaper over old wallcovering under some conditions, but it is usually best to remove old paper first. Moisture from the pasting process can loosen the old paper, spoiling the smoothness of the new layer. And the ink from the old paper can bleed through new paper unless you seal the old wallcovering with a special primer sealer formulated to seal stains. Vinyl paper can also reject the adhesive used to apply new wallpaper.

Only consider applying new over old if the old is smooth, just one layer thick, and in good condition, and the new is a porous type. To prepare a papered surface to receive the new wallcovering, repaste and roll any loose seams, apply spackling compound, and sand all nicks, rough spots, or overlapping seams. Starting from the bottom, wash the wall with a solution of TSP (trisodium phosphate)—or a non-phosphate substitute—or ammonia and water, and then let it dry.

To see if your old paper will bleed ink through the new wallcovering, moisten a small piece of the old paper with a clean sponge. If ink comes off on the sponge, apply stain-sealing primer. If the existing paper is nonporous, use vinyl-to-vinyl primer to ensure proper drying of the adhesive and prevent mildew.

removing wallpaper

With strippable wallpaper, start at a seam and gently pull off both the vinyl coating and the backing. With paper that can be peeled, the top layer will peel off easily but will leave a thin residue of paper and adhesive. Remove this backing and adhesive

REMOVING OLD WALLPAPER

1 Score the old wallpaper. If your wallpaper has a vinyl or foil covering, abrade the surface so moisture or remover can penetrate and help break down the adhesive. Score the surface with coarse sandpaper or an inexpensive wallpaper-scarifying tool.

2 Loosen old adhesive. After perforating the paper, apply a liquid or gel enzyme-based remover, taking care to follow label directions. Alternatively, adhesive can be loosened with a steamer or a fine mist of hot water, but these methods are usually more painstaking.

3 Remove the paper. Working from the top of the wall down, remove all paper and adhesive using a broad knife or wide putty knife (be careful not to damage wallboard). If there are multiple layers of paper, remove one layer at a time, following Steps 1 and 2.

with a wet sponge or an enzyme-based wallpaper remover. If the paper resists stripping or peeling, proceed as shown on page 85.

Once you have removed the paper and adhesive, repair any wall damage (see page 43), and then wash the wall with a solution of TSP (or a nonphosphate substitute) or ammonia and water. When the wall is dry, apply primer sealer.

preparing other surfaces

Most surfaces are easier to prepare than previously papered walls, but any irregular surface needs special attention.

painted walls Scrape and sand painted walls until they are smooth, and then dust them off. Degloss the walls by using sandpaper or an extra-strong solution of TSP (or a nonphosphate substitute) or ammonia and water. Repair and wash the walls (see page 85). Once the surface is dry, apply primer sealer unless you know the paint is alkyd.

mildewed surfaces If you are not sure whether you have mildew stains, try to wash them with a solution of detergent and water. If this is ineffective, the stains are likely mildew. Wearing eye protection and rubber gloves, sponge on a solution of half bleach and half water and then a solution of TSP (or a nonphosphate substitute) and water, and rinse well. Let the surface dry completely—at least 24 hours. Then apply a coat of alkyd primer sealer mixed with a fungicide additive.

new plaster walls Before papering, you will have to wait until the new plaster has cured thoroughly—this can take between one and four months. Consult with your contractor for the recommended time. Neutralize the new plaster by washing it with vinegar, and then apply two coats of high-quality primer sealer.

new wallboard All wallboard joints should be taped, spackling compound

applied, sanded, and then dusted with a short-napped soft brush. Remove the last particles of dust with a damp sponge. Finally, apply primer sealer.

uneven surfaces Cinder block, concrete, wood paneling, textured plaster, and textured paint can be uneven surfaces that will have to be smoothed before any wallpaper can be applied.

For light to moderate unevenness or for a small area, apply nonshrinking spackle or wallboard taping compound. When the wall is completely dry, sand the area and apply primer sealer. You can also smooth such a surface by hanging liner paper, available where you buy wallpaper. If a surface is severely uneven, it should be plastered over.

priming & sizing

Primers and sizing are formulated to ease application and make wallpaper adhere well.

priming This compound keeps the wall surface from absorbing moisture from the adhesive and also protects the wall from damage if the covering is removed. Walls painted with a high-quality flat alkyd paint may not need a primer.

Choose a primer sealer designed as a wallcovering undercoat. Apply it with a roller at least 24 hours before hanging the wallcovering to allow it to dry thoroughly.

When you are hanging a light-hued paper over existing wallpaper or a colored wall, use pigmented primer sealer that matches the paper's background color.

sizing This liquid coating is unnecessary in most cases because of advanced technology in primer sealers. You may want to consider sizing if you are hanging a porous or heavy paper, if the wall is textured or alkyd-painted, or if the paper is not sticking well.

Apply sizing with a roller or brush. It dries quickly, so you can begin hanging the wallcovering immediately unless the manufacturer recommends otherwise.

basic wallpaper techniques

WITH PROPER PREPARATION AND THE RIGHT TOOLS, YOU CAN MASTER THE BASIC techniques of cutting, pasting, and hanging wallpaper. Always thoroughly review the manufacturer's instructions that come with your wallpaper, and try to work during daylight hours—you will match patterns better and see seams more clearly. When you are done working for the day, cover wet wallpaper rolls and tools with plastic. (If possible, put them in a refrigerator.)

The first step in any wallpapering project is deciding where to hang the first and last strips. Because the pattern on the last strip you hang probably will not match that of the strip it meets, you may want to choose your end point first. The diagram below shows several possible starting and end points.

Because most house walls are not plumb—that is, at perfect right angles—you will need to establish a plumb line on each wall to properly align the first strips and then all succeeding strips. To draw a plumb line, use a plumb bob and a carpenter's level. Once you have determined your layout strategy and established plumb lines, you are ready to start papering.

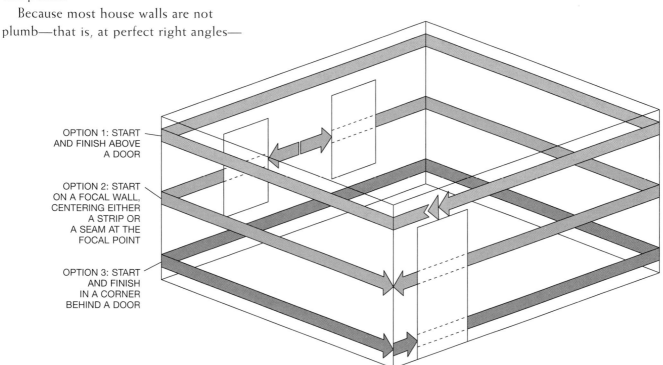

OPTION 1: START AND FINISH ABOVE A DOOR

OPTION 2: START ON A FOCAL WALL, CENTERING EITHER A STRIP OR A SEAM AT THE FOCAL POINT

OPTION 3: START AND FINISH IN A CORNER BEHIND A DOOR

PLANNING PROPER LAYOUT

The three main options for choosing starting and end points are: starting and ending above a door (see gold line), centering the first strip at a focal point in the room (see blue line), and starting and ending in a corner behind a door (see pink line). To determine which option is best for your situation, hold a wallpaper roll at the starting point and mark with a pencil where the seams will fall. Continue working your way around the room. Ideally, keep seams at least 4 inches away from the corners, as well as from the edges of windows and doors. In addition, try to plan seams so they will fall near the centers of windows and doors.

measuring, marking & cutting

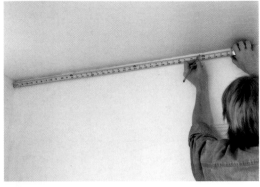

1 Start papering from one of three places, as discussed on page 87. For the room shown here, the first strip is being hung at the midpoint of the wall that separates the bathroom's vanity from the shower area. Measure and mark at the midpoint. Then mark the wall to the left side of the midpoint at a distance that is equal to half the wallpaper width; this mark is the starting point for the first strip.

2 Mark a vertical plumb line at the starting point to create a placement guide for the edge of the first strip. Use a carpenter's level to do this; never rely on wall edges or door casings to mark a vertical line because these edges are rarely plumb. Continue the line down the wall using a 6-foot straightedge and the level to keep the line plumb. Measure the height of the wall along the plumb line, from the ceiling to the top of the baseboard, using a measuring tape.

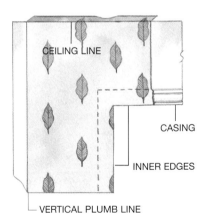

CEILING LINE

CASING

INNER EDGES

VERTICAL PLUMB LINE

3 To create a professional look, the wallpaper strips should be cut so that the pattern motifs align at the ceiling line around the room. On the wallpaper roll, find the point in the pattern that you want to start at the ceiling. Mark the starting point for measuring and for hanging on the paper. With a carpenter's square, measure 2 inches above that point, and mark a cutting line across the paper.

4 Measure and mark a strip that is equal to the wall height plus 2 inches. (Start measuring from the pattern starting point, not the cutting line.) Double-check to see that there are 2 inches above and 2 inches below the wall-height measurement. Using scissors, cut the strip on the marked lines. To accommodate a door opening, measure the distance from the vertical plumb line marked in Step 2 to the inner edge of the side casing. Measure the distance from the ceiling line down to the inner edge of the top casing. Trim the strip to these measurements.

hanging the first strip

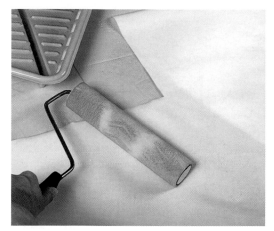

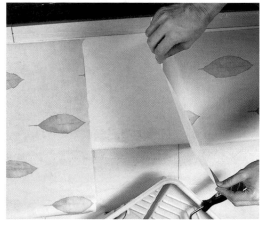

LOWE'S QUICK TIP
If you are booking several strips at a time, loosely roll each one and enclose in a plastic bag to keep them from drying out.

1 Turn off the power to the room at the circuit breaker or fuse box. Remove the switch plates and receptacle covers and then turn the power back on. Lay the first length of wallpaper, right side down, on your work surface. Using a paint roller with a foam roller cover, apply an even coat of adhesive to the back of the strip.

2 To ensure even adhesion of the wallpaper, "book" the strip by folding both ends to the middle. Then wait the amount of time recommended by the manufacturer (usually between 5 and 15 minutes) before hanging.

3 Unfold the top portion of the strip; allow the rest of the strip to drop down. Holding the strip by its upper corners, carefully align the left edge of the strip with the plumb line, and align the pattern starting point with the ceiling line.

4 Use a smoothing brush to adhere the paper at the ceiling line and to coax out any air bubbles. Wet a wallpaper sponge, wring it nearly dry, and lightly wipe away excess adhesive at the ceiling. Be gentle; wet wallpaper is fragile. Press the paper to the wall, working from the top down. With one hand, align the strip, being careful not to stretch the edge. With your other hand, smooth the paper. Use the smoothing brush to coax out any air bubbles. Wipe away the excess adhesive at the edges with the wallpaper sponge. Allow the wallpaper to "rest" for several minutes.

PROJECT CONTINUES ➡

5 Use scissors to cut a diagonal slit to the outer corner on a door casing, as shown.

6 Use a single-edged razor knife to slit an X in the wallpaper over any light switch or receptacle. Carefully fold back the cut pieces, and trim them even with the edges of the opening.

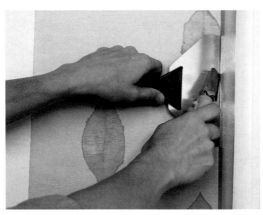

7 Hold down the wallpaper with a broad knife, and use a razor knife to trim the excess paper flush with the edge of the side casing. To avoid tearing the wallpaper when you're trimming, make continuous cuts, keeping the razor blade in contact with the paper while you move the head of the broad knife.

8 Trim the paper above the top casing in the same way. Wait 15 minutes, and then use a wallpaper smoother, held at a 30-degree angle, to smooth the surface of the paper.

9 Trim the excess paper at the ceiling line using a razor knife.

10 Trim the excess paper at the baseboard with the razor knife.

hanging subsequent strips

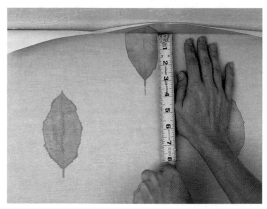

1 Measure, mark, and cut the next strip. (In this case, the second strip is short because it falls above the door.) Adhere the strip at the ceiling line. If necessary, measure a motif to make sure the pattern is positioned properly. Work the strip down the wall, aligning its edge with the edge of the first strip. Smooth, sponge, and trim the paper as you did with the first strip. Change the razor blade often.

2 Adhere the edges where the first and second strips meet with a seam roller. Use a light touch to avoid squeezing too much adhesive from under the seam. Continue hanging strips in the same manner.

3 When you approach a corner, measure from the edge of the most recent strip to the corner in three places and then add ¼ inch to the largest measurement. Mark and trim a new wallpaper strip to this width to allow the paper to turn the corner. Set aside the leftover piece.

4 Hang the strip. Smooth it with the brush, and wipe it with the sponge. Snip off the ¼ inch at the ceiling line and at the baseboard to make the strip fit around the corner. Measure the width of the leftover piece. Starting in the corner, measure and mark that distance on the adjoining wall. Using the level and the straightedge, mark a plumb line down the wall. Hang the piece, aligning one edge of the strip with the plumb line and butting the other edge into the corner. Continue hanging wallpaper strips around the room.

adding a wallpaper border

A WALLPAPER BORDER IS AN EASY ADORNMENT. BORDERS ARE AVAILABLE IN A wide array of styles and colors. Follow the same techniques for hanging a border as you would for hanging any other wallpaper. Surfaces should be clean and in good condition. The wallpaper border used in this project is prepasted, but, like wallpaper rolls, borders also come non-prepasted. If you are applying a border over existing wallpaper, coat the surface under the border with an opaque primer sealer and use vinyl-to-vinyl adhesive to hang it. Wallpaper borders are typically sold in 5-yard spools. To find out how much you need, measure the length of the surface you intend to border and add 10 percent for wastage.

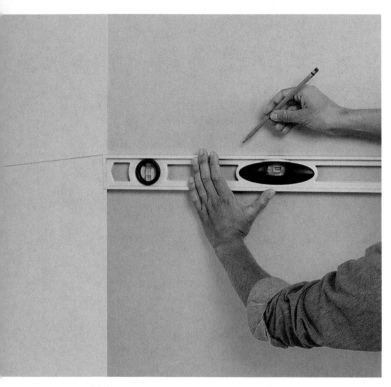

1 Make any necessary spot repairs. Wash the surface with a solution of dishwashing liquid and warm water, rinse it thoroughly, and allow it to dry. Draw a line along the wall at the desired height of the border with a carpenter's level.

2 Cut the border as needed into a manageable 4- to 6-foot strip with a utility knife and a trimming guide. For a prepasted border such as this one, fill a wallpaper trough about two-thirds full with warm water. Loosely roll the strip with the paste side out, immerse it in the water, and then allow it to soak for the time specified by the manufacturer. Lift out the strip by the top edge, and gently fold it into 6-inch pleats, paste side to paste side, without making creases. (This is called "booking.") Then let the strip sit for the time recommended by the manufacturer.

LOWE'S QUICK TIP
Before installing a border over a new wall covering, let the paper dry thoroughly so the weight of the border will not pull it away from the wall.

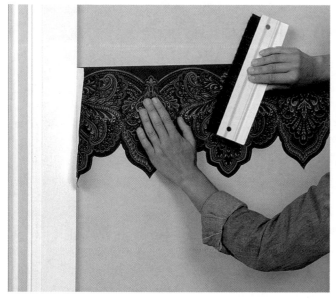

3 Hang the first strip against the frame of a door or window or in an inconspicuous corner. Align the strip with the marked guideline, and press the strip into place. Work out bumps and wrinkles with a smoothing tool. If necessary, trim the end of the strip to fit flush using a trimming guide and a utility knife.

4 To ensure a perfect pattern match without a gap, double-cut the seams. Hang a second strip so it overlaps and aligns with the pattern of the first. With a trimming guide and a utility knife, carefully cut through both strips. Lift off the end of the second strip, remove the waste pieces, and then press the strip back into place. Wait the amount of time recommended by the manufacturer, and then roll the seam with a seam roller.

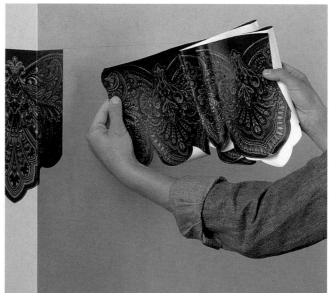

5 Cut a strip long enough to run an inch or two past the corner. Soak and book the strip, and then hang it. Press the strip into the corner with a damp sponge to crease it. Cut a strip for the opposite side of the corner so that strip overlaps and aligns with the pattern of the first.

6 Double-cut a seam at the corner to ensure the best possible pattern match. (Walls at an outside corner are seldom perfectly plumb—if you simply continue around the corner, the border is unlikely to be level on the other side.)

wallpapering below a chair rail

CHAIR RAILS GIVE YOU AN OPPORTUNITY TO USE TWO DIFFERENT DECORATING treatments on the same wall. In this example, the portion above the moulding is painted, and the section below will be covered with wallpaper. The chair rail can already be in place, as shown here, or can be installed afterward. Bear in mind that you can follow these same steps if you want to apply wallpaper to an entire wall that has no chair rail.

Preparation is the key to success with this project. Patch any cracks with spackling compound, and then sand the patches smooth. Wash the surface with a household cleaner to remove dirt, grease, and mildew. Set up a clean worktable large enough to hold a wallpaper trough, and cut all the wallpaper strips before you hang any of them.

Lowe's carries a wide variety of styles and types of wallpaper, including the kind shown here. Two main types of paper are commonly available: prepasted and unpasted. Soak prepasted paper in warm water, as in this project, or apply an activator according to the manufacturer's directions. Brush or roll wallpaper paste onto the back of unpasted paper.

1 Tack a finishing nail to the center of the wall just below the chair rail, and then hang a plumb bob from the nail to just below the baseboard. (It's better to work outward from the midpoint of the wall and end with equal strips at each end than to have a full strip at one end and a partial one at the other.) Mark two points on the wall in line with the plumb line. Remove the plumb bob and nail, and then draw a line between the points with a straightedge. Alternatively, use a carpenter's level to mark a vertical center line.

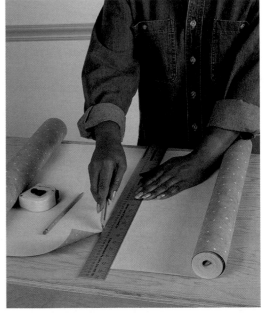

2 Measure the distance between the chair rail and the baseboard, and add about 3 inches. Unroll the wallpaper, pattern side down, and transfer your measurement to the back. Trim the paper to length with a straightedge and a utility knife. Turn the strip over so the pattern faces up, and then unroll the paper for the second strip beside it. Fold back the top edge of the roll so the pattern at the fold aligns with that of the first strip, and then cut the paper at the fold. Cut the second strip to the same length as the first. Cut the remaining strips as you did the second.

3 Fill a wallpaper trough about two-thirds full with warm water. Roll up the first strip, and set it in the trough, gently pressing down to remove air bubbles. Let the paper soak for the time recommended by the manufacturer. Lift the strip out by its top edge, allowing the water to drip back into the trough.

4 Allow the wet paste to activate for a few minutes before hanging the paper. Folding the wet wallpaper over on itself (booking it) will prevent it from drying out during this time: With the strip pattern side down on an absorbent cloth, gently fold each end of the strip to the center, taking care not to crease the paper. Cut and book two or three strips before applying them to the wall, arranging them on your work surface in order.

5 When the first strip is ready to be hung, gently lift it by the top edge, keeping the bottom half folded. At the wall, align one edge of the strip with the plumb line, and overlap the chair rail by about 2 inches. Pass a smoothing brush over the surface, creasing the paper at the chair rail. As you reach the middle of the sheet, open the bottom section. Continue smoothing the paper on the wall. When you reach the bottom of the wall, crease the paper at the baseboard, allowing the excess to overlap the moulding.

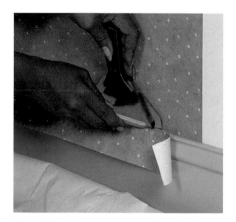

6 Trim the excess once the sheet is flat on the wall and the top and bottom are creased. Press a trimming guide into the crease at the baseboard, and then cut through the excess with a utility knife. Repeat for the crease bordering the chair rail.

7 Hang the second strip, gently butting its edge against the first. Shift the strip up or down as necessary to align the pattern, making sure to overlap the chair rail by about 2 inches. Smooth and trim the paper as you did the first strip. Hang several strips, and then smooth the seams with a seam roller. Avoid applying too much pressure, or you will force paste out from under the paper. Once you have hung all the paper, sponge the surface to remove any excess glue, and then pat the wall dry with a towel.

When wallpapering below a chair rail, always choose a darker color than the wall above.

covering switch plates & outlets

WHEN YOU ARE WALLPAPERING, THE COVER PLATES FOR SWITCHES AND OUTLETS threaten to stand out and interrupt the continuity of the pattern. The best approach is to proceed with your project, and then return to wallpaper the cover plates. Shut off electricity to the switches and outlets before removing the cover plates. With the cover plates out of the way, you can paper over the boxes and then trim the paper neatly along the edges of the boxes. As a final touch, paper the cover plates so the pattern aligns with that of the surrounding surface.

You'll only need a little extra wallpaper for cover plates. Shown here is the process for covering a switch plate; apply the same procedure for the cover plate of an outlet.

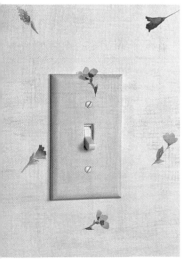

1 When removing the plate, turn off the switch, and then shut off the electricity to the circuit at the service panel. Next, undo the screws that hold the cover plate in place, and take the plate off.

2 Apply the paper to the wall, covering the box for the switch. With a utility knife, make diagonal cuts between the corners of the box, forming four flaps of wallpaper. Trim the flaps, running the knife blade from corner to corner along the inside edge of the box.

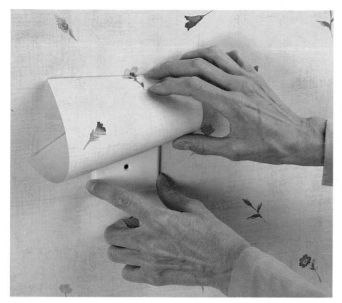

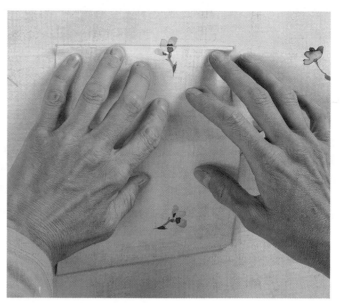

3 Cut a sheet of wallpaper large enough to cover the switch plate, and match the pattern to that of the surrounding surface. Hold the sheet over the box, align the patterns, and lightly mark the sheet with a pencil 1½ inches outside the edges of the box. Cut the sheet at the marks. Position the cover plate on the box, and lightly fold the sheet around the back of the cover plate's top edge.

4 To accommodate the plate's projection from the wall, position the cover plate on the wall, and slide the sheet down by about ⅛ inch. Once the patterns on the cover plate and wall are aligned, firmly crease the paper across the top, sides, and bottom of the cover plate.

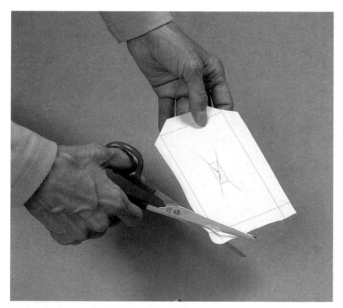

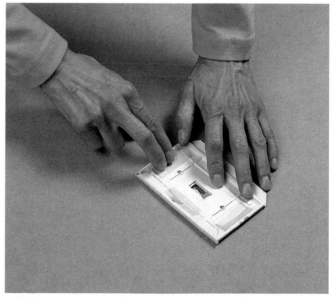

5 Trim the sheet of wallpaper to ½ inch outside the edges of the cover plate. Holding the cover plate and sheet together, outline the opening for the switch toggle on the sheet. Set the cover plate aside, and cut diagonally between the marked corners of the opening, forming flaps. With wallpaper scissors, trim the corners of the sheet to the creases.

6 Prepare the wallpaper sheet for gluing following the manufacturer's directions, and then set it facedown on a work surface. Position the cover plate facedown on the sheet, aligning its edges with the creases. Fold the edges of the sheet onto the plate back, and secure them with masking tape. Tape the flaps around the opening for the switch toggle in the same way. Allow the paper to dry, and then pierce holes through the sheet at the cover plate's screw-hole locations.

walls & ceilings

WALLS AND CEILINGS ARE INTERNAL HOUSE ELEMENTS THAT CREATE BOUNDARIES. Walls divide the large interior volume into smaller volumes, creating structure within the home, organizing public and private spaces, and creating traffic patterns. Ceilings enclose rooms in the vertical dimension, further defining the space.

However, these elements can be manipulated to create any number of effects. Walls can be used to hide or reveal, to entice, to frame a view. They can be pierced or partial. In establishing ceiling height, you create the sense of volume in a space and, in turn, how people feel in it. A large space can be made cozier by a low ceiling, while a small space can open up and soar with a high ceiling. Walls and ceilings need not be flat. Curved walls soften a home's hard edges, while recessed ceilings outfitted with hidden light wells add complexity and drama to any room.

Walls and ceilings can be dressed to complement any design style. Easily installed wood or composition mouldings—for example, crown moulding where the walls and ceiling meet and base moulding where the walls and floor meet, plus window and door trim, chair rails, and picture rails—provide distinctive period touches. Victorian-style pressed-metal panels, available in a wide variety of patterns and designs, are also a creative and inexpensive way to give a ceiling panache.

Beginning with construction basics, this chapter provides the information you need to work with walls and ceilings, including instructions on opening up and building walls, working with drywall and plaster, installing various types of trim, installing paneling, tiling a wall, and installing a suspended ceiling.

wall & ceiling basics

WALLS AND CEILINGS FORM THE LAYOUT WITHIN A HOME, CREATING INDIVIDUAL rooms and passageways. Walls are classified as either bearing or nonbearing. Bearing walls help carry the weight of the house, providing support to floors above and keeping the building rigid. All exterior walls are bearing. In addition, in most cases at least one main interior wall, situated over a girder or interior foundation wall, is also bearing. Especially in multilevel homes, many interior walls may be bearing.

Traditionally, walls have been built from 2-by-4 studs and plates, with studs placed on 16-inch centers. In recent years, 2-by-6 studs have been used increasingly to allow for more insulation in the walls. Sometimes studs are placed on 24-inch centers. Basic wall construction is the same with both types.

Nonbearing walls (which are also called partitions), while not essential from a construction standpoint, shape the interior by defining rooms within the house and also create cavities for essential plumbing and electrical systems. The framing for an opening (such as a door) in a nonbearing wall may be built from lighter materials than those needed for an opening in a bearing wall.

The standard ceiling height of interior spaces is 8 feet. But you will have trouble installing 4-by-8-foot gypsum wallboard or sheet paneling on walls unless you have framed the walls slightly higher to allow for the ceiling material's thickness: 8 feet, ¾ inch is the standard overall height of wall framing. When you subtract the thickness of the sole plate and doubled top plates, this leaves 7 feet, 8¼ inches (92¼ inches) for the wall studs. Lumberyards frequently stock studs that have been precut to this length.

types of construction

Typical homes have three basic types of construction. The most common, shown below, is platform framing (also known as

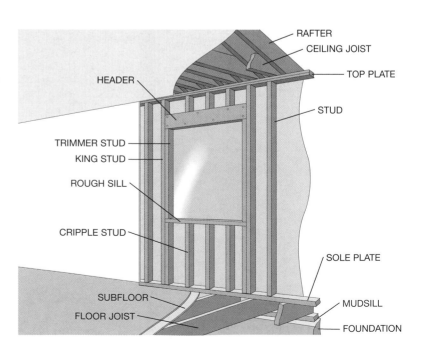

Platform framing utilizes a series of vertical wall studs, horizontal ceiling and floor joists, and roof rafters. Extra framing members help bear the loads where walls or ceilings have openings.

RAFTER
CEILING JOIST
HEADER
TOP PLATE
STUD
TRIMMER STUD
KING STUD
ROUGH SILL
CRIPPLE STUD
SOLE PLATE
MUDSILL
SUBFLOOR
FLOOR JOIST
FOUNDATION

Western framing). The simplest and safest house-building method in practice today, platform framing starts with the foundation and floor structure. The walls are built up from the subfloor with 2-by dimension lumber (in some regions, steel studs are used in place of dimension lumber). If the house is taller than one story, additional platforms and walls are stacked on top of the first-floor walls. The structure is completed with the attachment of ceiling and roof framing.

Balloon framing, where the wall studs extend in one piece from the mudsill above the foundation wall to the doubled top plate two stories up, was standard practice until about 1930 and is still used in some two-story houses, especially those with stucco, brick, or other masonry exteriors. A third, less-common construction method is post-and-beam, which utilizes heavy structural members at great intervals instead of smaller, closely spaced lumber.

Though some homes are now built from metal wall studs, most do-it-yourself construction calls for the use of wooden studs and framing members, nailed together and reinforced by metal framing connectors as required by local codes.

behind walls & ceilings

Most of a home's mechanical, electrical, and plumbing systems are contained inside the walls and ceilings. Plumbing-supply and waste pipes; electrical wires and telephone lines; and heating, ventilation, and air-conditioning systems are all installed after a house has been framed.

wall & ceiling finishes

Once a house has been framed, sheathed, and sided, and all of the necessary systems have been roughed in, windows as well as exterior doors can be installed. Then, wall and ceiling finishes can be completed.

Ceiling materials are fastened directly to the ceiling joists or to a metal or wooden grid suspended from the joists.

Gypsum wallboard or sheet paneling is applied directly to wall studs; solid board

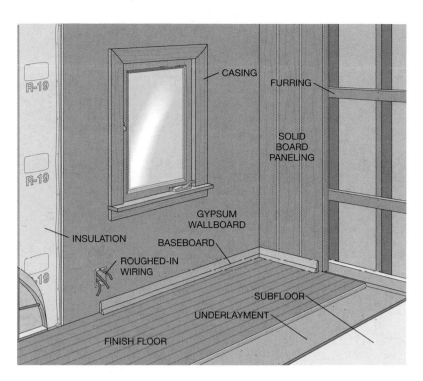

In a typical room, vertical studs fasten to a sole plate that is secured to the sub-floor. Wiring, ductwork, pipes, and insulation run between the studs. Here, one wall is finished with gypsum wallboard, and an interior wall is finished with solid board paneling attached to furring strips (lumber run horizontally between wall studs). Baseboard trim and interior window casings complete the room.

paneling may first require a wallboard backing or furring strips as a nailing base. Plaster walls need a gypsum, fiberboard, or metal lath backing. If you choose gypsum wallboard as a final covering for either ceilings or walls, you will need to tape, fill, and sand the joints between panels.

After the ceilings and walls are installed, the finish floor is put in place. Then interior trim—including baseboards, mouldings, and window or door casings as needed—completes the basic job.

STRUCTURAL INSULATED PANELS

Structural insulated panels (SIPs) are gaining in popularity as a fast and economical method of constructing interior and exterior walls. SIPs are typically constructed of oriented strand board, expanded polystyrene foam insulation, and sometimes gypsum wallboard. These materials are laminated together under pressure to produce panels having both structural and insulating properties. Channels for electrical wires are precut at the factory or can be made on site. Window and door openings are cut out, and the panels are set into place and secured as an entire unit.

BASIC TOOLS FOR WALLS & CEILINGS

Circuit tester	Combination square	Caulking gun	Chalk line
Corner taping tool	Power drill with bits and screwdriver tips	Bevel gauge	Putty knife	Pole sander
Carpenter's square	Claw hammer	Safety goggles	Contour gauge	Level
Handsaw	Measuring tape	Wallboard saw	Power circular saw	Perforated rasp
Stepladder	Prybar	Utility knife	Reciprocating saw	Drywall taping knife
	Screwdrivers	Stud finder	Plumb bob	Wood chisel

tools for walls & ceilings

BASIC CARPENTRY TOOLS, AS WELL AS A FEW TASK-SPECIFIC ITEMS, ARE USED TO construct walls. In addition to common tools such as hammers, tape measures, utility knives, and screwdrivers, specialty tools such as a combination square, taping knife, and stud finder can also improve results and reduce the time needed to complete tasks. In addition to the tools discussed here, you'll want to have on hand basic safety gear such as safety goggles and heavy gloves. In addition, if you intend to work with tile as a finish material, you'll need basic tile tools (see page 153).

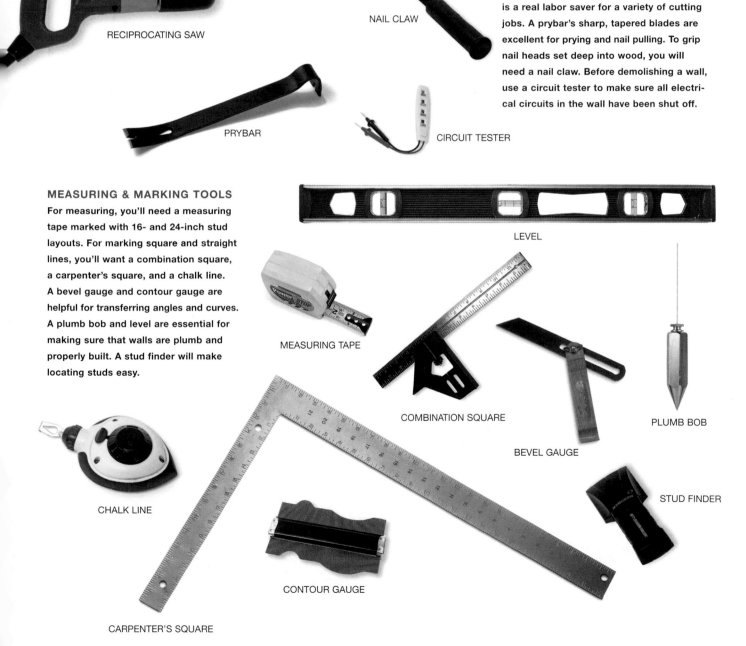

RECIPROCATING SAW

NAIL CLAW

PRYBAR

CIRCUIT TESTER

DEMOLITION TOOLS

For demolition work, a reciprocating saw is a real labor saver for a variety of cutting jobs. A prybar's sharp, tapered blades are excellent for prying and nail pulling. To grip nail heads set deep into wood, you will need a nail claw. Before demolishing a wall, use a circuit tester to make sure all electrical circuits in the wall have been shut off.

MEASURING & MARKING TOOLS

For measuring, you'll need a measuring tape marked with 16- and 24-inch stud layouts. For marking square and straight lines, you'll want a combination square, a carpenter's square, and a chalk line. A bevel gauge and contour gauge are helpful for transferring angles and curves. A plumb bob and level are essential for making sure that walls are plumb and properly built. A stud finder will make locating studs easy.

LEVEL

MEASURING TAPE

COMBINATION SQUARE

PLUMB BOB

BEVEL GAUGE

STUD FINDER

CHALK LINE

CONTOUR GAUGE

CARPENTER'S SQUARE

GENERAL CARPENTRY TOOLS

A claw hammer is one of the most useful tools of all. You will probably want two: a framing hammer for construction and a 16-ounce hammer for lighter work. A power circular saw is the tool of choice for cutting framing members (though a handsaw will work). A perforated rasp removes material quickly. Other miscellaneous tools that are helpful include screwdrivers, chisels, and a caulking gun. For additional tools required to install trimwork, see page 219.

CLAW HAMMER

POWER CIRCULAR SAW

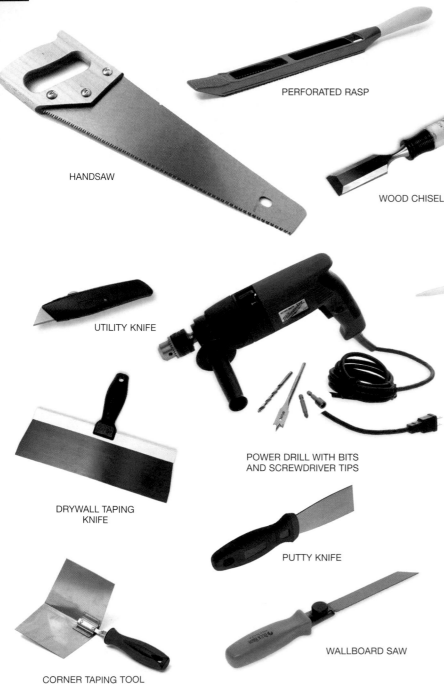

HANDSAW

PERFORATED RASP

WOOD CHISEL

SCREWDRIVERS

UTILITY KNIFE

POWER DRILL WITH BITS
AND SCREWDRIVER TIPS

CAULKING GUN

DRYWALL TAPING
KNIFE

PUTTY KNIFE

CORNER TAPING TOOL

WALLBOARD SAW

DRYWALL TOOLS

For measuring and cutting drywall, you will need the basic measuring and marking tools that are shown on page 103, a utility knife, a saber saw, and a wallboard saw. To hang drywall, plan to have on hand a wallboard hammer or a 16-ounce claw hammer, and a power drill with screwdriver tips. For taping and finishing the seams, you will need a putty knife and drywall taping knives with thin metal blades in a variety of widths, ranging from 3 to 10 inches. A corner taping tool, the companion to taping knives, has two blades at a 90-degree angle to shape and smooth plaster and joint compound on corners. A pole sander is essential for sanding taped joints.

POLE SANDER

fasteners

NAILS, SCREWS, BOLTS, AND A VARIETY OF OTHER SPECIALIZED FASTENERS ARE used for both constructing and fastening to walls and ceilings. Some are very familiar to many people, while others are a bit mysterious. Here you'll find basic information on how to select the right fastener and use it properly.

FROM LEFT: **Common nail, galvanized nail, finishing nail.**

nails Common nails, used for rough construction, have an extra-thick shank and a broad head. Drywall nails, a variation, have a thinner shank and a larger, slightly cupped head; annular-ring drywall nails, best used for installing drywall on ceilings, have a ribbed shank that grips better. Where you don't want a nail head to show, choose a finishing nail. (After you drive it nearly flush, sink the slightly rounded head below the surface with a nailset.) Use hot-dipped galvanized nails where they may be exposed to moisture.

screws Though they are more expensive than nails, screws offer several advantages for certain types of construction. They do not pop out as readily as nails do, and their coating is less likely to be damaged during installation. With screws, you do not have to worry about making hammer dents. Screws also are easier to remove when repairs are required.

Usually black, drywall screws (also called multipurpose screws) come in many sizes and can be driven in with a screw gun or an electric drill with an adjustable clutch and Phillips-screwdriver tip. Galvanized deck screws are longer and have a coarser thread; they are suitable for areas that will be exposed to moisture. Because drywall and deck screws are not rated for strength, use nails, lag screws, or bolts when engaging in heavy construction.

The lag screw (also called a lag bolt) is a heavy-duty fastener with a square or hexagonal head; it is driven with a wrench or a ratchet and socket. Before driving a lag screw, predrill a lead hole about two-thirds the screw's length using a drill bit that is $\frac{1}{8}$ inch smaller than the lag screw's shank. Slide a washer onto each of the lag screws before driving them.

FROM LEFT: **Drywall screw, deck screw, lag screw and washer.**

FINDING HIDDEN STUDS & JOISTS

Hidden studs and joists can be located in several ways. Most studs are spaced 16 or 24 inches apart, from center to center. To locate a stud or ceiling joist, measure out from a corner in multiples of 16 or 24 inches (depending on how the structure was built). Then lightly tap the area to find a section of wall with a solid backing (a stud or joist).

If you are unsure of the locations, you can buy a handheld electronic device called a stud finder. This device will beep or flash when it passes over a solid framing member; simply slide the finder along the surface until it signals the location of a wall stud or joist, and then find others by measuring (one will usually be located 16 or 24 inches from there). Find studs behind plaster walls by driving a small test nail just above the baseboard.

Often, the easiest way to find studs is to look for visible signs of the nails that hold wallboard to the studs—small dents or nail heads. Hold a strong flashlight at a sharp angle to the wall or ceiling to highlight them.

bolts For heavy-duty fastening, choose bolts, most of which are made from zinc-plated steel. Bolts go into predrilled holes and are secured by nuts. The machine bolt has a square or hexagonal head, a nut, and two washers; it must be tightened with a wrench at each end. The carriage bolt has a self-anchoring head that digs into the wood as the nut is tightened. Bolts are classified by diameter (⅛ to 1 inch) and length (⅜ inch and up). To give the nut a firm bite, select a bolt that is ½ to 1 inch longer than the combined thickness of the pieces to be joined.

wall fasteners You can hang heavy objects such as picture frames, plant hangers, and shelves on gypsum wallboard, plaster, or other hollow walls in several ways. The simplest solution is to hang items where a nail or screw can be driven into a stud or joist behind the finished wall or ceiling.

FROM LEFT: **Lag screw, washer, and expanding lead anchor; carriage bolt, washer, and nut; machine bolt, washers, and nut.**

You can use conventional nails to hang light objects from these walls (drill pilot holes first to avoid creating cracks), but picture hooks, which are rated in pounds, are often a better option. Determine the weight of the item to be hung, and purchase a hook that can support that weight or more. For example, a 35-pound picture frame should be secured by a 50-pound picture hook.

To secure shelf brackets and other heavy items, use only wood screws driven into studs.

When you can't drive into a stud, support medium-weight items with anchors or toggle bolts; once they are driven into the holes, they expand to distribute weight more widely than do screws. Be sure to buy the proper size fastener for the thickness of the wall and the weight of the object you are hanging.

Drill a hole, install the anchor, and insert the screw; then tighten it to spread the anchor.

When using a toggle bolt, slide the bolt through the hook or object to be mounted before inserting the toggle in a hole that is drilled into the wall; if you remove the bolt when the fastener is in place, you will lose the toggle. Don't fasten the bolt or screw too tightly; this only pulls the anchor or toggle into the wall material and weakens its grip.

masonry anchors For masonry walls, hang light objects from special tempered-steel masonry nails. Drive them in with a hammer (be sure to wear safety glasses). For heavier objects, use anchors that have a sleeve that expands to hold a screw or bolt in place.

The key to successful installation of masonry anchors is proper drilling of the hole to receive the sleeve and screw. Use an electric drill with a carbide-tipped masonry bit to drill the hole. Then push in the sleeve, insert the screw through whatever you are fastening, and drive the screw into the sleeve.

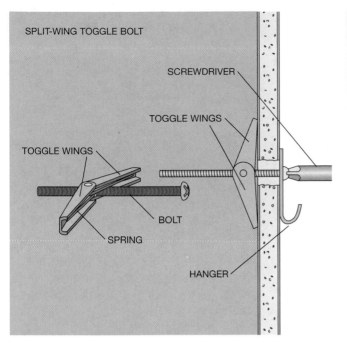

SPLIT-WING TOGGLE BOLT

SCREWDRIVER

TOGGLE WINGS

TOGGLE WINGS

BOLT

SPRING

HANGER

Drill a hole, and then insert the bolt through the hanger and toggle. Pinch the toggle wings together, insert the bolt with the toggle, and pull the bolt toward you. Tighten the bolt.

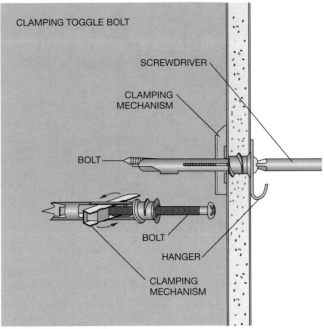

CLAMPING TOGGLE BOLT

SCREWDRIVER

CLAMPING MECHANISM

BOLT

BOLT

HANGER

CLAMPING MECHANISM

Drill a hole and insert the bolt. Press and turn the bolt with a screwdriver until you see that the bolt is flush with the wall and the arrows on the head are parallel to the wall stud. Add the hanger, and tighten the screw to engage the clamp.

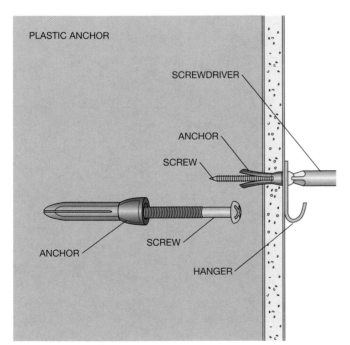

PLASTIC ANCHOR

SCREWDRIVER

ANCHOR

SCREW

ANCHOR

SCREW

HANGER

Drill a pilot hole slightly smaller than the anchor. Tap the anchor into the hole. Add the hanger, and then insert and tighten the screw.

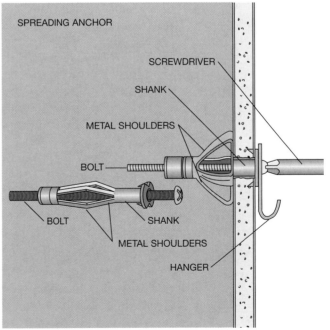

SPREADING ANCHOR

SCREWDRIVER

SHANK

METAL SHOULDERS

BOLT

BOLT

SHANK

METAL SHOULDERS

HANGER

Drill a hole, and then insert the anchor. Tighten the bolt until you feel resistance. Remove the bolt, add the hanger, and then reinsert and tighten the bolt.

opening up a wall

OPENING UP A WALL, WHETHER TO INSTALL A DOORWAY OR TO REMOVE AN INterior partition, is simple yet messy work. Before you remove any wall studs, you must find out whether or not the wall is a bearing wall, as discussed on page 100. If it is, you must engineer the opening with the proper beams or headers to carry the loads that will no longer be supported by the studs. If you are unsure whether an interior wall is a bearing wall, consult a local building professional before doing any demolition work.

Next, check for obstructions before opening the wall; extensive plumbing or wiring may cause you to rethink installing a doorway or pass-through at a certain location. (Always first shut off power to the receptacles and switches in the wall you are opening.) Then mask off the area with plastic sheeting to prevent the dust from permeating your home, and protect the floor with drop cloths. Wear work gloves, protective goggles, and a dust mask during the demolition process.

removing the surface Most walls are surfaced with gypsum wallboard. No matter how it is attached to the studs—with nails, screws, or adhesive—the removal procedure is exactly the same. Use a utility knife to slit through the taped joints. Then punch through the panel with a hammer or prybar, and pull off pieces.

Working from the center, use a prybar to pull the panel off the studs. Next, pull out any remaining nails with a hammer, or unfasten the screws. If you are removing the entire partition (for nonbearing walls only), take out any studs by cutting them with a reciprocating saw, and use a prybar to pull out any nails securing the top and bottom plates to the subfloor.

1 Pry any remnants of surface material off the studs of the wall you intend to take out. On the walls that adjoin it, remove the surface material back to the first stud. Pull out any remaining nails from all exposed studs.

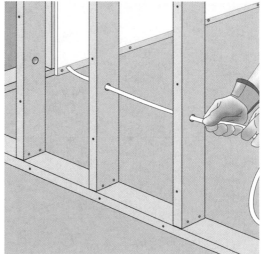

2 Make sure water and electrical circuits are turned off, and then remove any wiring or plumbing from the wall; properly cap pipes, and terminate circuits. If you are unfamiliar with this type of work, call an electrical or plumbing contractor. (See more about plumbing on pages 390–391 and wiring on pages 476–479.)

To remove plaster and lath, chisel through the plaster and then cut and pry the lath loose.

removing the structure If you are removing material for a new opening but leaving the majority of the partition intact, plan to create an opening large enough to accommodate the rough framing. Add an extra 1½ inches to each side and 3 inches at the top. It is often actually easiest to remove all of the wall covering from floor to ceiling between the two bordering studs that will remain in place. The best tool you can use to cut through the existing wall studs is a reciprocating saw.

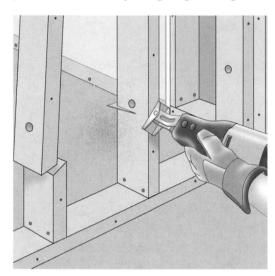

3 Knock out any fire blocks between the studs. Cut through all studs, except the end ones, a few inches up from the floor. Pull and twist the upper parts of the studs to free them from the top plate. Using a hammer, knock over the short stud blocks at the base, and pry them up. Pull out or cut off any remaining nails.

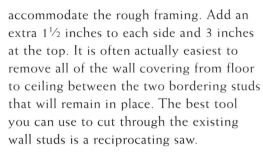

4 Make a diagonal cut through each end stud at a downward angle, and then pry out the two pieces beginning with the lower half. Pull them free from the top and bottom plates and the anchoring studs in the adjoining walls.

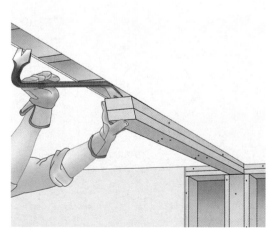

5 If the top plate goes through the adjoining wall, cut it flush with that wall's top plate. To remove the top plate, make a diagonal cut across it, wedge a prybar between the two halves, and pull down. Pull out any nails.

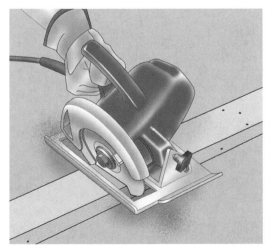

6 If the bottom plate goes through the adjoining wall, cut it flush with that wall's bottom plate. Then make an angled cut across it, taking care not to cut the floor. Pry up the plate, and pull out any nails.

building an interior wall

DURING THE COURSE OF A REMODELING PROJECT, IT OFTEN BECOMES NECESSARY to construct additional walls to create new spaces. Expect a fair amount of disruption in the work area. Depending on the finish flooring and ceiling material in the room, it may be necessary to do additional demolition work to uncover the subfloor and ceiling joists to provide secure attachment points for the new wall.

anchoring the plates The new wall should be anchored securely to the floor and ceiling joists. If you are unsure of joist locations, go into the attic and drive small nails through the ceiling on both sides of a joist to serve as reference points.

If one end of the new wall falls between the studs of the intersecting wall, remove existing wall materials, and install horizontal nailing blocks to receive the new wall's end stud.

On the ceiling, mark the ends of the new wall's centerline. Measure 1¾ inches on both sides of each mark; snap parallel chalk lines between the marks. Nail the top plate to either the ceiling joists or nailing

blocks. Hang a plumb bob from each end of the top plate, mark these points on the floor, and snap a chalk line to connect these points. Position and nail the bottom plate to the floor. With masonry floors, use a masonry bit to drill holes through the bottom plate and into the floor every 2 or 3 feet, and then insert expanding anchors.

install wall studs Attach one end stud (or both end studs) to existing studs or to nailing blocks between studs. To install each stud, lift it into place, line it up on the marks, and check plumb using a carpenter's level. Nail the stud to the top and bottom plates.

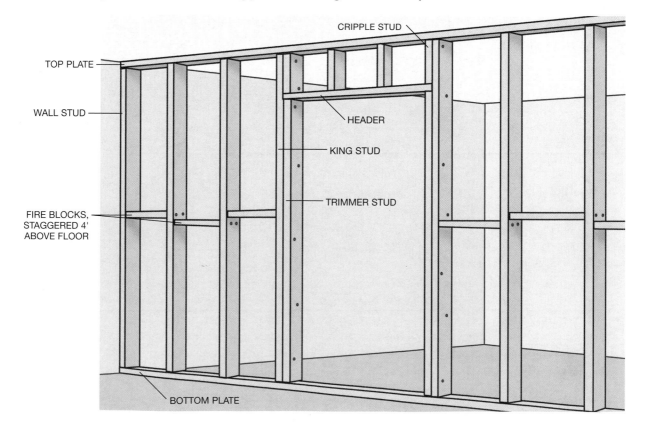

TOP PLATE

WALL STUD

FIRE BLOCKS, STAGGERED 4' ABOVE FLOOR

BOTTOM PLATE

CRIPPLE STUD

HEADER

KING STUD

TRIMMER STUD

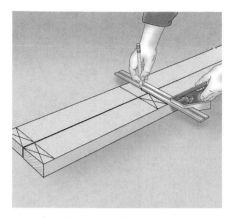

1 Lay the top and bottom plates side by side on the floor. Carefully measure where each wall stud will go, and then mark the locations across the plates using a combination square.

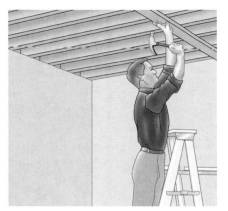

2 Locate the joists in the ceiling (the drawing shows the ceiling without the drywall for clarity). Hold the top plate in position along the guidelines marked on the ceiling (see the facing page), and nail through the ceiling material and into each joist with two 16d (3½-inch) nails. (If the new wall runs parallel to the joists, fasten the plate to nailing blocks installed between the joists.)

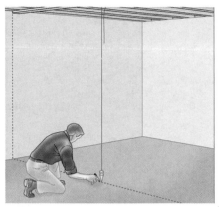

3 Hang a plumb bob from the edge of the top plate at each end, and then mark the floor to establish the bottom plate's location. Snap a chalk line along the floor between the marks as a guide for the corresponding edge of the bottom plate. Nail the bottom plate with 10d (3-inch) nails staggered and spaced every 16 inches.

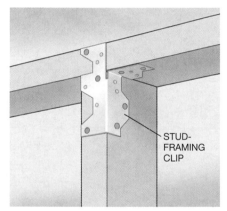

STUD-FRAMING CLIP

4 Use stud-framing clips to install each wall stud. Lift the stud into position, and line it up on its mark, flush with the edges of the top and bottom plates. Check plumb using a carpenter's level, and then nail the stud into place. Alternatively, you can toenail each stud to both the top and bottom plates with 8d (2½-inch) nails.

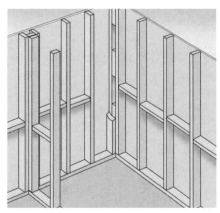

5 Double up studs to receive an intersecting wall. If the wall will turn a corner, frame with two full-length studs that have blocks sandwiched between them.

HOW TO FRAME A DOORWAY

■ Measure the rough opening for the door, and mark its center point. In each direction from that, measure half the door's width, and mark for the inside edge of each trimmer stud. Measure 3½ inches farther out to mark the inside edges of the king studs.

■ Cut the king studs to fit, and nail them to the top and bottom plates on each side of the doorway.

■ Cut the trimmer studs to the height of the door's rough opening, and then nail them to the king studs with 10d (3-inch) nails spaced about every 12 inches in a staggered pattern.

■ Cut the header, and nail it to the trimmers and king studs. Then cut the cripples, and nail them to the header and to the top plate.

■ Use a handsaw to cut through the bottom plate. Remove the piece within the doorway. Install the door frame.

hanging & finishing drywall

THE MOST COMMON FINISH MATERIAL FOR WALLS AND CEILINGS IS GYPSUM wallboard, or "drywall." Available in ½- and ⅝-inch-thick panels measuring 4 by 8 feet, drywall is straightforward to install, but the weight of full panels can be awkward to work with. The job will go much more smoothly with a helper or two.

If you are installing drywall on both ceilings and walls, apply the ceiling first; wall panels will support the edges of the ceiling panels. When handling wallboard, take care not to bend or break the corners or tear the paper covering; this will make finishing much easier.

You will need to finish the wallboard if the wall will be painted or wallpapered, but you may not need to hide joints and corners on installations that act as a backing for paneling, ceramic tile, or cabinets. Buy pre-creased wallboard tape and pre-mixed joint compound.

cutting drywall Mark the cutting line on the front paper layer with a pencil and straightedge, or snap a chalk line. Cut through the front paper layer with a utility knife. Next, turn the wallboard over, and break the gypsum core by bending it toward the back. Finish by cutting the back paper along the crease.

When fitting wallboard around obstructions such as doorways, windows, and outlets, carefully measure from the edge of an adjacent wallboard panel or reference point and up from the floor to the obstruction. Transfer the measurements to a new panel, and make the necessary cuts with a utility knife and/or wallboard saw, compass saw, or saber saw. For small cuts, such as those needed for outlets, cut the opening about ⅛ inch bigger than necessary. If the fit is too tight, trim the wallboard with a perforated rasp.

fastening drywall On ceilings, fasten drywall panels perpendicular to joists with annular ring nails or drywall screws. The easiest and fastest method is to drive in screws with a screw gun. Screw spacing is governed by local codes; typical spacing is every 8 inches along panel ends and at intermediate joists (called "in the field").

Another fastening method for ceilings is double-nailing. With this technique, space a first set of nails every 7 inches along the ends and every 12 inches in the field. Then place a second nail about 2 inches away

BELOW: **When you are cutting drywall, a T-square helps produce a straight, clean line.** FAR RIGHT: **Drywall nails should be nailed so their heads are slightly "dimpled" below the surface.**

from each nail in the first set. Nails should be spaced at least ³⁄₈ inch in from the perimeter.

On walls, nail or screw panels to studs, spacing nails according to code. Drywall nails go in faster, but they have a tendency to "pop" over time as the studs dry out. Set nail heads just below the surface into shallow dimples; recess screw heads.

application techniques
For the ceiling, position a pair of stepladders, or set up a couple of sturdy sawhorses, laying a few planks across them to serve as a short scaffold. Then you and a helper can hold each end of the panel in place with your heads. Put in fasteners at the center of each panel. Then place the next few fasteners at the edges to take the weight off your heads. When working alone, build one or two T-braces. The length of these braces should equal the height from the floor to the ceiling joists. When the panel is positioned, the extra thickness will help wedge the brace in place.

On walls, install the panels horizontally if possible and stagger vertical joints. This helps bridge irregularities between studs, results in a stronger wall, and makes finishing easier. Center panel ends or edges over studs.

finishing drywall
Concealing the joints with drywall tape and compound between panels and in corners demands patience and care. Apply joint compound and drywall tape to joints, and spread compound over the dimples left by the screws or nails. Continue as shown in Step 3 below and all of the steps on page 114.

INSTALLING DRYWALL

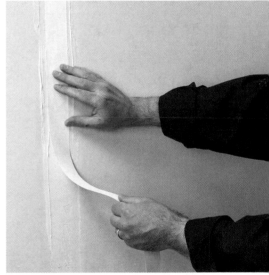

1 Measure for the first sheet of drywall, starting in a corner and centering the opposite end on a wall stud. If necessary, cut a sheet to fit. Install the sheets horizontally to make taping faster and easier. Plan to offset the sheets (stagger vertical joints) so taped joints will not be obvious.

2 Secure the sheet using either drywall nails or screws. The goal is to dimple the wallboard surface without puncturing the paper. If you are using screws, drive them in so they sit just below the surface, but do not break the paper covering. If you are using nails, use a bell-faced hammer. Normally, screw or nail spacing is every 8 inches along panel ends and edges and along intermediate supports. Fasteners must be at least ³⁄₈ inch from edges.

3 To conceal the joints between the sheets of drywall, apply drywall tape over the gaps. Tape may be self-adhesive or nonstick. With self-adhesive tape, just press it into place. To apply nonadhesive tape, first spread on a thin coat of joint compound, and then press the tape into the compound with a wide-blade putty knife.

PROJECT CONTINUES ➡

4 Apply a first coat of joint compound over the tape and the dimples left by the screws with a 4- to 6-inch-wide drywall knife. Make the compound as smooth as possible. Allow to dry, then lightly sand minor imperfections with sandpaper wrapped around a wood block.

5 Apply a second coat with a wider drywall knife. Work the compound gently away from the joint, feathering to create a smooth transition. You may have to feather in stages, allowing the compound to dry between coats. Give the walls a light sanding between coats with a pole sander (a tool with a sanding pad attached to a pole) to knock off imperfections. When the final layer is dry, rub the surface in a swirling motion with a slightly damp drywall sponge to remove any remaining imperfections.

FINISHING CORNERS

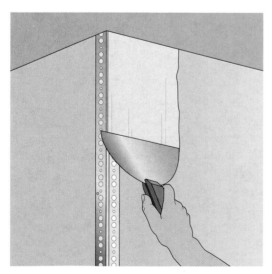

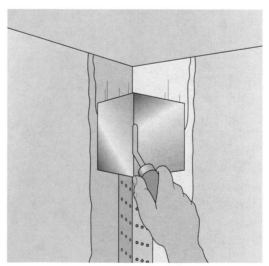

1 To finish outside corners, cover them with a protective metal corner bead that is cut to length. Nail every 12 inches through the perforations. Run the knife down the metal edge to fill the spaces with compound.

2 Apply a layer of compound to the wallboard on each side of an inside corner. Press precreased drywall tape into the corner with a corner tool or putty knife. Apply a thin layer of compound over the tape, and smooth the surface.

LOWE'S QUICK TIP
To create a crisp look, choose 90-degree metal corner beads. Or select rounded bullnose beads if you prefer a soft, plaster-like appearance.

repairing drywall

DRYWALL REPAIRS TYPICALLY INVOLVE REPAIRING DENTS AND POPPED NAILS, filling nail holes, and patching holes punched through the wall. These problems can usually be fixed simply, with just joint compound or spackling compound, a putty knife, and a few basic carpentry tools. After the repair, you must paint the repaired area to match the rest of the wall. If you do not have paint that matches, you will have to completely repaint the wall.

minor repairs To fix minor blemishes such as dents and small nail holes, sand the damaged area clean, and fill it with one or more layers of all-purpose joint compound using a flexible, narrow-bladed putty knife. Allow each layer to dry before applying the next. Fix popped nails by recessing the nail below the finished surface of the wall and driving another nail just beside it to hold it in. Cover the dimples with joint compound. When the repairs are dry, sand, prime, and paint the area.

repairing a large hole To repair a large hole, the damaged section of wallboard must be cut out and replaced with a new piece of gypsum wallboard of the same thickness. The key to a quality job is blending the repair with the surrounding surface. This is often done in three layers over a period of days. You will need ready-mixed all-purpose joint compound; 2-inch perforated or mesh wallboard tape; 4-, 6-, and 10-inch taping knives; and 400-grit silicon-carbide sandpaper.

Dip the edge of a clean taping-knife blade into the compound, loading about half the blade. Apply the compound across the joint. Then, holding the knife at a 45-degree angle to the wall, draw the blade along the joint. Let the compound dry for at least 24 hours, and then apply a second layer. When it is dry, apply a third. Using increasingly wider knives for each layer makes the joint smoother. When the last layer is dry, remove minor imperfections by wetting the compound with a sponge and sanding along the joints with sandpaper wrapped around a sanding block. Never sand the wallboard surface paper.

REPAIRING A LARGE HOLE IN DRYWALL

1 Cut out the damaged area by using a drywall saw or by making a series of progressively deeper cuts with a utility knife.

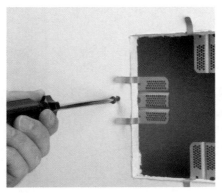

2 Slip the drywall repair clips onto the edges of the hole, and screw them into place. Be sure to drive the screw heads slightly below the surface of the drywall.

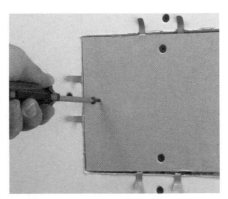

3 Cut a piece of drywall that will fit the hole. Drive screws through the patch into the clips. Finish the seams, and cover the clips using the method outlined above.

repairing plaster

PLASTER HAS A TENDENCY TO CRACK AS A HOME MOVES, WHETHER FROM EARTH-quakes or natural settling. Fine cracks, nail holes, and small gouges in plaster usually can be repaired with spackling compound. Widen hairline cracks to about ⅛ inch with the tip of a lever-type can opener; blow out dust and debris. With your finger or a putty knife, fill the crack with spackling compound. Sand the compound in a circular motion when dry, using a block wrapped with fine-grade sandpaper. Prime the patch with sealer.

REPAIRING HOLES

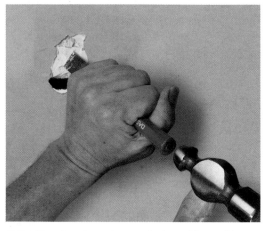

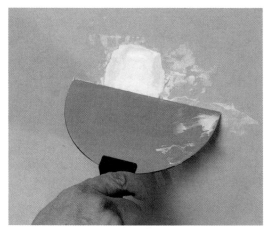

1 Knock out any loose plaster with a cold chisel and ball-peen hammer. Clean out the plaster in and behind the lath to provide a surface to which the new plaster can adhere. Brush the area clean, and dampen it with a sponge for better adhesion.

2 If the hole is smaller than 2 inches across (but larger than a fine crack, nail hole, or small gouge), fill it with a single layer of patching compound, and finish as described in Step 4. For larger holes, apply a first layer using a 6-inch broad knife.

3 Score the patch with a nail, and then allow the surface to dry. Moisten the patch, and then apply a second layer of patching compound, coming within ⅛ to ¼ inch of the surface. Score the patch, and let it dry.

4 Apply the final coat, feathering the edges an inch or so beyond the edges of the hole. Scrape a straightedge across the wet finish coat to remove any excess material. When the patch is dry, sand and spot-prime.

trim materials

COMMERCIAL MOULDINGS ARE MADE FROM A VARIETY OF DIFFERENT MATERIALS and come in a number of different profiles. Prices vary widely depending on the material itself and the complexity of the profile. Following below and on page 118 is a guide to your choices.

Trim made of wood is generally stocked in both softwoods and hardwoods. It is usually sold in lengths from 12 to 16 feet—often long enough to cover an entire wall. Paint-grade wood trim can be purchased pre-primed. If pieces of wood have been finger-jointed together (this is called PFJ, primed finger joint, trim) to form longer lengths, make sure the joints do not show through the primer.

You can buy wood trim off the shelf at a millwork supplier, lumberyard, or home improvement center, but availability varies from region to region. If your supplier does not stock the wood you want, you can request a special order, or you can investigate catalogs or Internet sites. Special orders will include setup and tooling fees, which will add significantly to your cost. Most trim dealers can also do custom runs for you.

Or, if you are skillful with a router, you can make your own trim. Poplar and straight-grained pine are fine for mouldings that will be painted. Make two or three shallow passes with the router, gradually working your way down to the final profile depth. For clear-finished trim, it is best to use hardwood. Be sure to rout cautiously and in several passes because any errors will show. If you are making many mouldings, a router table will hasten your work, increase safety and make your cuts more accurate.

If you are working in the Arts and Crafts, Modern, or Japanese styles, you can do much of your trim work with flat stock. Pine, maple, birch, beech, and bamboo are good species for light-colored trim. Douglas fir or oak is suitable for the stained trim typical of Arts and Crafts homes. When you are using flat boards for trim, look for the "S4S" (surfaced four sides) type, which means that the boards have been smoothed on all faces and edges so that any exposed side looks attractive.

Most boards are sold in nominal sizes. The names by which they are known indicate their size before milling, but actual sizes are smaller. Trim commonly uses 1-by stock, which was about 1 inch thick before milling; the finished thickness is about ¾ inch. For Arts and Crafts schemes, you will want ⁵⁄₄ and ⁴⁄₄ stock. A ⁵⁄₄ board is about an inch thick; a ⁴⁄₄ board is about ¾ inch thick.

softwoods Most interior trim projects are done with stock softwood mouldings. Clear, or stain-grade, mouldings are made from single lengths of lumber without knots and are meant to be clear-finished (stained or unstained). Paint-grade mouldings may have cosmetic flaws or be made up of many shorter pieces that are butt- or finger-jointed together. Pine, poplar, and basswood are all common species.

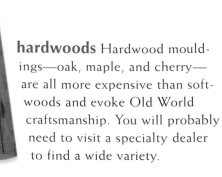

hardwoods Hardwood mouldings—oak, maple, and cherry—are all more expensive than softwoods and evoke Old World craftsmanship. You will probably need to visit a specialty dealer to find a wide variety.

medium-density fiberboard (MDF) This is a paint-grade trim that is less expensive than wood but is difficult to distinguish from the real thing when painted. Made by compressing wood fibers with resins, MDF trim has a smooth surface. Because it comes pre-primed, it can usually be finished with one coat of paint, and it requires little or no sanding. It will not split when it is nailed, and it is more resistant to dings and dents than most softwoods. But MDF is heavy (use a nail gun to fasten it) and will reflect every undulation in an uneven wall.

polyurethane trim If your trim will be painted, high-density polyurethane is a lightweight, inexpensive alternative to wood. It comes in many patterns, including ornate classical profiles that are extremely expensive to duplicate in wood. The one-piece mouldings, especially those that are joined together with corner blocks, are easy to install. Polyurethane can be cut and nailed without cracking, splintering, or splitting. It does not require predrilling for nails or screws, priming, or sanding before painting. It will not rot, and it expands and contracts much less than wood does when exposed to severe changes in temperature and humidity.

specialty pieces Sometimes a project cries out for a special accent piece. Such pieces, both molded and hand-carved, are available in hardwoods, softwoods, and composites to meet many requirements. Specialty pieces are usually expensive, but you do not need many to make a real difference in a room.

combination mouldings These mouldings are first milled from poplar. Then a composite material, carrying highly figured "carved" designs, is bonded to them. The result is an elaborate piece of trim that would be prohibitively expensive to produce by other means. When painted (they cannot be clear-finished), these mouldings lend great richness and style to a room.

flexible vinyl As the name suggests, these mouldings will follow curving walls to create an elegant effect. This is the only material that can make tight curves smoothly, as proved by the short length of baseboard shown here. Vinyl is cut and fastened just like wood, and it is impervious to water.

custom mouldings Sometimes stock mouldings don't quite create the look you are trying to achieve. Or you may need to match an older profile that is no longer made. For a setup charge, which includes grinding shaper knives for the profile you want, you can have a dealer make custom mouldings. Although this is expensive for a single room, the cost will be moderate when spread out over a very large job.

removing old trim

IF YOU ARE REPLACING EXISTING TRIM, IT'S OUT WITH THE OLD BEFORE IT'S IN with the new. In many cases, you can pretty much just rip out the old trim, taking care not to damage walls in the process. If, however, you want to reuse the old trim after remodeling, you will want to remove it carefully so as not to damage it.

If paint is binding the moulding to the wall, use a utility knife to score the paint along the edges of the moulding. Then use a stiff putty knife to slightly separate the moulding from the wall and create a space for prybars. To do this, slide the putty knife back and forth until you hit the finishing nails that hold the moulding in place.

After removing moulding that you intend to save, be sure to extract any nails from it.

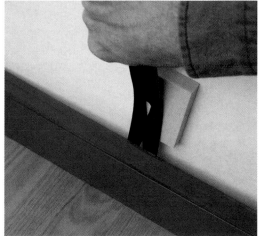

1 Insert a prybar at one set of nails, and place a scrap of wood behind the bar to protect the wall. Pry gently outward to bow the moulding away from the wall and loosen the nails. Move to the next set of nails, and repeat the process until you have loosened the moulding along its entire length.

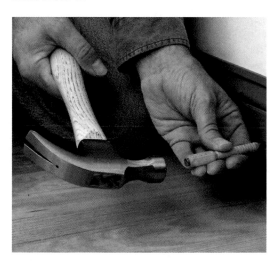

2 Sometimes the nails will not loosen, and prying will cause the nails to pull through the moulding. If the nails are stuck, use a nailset to drive them about three quarters of the way through the moulding's thickness. You do not need go all the way through.

3 Work with a pair of prybars and scrap blocks to remove the moulding, leapfrogging the bars in turn to gradually ease the moulding off without cracking or breaking it. After the moulding has been removed, use a hammer or prybar to remove any nails that remain in the wall.

LOWE'S QUICK TIP
If you are planning to reinstall moulding, label the back of each piece as you remove it to save time and confusion later on.

cutting & installing trim

BASE AND CROWN MOULDINGS AND CHAIR AND PICTURE RAILS USUALLY CONTINUE all the way around a room. The order in which you install the moulding pieces can make a difference in the effect, so plan your installation sequence carefully. Make a rough sketch of the room you are working on, and then consider the following points.

Stylistic consistency in crown mouldings, chair rails, wall paneling, door casings, and other trim gives a home's interior a finished look.

For a basic rectangular room, start with the most visible mouldings, the ones opposite the entry door. Square-cut the first mouldings where they meet adjoining walls. Once these starter pieces are installed, cut the adjoining pieces on either side, coping the corners that meet the first piece (see page 123). Cut the other ends square to butt against the adjacent walls. The final piece or pieces will be coped at both ends.

On very long walls, you may have to join shorter pieces with scarf joints (see page 123). Cut them so that they point away from you when you enter the room.

Some rooms have irregular shapes that involve outside and inside corners. The outside corners project into the room, and inside corners project away from the room. The former require mitered joints on trim (see pages 126–127), and the latter require coped joints. To remember which way the miter goes, keep in mind that with an outside corner, the cut trim pieces are longer on their outside surfaces (the ones facing the room). To cope an inside corner, always remember that the first cut is an inside miter cut, yielding a piece that is longer on the inside surface (the one facing the wall). Install the trim of the irregular area that requires the miters—such as a bay window, an alcove, or an L-shape—first.

When mounting mitered door and window casings (see page 122), lightly tack or clamp all the pieces in place first. You will probably have to make several adjustments to get everything lined up. Professionals generally put up the side casings first and then trim and fit the head casing, but this can be challenging for an amateur. A better approach is to start out with one side casing, temporarily fastened at the reveal line (the small amount of casing left uncovered), with the inner edge of the miter cut touching the head-casing reveal line. After that, position the head casing, trimming it to fit against the mitered side casing on one side and on the reveal line of the other side casing. Cut and fit the other side casing in the same way, keeping it a little long and then trimming the square-cut bottom until

you get a good fit. Once everything fits properly, take the pieces down, add glue at the joints, and nail the sections in place.

making secure attachments

For stability, all mouldings—especially weight-bearing mouldings such as picture rails and plate rails—should be attached to the wall studs. Finding studs can be a little tricky. Standard methods include tapping on the wall with your knuckle (you will listen for a solid rather than hollow sound) and using a stud finder (the indicator will show you). Or you can check the area around wall sockets and switches, which are nearly always attached to a stud on one side. A surefire way to find them is to drive small nails or drill 1/8-inch holes every inch or so along the wall in the area to be covered by the moulding until you hit the solid wood of a stud.

Once you have found a stud, the others should be 16 inches away from center to center on either side. After locating and marking the wall studs along the length of moulding you are installing, mark a level line, and position the moulding against it.

1 To attach the moulding, use finishing nails that are long enough to penetrate the stud to a depth equal to two times the combined thickness of the trim material and the wall material. Thus, for 1/2-inch-thick moulding and 1/2-inch wallboard, you will need 10-penny (3-inch) nails—1 inch to go through the moulding and wallboard and 2 inches to penetrate the stud. Sixteen-penny (3 1/2-inch) nails are usually necessary for thick mouldings and for those that must carry a lot of weight. For the best appearance (and to prevent splitting, especially at the ends of moulding pieces), drill pilot holes that are slightly smaller than the diameter of the nail. You can use construction adhesive with the nails to add strength, but be aware that if the mouldings ever need to be removed, you are likely to ruin the surface of gypsum wallboard.

2 Drive finishing nails at least 1/2 inch from the top and bottom edges of the moulding, where the nail heads will be easy to hide with wall patching compound. Hammer the nails to within 3/4 inch of the surface, and then use a nailset to drive them below the surface. Finish with wall patching compound if trim will be painted or with wood putty if trim will be clear-finished.

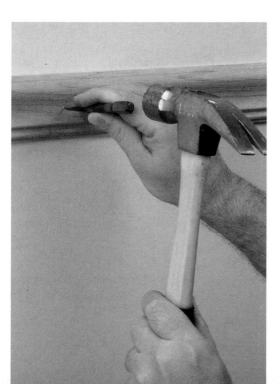

creating joints

Joinery lies at the heart of trim work. Good joints can make or break the effect. Often, the simplest joints—constructed using a few tricks of the trade—are the best, as the following guidelines explain.

butt joints

The simplest joint is the butt joint, where one piece is positioned flat against the other. Painter's caulk is applied to seal the edges of the moulding to the wall. Use a butt joint where two pieces of square-profile moulding meet at an inside corner; where side casings meet a window stool, plinth blocks, or the floor; and where a piece of thin moulding joins a thicker section. Avoid using a butt joint at an outside corner. The exposed end grain will be difficult to fill and cover with paint, and if the trim is intended to be stained later, the result will simply look unattractive.

A good butt joint must be gap-free, with a near-invisible line where the two pieces come together. Caulk may fill a tiny gap but may open up in time, so it is best to make the joint correctly in the first place. Test the fit of the pieces, and, if necessary, cut back the mating piece with a saw or block plane to achieve a tight fit on the face.

BELOW: **A butt joint is a simple but effective way of joining two square-profile pieces of trim at a corner that is nearly gap-free.** RIGHT: **Mitered corners for a window casing add dimension and a formal touch.**

mitered joints

Two pieces of trim meeting at an angle form a mitered joint. Miters can be cut across the face of the moulding (as shown below for a window casing) or across its thickness, as for the 45-degree cut used to turn a 90-degree corner (see pages 126–127). Compound miters, mostly confined to crown mouldings, are cut across both the face and the thickness.

An outside corner, which is formed by a projection into a room, requires outside miters in crown moulding, in a chair and picture rail, and in a baseboard. An inside corner will join seamlessly when you cope the joints; start the joint with a miter cut (see Step 1 on the facing page).

Flat miters, which are used at the corners of many door and window casings and in wall frames, are like the joints in a picture frame. If the wall is irregular, a flat miter may need to be cut back or otherwise trimmed to allow the joint to close without a gap.

For accuracy, the mating pieces must be cut at exactly the same angle, bisecting the total angle to be framed. To cut angles that are precisely or approximately 90 degrees, you can generally rely on your miter saw's angle guides for cutting and then trim to make minor adjustments. For other angles, measure with a bevel gauge, and divide the total angle in half with a protractor. Set your miter saw to this angle, cut the pieces, and then test their fit. Trim, if necessary, with the saw or a

block plane. You can cut back slightly to produce a tight face for the joint.

Test the fit of the pieces, predrill, and then nail them in place, putting one nail through from an edge to help keep the joint together. In the photo on the facing page, this "clinching" nail is on the left edge of the casing. To avoid splitting, keep nails approximately ¾ inch away from the ends of the joints.

coped joints

Coped joints are asymmetrical. One side is butted into the corner, and then the other side is cut to fit against the profile of the butted piece.

It is best to use coped joints at inside corners for baseboards, chair and picture rails, and crown mouldings. This is the only easy way to create a gap-free joint with complex mouldings and a joint that will remain tight when walls are out of square and when seasons change.

Although coped joints may seem complicated at first, they actually save labor. Once you have cut a few, you will find that they are easy to make—much easier than trying to cut and assemble accurate compound miter joints at inside corners.

scarf joints

When a wall is too long to be spanned by a single piece of moulding, you will need to join separate pieces. Do not just butt them together; the resulting line will show through even the best sanding and painting or staining job. Instead, use a scarf joint, centering it over a stud if possible.

Plan to point the joint away from the most likely viewing angle. First, cut the mating pieces at opposing angles. Cutting at a 30-degree angle is best if your saw can manage it; if not, you can cut the pieces at 45 degrees. Sand lightly to remove any roughness left by the blade. Carefully position the moulding along a marked line on the wall, supporting the joint with a tacked-on 1 by 4 or other light, straight board. Fasten the joint with glue and nails, and give it a light final sanding. Once it is finished, the joint should be nearly invisible.

A scarf joint appears almost seamless, especially when the cut is made away from view.

CUTTING A COPED JOINT

1 Miter-cut the moulding at 45 degrees, keeping the back edge longer than the front. To cope the back side, trim away the excess to create a mirror image of the moulding's contours. The front edge of the cut, which follows the moulding's profile (this is called "revealing the profile"), is the cutting line. Rubbing a pencil over this edge will make the cutting line more visible.

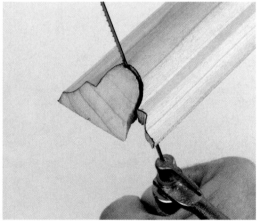

2 Hold the coping saw above the moulding with the blade perpendicular to it, as if you were going to cut the end squarely. Cut from top to bottom, following the curves of the front edge. In the middle of the cut, angle the blade so that it cuts back, and then return the blade to the perpendicular to finish the cut. Test the fit of the joint; it will probably require some adjustment. With a small rasp or file, carefully adjust the cut edge (thin edges can break easily) until you get a good, tight fit. Nail the moulding to the wall, and caulk any gaps.

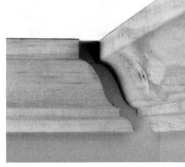

A coped joint is unparalleled for joining complex mouldings without gaps.

installing baseboard

BASEBOARD MOULDING PLAYS A KEY ROLE IN THE DECORATING SCHEME OF MANY rooms. If the baseboards you have now do not fit into your plans, replacing them is a relatively straightforward project. Many styles of baseboard, including the type shown here, come with matching corner blocks that greatly simplify running moulding around corners. The blocks are installed first, and then straight lengths are cut at 90 degrees to fit in between.

For corner blocks made of hardwood, drill pilot holes through the pieces before driving nails or the wood may split. If you plan to paint your new mouldings, apply a coat of primer before installation.

Some baseboards are combined with quarter-round shoe moulding, usually nailed to the baseboard or to the floor. Remove shoe moulding first, using the method shown in Step 1 below.

1 Remove the old baseboard. If the baseboard is fused to the wall with layers of paint, cut through the paint between the moulding and wall with a utility knife to open a gap large enough for a putty-knife blade. Slip the putty knife into the gap near one end of the baseboard, and push a wood shim behind the blade to protect the wall. Use a small prybar to pry the baseboard ½ inch away from the wall. Continue along the wall with the prybar and shim until you can pull off the entire length of moulding. Remove the nails.

2 Predrill the outside corner blocks. The outside corner block shown is to be nailed in place through the front corner. Drill pilot holes for the nails with the corner block clamped facedown to a work surface atop a scrap board. Fit an electric drill with a bit of the same diameter as the nails, and then drill two pilot holes straight through the block. Guide the drill so the bit exits at the front corner of the block. Locate the holes about 1 inch from the top and bottom of the block.

3 Fasten the outside corner blocks. Hold the outside corner block in position, making sure it is flat on the floor and flush against both wall surfaces. Drive a finishing nail into each hole to anchor the block to the wall. To avoid marring the wood, leave ¼ inch of the nails protruding, and then sink the heads below the surface with a nailset.

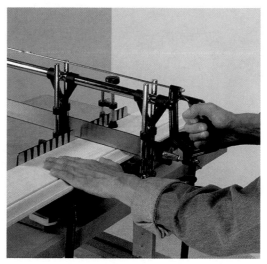

4 Anchor the inside corner blocks. Hold an inside corner block in position, and then drill two pilot holes through each face of the block, locating the holes about 1 inch from the top and bottom and offsetting them as shown. Drive a finishing nail into each hole to anchor the block to the wall, and then sink the heads. In case your walls are not perfectly square, check the angle of the corner blocks before cutting a straight length of baseboard to fit between them. Holding the handle of a bevel gauge against the floor, adjust the blade so it rests flush against the inside corner block. Adjust the angle of your miter box to the angle set on the bevel gauge.

5 Cut straight lengths of baseboard. Measure the distance between the inside and outside corner blocks, and transfer your measurement to a straight length of baseboard by marking two cutting lines. With the baseboard face up on the base of the miter box, align one of your cutting marks with the blade, and make the cut. Measure the angle of the outside corner block, as shown in Step 4, adjust the saw accordingly, and cut the other end of the baseboard.

6 Nail straight lengths of baseboard. With a stud finder, locate and mark the wall studs between corner blocks. Fasten straight lengths of moulding to the wall with a pair of 2-inch finishing nails at each stud, locating the nails 1½ inches from the top and bottom edges of the baseboard. Sink the nail heads with a nailset.

7 To finish the job, fill any gaps between the baseboard and the wall using a caulking gun and latex caulk. Conceal the nail heads with a non-shrinking latex hole filler. Let the caulk and filler dry according to the manufacturer's directions, use fine sandpaper to smooth the area, and apply a finish to the baseboard.

LOWE'S QUICK TIP
You can apply a finish to the moulding either before or after installation. If you are planning to wait until after installation, first finish the back face, which will keep the moulding from warping.

installing crown moulding

CROWN MOULDING IS NOW USED TO ADD A FORMAL LOOK TO A ROOM, BUT IT once played a practical role by concealing the joint between walls and ceilings. Widths and styles vary from simple flat moulding to the more commonly used decorative mouldings featured in this project. Wider, more elaborate mouldings tend to need larger spaces and higher ceilings to appear well-proportioned. For a room with 8-foot-high ceilings, choose a moulding that is about 3¼ inches wide.

Crown moulding is available in several materials, all of which are suitable for painting, including medium-density fiberboard (MDF) and polyurethane. Unlike wood, these materials do not contain knots and will not warp or twist. Of course, if you prefer a natural look, nothing quite equals the beauty of wood.

1 Measure the moulding projections. Before you can install your crown moulding, you must determine where the trim will rest on the walls and ceiling. Place a short length of trim against a carpenter's square so one arm of the square represents the wall and the other represents the ceiling. Record the vertical projection (how far down the wall the trim will extend) as well as the horizontal projection (how far along the ceiling the trim will extend). The 3¼-inch-wide moulding in this project has vertical and horizontal projections of 2⅜ inches.

2 Mark the moulding location. Beginning at one corner, measure and mark the vertical projection from the ceiling on both adjacent walls. Next, measure and mark the moulding's horizontal projection on the ceiling. Mark the same measurements at the opposite corners of the room. Attach a chalk line to a small finishing nail driven into the wall at one of the marks. Unwind the chalk line to the mark at the other end of the wall, and snap the line. Snap similar guidelines along the other walls and along the ceiling. With a stud finder, locate and mark the studs along the tops of the walls, marking the stud locations just above the guidelines. Also locate and mark ceiling joists that lie perpendicular to the walls.

3 Check the outside corners for square. Outside corners are not always 90 degrees—especially in older homes—and a standard 45-degree miter cut will not result in a tight joint if the corners in your home are not square. This step will help you cut a better-fitting corner joint. Cut a length of moulding, and hold it along the guidelines, extending it a few inches beyond the corner. Mark a line on the ceiling along the top edge of the trim, extending the line the full length of the piece. Repeat the procedure on the adjacent wall, intersecting the first mark.

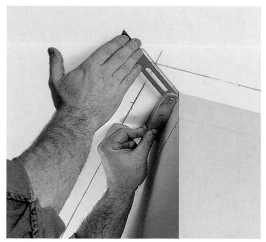

4 Determine the miter angle. Use a bevel gauge to measure the angle of the corner and to set up the cutting angle of your saw. Hold the handle of the gauge against one of the walls, and open the blade so it aligns with the corner and the point at which the lines drawn on the ceiling intersect. Lock the angle of the gauge, and lay the tool against the adjustable base of a sliding compound miter saw. Set the base, and tilt the blade of the saw to the angle on the bevel gauge.

5 Cut the moulding. Place the moulding upside down on the saw base with the bottom edge (the edge to be installed against the wall) flush against the fence. If it will be installed against the left of the corner, place it to the right of the blade. If the trim will be to the right of the corner, set it on the left side of the blade. Holding the moulding against the fence with your hands clear of the blade and aligning your cutting mark with the blade, saw the moulding.

6 Fasten the moulding in place. Align the moulding with the chalk lines keeping its mitered end toward the corner, and then fasten the moulding with a 2½-inch finishing nail at each wall stud and ceiling joist. For hardwood, first drill pilot holes. If the joists run parallel to the wall, fasten the trim to the ceiling with a nail at each end and construction adhesive in between. Spread wood glue on the mitered ends of both lengths of moulding, and then fasten the second piece. Drill a pilot hole for a 1¼-inch finishing nail through the joint from each side of the corner, and then drive in the nails. Sink the nails with a nailset.

7 Fasten trim at an inside corner. Adjust the bevel gauge to the angle of the corner, and then measure the angle with a protractor. Set the saw's angle to one-half that angle. Place the moulding right side up on the saw base, and miter the pieces as shown in Step 5. Fasten the moulding in place, driving 2½-inch finishing nails into the wall studs and ceiling joists. Use nails and construction adhesive if the joists run parallel to the wall. Sink the nails with a nailset as you go. Fill the nail holes with wood filler if you will be applying a clear finish; use a latex hole filler if you will be painting the moulding.

LOWE'S QUICK TIP
A pneumatic trim nailer, available at Lowe's, makes fastening trim a quick job and eliminates hammer dents.

adding a chair rail

CHAIR RAILS WERE ORIGINALLY INSTALLED, MAINLY IN DINING ROOMS, TO PROTECT plaster or paneled walls from being dented by chair backs. Although chair rails serve more of a decorative purpose than a functional one these days, they generally maintain their traditional profile: A length of flat, thin moulding features a rounded projecting element that serves as a bumper for chair backs. Other profiles are available—or you can create your own design by doubling up two styles of chair rail, installing one on top of the other.

Chair rails can be added to virtually any room of your house. Installed about 36 inches above the floor, chair rails divide walls visually, creating an ideal opportunity to employ two complementary wall treat-ments. Options include painting above the rail and wallpapering below or applying a different paint color on each side of the divide. The darker of the two should always be on the bottom.

1 Prime the trim if it will be painted. You can apply a top coat of paint or finish a chair rail before or after installing it. If you plan to cover the moulding before installation, apply an even coat of finish with a brush about the same width as the chair rail. Allow the pieces to dry.

2 Lay out level guidelines. Measure up 36 inches from the floor at both ends of each wall, mark these points, and then drive a finishing nail through each mark. Hook the end of a chalk line to a nail, and extend the line across the wall to the other nail. Snap a chalk line on the wall. With a carpenter's level, check that the chalk lines are level. If not, draw a level line above or below the chalk lines using the top edge of the level as a straightedge.

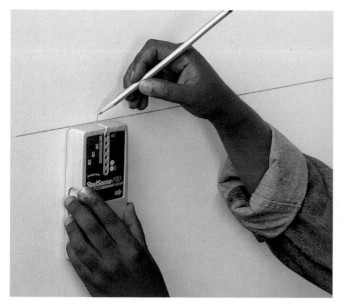

3 The chair rail should be fastened to wall studs, which are typically spaced at 16-inch intervals. Locate the studs with a stud finder. Using the electronic model shown, pass the device back and forth over the wall. The light at the top will indicate when the stud finder crosses the edges of a stud. Mark the center of each stud—which will be about 3/4 inch from the edges—on the guidelines.

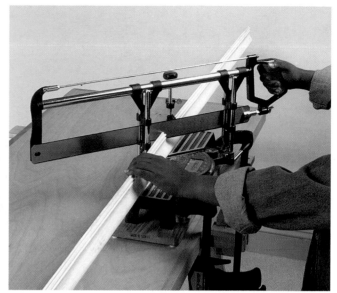

4 Miter the trim. For a chair-rail trim with a simple profile, such as the style shown here, the pieces can be joined at the corners with miters. For each wall, measure the distance between the corners, and then transfer this measurement onto the back face of the moulding. Set the chair rail upright in a miter box with the back face of the moulding pressed flush against the fence. Adjust the saw's blade angle for a 45-degree cut, and saw the chair rail.

5 Position the trim on the wall, aligning the top edge with the guideline and the mitered ends with the corners. Test-fit the corner joints—you may have to sand the mitered ends to close gaps. Fasten the chair rail to the wall with a pair of 2-inch finishing nails at each stud mark, locating the nails 1/2 inch from the top and bottom edges of the trim. To avoid marring the wood, leave 1/4 inch of the nails protruding, and then sink all heads below the surface with a nailset.

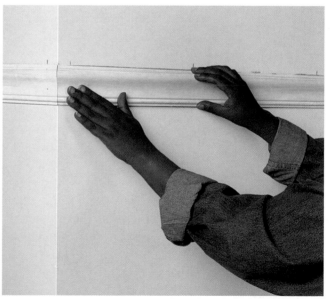

6 To ensure a snug fit at outside corners, drill a pilot hole for a 1 1/4-inch finishing nail through the joint from each side of the corner and then drive in the nails. Sink the nails, and fill all the holes with wood filler.

paneling a wall

THERE IS A PANELING STYLE FOR ALMOST EVERY DECOR. CHOICES INCLUDE RUSTIC boards, frame-and-panel designs with or without moulding, and elaborate raised panels. You can cover an entire wall or choose waist- or shoulder-high wainscoting. Paneling can be made from fine hardwoods or inexpensive pine. Finishes run the gamut as well. Panels can be given a clear finish or they can be painted, stained, or coated with any number of decorative finishes.

Paneling is sold in two main forms: sheets and boards. Sheets are typically 4 feet by 8 feet. Boards range from ⅜ to ⅞ inch thick, but the most common thicknesses are ½ and ¾ inch. Boards come in widths of between 3 and 10 inches and may have either square, tongue-and-groove, or shiplap edges.

Before installing paneling, place the materials in the room where they will be installed for two to five days to allow the wood to adjust to the home's humidity level. This will help eliminate any shrinkage or expansion problems once the panels are secured to the wall.

preparing a wall

When applying sheet or board panels over a finished wood-frame wall, you may be able to attach the material through the wallboard or plaster to the wall studs; otherwise, you will have to attach furring strips—1-by-3s or 1-by-4s—to the studs as a base for securing the panels. If the wall is new and without wallboard or plaster, you can attach sheets or boards directly to the studs or to 2-by-4 blocks nailed between the studs. Attach furring strips to wall studs with nails long enough to penetrate the studs by at least 1 inch. Fasten the strips to masonry walls using concrete nails or screws and shield-type masonry anchors.

To ensure that siding will sit flat on the wall, furring strips should be plumb and flat; you can make adjustments with cedar-shingle shims wedged behind the furring strips as needed. Leave a ¼-inch space at both the top and the bottom of the wall when applying the strips to allow for unevenness in the floor or ceiling.

Note that furring strips and paneling will add to the thickness of the wall. Window and door jambs must be built out to compensate for this. It is likely that you will have to add extensions to electrical switches and receptacle boxes, as well.

installing sheet paneling

Before installation, cut each sheet ¼ inch shorter than the distance from the floor to the ceiling. Apply adhesive to the framing in wavy lines. Drive four finishing nails through the top edge of the panel. Position the panel on the wall, leaving a ¼-inch space at the bottom, and drive the four nails partway into the wall. Pull the bottom edge of the panel about 6 inches from the wall, and push a block behind the sheet. Wait for the adhesive to become tacky. Remove the block, and press the panel firmly into place by knocking on the panel with a rubber mallet, or by hammering against a padded block. Drive the top-edge nails all the way in, and then nail the panel at the bottom and, if needed, through the grooves at stud locations. Cover the nail heads and the ¼-inch gap with moulding.

Fitting a panel around any opening requires careful measuring, marking, and cutting. Keep track of all the measurements by sketching them on a piece of paper.

Starting from the corner of the wall or the edge of the nearest panel, measure out to the edge of the opening or electrical box. Then, from the same point, measure out to the opening's opposite edge. Next, measure the distance from the floor to the opening's bottom edge and from the floor to the opening's top edge. (Remember that you will install the paneling ¼ inch above the floor.) Transfer these measurements to the panel, marking the side of the panel that will face you as you cut (face up for a handsaw, face down for a power saw).

1 With a helper, position the first panel at one corner of the room, but do not apply panel adhesive yet. Check the inside edge of the panel with a level to make sure it is plumb.

2 While your helper holds the panel in place, use a compass or scribe tool to scribe the corner edge of the panel so that it can be cut to fit snugly against the adjoining wall. Draw the compass along the adjoining wall so the pencil leg duplicates the unevenness onto the panel.

3 Cut the marked edge along the pencil line. A saber saw works best for this, but you will need to use a fine-toothed blade to avoid fraying the front of the panel. Or, you can transfer the mark to the backside of the panel and turn the panel over to cut it.

4 Attach the panel to the wall as detailed on the facing page. Place nails in the dark grooves where they're least likely to be visible. Stop hammering before the nail head reaches the surface, and set the head flush with a nailset.

5 When a panel must be cut for a switch or receptacle, hold the panel in position against the electrical box and mark the box's location. Snap chalk lines to the approximate place where the box will go. Then measure the distance from the edge of the adjoining installed panel to both sides of the box, and transfer these dimensions onto the panel between the chalk lines.

6 Make cutouts for electrical boxes using a saber saw equipped with a fine-cutting blade.

laying out **wall tile**

ONCE YOU HAVE MADE SURE THE WALL YOU WANT TO TILE IS PLUMB AND FLAT, it's time to plan exactly where the tiles will go. The main goal when laying out wall tiles is to avoid a row of very narrow-cut tiles. Narrow tiles look awkward and emphasize any imperfections in adjoining walls. A secondary goal is symmetry. Whenever it is possible, center the tiles on the wall so that the cut tiles at either side are the same size. An obstruction such as a window can make the layout much more complicated because you will also need to avoid having narrow tiles around its sides.

installing a batten

Decide how high above the floor the second horizontal row of tiles will be. If the floor beneath is fairly level and the bottom of the tiles will be covered with a base moulding, position the second row above the floor by the height of one tile plus an inch or so. If there will be no base moulding and the bottom row of tiles must meet the floor precisely, plan to cut all the tiles on the bottom row to about three-fourths of their full height.

Use a level to draw a horizontal working line for the second row. Draw a plumb vertical line in the exact center of the room. Attach a batten—a very straight board— with its top edge against the horizontal line. A long strip of plywood with one factory edge makes an ideal batten.

Position tiles in a dry run on top of the batten, starting at the centerline and running to one adjacent wall (below). If the tiles are not self-spacing, add spacers between them. If this layout leads to a particularly narrow-cut tile at the end, mark a corrected vertical line that will allow you to move the tiles the width of one-half tile in either direction.

handling obstacles

Small obstacles such as electrical receptacles or switches are not usually considered in the layout; an occasional narrow-cut tile does not present a problem. But a large obstacle, such as a window, may be the focal point of the wall. Avoid surrounding such an obstacle with narrow-cut tiles, and note that it is always preferable to make the cut tiles on either side the same size.

Measure to check whether there will be a narrow vertical row of tiles along either edge of the obstacle. If so, you may have to choose between placing narrow tiles there or putting them at the wall edges. Also determine whether there will be a narrow horizontal row of tiles just below or just above the obstacle. If it's clear that there will be, you may choose to raise or lower the batten.

If a room has more than one highly visible obstruction, you will probably have to make some compromises. If any of the obstructions is seriously out of plumb or level, try to place wide-cut tiles there.

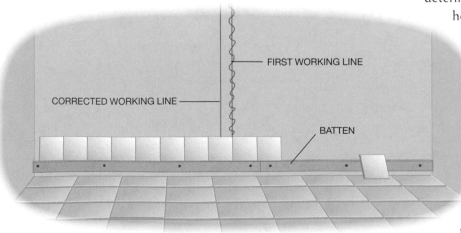

FIRST WORKING LINE

CORRECTED WORKING LINE

BATTEN

tiling a wall

IF THE WALL SUBSTRATE HAS BEEN WELL PREPARED, INSTALLING THE TILES WILL be a straightforward job. Double-check to see that the surface is flat and firm and that adjoining walls are plumb.

Organic mastic, which comes ready-mixed, is easy to apply and allows tiles to be adjusted up to 30 minutes after installation. Thinset mortar is more difficult to work with, but it is more resistant to water. Use mastic for walls that will stay relatively dry, and consider thinset for a wall that will often get wet, such as a tub enclosure (see pages 135–137).

  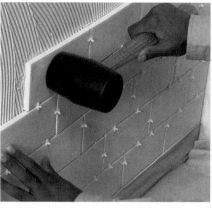

1 Using a trowel with notches recommended by the mastic manufacturer, scoop mastic out of the container, and spread it on the wall. Leave the working lines visible. As much as possible, apply the mastic with long, sweeping strokes. Continue to hold the trowel at the same angle to ensure a setting bed of consistent depth. The trowel teeth should lightly scrape the wall surface.

2 Press each tile into the adhesive. Avoid sliding a tile more than ½ inch. Add spacers as you go. Every 15 minutes or so, check the entire installation to make sure no tiles have strayed out of alignment. Using a cloth dampened with water or mineral spirits (depending on the type of mastic used), wipe away any mastic that squeezes onto the surface of a tile.

3 Tap the tile surface with a mallet to make sure the tiles are embedded in the mastic and form a smooth wall surface. If a tile's surface is raised noticeably above the surface of its neighbor, tap the raised tile against the wall using a rubber mallet. If this does not do the trick, you may have to remove some tiles, reapply mastic, and start over again.

cutting wall tiles

Most ceramic wall tiles are softer than floor tiles and can be cut easily with a snap cutter or rod saw. If a ceramic tile is too hard for a rod saw, use tile nippers, a wet saw, or both together. Stone tiles must always be cut with a wet saw, which is available for rent at many home centers.

To make a cutout with a rod saw, hold the tile firmly and allow the area to be cut to overhang the work surface (above). Saw with steady, moderate pressure. When turning a corner, take care not to twist the saw—you may crack the tile.

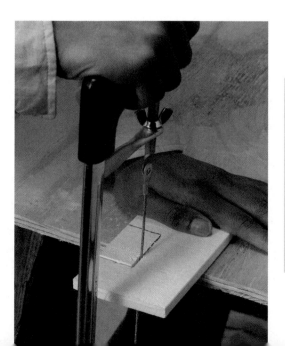

LOWE'S QUICK TIP
The moulding piece below a windowsill, called the apron, can be removed and then replaced after the tiles have been set. You can also remove it permanently and tile all the way up to the windowsill. No other window mouldings can be treated in this way.

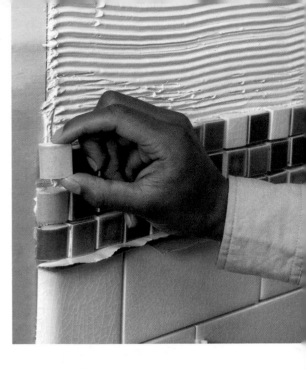

adding trim tiles

To finish off the unglazed edges of field tiles, add bullnose-tile pieces (also called caps), which have one finished edge. At an outside corner, use a corner-tile piece or a down-angle tile, which comes with two finished edges.

Bullnose tiles are supposed to have the same dimensions as the field tiles, but don't be surprised if you find they are slightly smaller. Leave a bit more space between them to maintain straight grout lines (right). If you have square tiles, you can compensate for this variation in size by positioning the bullnose tiles so that their grout lines do not line up with those of the field tiles.

grouting & finishing

Wait for the adhesive to completely harden before grouting (it can take a day or two). If you can move a tile to the side using your hand, you need to wait longer.

Use unsanded grout for joints less than ⅛ inch wide and sanded grout for wider joints. Unless the grout is fortified with powdered latex, mix it with liquid latex even if the directions say you can mix it with water only.

Prepare as much grout as you can use in 20 minutes or so. In a clean bucket, mix the liquid latex or water with the powder (a margin trowel works well as a mixing tool) until the grout is free of lumps and about as thick as toothpaste. Wait 10 minutes, and then stir again.

1 Tilt the float up, and use it like a squeegee to wipe away most of the grout from the face of the tiles. Be careful to scrape diagonally so that the edge of the float cannot dig into the grout lines between the tiles.

2 Dampen a sponge, and wipe the tiles gently. Rinse the sponge every few minutes with clean water. If you see a gap in a grout line, push grout into it using your finger, and wipe away the excess. Then wipe the surface two or three more times.

3 Run the sponge gently along the vertical and horizontal grout lines to make them consistent. If necessary, try running the rounded handle of a tool along each line. Allow the grout to dry, and then buff the surface of the tiles with a dry, lint-free cloth.

tiling a tub surround

A TUB SURROUND IS ONE OF THE MOST COMMON TILING PROJECTS. IN MOST cases, the tile extends about 4 feet above the tub. On the sides, you can either stop at the edge of the tub or extend the tile surface past the tub so a vertical row of trim tiles reaches the floor. Tiling a shower stall is nearly identical, except that you will run the tile to within a few inches of the ceiling. (Running the tile to the ceiling is usually avoided because ceilings are seldom perfectly level.) While similar to tiling a wall, tiling a tub or shower is more complicated because you will need to work around the faucet or shower control and amenities such as soap dishes, niches, and seats.

preparing the wall

To complete a long-lasting tile installation, use cement backerboard as a substrate. Remove all nails or screws from the studs. Measure to find out how thick the backerboard must be to match the surrounding wall surface. To cut backerboard, use a straightedge and a cement-board knife. The side-wall backerboard must be flush with the abutting wall surface.

Turn off the water supply, and remove faucet handles, the tub spout, and the shower arm. In most cases, you can remove a faucet head by prying off a decorative cover in the center of the handle, removing the screw that is underneath, and pulling off the handle. If there is an escutcheon (flange) behind the handle, it may simply lift off, or you may have to loosen a small setscrew first and pull off the handle.

To remove a spout, insert a wooden dowel into the opening, and then lever it counterclockwise. Or, wrap the faucet with tape or a rag, and use slip-joint pliers or a pipe wrench. Use the same technique to remove a shower arm.

INSTALLING BACKERBOARD

1 Place strips of ¼-inch plywood on the tub rim as spacers to prevent moisture from wicking up into the backerboard. Starting with the back wall, cut pieces of backerboard to fit, allowing a ⅛-inch gap between pieces. Drive a few backerboard screws through the backerboard and into the studs, sinking the heads of the screws just below the surface.

2 Measure and mark the backerboard for the center of each pipe. With a carbide-tipped hole saw, cut each hole about ½ inch wider than the pipe. Or, drill a hole in the center using a masonry bit, score the outline, and punch the hole out with a hammer. Drive screws every 6 inches into the studs. Press fiberglass mesh tape along each joint. Mix a little thinset mortar (see page 136); trowel a thin coat over the mesh tape. Feather the edges, and smooth any bumps.

applying thinset

In a 2-gallon bucket, combine thinset powder with latex additive to make enough thinset to last for 20 minutes or so. Hand-mix the solution with a margin trowel, or use a small mixer on an electric drill, until all the lumps are gone.

When it is properly mixed, the thinset should be almost thick enough to stick to a trowel held sideways. Let the mixture set for 10 minutes, and then stir again; it will be a bit thicker. The ideal mortar is just stiff enough to hold the shape of trowel lines on the wall but wet enough so that tiles will stick.

Using a ¼-inch-by-¼-inch square-notched trowel, spread thinset over about 10 square feet of the wall. Do not cover up the working lines.

installing the tiles

Check that the batten is level and the layout lines are plumb. Tiles set in organic mastic can be adjusted up to 30 minutes after setting them, but tiles set in thinset mortar should not be moved after 5 minutes. Check alignment every few minutes.

installing spacers To install irregularly shaped tiles, check every other horizontal row of tiles for level, and closely follow the plumb layout line in the center of the wall. Use scraps of cardboard as spacers, folding them if needed.

If you are installing regularly shaped tiles that are not self-spacing, place a plastic spacer at every corner, as shown below. Self-spacing tiles simply butt against each other. With either type of tile, once you have installed 10 tiles or so, there is no way to change the alignment.

Don't worry if the tiles go slightly awry from the layout line; it is more important that the tile corners align with each other. On the back wall, you have a margin for error; the cut tiles can be as much as ¼ inch short. Any such gaps will be filled in by the thickness of the side-wall tiles.

tiling the side walls On the side wall opposite the wall with plumbing fixtures, install the first two rows of full-sized field tiles, and then measure and cut pieces to fit at the corner. Cut them precisely; there should be no more than a ¹⁄₁₆-inch gap at

INSTALLING A TUB SURROUND

1 Work along the batten, pressing tiles firmly into the mortar or thinset. Add cut tiles on either side as you go. To be sure the tiles will stick, use a straight trowel to butter each piece with a thin coat of mortar.

2 Install the full-sized tiles closest to a pipe. Then hold a tile in place, and mark it for a cut. Use a square to mark both sides of the notch.

the corner, but you should not have to force a tile into position.

If a tile is slightly too wide, use a tile stone to shave off a little, or discard the piece and cut a new tile. Keep the tile-cutting guide in position so you can cut tiles for the next rows. You may need to adjust the cutting guide slightly as you move up the wall; few walls are absolutely plumb. Finish with the border and trim tiles as you did on the back wall.

On the side wall that has the plumbing, install as many full-sized tiles as possible. Temporarily prop any unsupported tiles in place so they will stay in horizontal alignment. Then measure for the tiles that must be cut to go around the pipes.

tiling around pipes

In most cases, you will need to cut a notch in a tile to wrap around a pipe, as shown in Step 2. If a pipe falls in the middle of a tile, measure to the center of the pipe, mark the cut on the tile, and bore a hole using a drill equipped with a carbide-tipped hole saw.

If you do not have a carbide-tipped hole saw and need to cut a hole in the interior of a tile, drill a series of closely spaced $\frac{1}{4}$-inch holes around the perimeter of the cut you have marked, and then gently tap out the center using a hammer.

tiling down to the tub

The bottom row of tiles should be $\frac{1}{8}$ inch above the tub; this will prevent cracking as the area expands and contracts with temperature changes. To install the bottom row, first remove the batten and scrape away any dried thinset. Cut tiles to fit, allowing for the $\frac{1}{8}$-inch gap above the tub's edge. If possible, spread thinset on the wall; otherwise, spread it on the backs of the tiles, and press them into place.

Cutting the tile located near the outer edge of the tub also requires special care. The bullnose tile at each outer corner of the tub can be cut straight like the others, but you will achieve a neater appearance if you cut it to follow the curve of the tub. Cutting this piece is tricky. Prepare a cardboard template with a utility knife. Trace the outline onto a bullnose tile, and then cut the piece carefully with a rod saw (see page 134).

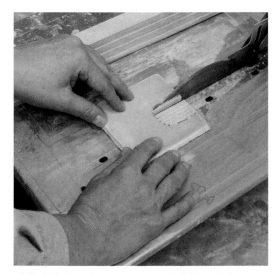

3 Most curved cuts in wall tiles can be made with a rod saw. A wet saw (shown above) or nibbling tool also works well. Make the cut about $\frac{1}{4}$ inch larger than it needs to be.

4 Test that no part of the tile ends up closer than $\frac{1}{8}$ inch to the pipe. If the mortar begins to harden while you are cutting the tile, scrape the mortar away, and back-butter the tile.

LOWE'S QUICK TIP
On the side walls, you may choose to extend the tiles past the tub by the width of a tile or two and run the outermost tiles along the tub all the way down to the floor. In that case, remove the baseboard trim, install the tiles, and cut and install the baseboard to meet up with the tiles.

installing a suspended ceiling

EASY-TO-INSTALL SUSPENDED CEILINGS CONSIST OF A METAL GRID SUPPORTED from above by wire or spring-type hangers. The grid holds acoustic or decorative fiberboard panels. In addition to the panels on display at Lowe's (and available by special order), look at some of the commercial offerings in manufacturers' catalogs and websites.

With suspended ceilings, light reflectivity (below) and acoustical control (right) are the two main functions to consider.

The most common panel dimension is 2 feet by 4 feet. Transparent and translucent plastic panels and egg-crate grills are made to fit the supporting grid and admit light from above. Recessed lighting panels that exactly replace one panel are available from some manufacturers.

All components are replaceable, and panels can be raised for access to wiring, ducts, and pipes. Panels are usually sold in packages containing a certain number of square feet of material. To estimate the quantity you need, measure the length and width of the room, eliminating areas that will not be covered with panels (a skylight or a ceiling fan, for example). Multiply these figures for the square footage, and add 10 percent for waste.

For a professional-looking job, plan to create equal-size borders on opposite sides of the room. To determine the nonstandard width of panels needed for perimeter rows, measure the extra space from the last full row of pieces to one wall and divide by two. This final figure will be the width of border pieces against that wall and the opposite wall. To complete your plan, repeat this procedure for the other room dimensions.

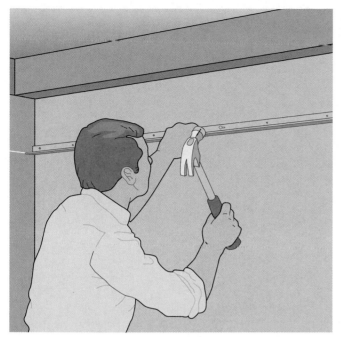

1 To install the track supports, first figure out the ceiling height—it should be at least 3 inches below plumbing and 5 inches below lights. Minimum ceiling height is 7 feet, 6 inches. Snap a chalk line around the room at your chosen level, and install right-angle moulding just covering the chalk line.

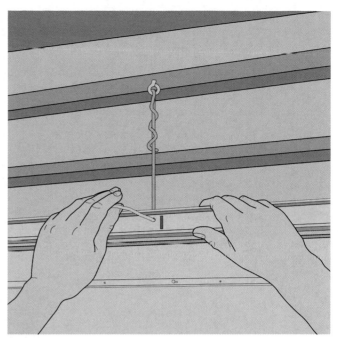

2 To hang the main runners for the panels, cut the main tees to length with tin snips or a hacksaw. Setting them on the right-angle moulding at each end, support them every 4 feet with #12 wire attached to small eye screws that are fastened into the joists above.

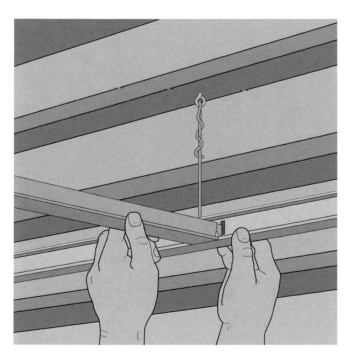

3 Lock 4-foot cross tees to the main tees by inserting the tabs into the slots in the main tees and then snapping them in place.

4 Slide the panels up diagonally through the grid openings, and lower them into place. Install any recessed lighting panels. Cut border panels as necessary with a sharp utility knife. Be sure your hands are clean when handling panels—smudges and fingerprints are hard to remove.

floors

FLOORS ARE OFTEN A HOME'S FOCAL POINT, AND FOR GOOD REASON. INSIDE
the house, nothing occupies as much continuous space. Most homes feature a variety
of flooring types—perhaps hardwood in the public rooms, carpet in the bedroom areas,
and tile or resilient flooring in the kitchen and bathrooms. Each of these materials has
its own strengths and weaknesses. To help you select the right one for your particular
circumstances and needs, this chapter starts with flooring basics and a buyer's guide.

Next come instructions for installing a variety of flooring materials (including wood,
engineered, resilient tile and sheet, ceramic tile, and stone). While installation of a new
floor does demand at least a certain amount of skill and self-confidence, new technologies and materials have made it possible for the less-experienced home improver to take
on floor-laying projects with greater ease and almost assured success.

A beautifully finished hardwood floor or cleverly done tile, stone, or laminate one is
an eye-catching asset that deserves fine care and maintenance. Particularly in the home's
traffic zones, floors are subject to continual wear and tear that is only exacerbated by
the presence of children and pets. Squeaks develop, boards swell, tiles crack, and surfaces become scuffed or scratched. Floor improvements can seem intimidating for even
ardent do-it-yourselfers, but they need not be; repair tasks can be easier
than you imagine. The chapter concludes with directions for
refinishing a wood floor and repairing tongue-and-
groove wood, laminate, and tile floors.

flooring basics

HAVE YOU EVER WONDERED WHAT IS UNDERNEATH THE FLOORING IN YOUR HOME? If you are going to be making repairs or improvements to your vinyl, wood, or tile floors, it is important to know your substructure. Here we look at typical floor construction.

The subfloor is typically constructed from 1-by-4 or 1-by-6 lumber or from plywood panels. In a lumber subfloor, boards are laid diagonally across joists. A plywood subfloor has panels that are laid in a staggered fashion, with the ends and edges butted together; panels are nailed (and sometimes also glued with construction adhesive) to the joists.

The thickness and stiffness of the subfloor determine the types of finished materials that can be put on top. If your house is built on a concrete slab, the slab can serve as a base for almost any type of flooring. But if your home has a plywood or board subfloor, it's important to check out the type and thickness of the material used to determine its limitations. For instance, a floor that is slightly flexible or springy is not suitable for rigid materials such as ceramic tile and stone (the grout or materials will crack with movement).

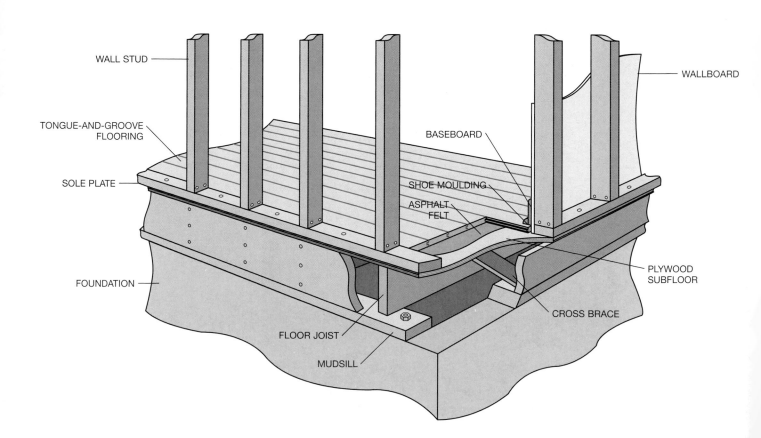

A typical wood-frame floor is raised up on a foundation. Floor joists provide the primary support. Here the subfloor is made from plywood, and the finished flooring is wood. An underlayment of asphalt felt is positioned between the two.

FLOORS

If your home has a crawl space or basement, you can go underneath to check out the underside of the subfloor. If you can tell that it is plywood, look for a grade stamp that designates the thickness.

A few minor dips in floors are common. Some settling results from stresses and fatigue. But if floors sag, the house could have a serious structural problem. Also look for evidence of rot. Discolored areas on the joists or subfloor usually indicate a plumbing leak. If you are faced with these kinds of problems, call a contractor.

ABOVE: **Stone flooring must be installed on a solid, rigid subfloor or the grout and tile may crack.** LEFT: **Wood flooring is typically installed over plywood subflooring.**

buyer's guide to flooring

AS RECENTLY AS THE '70S, WALL-TO-WALL CARPETING WAS A STANDARD SELECTION for homeowners who were purchasing new homes or new flooring. Linoleum was quite popular in the kitchen, and bathrooms were often covered with inexpensive vinyl tiles. These are still available, of course. In fact, linoleum has been rediscovered in recent years as an attractive, low-maintenance option, and vinyl tiles have exploded in colors that, when creatively arranged, can add a light, whimsical touch to a room. But nowadays, hardwood flooring, and ceramic and stone tile, are more often the preferred flooring materials.

many materials

It used to be that granite and marble surfaces were found only in office-building lobbies and banks. By the same token, rougher, more rustic stone materials were seen only in vacation cabins or backyard patios. Now, homeowners who like the

A classic material for bathrooms, ceramic tile is extremely durable and resistant to stains.

formal appeal of marble, perhaps in an entryway or bathroom, can install the tiles themselves. And those who prefer a casual or naturalistic decor can cover their floors with just about any material that was once reserved for outdoor spaces, including limestone. Often, strongly contrasting types of material are combined in the same house— perhaps even in the same room.

For decades, hardwood flooring meant strips of oak or maple installed in the traditional labor-intensive way—including the time-consuming process of sanding and applying multiple coats of protective finish. Now engineered-wood or laminate products (plastic that resembles wood) remove much of the hassle of installing a wood or wood-look floor. They come already stained and finished and are easy to maintain.

With so many choices, it can be hard to decide on a flooring product. Of course you want a floor that looks good and adds the right style for your home. But you also want to consider a material's durability, comfort, and ease of installation, as well as how simple it is to clean.

For a quick survey of products, see the chart on pages 147–149. It lists and describes a wide range of flooring products as well as the requirements for installation and maintenance.

Take your time as you make your selection. Visit Lowe's to review the available products and check out the manufacturers' recommendations for usage. How resistant

Nothing beats sheet vinyl flooring (left) and laminate strips (below) for ease of maintenance, imperviousness to water, and affordability.

is the material to stains and moisture? Is it durable enough for the level of traffic that the room will handle?

Your home is a special space. You will want to make a decision that will not only suit your style but will also be durable and easy to maintain so you can enjoy your new flooring for years to come.

choosing a style

The flooring you select should be compatible with the style of your house, whether it is contemporary, country, Victorian, or eclectic. Hardwood floors are a suitable choice in an old-fashioned kitchen, for example, and laminate strip flooring will work well in a contemporary family room. Slate can be stunning in a modern foyer. If your home has a Southwestern look, you might consider choosing terra-cotta

tiles. Or, if your home has elements of an Old World style, you might choose hand-painted Italian floor tiles as an accent in the dining room.

scale

In general, large-scale flooring works best in big rooms, while small rooms call for more delicacy. For example, large tiles can overwhelm a small room and mosaic tiles can be far too busy in a large room. It is wise to first buy a few samples of a material and then lay them in place to gauge their effect.

Remember, too, that a lengthwise pattern adds depth to a room, while a pattern running the width of a room makes the space look shorter and wider.

texture

Contrasting textures will add interest to a room. With tile flooring, texture can be expressed through different glazes and finishes. Stone can be honed, tumbled, or polished for a variety of appealing looks. And carpets offer a world of textural choices: closed or cut loops and sheared or carved pile, for instance.

design extras

Each type of flooring material comes with its own set of design accoutrements. Borders, medallions, and inlays now come premade for wood, tile, and stone floors. Even the grout between tiles can be a design element. Grout joints can be narrow or wide, plain or colored, depending on the desired look. Accent pieces can be used to break up a large expanse, to highlight a focal point, or to define one area of a room. In a multipurpose room, a good design plan may use different types of flooring to define two or more areas.

CHOOSING FLOORING

SURFACE	TYPE AND CHARACTERISTICS	INSTALLATION AND CARE
Bamboo	Made by laminating strips of split bamboo onto plywood planks, bamboo flooring is a hard, stable, and reliable flooring material with a pleasingly exotic appearance. Colors range from blond to medium-dark brown. Because bamboo grows quickly, it is an easily renewable, environmentally friendly product.	The subfloor need not be very strong or very smooth. Prefinished tongue-and-groove strips are stapled or glued down. Cut the pieces with a power saw. If the floor will get wet, apply an extra coat of polyurethane or wax following installation. Reapply finish after a few years if the floor gets worn or scratched. Bamboo cannot be sanded.
Carpeting	Carpet cushions the feet like no other flooring and helps keep a room quiet. It is most practical for living areas that receive light traffic and rarely get wet, but tightly woven types can work well even in a bathroom. Carpeting is available in a wide variety of styles and materials.	A slight degree of deflection in the subfloor is acceptable. Professional installers have specialized tools and experience, so they can install carpeting quickly. Padding is usually stapled to the subfloor, and tack strips are nailed around the perimeter. The carpet is stretched, attached to the strips, and trimmed. A high-quality carpet with stain protection is usually easy to keep clean. Ground-in soil and other stains require spot or steam cleaning.
Ceramic tile	Glazing gives tiles a hard surface that is impervious to water. Floor tiles are very hard and tend toward more muted colors than wall tiles, which are fairly soft and available in almost any color. The glazing can be slippery, so for floors, choose tiles with a bit of texture.	The substrate must be smooth and extremely strong; at least one layer of cement backerboard is recommended. Tiles are set in thinset mortar (for floors) or organic mastic (for walls). Cut the tiles with a snap cutter, wet saw, or nibbling tool. Joints must be filled with grout. The tiles themselves are easy to keep clean and otherwise virtually maintenance-free, but grout must be kept sealed.
Ceramic tile— porcelain	This product is extremely durable and resistant to stains. Many colors and styles are available. Porcelain can be manufactured to resemble ceramic tile and natural stone.	The substrate must be smooth and extremely strong. Tiles are set in thinset mortar and are most easily cut using a wet saw. Joints are filled with grout, which must be kept sealed.
Ceramic tile— quarry	These tiles are not glazed, so they are not slippery when wet. Quarry tiles have muted, natural colors that usually run toward grays and browns.	The substrate must be smooth and extremely strong. Set the tiles in thinset mortar; cut them with a snap cutter, wet saw, or nibbling tool. Grouted joints must be kept sealed. Vitreous types are fairly resistant to stains; semi-vitreous types are easily stained. Regular application of a sealer will make staining less likely.
Ceramic tile— terra-cotta	These are the softest of the ceramic tiles. Tiles vary slightly in color. Most are tan, brown, or reddish brown, their color reflecting the clay from which they were made. Some types are regular in shape, while handmade types (such as Mexican saltillos) are usually uneven in shape and irregular in size.	The substrate must be smooth and extremely strong. Set the tiles in a thick bed of thinset mortar; irregular tiles may need to be back-buttered—mortar applied to their backs—as well. Make all cuts using a wet saw. Terra-cotta tiles definitely need to be sealed.

CHOOSING FLOORING

SURFACE	TYPE AND CHARACTERISTICS	INSTALLATION AND CARE
Cork	Cork has a springiness that holds up for decades if the floor is well maintained. It creates a comfortable, warm surface and is hypoallergenic. It also has sound-deadening qualities. Cork is usually sold in plank form, unstained or lightly stained. Tiles 12 inches square are less common and may be natural in color or stained with muted to bold hues.	Like laminate flooring, cork planks are typically floated over a soft, rolled-out subsurface. Cut the pieces using a power saw. Most types snap together, so no glue is needed. Cork tiles require a very smooth subfloor. They can be cut with a knife and set in cork flooring adhesive. Cork comes prefinished; you may need to reapply polyurethane every year or so.
Hardwood flooring— engineered	Made by laminating a layer of hardwood onto a plywood strip, this product offers the warm look of natural wood but is much easier to install than a solid hardwood floor. Many wood species and stains are available.	The subfloor need not be very strong or very smooth. Most types are stapled onto the subfloor; some are floated over a sheet of underlayment. Cut the strips using a power miter saw. Engineered flooring comes with a durable polyurethane finish. It can be sanded only once.
Hardwood flooring— solid	This popular flooring material is available in random lengths with tongue-and-groove edges that fit tightly together. Oak strips are usually $\frac{3}{4}$ inch thick and $2\frac{1}{4}$ inches wide. Maple is usually $1\frac{1}{2}$ inches wide. Other species are available in various widths.	The subfloor need not be very strong or very smooth. Strips are fastened to the subfloor using a special tongue-and-groove stapler or nailer. Cut the strips using a power miter saw. Once installed, the floor must be sanded, perhaps stained, and then sealed with at least two coats of polyurethane or wax. Solid hardwood flooring can be sanded up to three times.
Laminate strips or tiles	This product has a laminate top coat that is far more durable than the type used on a typical laminate countertop. Available patterns often imitate hardwood or ceramic or stone tile. Some people object to the faux appearance, but others appreciate its ease of maintenance. Though the surface is hardy, it can be marred, so area rugs are recommended where traffic will be heavy.	The subfloor must be moderately strong and smooth. Laminate flooring is floated atop a layer of sheet underlayment. Cut the pieces using a power saw. Pieces snap together, making for a very easy installation. The surface is impervious to water, but standing water could seep into seams and damage the flooring.
Linoleum	Unlike vinyl sheet flooring, linoleum is a natural product made from oils, wood fiber, and bits of stone. This makes it environmentally friendly and lends a subtle, organic feel. There are many colors and patterns available.	The subfloor need not be very strong, but it must be smooth. Install linoleum much as you would vinyl sheet flooring, but use special linoleum adhesive. Keep the floor covered with coats of acrylic sealer. Tears and other damage can be repaired.
Mosaic tile	Made by adhering small pieces to a mesh backing, mosaic tile may be composed of ceramic or natural stone tile. An excellent range of colors and textures is available. Mosaics can be used on walls or floors. Because of the many grout lines, a mosaic floor is usually not slippery when wet.	The substrate must be smooth and extremely strong. Set the sheets of tiles in thinset mortar. Cut the sheets using a utility knife. Cut individual tiles using a nibbling tool or a handheld snap cutter. Grouting is demanding because there are so many grout lines. Apply tile or grout sealer regularly.

SURFACE	TYPE AND CHARACTERISTICS	INSTALLATION AND CARE
Stone tile—polished	Gleaming, smooth natural stone has an elegant and stately appearance. The tiles are cut precisely, but they will naturally vary from each other in color and pattern. Marble tiles tend to be veined. Granite is usually speckled. Travertine is mottled and veined. Inexpensive agglomerated tiles, composed of stone fragments held together with resin, have a rich pattern that includes several colors. Although it is a popular choice for bathroom floors, polished stone can be slippery when wet.	The substrate must be smooth and extremely strong. Set the tiles in white thinset mortar, and check for level periodically. Cut the tiles using a wet saw. Typically, grout lines are narrow. Marble, travertine, and other soft stone must be kept well sealed or it may stain. Apply a sealer made for natural stone. Granite is extremely hard and resistant to stains.
Stone tile—tumbled or rough	Marble that is tumbled has an entirely different appearance from the polished version. These tiles have a porous—sometimes even sponge-like—texture. There are variations in color, but veins and other patterns are generally absent. The result is a floor that feels relaxed yet sumptuous at the same time. Rough-cut stones such as limestone and slate have similar properties and appearance.	The substrate must be smooth and extremely strong. Set the tiles in white thinset mortar. The tiles may be somewhat irregular in shape, leading to grout lines of varying width, but this adds to the charm of the floor. Cut the tiles using a wet saw. Apply an acrylic sealer to the tiles before grouting so the grout does not seep into them. Left unsealed, these tiles will readily soak up stains, so keep them well protected with regular coats of sealer.
Vinyl sheet flooring	Sometimes mistakenly referred to as "linoleum," vinyl sheet flooring has a tough but flexible top layer with a pattern that is usually embossed on the surface. Patterns include wood tones, brick, tile, and geometric designs. The pattern is coated with a tough, shiny, no-wax coating. Because it is a continuous sheet rather than individual tiles, this product is excellent at repelling water.	The subfloor need not be very strong, but it must be smooth. Make a paper template of the floor, lay it on top of the sheet, and cut the sheet with a knife. For many types, spread adhesive over the entire floor; lay the sheet while the adhesive is wet. "Loose-lay" sheets are installed without adhesive; instead, you apply double-sided tape along the perimeter. The no-wax coating will last for years; eventually you will need to apply a sealer made for no-wax floors.
Vinyl tile—commercial	These 12-inch-square tiles are made of vinyl and other materials. Flecks of color, which run through the thickness of the tile, help hide dirt. Commercial tiles are a great value, offering durability and resilience for a small cost. Two or more colors can be combined in a pattern.	The subfloor need not be very firm, but it must be smooth. Spread vinyl adhesive, allow it to dry, and then set the tiles. Cut the tiles with a knife. Cover the tiles with acrylic finish or wax (even if they come prefinished) because bare tiles will stain easily.
Vinyl tile—self-stick	This is essentially the same material as vinyl sheet flooring in the form of individual tiles. Better-quality tiles are stiff, have a thick top layer, and are well protected with a solid no-wax coating.	The subfloor need not be very firm, but it must be smooth. Because the tiles are self-stick, you do not need to apply adhesive; simply peel off the paper backing and press the tile in place. Cut tiles using a knife. The no-wax coating will last for some years; eventually you will need to apply a sealer made for no-wax floors.

BASIC TOOLS FOR FLOORS

Rubber mallet

Claw hammer

Nibbling tool

Reciprocating saw

Masonry blade

Flooring roller

Chalk line

Laminated grout float

Carpenter's level

Cordless drill

Knee pads

Backerboard knife

Measuring tape

Power circular saw

Linoleum knife

Snap cutter

Jamb saw

Floor scraper

Prybar

Mixing paddle

Grinder

Tile stone

Utility knife

Wood chisel

Carbide-tipped hole saw

Nailsets

flooring tools

NO MATTER WHAT TYPE OF FLOORING YOU INSTALL, TO ACHIEVE HIGH-QUALITY results, you must use the right tools. For instance, when laying resilient flooring, it is important to apply the right adhesive using a properly sized notched trowel—otherwise, the flooring may not stick and form a smooth surface. When installing strip flooring, a power miter saw equipped with a sharp blade can ensure straight, tight joints. Some of the tools shown here and on the following pages are required for all flooring; others are needed only for a specific material, such as tile. Also be sure to have on hand the basic safety equipment, including safety glasses, work gloves, and dust masks.

TOOLS FOR PREPARING THE SUBSTRATE

A modest collection of tools will enable you to handle most of the work involved in preparing a subfloor or substrate for a new floor. You will want to wear knee pads throughout the project. A circular saw equipped with a carbide-tipped blade is best for straight cuts. A reciprocating saw will get into hard-to-reach places. Use a jamb saw to cut the bottom off door casings. A floor scraper quickly pries up ceramic or resilient flooring; finish the job with a straight scraper. To cut backerboard, use a backerboard knife. A prybar and cordless drill will come in handy for many tasks.

BACKERBOARD KNIFE

PRYBAR

RECIPROCATING SAW

POWER CIRCULAR SAW

KNEE PADS

STRAIGHT SCRAPER

JAMB SAW

FLOOR SCRAPER

CORDLESS DRILL

MEASURING TAPE

STRAIGHTEDGE

CARPENTER'S LEVEL

LAYOUT TOOLS

A successful floor installation starts with layout lines that are straight and square. Accurate measuring and marking are essential to getting the job done right. Shown here are the tools you will need.

CHALK LINE

CARPENTER'S SQUARE

TOOLS FOR CUTTING TILE

For most ceramic floor tiles, you can make straight cuts using a snap cutter, a wet saw (which can be rented), or a grinder in conjunction with a masonry blade. You will need a nibbling tool for small, irregular cuts and a hacksaw with a rod saw blade for curves and cutouts. To make a round hole, use a drill with a masonry bit or a carbide-tipped hole saw mounted in a power drill. Grind down rough edges or high spots with a tile stone.

TILE STONE

SNAP CUTTER

WET SAW

CARBIDE-TIPPED HOLE SAW

NIBBLING TOOL

HACKSAW WITH A ROD SAW BLADE

GRINDER

MASONRY BLADE

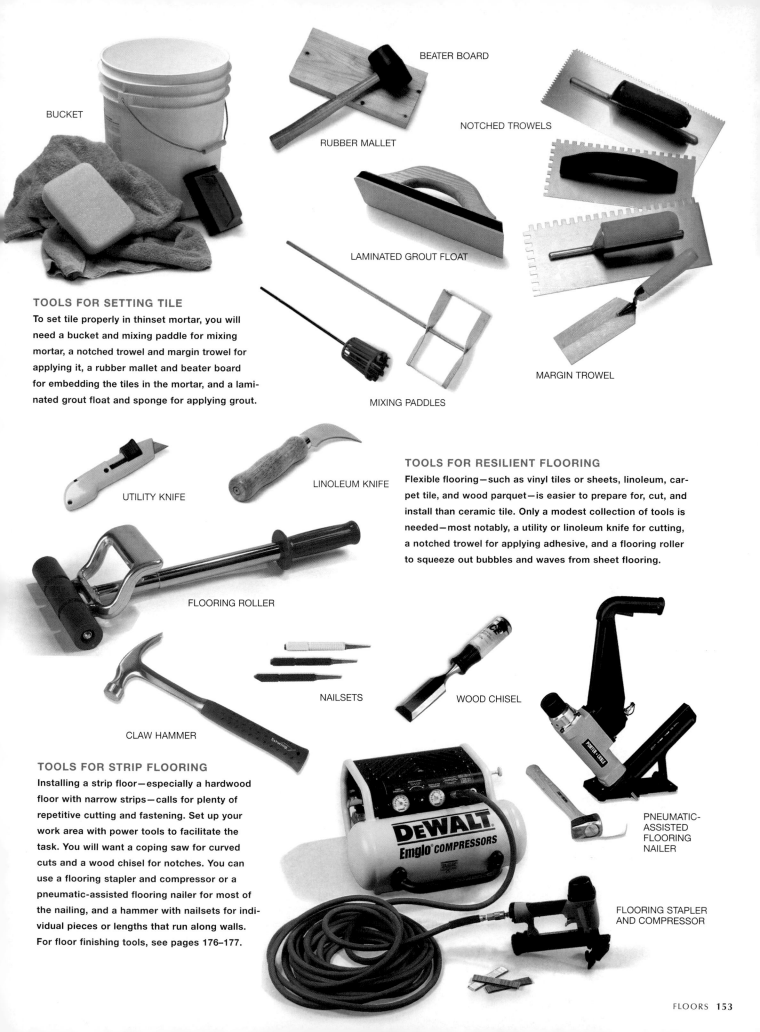

BEATER BOARD

BUCKET

RUBBER MALLET

NOTCHED TROWELS

LAMINATED GROUT FLOAT

MARGIN TROWEL

MIXING PADDLES

TOOLS FOR SETTING TILE

To set tile properly in thinset mortar, you will need a bucket and mixing paddle for mixing mortar, a notched trowel and margin trowel for applying it, a rubber mallet and beater board for embedding the tiles in the mortar, and a laminated grout float and sponge for applying grout.

UTILITY KNIFE

LINOLEUM KNIFE

FLOORING ROLLER

TOOLS FOR RESILIENT FLOORING

Flexible flooring—such as vinyl tiles or sheets, linoleum, carpet tile, and wood parquet—is easier to prepare for, cut, and install than ceramic tile. Only a modest collection of tools is needed—most notably, a utility or linoleum knife for cutting, a notched trowel for applying adhesive, and a flooring roller to squeeze out bubbles and waves from sheet flooring.

NAILSETS

WOOD CHISEL

CLAW HAMMER

PNEUMATIC-ASSISTED FLOORING NAILER

TOOLS FOR STRIP FLOORING

Installing a strip floor—especially a hardwood floor with narrow strips—calls for plenty of repetitive cutting and fastening. Set up your work area with power tools to facilitate the task. You will want a coping saw for curved cuts and a wood chisel for notches. You can use a flooring stapler and compressor or a pneumatic-assisted flooring nailer for most of the nailing, and a hammer with nailsets for individual pieces or lengths that run along walls. For floor finishing tools, see pages 176–177.

DeWALT Emglo® COMPRESSORS

FLOORING STAPLER AND COMPRESSOR

firming a floor

A FLOOR THAT FLEXES CAN CAUSE RIGID, BRITTLE FLOORING MATERIALS SUCH AS tile and stone to crack. Flexing may occur if the subfloor is too thin, inadequately attached, or poorly supported by joists and beams. Sometimes the solution may be as easy as driving screws through the subfloor and into the joists. Other times, however, it may involve extensive structural work. Following are common methods of improving a floor's rigidity.

adding a sister joist

If a joist has sagged, driving additional screws may have the unfortunate effect of pulling the floorboards down, doing nothing to strengthen the weak joist. When the problem involves multiple joists, call in a carpenter. To shore up one or two joists, install a "sister" onto each (right). Cut the sister out of 2-by lumber, making it as long as possible. Press it up against the bottom of the floor, and hold it temporarily in place by wedging a 2-by-4 support under it. Drive pairs of 3-inch wood screws every 8 inches or so to secure the sister to the joist.

installing blocking

To strengthen an entire floor, install blocking. From 2-by stock that is the same width as the joists, cut pieces to fit tightly between the joists. Tap the blocking into place between the joists (right) offsetting

each piece from the one next to it by 1½ inches to simplify nailing. Drive 3-inch screws or 16d nails to anchor the blocking to the joists.

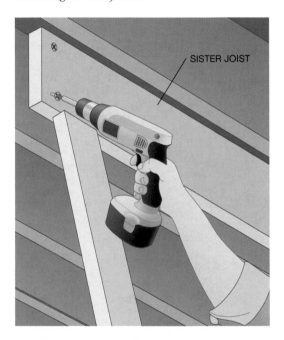

SISTER JOIST

BLOCKING

ARE THE JOISTS STRONG ENOUGH?

If a floor seems generally weak even though the subflooring is thick enough, the joists may be undersized. Local building codes vary, but in general, if joists are spaced 16 inches apart, they should follow these guidelines. If you find that your joists are too small for their spans, install a sister joist onto each of them.

Joist Size	Maximum span
2-by-6	8'6"
2-by-8	11'
2-by-10	14'
2-by-12	17'

adding metal bridging

Steel bridging (right) will not add as much strength as blocking. But it will provide reinforcement to some extent and cut down on squeaks, and it is easier to install. Purchase bridging pieces that are made to fit the spaces between your joists, typically 14½ inches. Wedge each piece tightly into position, and drive a nail or screw through each hole. Where the spacing is smaller, install a piece of blocking instead.

installing shims

If a joist sags or you see a space between the subfloor and the joist, purchase some wooden shims. Drive them into the gap by tapping with medium pressure—hitting them too hard will cause the floor to rise. Drive shims every 2 inches or so (right). After you have driven a group of shims, go back and tap them all to make sure they are snug. From above, drive a series of fasteners through the shims into the joist.

firming from on top

Adding more than one layer of subflooring that is ½ inch or thicker will strengthen your floor substantially. Ideally, use plywood for lower layers and either cement backerboard (if you are installing ceramic or stone tile) or ¼-inch underlayment (for vinyl tiles or sheet flooring) for the top layer. The structure will gain even more strength if you use plenty of fasteners— drive long screws every 6 inches into joists, and drive shorter screws (just long enough to penetrate all the way through the subfloor) in a grid every 8 inches between the joists. Setting backerboard in a bed of mortar, or fixing plywood in flooring adhesive, will also add firmness.

silencing squeaks

You can solve most floor squeaks simply by driving in additional nails or screws. If you plan to remove the existing flooring (see pages 158–160), do so before fixing the squeak. Stand over the source of the squeak, and examine the floor closely as you shift your weight and step around;

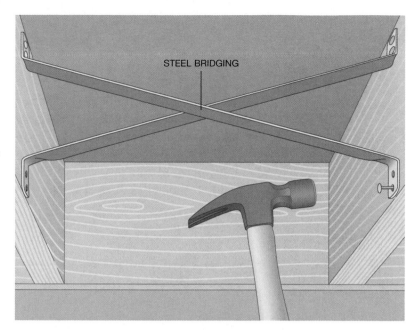

STEEL BRIDGING

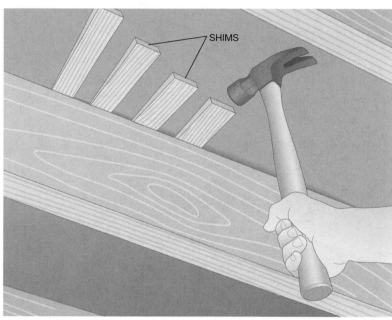

SHIMS

most likely you will see an area that moves up and down. Use a stud finder or drill a series of test holes to find the closest joist, and drive a series of 2½-inch screws (use only wood or deck screws) or 8d nails into the joist.

If driving in fasteners causes the floor to dip noticeably, the joist below has probably sagged; if this is the case, drive in shims as shown above. If a squeak emanates from a place between joists, try fastening the top piece of plywood to the underlying piece (or planks) by driving in a grid of 1⅝-inch screws.

removing mouldings

MANY A HOMEOWNER HAS TRIED TO SAVE TIME BY LEAVING MOULDINGS IN PLACE and cutting the flooring material to fit. Don't make this mistake. Systematically remove all mouldings, and plan your layout so that all flooring edges will be covered once the mouldings are back in place. The only exception is wood baseboard without a separate "shoe" piece. If you have this type of moulding, you may choose to leave the baseboard alone and install shoe sections after laying the floor. But if any of the existing moulding looks worn, remove and replace it.

vinyl cove base Pry cove base off the wall using a stiff putty knife. To avoid damaging the wall above the moulding, insert the knife at the top of the base and push down. If the moulding is stuck tight, use a heat gun to soften the adhesive as you pry (right). Scrape any protruding globs of adhesive off the wall. Install a new cove base after laying new flooring.

LOWE'S QUICK TIP
Old mouldings that look fine now may seem shabby when positioned against new tiles or other flooring. If your mouldings are dented or otherwise marred, achieve a total finished appearance by replacing them—or at least painting them.

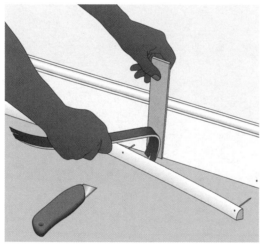

wood base shoe and baseboard If a room has a wood baseboard with a smaller bottom shoe piece, you only need to remove the shoe. Using a utility knife, slice through the paint along the top of the shoe. Pry the shoe off using a flat prybar and a scrap of wood to protect the baseboard (left). If the shoe is in good shape, write numbers on the back of the pieces so you can easily replace them later.

If there is only a baseboard and no shoe, you can leave the baseboard in place, lay new flooring to within ½ inch of the moulding, and then cover the gap by adding a base shoe.

If you plan to reuse mouldings, pull the nails through the back side (left) to prevent marring the surface. Firmly grab each nail with a large pair of slip-joint pliers, and then roll your hand over to pull the nail through.

cutting door mouldings If you will be installing backerboard or plywood underlayment, set a piece of the material on the subfloor and use it as a guide for your saw cut. Then, before installing the finish floor material, repeat this process. This will allow you to slide the flooring under the moulding, which will save you from making complicated cuts. If the flooring will extend on both sides of the door, also cut the bottom of the door-jamb and stop, using the same technique.

CHOOSING AN UNDERLAYMENT

If a floor is solid or smooth, it may be possible to lay new flooring directly over it. If the existing surface is not up to the task, or if the area will get wet, install materials designed specifically for your type of flooring.

Plywood is the best underlayment for non-ceramic flooring such as vinyl tile, cork, wood parquet, and laminate tiles. Plywood is inexpensive and easy to cut and install, and it can form a very smooth surface—an important consideration when applying thin resilient tiles that show every imperfection in the subfloor. Plywood designed for underlayment has a series of cross-shaped marks to guide you when you drive screws or nails in a grid pattern.

Ceramic or stone floor tile can also be installed on plywood, as long as the floor structure is firm and the tiles will not get very wet. Plywood, however, is more flexible than cement backerboard, and it swells when moistened. For ceramic or stone tile, cement backerboard is the better choice.

Some pros install tile the old-fashioned way, by pouring a thick slab of mortar and setting the tiles directly in it—a time-consuming operation that requires skill. Today, homeowners can achieve acceptable moisture tolerance and strength by attaching sheets of cement backerboard before setting the tiles.

Cement backerboard comes in two varieties, both made primarily of Portland cement, which retains its strength even when soaked in water. Mesh-reinforced cement backerboard is basically made up of a slab of cement held together by embedded fiberglass mesh that wraps around both sides. Fibrous cement backerboard has fibers running through-out and is smoother and a bit easier to cut. Both types are available in thick-nesses ranging from $\frac{1}{4}$ inch to $\frac{5}{8}$ inch and in sheets of various sizes.

Attach either type of cement backer-board using special backerboard screws, which are strong and can be easily driven flush with the surface of the board. Stan-dard drywall screws are much more difficult to drive flush and are prone to break. Seal joints in the backerboard with fiberglass mesh tape and thinset mortar. Cement backerboard stays strong when it gets wet, but it does not repel water. If a floor is often subjected to standing water, the water could seep through the grout, through the backerboard, and into the plywood below. To protect the wood below the backerboard, install a water-proofing membrane.

removing flooring

DEPENDING UPON YOUR EXISTING FLOOR'S CONDITION AND THE TYPE OF NEW flooring you intend to install, it may be necessary to remove the old flooring before putting in new material. Carpeting always requires removal. Ceramic tile must be removed unless you're installing ceramic tile or stone over it and its added thickness and weight won't create a problem. Resilient flooring is usually best removed, but a single flat, firmly attached layer can be left in place beneath tile and some types of laminate, resilient, and wood flooring (you generally install backerboard directly on top before the finished flooring).

ceramic tile Removing ceramic tile can be very difficult, especially if the tiles are set in an old mortar bed. Start by chipping at them with a cold chisel and hammer

If you need to remove the underlayment as well as the flooring, you can remove both at the same time (see page 160).

(below left). Once the bulk of the tiles has been removed, use a floor scraper (facing page, above right) to clean up any of the remaining mortar.

You can install new ceramic or stone tile directly on top of firmly attached ceramic or stone tile. If the old tile is glazed, rough up the surface using a belt sander, a tiling stone, or a grinder to ensure that the thinset will adhere.

When the existing surface has deep-set grout lines, you can probably set large tiles on top with no problem, but small ones may be uneven. Experiment first by laying the new tiles down without adhesive; if they form an uneven surface, fill the grout lines with thinset to level the surface. Allow the thinset to dry before starting the tiling job.

vinyl tile If a single layer of vinyl tile or non-cushioned resilient flooring is flat, smooth, and firmly attached, you can install ceramic or stone tile, laminate, and some types of resilient and wood flooring directly on top. For vinyl with a shiny surface, rough up the vinyl with a sanding block first. Where there is more than one layer of resilient flooring or where the flooring is cushioned, remove the flooring.

Remove vinyl tiles with a floor scraper, a straight paint scraper, or a drywall taping blade. If the going is rough, soften one or two tiles at a time using a heat gun (left). Scrape up the adhesive as you remove the tiles.

sheet flooring Using a utility knife, make long cuts about 8 inches apart through the flooring. Use a scraper to pry the edges, and pull up a series of strips. Where the paper backing does not come up, use a pump sprayer to wet it with a weak solution of soap and water. Allow the liquid to soak in for a few minutes, and then use a floor scraper or paint scraper to rough up the rest. It may take several applications of liquid before the backing becomes soft enough to remove.

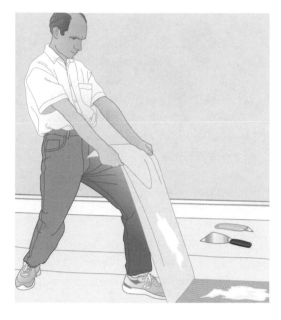

carpeting Most carpets are held in place by barbed strips nailed along the base of the walls. To remove, grab a corner with a pair of lineman's pliers and pull (below). Use a utility knife to cut the carpet into manageable strips, and then roll up each strip to be discarded.

Remove the padding, and pry up any staples from the floor using a small screwdriver, utility knife, or lineman's pliers. Use a flat prybar to remove the barbed strips (below). Gather them together carefully—they have lots of sharp tack points—and discard.

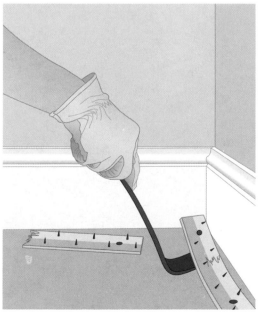

removing underlayment

Removing underlayment and resilient or laminate flooring in one step can be quicker and easier than removing flooring alone, especially if the two are firmly adhered. Be sure to wear gloves and protective clothing during removal.

Determine how small the pieces need to be to fit into your garbage container. Snap a grid of chalk lines on the floor. Equip a circular saw with a carbide blade that is set to cut through just the flooring and the underlayment. Cut along the chalk lines (right). Where the circular saw cannot reach, accomplish the cuts using a hammer and chisel.

Pull up the cut pieces with a prybar (below left). Carry out and carefully discard the pieces. Next, use pliers to remove any nails that may have remained embedded in the subfloor.

If the underlayment was installed using screws rather than nails, removal may be a bit more painstaking. First, try prying up pieces; this may work if the screws are not too long. If the screws are too difficult to pull up, remove the flooring first (see pages 158–159). You may need to expose screw heads by scraping them with a putty knife or screwdriver. Remove the screws using a drill equipped with a screwdriver bit (below right). If a bit becomes stripped, replace it or you'll damage the screws' heads, making them even more difficult to extract.

creating a level surface

IF A SUBFLOOR HAS UNEVEN AREAS OR DIPS THAT NEED TO BE FILLED, OR IF YOU need to smooth a slightly bumpy surface, you can generally use a leveling compound to repair the problem. Consult with a flooring expert at Lowe's to find the right product for your needs.

embossing leveler

Some resilient flooring, such as vinyl tiles and sheet flooring, will show even the slightest imperfections in the material they are adhered to. If you are installing these products over embossed vinyl tile or sheet flooring, or over ceramic tile, first apply embossing leveler. Paint the area with latex bonding agent to ensure that the embossing leveler will bond to the substrate. Mix the leveler with water or a latex additive as directed by the manufacturer. The solution should be pourable but still fairly thick. Pour it onto the floor, and spread it by scraping lightly with a flat trowel. Use long, sweeping strokes. Work quickly because the leveler will set in 15 minutes or less. Allow the leveler to dry, and then scrape it lightly with the trowel to assure bonding with the tile adhesive. Do not press too hard; you may dig up chunks of dried leveler. You may need to use a sanding block in spots.

leveling compound

Thinset can be laid thickly to correct a dip up to $3/8$ inch in depth, but use leveling compound where the depressions are deeper and for large areas. Bear in mind that it will not add to the floor's strength. If you install it on a floor that is springy, it may crack. Some leveling compounds are considered patching compounds. Others are self-leveling, meaning they will achieve a smooth surface with little or no troweling.

1 If the area to be filled is bordered by other flooring, as shown, attach a board temporarily to act as a dam. (If you are filling an isolated dip, you will not need a dam.) To ensure adherence to the underlayment, many leveling compounds require a bonding agent. The type shown is made of two parts mixed together and rolled onto the underlayment.

2 Mix the leveling compound with water or latex additive as directed by the manufacturer until you achieve a lump-free solution that can be poured. Pour the leveler onto the floor, and spread it with a straight-edged trowel. Don't overwork the surface. Just spread the compound so it is generally at the right thickness, and then allow it to settle to a uniform smoothness.

3 Use a drywall taping blade or a flat trowel to feather the edges. If you know that you will be installing thin vinyl tiles or sheets, sand the edges of the compound with a drywall hand sander before applying the adhesive.

installing plywood underlayment

PLYWOOD THAT IS 4 FEET SQUARE AND HAS A GRID OF X MARKS IS AN IDEAL underlayment material for all floorings other than ceramic or stone tile. Such plywood is ¼ inch thick; if you need a thicker underlayment, use 4-by-8 sheets of the AC- or BC-grade plywood. Make sure the surface is free of knots and other imperfections.

fastening options

You can install plywood using nails or screws, but an underlayment stapler drives in fasteners more quickly (and staples are easier to cover with patching compound). For a big job, rent a pneumatic stapler or a hand-powered stapler that you can pound firmly with a mallet.

keeping it smooth

As you work, keep in mind that any uneven seams, protruding fasteners, or other imperfections will eventually show up in your final flooring if you do not deal with them. This will likely be the most demanding and time-consuming step in your flooring project.

1 Drive screws where necessary to secure the seams of the subfloor materials. If the floor is spongy or wavy, see pages 154–155 for ways to solve those problems. Go over the subfloor with a straight trowel, making sure no fastener heads are sticking up.

2 Starting at a corner of the room, lay several full-sized sheets of underlayment on the floor. Use scraps of plywood to keep the sheets about ¼ inch away from the walls and to allow for expansion. See that the joints are offset from the subflooring joints below by at least 3 inches at all points. Measure to see how you will need to cut subsequent pieces; you may choose to reorient the sheets to minimize cutting.

LOWE'S QUICK TIP
Some 4-by-8 sheets of lauan plywood, often sold for use as flooring underlayment, are made from a wood species that has a heavy oil content. Thinset mortar and even organic mastic may come unstuck from this product in a year or less. Before applying adhesive, scrub the sheets with a weak soap-and-water solution, and then allow the boards to dry.

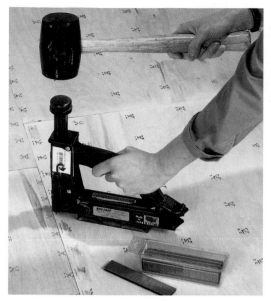

3 Starting at one end and moving across, drive underlayment staples, underlayment nails, or deck screws into each of the X marks on the sheet. Make sure all fastener heads are slightly below the plywood surface by scraping the surface with a flat trowel or drywall blade. Where sheets butt together, make sure that they are at exactly the same height. If they are not, drive in extra fasteners to force down the raised edges.

4 After installing several full-sized sheets, measure and mark the sheets that will require cutting. Position any cut edges against the walls; a cut edge should never be in the middle of the room. Use a drywall square to mark the cut lines. Where a sheet needs to be cut at an angle, mark each end of the cutting line, and snap a chalk line. Place two 2-by-4 boards across a pair of sawhorses or on a worktable, and rest the sheet on top of the 2 by 4s. Adjust the blade of a circular saw to cut about ¼ inch deeper than the thickness of the plywood sheet.

5 Mix a small quantity of acrylic- or latex-reinforced flooring patch until it reaches the consistency of toothpaste. Use a flat trowel or a drywall taping blade to cover all the seams and the fastener heads.

6 Once the patch has dried, sand the entire floor smooth using a drywall-type hand sander. Keep sanding until the floor feels smooth when you run your hand or a flat trowel over it.

installing wood strips or planks

STRIP FLOORS FIT TOGETHER BY MEANS OF A PROTRUDING TONGUE ON ONE SIDE of each strip that fits into a groove in the next board. Most solid flooring is 2¼ inches wide and ¾ inches thick. Nails, or flooring staples, are driven through the tongue into the subflooring. Once a conventional wood floor is installed, it must be sanded smooth and finished (see pages 176–179).

A solid wood floor (unlike a laminate or engineered one) expands and contracts widthwise—not lengthwise—with changes in temperature and humidity. It is essential to have a ½-inch gap between the flooring and the wall to allow for this movement.

Wood flooring imbues a room with warmth and natural beauty.

preparing for the job

The subfloor should be made of plywood or planks that are at least ⅝ inch thick and in sound condition so nails or staples will grab firmly. It should be reasonably smooth and free of squeaks; new strip flooring may eliminate some squeaks, but you cannot count on it. A single layer of ¾-inch plywood over joists spaced 16 inches apart is a typical base. See pages 154–163 for preparing a floor surface. Installing flooring is a major project, so you will need to plan carefully, taking the following into account:

- Flooring boards should be stored in the room where they will be installed to adjust to the ambient temperature and humidity. Consult with a Lowe's flooring expert and check the manufacturer's directions to see how long the flooring should lie in the room prior to installation. Installing the boards too early can result in shrinkage and gaps or in boards that swell and buckle. You may need to remove packaging so the flooring can breathe. If this is the case, stack the boards carefully so they do not warp as they dry out.

- You will need to cut boards one at a time as you reach the end of each row. It will most likely take two days to cut and nail all the boards.

- Once all the boards are installed, it will take a week or so to sand and seal the floor. This will typically involve three passes with a sanding machine, an

---

A SENSE OF DIRECTION

When installing over existing planks or strip flooring (often used in older homes to make the subfloor), it is important that the new flooring runs in a different direction. If it does not, the new floor will almost certainly develop unsightly waves. Run the new flooring in a different direction (perhaps at a 45-degree angle), or install underlayment on top of the old strip flooring (see pages 162–163).

LOWE'S QUICK TIP
Solid wood flooring must be well cured and dry; if the boards are a little green, they will shrink, creating unsightly gaps.

FLOORS

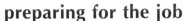

application of stain (if you choose), and two or three coats of finish (see page 179). This process will produce considerable dust, as well as unpleasant odors. You may choose to hire a professional to speed up this stage.

■ Mouldings can be installed after sanding if they will be stained the same color as the floor. Otherwise, wait to install them until you have completely finished the floor.

■ Rent a pneumatic flooring stapler, and buy plenty of staples. You may be able to return any boxes you do not use.

prepare the room

Remove obstructions and the base shoe or base moulding. Cut the door casings (above right) so you can slip the new flooring under them. Run a trowel over the floor, and remove or drive down any protruding fasteners. Walk over the floor to identify any squeaks, and drive in screws to eliminate them.

Roll 15-pound roofing felt (tar paper) onto the floor, and cut the felt to fit. (You can use rosin paper—also called kraft or construction paper—but tar paper is better at reducing squeaks.) Spread it flat, removing waves and bubbles. Staple it at 12-inch intervals. A roofer's stapler (shown right), which drives in the fasteners as quickly as you can hammer, is easier to use than a standard stapler.

TOP: **Under-cut the door casing, using a piece of new flooring as a guide.** ABOVE: **Staple roofing felt to the subfloor to serve as an underlayment.**

LEVELING A FLOOR WITH SLEEPERS

In older homes, hardwood flooring is often installed atop "sleepers": 1-by boards laid flat on top of the subflooring and spaced about 12 inches apart. If your floor is uneven, sleepers can straighten it out. You will need materials of several thicknesses, as well as a bundle or two of shims. Set the sleepers every 10 inches or so. Use a carpenter's level to check that they are at the correct height. Drive screws to attach the boards firmly to the floor.

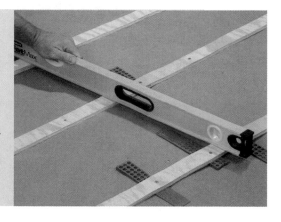

INSTALLING WOOD STRIP FLOORING

FLOORS

1 Start your layout on a long wall in the most visible part of the room. At each end of the wall, measure out the width of a board plus ¼ inch, and make a mark. Snap a chalk line between the two marks. Measure to see that the line is a fairly consistent distance from the wall at all points, and make sure the first board will be close enough to the wall for base moulding to cover it. Also measure from the opposite wall to the chalk line. If the opposite wall is not parallel to the line, the flooring will not be parallel to the wall. You may be able to adjust the chalk line slightly to improve the outcome or plan so that a sofa or other piece of furniture will cover any nonparallel flooring area.

2 Make your cutting station comfortable and easy-to-use. A power miter saw is ideal, but you can also cut using a circular saw and a square. For long boards, be sure to support both ends to avoid binding. For consistently smooth cuts, equip your power saw with a carbide-tipped blade that has at least 20 teeth. Always let the saw come to full speed before cutting. Also, make sure the blade stops completely before removing the board.

SPACER

LOWE'S QUICK TIP
Early on, open all the bundles of flooring, and make sure the colors are fairly consistent from bundle to bundle. If not, combine the boards from several bundles.

3 Choose very straight boards for the first row. Match the tongue and groove when installing the second and subsequent boards of the row. At the end of the row—and only then—cut the last board; be sure it falls ½ inch short of the end wall to allow for expansion.

4 Fit the last board in place, carefully aligning it with the chalk line. Maintain the expansion gap by inserting a ½-inch-thick spacer. Check the joints for a tight fit. Drill pilot holes approximately every 12 inches in the face of each board and, if possible, into the joists below.

5 Working from one end of the row to the other, drive finish nails or hard trim nails into the holes. Use a nailset to drive the nail heads at least ¼ inch below the surface. (If a nail is not driven deep enough, it will rip the sandpaper when you sand the floor.)

6 Lay out the next seven or eight rows of boards in the order you want to install them—a process called "racking." Keep in mind the "1½-inch rule" (see Step 8) for staggering joints, and aim for an even distribution of various colors and grain shapes in the pieces you select.

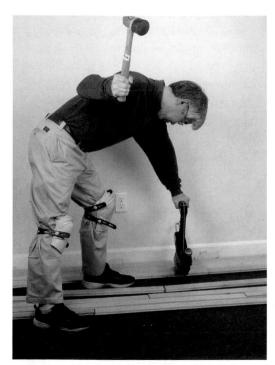

LOWE'S QUICK TIP

"Hard trim" nails cost a bit more than standard finish nails, but they are worth the cost. They are thinner, so you end up with a smaller hole to fill. They are also less likely to bend.

7 Use a flooring stapler instead of face nailing as soon as the tool will fit. The manual flooring stapler (shown) drives in a staple when you hit it with a mallet. The head of the staple should be sunk slightly into the wood. Adjust the tool if it is driving in the staples too shallow or deep.

8 As you continue to lay the strips, make sure no joint is closer than 1½ inches to a joint in either of the two adjoining rows. This time-tested rule makes for a professional appearance; closely spaced joints simply do not look right.

PROJECT CONTINUES ➡

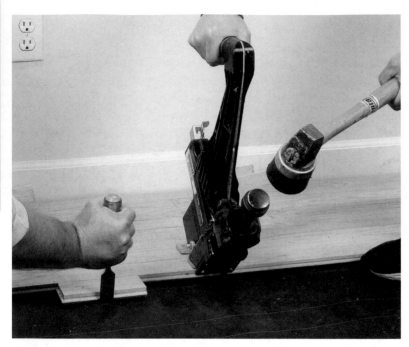

9 If a board is slightly warped, you can often straighten it by whacking the stapler hard when you drive in the staple; you may need to drive several staples very close together. For extra bending power, place a narrow scrap with a groove against the piece, drive a chisel into the subfloor next to it, and have a helper pry while you drive in the staple. Straighten a board by driving in several staples only if you are confident of success; otherwise, if you fail to fix the problem, you will have to pry out the bunch.

10 At a doorway or an outside corner, most if not all of the cuts will be covered with moulding, but the cut must be exact where it meets the jamb. Usually, it works best to measure for the rip cut (along the length of the board) using a tape measure and, for the crosscut (at a right angle to the board), by holding the piece in place and making a mark. Once the board is cut, fit it against its neighbor, and tap it into position.

FLOORING AROUND A HEARTH

At a hearth or other decorative obstruction, a frame made of mitered flooring pieces looks better than flooring simply cut to fit. Whenever possible, position the frame pieces so the flooring will fit onto a tongue or into a groove. In some cases, you may need to cut off the tongue of a frame board.

When you butt flooring pieces to the mitered frame, you will probably need to make rip cuts on some of the pieces using a circular saw or a table saw. Wherever the frame and flooring pieces meet without a mitered joint, drill pilot holes, and drive in face nails to secure the boards.

11 You will probably need to make rip cuts on the final row of strips in addition to making small rip cuts to fit flooring against jambs (see Step 10). Be sure to allow for a ½-inch expansion space between the flooring and the wall. A table saw is the ideal tool for this, but a circular saw with a ripping fence will also work. (You may want to practice a few of these on scraps of flooring.) When all the boards are fastened in place, don't be surprised if some strips are slightly higher or lower than the pieces they abut. This will be smoothed out when the floor is sanded (see page 178).

(see page 178)

ADDING A SPLINE

If you are installing continuous flooring in two adjoining rooms or in a room and a hallway, you may come to a point where will you need to turn the boards so that the tongues face in the opposite direction. Two boards will then meet groove to groove. To make the floor strong at this point, rip-cut a spline, a thin strip of wood that simulates a tongue. Once you are certain the spline will fit, squirt glue into one of the grooves, and tap in the spline.

12 Drill holes when you get too close to the wall to use the stapler, and drive in face nails as shown in Steps 4 and 5 on pages 166–167. Use a prybar and wood scraps of various sizes to pry the boards tight against their neighbors while you drill and drive.

13 Install the base shoe or the base moulding once the floor is sanded, stained, and finished. Attach all mouldings by driving nails into the wall only—not into the flooring or the subflooring—to allow the flooring to expand and contract with changes in humidity.

stapling an engineered wood floor

IN MOST CASES, ENGINEERED FLOORING PLANKS THAT ARE 3 INCHES WIDE OR smaller should be stapled; wider planks should be either glued down or floated. Check the flooring's packaging for installation requirements.

Stapling an engineered floor is much like applying a solid strip floor; see pages 164–169 for tips on laying out the job and cutting pieces to fit. Engineered planks are easier to install than solid strips, because they are far less likely to warp.

preparing the subsurface

See pages 156–163 for instructions on how to prepare the floor. The subsurface should be reasonably firm and free of any squeaks. Remove all obstructions, as well as the base shoe or the baseboard. Undercut the door casing, using a jamb saw with a scrap of the new material as a guide, to allow the flooring to slip under the casing (see page 165).

For the firmest installation, run the flooring perpendicular or at a 45-degree angle to the floor joists, and drive long staples into the joists. If that is impossible, you can drive 1-inch staples into the subfloor as long as it is made of plywood or planks that are in good condition and that are at least $\frac{5}{8}$ inch thick.

laying the floor

Scatter packages of the flooring throughout the room, and then wait a minimum of 3 days before installation to give the planks time to adjust to the ambient temperature and humidity.

Plan to leave a $\frac{1}{4}$-inch gap between the flooring and the wall; it will be covered by a baseboard (or a base shoe). Drive in exploratory nails or screws to locate the joists under the subfloor; mark the walls to indicate joist centers.

LOWE'S QUICK TIP
If the subfloor may be subjected to moisture, staple down plastic sheeting before you install the roofing felt or rosin paper.

1 Cover the floor with 15-pound roofing felt (tar paper) or rosin paper (also called kraft paper). Roll and spread the paper neatly, eliminating any bubbles or waves. Attach the paper with staples every 16 inches or so. Overlap the edges by about 4 inches. Snap chalk lines between the joist marks, so you can drive staples into joists when you install the planks. Install a test plank next to a long, highly visible wall. At either end of the wall, measure out from the wall the width of a flooring plank, including its tongue, plus $\frac{1}{4}$ inch (or the gap recommended by the manufacturer), and make a mark.

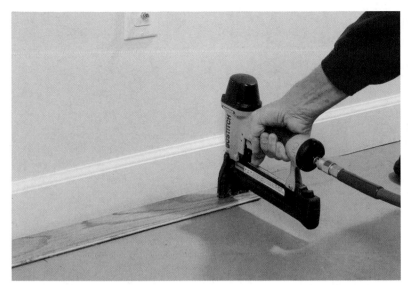

2 Snap a chalk line between the two marks. Measure from each end of this line to the opposite wall. If the measurements differ by more than ½ inch, one end of the final piece on that wall will be visibly narrower than the other end. You may choose to split the difference and make the first row slightly unparallel with its wall. Align the first plank so its tongue is directly over the chalk line. If the wall is wavy, you may need to trim the plank to maintain a gap of at least ¼ inch at all points, or you may choose to snap another line a bit farther out from the wall. Some staplers can be adjusted to shoot staples through the face of the plank. Otherwise, drill pilot holes, and face-nail and set 6-penny (6d) or 8-penny (8d) finish nails.

3 When you come to the end of a row, measure and cut a piece to fit, allowing for a ¼-inch gap between the board end and the wall. You will need to cut plenty of planks, so consider renting a power miter saw if you don't own one. If you cut with a circular saw (shown), use a small square for a guide, and cut the planks upside down to prevent splintering.

LOWE'S QUICK TIP
The staple's head should sink slightly below the wood surface. If it is not buried in the wood, the next piece will not be able to fit tightly; if it sinks more than ¼ inch or so, it will not hold the board securely. Adjust the nailer's air pressure until you get it just right.

4 Slip the end piece into place. Use shims or a prybar to hold the piece tightly against its neighbor as you drill pilot holes and drive in nails. Walls are easily damaged by prybars, so always protect the wall with a scrap of wood before using this tool.

5 Add the second row using a scrap of flooring to tap the planks together. It is normal for a plank to be slightly warped lengthwise; you may have to kneel on one end as you tap the other end into place. Then work your way down the plank to set the groove onto the tongue.

PROJECT CONTINUES ➡

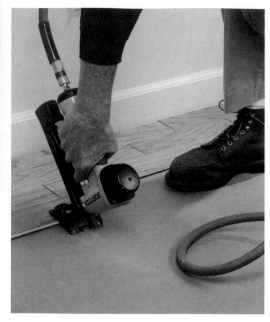

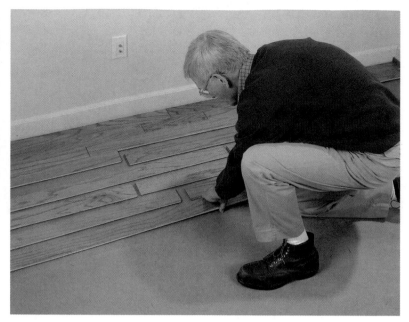

6 Once you are two or three rows away from the wall, you can stop face-nailing and can adjust the stapler to fasten at an angle through the tongue of each plank. Drive staples into joists whenever possible.

7 To save time, rack three or four rows of planks before stapling and cutting them to fit. Lay them out in the order you will install them. Check joint spacing as you work. If planks are 3 inches wide, joints should be no closer than 2 inches to an adjacent joint or a joint that is one board away. If planks are 5 inches wide, joints should be at least 3 inches apart.

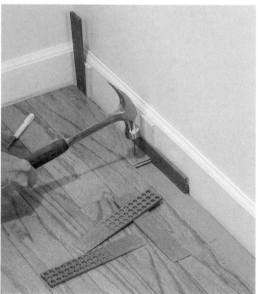

8 Pieces in the last row will probably need to be cut to width. To measure, place spacers against the wall, lay a plank upside down and pressed against the spacers, and make a mark. If the wall is not wavy, you can simply adjust the rip guide of a tablesaw or a circular saw and cut all the pieces to the same width. If the wall has waves or the planks are not parallel to the wall, you will need to measure and cut each piece individually.

9 You will probably need to face-nail the last two or three rows because the stapler will not fit against the wall. Use shims and a spacer (shown) or a prybar to press each plank firmly against its neighbor before driving in nails. Set the nails, and fill the holes with colored putty.

gluing down engineered flooring

BECAUSE IT IS ALWAYS STRAIGHT AND UNIFORM, ENGINEERED FLOORING CAN BE glued rather than nailed or stapled. Gluing can be done on any clean, firm substrate. The adhesive, however, is so messy to work with, this method is usually reserved for concrete, where nailing or stapling is not possible.

preparing the subsurface

If moisture is a slight problem, glue down sheets of pressure-treated plywood as the underlayment, and then glue the flooring to the plywood (it's not thick enough to receive nails or staples). If the floor may actually get wet from time to time, install ceramic or stone tile rather than wood or laminate flooring.

Beware: A concrete floor that feels dry may actually be moist enough to ruin a wood floor. Perform a test during the most humid part of the year using duct tape to attach pieces of plastic sheeting to the floor in several places. Make sure the tape seals completely all around the plastic.

Wait several days, and then remove the plastic sheeting. If the floor or the underside of the plastic is wet, then the area is too moist for a wood floor. To conduct a more precise test, purchase a calcium chloride moisture tester and follow the manufacturer's instructions.

If the floor is finished with paint, wax, or any other product, the adhesive will stick to the finish—not to the concrete. Unless the finish is strongly bonded to the concrete, it may be necessary to remove it before installing new flooring. Use paint stripper or a muriatic acid solution, and then degloss the surface by sanding it or cleaning and rinsing it thoroughly.

1 Start at the most visible wall. At either end, measure out the width of a flooring plank, including its tongue, plus ¼ inch (or the gap recommended by the manufacturer), and make a mark. Snap a chalk line between the two marks. Place a straightedge—you can use the factory edge of a piece of plywood—along the line, and use shims (as shown) or masonry screws to hold it in place so you can press against it when installing the flooring.

PROJECT CONTINUES ➡

LOWE'S QUICK TIP

Keep the work site, the flooring, and your clothing free of errant adhesive. Otherwise, you will have a cleaning headache after the floor is laid. When adhesive gets on your hands, always wash them immediately.

2 Use the flooring adhesive and the notched trowel recommended by the manufacturer. Spread a line of adhesive wide enough for two or three planks by either pouring out dollops of adhesive or scooping the adhesive out of the bucket using the trowel. To maintain a consistent thickness, keep the trowel at a 45-degree angle. Comb away any thick areas, which could ooze up through the planks.

3 Press the first piece into the adhesive, and sandwich a spacer between the end of the plank and the wall to maintain an expansion gap of about ¼ inch. Then pull up the piece, and examine its underside. If the adhesive does not cover at least 80 percent of the surface, spread the adhesive thicker. But if the adhesive is so thick that it oozes out the sides of the plank, spread it thinner.

4 If the amount to be cut off from the last plank is more than 1 foot, save the piece to be the first plank of another row. Use spacers to keep the end of the last plank ¼ inch or so from the wall. To install the next row without creating a mess, hold the plank at a 45-degree angle to the floor and press its groove slightly into the tongue of the preceding plank all along its edge. Then lay it down onto the adhesive, and press it against the preceding plank until the seam is fairly tight.

5 For planks that are 3 inches wide, make sure that no joint is more than 2 inches from an adjoining joint or from a joint that is one board away. If the planks are 5 inches wide, see that the joints are no more than 3 inches apart. Every few rows, use a plastic tapping tool or a scrap of the flooring to tap the pieces together tightly. Use a rag dampened with either water or mineral spirits (depending on the type of adhesive) to wipe up any spills or oozed-out adhesive.

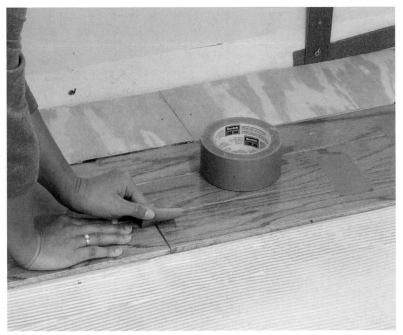

6 To ensure that the end joints, which also attach via tongue and groove, are tight, pull up either end using a flat prybar (protect the wall with a scrap of wood.)

7 Every three or four rows, check all the previous rows to make sure they have not spread apart. If they have spread, tap all the planks together tightly, and use pieces of painter's tape to hold the joints together.

8 You will most likely need to rip-cut the last row. Make sure that the last row will be at least ¼ inch away from the wall. Firmly clamp the strip you are ripping. One good method is to clamp the end of the strip farthest from where you begin your cut. Halfway through the cut, move the clamp to the opposite end of the plank.

9 After installing the last row, use a flat prybar to tighten all the joints. Then tap in shims to hold the seams tight. On the following day, return to the opposite wall, where you began the installation. Remove the straightedge and shims, and glue in place strips of flooring to complete the job.

LOWE'S QUICK TIP
Some manufacturers recommend that you use a flooring roller to ensure good adhesion. But simply walking all over the floor does nearly the same job.

refinishing a wood floor

A DAMAGED OR DINGY HARDWOOD FLOOR CAN BE REJUVENATED BY SANDING and refinishing. A medium-sized room can be sanded and stained in a day; allow several more days to apply coats of protective finish. This is a job often tackled by homeowners, but be aware that you will need to work carefully, especially when using a drum sander with heavy-grit paper, to avoid gouging the floor.

FLOORING BUFFER

RANDOM-VIBRATING SANDER

when to sand

Make sure your floor is a valid candidate for a thorough sanding, which typically removes up to ⅛ inch of thickness from the flooring. If the floor has only surface damage, consider the alternatives to drum sanding (see box below).

LOWE'S QUICK TIP

Carefully examine the entire floor for any raised fastener heads. Countersink any you find at least ¼ inch below the surface of the board. A single nail head that is not adequately sunk can catch the sanding belt and destroy it.

■ Solid, ¾-inch-thick flooring can usually be sanded up to three times. In an older home, the floor may have already been sanded once or twice. To check for this, examine the top of the flooring in several places in the room. (Signs may be visible in a damaged section or at the end of a board.) If you have less than ⅛ inch of thickness above the tongue (or the groove), there is not enough left to sand with a drum sander.

■ High-quality engineered flooring can be sanded once but not more. Consider using a random-vibrating sander (see box below) instead of a drum sander.

■ Water or pet-urine stains on a portion of the floor that is unfinished (lacking a glossy coat) are most likely too deep to be sanded away. You can try sanding the area, but you may find that you need to replace the flooring.

■ If a hardwood floor was covered with underlayment and another flooring material, removing the underlayment will reveal a grid of nail or staple holes. These holes are likely to remain somewhat visible after the floor has been sanded and finished.

ALTERNATIVES TO DRUM SANDING

If the damage to your floor is not severe and you do not need to remove a water or pet-urine stain, consider this pair of options.

To remove a floor's finish and perhaps some shallow scratches, rent a janitor-type flooring buffer (far left). Buy some flooring screens and a pad to hold them. Start with a heavy screen, such as 60-grit, and finish with a lighter 80- or 100-grit screen. You may find it takes 15 minutes or so to get the hang of operating the buffer. Replace a screen once it stops removing material from the surface of the floor.

A random-vibrating sander (left) removes shallow scratches as well as the finish. It is safer to use than a drum sander because there is no danger of gouging the floor. Begin with 60-grit paper, then use 80-grit, and finally 100-grit.

what you'll need

Rent a drum sander designed for finishing floors. A machine that runs on 220-volt current will work quickly, but you will need to be extra careful or you could pit the floor, and your home will have to have a 220-volt receptacle. (An electric stove and older window air conditioners require such a receptacle.)

A sander that runs on standard 120-volt current is slower and safer to use. You can buy drum sanding belts in three grits: typically, 40, 60, and 80 (or 100).

You will also need an edge sander to get near the wall and a pull-type paint scraper for tight spots and corners. It is important to clean up the dust as you go along to prevent it from settling in cracks, so have a shop vacuum on hand. To apply the stain and finish, use an applicator made from lamb's wool (a paintbrush is also handy for hard-to-reach areas). A pole sander equipped with 100-grit sandpaper speeds the job of sanding the finish between coats.

DRUM SANDER

EDGE SANDER

PAINT SCRAPER

SHOP VACUUM

LAMB'S-WOOL APPLICATOR

POLE SANDER

1 Make any necessary repairs to the floor. (If some boards are damaged and need to be replaced, see pages 198–199 for how to patch these areas.) To silence squeaky boards, drill pilot holes and drive in screws or nails. Fill holes with wood putty that is either stainable or close to the desired finish color of the floor.

2 Remove the base shoe or, if absolutely necessary, the baseboard. Sanding can create an immense quantity of fine dust that can work its way through even small openings. Open a window and point a fan outside to expel the dust and make the air breathable. Seal doors using masking tape and plastic.

LOWE'S SAFETY TIP

PROJECT CONTINUES ➡

3 Ask at the rental store for detailed instructions on the use of the drum sander. To load a drum sander with a sanding belt, unplug the machine and tip it up so you can get at the underside. First, loosen one or two mounting nuts, slip the sanding belt onto the rollers, and then tighten the nut(s). For serious sanding, start with very coarse paper such as 36- or even 20-grit. Begin sanding in an inconspicuous place—where a sofa will cover the floor, for example.

4 Tip the sander up so the sanding belt is off the floor, and turn the sander on. Slowly lower the belt onto the floor, and allow the machine to pull forward; do not allow the sander to stay in one place for even a second or the belt will dig into the floor. Depending on the type of machine you have rented, you may need to work the sander both forward and backward. Overlap your passes by several inches. When the sander no longer removes material effectively, change sanding belts.

LOWE'S QUICK TIP
Some professionals start by sanding at a 45-degree angle, but sanding along the wood grain is a safer method. If you find the machine is not removing enough material, however, you may want to try sanding at an angle—for the first sanding only. For the second and third sandings, sand in the direction of the grain.

5 Vacuum the floor thoroughly after each sanding. After vacuuming, examine the floor for any fastener heads that may have become exposed. Countersink them to prevent damaging a sanding belt. Resist the temptation to skip one of the sandings. If you omit the medium- or fine-grit sanding, the floor will probably show visible sanding marks. Sand the surface a second time using a medium-grit paper.

6 Use an edge sander to reach most of the areas not covered by the drum sander. Wear a face mask and ear protectors when using an edge sander; this tool creates a lot of dust and is very noisy. Equip the sander with 60-grit sanding disks for the first sanding. It will take a few minutes to get the knack of keeping the machine flat and steady as you work—it can run away from you if you are not careful.

7 Where the edger cannot reach, use a pull-type paint scraper equipped with a very sharp blade. Apply strong downward pressure as you pull the scraper toward you, pushing down on the knob with the heel of your hand if necessary. Whenever possible, scrape with the grain, not across it. When you must go against the grain, bear down with less force to avoid splintering the wood. Change the blade (or rotate it if you have a four-sided blade) as soon as the going gets tough.

8 After the second sanding, vacuum the floor thoroughly. Fill any holes with wood putty, removing as much excess putty as possible with the blade. Choose putty that is stainable and close to the desired finish color of the floor or, if you are not going to apply stain, close to the color of the raw wood. When the putty is dry, sand the floor one final time using 80- or 100-grit paper. At corners where you used the scraper, smooth the floor using a hand sander.

9 The floor must be dust-free. Vacuum thoroughly, wait a bit, and vacuum again. Run your hand over the surface; if you pick up dust, vacuum again. If you choose to apply stain, mix it thoroughly. Apply the stain with an applicator to an area of about 10 square feet. Wipe away any excess with a rag. Work quickly and systematically so you never apply stain to an area abutting a space where stain has already dried.

10 After the stain has dried, apply two or three coats of polyurethane finish. Apply the finish carefully, using smooth strokes, to avoid creating bubbles. An applicator made from lamb's wool is the best tool for this job. Allow the finish to dry, and then sand lightly using 220-grit sandpaper. (A pole sander makes the job easier.) Vacuum thoroughly. Apply one or two additional coats of finish.

installing a laminate floor

LAMINATE FLOORS ARE NOT ATTACHED TO THE SUBSTRATE. INSTEAD, THEY FLOAT above it on a sheet of foam underlayment. Flooring that floats must be extremely stable and resistant to warping.

Laminate flooring, which has a hard surface that imitates the look of wood, simply snaps and/or glues together for easy installation. The flooring manufacturer may offer an installation kit that includes glue, a plastic tapping tool, and a prybar. Such a kit is worth the modest cost.

preparing the room

See pages 156–163 for instructions on how to prepare the subfloor and the room. The subfloor must be reasonably strong, level, and free of squeaks, but it does not need to be rock-solid. Remove all obstructions in the room, undercut the casing moulding at the doors, and remove either the base moulding or the base shoe.

Laminate flooring has the look of wood but at a fraction of the price. In addition, installation is a relative snap.

mapping the layout

On a floating floor, it is important that all planks are at least 2 inches wide; a narrower piece is likely to buckle. Measure the width of the room at several places, taking into account the $\frac{1}{4}$-inch expansion gap you need to leave between the flooring and the wall, and then make some careful calculations. Divide the width of your room by the width of your planks. If the remainder is less than 2 inches, you will need to rip-cut the first piece.

For example, if the room is 120 inches wide and the planks are 7 inches wide, the room will hold 17 pieces, with 1 inch left over ($17 \times 7 = 119$). In that case, plan on using only 16 full-width pieces, which will leave you with 8 inches of leftover space ($16 \times 7 = 112$). Rip-cut both the first and last pieces at 4 inches.

Install the first board at a long, highly visible wall. At each end of the wall, measure out from the wall the width of the first plank plus $\frac{1}{4}$ inch, and make a mark. Working with a helper, snap a chalk line between the two marks. Measure to see that the line is a fairly consistent distance from the wall at all points. Make sure the first board will be close enough to the wall for the base moulding to cover the gap.

installing the flooring

These instructions show how to install a glue-together laminate floor. If you are installing a snap-together laminate floor, ignore the instructions for applying and wiping glue.

Like other flooring types, laminate flooring should sit in the room for several days prior to installation so it can adjust to the room's temperature and humidity.

1 Roll out the foam underlayment that is recommended for your flooring. Some manufacturers recommend that you overlap the seams of the underlayment, while others say you should not overlap the seams. Follow your manufacturer's instructions. Staple the material firmly in place, and mark your layout.

2 Install a starter strip that aligns with the layout chalk line. A strip of plywood works well, as long as you place the factory edge (or an edge that has been very carefully cut with a table saw) against the chalk line. Drive screws to hold the starter strip firmly; you will be tapping the boards against it, so it is important that it not move.

3 Install the first row with the tongue facing out. Use spacers to keep the end of the first plank ¼ inch away from the wall. Glue the pieces together by applying a smooth bead of glue to the top side of the end tongues. Press the pieces together to form a fairly tight seal; use the tapping tool if needed.

4 Measure the last piece in the row for cutting, taking into account the ¼-inch space you must have between the floor and the wall to allow for expansion. Cut the plank using a power miter saw, table saw, or circular saw (shown). Cutting a plank upside down helps prevent splintering the top surface.

LOWE'S QUICK TIP
If your underlayment is transparent, you can mark your layout before rolling it out. If the underlayment is opaque, you will roll it in place and then mark your layout.

PROJECT CONTINUES ➡

5 Use a tapping tool or a prybar to tighten each row. Slip one end over the end of the last board, and tap on the rear of the tool with a hammer. Then insert a spacer, and tap a shim in front of it to hold the joints tight.

6 Rack a couple of rows. If the cutoff from the first row is at least 12 inches long, you can use it as the first piece of the second row, but you must start from the opposite end of the room. Apply glue, and tap the rows into place.

LOWE'S QUICK TIP

As you continue to lay strips, make sure that no joint is closer than 1½ inches from an adjoining joint—or from a joint that is one board away. While closely spaced joints don't affect the floor's integrity, they look unprofessional.

7 Install the next rows of planks. Working systematically, set spacers against the end wall, ensure that the joints are offset, apply the glue, and then press the planks together. Press the planks against each other to produce tight joints, using the tapping tool as needed.

8 Have several damp rags on hand, as well as a bucket of clean water, so you can rinse the rags quickly. Wipe away squeezed-up glue after installing each row of planks.

LOWE'S QUICK TIP
When installing baseboard over a floating floor, never drive nails into the flooring. Drive nails into the wall only. Install a base shoe by driving nails into the baseboard only. That way, the floor will be able to move slightly as it expands and contracts with the changes in humidity.

9 Every few rows, check the entire floor to make sure no joints have separated. In most cases, you can tighten joints several rows away by firmly tapping them. If a joint is widely separated, ask a helper to stand on one or both planks while you tap.

10 For the last row, if the wall is straight with the flooring, simply adjust the rip guide of a table saw or a circular saw and cut all the pieces to the same width. If the wall has waves, or if the planks are not parallel with the wall, measure the pieces individually. For a precise measurement, place the piece to be cut upside down and against the wall. Cut a scrap of wood to the width of the opening minus ⅜ inch, and use it to scribe a cut line.

SNAP-TOGETHER LAMINATE FLOORING

To attach a piece of snap-together laminate flooring, hold it at an angle, slide its groove against the tongue of an installed board, make sure that it is tight all along its length, and push down. Double-check that the joint is tight before moving on to the next piece.

In an area that will get wet, such as a bathroom, apply a bead of glue or silicone caulk to the top edge of the tongues.

11 Install the last row, and use spacers and shims to wedge it tight. Remove the starter strip, and install the first row in the same way. Avoid walking on the floor for 8 hours or so before removing the spacers and shims.

installing resilient tile

INSTALLING RESILIENT TILE IS A MANAGEABLE PROJECT FOR DO-IT-YOURSELFERS with moderate skills. The small squares of resilient tile are easy to handle, cut, and glue into place. The project shown here utilizes commercial-grade vinyl composition tile, known as VCT, which is 12 inches square and comes in boxes of 45 pieces of the same color. Be sure to use a trowel designed just for VCT adhesive; other trowels apply too much adhesive, preventing it from setting properly.

A blue-and-white checkerboard pattern creates the illusion of space in this small bathroom.

If your underlayment is not perfectly smooth, which it will not be if you rip out existing sheet vinyl, you will need to replace it or have it replaced by a flooring installer.

It is usually best to start at the room's center and work toward the walls. Using a steel tape, carpenter's square, and long metal straightedge, carefully measure and draw reference lines on the underlayment that intersect at a 90-degree angle, indicating the center of the first tile. Lay the darker tile over the center so its corners align precisely with the reference lines.

1 Hold the tile firmly in place—or, better yet, have a helper stand on it. Using a metal straightedge, draw guidelines along two adjoining edges of the tile; extend the lines 24 inches in both directions. These will be your initial placement lines for the diagonal pattern. Make the lines dark so that you will be able to see them through the adhesive.

> **LOWE'S QUICK TIP**
> When planning the layout for diagonal tile, start with an interior tile and work outward. In this small bathroom, the first tile was centered on the doorway and down the galley portion of the room.

2 Put the tile aside. Wearing gloves and knee pads, spread adhesive thinly and evenly with a notched trowel, covering the area marked by the placement lines. Allow the adhesive to set according to the manufacturer's instructions before installing the tile.

3 Lower the dark tile into place, lining up its edges precisely with the placement lines. Press it firmly into the adhesive.

4 Lay a lighter-colored tile, lining it up snugly against the first tile and precisely along the placement lines.

5 Lay a dark tile and follow with a light tile to complete a unit of four tiles. (It's easiest to work in modules of four tiles.)

PROJECT CONTINUES ➡

6 Continue spreading adhesive and laying full tiles until you reach the point where you must cut tiles to fit. Clean excess adhesive off the tiles with a clean cloth and warm, soapy water. (If the adhesive has dried, see Step 9.) Go over the laid tiles with a rolling pin to set them.

7 To cut a tile, first warm it using a hair dryer. Then cut it carefully with a utility knife. For a diagonal cut, line up the tile to be cut with the 45-degree-angle lines on the rotary cutting mat, as shown. Tape two adjoining edges to the mat using blue painter's tape. Lay a steel tape over the tile, aligning your measurement with the point of the tile. Lay a metal straightedge perpendicular to the end of the tape, using the cutting lines on the mat as a guide. Mark the tile along the straightedge.

8 Using the metal straightedge and the utility knife, firmly score the tile along the marked line. Snap the tile. Smooth the snapped edge against a scrap tile. The snapped edges on most partial tiles need not be perfect—baseboards will cover them.

9 Spread adhesive on the area, being careful not to get the substance on the already-set tiles. Allow the adhesive to set, and lay the cut tile. Continue cutting and setting partial tiles to complete the floor. Go over the tiles with a rolling pin. Clean up dried adhesive on the tiles with mineral spirits and a clean cloth. To remove the residue, lightly wash the surface with mild soap and water. Allow the tiles and adhesive to "cure" overnight. Apply the acrylic floor finish according to the manufacturer's instructions. Finally, reattach the baseboards.

installing vinyl sheet flooring

SHEET VINYL IS MADE OF BASICALLY THE SAME MATERIAL AS HIGH-QUALITY surface-printed vinyl tile. Better-quality products are ⅛ inch thick and have a strong coating, so they will not tear easily during or after installation. Installing vinyl sheet flooring is more difficult than installing vinyl tiles. With vinyl tiles, if you make a mistake while cutting a tile, you can simply discard it and install another one. With sheet flooring, however, a mistake ruins the entire sheet.

The flooring shown is laid in a continuous bed of troweled adhesive. A "loose-lay" vinyl sheet is adhered to the floor only around the perimeter of the room, using either a narrow strip of troweled adhesive or double-sided tape.

getting ready

Remove any obstructions, as well as the base shoe or the base moulding. Prepare the floor as you would for vinyl tile, either by installing underlayment or by patching the existing flooring. Sand the floor until it is smooth, then sweep and vacuum.

Sheet vinyl is easy to cut. However, you should plan your layout to minimize the need for complicated cuts.

creating a template

Because you get only one chance to cut the vinyl sheet correctly, it is vital that you make an accurate template (though base moulding will overlap the edge of the vinyl around the room's perimeter). Some flooring sheets are rolled up with a heavy paper sheet that can be used as a template. If yours does not come with such a sheet, use rosin paper or kraft paper.

1 Undercut door casings and other mouldings so you can slip the vinyl under the obstruction rather than cut the vinyl to fit. A trim saw (shown) makes the job easy.

2 Roll out a sheet of rosin paper lengthwise in the room. Try to avoid tearing the paper. (If necessary, you can mend tears with masking tape.) Cut the paper a bit longer than needed.

3 Place the template about ¼ inch away from the wall if the moulding is wide enough to cover the gap at all points and the wall is fairly straight. If the wall is wavy, use a short straightedge to scribe a line that parallels the wall. Cut along the line, and then slide the template so that it is ¼ inch away from the wall.

PROJECT CONTINUES ➡

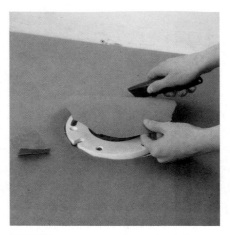

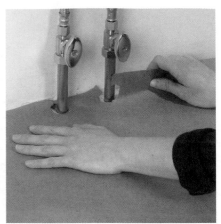

4 Once you have a piece of the template correctly positioned, cut out a series of triangles that are about 2 inches wide and spaced about 16 inches apart. Press masking tape over the triangles to hold the template in place. Roll out another sheet, overlapping the first by an inch or so. When it is correctly positioned, cut and tape triangles to hold it in place. Do not tape the seams yet.

5 When you come to a raised obstruction (like this toilet flange), cut the hole a little small and then enlarge it to fit. If you make a mistake, simply cut a piece of rosin paper and tape it so it covers the gap. Be sure that any patching pieces are firmly adhered.

6 When you encounter a pipe, pull the paper back and make a slice long enough to extend from the front of the pipe to the wall. Then cut a circle to accommodate the pipe, and push the paper into place. The paper should be about $1/4$ inch away from the pipe.

LOWE'S QUICK TIP
To be accurate, the template must lie flat on the floor at all points. If there is a bubble or a wave, slice through it with a utility knife, lay the two sides flat, and cover the slice with a strip of masking tape.

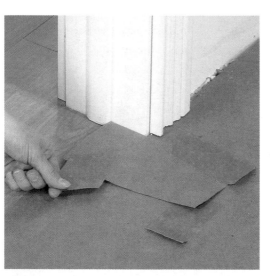

7 At a door opening, the vinyl will slip under the casing, but it must fit snugly against the jamb, where moulding will not cover it. Slip the template under the casing, and use a patch piece to butt it against the jamb. The template should end at a point that will be under the door when the door is shut.

8 Tape the succeeding sheets of rosin paper firmly together so the template becomes a single sheet that will not come apart when you roll it up. Examine the template carefully at all points to make sure that it fits around the perimeter.

cutting & laying sheet vinyl

Once you are satisfied with the template, remove the masking tape covering the cutout triangles. Roll up the template, taking care not to rip it or pull apart the pieces.

To cut the vinyl, you will need a work area large enough to lay out the entire sheet. An adjoining room is best, but a deck, garage, or driveway is also an option. Sweep the surface clear of all debris; even a small stone could poke a hole through vinyl if it is stepped on. Check the sheet as you roll it up to make sure no debris has stuck to it.

1 To get the vinyl to lie flat, roll it backward and then unroll it. Lay the vinyl with the finished surface facing up, and smooth out any bubbles or waves. Place the template on the vinyl, and adjust its position for the best appearance. You may want to avoid having a pattern line come very near a wall, or you may want to center the pattern on the floor. Secure the template with pieces of masking tape every 12 inches or so around the perimeter and with tape over the cutout triangles.

LOWE'S QUICK TIP
Some vinyl sheets may become permanently stained if you draw on them with a marker. Test a scrap piece to make sure you will be able to erase the line; you may need to use a pencil instead.

2 Trace the outline of the template onto the vinyl sheet. To be sure you are drawing a straight line, lay a framing square or straightedge along the edge of the template.

3 Before cutting, slip a piece of scrap wood or plywood under the vinyl. Use a utility knife equipped with either a hook blade or a standard blade. Where the vinyl will be covered with moulding, you can cut freehand, although you may find it easier to use a straightedge. Where the vinyl must be cut precisely, use a straightedge.

4 To cut a hole for a pipe, first use a speed square to cut a straight line from the edge of the sheet to the front of the pipe. Then cut the hole freehand. Plan to use a pipe flange (also called an escutcheon) to cover the gap between the vinyl and the pipe.

PROJECT CONTINUES ➡

5 To determine which end of the vinyl sheet you should roll out first, assess the shape of the room and how you can most easily get the roll into the room. Roll the sheet up so that the finish side is facing up. Work carefully to avoid tearing the sheet; inside corners are easily torn during the installation process. To strengthen an inside corner, apply a strip of duct tape at a 45-degree angle.

6 Sweep the floor, vacuum, and then wipe the area with a damp cloth. Unroll the vinyl sheet, pushing the edges into the corners as you go. Run your hand along the surface to make sure there is no debris underneath. If you find a bump, reroll the sheet and remove the debris immediately. Make sure the vinyl lies flat at all points, with no bubbles or waves. Pay special attention to any places, such as doorjambs, where the vinyl must be positioned exactly.

7 If the gap between the vinyl sheet and the wall is less than ¼ inch at any point, use a straightedge as a guide while you slice off a sliver with a utility knife.

8 Roll up one half of the vinyl, apply adhesive to the floor (see Step 9), and lay the vinyl back onto the adhesive. Then do the same for the other half. (Take care not to tear the vinyl.) To keep the vinyl from shifting, place two or more heavy objects on the part you will roll up next. Or, if the shape of the room makes it necessary, fold the vinyl back on itself. Do not step on the fold, or the vinyl could crack.

9 Using the notched trowel called for by the manufacturer, spread the recommended adhesive onto the floor. Aim for even coverage, with no blobs or gaps. If you purchased "loose-lay" flooring, apply the adhesive—either a strip of troweled adhesive or double-sided tape—only around the perimeter of the room. Carefully unroll the vinyl onto the troweled adhesive, smoothing it with your hand as you go. Check that the vinyl is positioned correctly.

10 Starting near the middle of the adhered section and moving outward, run a floor roller over the entire surface to remove any air bubbles. Once the first half of the floor is installed to your satisfaction, repeat Steps 8 through 10 for the second half. Once the floor is laid, clean off any adhesive on the surface using a solvent recommended by the flooring manufacturer. You may want to wait a day before installing the base moulding so you will not run the risk of getting sticky adhesive on the mouldings.

JOINING TWO PIECES OF VINYL

If the floor is wider than a single sheet of vinyl, you will need to create a waterproof seam between the two sheets. Following the instructions on the previous pages, make two templates, one for each sheet, that overlap each other by 2 inches. Before cutting the two pieces of vinyl, spread them out with one overlapping the other, and see that the pattern matches. Set the templates on top, and cut the pieces.

Lay the pieces on the floor. Once you are satisfied with the alignment of both pieces, use a straightedge to cut through both at once (top right). Hold the blade of the knife in a straight vertical position as you cut to ensure a tight seam. Remove the two thin scrap pieces that are produced.

Adhere the sheets to the floor. As a last step, focus on the seam line. Take care to keep everything perfectly clean as you work, and clean the seam completely using seam cleaner. Use a special applicator (bottom right) to apply seam sealer to the joint. Avoid touching the seam for several hours; any dirt that gets into it before it dries completely will become a permanent part of the floor.

setting ceramic tile

OF THE VARIOUS FLOORING MATERIALS, CERAMIC TILE IS ONE OF THE MOST difficult to install. On the flip side, however, when the job is done, the results are usually well worth the effort. The methods shown on these pages are for laying tile in a thinset mortar base, the method recommended by most professional tile setters (tile can also be installed with adhesive).

preparing a base

Ceramic tile must be laid on a base that is firm, solid, and flat. Several types of existing floors can provide such a base; these include concrete slab and wood or plywood subflooring. A wood or plywood base, which must be strong enough not to flex when you jump on it, is typically covered with ½-inch tile backerboard or ½-inch plywood underlayment (over the subfloor) as a substrate for ceramic tile. The combined thickness of the subfloor and the underlayment should be at least 1¼ inches.

Wood strip and plank flooring are not smooth enough to serve as a backing for ceramic tile; cover these flooring types with ½-inch plywood underlayment.

Similarly, cushioned resilient flooring is too springy to serve as a base; it should be removed or covered with plywood underlayment, as should badly damaged flooring. Note: Your old resilient floor may contain asbestos; refer to the information in the Lowe's Safety Tip on page 159.

New ceramic tile can be applied over old tile that is in good condition. To improve adhesion of the thinset, roughen the old tile's surface with an abrasive disk mounted in an electric drill (wear a dust mask), and then clean the surface with a commercial degreasing agent.

Gently pry up the quarter-round shoe moulding along the base of the walls before putting in the new floor (see page 156).

INSTALLING BACKERBOARD

1 Lay down the sheet to be cut. Measure for the cut, and subtract ¼ inch for the rough edge. Cut the panel with a cement-backerboard knife, guiding the blade along a drywall square.

2 Turn the sheet upside down, and, holding it down on one side of the scored line, snap the other side upward. Pick the sheet up on its side, score the back of the cut, and snap the sheet back to free the cut piece. Smooth the rough edge with a tile stone.

3 Sweep the floor free of debris, mix thinset mortar according to label directions, and spread the mortar on the floor using a ¼-inch square-notched trowel. Lay the sheet in the mortar carefully. Drive screws through the sheet into the joists every 6 inches (or as recommended by the manufacturer).

Baseboards do not need to be removed unless there is no shoe moulding. As you remove the moulding, number the pieces with a pencil so you can easily replace them later.

installing backerboard

Stagger the joints between sheets of backerboard or underlayment so they do not fall directly over joints in the subflooring, and stagger corners to avoid having four pieces come together in one place. If you are using plywood, interlock the edges; leave a ⅛-inch space between panels if you are using backerboard. Allow a ¼-inch gap between plywood or backerboard panels and the wall or baseboard. Drive a screw or pneumatically shoot a flooring staple at every cross mark on plywood underlayment. Fasten backerboard with special backerboard screws, setting all of the screw heads below the surface.

layout tips

You can begin either from perpendicular working lines at the center of the room or from along one wall. Begin at the center

4 Lay fiberglass mesh tape over the joints, and, using the flat edge of a trowel, spread a thin layer of thinset mortar over the tape. Feather out the mortar on either side, and smooth away any high spots. After the thinset has hardened, the surface is ready to tile.

if the room is badly out of square or if you have chosen tile with a pattern or design. You will have to cut tiles along all four walls, but the cut tiles will be of equal size. Start at one wall only if adjoining walls meet at an exact 90-degree angle. Then you will only have to cut tile on two walls. Plan your tiling so you will never have to step on recently laid tiles; this may mean starting at the far end of the room and working toward the door.

Once you have settled on a layout, it is time to establish the working lines that you will use as guides for the first tiles you lay, as shown above. Then you will butt the first row of tiles up to a batten that is fastened along one of the lines. Once the mortar starts to harden, remove the batten.

cutting tile

Mark a cutting line using a pencil or marker. For 90-degree marks, use a combination square. Angles can be transferred from a wall to a tile using an adjustable bevel guide, and irregular shapes can be transferred with a contour gauge.

Always wear eye protection when cutting. Cut straight lines using a snap cutter, or, if you have a lot of cutting to do, consider renting a wet saw with a diamond blade—you will find it well worth the relatively small expense. Stone, terra-cotta, cement-body, and some porcelain tiles should be cut only with a wet saw. Cut curves or small cutouts with a nibbling

Snap two perpendicular chalk lines where you want to begin. Then, to ensure that your first line of tiles will be straight, temporarily screw a batten, or a long, straight board, next to one of the working lines.

Nibbling cuts, though not crisp and precise, are sufficiently accurate for most purposes. First score the lines using a snap cutter or a glass cutter, and then use a nibbling tool to take small bites out of the cutout area.

tool. For interior cuts, first drill a hole using a masonry bit, and then enlarge the hole with a rod saw (this can also be used for cutting curves).

installation tips

Before beginning, open all tile boxes to check for uniform color. If the tile is dusty, wash and dry it before beginning because dust keeps the adhesive from forming a strong bond.

Pay attention to the mortar's open time (the duration of time it remains workable) so you don't end up racing to set the tile before it dries. Once the mortar begins to harden, adjusting tiles is almost impossible. First make a dry run before you begin setting tiles in thinset. The dry run will keep the number of cut tiles to a minimum and will prepare you for the unexpected.

For most tile, use gray thinset mortar with a liquid latex additive. For glass tile, marble, or other translucent tile, use white thinset mortar. Check with your dealer for

the proper mortar. Mix only as much as you can use in about 30 minutes (less if the weather is dry and warm). Be sure to follow label directions. The mortar should be wet enough to pour and also just thick enough to stick to a trowel for a second or two when held upside down.

Maintain properly sized grout joints by using tile spacers; remove these spacers as soon as the mortar begins to set. About every 10 minutes or so, pick up a tile that you've just set; mortar should adhere to the entire surface. If it doesn't, scrape the mortar off the floor and reset the tile with new mortar. After installing all the tiles, remove the spacers, clean up excess mortar, and allow the tiles to set for at least 12 hours before walking on the floor.

Prepare grout by adding water sparingly to dry powdered grout, mixing a small quantity at a time. Be sure all particles are thoroughly moistened and there are no lumps. For areas of the floor that will be exposed to water, mix in a liquid grout

A wet saw typically has a rotating diamond blade that is submerged or drenched with water from a pump (it must be underwater when cutting or it will become dull). Slide the tray all the way back toward you, and position the tile, pressing it firmly against the guide. Turn on the saw. Holding the tile firmly in place, slide it gently forward against the blade.

sealer. Always wear rubber gloves when mixing grout, as the lime in it is caustic.

Let the grout cure for the time specified by the manufacturer. Then, if you have used a cement-based grout and the floor is likely to be subjected to standing water, apply a grout sealer for extra protection. Wipe sealer off the tiles before it hardens Unglazed tile (except porcelain) should also be sealed. Use a sealer intended for tile, and follow the manufacturer's instructions for applying it.

LAYING A TILE FLOOR

1 Spread mortar on the floor, next to a batten, using the smooth edge of a notched trowel. Then comb it with the notched edge, holding the trowel at a consistent angle, as shown. Use sweeping strokes to create an even bed.

2 Align the first tile with the working lines, and set it in the mortar without sliding it more than about 1 inch. Set several more tiles, inserting spacers at every corner. Avoid pressing down on the tiles when placing them.

3 When you finish a section of floor, bed the tiles by setting a short block over two or more tiles and tapping it with a rubber mallet. Periodically glance across the tiles to make sure they are forming a level plane.

4 To mark a border tile for a straight cut, place a spacer equal in thickness to the grout lines against the wall. Set the border tile on top of the adjacent whole tile, and precisely align the edges of the two tiles on all four sides. Set another whole tile on top, and then slide the top tile against the spacer. Use the top tile to draw the cutting line across the border tile.

5 Pour about 1 cup of grout onto the floor at a time. Holding a laminated grout float nearly flat, use sweeping back-and-forth strokes in two or more directions to force the grout into the joints. Then tip the float up, and, using it like a squeegee, clear away most of the grout by dragging the float diagonally across the tiles. Do not allow its edge to dig into the grout lines.

6 Before the grout dries, lightly wipe the tiles with a damp sponge (rinse frequently), using a circular motion. Smooth and level the grout joints with the tiles. Let the grout dry until a haze appears on the tiles, and then polish the tiles with a soft cloth. Apply a grout sealer after waiting the period specified by the grout manufacturer.

installing a stone floor

BOTH POLISHED AND ROUGH STONE TILE CAN USUALLY BE INSTALLED WHEREVER ceramic tile is used employing basically the same methods (see pages 192–195). Take extra care that the substrate is firm because stone tiles, although hard, are easily cracked. You will probably have to make all the cuts with a wet saw rather than with a snap cutter or nibbling tool.

Though they may not appear so, light-colored marble, travertine, and other natural stones are actually somewhat translucent. Gray thinset adhesive can show through enough to muddy their appearance, so use white thinset instead.

rough stone tile

Tumbled marble and other porous stones usually are installed with wide grout lines; the finished floor is not expected to be perfectly smooth. As a result, installation is much less nerve-wracking than it can be for polished stone. A wide choice of borders and decorative insets is available for use with porous stone.

It can be difficult to clean grout from porous stone. In most cases, you should seal the tiles before applying grout. When you apply the grout (below), wipe the tiles with a clean, wet sponge early and often (bottom) using clean, cool water.

Most polished stone tiles, such as this marble, require fine grout lines to complement the elegance of the material.

FLOORS

If the tiles are irregular in shape, use the grid method to lay out and install them (see page 193). Some types look irregular but are actually precise squares; check to see whether you can use spacers when installing them.

polished stone tile

Typically, formal-looking polished stone tiles such as marble or granite are installed with thin grout lines. Use $\frac{1}{16}$-inch spacers and unsanded grout. Because these tiles are placed so closely together, even the slightest height discrepancy between tiles may be very noticeable. Be sure to start with a substrate that is absolutely smooth, level, and clean.

Some natural stone tiles have a slight warp. Before applying mortar, lay a number of tiles next to each other to test for imperfections in size. Also take extra care while combing the mortar to achieve a very even surface. When you set the tiles, check periodically for changes in level; use a beater board (right) to make corrections.

INSTALLING MOSAIC TILES

With small mosaic tiles, every square inch must nestle firmly in the mortar or else one of the individual tiles may come loose. Achieving this can be tricky because the paper or mesh backing that holds mosaics together interferes with the ability of the mortar to adhere. To make sure that all the tiles stick, a sheet of mosaics must be pressed firmly into the mortar, which causes mortar to ooze up through the many grout lines and makes installation a messy operation.

To ensure firm adhesion, spend a little more for epoxy thinset. Or use standard thinset mortar mixed with liquid latex, and work carefully. In either case, mix the mortar so that it is a little wetter than it would be for regular tiles; it should be just firm enough for the ridges made by a notched trowel to hold their shape. The job will go slowly, so mix small amounts at a time. As you lay the sheets in mortar, check often to make sure all the tiles are sticking. Tap the tiles firmly into the mortar using a beater board. When mortar oozes up between the tiles, wipe it off with a damp—not wet—sponge; getting the remaining mortar wet could weaken it. Wiping the mortar away to a depth of at least $\frac{1}{4}$ inch is a tedious but necessary job.

If the individual tiles are large enough, you can cut mosaics using a snap cutter, but a nibbling tool is usually easier to use.

To make a precise cut in a small tile, first score the line with a snap cutter, and then cut with a nibbling tool. (For instructions on cutting tile, see page 194.)

When you apply the grout, you will not be able to tool every line as you would with larger tiles. Keep wiping the surface lightly, over and over again, until the grout lines are consistent.

repairing tongue-and-groove flooring

TOO OFTEN, A REPAIR TO DAMAGED TONGUE-AND-GROOVE FLOORING RESULTS IN a rectangular patch that stands out like a sore thumb because its joints are not staggered as all the others are. A better approach is to remove boards or portions of boards so that their ends are staggered in a way that blends in with the surrounding floor. Because the pieces interlock, however, removing and patching tongue-and-groove flooring in this way is a time-consuming task that requires some skill.

preparing for the repair

Buy replacement boards that match the existing flooring in size and color. These pages show how to repair a floor made of ¾-inch-thick solid oak planking, but essentially the same techniques can be used to repair engineered wood flooring. On a solid hardwood floor, strip the finish off a piece of the removed flooring to determine what sort of wood to buy.

With a solid hardwood floor, staining and finishing may require more work and time than the actual repair. You can try to finish the new boards before installing them, but it is difficult to achieve an exact match. It may be necessary to sand and refinish the entire floor.

To repair squeaks or to prepare the area for the installation of a new type of flooring on top, see pages 156–163. If you need to replace more than one board, plan the complete patch so that you end up with staggered joints. You may choose to remove full-length boards. If a damaged board is very long, however, you may choose to replace only a portion of it.

1 Use a square and a knife to mark the cut line; this will prevent splintering when you cut the board. If you are skilled with a circular saw, make a plunge cut (see the box on the facing page). If you are not confident making this type of cut, make the cut with a hammer and chisel. Hold the chisel with the bevel facing the area to be removed.

2 Bore a series of ⅜- or ½-inch holes across the width of the board in two places, spaced 4 to 6 inches apart, near the center of the damaged plank. Be careful to avoid adjacent flooring. These rows of holes will enable you to remove a section from the middle of the board.

3 Split the area between the holes, and pry out the pieces. With a hammer and chisel, slide both end pieces toward the middle to disengage the tongues and grooves on the ends. Split and remove the end pieces with the chisel.

4 Cut replacement boards. Use a scrap of flooring to protect each replacement board's tongue or groove as you tap it into place. Drill pilot holes, and then drive screws or nails at an angle through the tongue to fasten the board to the subfloor.

5 Many times, you will need to cut off the end tongue of a replacement board. For the last replacement board, you will likely also need to remove the lower lip on the grooved side. You can chisel this lower lip off (as shown) or cut it with a table saw or circular saw.

6 Tap the last piece in place. Drill pilot holes, and drive nails or trimhead screws through the face of the board. Set the fastener heads, and fill them with putty. Use a power sander or a hand sander to bring the patch even with the level of the surrounding floor.

LOWE'S QUICK TIP

For this work, it is important to have a high-quality, sharp chisel. Use a ¾- or 1-inch-wide wood chisel. Have a sharpening stone available because hardwood will quickly dull the chisel.

ALTERNATIVE METHOD

Here is an easy way to remove a single piece of damaged flooring:

Using a circular saw, make two lengthwise plunge cuts into the middle of the damaged board, cutting from one end of the board to the other. (Be careful not to cut into the adjacent boards.) Chisel down far enough to release each end. Pry out the central cutout section using the chisel. Now you can carefully pry out the grooved side and the tongue side.

repairing laminate flooring

LAMINATE FLOORING IS NOT EASILY SCRATCHED, BUT ONCE SCRATCHES DEVELOP, you cannot completely erase them. To prevent scratches, keep the floor well vacuumed and place rugs in heavy-traffic areas.

patching a puncture

Small areas of damage can be filled with patching putty. If possible, bring a scrap of flooring to Lowe's so you can choose the right color putty. Use a utility knife and chisel to cut the hole (at least ¼ inch deep) and square up its edges. Squeeze putty into the hole. Then, using a putty knife, force putty down and scrape the surface (left). Wait for an hour or so, and then wipe the area with a damp cloth.

replacing a strip

Laminate strips are very long, so you will probably want to replace only part of a strip. Follow the steps below to remove and replace a damaged section.

LOWE'S QUICK TIP
Because laminate flooring has a slippery surface, take extra care when cutting with a circular saw to make sure the saw does not skate away and damage an adjacent strip.

1 Mark the section you want to remove, and then use a circular saw to cut out a portion from the middle that is about 1 inch away from all four edges. Pry this middle piece out. Cut the end lines with a circular saw, and complete the cuts with a sharp chisel. Next, make four short, angled cuts running from the cutout area to each of the corners; complete the cuts using a chisel. First, pry out the end scraps, and then remove the tongued strip and the grooved strip.

2 Cut a new piece of laminate flooring to fit snugly into the cutout area. Turn the piece upside down, and use a circular saw or table saw to cut off the lip below the groove. Test that this patch will fit, and then remove it. Apply glue to the top of the patch's tongue as well as to the top of the tongue that is exposed in the floor. Also apply glue to the ends of the opening in the floor. Slip the patch into place, and weight it down for a day before walking on it.

replacing tiles

METHODS OF REPLACING TILES DIFFER GREATLY BETWEEN VINYL AND CERAMIC OR stone. Generally, replacing resilient tile is far easier because the new piece is simply glued into place, as discussed below. If more than one or two ceramic or stone tiles are broken, look for an underlying problem. Jump on the floor. If you feel any flex, the substrate needs to be repaired or shored up. Install a patch of new cement backerboard or underlayment before reinstalling the tiles.

ceramic or stone tile

Removing and replacing a ceramic or stone tile is not usually difficult, but searching out and finding matching replacement tile and grout can be time-consuming.

If the manufacturer's name is printed on the back of the damaged tile, you can conduct most of your search by telephoning suppliers. If not, you will have to visit tile dealers with the old tile in hand to check for one that matches.

Even if you get the correct brand and color of grout, chances are your existing grout has slightly darkened over the years. Clean the old grout using grout cleaner. Chip off a piece of the cleaned grout, and take it to a tile dealer to find a close match.

vinyl tile

If you cannot find an exact replacement for a damaged resilient tile, remove a tile from under the refrigerator or some other inconspicuous place.

If the damaged tile has started to curl up or is cracked, use a putty knife to pry it up. You can also heat it with a clothes iron to soften the mastic, keeping a cloth between the iron and the tile to avoid dirtying the face of the iron.

Scrape the area absolutely clean, and then vacuum away all dust. Test to make sure the new tile will fit. Apply mastic to the floor, allow it to dry, and set the tile. Use a kitchen rolling pin to press the tile firmly into the mastic.

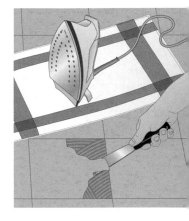

A clothes iron can be used to soften the mastic and ease removal of a damaged tile.

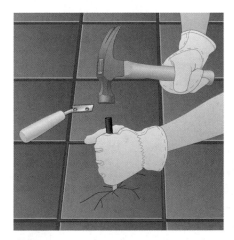

1 All around the damaged tile, scrape out the grout using a grout saw. With a hammer and cold chisel, strike the center of the tile until it cracks. Pry out the tile shards.

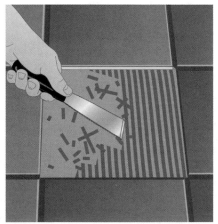

2 Use a putty knife or margin trowel to pry away the mortar. Scrape out all the mortar remnants. Gently use the putty knife (and perhaps a hammer) to chip remaining grout from around the area. Vacuum away the debris, and clean the area thoroughly with a damp cloth.

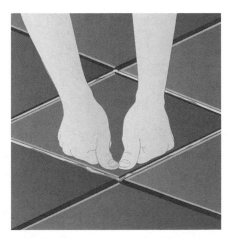

3 Back-butter the replacement tile, and press it into place. Check that it is level with the surrounding tiles, and wipe away any mortar that oozes out. Make sure all the grout lines are the same width. Allow the mortar to set overnight, and then apply grout around the new tile.

windows & doors

IF A HOUSE IS A SHELTER FROM THE ELEMENTS, ITS WINDOWS AND DOORS ARE ITS links to the world outside, allowing light and air to penetrate and people to enter and exit the house and its rooms while maintaining protection. Doors and windows must function at high levels of efficiency, shutting out noise and drafts, keeping in heat or cooled air, and filtering harmful ultraviolet rays. They must fasten securely, keeping intruders out and inquisitive toddlers in. And they not only must provide these basic services but also need to be attractive design elements. Achieving this balance is no easy feat, but technology has provided today's homeowners with a wide and wonderful selection in a variety of price ranges. This chapter offers a buying guide to new windows and doors and reveals how to frame and install them, including tips on how to add interior doors to improve a home's traffic flow.

The new generation of windows and doors can offer many energy-saving advantages for remodelers or new builders. For those with older or period homes, the reality of existing elements is less efficient, and occasionally balky, windows and doors. Sashes and doors get stuck, panes break, and weather stripping weakens. Window and door repairs can be handled by most homeowners without too much time, trouble, and expense. You will find here information on freeing a stuck sash, repairing broken window mechanisms and screens, and fixing loose or binding doors or problematic sliding doors.

Finally, the chapter offers information on installing and repairing lock sets, deadbolts, and other window and door security mechanisms.

buying windows

WINDOWS HAVE A TREMENDOUS ENVIRONMENTAL INFLUENCE ON A HOUSE, affecting the light, ventilation, and temperature of the interior—and the comfort of the occupants. In addition, windows are part of a home's architectural identity, immediately conveying period and style. When you are choosing new windows, make sure the styles you select will suit your home both practically and aesthetically.

window styles

Windows come in many shapes, sizes, and types and are made from a variety of materials. How do you select the right ones?

There are several criteria to consider: your budget, your home's style, and your needs for a given window's performance. Think about the relative importance of ventilation and security; consider what you need in terms of ease of maintenance. And decide whether you want to emphasize

the window as an architectural focal point or simply have it serve in a predominantly practical manner.

Windows are either fixed or operable. The photographs on this and the following three pages show some common varieties, and the chart on page 206 provides basic information about characteristics and performance of the key types.

window orientation

In addition to their size, where your windows are placed and what type they are have a significant effect on the amount of light and ventilation they provide. A south-facing window lets in the most light and is desirable in all but the hottest climates; a north window provides soft, diffuse light. Because of the low angle of the sun in the morning and late afternoon, light and heat from east- and west-facing windows can be too intense.

The view out a window is just as important as the light and ventilation the window provides. Windows connect us to the outdoors and enhance our sense of interior space. Consider the view before you decide the placement and size of your windows.

materials

Windows are made from wood, aluminum, steel, vinyl, or fiberglass—or from a combination of these materials. In general, those that offer better weather protection cost more, but they pay off in low maintenance and energy savings.

wood Wood tends to be the most popular window material, particularly for the parts

This window wall offers the warmth of wood inside and the durability of aluminum cladding outside.

of a window seen from indoors. Wood does not conduct cold or allow condensation as much as other materials do. However, wood is subject to shrinkage and swelling, so it will warp and rot over time—especially on the exterior—unless it is protected.

Wood windows typically come unfinished unless you order them otherwise. If you intend to paint them, you can save work by purchasing them already primed on the exterior and/or interior surfaces of the frame and sash. Or you may be able to eliminate painting altogether—some manufacturers offer pre-painted windows in a number of standard colors.

clad wood You will find that many of today's windows have wood inside and a tough, attractive exterior jacket of extruded aluminum or vinyl on the outside. The cladding, available in a few stock colors, covers both the sash and frame; it will keep windows virtually maintenance-free for years. With vinyl, the color permeates

the material so scratches do not show. Aluminum will scratch, but it is tougher and easier to paint, and it comes in a wider variety of colors (though neither vinyl nor aluminum should require painting). Both types will resist rust and rot.

vinyl Vinyl windows are made from rigid, impact-resistant polyvinyl chloride (PVC) and have hollow spaces inside that make them resistant to heat loss and condensation. Inexpensive vinyl windows have a tendency to distort when exposed to extremes of heat and cold, making them

ATTACHMENT TYPES

When you buy windows, consider how they will be attached. Most wood windows come pre-hung in complete frames that fit into a rough opening in the wall. They are attached with nails driven through the exterior casing, on the outside and through the jambs on the inside. Vinyl or aluminum windows and some wood windows with a vinyl or aluminum cladding are even easier to install. They have a nailing flange on the outside that you attach to the sheathing around the window's opening.

harder to operate and allowing air leakage. Vinyl windows cannot be painted, and darker shades may fade over time.

steel Steel is more resistant to the elements than both aluminum and wood. But because of their expense, steel windows generally are not used in homes. If you have the budget, however, these attractive, low-maintenance windows will last for years.

aluminum Aluminum windows are more durable than bare wood and are also thinner, lighter, and easier to handle. They are insulated with a thermal break of extruded

RIGHT: **Double-hung windows offer ventilation at both top and bottom.**

TYPES OF WINDOWS

Double-hung	Classic in style, double-hung windows have an upper outside sash that slides down and a lower inside sash that slides up. Hidden springs, weights, or friction devices help lift, lower, and position the sash. With certain types, the sash can be removed, rotated, or tilted for cleaning. If only one sash slides, the window is called "vertical sliding" or "single-hung."
Casement	Hung singly or in pairs, casement windows are side-mounted on hinges and operated by cranks that swing the sash inward or, more commonly, outward. They open fully for easy cleaning and offer excellent ventilation because they can "scoop" in breezes.
Horizontal slider	These work well at sealing in energy. They may have one or more fixed panels in addition to one or more panels that slide in horizontal tracks. Only half of the total window may be opened for ventilation at a time.
Awning and hopper	An awning window is like a horizontal, top-hinged casement—it tilts out at the bottom, offering partial ventilation, an unobstructed view, and reasonably good security. A top-opening style, typically placed low on a wall, is called a hopper window.
Jalousie	Jalousie windows, also called louvers, are made of glass slats set in metal clips that can be opened and closed in unison. These offer good ventilation but are chilly and drafty in cold climates.
Bay	This style projects out from the wall; a center window parallel to the wall is flanked by two windows attached at an angle, usually casement or double-hung styles. Box bays have side windows at a 90-degree angle.
Bow	A bow window projects like a bay but has more than three sections that join to form a gentle curve. Center windows are generally fixed; side sashes are typically casement windows.
Tilt-turn windows	Tilt-turn windows offer distinctive European styling and have a special advantage over conventional double-hung windows: They tilt in toward the room at the top and also turn a full 180 degrees for easy cleaning. This feature also makes them excellent emergency exits. Look for a multipoint locking system; this adds security and helps keep the window tightly closed.

vinyl and sometimes also foam, which reduces heat loss and condensation. Finishes protect the aluminum from corrosion but deteriorate in coastal areas because of the moist, salty air.

window hardware

All operable windows come equipped with hardware, the mechanisms used for opening and closing the sash, the latches, and so forth. Here is a closer look at the key types of hardware.

cranks Casement, awning, and hopper windows utilize cranks for opening and closing. (Older types used push-bar operators.) Some manufacturers offer cranks in nonmetallic finishes (notably white), and some new types have fold-down handles that are relatively inconspicuous.

latches & locks Latches are used to hold the window tightly closed. Two are recommended on tall or wide hinged windows. On double-hung windows, sash locks pull together the upper and lower sash. Keyed sash locks can improve security. On sliders, look for security locks so the operable sashes cannot be jimmied open.

hinges The best casement, awning, and hopper hinges pivot to allow arm space between the sash and the window frame so washing exterior glass is an easy job. You can even find special European hardware that turns a casement window into a hopper window. Because the hardware locks tightly in several places around the frame, the windows have very low air infil-

tration. But, unlike American casement windows, the European style window mechanism swings into the room. This feature can interfere with draperies. See related information about tilt-turn windows on the facing page.

counterbalances On double-hung windows, the sash is counterbalanced on the sides by weights or mechanisms such as torsion screws.

sliding mechanisms The sashes of most aluminum and vinyl windows are lightweight enough to slide in the sill tracks. But large, door-height sashes must be supported by heavy-duty rollers on their bottom edges.

LEFT: **Typical casement windows swing out and are operated by a crank.** TOP: **Some casements feature cranks that fold flat.** ABOVE: **Today's window latches offer both security and style.**

buying doors

WHEN SHOPPING FOR NEW DOORS, YOU WILL DISCOVER HUNDREDS OF TYPES AND sizes, ranging from conventional wood models to steel and fiberglass composite entry systems. Once you have a basic understanding of how doors are made and know whether you want an exterior entry door or an interior door (there are distinct differences between the two, as explained below), you are ready to explore the many options within that category to find the perfect door for your needs.

door construction

Regardless of whether they are made from wood or another material, doors are either "flush" or "paneled." These terms describe how a wood door is built or, in the case of nonwood doors, simply refer to the door's general style and appearance.

Paneled doors have rectangular recesses (panels) framed by horizontal rails and vertical stiles. They are sometimes called stile-and-rail doors. Superior strength and traditional looks make this type a wise choice for exterior doors and for the interior doors of homes with traditional decor. Panel construction on a wood door also minimizes cracking and warping because panels have room to shift as they expand and contract with changes in moisture.

Flush doors are flat and smooth on both faces. Wood ones are covered with birch or other wood veneer that is easy to stain and varnish or paint. Nonwood doors are clad with fiberglass or steel. Flush doors may have a solid-wood or a foam-filled core,

This four-panel exterior door is mounted to the jambs with three hinges. The stops are wood strips that the door fits against when closed. The sill fits between the jambs, forming the frame bottom. Casing covers the space between wall materials and the jambs and strengthens the frame.

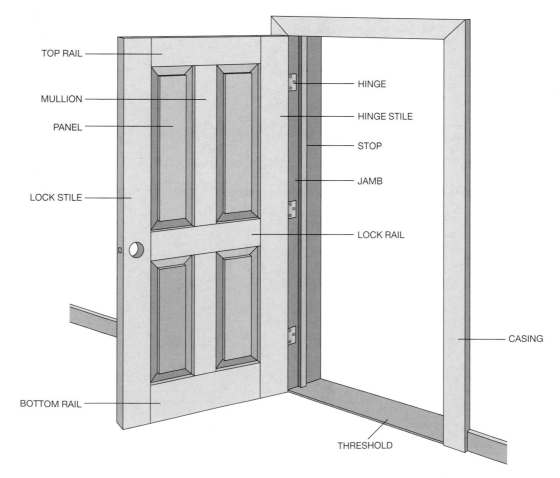

TOP RAIL

MULLION

PANEL

LOCK STILE

BOTTOM RAIL

HINGE

HINGE STILE

STOP

JAMB

LOCK RAIL

CASING

THRESHOLD

FAR LEFT: **Both practical and stylish, this single-light wood door is fitted with a chalkboard on one side. LEFT: Though it looks like a panel door, this sturdy model is actually surfaced with steel, making it an excellent choice for safety between the garage and interior rooms.**

or, in the case of interior doors, they may have a hollow core filled with a light-weight baffle, such as a honeycomb of dense cardboard. The latter type is relatively inexpensive and lightweight.

The door frame consists of jambs, casing, stops, and a threshold (and a sill in the case of an exterior door), as shown in the illustration on the facing page. All swinging doors are attached to the jambs with two or three hinges. On exterior doors, the hinges are on the inside of the house to prevent removal of the hinge pins by a potential intruder.

Glass sections of doors are called lights. A six-light door, for example, has six glass panes, separated by muntins. You can buy true divided-light doors from some companies or, if you just want the look of divided lights, you can buy snap-in muntins that do a fair job of mimicking the look but are

much less expensive (and they make the glass easier to clean).

What we refer to as French doors are simply multiple-light, hinged doors that are paired together. Patio and sliding doors may have a single light (a full-sized glass panel) or multiple lights, but these doors slide rather than swing. See more about sliding doors on pages 212–213.

This door's flush surface is clad with a natural lauan wood panel.

The most common height for doors is 6 feet, 8 inches, but you can buy styles up to 8 feet tall. Widths of interior doors vary from 12 inches up to 36 inches or more. Typical exterior doors range from 30 to 36 inches; a 34-inch door—the minimum to accommodate a wheelchair—will make it easier to move furniture indoors and out. Thickness is $1\frac{3}{4}$ inches for exterior doors.

Interior doors do not have to meet the same standards for weatherization as exterior doors. Both panel and flush doors are thinner ($1\frac{3}{8}$ inch) and lighter-weight. There are also a variety of interior doors that can be used for specialty needs: bifold, accordion, and bypass doors for closets and storage spaces, and pocket doors that help save space by sliding into a cavity in the wall, for example.

Interior doors typically are hinged to swing in toward a room, with the exception of closets and other storage rooms, whose doors are hinged to swing outward. Jambs, casing, and stops are the same as for exterior doors. Unlike exterior doors, interior doors do not have a sill, but some have a threshold that hides the transition between two different flooring materials.

entry doors

You can buy an entry door singly (as a door ready to be mounted in an existing frame) or "pre-hung"—attached to a frame. A pre-hung door usually comes as a complete entry system, with an integral interlocking threshold and weather stripping encircling the door's perimeter. With an entry system, side lights may flank the door on each side

French doors with side lights and an array of second-story fixed windows give the facade of this home stately appeal.

and a transom window may cap the top. Because the hinges and lock set are designed as part of the whole entry system, the doors tend to be very weather-tight and to function extremely reliably.

wood entry doors

Wood has the warm, natural look and feel that most people prefer, but wood will eventually warp, crack, and bow when exposed to the elements. Because of this, wood doors must be maintained with a durable finish. Solid wood doors tend to be more expensive than those made from other materials. Typical species include oak, cherry, walnut, mahogany, maple, fir, pine, or paint-grade doors from any of several softwoods.

Most mass-produced doors are not solid wood. Instead, they are made with an engineered-wood core that is faced with a veneer, a construction that minimizes warping and movement and makes a door more affordable to build. Be aware that surface veneers on doors are easily damaged, particularly if they are thinner than about $1/16$ inch.

fiberglass-composite doors

Where it will be exposed to weather or a particularly harsh or humid climate, a door made of fiberglass composite is a smart choice. These doors realistically imitate the look of wood, thanks to surfaces that are a combination of molded wood-grain texturing and a wood-like cellulose coating that can be stained. A fiberglass door's framework is usually made of wooden stiles and rails that are filled with a core of foam insulation.

Fiberglass doors, like wood doors, are sold as single units or as complete entry systems with stainable wood jambs, a variety of glazings, adjustable sills, and security lock sets. Many fiberglass door entry systems are guaranteed for as long as you own the house.

steel entry doors

Steel doors are extremely rugged and durable. Although some steel doors have traditional panel styling, they are not true panel doors. They have a steel or wood frame and are filled with energy-saving foam insulation.

LEFT: **Leaded-glass windows in this wide, handsome entry door—and the side lights that flank it—give this home Craftsman-era style.**

ABOVE: **These divided-light doors, side lights, and transom windows are clad with aluminum for high durability.**

ABOVE: **A steel entry door provides high security and permanence at a relatively low price.**
BELOW: **Entry doors can be made to order from hardwoods; the sky is the limit in both possibilities and price.**

Steel doors are not as industrial-looking as they sound; most varieties have surfaces of heavy-gauge galvanized steel that have been embossed with a wood-grain pattern. Most come factory-primed with a baked-on polyester finish that may need periodic repainting. Some are given a vinyl coating

for greater weather resistance. If you want the look of wood, you can opt for a steel door that has been embossed with a wood-grain pattern or choose a type that has been given a wood-fiber coating or a real-wood veneer that can be stained.

buying tips When replacing just the door, measure the door's actual height, width, and thickness. When buying a pre-hung door, measure the width of the existing jamb, from the inside of the exterior moulding to the inside of the interior moulding. Note which side the knob is on from inside the room. If the knob is on the right, the door is a "right-hand" door; if it is on the left, it is a "left-hand" door.

When buying an entry system, be sure all of the components are from the same manufacturer—not assembled by distributors from a variety of products—to ensure the parts will work together effectively.

buying sliding doors

Contemporary sliding or "gliding" doors have come a long way since yesteryear's aluminum sliders, infamous for their stark appearance, sweating frames, and cold glazing. Today, a new generation of high-quality models offers energy efficiency, durability, safety, and style.

Though conventional aluminum sliders maintain a strong foothold in the market, sliding doors made of wood and other materials have given the genre an entirely new identity. The most popular sliders offer the warm look of wood on the inside along with the durable cladding of vinyl on the outside. These are made just like the clad-wood windows that are discussed on page 205.

Because wood is vulnerable to moisture and sun, it must be given a durable finish. You can buy all-wood sliders that have been factory-primed or pre-painted in standard colors; some manufacturers will also custom paint them for a premium.

As alternatives, there are doors made from fiberglass composites that resemble wood but will not crack or warp, as well

as rugged steel sliders, usually less expensive. Still other doors are faced on both sides with a vinyl or aluminum skin; a polyurethane foam insulation core fills the shell, offering six times the energy efficiency of wood.

sliding door glazing Of course, the largest part of a sliding glass door is glass. To make such a door truly energy efficient, high-performance glazing is key. Fortunately, this is standard with most high-quality sliders. You will find dual glazing, or more typically—double-paned glass with low-emissivity (low-e) coating and, in some cases, argon gas filling. (See pages 214–215 for more about types of glazing.)

In addition, some companies offer decorative stained or beveled glass with true brass caming (leading). Like other types of doors and windows, sliders are available with real or false divided lights. Most manufacturers let you specify the glazing you want when you order.

sizes & options Beyond the standard 6-feet, 8-inch height, sliding doors are made 6 feet, 11 inches or 8 feet tall. You can also buy three- or four-door-wide configurations that run up to about 16 feet wide. Sliders are made in single-opening and double-opening styles. To extend your design options, most manufacturers provide matching rectangular and circle-head transom windows intended to fit above doors.

Some companies offer top-mounted insect screens that are easier to use than rolling screens. With these, debris along the bottom glide rail is much less likely to interfere with smooth operation.

RIGHT: **The handles and latch are elegantly integrated into this vinyl sliding door.**

ABOVE: **Aluminum-clad sliding doors are sold prefinished in white with a choice of integral, simulated, or inside-the-glass muntins.**

LEFT: **The height of these wood sliders is extended by the insertion of a long transom window across the top.**

glazing

UNFORTUNATELY, GLASS IS NOT NEARLY AS GOOD AT CONSERVING ENERGY AS an insulated wall, so glazed doors and windows can be responsible for a major part of a home's energy loss if they are not well chosen. Storm windows and doors and certain window coverings can help retard heat movement, but the surest and most effective way to save energy is to utilize high-performance glazing.

Two important ratings to check when buying windows and glazed doors are the R-value and the U-value. An R-value measures a material's resistance to heat transfer; the higher the R-value, the better the insulating properties of the glazing. U-value measures overall energy efficiency. It tells you the rate at which heat flows through the entire window or door, frame and all. The lower the U-value, the more energy-efficient the window or door. An average U-value is fine for warm climates; in cold climates, a lower U-value is worth the premium you are likely to pay for it.

Insulating glazing typically has two, or sometimes as many as three, panes of glass sealed together with either air or argon gas trapped between them to act as an insulator. Some units have a plastic film suspended between two glass panes. If the unit is properly sealed, condensation shouldn't occur between the panes; sometimes a drying agent (called a desiccant) is used in the spacer (the strip inside the panes that helps keep them apart) as added insurance against condensation. There is no easy way to get rid of condensation in dual glazing, so one very important reason for buying windows and doors with a strong warranty is to ensure that they will be backed if the seal fails and condensation does occur.

You will discover that there are also a number of glass products on the market for special situations and uses, including safety glass and stained glass. Here is a closer look at both high-performance and specialty glazing.

low-emissivity glass Low-emissivity, or low-e, glazing has a film applied to one of the glass surfaces or suspended between the panes. This coating or film allows light in but also prevents some solar rays from being transmitted through the glass. A low-e coating can help keep your home cool on a hot day by blocking longer-wave radiant heat from entering, and on a cold day it can prevent the radiant interior heat from escaping through the glass. Low-e coatings also block ultraviolet rays, which reduces the fading of floors, floor coverings, drapes, and upholstery.

tinted glass Usually given a bronze or gray cast, tinted glass dramatically cuts glare and heat from the sun (solar gain) yet only slightly reduces the amount of light admitted into your home.

This cross-section of high-performance glazing shows two panes of glass with a space in between. In some cases, the space is filled with argon or a similar inert gas, which serves as an insulator. In addition, a low-emissivity coating deflects ultraviolet rays while retaining indoor radiant heat.

Where sun-caused fading or damage may be a serious problem, such as at unprotected south-facing windows, you may want to opt for glass with a solar bronze or solar gray tint to reject UV rays.

reflective glass Like tinted glass, reflective glass reduces solar gain. From outside, it appears to be a mirror, obscuring the view in.

safety glass Required by some local building codes for certain situations, safety glass is always a good choice if there's any risk of a person walking through a window. Safety glass is available tempered, laminated, or wire-reinforced. Tempered glass is heat-treated during the manufacturing process and crumbles (instead of shattering) if it is broken. Laminated glass has a film of plastic that holds the glass together if broken. Wire-reinforced glass clings to its wire mesh if broken.

stained glass Before choosing a stained-glass window, don't just consider its design and size—think about the color scheme of the room, the direction the panel will face, and the amount of outdoor view you'd like. A rectangular or curved stained-glass frame around a clear pane can focus attention on the view. A stained-glass panel the size of the window will block out an undesirable view. Stained glass also can be lovely around doors, but check to see if this is permitted by your local codes. Do not use stained glass where people could walk into it.

You can install small stained-glass panels in the same way you would install ordinary clear panes (see page 226). Large panels will need additional support for a permanent installation; for example, you may need to fit them into routed wood frames or block their edges on both sides with wood strips nailed to the sill and window frame. Be sure to set a stained-glass panel in glazing putty, and caulk all outside joints.

BASIC TOOLS FOR WINDOWS & DOORS

Block plane

Measuring tape

Caulking gun

Chalk line

Claw hammer

Combination square

5-in-1 tool

Power drill with bits and screwdriver tips

Hand stapler

Reciprocating saw

Pliers

Perforated rasp

Miter box and backsaw

Level

Glass cutter

Safety goggles

Putty knife

Power circular saw

Stud finder

Sanding block

Screwdrivers

Stepladder

Prybar

Tin snips

Utility knife

Wood chisel

Coping saw

tools for windows & doors

MOST WORK ON WINDOWS AND DOORS REQUIRES A HOST OF CONVENTIONAL carpentry tools. Of course, you do not need all of these for every job; some repair jobs require just two or three tools. Be sure you have appropriate safety equipment such as safety glasses, gloves, and a dust mask. For many jobs, you will also need a stepladder—and you may need a pair of sawhorses to hold a door or window that is not installed. For touchup work, you will most likely need drywall tools (see page 104) and a variety of paintbrushes and painting tools (see pages 34–39).

NAIL CLAW

RECIPROCATING SAW

COLD CHISEL

PRYBAR

WRECKING BAR

DEMOLITION TOOLS

Window and door installation often requires a bit of minor demolition work. For chipping away masonry, you will need a cold chisel (be sure to wear safety glasses). A prybar is useful for various tear-out jobs, and a nail claw helps pull out stubborn nails. A reciprocating saw makes it easy to cut away wall materials.

MEASURING & MARKING TOOLS

The tools shown here are necessary for the various layout and measuring tasks involved in new window and door installation. Choose a measuring tape that is at least 16 feet long and has markings for stud layouts along its blade every 16 and 24 inches. A stud finder is helpful for locating wall studs.

LEVEL

COMBINATION SQUARE

CARPENTER'S SQUARE

MEASURING TAPE

CHALK LINE

STUD FINDER

CUTTING TOOLS

A power circular saw allows you to cut wood quickly; a handsaw gives you more controlled cutting. For other wood cutting, you will need wood chisels in two or three sizes. A block plane and perforated rasp help shave down wood—for example, when you need to trim a door to achieve a better fit. A saber saw is used for making curved cuts. Tin snips cut metal flashing during window and door installation. A utility knife is handy for many jobs.

HANDSAW

POWER CIRCULAR SAW

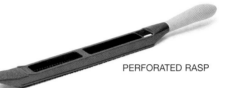

TIN SNIPS

BLOCK PLANE

SABER SAW (JIGSAW)

WOOD CHISEL

UTILITY KNIFE

PERFORATED RASP

HOLE SAW

CONSTRUCTION TOOLS

When installing doors and windows, you will need a variety of basic carpentry tools, including those shown here. In addition to the electric drill, be sure you have a set of drill bits, Phillips-head screwdriver bits, and—if you intend to install a lock set or deadbolt— a hole saw. A hand stapler fastens building paper and insulation during window and door installation. A caulking gun is used to seal joints between materials.

POWER DRILL WITH BITS
AND SCREWDRIVER TIPS

HAND STAPLER

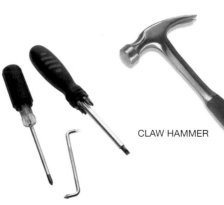

CLAW HAMMER

CAULKING GUN

SCREWDRIVERS

HEAVY-DUTY SCISSORS

PLIERS

PUTTY KNIFE

GLASS CUTTER

SCREEN-SPLINE ROLLER

5-IN-1 TOOL

REPAIR TOOLS

Window- and door-related repairs call for some of the tools shown here. To cut replacement glass for a window pane, you'll need a glass cutter. To repair window screens, be sure you have heavy-duty scissors for cutting screening and a screen-spline roller for installing it. Pliers may be necessary for repairing your double-hung window mechanisms.

TRIMWORK TOOLS

Used with a common backsaw, a miter box eases the task of cutting angles. A coping saw features a fine-toothed blade for making precise cuts by hand on trim. A nailset is used for recessing the heads of finishing nails slightly below the surface of trim. A sanding block and sandpaper prepare trim for paint. For more about painting trim, see page 71.

COPING SAW

NAILSETS

SANDING BLOCK
AND SANDPAPER

MITER BOX AND BACKSAW

framing a window

BEFORE YOU ADD OR REPLACE A WINDOW (OR A DOOR—A VERY SIMILAR PROCESS), you must prepare the proper rough-frame opening in the wall. To do this, you need to understand wall construction and the techniques involved in opening a wall, installing new framing, and then closing up the wall. You will find information on each of these topics—wall framing, drywall, and so forth—in their respective sections in this book. Here, we will look at rough-framing a window. For information on inserting a door, see page 236.

This diagram shows the anatomy of window framing. The blue arrows identify the finished opening; the green arrows define the rough opening. King studs are installed first, followed by trimmer studs and the header. The opening is completed by adding the cripple studs.

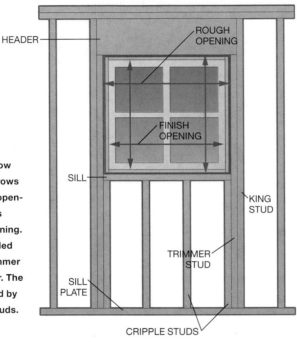

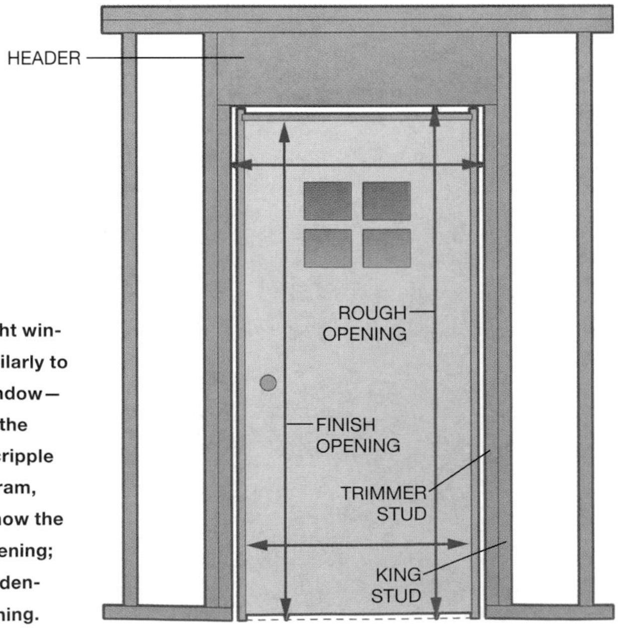

HEADER

ROUGH OPENING

FINISH OPENING

SILL

KING STUD

TRIMMER STUD

SILL PLATE

CRIPPLE STUDS

A door or full-height window is framed similarly to a conventional window— you just leave out the sill and the short cripple studs. In this diagram, the blue arrows show the door's finished opening; the green arrows identify the rough opening.

HEADER

ROUGH OPENING

FINISH OPENING

TRIMMER STUD

KING STUD

The frame you construct around a window opening supports the new window and may support loads from above, including a second-story floor, ceiling, and the roof. Do not compromise your home's structure. Find out whether the house is built with balloon framing or Western framing and whether the wall is nonbearing or bearing (see pages 100–101). If it is a nonbearing wall, you may be able to use lighter construction than that used in bearing walls and will not have to temporarily support the ceiling. If your house is balloon-framed, consult a professional for structural advice.

Bearing walls require structural headers to support the weight above them. These headers are short beams, made from lumber heavier than the studs—typically two 2 by 4s nailed together with a $\frac{1}{2}$-inch plywood spacer, or larger materials such as 4 by 6s, 4 by 8s, or even 4 by 12s. Headers transfer weight to the studs on each side of the window opening. Nonbearing walls do not require load-bearing headers; you can build them from a single piece of 2-by-4 lumber placed flat.

Before you open the wall, check for obstructions as discussed on page 237.

marking the location Mark the manufacturer's rough-opening specifications on the wall, using a framing square to ensure square corners. If possible, plan it so that at least one existing wall stud can serve as a king stud. (See pages 236–237 for information on locating wall studs and removing the wall covering.)

Using a combination square, mark the total height of the opening on the king stud or studs, marking each stud on the edge and one side. Then, from the marks you have just drawn, measure down to the height of the rough opening (equal to the height of the unit plus $3/8$ inch), then add $1\frac{1}{2}$ inches for the thickness of the rough sill. Mark the studs again.

framing the opening Nail trimmer studs to king studs with 16d ($3\frac{1}{2}$-inch) nails. To narrow the width of the opening, toenail a doubled trimmer on one side, allowing enough shimming space for the window. (If you use a 2-by-12 header, be sure to place it tight against the top plate; otherwise, toenail short cripple studs above the header.) Set the header on top of the trimmer studs and, using 8d ($2\frac{1}{2}$-inch) common nails, toenail the ends of the header to the king studs.

If you do not have a helper, you can prepare the header, cut trimmers to the required length, mount one trimmer and nail it to the king stud, load one end of the header onto it, and wedge the header into place with the second trimmer.

finishing up On a dry day, drill holes through the wall from inside at each corner of the rough opening, and stick nails through to the outside to mark the outside wall for the window's placement. Turn to pages 222–224 for installation information.

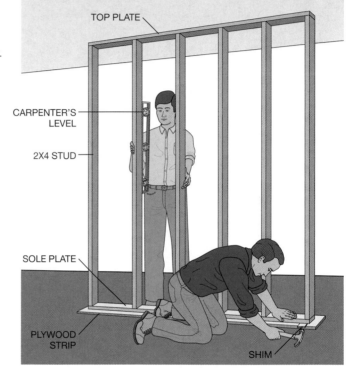

SUPPORTING A CEILING

If the wall is a bearing wall, before removing any studs, build a temporary wall perpendicular to ceiling joists. Build it slightly wider than the width of the opening and about 4 feet away from the existing wall. Protect flooring with $\frac{1}{2}$-inch plywood. While a helper holds the wall plumb, drive shims between the sole plate and plywood until the plate is tight against the ceiling.

TOP PLATE

CARPENTER'S LEVEL

2X4 STUD

SOLE PLATE

PLYWOOD STRIP

SHIM

CUTTING IN A WINDOW

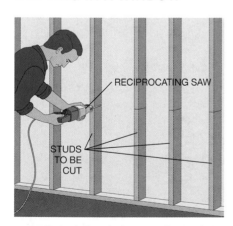

RECIPROCATING SAW

STUDS TO BE CUT

1 To install a window, cut the studs to be removed at the lines marking the bottom of the rough sill and the header's top edge.

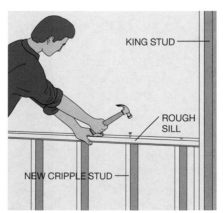

KING STUD

ROUGH SILL

NEW CRIPPLE STUD

2 Measure the distance from the sole plate to the line marking the sill on each king stud. Cut two cripple studs to this length. Install the cripple studs. Measure the distance between the king studs, cut the rough sill to this length, and nail it to each cripple stud.

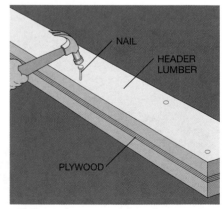

NAIL

HEADER LUMBER

PLYWOOD

3 Assemble a header. With a helper, if necessary, position the top of the header on top of the trimmers, and nail it in place as described above.

installing a window

ONCE YOU HAVE PREPARED A ROUGH OPENING, AS DISCUSSED ON PAGES 220–221, installing a pre-hung window is relatively easy. The exact methods depend on the type of window you are putting in and vary from one manufacturer to the next. The directions offered here are intended as helpful guidelines, but be sure to follow the specific instructions that come with your new window.

Pre-hung windows are blocked and braced to prevent damage during shipping; in most cases, you should not remove the bracing until the window is fastened in place. After you have installed the unit, be sure the sash operates freely (for an operable window) before you install the interior trim or caulk the exterior.

installing a pre-hung window

A pre-hung window comes complete with a sash, a frame, a sill, hardware, and most of the trim. When ordering a window, you will need to know the exact depth of the wall it will fit into so that the jambs will be the proper size to fit flush with the wall.

It is best to install the window from the outside, although you can maneuver an operable window through the opening from the inside, open it, and lean through to fasten it. If you want to install the window from the inside, make sure you are safely anchored so you don't fall out.

cutting the exterior opening
After laying out where you want to put the new window from inside the room, drill holes at the corners, and then drive nails through the holes so they are visible from the outside. With a carpenter's level, mark lines on the outside connecting the corners.

From the outside, using a circular saw, jigsaw, or reciprocating saw, cut through the siding and the sheathing along the lines; lay the cut material aside. For stucco, use a circular saw fitted with a masonry-cutting blade. Always wear eye protection. Inside, remove drywall as discussed on pages 108–109.

If necessary, assemble the mounting flanges and flashing of your window; make sure to follow the window manufacturer's instructions carefully.

After holding up the window and marking its placement on the siding, take the window down and widen the cuts through the siding, but not the sheathing, to allow for the brickmold or flange that runs around the outside perimeter of the frame.

mounting the window
Prepare the opening, as described in Step 2 on the facing page. Pre-set shims along the rough sill as shown in Step 3, making sure the pairs of shims are not so thick that they will prevent the window from fitting into the opening. Inside, trim the shims flush with the jambs. For nailing the flange or brickmold to the sheathing, use 4d (1½-inch) roofing nails (for a flange) or 8d (2½-inch) galvanized casing nails (for brickmold).

trimming a window

To complete your window project, you may need to install slivers of wallboard to fill the gap around the edges of the window (see pages 112–114); fit the new pieces as close as possible to the jambs on all sides.

You will also need to finish the inside edges of the window with moulding. On a single- or double-hung window, this involves fastening a stool to the windowsill, attaching an apron to the wall underneath the sill, and fastening casings to the sides and top to cover joints between the wall and window. Other types of windows—casement, awning, and hopper—are usually finished just with casings on all four sides.

LOWE'S **QUICK TIP**
Do not nail vinyl and aluminum windows through the jambs—just nail the window's flange to the sheathing (over building paper or house wrap) with 1-inch roofing nails. The finished siding will butt against the outside of the window, concealing the flange. Apply a bead of caulk around the window to weatherproof it.

1 On the wall outside the new window's location, mark the outline of the rough opening on the siding, using a carpenter's level. Here, nails have been driven through at the corners from inside; these are used to mark the placement. Using a saw equipped with the appropriate blade, cut through the siding and sheathing along the lines. Hold the window in place, mark its perimeter, and cut again—this time through the siding only.

2 Apply 8-inch-wide strips of moisture seal around the perimeter of the window opening, sliding it behind the siding. Make diagonal slits at the corners, using a utility knife; fold the moisture seal back over the rough framing and then staple it. The strips should stop just before the inside edge of the opening.

3 Place pairs of shims at the base of the rough opening, and adjust them until they are level. Drill pilot holes (to prevent the shims from splitting), nail them with two 6d (2-inch) nails per pair, and then cut them flush with the exterior wall.

4 Center the window in the opening. While holding the window in place, partially drive a nail through the flange or trim at one of the top corners. Check to make sure the window is level. If it isn't, adjust the shims. When it is level, nail through the flange or trim at the other corners and then around the perimeter.

PROJECT CONTINUES ➡

5 Nail on the outside trim, and thoroughly caulk the joints between the siding and window. Make sure to pay special attention to the manufacturer's instructions for flashing and/or caulking around the window trim.

6 From inside, shim the sides of the window so it fits snugly in the opening. Nail through the jamb and each set of shims into the trimmer studs with 8d (2½-inch) finishing nails; set the nail heads just below the surface with a nailset. Stuff the space between jambs and trimmer studs with insulation. Finally, cut off the shims flush with the wall, and install the trim around the window.

USING SASH REPLACEMENT KITS

If you have old, drafty, and inefficient single- or double-hung windows, you may be able to replace them without completely tearing out the frames and preparing a new rough opening. Instead, you may be able to install a sash replacement kit in the existing frame. These kits allow you to change an unsightly or poorly insulating sash window relatively easily. You can order a number of standard sizes and styles that fit most frames.

Sash replacement kits come with all necessary hardware and instructions. Basically, this is how they work:

1) You remove the old stops and the existing window from the frame and take up all the jamb hardware.
2) You fasten metal brackets, spacing them evenly along both sides of the window, and then install new jamb hardware for the replacement sash.
3) You install the new sash in the opening according to the kit directions.
4) Last, you tack the original stops back into place.

freeing a stuck sash

A SIMPLE SASH OR STOP REPAIR CAN OFTEN RESTORE A WINDOW TO GOOD WORKING order. If a sash is temporarily stuck because of high humidity, a change of weather may correct the problem. If a sash moves reluctantly, clean the sash channels. Windows that have been painted shut require a little more effort but can be opened, too.

If windows stick, chisel any dirt or large globs of paint from the channels, and then sand the channels smooth with sandpaper wrapped around a wood block. It also helps to coat the surfaces of the channels with wax so the sash will move easily. If the window binds against the channel, widen the channel by inserting a wood block inside the channel at the point that binds and tapping it with a hammer.

1 Score the painted edges of the sash with a utility knife. Work a wide putty knife between the sash and frame. Tap the knife with a mallet.

2 From outside, wedge a prybar between the sill and sash; work alternately at each corner so the sash moves up evenly. Protect the sill with a wood block.

LOWE'S QUICK TIP
A few hours after you have painted a window, score along the movable parts with a utility knife, and then operate it a couple times to keep it from becoming stuck.

3 Chisel any built-up paint off the edges of the sash, stops, and parting strip. Sand the edges smooth, and apply paraffin to them.

TIGHTENING A SASH

A sash that is too loose can be tightened. If the gap is not too wide and the stop is nailed rather than screwed, you can adjust the stop slightly without actually removing it. Score the paint between the stop and jamb, and place a cardboard shim between the stop and sash. Protect the stop by holding a block of wood against it, and hammer toward the sash along the length of the stop until the paint film breaks and the stop rests against the shim. Then secure the stop with finishing nails. For wide gaps, reposition the stops.

replacing a broken pane

REPLACING BROKEN GLASS IN A SINGLE-PANE WOODEN WINDOW, ESPECIALLY a small one, is not difficult. Wear heavy gloves and safety goggles. Before removing broken glass, tape newspaper to the inside of the sash to catch splinters. Then, pad glass shards with layers of newspaper to transport the debris to the garbage.

To bed the new glass, you can use conventional glazing compound, which is like a thick paste and is applied with a putty knife, or a newer caulk-like compound that is applied with a caulking gun (this can be a little trickier to apply).

Because panes of glass larger than 2 by 3 feet are awkward and dangerous to handle, replacing them is best left to a professional installer.

1 Tape the cracked pane with a cross-hatch of duct tape to prevent glass shards from falling out as you work. Be sure to wear safety glasses during this task. When you're finished, you can tape newspaper to the inside of the window to help catch broken glass.

2 Use a 5-in-1 tool to remove the old window putty. If necessary, warm the old putty with a heat gun, but be very careful not to scorch the frame (keep a fire extinguisher nearby). Wear heavy work gloves.

SEALS, GASKETS, OR MOULDINGS

To replace glass secured with rubber seals, unscrew the two sash halves and remove the inside one. Brush out glass fragments, set a new pane against one sash half, replace the other half of the sash, and secure the sash parts with screws.

If the glass sits on a continuous rubber gasket (or four separate ones), remove the screws from a vertical end of the sash, and pull the end away from the sash. Clean out the old glass, and then pull the gasket around the new pane; slide the pane into the sash, and secure the end.

To replace glass in a sash with snap-out mouldings, loosen one end of a piece of moulding by inserting the tip of a putty knife where two ends meet. Pry gently, using the frame for leverage. Pull out the loosened strip of moulding. When you have replaced the pane, push each moulding piece into place with your hands. Pieces damaged during removal should be replaced.

LOWE'S QUICK TIP
When buying a replacement pane of glass, have it cut to fit ahead of time. Size it 1/8 inch smaller in height and width than the opening.

3 Remove any broken glass, and then pry out metal glazier's points. Use a wire brush to scrub the rabbeted area of the window frame. Dust it off, and then apply linseed oil to the rabbet, using a small brush.

4 Soften the glazing compound by warming it. Then roll it into a thin rope with your hands, and use a 5-in-1 tool and your fingers to press this rope around the opening where the glass will go.

5 Press the new pane into place, and remove excess putty. Secure the pane by pressing glazier's points into place with a 5-in-1 tool (use two points on each side for small panes and one point every 4 to 6 inches for larger ones). Be careful not to push against the glass; this could crack it.

6 Roll more putty into a rope about ¼ inch thick; apply it around the outside edges. With a putty knife, smooth and bevel the putty at about a 30-degree angle, keeping the top edge even with the inside edge of the muntin. Once the putty is dry, paint it to match the wood.

window mechanism repairs

IF A DOUBLE-HUNG WINDOW SASH REFUSES TO REMAIN OPEN OR CLOSED, OR IF IT jams in one position, repairing or replacing the balance system is the only way to fix the problem. The type of repair depends on the type of system: pulley and weight, spiral-lift, tension-spring, or cord. Take off any interlocking weather stripping, and then remove the sash. If just the lower sash is affected, remove only that sash. If the repair involves the upper sash, remove both sashes.

pulley & cord systems Pulleys and weights operate most older double-hung windows. The weights are suspended on cords or chains located behind the side jambs. If you are replacing a broken cord, it is a good idea to replace all the cords in the window at the same time, preferably with long-lasting chains or nylon ropes.

To replace a defective chain, follow the instructions for cords below. Before trying to detach the old chain, be sure to immobilize the sash weights: Draw up the chains until the weights touch the pulleys. Then slide a nail through a link at each pulley to hold the weights in place. Last, detach the chains from the sash.

spiral-lift system In a spiral-lift balance system, a spring-loaded spiral rod encased in a tube rests in a channel in the side of the stile. The top of the tube is screwed to the side jamb; the rod is attached to a mounting bracket on the bottom of the window sash.

Adjusting the spring tension may be all that is needed to make the window operate properly. If the sash creeps up, loosen the spring by detaching the tube from the sash channel and letting the spring unwind a bit. If the sash keeps sliding down, tighten the spring by turning the rod clockwise a few times. If this does not help, replace the entire unit as shown opposite top.

REPLACING CORDS OR CHAINS

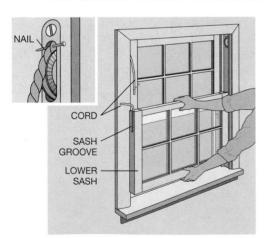

1 Remove the inside stops, and angle the lower sash out. Remove the broken cord from the grooves in each sash (a nail keeps the cord from slipping through the pulley).

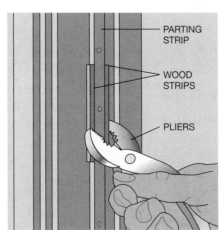

2 Pull out each parting strip with pliers (use wood strips to protect the parting strips). Angle the upper sash out of the frame; disconnect the cords.

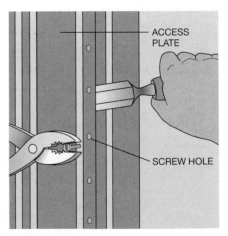

3 Remove the screws holding the plates, and remove the plates using a chisel. Tape the new sash cord or sash chain to the old, and then feed it through the pulley. Slip a nail through the chain's other end. Untie the weights, and pull the new cords out of the openings.

REPLACING A SPIRAL LIFT

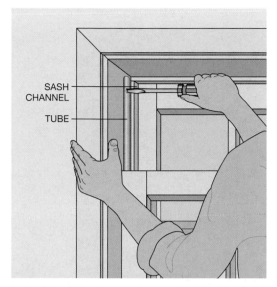

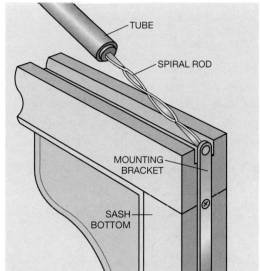

1 Pry off the stop, and unscrew the tube where it is fastened to the top of the side jamb. Let the spring unwind. Raise the sash 6 to 8 inches, and angle it out of the frame. If the rod is attached to the bottom of the sash with a detachable hook, unhook it. Support the sash in a raised position with a wood block, and then unscrew and remove the mounting bracket.

2 Position a new tube in the channel, and then screw it into the top of the side jamb. Pull the spiral rod down as far as it will go, and tighten it by turning it clockwise about four complete turns. Let the rod retract into the tube far enough so you can fasten the mounting bracket to the bottom of the sash. Replace the sash, adjust the tension, and reposition the stop.

tension-spring & cord systems In a tension-spring balance system, each window sash is operated by two balance units with spring-loaded drums inside; both of the units fit into the side jamb close to the top. A flexible metal tape hooks onto a bracket screwed into a groove routed in the sash.

A cord balance system has two spring-loaded reel units that fit into each corner of the top jamb. Nylon cords connect the units to each sash and plastic top, and side-jamb liners conceal the parts. If any component of a tension-spring or cord-balance system breaks, you must remove the unit and install a new one as shown right.

To access the spring-loaded drum, remove the screws from the drum plate, and pry the unit out of the jamb pocket. Insert the new balance into the pocket, and secure it with wood screws. Using long-nosed pliers, pull the tape down, and hook the end onto the bracket on the sash.

REPLACING A TENSION SPRING UNIT

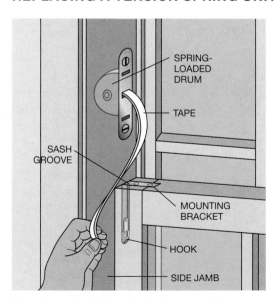

To replace a tension-spring unit, remove the stop and ease out the sash. Unhook the tape from the bracket, and let it wind back slowly on the drum.

repairing screens

WHEN WINDOW AND DOOR SCREENS ARE TORN, THEY ALLOW BUGS INTO YOUR
home. When they're sagging or rusty, they look terrible and darken rooms. Fortunately,
most screens are easy to remove and replace. The frames will be either wood or metal,
and the screens will be either metal (typically aluminum) or fiberglass. Chances are the
frames themselves will not need attention nearly as often as the screens.

1 Use a screwdriver to pry up the spline that
runs around the perimeter of the frame. Pull
out the spline, and remove the old or damaged
screen fabric.

2 Lay the new screen fabric over the frame,
and, using sharp utility scissors, trim it so
that it is just slightly larger than the frame. Then
snip off the corners as shown.

3 Using the convex wheel of a screen-spline
roller, force the screen into the spline channel. Then push the spline back in, and, using the
roller's concave wheel, force the spline into place,
stretching the screen fabric taut. Cut off the excess screen fabric with a utility knife.

LOWE'S QUICK TIP
If your screen frames
are bent or damaged,
consider replacing
(rather than trying
to repair) them.

weather stripping

HEATING AND COOLING SYSTEMS DON'T DO MUCH GOOD IF THE AIR LEAKS RIGHT out of your home. Weather stripping and caulking are simple, cost-effective ways to keep heated or cooled air where it belongs: in the house. Weather stripping is used to seal gaps around moving parts such as doors and windows; caulking seals gaps around stationary objects such as siding and window frames.

weather-stripping options

There are numerous types of weather stripping for windows and doors. These products can be classified in two groups: self-stick tapes and nail-on strips. Self-stick tapes are rubber, foam, or vinyl and come with an adhesive covered with a peel-off backing. These are good choices for metal or vinyl windows where nailing isn't an option, especially for where the parts of doors or windows press together rather than slide against one another. Self-stick tapes can easily be cut with scissors and take only minutes to apply.

The highest-quality and longest-lasting type of self-stick tape is EPDM (ethylene-propylene-diene-monomer) rubber. EPDM retains its elasticity and insulating qualities even after years of exposure to sub-zero temperatures. Another good choice is high-density foam, which is also durable and long-lasting. Closed-cell foam is waterproof, weather-resistant, and inexpensive, but it does break down, so will need to be replaced regularly. Open-cell foam can be compressed the most to seal even the narrowest of gaps, but it is only for indoor use, as it quickly degrades when exposed to the elements. Vinyl V-strips are extremely easy to install but also wear out quickly.

Nail-on strips are the best choice for wood windows because they do not rely on adhesive and thus tend to stay in place over time. The type of nail-on strip you choose will depend on the gaps you need to seal. Gaps that are less than ¼ inch wide and relatively consistent in width can be best sealed with spring bronze—a metal flange that is nailed in place and then "sprung" open to close the gap. This material is well suited for filling the gaps between a window sash and its jambs because it is out of view when the window is closed.

A vinyl tubular gasket works well where the gaps are large or inconsistent in width. This product is made up of rubber tubing with a flange for nailing. The flange is often reinforced with metal to prevent the soft vinyl from tearing.

Felt weather stripping is also available, but it is only suitable for indoor use because it rots quickly when it gets wet.

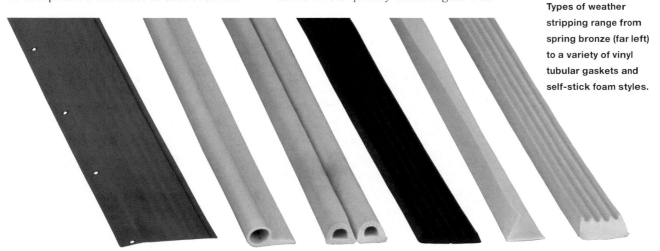

Types of weather stripping range from spring bronze (far left) to a variety of vinyl tubular gaskets and self-stick foam styles.

seals for a double-hung window

The double-hung window is one of the most common in home construction. But, with its two sliding sashes, it is also the most difficult to seal. While newer windows have built-in weather stripping that creates an excellent seal, older windows often need some attention.

Installing spring bronze nail-on strips is the best way to weather-strip wood windows. To seal the window completely, insert metal strips between the sashes and jambs, and attach the strips to the top edge and bottom face of the upper sash, and to the lower sash's bottom edge.

other weather-stripping options

There are some instances in which you can't or won't want to use spring bronze to seal a double-hung window. If the window is made of metal or vinyl, nailing isn't an option and you'll need to use self-stick products. When gaps at the top or bottom of the window are large or uneven, use self-stick foam, which will seal better than spring bronze. Finally, on windows where the gap between the sash and the jamb is too tight for spring bronze, tubular vinyl is an adequate substitute. In all cases, make sure the surfaces are clean and dry to ensure proper adhesion.

WEATHER STRIPPING FOR DOUBLE-HUNG WINDOWS

1 Before applying weather stripping, scrape away loose paint or old weather stripping. With double-hung windows, also check the sash lock, making sure it is pulling the upper and lower sashes together to form a tight seal. You can correct a loose seal by repositioning one or both halves of the sash lock.

2 Measure the side channels for both sashes, and then cut spring bronze strips to length with tin snips. Slide the pieces up between the sash and jamb so the nailing flange butts up against the sash stop. Push the strip up until it hits the top of the window or the pulley. If your window has pulleys, cut the strip into two pieces so the bottom strip is flush with the bottom of the pulley, then cut a shorter piece to fit above the pulley. Attach the strips to the jambs with brads. You can increase the tension on the strip by slipping a putty knife under the open end and prying gently upward a little at a time.

3 Measure for the horizontal strips (three in all), and cut them to length so they extend the full width of the window. Attach one piece to the bottom of the lower sash so that the nailing flange is flush with the inside edge of the window. Hammer gently so that you avoid cracking the window. Attach the second piece to the top of the upper sash. Attach the third piece to the bottom face of the upper sash to create a seal between the sashes when the window is closed. Adjust the tension on these strips as you did for the vertical pieces.

Self-stick foam is easy to apply. The only requirement for a good bond is a smooth, clean surface. Remove any loose paint, clean the surfaces with a mild detergent, and allow them to dry. Measure strips, and cut them to length with scissors. Peel off the backing, and press the foam in place.

Tubular gaskets are applied outside of the window and are thus somewhat more obvious. Measure the strips, and cut them to length with scissors (or tin snips if they're reinforced with metal). Butt the tube section snug up against the part to be sealed, keeping tension on the strip as you drive in the brads.

When installing plastic self-adhesive V-strips, take particular care to clean the surfaces so the adhesive will stick well. Measure the pieces, and cut them to length with scissors. Peel off the backing, and press them in place.

weather-stripping doors

Because doors have fewer moving parts than windows, they're generally easier to seal, presuming they are in something close to their proper alignment. To add weather stripping so it doesn't cause binding, it's best to even out the gaps around the door before starting work by resetting and shimming hinges as needed to create uniform spaces (see pages 248–249).

A gap of ¼ inch along the bottom of a 36-inch-wide door is the equivalent of having a 3-inch-square hole in the door. Fortunately, there are straightforward solutions to sealing such gaps.

The weather stripping used to seal door-jambs is the same as that employed for a window. Spring bronze or plastic V-strips do a good job for the top and sides. However, the door bottom presents a different challenge, especially where foot traffic is heavy. Standard weather stripping, even metal strips, would wear out quickly under heavy use. Special seals designed for door bottoms include door sweeps, door shoes, and metal thresholds.

A door sweep attaches to the bottom face of the door; its rubber blade presses along the threshold to create a seal. A door shoe fits on the door's bottom edge with a flexible gasket pressing tightly against the floor or threshold. A metal threshold with a rubber gasket, on the other hand, presses against the bottom of the door so as to stop drafts. These various components can be used independently or in combination when necessary. For example, when the gap below a door is too large to be spanned by a single gasket, a door shoe and a threshold can be combined to create a seal.

Garage doors have their own special seals, typically rubber gaskets that attach to the bottom of the door and to the side and top jambs.

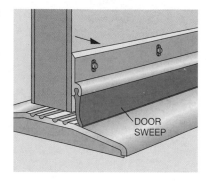

A door sweep, which is screwed to the bottom of the door, has a rubber blade that seals against the threshold.

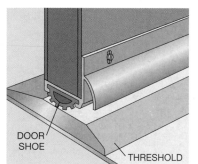

A door shoe's flexible gasket seals against the threshold.

DOOR SHOE

THRESHOLD

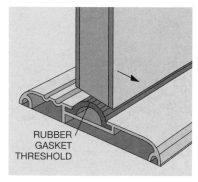

A metal threshold may have a rubber gasket that presses against the door's bottom end.

RUBBER GASKET THRESHOLD

APPLYING WEATHER STRIPPING

To weather-strip a door, begin by cutting a short strip of spring bronze for the latch area. This piece fits behind the strike plate up against the door stop. In most cases, you will need to bend or trim this piece to keep it from interfering with the strike plate or latch mechanism. Attach the strip with brass brads. Measure and cut strips for the rest of the latch side and then for the top and the opposite side. If you are working with vinyl V-strip, you can often apply the latch strip to the stop because these strips are narrower than spring bronze.

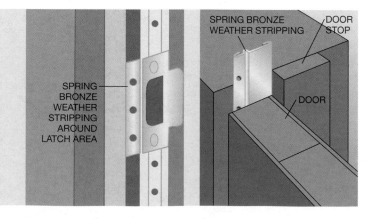

SPRING BRONZE WEATHER STRIPPING AROUND LATCH AREA

SPRING BRONZE WEATHER STRIPPING

DOOR STOP

DOOR

installing a door sweep

A door sweep is the simplest seal to apply to the bottom of a door because you can leave the door on its hinges.

Just measure the width of the door, and cut the sweep to match. Then screw it to the base of the door, positioning it so it contacts the threshold while still allowing the door to swing freely.

installing a door shoe

Door shoes require a little more work than door sweeps but create a better seal against a threshold. You will likely need to trim the door to allow for the shoe's thickness.

To determine how much you will need to trim, open the door and slip the shoe into place. Then measure from the bottom of the shoe to the bottom of the door. Remove the shoe, close the door, and transfer this measurement to the bottom corners of the door, measuring from the top of the threshold. Take the door off its hinges, lay it across sawhorses, and draw a line to connect the marks. Clamp a straightedge to the door to guide a circular saw in cutting along the line. Remove splinters with sandpaper. Cut the shoe to length, slip it on, and

A door sweep is simply screwed to the bottom of the door.

Screw a door shoe along the bottom edge after removing and trimming the door.

attach it with screws. Hang the door, and check to make sure it seals without binding.

installing a threshold

To replace an old wooden threshold with a metal-and-rubber one designed to seal the door's bottom edge, start by cutting the old in two, taking care to protect the adjacent flooring. Pry up the pieces, and save them to serve as templates for marking the length on the new threshold. Place the pieces on the new metal threshold's frame. Allowing for the thickness of the blade you used to cut them, mark the new threshold and cut it to length with a hacksaw. Test the fit. When the threshold is snug, remove it and apply two beads of silicone to the flooring. Reposition the threshold, and attach it with the screws provided. Finally, trim the threshold's rubber gasket to length if needed, and fit it into the threshold.

cutting in a doorway

OPENING UP A WALL WITH A NEW DOORWAY CAN PUT A WHOLE NEW SPIN ON THE way traffic moves through your home, sometimes making rooms immeasurably more accessible and usable. But before you cut a hole in a wall to add a doorway, be clear about what you might encounter.

Walls conceal a host of surprises, including wiring, pipes, and ducts that almost inevitably turn out to be just where you want to place the door. Investigate to discover where these or similar obstructions are located before determining where your new opening will go (see "Locating Wires, Pipes, and Obstructions" on the facing page). If you find pipes, ducts, or extensive wiring in the way, the easiest and least expensive option may be to modify your plan for the door's location. Rerouting utilities can be quite involved and is generally a job for a contractor, unless you are comfortable with a variety of do-it-yourself tasks. This type of construction usually requires a permit and is regulated by local building codes.

It is relatively easy to replace a window with a door. For instance, if your breakfast room has a 6-foot-wide sliding window that overlooks the backyard, you could replace it with a 6-foot sliding door. The framing, hidden behind the drywall, is already nearly complete. To prepare the area, you would just remove the window, the wall's surface material, and the studs below the window.

It is also fairly simple to install an interior door if the wall is not a bearing wall (see pages 100–101). Most interior walls, called partition walls, do not carry the weight of the roof framing, though a major central wall, such as that along a hallway, is likely to be bearing. The project on these pages shows the installation of a door in a non-load-bearing partition wall.

Doors are sold individually or as prehung systems, which come already hinged in a jamb and frame. The latter one is the

1 After covering the floor with a drop cloth, use a sharp utility knife to score deeply into the drywall along your vertical layout lines. Make several passes if necessary to cut all the way through the material. Remove the drywall.

2 Use a reciprocating saw to cut off the studs that are located within the new opening. (Note: If the wall is a bearing wall, the ceiling must be supported first. For more information about removing a bearing wall, see page 221.) Twist the stud pieces, and pry them away from the plates.

3 Mark the placement of new studs on the plates, using a pencil and a square. Where the doorway will go, cut away the plate, using a reciprocating saw. Be sure the remaining parts of the plate are fastened firmly to the floor.

easiest type to install. When you buy a pre-hung door, the manufacturer can provide you with the rough opening dimensions necessary for the structural framing. Normally, you will need to remove the wall covering for at least the rough opening plus 3 inches on each side and across the top for framing. If the door is going into a bearing wall, the rough opening may need to be even taller to allow for a header.

Often it is best to remove the wall covering from floor to ceiling between two bordering studs that will remain in place. Add 6 inches to the rough opening width, center this dimension on the wall where you want the door, and mark both sides. From those marks, tap a nail through the wall covering, working away from the center, to find the nearest studs (the new king studs). Lay out vertical cuts centered on these studs.

To remove drywall, just cut along your outline with a utility knife and pry the cut panels off the studs. To remove plaster and lath, cut through the lath with a saber saw or reciprocating saw equipped with a blade made for the job; be sure to wear safety glasses, a dust mask, and gloves. (Check first to see that there are no pipes or wires inside the wall where you will be cutting.)

To prevent unnecessary vibration, hold the saw's foot plate firmly against the plaster. Then you can use a prybar to pull down chunks of the plaster; remove the lath from the studs.

Finally, be aware that when you remove a section of wall to install a new doorway, the floor must be finished where the wall once stood (see "Floors & Stairs," beginning on page 140).

LOCATING WIRES, PIPES, AND OBSTRUCTIONS

On plan-view and elevation-view sketches of the wall, show the position of the nearest intersecting wall, and note clues to what lies behind the wall.

From outside the house, look for pipes coming through the roof directly above the proposed door opening. Pipes projecting above the roof indicate drainpipes in the wall directly below; you may find water pipes nearby, as well.

Check the rooms above and below the proposed opening, too. Is there a radiator against the wall? If so, there may be a hot-water or steam pipe below. A hot-air register in the wall under the proposed opening may mean there is a heating duct in the wall. Removing the register's grille and reaching into the duct can help you determine where it goes.

On your sketches, mark the locations of receptacles, switches, and wall lights, and then figure out the likely route for wires running between them. If you have an attic, go into it with a light, and locate the top plate of the wall you propose to open. Measuring from the nearest side wall, mark on your sketches the locations of any wires, pipes, or ducts coming through the top plate. If your house has a basement or crawl space, repeat the process.

4 Toenail the new king studs to the plate (cut them for a tight fit). It's easiest to pin the stud in place with 8d nails at the front and back edges before toenailing each side with two 10d nails. Make sure the studs are plumb before nailing them at the top.

5 Nail the trimmer studs to the king studs, and then nail a flat 2-by-4 header across the top, driving two 16d nails down through each end and into the tops of the trimmers.

6 Measure for short cripple studs between the header and the top plate. They should be positioned to maintain the typical stud spacing of 16 inches from center to center.

installing a door

WITH A FACTORY-MANUFACTURED PRE-HUNG DOOR, HINGES ATTACH THE DOOR to the preassembled jambs, and the sill and jambs are braced to keep the whole assembly square until you install it. For more about the types of doors available, see pages 208–213.

Pre-hung interior doors normally have a piece of scrap trim stapled to the bottom of the door and jambs. After carrying the door to where you intend to install it, remove this temporary brace. (You must be able to open and close the door as you place shims between the studs and jambs, drive in nails to hold the jambs, and check the alignment of jambs.)

When you are ordering a pre-hung door, make sure you specify the wall's overall thickness. The jambs ordered for plaster-covered walls are different than those for walls finished with drywall. When you fit the jamb into the rough opening, you will see that the jamb is wider than the rough framing and that it sticks out on either side. Be sure the distances are proper to allow for drywall, plaster, or—in the case of an exterior door—sheathing and siding.

For information on how to prepare the rough opening, see pages 220–221.

position the door properly
Place the door in the rough opening, centering it in the frame and fastening it as discussed in the steps on the facing page. Using a piece of drywall (or other finish material) as a spacer against the trimmer studs, slightly adjust the unit until it is flush with the spacer. (If the finish floor has not yet been installed, raise the side jambs to the correct level with blocks; you want to avoid cutting off the bottom of a new door if possible.)

Before nailing the jambs, it's very important to make sure the door fits squarely in the opening and that the jambs are plumb, both from side to side and from front to back. Drive pairs of tapered wooden shims between the jambs and the trimmer studs (if the casing is attached to the jambs, insert shims from the open side) to adjust the unit and hold it in place until you nail it.

secure the door hinge-side first
Start by shimming the lower hinge side of the door. Nail through the jamb and shims partway (1 inch) into the stud with a 10d finishing nail; position the nail where the stop moulding will cover it. Insert shims next to the upper hinge location, check the jamb for plumb, and nail partway. Again, shim, plumb, and nail halfway between the top and middle hinge positions. Repeat this process between the middle and bottom hinges. Check to make sure the jamb above the doorway is level. Now shim the opposite jamb at similar locations, but do not nail where you will need to cut for the latch.

complete the installation
Remove any bracing or blocking tacked to the unit. Close the door, and check that there is the same amount of space ($1/16$ to $1/8$ inch) between the edges of the door and the jambs. If the door sticks or is out of alignment, pull out nails in the area that seems to be the problem, using a block to protect the jambs from your hammer. Adjust the shims and re-nail. Install the lock set as discussed on pages 242–243. Drive the nails almost flush, and then set the heads with a nailset. Using a handsaw, cut off the shims flush with the jambs (you can just break off short, thin pieces). Finish with door casing or other trim.

For exterior doors, nail the threshold between the jambs, shimming below if the threshold does not rest securely on the subfloor. Finally, install the stop moulding with 4d finishing nails.

LOWE'S QUICK TIP
Be sure the door jambs are perfectly plumb; otherwise, the door may hang partially open.

1 If you're replacing an existing door, pry off the old trim, and pry out the side and head jambs. If you're installing a door in a newly framed opening (see page 236), be sure the framing is sized properly.

2 Set the pre-hung door into place with the hinges positioned on the proper side, and tilt it up into the opening. It's a good idea to have a helper on the other side of the door to receive it and help shift it so that the jambs are flush with the walls.

3 Push wooden shims between the jambs and trimmer studs on both sides while checking the jambs for plumb with a level. Tap the shims with a hammer until they're snug.

4 Nail through the jambs and sets of shims with 10d finishing nails. To avoid denting the jambs with the hammer head, stop nailing before the heads reach the surface and finish with a nailset.

5 Install new trim around the door, using 6d (2-inch) finishing nails. For more about working with trim, see pages 120–123.

installing a storm door

STORM DOORS BLOCK DRAFTS IN THE WINTER, HELPING TO MINIMIZE ENERGY LOSS. Many have clip-in tempered glass panels you can remove and replace with insect screen panels for summer. In addition, storm doors protect the main door from rough weather, and newer models are so attractive they can add to your home's curb appeal.

choices Sturdy storm doors that don't rattle, twist, or dent are made of a solid particleboard core that has an outer aluminum skin with a baked-on finish. They are sold as pre-framed units that are easily screwed into existing doorjambs. Both storm and screen doors come in standard door widths of 30, 32, 34, and 36 inches and may be hinged on either side. (When buying one, be sure you get the right size; measure the door's opening between the doorjambs, not the size of the door.) Some are made so that the unused glass or screening panel stores inside the door. Those designed for security often have a heavy-duty aluminum or steel frame with a foam or solid wood core and a tamper-proof deadbolt and hinges.

If you want to display your front door or maximize light and views, choose a storm door with a full-height glass panel. The mid-view type has a solid panel in the bottom third of the door. A high-view door has a glazed section that is about half the door's height.

If you know the brand of door in your home, check to see if the manufacturer also provides a door kit for storms and screens. This is an especially good idea if you have a sliding or French door. The kit will match the design of the door and will fit properly over the threshold.

about installation Storm doors come with full instructions and a template for mounting the hardware. Major manufacturers offer assistance by phone as well as instructions or troubleshooting information online. There are two mistakes you can make that will be difficult to fix. The first can occur when you are cutting vertical mounting frames. These must fit your openings; do not cut them too short. Also, when you are drilling holes to fit hardware on a wood-core storm door, be precise. Most manufacturers supply a template to make this job easier. Take your time, and follow the instructions.

door closers To automatically close the storm or screen door smoothly and to prevent it from being opened too wide or with too much force, install a simple door closer, as shown at left. Before you begin, check that the door operation is smooth and that the door hardware is in good working order. For a pneumatic closer, install the door mounting bracket on the top rail of the door, mount the closer in the bracket, and fasten the jamb mounting bracket to the hinge jamb. Then adjust the tension.

To ensure an exterior door closes automatically, you can install a hydraulic closer. Some types fit only a right-hand or left-hand door. Others can be adjusted for either type by inserting a screwdriver in the adjustment screw, pushing in, and turning the screw 180 degrees. A slight adjustment to the screw changes the door's closing speed.

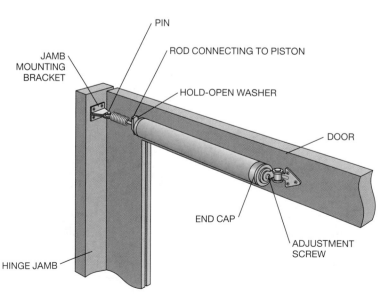

PIN

ROD CONNECTING TO PISTON

JAMB MOUNTING BRACKET

HOLD-OPEN WASHER

DOOR

END CAP

ADJUSTMENT SCREW

HINGE JAMB

1 Place the door interior side up, and position the vertical hinge mounting frame on the hinge side so that the top of the track extends beyond the door by 3/32 inch. Then drive one mounting screw through the hinge into the predrilled hole in the door. Line up the hinge holes along the edge of the door. Next, center-punch and drill a pilot hole for each remaining screw, and drive in the screws.

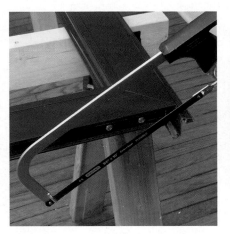

2 Measure the height of the opening where the door will hang, both at the face of the jamb and at the stop. Turn over the door, and transfer these dimensions onto the hinge mounting frame. Using a hacksaw, cut the bottom of the hinge mounting frame at the angle that will fit your door's sill. If the bottom of your door includes a sweep, temporarily install it on the door. (Adjust and screw it tight after the door is hung.)

3 With a helper, stand the door in the opening, position it, and screw it in place. With the door open, place the top mounting frame on the hinge mounting frame. Then close the door, adjust the top mounting frame's position, and screw it in place. Then mount the latch-side frame using the same methods.

4 Close the door, adjust the sweep so that it presses lightly against the sill, and screw it in place. Install the handle hardware according to the directions provided by the manufacturer.

5 Screw the door closer's bracket to the top of the jamb. The type shown is spaced 1 inch down from the top of the jamb and 1/4 inch back from the hinge side. Assemble the closer, attach it to the jamb bracket, and close the door. Holding the closer level, place the bracket on the door and mark for screws. Predrill screw holes, and attach the closer. If the door has a closer at the bottom, attach it the same way.

6 Close and latch the door, and then install the screen or glass panels. The system shown utilizes retainer strips. Hold the glass or screen in place, and then install the top retainer, horizontal retainers, and vertical strips.

installing a lock set

WHEN DOORKNOBS OR LATCHES CEASE TO WORK PROPERLY, REPLACEMENT IS OFTEN the easiest and fastest answer to the problem. In addition, replacing hardware can be an effective way of dressing up a door, giving it just the type of visual detail that adds character and style to a home.

Many exterior doors have a standard cylindrical lock set of the type shown on this page. This variety has a round body that fits into a hole drilled into the door. Some exterior doors, especially front doors, have a mortise lock set, with a squared body that slides into a deep notch into the door's edge. The latter type may have a combined latch and deadbolt mechanism. In addition to the lock set, exterior doors may have a deadbolt lock or a surface-mounted rim lock (see pages 244–245). Interior doors have either a cylindrical lock set operated

with a push button or a tubular lock set, which is similar to the cylindrical type but is simpler and less rugged.

Here we look at how to replace a lock set and how to prepare a new door to receive a lock set. If you need to drill holes in the door to install a new lock set, be sure that you have the right size hole saw and spade bit on hand (usually a $2\frac{1}{8}$-inch for the lock hole and a 1-inch for the latch hole). In addition, you will achieve the best results if you use a hole saw with an integral guide bit.

REPLACING A LOCK SET

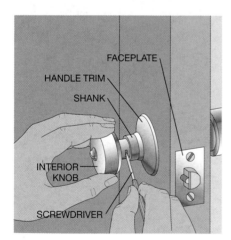

FACEPLATE
HANDLE TRIM
SHANK
INTERIOR KNOB
SCREWDRIVER

1 To remove the interior knob, take out screws from the inside face. If there are none, look for a small slot in the shank. Push the tip of a small screwdriver or nail into the slot, and then remove the interior knob and trim.

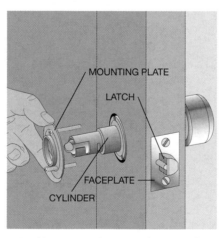

MOUNTING PLATE
LATCH
FACEPLATE
CYLINDER

2 Unscrew and remove the mounting plate; slip out the cylinder. Unscrew and take out the faceplate and latch assembly, and then remove the strike plate from the doorjamb.

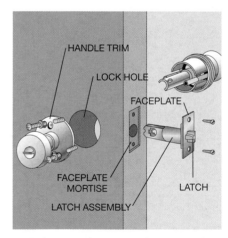

HANDLE TRIM
LOCK HOLE
FACEPLATE
FACEPLATE MORTISE
LATCH ASSEMBLY
LATCH

3 Insert and screw on the new latch assembly and faceplate. Holding the exterior knob and cylinder, slide the cylinder in, and engage it with the latch assembly. Attach the mounting plate, handle trim, and knob. Then screw on the new strike plate to the side jamb, making sure the latch engages in it. (See page 246 if it does not.)

DRILLING A DOOR FOR A LOCK SET

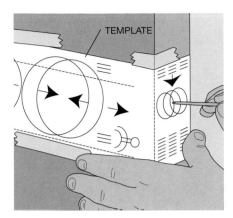

1 A template and instructions should be included with your new lock set. Plan to place the knob 36 to 37 inches above the floor. Tape the template to the door, and then use a nail or awl to mark the centers of the lock and latch holes.

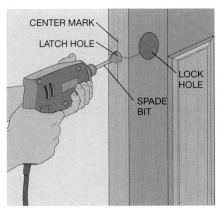

2 Using a hole saw, bore the lock hole. As soon as the guide bit exits the opposite side of the door, stop and continue from the other side. This will help prevent tear-out when the hole saw exits. Use a spade bit to bore the latch hole, as shown. Take care to drill straight, level holes.

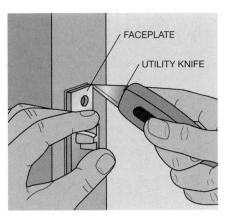

3 Insert the latch assembly. Holding it square, trace the outline of the faceplate with a sharp pencil. Then use a utility knife or awl to score the outline. Alternatively, trace around the faceplate with a utility knife, as shown.

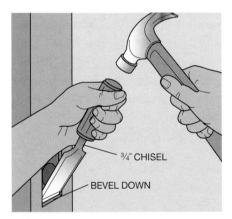

4 With a ¾-inch chisel and hammer, score the two long sides; hold the chisel at a 45-degree angle, with the beveled edge toward the wood. Working from the center of the mortise, tap the chisel to the bottom and then to the top. The finished mortise should be about ³⁄₁₆ inch deep. Insert the latch. If necessary, shave off a bit more wood.

5 With the lock set installed and screws tightened, close the door until the latch just hits the jamb. With a pencil, mark the spot where the center of the latch contacts the jamb.

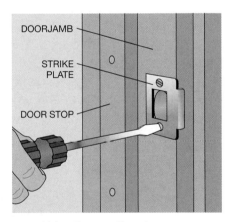

6 Using the pencil mark as your guide, hold the strike plate against the jamb, and trace its outline with a pencil. Score the outline, and then chisel the mortise as described in Step 4. Note that you may have to cut the mortise all the way to the edge of the jamb. After checking the alignment, attach the strike plate to the jamb with screws.

CUSTOM-DRILLING DOORS

Lock manufacturers provide all the hardware for lock sets. If you are ordering a pre-hung door and know the measurements of the lock you will be installing, give the template and specifications to the door manufacturer. The company will bore the necessary holes for the door and jamb, which will make installing your lock much easier. In other cases, you will have to drill the holes yourself.

installing a deadbolt

DEADBOLT LOCK SETS PROVIDE AN ADDITIONAL MEASURE OF SECURITY ON EXTE-rior doors. As a general rule, a deadbolt is stronger and more difficult to tamper with than a conventional lock, and the bolt's "throw" (the distance it extends) is generally longer. Replacing a deadbolt lock set is easy if you buy one similar to your original model.

single-cylinder deadbolts Opened from the exterior with a key and from inside the house by hand with a thumb turn, single-cylinder deadbolts are often keyed differently from the knob and latch set on the door.

double-cylinder deadbolts These locks are opened by a key on both sides. While these are the most secure on doors with windows, local building and fire codes may prohibit them because they can make it difficult to exit the building in an emergency. Check your area's regulations before installing one.

surface-mounted locks Surface-mounted locks (also known as rim locks or vertical deadbolts) can be used as the only lock set on an exterior door or in conjunction with other locks for added security. They are easier to install than deadbolt locks, but they are also less visually appealing from the interior. The lock has a bolt that fits through the strike plate, which is screwed to the doorjamb; it is controlled by a key on the outside and a thumb turn or key on the inside. This type can improve security on secondary entry doors such as those to basements and back porches.

If you are replacing a surface-mounted lock, buy a new one of the same type and size. For a new installation, tape the template to the door according to manufacturer instructions. Mark guide holes with a nail or awl, and then drill the holes.

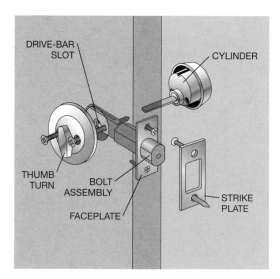

A single-cylinder deadbolt lock set has a thumb turn on the inside and a keyed cylinder on the outside. On a double-cylinder deadbolt, a second keyed cylinder replaces the thumb turn.

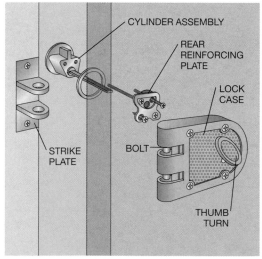

A surface-mounted lock set adds security, if not beauty, to a door. Use the lock set's template and follow package instructions to install the lock.

INSTALLING A DEADBOLT

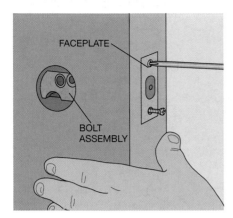

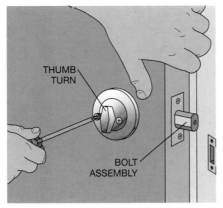

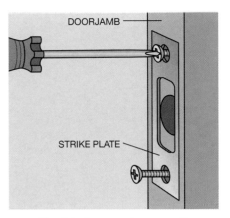

1 Using the manufacturer's template as a guide, drill holes in the door (unless you are replacing an old deadbolt). Insert the bolt assembly, and screw the faceplate to the edge of the door.

2 Mount the cylinder assembly by carefully and precisely inserting the drive bar into its slot. Attach the cylinder to the thumb turn with two mounting screws. Test the bolt to ensure that it moves in and out.

3 Use 3-inch screws to secure the strike plate to the doorjamb. If this is a new installation, first cut a mortise for the strike plate according to the instructions in Step 4 on page 243. Then drill a recess hole for the bolt.

INSTALLING A SURFACE-MOUNTED LOCK

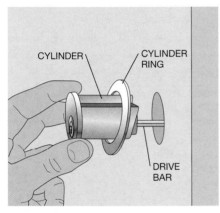

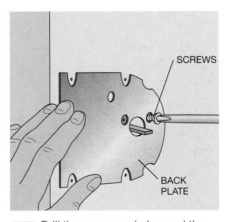

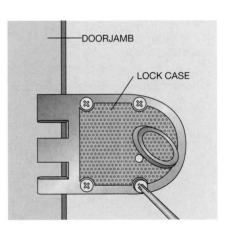

1 Slide the ring over the cylinder. From the outside of the door, insert the cylinder and drive bar into the hole so that the keyhole is on the outside and the bar is in the horizontal position.

2 Drill the necessary holes, and then place the back plate ⅛ inch from the door edge on the inside. Drive screws through the plate and into the screw holes in the cylinder.

3 Place the bolt in the unlocked position. Fit the drive bar into the slot on the rear side of the lock case, and attach it to the inside of the door using the screws provided.

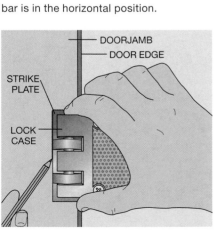

4 Hold the strike plate in position, and measure and mark it when the bolt is in the locked position. Cut a mortise, if necessary, and screw the strike plate in place on the jamb.

LOWE'S QUICK TIP
When buying a deadbolt or surface-mounted lock, choose one with a finish that will match the existing lock set.

fixing lock sets & knobs

MANY LOCK-SET PROBLEMS CAN BE CORRECTED BEFORE THEY BECOME SO SERIOUS that the lock set will not work. Often, a malfunctioning latch assembly or lock mechanism causes the problem. An improperly functioning latch may be the result of a poorly fitting door. The lock mechanism may not work simply because the lock is dirty or dry and needs to be lubricated with graphite (do not use any type of oil).

For serious lock problems, it is usually best to call a locksmith or to replace the lock entirely. If your problems require professional help, keep in mind that removing the lock and taking it to a locksmith is far less expensive than having the locksmith come to you. For information on how to replace a lock set, see pages 242–243.

If a door latch does not operate smoothly, the latch bolt on the door may not be lined up properly with the strike plate on the doorjamb. Repairs range from making minor latch adjustments to repositioning the door.

If the latch does not catch, close the door slowly to watch how the latch bolt meets the strike plate. The bolt may be positioned above, below, or to one side of the strike plate. (Scars on the strike plate show where it is misaligned.) It is also possible the door has shrunk and the latch no longer reaches the strike plate. Once you have figured out the problem, try one of the methods shown on this page.

For less than a ⅛-inch misalignment of the latch bolt and strike plate, file the inside edges of the plate to enlarge the opening.

If the latch does not reach the strike plate, shim out the plate, or add another strike plate. If the latch still will not reach, shim out the door's hinges (see page 248). Replace the door with a wider one only as a last resort.

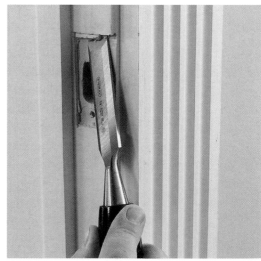

ABOVE: **For more than a ⅛-inch misalignment, remove the strike plate, and extend the mortise higher or lower as necessary. Replace the plate, fill the gap at the top or bottom with wood putty, and refinish.**

On mortise lock sets (the type that fit into a large slot in the edge of the door), doorknobs may become loose over time. To tighten them, loosen the setscrew on the knob's shank. Hold the knob on the other side of the door, and turn the loose knob clockwise until it fits snugly. Then tighten the screw until you feel it resting against the flat side of the spindle. The knob should turn freely. If this does not help, remove the knob and check the spindle; if the spindle is worn, it must be replaced. If the whole lock set is worn, it is best to replace it entirely.

A setscrew on a doorknob locks the knob to the spindle. To loosen the setscrew, turn it counterclockwise with a screwdriver; to tighten the setscrew, turn it clockwise.

TROUBLESHOOTING A PROBLEM LOCK SET

PROBLEM	POSSIBLE CAUSE	REMEDIES
Latch sticks or responds slowly	Gummed-up or dirty lock mechanism	Blow a pinch of powdered graphite or pencil lead into the lock mechanism or keyway.
Key does not insert smoothly	Dirty keyway and tumbler area Foreign object in keyway	Blow a pinch of graphite or pencil lead, or put silicone spray into the keyway (don't use oil). Attempt to dislodge the object with a thin, stiff wire.
Key doesn't insert at all	Ice in the keyway	Chip the ice from the opening, carefully heat the key with a match, and then insert the key in the lock and work it gently until the ice melts.
Key is broken in lock	Improperly inserted key, ill-fitting replacement key, or wrong key forced into lock	Remove the broken key with a thin, stiff, hooked wire or with a coping saw blade; if this doesn't work, remove the lock cylinder, and push the key fragment out from the other side with a thin, stiff wire.
Key won't turn in lock	Cylinder is turned in faceplate Poorly duplicated key Damaged tumblers	Move the cylinder to its proper position. Check the key against the original; replace it if necessary. Replace the cylinder or the entire lockset.
Key turns but does not operate locking mechanism	Broken lock mechanism	Repair or replace the lock set.

fixing loose or binding doors

AGE AND CONTINUAL USE CAN CAUSE EVEN A WELL-FITTED DOOR TO LOOSEN, bind, or warp. Binding or loose doors are relatively easy to fix. On the other hand, a door that is badly warped will have to be replaced.

You do not necessarily have to remove a door to fix it. If you are working on just one hinge at a time or on the top of a door, you only need to open the door partially and drive a wedge underneath the latch side to hold the door steady. But for other repairs, including sanding or planing the side or bottom of a door, you will need to remove it from its hinges to do the repairs.

tightening a loose door If a door is too small for its frame, an easy though somewhat obtrusive solution is to install weather stripping on the latch side of the jamb. A more attractive fix is to shim out one or more of the door's hinges. To do

this, you'll need to remove the hinge pins and remove the door. Unscrew the hinge leaf from the jamb. Cut a piece of thin sheet brass or dense, hard-surface cardboard to fit beneath it. Double up shims if you need more thickness. Then screw the leaf back in place.

Often, simply tightening loose hinges gets a sagging door back in alignment. You can try tightening loose hinge screws or replacing them with longer ones. If the holes are so badly stripped that the screws won't hold, repair the screw holes as shown below.

If a loose door isn't latching properly, see page 246 for how to align the latch.

STRENGTHENING A LOOSE HINGE

1 If hinge screw holes are stripped, remove the screws and hinge leaf from the jamb. Coat small wood dowels or wooden matchsticks with glue, and pack them in the holes. Wipe off the excess glue, and trim the resulting plug flush.

2 After allowing the glue to dry, hold the hinge leaf in position, and drill new pilot holes for screws. Then drive in the screws. For extra strength, you can substitute longer screws for the original ones.

PLANING A DOOR THAT BINDS

1 Using a pencil, mark the area to be planed on both faces of the door. Typically, you should be able to slide a dime between the door and the jamb along both sides and the top.

2 Set the door on edge, and, using a plane with a sharp blade set to make a very shallow cut, shave off small portions. Work in line with the grain, holding the plane at a slight angle and flat against the surface. At the door's top and bottom, plane from the corner toward the middle to avoid splitting the ends of the stiles.

adjusting a warped door To fix a slightly warped door, try adjusting the stop, partially shimming the hinges, or adding another hinge. Where there is a slight bow on the hinge side, centering a third hinge between the top and bottom ones often pulls the door back into alignment. If the bow is near the lock side and the door latches only when it is slammed, first try adjusting the latch (see page 246). Then try repositioning the stop, as you would for a window (see page 225). If necessary, adjust the strike plate as shown on page 246. If the top or bottom of the door does not meet the stop on the lock side, try repositioning the stop and the strike plate.

You may also have to shim the hinges to change the angle of the door's swing. You can move a door closer to the lock side of the jamb by inserting shims under the hinge leaves. Depending on the direction of the warp, place a half shim under each hinge leaf either on the side of the leaf that is closest to the pin or on the opposite side. Usually, the other hinge is shimmed in the opposite way.

binding doors If a door binds or rubs against the jamb, identify the spots where it binds by sliding a thin strip of cardboard or wood between the door and the jambs. Look for a buildup of paint, which usually is the culprit. Hold a sharp wood chisel flat against the surface, and slice off the excess. Then smooth the surface with fine-grit sandpaper. Coat the door edges and the jambs with paraffin.

If you must remove excess wood from the door edges, before planing first try sanding the areas with coarse, followed by finer, sandpaper. When sanding or planing the stiles, concentrate on the hinge side; not only is the lock side usually beveled to allow for a tight fit, but planing it can also intrude on the way the lock set fits.

repairing sliding doors

THOUGH HARDWARE VARIATIONS ARE ALMOST UNLIMITED, ALL SLIDING, BYPASS, and pocket doors operate in basically the same way. Some lightweight sliding doors, including bypass closet doors and pocket doors (which slide into walls), are hung from the top rail. Moderately heavy doors such as patio doors rest on the bottom rail. Plastic guides at the top or bottom keep the doors vertical and aligned with their tracks.

Removing a sliding door for repair or maintenance is simple, but you should keep in mind that the door can be very heavy, especially if it is one with double- or triple-pane glass. If you're just cleaning out dirty tracks, use a vacuum cleaner with a wand attachment rather than taking out the door.

All tracks, especially the one that supports the rollers, must be kept free of dirt, debris, and foreign objects. Occasionally applying a little graphite or paraffin to the track and a drop of oil to each roller bearing will help keep the door moving smoothly and quietly.

Sliding doors glide on rollers that need periodic adjustment. Tighten any loosened

Lift a bottom-supported door straight up to clear the track. To remove it, sharply angle the lower part of the door outward. You may need a helper to hold the door if it is extremely heavy.

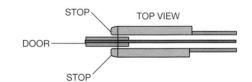

Lift a top-hung door straight up, and angle it to lift the rollers out of the track. (Some doors have notches on the track that you must align with the rollers before you lift out the door.)

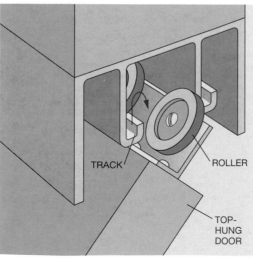

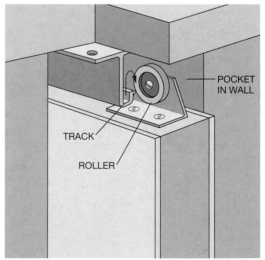

ABOVE: **On a pocket door, remove both stops from the head jamb. Take off one side-jamb stop to allow the door to swing out. To remove the door, angle the bottom out and then carefully lift it up.**

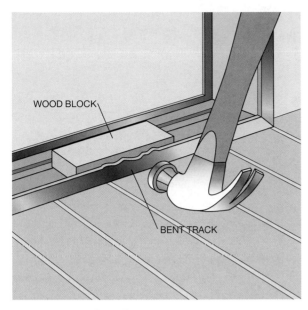

WOOD BLOCK

BENT TRACK

Use a hammer and wood block to straighten a bent metal track. Replace a track that is badly bent or broken.

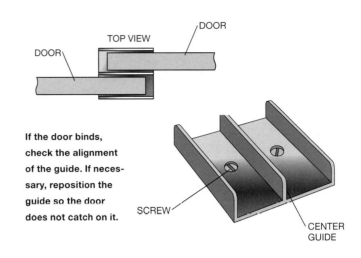

TOP VIEW

DOOR

DOOR

If the door binds, check the alignment of the guide. If necessary, reposition the guide so the door does not catch on it.

SCREW

CENTER GUIDE

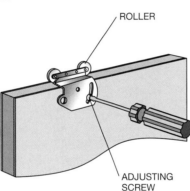

ROLLER

ADJUSTING SCREW

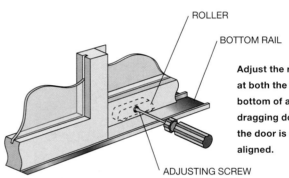

ROLLER

BOTTOM RAIL

ADJUSTING SCREW

Adjust the roller height at both the top and the bottom of a tilting or dragging door until the door is correctly aligned.

screws in the frame or track and replace any part that is worn, broken, or missing. If a door jumps off its track, check for a dirty track, a section that is worn or bent, or a guide that is out of alignment. A door tilted in its frame usually needs a roller adjustment. (There should be a ³⁄₈-inch clearance between the bottom of the door and the floor or rug.)

Pocket doors and bypass closet doors may warp, which can cause them to jam. You can compensate for a minor warp by adjusting the rollers to make the door higher or lower. You may also need to change the alignment of the door guide. If a door is badly warped, you must replace it. Make sure the new door is sealed with paint or varnish on all sides and edges to prevent the problem from recurring.

New high-quality sliding doors are virtually maintenance-free. This door has a multi-point locking system, and aluminum-clad exterior surface, and a trouble-free track design.

installing door trim

FEW DECORATING PROJECTS ARE AS EFFECTIVE AT TRANSFORMING THE LOOK OF your home's doorways as replacing the door trim, also known as door casing. If the trim framing your doors is banged up or simply visually uninteresting, you can easily remove it and install new trim that suits your decorating scheme.

Lowe's stocks various types and styles of door trim, from simple to ornate. It is a good idea to choose a style and size that complement the adjoining baseboards. The trim featured here, for example, comes with plinth blocks for the bottom of the doorway and rosettes for the top that match the trim. These accents have a traditional Victorian look, and the rosettes eliminate the need to make tricky miter cuts at the top corners: Lengths of trim that butt against the rosettes can simply be cut at 90-degree angles.

The trickiest part of this installation is keeping the trim level and plumb in relation to the door frame. Marking a "reveal" line around the frame (see Step 2 below) will give you the same professional advantage that finish carpenters enjoy.

If you are installing hardwood door casing, it is best to predrill pilot holes before driving in the nails to avoid splitting the wooden stock.

If you plan to paint the trim, apply a coat of primer to the pieces before installation to make the job easier.

LOWE'S QUICK TIP

To break any paint bond between the old trim and the wall, cut along the seam with a utility knife, opening a gap large enough for the putty knife.

1 Wearing goggles, pry up a length of side casing with a putty knife, and slip in a wood shim. Remove the knife, and slip in a small prybar, using the shim to protect the wall. Pry away the trim, gradually moving along its length. Pry off the other length of side casing and the head casing in the same way. Remove the nails from the door casing and wall.

2 A reveal line serves as a guideline for fastening door casing just inside the door frame, revealing a narrow portion of the frame (typically ¼ inch). Adjust the end of the ruler on a combination square ¼ inch from the handle. Then, holding the handle flush against one side doorjamb and a pencil against the end of the ruler, slide the handle and pencil along the edge of the jamb, marking the reveal line. Mark the head jamb and the other side jamb in the same way.

3 Place one of the plinth blocks on the floor, lining up its inside edge with the edge of one side jamb. Drive a 6d finishing nail through the block, about 1 inch above the floor, into the jamb. Fasten the three other corners of the block in the same way. To avoid marking the block, leave about ⅛ inch of the nails protruding. Then, with a nailset, sink the nail heads just below the surface. Install the other plinth block on the opposite side of the doorway.

4 Align one of the rosettes with a top corner of the frame. Drive a 6d finishing nail through the bottom corner of the rosette into the jamb. (The three remaining corners will be fastened to the wall in Step 5.) Attach the other rosette on the opposite side of the door in the same way. Measure the distance between the rosettes. Transfer the measurement to the casing, and then cut the trim in a miter box.

5 Aligning the bottom edge of the head casing with the reveal line along the head jamb, fasten the casing's midpoint to the jamb with a 6d finishing nail at the bottom edge. Drive two more nails into the trim and jamb, each about 1½ inches in from the end of the casing and along the bottom edge. Then drive three more nails along the casing's top edge, opposite those along the bottom. Holding the rosettes flush against the head casing, fasten each one's three remaining corners. Sink all the nail heads with a nailset.

6 Measure and cut lengths of side casing to fit between the rosettes and the plinth blocks. Affix the casings one at a time, aligning their inside edges with the reveal line. Nail the side casing to the jambs and wall as you did with the head casing. Fill the nail holes with spackling compound, let it dry, and lightly sand the areas. Wipe the trim with a clean, dry rag, and then apply a finish to the wood.

creating window stools & aprons

A TRIM PROJECT MAY INVOLVE INSTALLING A NEW WINDOW STOOL (THE HORIZONTAL "table" that sits on the sill and extends into the room) and a new apron (the moulding that supports the stool from beneath and is attached to the wall). If you are replacing trim, you may be able to leave the stool in place, changing only the apron and casing.

The stool is a single piece cut to fit within the window opening, with "horns" that extend in front of and beneath the window casing and beyond it at a distance equal to the casing's thickness. You can make the stool out of molded $1\frac{1}{16}$-inch stool stock or use clear, straight-grained lumber, routing or chamfering the edges. The stool is installed before the casings.

Before beginning installation, precut the stool. To mark its width, hold a piece of casing against the reveal line along one side of the window and mark the casing's outer edge on the wall; repeat for the other side (for more about establishing a reveal line, refer to Step 2 on page 252) . Then measure the thickness of the casing stock, and

mark that amount outside the casing lines. Measure between these outer marks, and cut the stool to this measurement. For the best appearance, cut the ends of the stool at 45 degrees (see Step 2). Next, measure from the sash to the edge of the sill. To this measurement add twice the thickness of the casing, and then subtract $\frac{1}{16}$ inch (this is the stool's depth measurement). Rip the stool to this size, and cut the notches that create the horns of the stool. After assembly (as shown below), countersink all nails. If you are painting, fill the nail holes with wall patching compound. If you are using a clear finish or stain, apply the complete finish first, and then use a matching putty stick to fill the nail holes.

1 Center the stool within the window opening, and mark the points where the side jambs intersect it. With a square, extend these marks across the stool, and, from there, figure the length of the stool. Then cut out the notches with a jigsaw or coping saw. Glue and tack the stool to the sill with 4d finishing nails placed every 10 inches, predrilling for the nails.

2 To finish the stool, cut and fit a return piece at each end. Fasten the return pieces with glue. Alternatively, you can shape the ends of the stool to match its front profile, although this will leave end grain exposed.

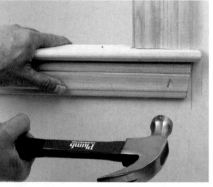

3 Cut and attach the casings (see pages 252–253). Cut and attach the apron, aligning its edges with those of the casing. Miter or cope the edges (see pages 122–123) to match the apron's face profile. Glue and nail the apron to the stool and wall with 6d finishing nails. When the glue is dry, predrill and then drive 4d finishing nails through the stool into the apron every 10 inches.

security for windows & doors

KEEPING WOULD-BE INTRUDERS OUTSIDE IS AN IMPORTANT CONCERN FOR MOST homeowners. Though hinged doors are relatively easy to protect with proper latches and deadbolts (see pages 242–245), windows and sliding glass doors are not as simple to secure. Windows and doors that slide can be forced open or lifted off their tracks, and glazing can be broken.

In addition to installing locking devices, you can enhance security by replacing all ordinary glass with tempered, laminated, or wire-reinforced glass or with plastic, as well as by installing perimeter alarm systems.

Several ready-made devices are available at Lowe's to make prying open a window and/or removing a sliding glass door from its track more difficult. The right locking device to choose will depend on whether you need to secure a sliding window or door, or a double-hung window.

To keep a panel from sliding, use track grips, tightened by a thumbscrew or key, or metal stops that straddle the lower track and are secured with a lever or thumbscrew that clamps them in place. Or use a spring bolt, which is screwed to the base track or sill and has a pin that snaps through a hole drilled into the edge of the lower track and bottom of the sash. Even more secure is a bar that screws to the doorjamb and swings up into a saddle on the edge of the door to lock it in place; an advantage of this type of bar is that it can be adjusted to allow the door to be partially open. The easiest way to keep an inside panel from sliding is to drop a dowel or a piece of tubing into the empty portion of the lower track. Cut it ¼ inch shorter than the distance between the panel and the jamb.

Double-hung windows can be locked with wedge locks, key-operated latches, or locking pins that go through one sash and into the next.

ABOVE LEFT: **A spring bolt, screwed to the sill, will secure almost any sliding window or door.**

ABOVE: **A locking pin is designed for a double-hung window. The pin hangs from a short chain when not in use.**

FAR LEFT: **This keyed device is designed for securely locking a double-hung window sash.**

LEFT: **This quick-release track grip can be positioned anywhere along a sliding door's track.**

cabinets & storage

FRESH PAINT AND FINE DECORATING MAY GIVE YOUR HOUSE ITS POLISH, BUT the backbone of any comfortable, organized home is its cabinetry and storage. If you are like most homeowners, your most common complaint is that there is never enough storage space to stash all your belongings in a manner that makes them easy to access. Well-planned, ample storage can be a great tonic to constant clutter, improving a family's quality of life in a very real sense. Well-built cabinetry does not come cheap, but if you are remodeling or building from scratch, you should purchase the best quality that your family's budget will allow. Not only will it be more satisfactory, but it will also add value to the house.

Cabinets have become more and more specialized to handle the increased complexity of today's storage needs. Beyond cabinets, however, it pays to think creatively. As needs have grown, so have the number of products specifically designed to tackle such difficult-to-control areas as the garage, laundry, and bedroom closet. A stroll through your nearby Lowe's will reveal a great variety of clever, efficient, and easy-to-install systems that allow you to add new capacity as well as to upgrade or modernize existing storage.

In this chapter, we tackle choosing cabinetry and countertops, installing and repairing cabinets, installing a kitchen island, tiling a countertop, installing laminate countertops on new cabinetry, adding a built-in closet and assembling a closet system, and hanging a simple shelf.

buyer's guide to cabinets

BECAUSE CABINETS CAN DOMINATE A ROOM'S DESIGN AND USUALLY ACCOUNT FOR a significant portion of remodeling costs, it pays to do your homework before making a purchase. Whether you're hunting for cabinets for your kitchen, bathroom, home office, or another room, you'll find a staggering array of types, styles, and prices. Streamline the process by determining the look you like and the price point that is comfortable for you.

Regarding price, you can choose relatively affordable mass-produced stock cabinets, pricey made-to-order custom ones, mid-range "semi-custom" hybrids—or perhaps a mix of these. Lowe's design specialists can help you stretch your dollars to achieve what you want.

Be sure to order cabinets early; many types will take weeks or months to receive. In a kitchen, appliances and countertops cannot be installed before the cabinetry.

cabinet construction

There are two basic types of cabinet construction: "faceframe," in which the front edge of the cabinet box is concealed by a 1-by-2-inch hardwood frame, and "frameless," also known as "European style."

About 80 percent of the cabinets made by American manufacturers are of the faceframe variety. Because the structural frame makes it possible to use lower-quality wood for the cabinet sides, faceframe cabinets

ABOVE: These handsome multi-depth bath cabinets add dimension, style, and plenty of storage to this bathroom. RIGHT: Glass doors, plate racks, full-usage corner cabinets—these are the types of options that can enhance the function of a kitchen cabinet system.

can be less costly than comparable frameless ones. But the frame also narrows the openings of drawers and doors, which means you will have slightly restricted access to storage space. Faceframe cabinets are a good option if your room's walls are not quite straight because the frame can be shaved to fit an irregular space. Faceframe cabinets have an integral toe kick at the bottom. Shelving is not movable.

European-style cabinets are constructed of panels that are finished on both sides, so they can be freestanding or have one side exposed. A separate toe-space pedestal (plinth) allows you to vary counter heights or stack base cabinets to make tall cabinets. Most frameless cabinets use the "32-mm system," which means that holes are drilled at intervals of 32 millimeters along each side panel so that hardware such as door hinges and shelf pins can be plugged in anywhere you like.

stock cabinets

If your budget or schedule is tight, stock cabinets offer many advantages. Because they are mass-produced, stock cabinets cost at least one-third less than those that are custom-made or configured to order, and they are usually delivered in less than three weeks.

But stock cabinets do have limitations. Because they are manufactured in standard sizes, they may not be the ideal choice for an unusual space. Your selection of styles and finishes is relatively restricted, and in the case of kitchen cabinets, special accessories such as breadboards, wine racks, and roll-out shelves might not be readily available, or available at all.

That said, stock cabinets can be used in just about any situation. There are so many standard sizes that it is usually possible to accommodate even an unusual installation. Widths vary by 3-inch increments, from 9 to 48 inches; upper cabinets are available in heights of 12, 18, 24, 36, and 42 inches for use over sinks, stoves, and countertops. Manufacturers also offer a wide variety of designs, features, and finishes. For an extra

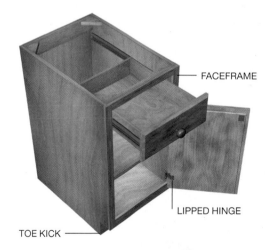

FACEFRAME

LIPPED HINGE

TOE KICK

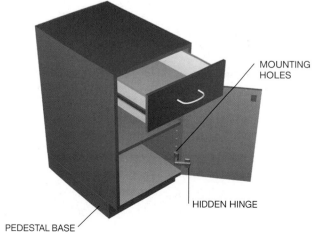

MOUNTING HOLES

HIDDEN HINGE

PEDESTAL BASE

ABOVE: **These dramatic face-frame cabinets reach far beyond the utilitarian to become the focal point of the bathroom's style. The hickory raised-panel doors feature glass inserts with Prairie-style motifs. LEFT: Faceframe cabinet construction allows for greater variation in wood quality and pricing. BELOW: Frameless cabinets have more spacious interiors.**

RIGHT: Adjustable, low-profile hinges give a clean, uncluttered appearance to cabinetry.
FAR RIGHT: Solid ½-inch wood drawers feature dovetail joinery, a sign of fine construction.

cost, some will even make certain modifications to their cabinets, allowing you (within a particular range) to increase or decrease cabinet depths, alter toe kicks, and upgrade interiors or doors.

A trip to your local Lowe's will give you an idea of the many choices available in stock cabinetry. You will find dozens of styles, from country cottage to contemporary, plus hundreds of decorative touches

and hardware options such as door pulls for personalizing your cabinet installation.

custom cabinets

Custom cabinets are designed and built from scratch to fit a particular situation. Consequently, they cost a great deal more—five to 15 times more, depending on the materials and the sizes—than stock cabinets. You may also spend six weeks to three

CABINET WOODS & MATERIALS

Maple
- A hard, close-grained wood
- Fine and evenly textured
- Predominantly off-white in color with yellow-brown hues
- Can feature "bird's-eye" dots; grain is mostly straight but may be wavy

Cherry
- A warm, close-grained hardwood that mellows in hue as it ages
- Uniform texture
- Color can vary from pale yellow to deep reddish brown within one panel
- Natural or light stains accent color variations; streaks and small knots are common

Oak
- A tightly grained, extremely hard wood
- Grain patterns run from straight to widely arched
- Color ranges from white to brown; variation can be strong within a panel
- May have color accents of cream or black; knots may be present

Hickory
- A strong, open-grained wood
- Dramatic, flowing grain patterns
- Wide variation in color, from blond to deep brown
- Distinctive burls, streaks, knots, and wormholes

Laminate
- A very smooth surface made of high-impact plastic
- Uniform color and texture
- White or shades of cream; color may change over time
- Durable finish and easy to maintain

LEFT: This generous wrap-around kitchen is designed from a variety of semi-custom cabinet components. Raised-panel doors completely overlay the faceframes.
BELOW: These hickory cabinets combine bead-board doors and detailed mouldings to create a custom look.

months waiting for them to arrive. It is worth the wait and the money, however, if your goal is to transform a room into a showpiece. Skilled cabinetmakers can create heirloom-quality woodwork that cannot be made by machine.

semi-custom cabinets

If you want special sizes, configurations, or finishes, semi-custom cabinets may serve your needs without breaking the bank. Semi-custom cabinets are manufactured, but you have as many as 2,000 standard options from which to choose. If you still cannot find what you want, you can ask for just about any modification imaginable, including oddball sizes, specialty accessories, and custom colors or finishes.

You will pay more for semi-custom cabinets than you would for stock cabinets, of course, but you will also get higher-quality workmanship and materials. For example, the semi-custom cabinets designed for Lowe's customers feature solid wood dovetail construction, super-tough finishes, and

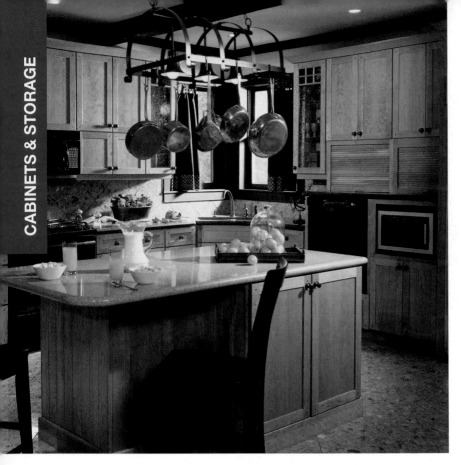

Square veneer recessed panel doors, walnut peg detailing, and a touch of glass lend character and visual interest to these faceframe cabinets.

extra-thick shelves that exceed cabinet industry standards.

Delivery of semi-custom cabinets can take a couple of months, so place your order well in advance.

ready-to-assemble cabinets

A less-costly cousin of stock cabinets, ready-to-assemble (RTA) cabinets are sold knocked-down in flat boxes for assembly by the customer. Despite their rock-bottom prices, RTAs can be quite stylish and versatile. Most are frameless European-style cabinets that are relatively easy to put together and modify. You will only need basic tools and respectable do-it-yourself skills to tackle the job.

cabinet hardware

Although hardware is often an afterthought, it can make a big difference in the way your cabinetry looks and functions. Make sure your hardware selection has a durable finish that will not wear off with repeated use, and remember that pulls will look especially prominent because they occupy more cabinet surface than knobs. If you are simply replacing your hardware, look for knobs or pulls that fit the existing holes in your cabinet doors. If your new hardware does not match your old, fill the holes with wood putty.

hinges
The hinges inside your cabinets ensure that the doors remain stable and easy to operate. Before you go shopping for hinges, make sure you know whether you have faceframe-type cabinets or European-style frameless ones (see page 259). You will also need to determine what type of cabinet doors you have. Some hinges are made to fit only one type of cabinet and one style of door; others are more versatile.

A partial wraparound hinge can be used on all faceframe cabinets and also has a

BASE CABINETRY FEATURES

Base cabinets offer such specialty options as sliding trays (shown), storage compartments for dry staples, or a built-in lazy Susan. Look for interiors with easy-to-clean laminate surfaces. Adjustable board shelves also come in handy. Standard base cabinets range in width from 9 to 48 inches and are 24 inches deep and 34½ inches high. The box construction on the base cabinet shown here features ⅜-inch-thick plywood, which wraps around the entire case. The plywood shelves are ¾ inch thick. The veneered surface of the cabinet is durable and non-peeling. Solid wood doors and drawer fronts are available in maple, cherry, and other hardwoods.

CREATING A CUSTOM LOOK

With a little creativity, you can achieve a made-to-order look using affordable stock cabinets. Here are a few tips for creating a custom-made appearance without spending a fortune:

- Add options, such as glass doors, display shelves, or plate racks.
- Order specialty accessories through an independent cabinetmaker.
- Ask the manufacturer to sell you some pre-finished plywood and hardwood pieces that match your cabinets. It is also possible to have pieces fabricated to create special cabinet parts such as fillers, soffits, and angled connections.
- In a kitchen, outfit your refrigerator and dishwasher with decorative panels that match the cabinets.
- Vary cabinet heights.
- Replace stock door and drawer pulls with more interesting varieties.

ABOVE: Exclusive to Lowe's, these oak cabinets feature raised-panel doors, glass inserts with frosted edges, and crown moulding across the top.

RIGHT: A combination of a colorful semi-transparent stain and whimsical door and drawer pulls gives these kitchen cabinets a bright, spirited look.

ABOVE: Dark-stained wood, leaded glass, and detailed mouldings imbue these traditional wall cabinets with a time-less quality.

large surface area that improves door stability. Self-closing European hinges can be used on both faceframe and frameless cabinets and can be adjusted to align and level cabinet doors. Ease of installation and the ability to handle heavy doors make European hinges the most popular.

Hinges come in different sizes to support different door weights. In addition to choosing the proper hinges, be sure you install enough to stabilize each door, based on its height.

Unless you have chosen self-closing hinges, you will need to outfit your cabinet doors with catches. Catches use either magnets or tension to hold doors closed. Magnetic catches work well on irregular or warped doors. Spring-roller and friction catches close quietly and keep doors securely shut.

drawers

For drawers that function smoothly, choose hardware that is sturdy enough to support the drawer and its contents. Drawer slides have load ratings of light, medium, and heavy, so make a note about each drawer's likely contents before you shop. Also measure the length of each drawer to determine how long your slides should be. Drawer slides come in side-mounted or center-mounted styles; while

center slides are more affordable, side styles are considerably more durable. If you choose side-mounted slides, you can add options such as drawer stops, ball-bearing or nylon rollers, self-closing designs, and slide extensions that allow access to the entire drawer.

FAR RIGHT: A tall, slim pull-out turns a space that would otherwise be too narrow to be useful into convenient storage.

RIGHT: Storage space that is oftentimes lost in the corners of an L-shape or U-shape kitchen can be reclaimed with corner drawers like these. FAR RIGHT: Hinges come in a wide range of styles and finishes. Clockwise from top left are a concealed hinge for frameless cabinets; an offset hinge and surface hinge for faceframe cabinets; and an invisible hinge for frameless cabinets.

CABINET REFACING

The fastest, thriftiest way to update your cabinets is to reface them rather than replace them. With refacing, the cabinet boxes stay in place and are simply repainted. Then new doors and drawers are added. The process is economical not only because you do not incur the expense of new cabinets but also because countertops, wall coverings, plumbing, and wiring are left untouched. Refacing is relatively simple for experienced do-it-yourselfers; if you do not have the talent or time, you can arrange for Lowe's to do the work. Consider refacing only if your cabinet boxes are in good shape and you are satisfied with the room's layout. There is a wide selection of materials available for stylish resurfacing jobs. Lowe's specialists will carefully craft hardwood or laminate cabinet doors and drawer fronts to custom-fit the precise measurements of the old cabinetry.

BEFORE

AFTER

buyer's guide to countertops

AS THE FINISHING TOUCH TO CABINET STORAGE UNITS, COUNTERTOPS PROVIDE a functional work surface while helping to establish a room's decorative style. Today, an eye-popping array of countertop materials in just about every imaginable color and style awaits you. Once wood and ceramic tile were the only choices, but now plastic laminate, solid surface, stone, stainless steel, glass, and even cast concrete have joined the selection. Some of the priciest countertops, such as stone and solid surface, are most effectively used in areas that take full advantage of their ruggedness and stain- and heat-resistant

A COMPARISON OF COUNTERTOPS

MATERIAL	ADVANTAGES
Ceramic tile	A kitchen and bath classic, ceramic tile comes in a multitude of colors, sizes, textures, and patterns—and a range of prices. Tile is made either by hand or by machine, with the former popular for rustic-style design. Installed correctly, it is heat-proof and scratch- and water-resistant. Grout is also available today in a number of colors to blend in or add contrast. Because some tile is meant for floors, be sure to buy a tile rated for countertop use.
Solid surface	Durable, nonporous, heat- and stain-resistant, and a breeze to clean, this marble-like material is made of cast acrylic or polyester plastic with mineral fillers. It can be shaped and joined seamlessly. A sink and countertop can be fashioned from one continuous piece for a sleek look. Any blemishes and scratches can be sanded out easily.
Plastic laminate	Laminate, composed of layers of paper soaked and stacked in plastic, comes in a wide range of colors, textures, and patterns. It is durable, easy to clean, water-resistant, and relatively inexpensive. Ready-made molded versions are called postformed, while custom countertops are built from scratch atop particleboard or plywood substrates. With the proper tools, laminate is the easiest material to install.
Stone	Few materials beat the elegance and outright beauty of natural stone countertops, particularly multihued granites and marble. Stone is heat-proof, water-resistant, easy to clean, and hard as a rock—because it is rock. The countertop's cool surface is perfect for working with dough or making candy. Granite is almost impervious to stains. Stone can be purchased as cut tiles in a variety of sizes or as solid slabs. The variety of colors and internal patterning makes for intriguing looks.
Synthetic marble	These manufactured products, collectively known as cast polymers, include cultured marble, cultured onyx, and cultured granite. Primarily sold for bathroom use. Easy to clean.
Wood	A wood countertop adds warmth to any kitchen. Wood is handsome and comes in shades ranging from dark to light. It is easily installed and is gentle on glassware and china. Maple butcher block, the most popular and functional choice for kitchens, is sold in 24-, 30-, and 36-inch widths. Installation costs are comparable to ceramic or top-of-the-line laminate.
Stainless steel	Stainless steel is ultra-hygienic, easy to clean, waterproof, heat-resistant, and very durable. Stylistically, it is perfect for a modern look.

qualities. Some of the best designs, however, employ a mix of countertop materials—for example, solid surface for the work areas, ceramic tile backsplash and wall murals for flair, and a baker's insert of cool marble or granite for dough preparation.

Not surprisingly, with the vast array of countertop surfaces, materials vary greatly in properties and price. Each has its advantages and disadvantages.

Plastic laminate, which offers perhaps the greatest range of styles and colors, is relatively inexpensive and can be purchased in prefabricated lengths ready for installation. The downside of plastic laminate is that it shows wear and tear faster than most other materials. Ceramic tile is a perennial favorite and, depending on the tile chosen, can be a bargain. Grout lines can stain and collect dirt, however, and need upkeep and repair. Solid surface is one of the most expensive materials on the market and requires a professional installer, but those who own it sing its praises for durability, ease of cleaning, and resistance to stains and heat.

DISADVANTAGES

Some tile glazes can react adversely to cleaning chemicals, so be sure to ask the dealer about care. Handmade tiles, especially Mexican tiles formed from soft clay, are prone to chipping. Light-colored grout lines stain and can be tough to keep clean, particularly as they wear down. Handmade tiles usually take thicker grout lines, which can exacerbate the problem. Using stain-resistant epoxy grout and machine tiles that take thin grout lines can mitigate grout trouble.

Solid surface is one of the most expensive countertop materials available today. Fabrication and installation are best left to—and sometimes require—a professional. The material needs very firm support. Add to the basic cost the high price of contrast lines, wood inlays, and other interesting edge details. Dark-toned surfaces tend to show blemishes faster.

It can scratch, chip, and stain. Once marred, it is difficult to repair. Ready-made postformed countertops can look uninspired. Conventional laminate has a dark backing that shows at the seams, while new solid-color laminates, designed to hide these lines, are somewhat brittle and more expensive. High-gloss laminates show every smudge.

The price. Granite especially can be worth its weight in gold, and solid stone slabs are among the most expensive countertop materials on the market. Stone tiles, particularly slate and limestone, are less expensive than slabs. Stone also needs strong support. Oil, alcohol, and any acid such as lemon or wine will stain marble or at least damage its high-gloss finish. There is usually a wait time for custom-cut solid slabs, and you should let a professional install them.

Cast polymers may look cheap and are not very durable. They tend to scratch and ding and are tough to repair. Quality varies widely. Look for Cultured Marble Institute certification.

Wood can scorch and scratch and may blacken when near a moisture source such as a sink. Sealers such as mineral oil and polyurethane are available, but neither is ideal. If you use mineral oil, you must coat both sides, top and bottom, of the wood slab, or it will warp. If you choose polyurethane, which is a permanent protective sealant, you cannot cut on the bare counter.

If you cut on it, you will ruin both the surface and your knives. Fabrication can be expensive. Custom touches and high chromium content add significantly to the cost.

BASIC TOOLS FOR CABINETS & STORAGE

Bevel gauge	Block plane	Power drill with bits and screwdriver tips	Caulking gun
Chalk line	Router	Combination square	Compass	Contour gauge
Coping saw	Drop cloths	Handsaw	Level
Nail claw	Prybar	Power circular saw	C-clamp	Perforated rasp
Reciprocating saw	Stepladder	Claw hammer	Saber saw (jigsaw)	Sandpaper and sanding bloc
Screwdrivers	Stepladder	Stud finder	Utility knife	Wood chisel

tools for cabinets & storage

WORKING ON CABINETRY, COUNTERTOPS, SHELVING, AND CLOSETS CALLS FOR quite a few conventional carpentry tools. You do not need all of the tools shown here for every storage-related project, but you will find this is a good selection to have on hand, particularly if you will be doing much finish carpentry work. Be sure you also have basic safety equipment, including safety glasses, gloves, and a dust mask.

In addition to the tools shown here, you may need electrical and plumbing tools if your work will involve moving receptacles, switches, or plumbing fixtures. For any job that requires you to work with walls, you will need some of the tools discussed on pages 102–104. If you take on tile work, you will need tile tools, as discussed on pages 152–153. And, of course, if you intend to do any painting or finishing, you will need tools for those jobs, too (see pages 34–39).

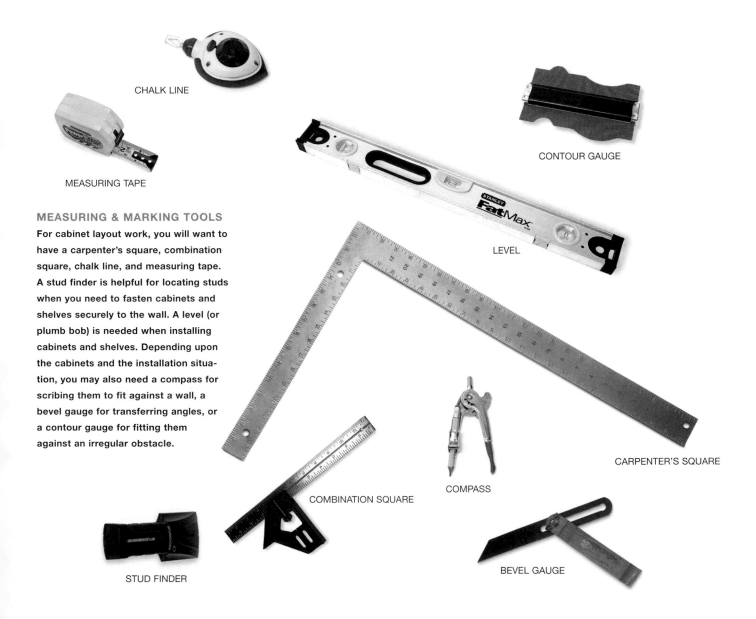

CHALK LINE

MEASURING TAPE

CONTOUR GAUGE

LEVEL

MEASURING & MARKING TOOLS

For cabinet layout work, you will want to have a carpenter's square, combination square, chalk line, and measuring tape. A stud finder is helpful for locating studs when you need to fasten cabinets and shelves securely to the wall. A level (or plumb bob) is needed when installing cabinets and shelves. Depending upon the cabinets and the installation situation, you may also need a compass for scribing them to fit against a wall, a bevel gauge for transferring angles, or a contour gauge for fitting them against an irregular obstacle.

CARPENTER'S SQUARE

COMBINATION SQUARE

COMPASS

STUD FINDER

BEVEL GAUGE

CABINET REMOVAL TOOLS

For removing existing cabinets, you will need a prybar. In addition, you may need a heavier-duty wrecking bar, a nail claw for pulling balky nails, and a reciprocating saw for cutting through the old cabinets.

RECIPROCATING SAW

NAIL CLAW

PRYBAR

WRECKING BAR

CUTTING TOOLS

A handsaw and power circular saw help you cut straight lines; a coping saw and saber saw cut curves. Chisels, a perforated rasp, and a block plane assist in removing small amounts of wood for fine fitting. A utility knife is very handy for many jobs. A router is essential if you intend to laminate your own countertops.

POWER CIRCULAR SAW

BLOCK PLANE

ROUTER

HANDSAW

UTILITY KNIFE

WOOD CHISEL

COPING SAW

PERFORATED RASP

SABER SAW (JIGSAW)

POWER DRILL WITH BITS
AND SCREWDRIVER TIPS

STEPLADDER

CAULKING GUN

C-CLAMP

SCREWDRIVERS

SANDPAPER AND SANDING BLOCK

DROP CLOTHS

GENERAL CARPENTRY TOOLS

For the basic construction tasks related to cabinets and
shelving, you will need a good selection of general construction tools, including a claw hammer, screwdrivers,
a power drill with bits and screwdriver tips, a couple of
clamps, a caulking gun, and a stepladder. For additional
tools that can be helpful for finish carpentry, see page 219.

CLAW HAMMER

installing cabinets

NEW CABINETS CAN TRANSFORM A KITCHEN OR BATHROOM BOTH IN FORM AND IN function. In a kitchen, especially, cabinets are by far the most important and visible elements. With this in mind, careful attention to detail and craftsmanship during installation is very important.

Though many homeowners choose to have cabinets designed and installed by professionals such as the specialists at Lowe's, installation can be handled by do-it-yourselfers with some experience.

Plan to put in cabinets after you install rough wiring and plumbing but before you install finish flooring. This way, you will not use more flooring material than necessary and you will also not be in danger of damaging new floors. You will, however,

need to protect the new cabinets during flooring installation and painting.

Most kitchen and bath cabinets are fundamentally the same; they just come in various sizes and are designed for slightly different storage. Here you will find information on installing cabinets in a kitchen. For information on installing bathroom cabinets, see pages 278–279.

Some cabinets are sold unassembled. If this is the case with yours, put them

1 Identify the floor's high spot, using a straight-edge and level. Mark the base of the wall where the high spot occurs. At the high spot, measure up 34½ inches, and draw a horizontal line to mark the top of all base cabinets.

2 Draw another horizontal line where you want the bottom of the wall cabinets to be (typically 54 inches up from the floor). Locate studs with a stud finder, and then mark their placements on the wall's surface. Use a level and pencil to mark all base and wall cabinet locations.

together according to the manufacturer's directions. Regardless of whether your cabinets are assembled or not, remove (or do not install) doors, shelves, and drawers. Label them so you will know where they go when it is time to put them in place.

If you are installing both wall and base cabinets, hang the wall-mounted cabinets first so the base cabinets will not be in your way as you work. Check the smoothness and flatness of the wall behind the cabinets by placing a long straightedge against it. Mark any bumpy or bulging areas so that, during installation, you will know where to tap in wood shims to make slight adjustments.

It is particularly important to install the first wall and base cabinets level and plumb, both from side to side and from front to back, because all other cabinets will be aligned with the first one.

REMOVING OLD CABINETS

Before you begin, turn off the water supply and any electrical circuits that will be affected. If you intend to save the floor, protect it by taping down a layer of ¼-inch plywood. Remove everything from the cabinets, including the shelves and drawers.

Next, unscrew all of the hinges, and remove the doors. From underneath, loosen any brackets used to attach the sink. Disconnect the supply and drain lines, and lift out the sink. If the sink is an integral part of the countertop, you will need to remove the countertop along with it (see page 282).

Once the countertop has been removed, locate the screws attaching the backs of the base cabinets to the wall. Remove the screws, and pry the cabinets away from the wall. Then, with a helper, unscrew and take down the wall cabinets.

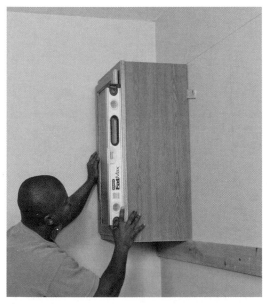

3 Screw a level temporary support rail to the wall, aligning its top edge with the line for the bottom edge of the wall cabinets.

4 While a helper holds the first cabinet in place, drill pilot holes either through the sturdy cabinet back or through its support rail into the wall studs. Shim and fasten the cabinet, checking to make sure it is plumb.

LOWE'S SAFETY TIP
Because upper cabinets are extremely heavy when they are filled, they must be fastened very securely to wall studs. Screw through a strong part of the cabinet with at least 3-inch screws that enter the studs by at least 1½ inches.

PROJECT CONTINUES ➡

5 Shim and fasten the second cabinet and adjoining wall cabinets, securing each to its neighbor with clamps. Make sure the cabinets are plumb, and then screw them together and to the wall. On faceframe cabinets, first drill two ⅛-inch pilot holes through the sides of the faceframe for the screws. With frameless cabinets, predrill bolt holes through shelf-peg holes you won't be using, and bolt the cabinets together.

6 Position and shim a corner base cabinet. Make sure its top edge aligns with the level line on the wall. Once the cabinet is level, plumb, and securely against the side wall, drive screws through the cabinet back and shims into the wall studs. Use a knife or sharp chisel to trim any excess material from the shims.

7 Set the adjoining cabinet in place, shimming and leveling it in the same way. Clamp it to the first cabinet, and fasten it to the adjoining cabinet as you fastened the wall cabinets together. Be sure to cut out cabinet backs as required for plumbing or electrical outlets.

8 Fasten the cabinets to the wall. Once all the base cabinets are positioned, attach each cabinet to the wall studs with at least two 2½-inch (8d) screws driven through the mounting rails. Last, install all shelves, drawers, and doors.

cabinet repairs

SOMETIMES ALL YOU NEED TO GIVE YOUR ROOM A WHOLE NEW LEASE ON LIFE is a bit of basic cabinet repair or improvement. Changing your pulls, for example, can completely alter the look of your cabinets. Remember to measure the distance between the existing screw holes in the cabinet face because you will not want to drill new holes.

hinges

If your cabinet doors droop or shut poorly, consider repairing or changing the hinges. First, try tightening the screws. If a screw will not tighten, remove it, squirt a little white glue into the screw hole, and fill up the hole with some wooden toothpicks (wipe off any excess glue). After the glue dries, use a utility knife to cut the toothpicks flush with the surface, and drive the screw into the refurbished hole. (You may have to drill a small pilot hole first.)

If it seems that your cabinet doors are perpetually hanging open, you may want to switch to self-closing hinges, which do not require a separate catch to keep the door closed. Many types of hinges are available in self-closing styles.

catches

Hinges alone may not be adequate to keep wayward doors closed. If you think you would like extra holding power—perhaps because of the presence of a small child or the likelihood of earthquake rattling—catches, latches, and locks may add an extra measure of security.

Magnetic catches work well in most conventional situations because they are less dependent on strict alignment than other types and they do not wear out. Alternatives include friction catches, which have a metal protrusion that catches or clicks into a metal opening, and double and single rollers, which have spring-loaded arms that close over a strike plate or screw.

drawers

Another common and easily accomplished repair involves misaligned drawers, or drawers that do not close easily or well. You can usually fix this problem by re-attaching or replacing the drawer's glides. For the smoothest, most trouble-free drawer operation, purchase prefabricated metal ball-bearing glide sets that attach to the drawer bottom or sides. If you want to use side glides in a faceframe cabinet, you will need to bring the mounting surface flush with the edge of the faceframe stiles by gluing and screwing filler strips to the inside of the cabinet's sides. The manufacturer's instructions will detail installation.

Ball-bearing side glides offer strength, smooth operation, and full extension.

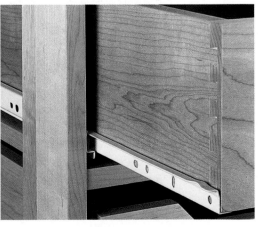

Undermount side slides are relatively inexpensive, barely visible when drawers are open, and easy to install.

installing an island

THE ISLAND HAS ENJOYED GROWING POPULARITY IN THE KITCHEN OVER THE LAST decade, and for good reason. It's doubtless one of the kitchen's most versatile elements. It expands usable counter space, providing both preparation and serving area, and increases the kitchen's storage capacity with base cabinetry.

An island can be shaped or sized to fit practically any kitchen's contours. The best kitchen layouts for an island are one-wall, L-shape, and U-shape floor plans.

A new island should be sized in proper proportion to the kitchen. You will need to leave a 48-inch clearance from the island to counters for safe passage—more if two cooks will be working simultaneously. Most islands are 36 to 42 inches high, 24 to 48 inches deep, and 3 or more feet long.

Generally, islands are assembled from the same materials and installed using the same basic techniques as those for the other kitchen cabinets and counters (see pages 272–274 on installing cabinets as well as 280–283 on tiling a countertop). But there are a couple of exceptions. Island cabinets cannot be fastened to a wall, so they must

be secured more firmly to the floor. And, because their backs are unfinished, island cabinets are either placed back to back so that doors, drawers, and shelves are accessible from both sides, or their backs and ends are faced with finished panels such as the beadboard shown on the facing page. The back-to-back method works well for creating an island that is 36 inches deep (a 24-inch base plus a 12-inch base) or 48 inches deep (two 24-inch bases). Or, island cabinets may be custom-built to the desired sizes and configurations.

Before installing island cabinets, be sure to rough-in any plumbing needed (for a bar sink, for example) and all electrical wiring for outlets. For more about plumbing, see pages 376–463, and for wiring information, see pages 464–519.

1 Position one cabinet in place, and mark its inside edges on the floor. Tip the cabinet over, and screw two cleats in the floor where they will sit just inside each side panel. Tip the cabinet back in place and nail it to the cleats on both sides with 8d finishing nails.

2 Position the second cabinet, and temporarily clamp it to the first one. Mark the floor for one cleat inside the second cabinet's outside edge. Tip that cabinet out of the way, and screw the third cleat in place.

3 Tip the second cabinet back into place, screw it to the first cabinet, and nail it to the cleat. Before putting a countertop in place (see pages 280–283), add a decorative panel to cover the backs or add a second set of cabinets back to back with the first ones.

beadboarding an island

THE HOMEOWNERS MADE THIS ISLAND USING STOCK CABINETS (ONE 2 FEET LONG, the other 3 feet long) to match their fitted cabinets. To give it a custom look, they added medium-density fiberboard (MDF) beadboard to the backs and exposed sides of the stock components. One edge of each beadboard sheet needs to be mitered at a cabinet shop, home center, or lumberyard; you can measure and cut the other edges at home.

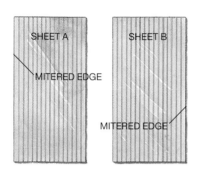

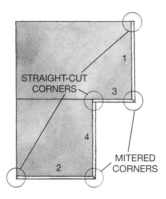

1 Most islands will require two sheets of MDF beadboard. Miter one edge on each sheet as follows: With the sheets arranged in the same orientation, miter the left edge on the first sheet (label it Sheet A) and the right edge on the second sheet (label it Sheet B).

2 Before you start cutting the panels, it is important to understand which edges are mitered on the island. Set them in place, oriented properly.

3 On Sheet A, measure and mark the Piece 1 panel of beadboard. Cut it using a circular saw, and cut out any openings with a saber saw. Dry-fit the piece against the cabinet. Measure, cut, and dry-fit the remaining pieces in the following order: Piece 2 from Sheet B, Piece 3 from Sheet B, and then Piece 4 from Sheet A.

4 Prime the beadboard pieces, and sand them lightly with 100-grit sandpaper. Paint them with white latex paint, allow them to dry, and apply wood glue to the island where Piece 1 goes. Making sure the mitered edge is on the left, adhere the panel to the island's side.

5 Using a brad nailer and ½-inch nails, attach the beadboard piece to the side of the island by nailing the edges, placing a nail approximately every 6 inches. Next, glue the Piece 2 panel, facing its mitered edge toward the right. Brad-nail the piece into place.

6 Glue the Piece 3 panel, facing its mitered edge to the right, against Piece 1. Brad-nail it. Glue the Piece 4 panel, facing its mitered edge to the left, against Piece 2, and brad-nail it. Fill the nail holes with putty, and sand. Apply a second coat of paint.

installing bathroom cabinets

SOME BATHROOMS HAVE ENTIRE CABINET SYSTEMS, WHILE OTHERS HAVE SIMPLE base and wall cabinets. In the step-by-step sequence offered here, you will find the techniques for installing the latter. If you will be implementing a more comprehensive cabinet system, refer to the instructions for installing kitchen cabinets on pages 272–274; the same principles and techniques apply. Install bath cabinets such as the ones shown here after wiring and plumbing have been roughed in and flooring has been laid.

INSTALLING A BASE CABINET

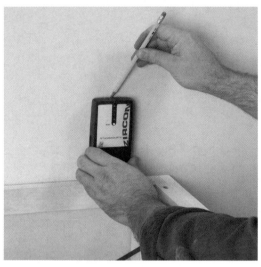

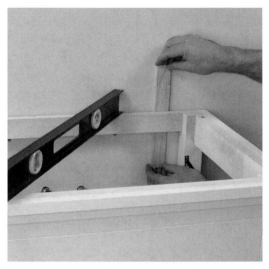

1 Using a stud finder, locate the wall studs to which the cabinet will attach. With a pencil, mark the stud locations on the wall (make sure you will be able to see the marks after the cabinet is in place). Draw straight vertical lines to indicate the center of the studs.

2 Level the cabinet from front to back and from side to side. (If necessary, use shims to raise it to the high point of the floor or otherwise change its position.) Note that on some vanities, adjustable levelers built into the legs eliminate the need for shims on the floor.

3 Drive screws through the cabinet back rail (and shims) into the wall studs. Trim the shims with a sharp chisel or knife so they will not be visible when the countertop is in place. With the sink and faucet set installed, position and attach the countertop to the cabinet from underneath.

LOWE'S QUICK TIP
A scribe rail is a length of wood shaped to serve as a buffer between a wall with an irregular surface and a cabinet. Use a simple compass to trace the surface of the wall onto the rail, and then trim the rail to ensure a tight fit.

HANGING A WALL CABINET

1 To install wall-mounted cabinets, start by determining their positions and drawing a level horizontal line on the wall where the bottom of each cabinet will be located. Double-check your layout by lightly penciling the cabinets' dimensions and placement on the wall.

2 Align the top edge of a temporary 1-by-3 support rail with the line for the bottom edge of the cabinets, and drive three or four 2-inch screws through the rail and into the wall studs.

3 Drill pilot holes through the sturdy part of the cabinet back or its support rail and into the wall studs. Screw the cabinet to the wall using two screws that are long enough to penetrate the studs by at least 1½ inches.

A wall-mounted cabinet can provide generous storage without taking up floor space; it must be fastened securely to the wall studs.

tiling a countertop

RESISTANT TO HEAT, MOISTURE, AND STAINS, CERAMIC TILE IS AN EXCELLENT choice for a countertop. If you have never worked with ceramic tile before, tiling a countertop is an ideal first-time project because a countertop is a horizontal and relatively small surface. The keys to a successful tile job are planning and surface preparation.

Before selecting your tile, carefully measure your countertop. When calculating the number of tiles required to cover it, make sure you allow for any specialty tiles, such as those needed for edging or a backsplash. (Manufacturers make a number of edge tiles, the most common being the bullnose shown in Step 4 on page 283.) To allow for cutting and breakage, order slightly more than you need; the rule of thumb is to buy 10 percent extra. Once you have made your purchase, lay out the tile on the countertop to make sure you have enough for the job and to see in advance where you will need to make cuts.

building a substrate

Countertop tiles should rest on a surface that is solid and capable of withstanding moisture. The front edge must be thick enough to accommodate the edging you have chosen, and the substrate needs to be level in both directions.

In most cases, a layer of ³/₄-inch plywood topped with ¹/₂-inch or ¹/₄-inch cement backerboard will do the job. Although a standard kitchen countertop is 25 inches deep and a backsplash is commonly 4 to 6 inches high, you may want to modify those dimensions slightly to minimize the amount of cutting that will be required.

Before you begin, cover the base cabinets with plastic sheeting or heavy-duty con-

struction paper; position a drop cloth on the floor.

And do not forget about the kitchen sink (see pages 418–419 for installation instructions). Install a flush-mounted sink before adhering the backerboard. If you are planning on installing an undermount sink, put it in after the backerboard or the backerboard and tiling. A typical self-rimming sink is installed after the countertop, as discussed on pages 418–419.

Cut the plywood pieces so they overlap the cabinets by about an inch, and install

LOWE'S QUICK TIP
Use a fine-point permanent marker to mark cutting lines on tile surfaces.

PREPARING A BASE FOR TILE

1 Attach the plywood to the top of the cabinets by driving 1⅝-inch deck screws (which resist rusting) through the plywood and into the cabinet top every 6 inches or so. Cut a hole for the sink following the manufacturer's instructions. (Attach a flush-mounted sink before adding the backerboard.)

2 Cut backerboard pieces to fit. Offset any seams from plywood seams by at least 3 inches. Lay out the pieces in a dry run, and make sure the edges line up precisely with the plywood. Check the sink for fit. For a flush-mounted sink, bring the backerboard right up to the sink edge.

3 Mix a batch of latex-reinforced or epoxy thinset mortar. Spread thinset over the plywood with a ¼-inch notched trowel, spreading only enough for one backerboard piece at a time. Lay the backerboard in the thinset, and drive 1¼-inch backerboard screws in a grid, spaced approximately 6 inches apart across the material.

4 If you plan to tile the backsplash with radius bullnose or quarter-round trim at the top, cut pieces of backerboard to accommodate the thickness and width of the backsplash. Butter the back of the strips with thinset, and press these into place against the wall.

5 Apply fiberglass mesh tape to the backerboard joints. Also wrap the front edges of the backerboard and plywood with the tape. Do not apply tape where the backsplash meets the countertop. (Install an undermount sink before tiling.)

them with the factory edges facing out. Check the entire surface to make sure it is level as you attach the plywood; if necessary, remove screws, install shims, and then re-drive the screws.

Backerboard is easy to cut and install. You simply scribe and snap it, and then attach it to the plywood foundation with special galvanized screws. For more about installing backerboard, see pages 112–114. Once backerboard is in place, cover the screw heads with thinset mortar, tape all of the seams with fiberglass mesh tape, and fill in with thinset mortar.

tiling the surface

A tile cutter does an excellent job of scoring and snapping tile to fit. If your tile is particularly hard, you may need to cut it with a wet saw, which can be rented. When you cut a tile, the result is a sharp edge that is not only easily damaged but is also difficult to wipe clean. If possible, you should position all cut edges at the back of the countertop, where the backsplash tiles will cover them.

For fine-tuning, tile nippers can break off tiny pieces to create curved or complicated profiles. For more about cutting tile, see page 194.

Before preparing the mortar, place the tiles where they will go on the substrate in a dry run, using plastic spacers for grout lines. Make adjustments as needed. Aim for

LOWE'S SAFETY TIP

a symmetrical look, with no narrow slivers of cut tiles.

For a countertop that turns a corner, start the layout at the inside corner. If the layout ends with a very narrow sliver, then slightly widening the grout lines may solve the problem. When cutting the tiles, take into account the width of the grout lines on either side.

When mixing grout for the installed tile, follow the label instructions. Use a laminated grout float to scoop some grout onto the tile surface. Push the grout into the joints, holding the float diagonally and sweeping it back and forth across the surface.

Once the grout becomes firm, wipe off the excess with a damp sponge. Allow residual film on the surface to dry to a haze, and then buff the area with a clean, soft cloth. Apply a sealer after waiting the time specified by the manufacturer (typically two to four weeks).

TILING A COUNTERTOP

1 If you are using edging tiles, mark a line on the edge of the countertop that allows for the tiles plus a grout joint. Then temporarily attach a guide strip along this line with nails. Lay out the field tiles from the edge of the strip to the back of the countertop, using a straightedge to align them.

REMOVING AN OLD COUNTERTOP

The right methods for removing a countertop depend upon the material and its construction. The first step is to determine how it was made and attached to the cabinets. Using a flashlight, look underneath to find the fasteners. Laminate countertops and tile, which have a plywood base, are usually screwed to the cabinets from underneath; remove the screws, and pry up the countertop using a flat prybar. For tile, be sure to have a helper on hand because the countertop will be very heavy. A solid-surface countertop may be siliconed to the cabinet's top rails—this can be very difficult to remove without cutting the support rails from underneath. Depending upon the material, you may be able to break and/or cut the countertop into several pieces to make removal easier. If you intend to save the cabinets, be careful! Pounding or prying too hard can render them unusable.

2 Mix up enough thinset mortar for the entire countertop, and allow the substance to rest for the amount of time specified by the manufacturer. Starting in a corner, apply the mortar to the backerboard with the appropriate-sized notched trowel, working in an area no larger than 2 to 3 square feet.

3 Working out from the corner, begin laying tiles. Press a tile firmly into the mortar, wiggling it slightly as you press down. Continue filling in tiles on either side of the first tile; use plastic spacers to create even gaps for the grout that will be applied later. Once all the full tiles are in place, cut tiles to fill in the remaining space. Then, remove the spacers.

4 Once all the tiles are set, remove the guide strip, and add the edging pieces. The simplest way to do this is by "back buttering," which means smearing thinset mortar on the back faces of the edging tiles as if buttering a piece of bread. Then position the edging so it butts against the full tiles, press down, and wiggle to set the pieces.

5 Allow the mortar to set overnight. Then mix up sufficient grout to fill in the gaps between tiles, following the manufacturer's directions. Apply the grout with a grout float held diagonally to the surface, forcing the grout between the tiles. To remove the excess, hold the float at a 45-degree angle and scrape the surface.

making a laminate countertop

THERE ARE HUNDREDS OF COLORS AND TEXTURES OF PLASTIC LAMINATE, BUT VERY few are available in stock prefabricated countertops. The less common colors are expensive to special order, but if you laminate your own, you can save money and get the exact look you want. Plastic laminate is a thin sheet of plastic that is glued down to a substrate. The project shown here uses "shop-grade" hardwood plywood as the substrate. The edges of the top shown here have been finished with wood trim. You can apply plastic laminate to the edges, but that job can be a tricky procedure.

1 Cut ¾-inch plywood to the desired length and width. In order to make the countertop thicker than a single sheet of plywood, cut four 4-inch- wide strips of plywood to build up the edges. Apply yellow glue to the faces of the strips and the underside edges of the top. Then, with all edges flush, screw the strips to the plywood sheet, using 1¼-inch screws. Also install three 4-inch-wide crosspieces between the edge strips for added strength. On a clean, flat surface, unroll the laminate face down, and lay the plywood base on top of it (also face down). Mark cutting lines on the laminate's under-side so it measures ¼ to ½ inch wider than the length and width of the plywood substrate (to allow for trimming later).

2 Cut the sheet of laminate face down using a circular saw equipped with a laminate-cutting blade, or, alternatively, cut it face up using a laminate knife or a table saw with a laminate-cutting blade. Lay the laminate and substrate face down, side by side, on a clean, flat surface, and clean them both. Pour contact cement in a paint tray and, using a smooth-nap roller, apply a coating of contact cement to both surfaces according to the manufacturer's recommendations. Let the cement dry to the touch.

LOWE'S | QUICK TIP
Stick masking tape along the cutting line on the laminate. This will make the line much easier to see and will minimize chipping.

3 When both surfaces are dry, lay ¼-inch wood dowels along the top of the plywood substrate every 12 inches to keep the two materials apart until you have positioned them perfectly. (Once they have bonded, you may not be able to pull them apart.) With a helper, carefully lay the sheet of laminate finish side up on top of the dowels, being careful not to allow the two cemented surfaces to touch. Starting at one end, roll each dowel along the substrate to allow a section of laminate to make contact with the substrate. Do not allow any bulges. Finally, remove the dowels.

4 Using a laminate roller, apply pressure to the entire surface of the countertop (this will secure the bond and eliminate any air bubbles). Don't expect to fix bulges at this point; it's too late. Roll in all directions to maximize the contact between the laminate and plywood.

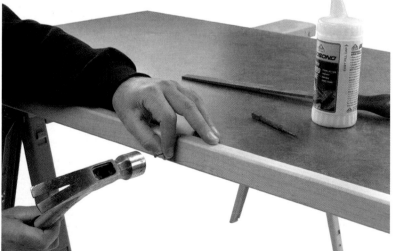

5 Using a router equipped with a self-piloting trim bit or a laminate trimmer, trim the excess laminate so it is flush with the edge of the top. You can also use a file set at a slight angle or a sharp block plane. Whatever trim tool you use, touch up the edges slightly with a file or sharp plane.

6 Cut strips of hardwood trim to frame the edges of the top. Sand them and nail them into the plywood edges with finishing nails. Countersink the nail heads, and fill the holes. Sand the wood, and finish it to your liking. Immediately wipe away any finish that gets on the laminate.

adding a built-in closet

AT THE TOP OF MANY A HOMEOWNER'S WISH LIST IS MORE CLOSET SPACE. IF YOU have adequate floor space and some carpentry skills, you can add a closet—in a bedroom, guestroom, den, or hallway—that will look like it has been there all along.

The first step is to build the closet frame and fasten it to the surrounding walls. Next, you will trim the door opening and install the doors of your choice. Then you will hang the closet rods or customize the interior with rods, shelving, drawers, and any other accessories you desire.

framing the closet walls Plan to build the closet frame from 2 by 4s, allowing an inside depth of at least 27 inches. You can construct the frame in one of two ways: Either build the walls flat on the floor and then raise them up into position, or build them in place. It is much easier to nail the framing members together on the floor if the room has a large, clear area to accommodate this. But using this method, you

will have to make a slight modification in the height of the closet walls because it is impossible to tilt an 8-foot-tall wall up into an 8-foot-high space (as you angle the wall into position, it is actually about $\frac{1}{4}$ inch taller). Build the wall about $\frac{1}{4}$ inch shorter than the height of the ceiling, and then place shims or thin blocks between the top plate and the ceiling.

First, mark the positions of the top plate and the sole plate. On the ceiling, mark both ends of the center line of the new closet wall. Measure $1\frac{3}{4}$ inches (half the width of a 2-by-4 top plate) on both sides of each mark. Snap parallel lines between corresponding marks with a chalk line to show the position of the top plate.

Next, hang a plumb bob from each end of the lines, and mark these points on the floor. Snap two more chalk lines to connect the floor points, marking the sole plate's position. If the closet has a side wall return like the one shown at left, lay out the top plate and sole plate in the same way; use a framing square to make sure this will be perfectly perpendicular to the front wall. Cut each sole plate and top plate to the desired length.

marking stud positions Lay each top plate edge to edge against its sole plate and flush at both ends. Beginning at an end that will be attached to an existing wall, measure in $1\frac{1}{2}$ inches (the thickness of a 2-by-4 stud), and draw a line across both plates using a combination square. Starting from that end, measure and draw lines at $15\frac{1}{4}$ and $16\frac{3}{4}$ inches. From these marks, advance 16 inches at a time, drawing new lines for stud locations until you reach the far end of both plates.

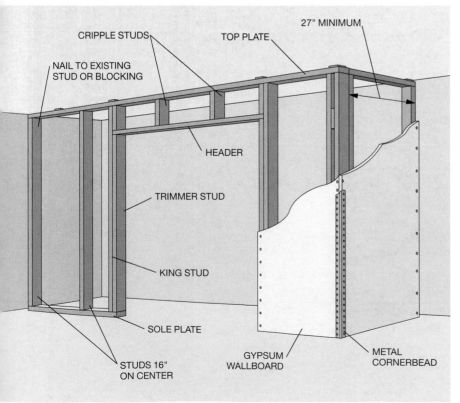

CRIPPLE STUDS

NAIL TO EXISTING STUD OR BLOCKING

TOP PLATE

27" MINIMUM

HEADER

TRIMMER STUD

KING STUD

SOLE PLATE

STUDS 16" ON CENTER

GYPSUM WALLBOARD

METAL CORNERBEAD

framing each wall Frame each wall according to the drawing on the opposite page. Note that the sole plate has been cut out where it spans the door's opening—you will cut this after erecting the wall. The rough opening for the door requires a king stud and a trimmer stud on each side, a header across the top, and cripple studs between the header and top plate.

Cut the full-length studs to a length equal to the ceiling height minus 3¾ inches (for the 1½-inch-thick top and sole plates and the needed ¼-inch clearance).

Nail short "cripple" studs into the top plate at appropriate intervals, or, if you have nailed in studs across the doorway, cut these to size. Measure and cut the header, and then nail it to the bottoms of the cripple studs with 16d nails. Using 8d nails, toenail the header to the king studs. Measure and cut two trimmer studs, and nail one to each king stud with 10d nails in a staggered pattern. You will probably need to adjust the width of the opening by adding a pair of trimmers on one side.

building the walls Once the walls are built, lift them into place, and shim between the top plate and the ceiling joists. Anchor the end studs to existing wall studs or to the blocking that is inserted between the wall studs.

Lay each sole plate between the lines on the floor, and nail them in place with 10d nails spaced every 2 feet. Do not nail the portion of the sole plate that runs across your planned closet doorway. Nail them to the header and sole plate. Cut out the sole plate, taking care not to damage any flooring beneath it, to match the width of the rough opening. Pry the sole plate away from the subflooring or flooring.

finishing Add wall coverings to match the room. If you are installing gypsum wallboard (see pages 112–114), tape the seams between the new and old wallboard, and protect any outside corners with metal cornerbead. For information on painting, see pages 24–75.

Next, hang the doors. Bifold doors move in metal tracks mounted to the bottom of the head jamb. Pivots turn in top and bottom brackets, and a center guide at the top runs in the track. Sliding doors run on rollers inside metal tracks with floor guides below that keep the doors in line. Tracks are available to fit standard 1⅜-inch interior doors. A trim strip usually hides the track. Most doors come with all the necessary hardware.

To install a rod inside a closet, a good option is to use pole sockets. First, screw one socket in place. Then insert the rod; level it before fastening the other socket. If the closet rod is very long, provide additional support by fastening a hook to the top or back of the closet near the middle of the rod.

Bifold doors push out of the way to offer generous access to a closet or, in this case, a hideaway laundry.

organizing your closet

WHEN IT COMES TO STORAGE, IT IS NOT NECESSARILY HOW MANY CLOSETS YOUR home has that counts but how well-organized and efficient those closets are. Good storage means maximizing space and storing items in an easy-to-access fashion. Modular closet organizers featuring shelves, drawers, and rods can turn the messiest area into perfectly functional storage space.

If you want a fast route to organizing a closet, purchase one of the ready-made storage systems sold at Lowe's. If you like a cabinet-style approach, choose ready-to-assemble (RTA) kits made of melamine or wood-veneered panels. They are connected with a combination of easy-to-install cam studs and locks that fit into pre-bored holes in the panels. Or, if you prefer something a bit more open, you can select one of the many popular chrome- or vinyl-coated wire systems, which are a snap to install (see the step-by-step sequences on pages 290–291 for more information). Yet another alternative is to mix the two types and create your own combination of shelves, drawers, baskets, doors, hanging rods, and slide-out tie and belt racks.

If you need to have shelving that is cut to fit your closet, take your measurements

Shelves, rods, cubby-holes and drawers, constructed from a wood-veneer panel system, maximize this closet's space.

LEFT: In this closet reno-
vation, sliding doors and
a single hanging rod were
replaced with fabric-lined
French doors and a cus-
tom storage system of
rods, shelves, and hooks.
BELOW: This wall-mounted
wire closet system em-
ploys shelves, rods, and
baskets for highly effi-
cient organization of a
child's closet space.

to your local Lowe's. A sales specialist will custom-cut a unit for you. If you would rather not install your own closet system, you can pay a bit more to have one put in by a Lowe's-approved installer. This is a sure way to get a customized system that fits your closet and storage needs exactly.

When deciding on the components for a closet storage system, consider the types of items you want to store and their general dimensions, such as the hanging length of dresses, coats, shirts, blouses, and pants. Calculate how many lineal feet of hanging rods and shelves you will need. Be aware that drawers add considerably to the cost; consider whether a shelf or another type of open storage might work better. Place any items you want to access quickly on open shelves. Bulky clothing articles, including sweaters and hats, usually fit best on top of shelves. If you keep the closet area neat, such open storage can be decorative as well as functional.

assembling a closet system

ONE EASY WAY TO SOLVE A STORAGE PROBLEM WITH A MINIMUM OF FUSS AND expense is to put in a wire closet system. These systems, made of vinyl- or chrome-coated wire, are easy for the do-it-yourselfer to install—in fact, you can probably organize an entire closet with one of these in a single afternoon.

Methods for installing two types of systems are shown here. The style below is a simple wire shelf that is attached to the wall with a small hook made for that purpose and supported by a diagonal metal brace. You can hang just one of these or outfit an entire closet with them.

On the facing page, you can see how to install a system of wire shelves that mount on standards hanging from a horizontal track. With this type of system, because all the standards attach to a single, level track, you do not have to level each shelf as you install it. Every shelf that sits on brackets

inserted into the standards will automatically align properly.

The systems shown are fastened to the wall studs using screws. Use an electronic stud finder to locate stud positions. If there are not studs where you need them, you can fasten the systems to the walls with toggle bolts or expanding anchors, but be aware that these methods are not as strong as attaching to studs.

You can have your Lowe's sales specialist cut shelves and tracks to length, or cut the pieces yourself using a hacksaw (you can also use a bolt cutter to cut the wire).

INSTALLING A WIRE SHELF

1 Using a level as a guide, mark a level line along the wall where you want the shelf to go. Drill a pilot hole for the special expanding anchor hook that is designed to grip the back of the shelf (size this hole according to the manufacturer's recommendations).

2 Insert the expanding anchor hook, and drive in its screw. Check it to make sure it is secure. Install another at the other end.

3 Hang the back of the wire shelf onto the pair of anchors. At each shelf end, attach a diagonal support to the front of the shelf using a bracket. Then raise the shelf until it is level, and drill a pilot hole through the hole at the bottom of the diagonal support. Insert an expanding anchor into the hole, and then screw the support to it.

INSTALLING A TRACK-MOUNTED SHELVING SYSTEM

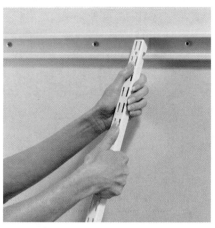

1 Position the top of the hang track on the wall. It should be level and mounted where you want the top of the unit to be. Most people choose to mount the highest shelf 85½ inches from the floor and the hang track about 6 inches higher. Drive screws through the hang track and drywall into the wall studs. Be sure to mount the track securely—it will carry most of the system's loaded weight.

2 Lock the first shelf standard onto the hang track, centered over the location of a wall stud. Check it with a level for plumb, and then screw through the center of the track into the stud. Add additional standards, using the same methods. Space the standards no more than 24 inches apart; place the two at the sides no more than 4 inches from where the ends of the shelves will be.

3 Insert the shelf brackets into the tracks. Count down the number of slots from the top of the standards to be sure the brackets for each shelf are level with each other.

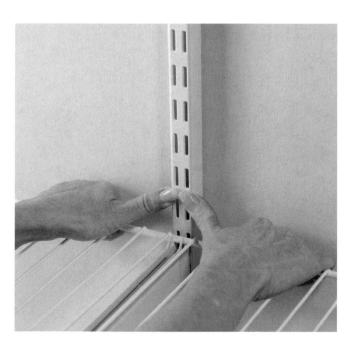

4 Lock the wire shelves onto each set of the shelf brackets. If your system includes hanger bars, add the supports for them to the fronts of the shelves.

5 Use a level to make sure the shelf standards are perfectly plumb, and then attach the standards to the wall with additional screws. To finish the system, add end caps to every wire at both ends of the shelving unit and to the hanger track.

installing a wall shelf

DECORATIVE WALL SHELVES ARE A TRADITIONAL FAVORITE FOR DISPLAYING ANYTHING from books to bric-a-brac, and give your walls an attractive focal point. Installing shelving is not complicated, but there are a few pitfalls to avoid.

First, be sure to provide adequate support. It is best to secure shelf brackets to wall studs, which are located at 16-inch intervals. If, as in this project, the brackets are installed less than 16 inches apart, fasten one to a stud and the other to the wall with a plastic wallboard anchor. Second,

make sure the shelf is level. For best results, work with a level; do not try to eyeball the height of the shelf brackets.

This project features a rectangular "trophy shelf," but Lowe's carries many other styles of decorative shelving, including semicircular corner shelves.

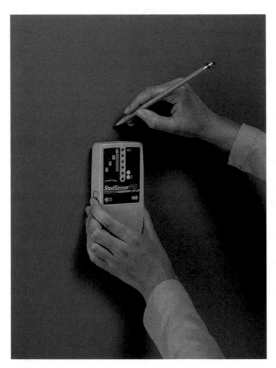

1 Select the location and height of your shelf, and then find the nearest wall studs with a stud finder. For the electronic type shown, pass the finder slowly back and forth over the wall. The light at the top will glow when the stud finder crosses the edges of a stud. Mark the center of the stud, about ¾ inch from the edges.

2 Place a level against the wall 1 inch below the shelf location, crossing the stud marks. Lightly mark a line on the wall along the top edge of the level.

LOWE'S QUICK TIP
Shelving brackets should rest squarely against the wall. If they do not, remove the brackets, and adjust the screws, easing them out a bit or driving them deeper into the wall.

3 For the shelving unit shown here, the brackets are located 10 inches apart and 3 inches in from each end of the shelf. Mark a point on the level line, aligned with a marked stud location. Mark another point 10 inches from the first, again on the level line.

4 Choose a plastic wallboard anchor to fit the screws provided with the shelving unit. Fit an electric drill with a bit that is the same diameter as the anchor, and then drill a hole into the wall at the second point you marked in Step 3.

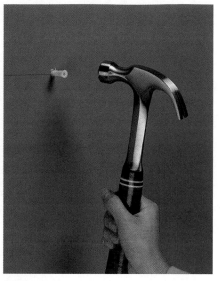

5 Insert the plastic anchor into the hole, and lightly tap it with a hammer until the sleeve of the anchor is flush with the wall.

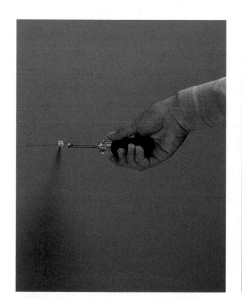

6 With a screwdriver, fasten one of the screws supplied with the shelving unit into the anchor, leaving 1/4 inch of the screw projecting from the wall. With the drill, drive a second screw directly into the wall at the marked stud point, again leaving 1/4 inch protruding.

7 Engage the metal fitting in each shelf bracket with a projecting screw head, and then tug the brackets downward to secure them.

8 Set the shelf on the brackets, centering it so the ends extend past the brackets by about 3 inches.

LOWE'S QUICK TIP
A 2-foot level is an ideal tool for leveling short shelving units.

siding

AFTER THE ROOF, THE MOST IMPORTANT STRUCTURES STANDING BETWEEN YOUR home and the elements are its exterior walls. Those walls are clad with siding, sometimes constructed of wood or metals and other times made of brick, stone, stucco, vinyl, or a combination of these materials.

Attractive, well-maintained siding ensures that your house always has its best face forward. Siding that is free of cracking, peeling, or sagging announces to the world that this home is well cared for by its vigilant owners. A bedraggled exterior, however, not only is unsightly but also is a sure sign of internal trouble brewing. Rain can penetrate small cracks in siding to seep into the wall's interior, creating mold and mildew, causing interior paint to blister and peel, and perhaps even damaging the wood frame. Exterior paint will blister and peel as well, allowing more water to penetrate, and the problems can escalate from there to potential structural damage. Regular maintenance, much of which can be done by a moderately experienced do-it-yourselfer, can spare you a large and painful repair bill at a later point.

In this chapter, you will learn all about siding, starting with guidance on buying it. Along with information on typical wall construction, you will learn about preparing to re-side your house and installing lap, vinyl, aluminum, and shingle siding. You will also be advised on how to diagnose various siding problems—an important skill— and on how to repair wood, synthetic, and masonry siding as well as soffits.

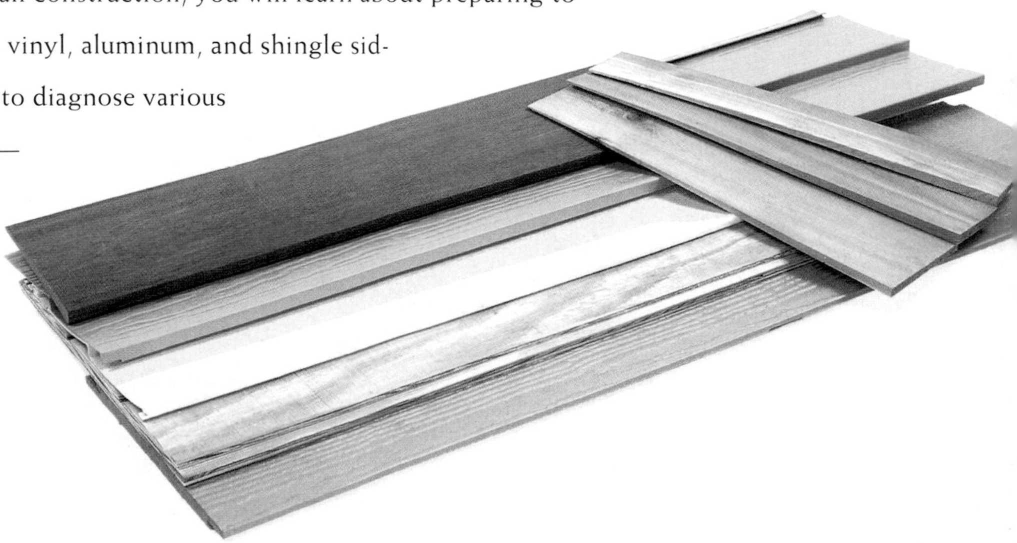

buying siding

BECAUSE SIDING COVERS MUCH OF A HOUSE'S EXTERIOR SURFACE, IT GREATLY affects a home's overall look, setting its tone and character. When choosing siding materials, the key is to look for beautiful, durable products that harmonize with the style of your house. The following offers a look at key options.

siding choices

Siding comes in a wide array of styles and materials. The type that is right for your home depends on your house's architecture, your budget, and the amount of maintenance you are willing to do.

wood For beauty and versatility, nothing beats wood siding. Typically made from cedar (although you can also get pine, spruce, redwood, cypress, and Douglas fir),

This home's fiber-cement siding mimics the look of wood while offering unmatched durability.

wood siding is sold in boards, shingles, or shakes. Wood lap siding, formed by overlapping horizontal clapboards, is a classic feature of American architectural styles such as Colonial and Craftsman, and it is still a top choice among designers of upper-end houses. Board-and-batten siding, a less common style in which boards are installed vertically, is more suited to contemporary designs. Shingle siding, typical of country-cottage and Victorian styles, comes in a variety of configurations for maximum design flexibility and decorative flair. Wood shakes have a rustic look.

Though unmatched as a design element, wood requires vigilant maintenance; it must be sealed on both sides before installation and then resealed every few years to prevent deterioration. It is also expensive, and high-quality products can be difficult to obtain.

composite Composite-wood products are less expensive than solid wood. Plywood siding is the least costly and easiest to install. Pre-priming panel edges and caulking seams, especially in harsh climates, where moisture can cause plywood panels to delaminate, is wise. Oriented strand board (OSB) and hardboard products are sold as 4-by-8-foot sheets or are molded to look like clapboard. Although hardboard sidings failed on many homes in the '80s and '90s, manufacturers have taken steps to improve their products with better preservatives, primers, and adhesives.

vinyl The most popular wood-siding substitute is vinyl. Available in both shingle and lap styles, vinyl is much less expensive than wood, but in appearance it is no

LEFT: **Red cedar siding presents a natural, warm, and rustic look.**

soft to weather natural hazards such as hail and high winds (although aluminum may be the better choice if you live in an area where salty ocean breezes or air pollution cause steel to corrode). An experienced installer is a must if you choose steel because newly cut ends will rust if not properly protected from the elements.

stucco Stucco continues to be a popular siding material, particularly for homes of Southwestern, Mediterranean, or contemporary architecture. Once considered a high-maintenance exterior finish, stucco is now formulated with epoxy, making it

substitute for the real thing. For many people, vinyl's major attraction is reduced maintenance. It never needs painting, and because it is colored all the way through, it will not show nicks and scratches. It does need to be cleaned regularly, and it can be damaged by impact, severe wind, and extreme temperatures. For maximum durability and a realistic look, be sure to buy a top-quality product. An experienced contractor is crucial because even the most expensive vinyl siding will buckle and warp if installed incorrectly.

Fiber-cement (sometimes called "cementious") siding is another wood look-alike that is sold as planks, panels, and shingles. It will not rot, burn, or attract insects; additionally, it inhibits fungus growth. Like wood, it requires regular topcoat maintenance, but manufacturers claim that it can hold paint five times longer than wood. Fiber-cement siding costs about half as much as cedar, and the top brands carry a 50-year warranty.

metal Aluminum and steel siding are fireproof, affordable, and, in most cases, easy to install over existing siding. Styles include lap, shingle, and board-and-batten, and many manufacturers offer matching trim. Color choices, however, are limited, and metal siding is prone to denting. In all but the most temperate climates, steel siding is preferable to aluminum, which is too

Though this home's walls appear to be clad with board siding—appropriate for the architecture—they're convincingly covered with more durable vinyl siding.

simpler to clean and less prone to cracking. Traditional stucco is applied by hand and can be tinted to produce a surface that will not need to be painted. Chips and cracks can be repaired by a skilled do-it-yourselfer (see page 316).

So-called synthetic stucco, technically known as exterior insulation and finishing system (EIFS), consists of flexible panels covered with an acrylic coating that mimics the appearance of plaster. EIFS has been plagued by moisture-related problems; proper installation is essential to avoid water damage.

Stucco siding, whether synthetic or traditional, is relatively inexpensive, about 20 percent less than cedar clapboard for a hand-applied finish.

brick & stone Brick and stone are both handsome, timeless siding materials that

BUYER'S GUIDE TO SIDING MATERIALS

MATERIAL	TYPES & CHARACTERISTICS	DURABILITY
Solid boards	Available in many species; redwood and cedar resist decay. Milled in various patterns. Nominal dimensions are 1" thick, 4"–12" wide, random lengths to 20'. Sold untreated, treated with water repellent, primed, painted, or stained. Applied horizontally, vertically, or diagonally.	30 years to life of building, depending on maintenance.
Exterior plywood	Most siding species are Douglas fir, Western red cedar, redwood, and Southern pine. Broad range of textures and patterns. Sheets are 4' wide, 8'–10' long. Lap boards are 6"–12" wide, 16' long. Thicknesses of both are $3/8"$–$5/8"$.	30 years to life of building, depending on maintenance.
Hardboard and OSB	Available smooth or textured: rough-sawn, board, stucco, others. Sheets are 4' wide, 8'–10' long. Lap boards are 6"–12" wide, 16' long, $3/8"$–$5/8"$ thick. Sold untreated, treated with water repellent, or opaque stained. Sheets are usually applied vertically.	30 years to life of building, depending on maintenance. Prepainted finish guaranteed to 20 years.
Shingles and shakes	Cedar shingles are graded: #1 ("blue label") are best; #2 ("red label") are acceptable as underlayment when double-coursing (applying two layers). Also available in specialty patterns. Widths are random 3"–14". Lengths are 16" (shingles only), 18", and 24". Shakes are thicker than shingles, with butts $3/8"$–$3/4"$ thick. Primarily sold unpainted, but also available prestained, painted, and treated with fire retardant or preservative.	20 to 40 years, depending on heat, humidity, and maintenance.
Vinyl	Extruded from polyvinyl chloride (PVC) in white and light colors. Smooth and wood-grain textures are typical. Horizontal panels simulate lap boards. Vertical panels simulate boards with battens. Standard length is 12', 6".	40 years to life of structure.
Aluminum	Extruded panels in a wide range of factory-baked colors, textures. Types and dimensions are the same as vinyl. Also sold as 12"-by-36" or 12"-by-48" panels of simulated cedar shakes.	40 years to life of structure.
Steel	Extruded panels in a wide range of factory-baked colors, smooth and wood-grain textures. Types and dimensions are the same as vinyl.	40 years to life of structure.
Brick and stone veneers	Thin bricks or stones or cultured synthetic masonry materials $1/2"$–4" thick. Sold in individual units or panelized. Applied over wood framing.	Life of structure.
Stucco systems	Traditional compound made from fine sand, portland cement, hydrated lime, and water. Applied wet over wire lath in two or three coats. Pigment added to final coat, or surface can be painted when dry. Newer polymers are sprayed onto foam- or fiber-cement board sheathing.	Life of structure.

complement many architectural styles. Exceptionally resistant to pests, fire, and impact, they require little maintenance. Because of their high cost, masonry materials are often used to provide a decorative accent to less expensive sidings. For about half the price of real stone, manufactured stone offers a similar look and easier installation. It can be installed directly over many types of siding.

MAINTENANCE	INSTALLATION	ADVANTAGES & DISADVANTAGES
Before using, seal all edges with water repellent. Needs painting every 4–6 years, transparent staining every 3–5 years, or finishing with water repellent every 2 years.	Difficulty varies with pattern. Most are manageable with basic skills and tools.	Easy to handle, tool, and finish. Burns. Prone to split, crack, warp, peel (if painted). Any species other than cedar and redwood must be finished to protect against termites and rot.
Before using, seal all edges with water repellent, stain sealer, or exterior house paint primer. Restain or repaint every 5 years.	Sheets go up quickly. Manageable with basic carpentry skills and tools.	Can add great structural support to a wall. Burns. May "check" (show small surface cracks). Susceptible to termite damage when in direct contact with soil and to water rot if not properly finished.
Before using, seal all edges with water repellent, stain sealer, or exterior house paint primer. Paint or stain unprimed and pre-primed hardboard within 60 days of installation; repeat every 5 years.	Sheets go up quickly. Manageable with basic carpentry skills and tools.	Uniform appearance, without defects typical of wood. Many textures, designs. Accepts finishes well. Lacks plywood's strength. Susceptible to termite damage when in direct contact with soil, and to water rot and buckling if not properly finished.
In hot, humid climates, apply fungicide/mildew retardant every 3 years. In dry climates, preserve resiliency with oil finish every 5 years.	Time-consuming but manageable with basic carpentry skills and tools plus a roofer's hatchet.	Rustic wood appearance. Easy to handle, install, and repair. Adapts well to intricate architectural styles. Burns. Prone to rot, splinter, crack, and cup. May be pried loose by wind. Changes color with age unless treated with stain or preservative.
Hose off annually.	Manageable with basic skills and tools.	Won't rot, rust, peel, or blister. Easy to apply. Light colors only. Sun may cause fading.
Hose off annually. Clean surface stains with nonabrasive detergent. Refinish with paint recommended by the manufacturer.	Manageable with mostly basic skills and tools.	Won't rot, rust, or blister. Fireproof. Impervious to termites. Lightweight and easy to handle. Dents, scratches easily. May corrode.
Hose off annually. Paint scratches to prevent rust.	Best reserved for professionals.	Won't rot, blister, burn, or be eaten by bugs. Difficult to handle and cut. Rusts if scratched.
Hose off annually.	Professionals only.	Fireproof, durable, and very solid. Professional installation is expensive.
Hose off annually. If painted, repaint as condition requires.	Professionals only.	Fireproof, durable, solid, and seamless. Can be painted any color. Professional installation is expensive. Real stucco can crack with building movement.

exterior wall construction

IF YOU ARE REPAIRING OR REPLACING SIDING, IT IS IMPORTANT TO UNDERSTAND how exterior house walls are built. Here we look at how exterior wood-frame walls are clad with a variety of siding materials.

Wall construction varies slightly, depending upon the type of material that is to be applied as a siding. Various available sidings are discussed on pages 298–299, but for an overview of construction methods, this book divides these types into three categories: 1) wood and manufactured sidings such as vinyl and aluminum, 2) stucco and related coatings, and 3) brick and masonry sidings.

Wood-frame walls are usually constructed from 2-by-6 or 2-by-4 studs. Insulation is placed between the studs, which are then covered with a sheathing of wood-based panels or insulation board. Depending on the type of siding to be used, building paper or house wrap may be applied over the sheathing to provide an additional layer of weatherproofing.

Finally, the siding is nailed on. Or, in the case of masonry walls, a veneer of brick or stone is applied. With masonry, each course of bricks or stones is attached to the underlayment with short metal strips called ties, and the bricks or stones are mortared in place.

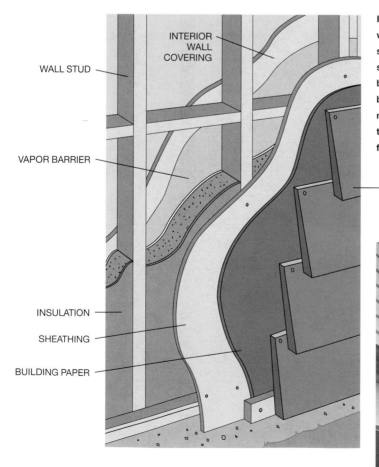

INTERIOR WALL COVERING

WALL STUD

VAPOR BARRIER

INSULATION

SHEATHING

BUILDING PAPER

SIDING

If walls are to be finished with wood, aluminum, steel, or vinyl siding, the sheathing is covered with building paper. The siding boards or panels are then nailed on, lapped from the bottom up to allow for water runoff.

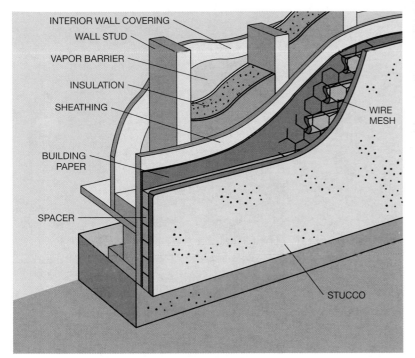

Labels (top diagram):
INTERIOR WALL COVERING
WALL STUD
VAPOR BARRIER
INSULATION
SHEATHING
BUILDING PAPER
SPACER
WIRE MESH
STUCCO

For standard stucco siding, wire mesh is nailed directly to sheathing covered with building paper and, sometimes, to spacers. Stucco is applied over the wire mesh in three layers. In a contemporary variation of this time-honored method, many contractors now install EIFS, stucco-like systems that use special backer-boards with polymer-based coatings.

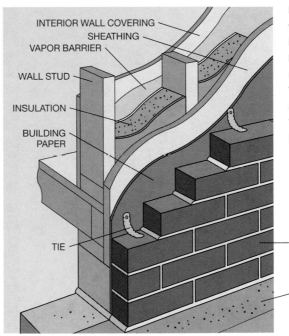

Labels (masonry diagram):
INTERIOR WALL COVERING
SHEATHING
VAPOR BARRIER
WALL STUD
INSULATION
BUILDING PAPER
TIE
BRICK
FOUNDATION

For masonry walls, a veneer of brick or stone is attached outside the building paper with short metal strips called ties. Then the bricks or stones are mortared in place. Their weight is supported by part of the foundation.

WOOD-SIDING VARIATIONS

Most wood-siding patterns are milled with special overlapping or interlocking edges and in beveled or tapered profiles. The types that lock together, such as tongue-and-groove, do not allow for expansion or contraction and so are prone to problems. Though most patterns are meant to be installed horizontally, some are milled for vertical installation. Widths run 4, 5, 6, 8, 10, and 12 inches; boards are given nominal dimensions before drying and milling, so each size is actually about 1/2 inch smaller than its proclaimed width. Widths of 8 inches or narrower shrink less than larger sizes and do not have the same tendency to cup.

BASIC TOOLS FOR SIDING

Ball-peen hammer

Bevel gauge

Block plane

Brick trowel

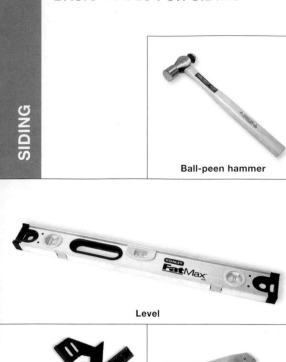
Level

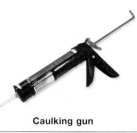
Caulking gun

Claw hammer

Cold chisel

Combination square

Hand stapler

Chalk line

Hawk

Handsaw

Jointer

Measuring tape

Nail claw

Power circular saw

Prybar

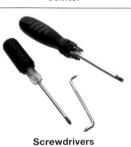
Screwdrivers

Stepladder

Pneumatic stapler or nailer

Wood chisel

Roofer's hatchet

Saber saw (jigsaw)

Stepladder

Tin snips

Utility knife

Zipper (for vinyl siding)

siding tools

FOR MOST SIDING INSTALLATION WORK, YOU NEED QUITE A FEW CARPENTRY tools, as well as protective gear such as gloves and safety glasses. At least one ladder and, particularly if you will be working up high along walls, scaffolding are required (for more about ladders and scaffolding, see page 38).

Most of the tools on these pages are needed for installation and repairs to wood siding. Depending upon the work you are tackling, you may also need a few of the specialty tools shown. For removing shingles, a shingle ripper is a very helpful tool. For cutting sheet metal, use tin snips. For bricks or other masonry siding, you will likely need a ball-peen hammer and a cold chisel—along with a hawk, a trowel, and a jointer. Working with vinyl and aluminum calls for a special tool called a zipper. To prepare siding for repainting, use the equipment discussed on pages 68–69.

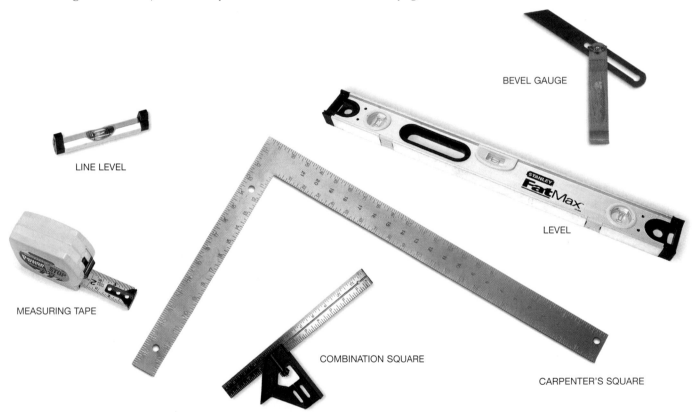

BEVEL GAUGE

LINE LEVEL

LEVEL

MEASURING TAPE

COMBINATION SQUARE

CARPENTER'S SQUARE

CHALK LINE

STUD FINDER

MEASURING & MARKING TOOLS

For basic layout and measuring during siding installation, you will need some or all of the tools shown here. For measuring, use a measuring tape that has markings for stud layouts along its blade every 16 and 24 inches. A carpenter's square and combination square are important for marking and checking square cuts, and a bevel gauge is helpful for transferring angles to be cut. For establishing level across a long distance such as an entire wall, use a line level; a conventional level works better for checking level and plumb as you work. Use a chalk line to snap long, straight lines for layout or cutting.

CUTTING TOOLS

For cutting wood siding and sheathing, use a power circular saw; a handsaw also comes in handy for places where the power saw will not easily go. Use a saber saw to cut curves. Use a block plane and perforated rasp to shave down boards for a tight fit. One or more chisels are handy for cutting out notches; you can use a cold chisel for chipping or cutting masonry. Tin snips are necessary for cutting metal flashing. Use a utility knife for marking lines, cutting building paper, and other jobs.

POWER CIRCULAR SAW

UTILITY KNIFE

HANDSAW

CONSTRUCTION TOOLS

Installing siding calls for a variety of basic carpentry tools, including those shown here. In addition to a claw hammer, a roofer's hatchet is excellent for installing shingle siding. For the power drill, be sure you have a set of drill bits and Phillips-head screwdriver bits. A hand stapler is utilized to fasten building paper and insulation. A pneumatic stapler or nailer can greatly speed up siding installation. If you are installing or repairing vinyl siding, you will also need a zipper for locking the pieces together. If you are working with masonry or brick siding, your work will require a ball-peen hammer and cold chisel for cutting the masonry. For holding, applying, and finishing mortar, you will need a hawk, a trowel, and a jointer.

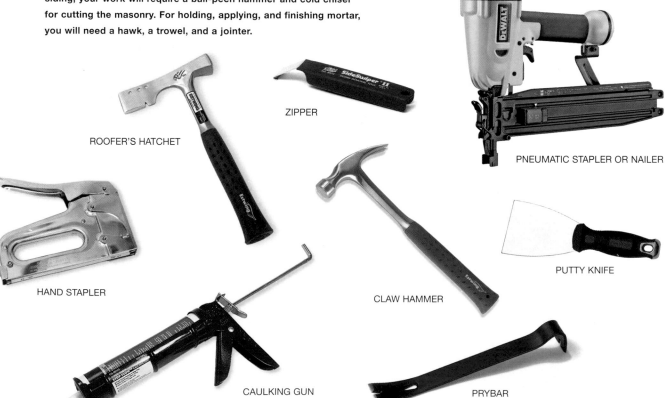

ROOFER'S HATCHET

ZIPPER

PNEUMATIC STAPLER OR NAILER

HAND STAPLER

CLAW HAMMER

PUTTY KNIFE

CAULKING GUN

PRYBAR

PERFORATED RASP

SABER SAW (JIGSAW)

WOOD CHISEL

COLD CHISEL

TIN SNIPS

BLOCK PLANE

SCREWDRIVERS

BRICK TROWEL

JOINTER

NAIL CLAW

HAWK

BALL-PEEN HAMMER

POWER DRILL WITH BITS
AND SCREWDRIVER TIPS

STEPLADDER

preparing to re-side

SIDING A HOUSE IS A BIG JOB. THOUGH YOU MAY BE ABLE TO SAVE ABOUT HALF THE job's cost by doing the work yourself, be realistic about what is involved. You should be willing to take on the heavy labor, and you should be careful, competent with tools, adept at following instructions, and able, if necessary, to adapt instructions to the eccentricities of your house. If you live in a large house or a tall one perched on a hillside, seriously consider hiring a contractor to install siding.

SIDING

estimating your needs

Figuring the amount of siding you will need to cover your house is usually just a matter of measuring exterior walls, calculating the square footage, and adjusting the resulting figures for waste. A easy way to do this is to divide the surfaces to be covered into rectangles, and calculate the area of each by multiplying its length by its width.

Add together all the areas you have computed. Then (except for sheet sidings, such as plywood—see below), subtract the areas of windows, doors, chimneys, and other places the new siding will not cover. The result is approximately how many square feet of siding you need; add 10 percent for waste. If your house has steep angles at its gables or other features that will require a lot of cutting, add another 15 percent to the total amount.

Be sure to take into account the overlap of most board sidings. It takes about 1,240 square feet of 8-inch horizontal bevel siding, for example, to cover 1,000 square feet of wall space. Manufacturers offer charts, based on their specific patterns, to help you estimate your needs.

Vinyl and aluminum sidings are usually sold by the number of square feet a given amount covers. When ordering, you must also estimate how many linear feet of various trim pieces you need.

Plywood and hardboard sheets are sold in sizes that correlate directly with square footage. Add 10 percent for normal waste and, if your house has sharply angled walls, another 15 percent for extra cutting.

preparing the walls

If you are siding over an existing wall that is flat and sound, you may be able to nail new siding directly over it. On the other hand, if the existing siding is metal, vinyl, or masonry, or is irregular, you must either strip it off or provide a nailing base of furring strips on top of it (see pages 308–309).

For siding removal, use a claw hammer and a flat prybar for prying, and a "cat's paw" and a pair of locking pliers for pulling nails. When removing most types of siding, start at the top and work your way down. If you want to avoid marring the wood, use the cat's paw on the first board, and then use a prybar to pry up subsequent boards and pull the nails.

To remove shingles and shakes from a wall, insert a square-bottom shovel underneath them, lift them up, and pull them off, working from the top down on the wall. Pull out any remaining nails.

Removing stucco is hard work; if at all possible, apply new siding over the old surface. For an extensive removal job, call a demolition contractor.

ASBESTOS-CEMENT SHINGLES

Because of cancer risks associated with airborne asbestos particles, asbestos-cement shingles should only be removed by an asbestos-abatement contractor. The Environmental Protection Agency and the Consumer Product Safety Commission recommend leaving inert asbestos alone unless it is flaking or crumbling. To find out your state and local regulations, contact public health agencies. Some experts recommend leaving asbestos shingles in place and covering them with vinyl or aluminum siding.

sheathing the walls

Most new walls need sheathing to strengthen them, to act as a nailing base for siding, and/or to boost insulation. Existing walls usually do not require sheathing unless you are stripping off the old siding and applying a different type that calls for sheathing. Be sure to check the siding manufacturer's directions and local codes to determine whether sheathing is required.

There are two types of sheathing: structural and nonstructural.

structural sheathing This type is integral to the house's framing. It ties together wall studs, contributing shear strength and rigidity and forming a solid nailing base for siding materials. Most structural sheathings do not add much insulation value.

Common structural sheathings include plywood, oriented strand board (OSB), waferboard, and exterior gypsum board.

When choosing plywood, OSB, or waferboard panels, be sure they are rated as wall sheathing, and choose an appropriate thickness. Although you can use panels as thin as $5/16$ inch for some applications, it is usually a good idea to spend a little bit more for sturdier $1/2$-inch panels. The most common panel size is 4 by 8 feet, but you can also get some products in 4-by-9- and 4-by-10-foot sheets.

Using 6d (2-inch) galvanized nails, fasten panels (usually horizontally) to wall studs, spacing nails 6 inches apart along the panels' edges and 12 inches apart mid-panel (or as specified by your local building codes). Allow an expansion gap of $1/16$ inch between panel ends and $1/8$ inch between panel edges.

nonstructural sheathing This type of sheathing does not add significantly to a wall's strength but can greatly increase its insulation value. Rigid foam and cellulose-fiber panels may be attached directly to wall studs or masonry walls, under or over structural sheathing (depending upon nailing requirements), or, in some cases, over existing siding before re-siding.

ABOVE: **This exterior gypsum board sheathing is faced with fiberglass mats instead of paper for excellent resistance to moisture and mold.**
LEFT: **Plywood sheathing is often the material of choice because of its strength and the ease of handling it.**

The two most common types of foam board sheathing materials are extruded polystyrene or polyisocyanurate. Polyisocyanurate has higher per-inch insulation (R) values—up to R-8.7 per inch—than polystyrene. For more information about R-values, see page 543.

Foam board thicknesses range from $3/8$ inch to $4 1/4$ inches. For covering existing siding, $1/2$-inch and $3/4$-inch thicknesses are commonly used. Standard panels are 2 by 8, 4 by 8, and 4 by 9 feet, though some can be purchased in fan-folded panels that run up to 50 feet long.

Which type of panels to choose, and which side to face outward, depends upon the makeup of your walls and the siding you are applying. As a rule, use panels with either reflective aluminum or matte facings beneath brick, stucco, and certain wood sidings. Non-foil-faced panels are generally recommended beneath aluminum, vinyl, and wood-based sidings.

Most foam and cellulose panels are extremely lightweight and capable of being cut with a utility knife. Nail the panels to wall studs with large-headed galvanized nails long enough to penetrate studs by at least 1 inch. Space nails according to the manufacturer's instructions. (Because these panels are not structural, 12-inch spacing is usually sufficient.) Drive nails flush, being careful not to crush the panels with your final hammer blow.

Fire codes and safety may affect how nonstructural panels are applied because of combustibility. Be sure to follow manufacturer's instructions in this regard.

applying building paper

Building paper, a black felt or kraft paper impregnated with asphalt, is applied between the sheathing (or the unsheathed studs) and the siding to resist wind and water without trapping moist air. It comes in rolls that are 36 to 40 inches wide and long enough to cover 200 to 500 square feet (allowing for overlap).

Though some building codes require the use of building paper, others do not. You may want to apply it anyway if your siding will be subjected to either heavy winds or wind-driven rain or snow. You should especially consider this if your siding consists of boards or shingles that present numerous places for wind and water to penetrate.

applying house wrap

Air infiltration typically causes more than 20 percent of a house's heat loss. To protect against this, many builders now apply house wrap before installing siding. This spun-bonded or woven polymer material keeps water and drafts out yet breathes so it does not trap moisture in the walls.

It comes in 8-foot-wide rolls and is easy and quick to install. On a still day when you have a helper, start at one corner of the house and, holding the roll vertically, unroll about 6 feet of the material. Let it overlap the corner by about 12 inches, and fasten it in place with "cap nails" (roofing nails that have a plastic or metal washer-type head). Keep the material plumb and the bottom edge aligned with the foundation line. Secure the material every 12 to 18 inches along the studs. Most types of house wrap have stud lines marked on the fabric; align the first sheet, and the others should automatically fall on subsequent studs. Lap the wrap by about 2 inches between sheets, and seal seams with special house-wrap tape. Finally, cut out the window and door openings.

attaching furring strips

If your present siding is masonry or is otherwise bumpy and irregular, you may need to install a base of furring strips, generally a grid of 1-by-3 boards or strips placed to provide flat nailing support for the new siding at appropriate intervals. Be aware that furring out a wall or applying siding directly over the top of old siding will add to the

Cut building paper with a utility knife. Staple the paper to studs or sheathing to hold it in place until the siding is installed. Apply the paper in horizontal strips, starting at the bottom of each wall and working up. Overlap 2 inches at horizontal joints and 6 inches at vertical joints. Wrap the paper at least 12 inches around each corner.

PLYWOOD SHEATHING

BUILDING PAPER

STRIPS STAPLED AROUND WINDOWS AND DOORS.

2" OVERLAP

6" OVERLAP

LEVEL CHALK LINE

8" MINIMUM

wall's thickness, which will affect how window jambs and doorjambs are trimmed at the surface (see below).

Use a long, straight board or taut line to determine where it is necessary to shim furring strips in order to create a flat plane. To shim, tap wood shingles between the wall and furring strips. Check furring strips for plumb before you nail them in place, and adjust them if necessary.

Secure the strips every 12 inches with nails that are long enough to penetrate studs by at least 1 inch. If the existing walls are masonry, you will need to use concrete nails or masonry anchors.

preparing windows & doors

Unless you strip the walls first, furring strips and new siding will add to your walls' thickness. For both weatherproofing and appearance, it is usually necessary to build up the jambs and sills of windows and doors to compensate for the added thickness. Depending upon your particular situation, it may be easier to add jamb extensions after applying the new siding, as shown in the illustration at top right. (For synthetic sidings, special add-on trim pieces are provided to handle this.)

flashing siding

Flashing prevents water that runs down a wall from penetrating the joints between materials. Standard galvanized and aluminum flashing is available at Lowe's home improvement centers. Types made for vinyl and metal sidings are sold by siding manufacturers. Specialty flashings and flashings made of copper are usually custom fabricated at sheet-metal shops.

Use only galvanized nails for galvanized flashing, aluminum nails for aluminum, and bronze nails for copper flashing. Combining differing metals can cause corrosive electrolysis that may weaken nails as well as stain siding.

establishing a baseline

No matter what siding you install, you must align its lowest edge along the base

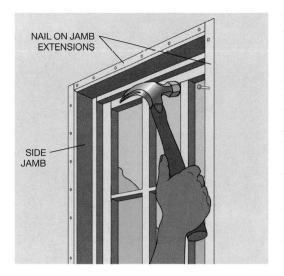

NAIL ON JAMB EXTENSIONS

SIDE JAMB

To add a jamb extension, first gently pry off the old exterior trim. Extend wood jambs by adding small wood strips to them. Cut extenders to the same width as the jambs and deep enough to be flush with the siding's surface. Nail on the top piece, then the sides, and finally the sill. Fill any gaps between old and new with wood putty. Sand the area flush.

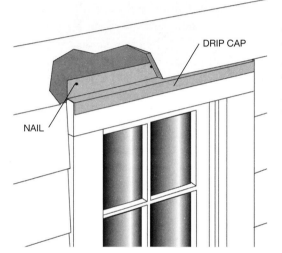

DRIP CAP

NAIL

Before applying siding, be sure L- or Z-shaped drip caps protect the tops of wood window and door frames. Cut them with tin snips. Position nails where siding will cover them.

of each wall by snapping a level chalk line no less than 8 inches above grade (ground level). When applying new siding over old, the line is usually set 1 inch below the lower edge of the existing siding.

Excavate any surrounding soil that interferes with this 8-inch clearance, sloping the grade away from the house so water will not pool by the foundation. You may find it necessary to step the siding (adjust the baseline up or down) to conform to a hillside or irregular grade. If you are applying horizontal siding, shingles, or shakes, work out the sizes of the required steps so they correspond with the planned exposure for each course.

If you do not have a helper, stretch the chalk line from a concrete nail pounded into the foundation wall. (Use one at each end if necessary.)

applying lap siding

BEFORE YOU START NAILING UP SIDING BOARDS, BE SURE TO READ THROUGH THE information on preparing the wall, beginning on page 306. When you have the siding delivered, allow the wood to acclimate to local humidity. Store boards flat, raised above the ground on blocks or scraps. To make painting or staining the siding easier later on, prime or pre-finish it before installation and then touch up the cut ends as you work.

Plan your layout, and decide how you will treat the corners. When working out your layout, try to allow the siding boards to fit seamlessly around windows, doors, and other openings. With horizontal siding, a slight adjustment to your baseline may do the trick. Where you must butt board ends together, stagger the joints.

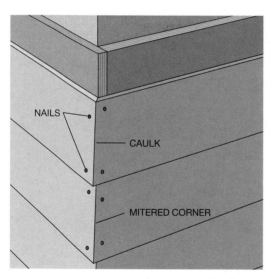

For an outside corner, you can miter the board ends so that no end grain is visible or exposed to the elements. This method takes a fairly high degree of craftsmanship but, when done well, looks great.

One easy way to handle an outside corner is to butt the siding boards against a vertical 1 by 3 and 1 by 4. When joining these vertical boards end to end, miter the joint at a 45-degree angle, with the cuts sloping downward to ensure proper water runoff.

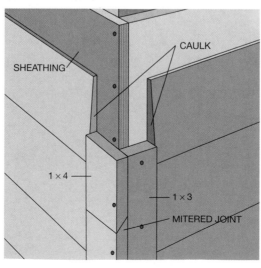

nailing Nail each board individually; do not nail through overlapping parts. Be careful not to dent the board's surface when nailing. Use stainless-steel, high-tensile aluminum or hot-dipped galvanized siding or box nails. Spiral or ring-shank nails offer the best holding power.

Choose nails that are long enough to penetrate the studs by at least $1\frac{1}{4}$ inches. Boards that are 6 inches wide and narrower require only one nail per stud; wider boards require two.

cutting Mark all 90-degree cuts using a combination square. Then do the cutting with a power circular saw, a handsaw, or (if available) a table saw or radial-arm saw.

first board The first board goes at the bottom. Most types require a 1-by-2 starter strip beneath the board's lower edge, along the wall's base, so the first board's angle will match the angle of the other boards.

successive boards To lay out horizontal board siding, you will need to use a "story pole," made from a 1 by 2 that is as long as your tallest wall's height (unless that wall is more than one story). Make it as shown in Step 3 on page 312.

corners & tops of walls When you are installing horizontal siding, determine whether the cornice will be open or closed (see page 317) before nailing the last board in place at the top of the wall. Where the boards must be cut at an angle to match the roofline, figure out and cut the angle as shown in Step 7 on page 312.

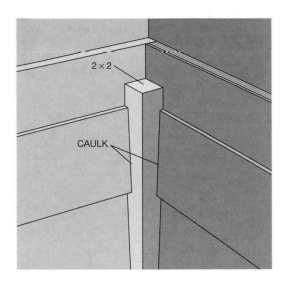

2 × 2

CAULK

At inside corners, run a length of 2 by 2 vertically, and butt the siding board ends against it. Caulk along the joints.

USING A STARTER STRIP

Establish the proper angle for the first board by running a 1-by-2 starter strip beneath the board's lower edge, along the base of the wall.

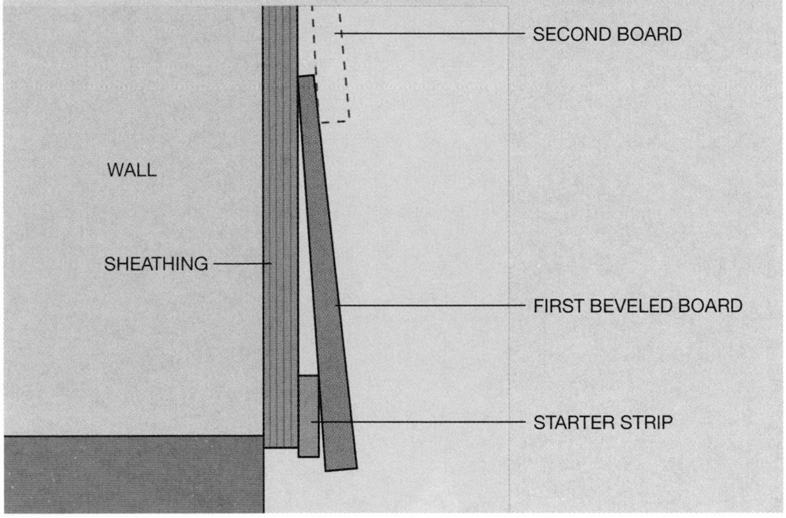

WALL

SHEATHING

SECOND BOARD

FIRST BEVELED BOARD

STARTER STRIP

open & closed cornices Cornices (sometimes called soffits) are often left open with wood-board siding so that the boards extend to the tops of the rafters. For this method, notch the board ends where they intersect rafters, and caulk the ends thoroughly once they are in place. Trim along the top edge, between the rafters, using quarter-round moulding or a narrow trim board (called a "frieze board").

If you prefer a closed cornice, you can build one using a special wood board called a plowed fascia board plus roofing material. A plowed fascia board, nailed over the rafter ends or existing fascia, has a routed groove near one edge for holding soffit boards or panels, as shown in the drawing on page 317.

1 Build a corner trim from a 1 by 3 and a 1 by 4, and then snap a level chalk line to indicate the top edge of the first length of siding. Next, measure down the width of your siding, and run a 1-by-2 starter strip along the wall's base to hold the first siding board at the proper angle.

2 Butt the first siding board in place against the corner, so that its top edge is aligned with the chalk line. Have a helper hold one end as you nail the other. Drive galvanized nails through the siding into the starter strip, spacing them 6 inches apart.

LOWE'S QUICK TIP
If siding boards tend to split, try blunting the nail tips with a hammer. Otherwise, predrill nail holes, using a drill bit that is slightly smaller than the nails' diameter.

PROJECT CONTINUES ➡

3 Make a story pole for transferring measurements from one corner to the next and to window and door frames. To make this, mark a 1 by 2 at intervals equaling the width of the siding boards. Then transfer these marks to each corner.

4 Overlap 1 inch of the first siding board with the second one, aligning the ends of the second board with the story-pole marks at the corners. Be sure the board fits snugly up against each corner, straight along its length and level, and then nail it in place. Place the nails about 1 inch up from the lower edge.

5 Repeat this process as you apply the other siding boards up the wall. Use the story pole to transfer the marks for siding placement onto the door and window frames.

6 Where two siding boards must be joined end-to-end, plan to center the joint over a framing member. Make very straight cuts to form a snug butt joint. Apply caulking compound to the board ends, nail them in place, and wipe off excess caulk.

7 If you'll be applying siding under gabled eaves (where the roofline is angled like the one shown), use a bevel gauge to establish the proper angle for cutting the boards. Transfer this angle to each board end, and then cut.

repairing wood siding

IN TIME, EVEN THE BEST-MAINTAINED WOOD SIDING BEGINS TO SHOW SIGNS OF deterioration. The most common problem you are likely to come up against is rot. If the damage is limited, you can dig out the bad wood with a scraper or old screwdriver and fill in the hole with vinyl exterior spackling compound or wood filler.

1 Mark the cuts you will make at each end of the damaged section. Drive small wedges up under the board directly above the damaged one on each side of the two marked lines. Using a keyhole saw, make straight cuts across both ends of the damaged board as shown.

2 Use a miniature hacksaw to cut off any nails holding the damaged piece in place. Alternatively, you can split the damaged section with a chisel, pull out the pieces, and then pry out the nails. Repair any tears in the building paper with roofing cement.

If the damage is spread across an entire siding panel or there is not enough wood left to hold a repair, the entire section of siding will have to be replaced.

Before you repair any damage, you will want to determine the cause of the problem, which is most likely moisture. Leaks in gutters or roofing are common culprits, so repair them before painting (see the Roofing chapter, starting on page 330).

When the source of moisture is not obvious, look into hiring a professional. If you do not remedy the cause of the problem, the repaired surface will only begin to disintegrate again.

3 Cut the replacement piece to fit, and then drive it up into position with a hammer. Protect the edge of the piece from being damaged by the hammer by holding a scrap block against it as shown. Nail the new piece through the existing nail holes and along the bottom edge. Putty the nail holes and the board ends with wood filler, and then sand the area before painting.

applying panel siding

PLYWOOD AND HARDBOARD SIDING PANELS ARE POPULAR BECAUSE THEIR LARGE 4-by-8-, 4-by-9-, or 4-by-10-foot sizes give quick coverage. And, plywood's strength can eliminate the need for bracing and sheathing on a new wall's frame (check your local building codes). Hardboard panels, nailed on according to the manufacturer's specifications, can also provide shear strength.

Though codes may not demand the use of building paper or house wrap beneath plywood, it is a good idea to install this extra barrier under either plywood or hardboard sidings, particularly if the panel edges do not interlock or are not covered with battens. It is also important to brush all siding panel edges with a water sealant prior to installation.

Plywood panel siding, mounted vertically, accents this home's architectural lines.

Panels may be mounted either vertically or horizontally. The preferred method is vertical installation because it minimizes the number of horizontal joints, which provides for better waterproofing and also is more aesthetically pleasing. If you choose a horizontal pattern, stagger vertical end joints, and nail the long, horizontal edges into fire blocks or other nailing supports. In most cases, these joints must be flashed or caulked. (To learn more about wall framing, see pages 300–301.) Because hardboard is not as strong as plywood, it often is applied over sheathing.

Plywood and hardboard lap sidings (as opposed to panels) are installed with methods similar to those used for installing board sidings. For more information, see pages 310–311.

nailing Fasten the panels with 6d (2-inch) or 8d (2½-inch) corrosion-resistant common or box nails, depending upon the manufacturer's recommendations for application to your nailing base. For re-siding over wood boards or sheathing, use hot-dipped galvanized ring-shank nails. Do not use finishing nails, staples, T nails, or bugle-head nails. Hardboard manufacturers sell nails with heads colored to match factory finishes on the panels.

The nails should be long enough to penetrate studs or other backing by at least 1½ inches. For new siding nailed directly to the studs, use 6d (2-inch) nails for ⅜-inch or ½-inch panels and 8d (2½-inch) nails for ⅝-inch panels. Nail every 6 inches around the perimeter of each sheet and every 12 inches along studs or furring. If hardboard panels are meant to supply shear strength where not applied over sheathing, space nails every 4 inches around the perimeter and intermediately every 8 inches along studs.

When driving in nails, be very careful not to dimple the panel's surface with the last hammer blow. Do not set nail heads below the surface.

When you nail a panel, first tack it in position with nails at each corner (leave these nail heads protruding so you can pull them if necessary). Then nail from top to bottom along one edge (the edge adjoining the preceding panel). Move on to the next stud or furring strip and nail along it, move to the next support, and then continue on. This method prevents the panel from buckling in the center.

measuring for height Before you begin putting up panels, decide how long they should be. To do this, measure from the base chalk line to the soffit. If you plan to create a closed cornice, it may be simpler to install the soffit before the siding panels. If you find the distance from baseline to soffit is longer than the siding sheets, you will need to join the panels end to end, using one of the methods for horizontal joints shown on page 316.

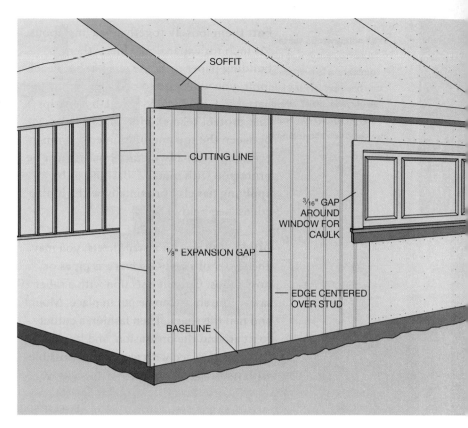

SOFFIT

CUTTING LINE

3/16" GAP AROUND WINDOW FOR CAULK

1/8" EXPANSION GAP

EDGE CENTERED OVER STUD

BASELINE

the first sheet Position the first sheet at an outside corner, keeping its bottom edge flush with the baseline and the inside vertical edge centered over a stud, furring strip, or other firm backing. Use a carpenter's level to make sure the vertical edges are plumb. If the corner is not plumb, you will need to trim the panel edge to align with it. Hold or tack the sheet in place, flush with the baseline, and trace along the outermost points of the existing siding or framing from top to bottom.

Take the panel down, and cut along the line you traced, using a circular saw or handsaw. Nail the trimmed panel in place.

successive sheets The next sheet butts against the first sheet, often with an overlapping shiplap vertical edge (see more about edge details on page 316). Leave a 1/16-inch expansion gap at all joints (in humid climates, leave 1/8 inch). Sheets must join over studs, blocking, or other sturdy backing. Be careful not to nail through both parts of the laps.

If your panel does not have a shiplap edge, caulk along the vertical edges, and

When installing panel siding, tack the first sheet in place, so that it is flush with the baseline and inward edge. Be sure it is perfectly plumb and centered over a wall stud. Align the second panel with the edge of the first. Cut panels to fit around windows or doors, allowing a 3/16-inch gap for a bead of caulk.

PLY

handling corners & trim

With aluminum and vinyl systems, the trim is installed first, around the house baseline and window and door frames and against soffit or gable edges. Panels are then fitted into it. (See the drawings on page 318 for a typical system, its basic components, and how all the various corner posts and trim pieces fit in place.)

installing posts

Position each post by driving two nails through the top of the uppermost slots; the post should hang from the nails. Use a level to check for vertical alignment. Then fasten the posts with nails every 12 inches. If you must stack one corner post above another, trim 1/4 inch from the nailing flange at the bottom end of the top post. Then mount the top post so it overlaps the lower one by about 1 inch.

installing a starter strip

Install the starter strip (for horizontal siding) or vertical base trim (for vertical siding) along the base chalk line.

Align the upper edge of the base trim with the chalk line, and nail every 6 inches. When you come to an outside corner, allow 1/4 inch (vinyl) or 1/8 inch (aluminum) for expansion between the starter strip or base trim and the corner post.

installing door & window trim

Your next step is to mount strips of appropriate trim around window and door openings. To reduce moisture and air flow, however, first run a bead of caulk around the openings, forming a seal.

When you install door and window trim, do the top first, then the sides, and finally the under-sill trim. Aluminum fittings are often folded, while vinyl is not.

Along the tops of doors and windows, install J-channel trim (when using horizontal siding) or vertical base trim (when using vertical panels). Use lengths of trim that measure two channel widths longer than the top of the opening; either miter the ends or cut tabs at each end. Nail 12 inches on center.

Along the sides, use mitered trim if the top trim is mitered. When fitting the side pieces, position the top nail at the top of the nailing slot, but drive all of the remaining trim nails every 12 inches into the slots' centers.

To avoid problems when fitting horizontal panels into narrow places, fasten down the trim along only one side. Trim on the other side of the area can be fastened as panels are put in place. Under windows, install under-sill trim for horizontal siding or J-channel trim for vertical. Add furring strips where necessary to maintain the slope of the siding.

installing trim under eaves & rakes

If you are installing horizontal siding, use F-channel trim at the soffit and gable rake. For vertical panels, use J-channel trim. Nail 12 inches on center. Add furring strips if they are needed.

working with horizontal panels

Allowing for expansion (1/4 inch for vinyl and 1/8 inch for aluminum) where the panel falls into the J channel, fit and securely lock the starter panel into the starter strip. If you are installing the insulating backerboard that comes with some sidings, drop it behind the panel, with its beveled edge down and toward the wall.

Fit the soffit panels into F channels installed both along the wall and along the fascia.

SOFFIT PANELS   FASCIA

F CHANNELS

WALL

fitting end joints Where panels meet, overlap the ends by 1 inch. Run overlaps away from the most obvious focal point on each wall so joints will be less obtrusive. When overlapping, cut 1½ inches of the nailing flange away from the end of one panel to allow for expansion.

Some vinyl and most aluminum horizontal sidings use backer tabs at joints to make the material more stable over long spans. Slip the backer tabs, flat side out, behind the joints, and try to offset the joints at least 24 inches from one course to the next.

fitting panels around openings To trim panels around windows and doors, use a sharp knife, tin snips, or a power saw. Do not use the tin snips to cut the locking detail at the panel's lower edge.

Measure window and door openings, and cut panels to fit, allowing ¼ inch (for vinyl) or ⅛ inch (for aluminum) for expansion. Before fitting cut vinyl panels to the under-sill trim, use a snap-lock punch to crimp nubs or "ears" along the trimmed edge. The ears, spaced 6 to 8 inches apart, should face outward so they can hook onto the under-sill trim.

With aluminum siding, gutter-seal adhesive holds panels under windowsills and at soffits. The gutter seal serves the same purpose as the ears crimped on vinyl.

To fit horizontal panels into narrow places, slip each panel into the trim along one side; as successive panels go into place, nail down the trim along the other side.

installing top panels at eaves First, measure from the bottom of the top lock to the eaves, and subtract ¼ inch (for vinyl) or ⅛ inch (for aluminum) for expansion. To determine the width of the final panel, measure in several places along the eaves.

Cut the panel, and use the snap-lock punch to crimp ears every 6 to 8 inches along the upper edge. Tuck the panel into the trim. At the gables, cut panels at an angle to fit into the J channels, F channels, or quarter-round mouldings along the gable rake. Crimp ears as for window trim.

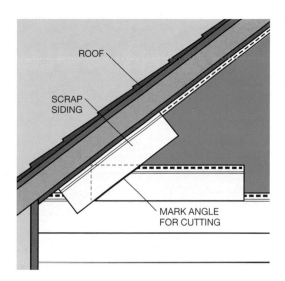

ROOF

SCRAP SIDING

MARK ANGLE FOR CUTTING

To mark the angled roofline on a panel for cutting, hold a piece of scrap siding in line with the roof and then use it as a guide.

handling vertical panels

Once the corner posts and trim are positioned, locate the center of each wall, and, using a level and a straightedge, draw a line down the center. Allowing ¼ inch (for vinyl) or ⅛ inch (for aluminum) for expansion at the top, center the first panel over the line. Fasten it every 8 inches with nails at the top of the nailing slots.

Working from this starter panel, install successive panels. These should each be long enough to fit between the trim strips, minus ¼ inch (for vinyl) or ⅛ inch (for aluminum) for expansion. Panels should rest on the vertical base trim. Insert each panel into the J channel along the top of the wall. Letting the panel rest on the vertical base trim, lock it into the previous panel.

Position nails for successive panels in the slot centers. Space them every 8 to 16 inches (depending on the manufacturer's recommendations).

When fitting vertical panels around windows and doors, follow the instructions on the facing page.

Before you insert the last panels into the corner posts, be sure to install J or U channels or under-sill trim in the corner-post slots (manufacturers' instructions vary). To keep panels on the same plane, raise the J channels with ⁵⁄₁₆-inch shims. Then insert uncut panel edges into the J channel. Cut edges of flat sections should be inserted between the J channel and the post's outer flange.

LOWE'S QUICK TIP
If you intend to put vinyl covers on windowsills and casings, do so before installing accessory trim.

repairing synthetic siding

ALUMINUM AND VINYL SIDING PANELS HAVE INTERLOCKING FLANGES ALONG BOTH edges. The panels are nailed to the sheathing through slots along one flange; the other flange interlocks with the adjacent panel. Though a few simple repairs can be made to aluminum siding, large repairs and nearly all repairs to vinyl call for replacing a small section of the material. For more about vinyl and aluminum siding, see pages 318–321.

making small repairs To remove a dent in aluminum siding, drill a hole in the center of the dent and screw in a self-tapping screw that has two washers under the screw head (the screw cuts its own thread as it is driven in). Gently pull on the screw head with pliers until the surface is even. Remove the screw, and fill the hole with plastic aluminum filler (following the directions on the tube). When the area is dry, sand it smooth, and, finally, touch it up with matching paint.

You can fix corrosion in aluminum siding by cleaning corroded areas with fine steel wool, applying rust-resistant metal primer, and then coating the surfaces with acrylic house paint. Conceal scratches with primer and paint.

replacing synthetic siding If a section of your synthetic siding is damaged beyond a simple surface repair, replace it by cutting out the damaged part of the panel, leaving the nailed portion in place. Use tin snips for aluminum and a utility knife for vinyl to cut the new section of siding, and then install it.

Cut a replacement piece slightly longer than the section you just removed to allow for a slight overlap on each end. (Cut only 1 inch longer if the damaged section ends at a corner or joint.) For aluminum, snap the top edge of the new section in place, and nail it with aluminum box nails that will penetrate 1 inch into the studs. For vinyl, adhere the piece as shown in the steps below.

> **LOWE'S QUICK TIP**
> Vinyl and aluminum siding are installed with interlocking flanges. You can use a special tool called a "zipper" to assist in separating the panels.

1 To replace a section of vinyl siding, use a utility knife to cut through the center of the panel to just beyond both edges of the damaged area. Make vertical cuts on both ends, and then remove the lower half of the damaged section.

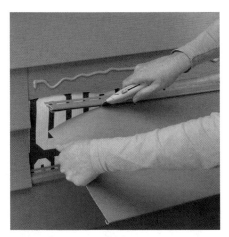

2 Cut the nailing strip off the replacement with a utility knife. The new piece should be 6 inches longer than the damaged section, or 3 inches longer if one end is at a joint or corner.

3 Generously apply polyurethane caulk or lap seal to the damaged panel. Press the new piece in place so that each end overlaps the existing siding by 3 inches. Hold or prop it there until the sealant is dry.

repairing a fascia

FASCIA BOARDS TAKE THE BRUNT OF HARSH WEATHER AND, AS A RESULT, OFTEN become damaged or badly worn. Fortunately, making repairs is a relatively easy job on a low, single-story house if you are comfortable being on a ladder and have basic woodworking skills. If your home does not have eaves that are easy to work on, you will be better off hiring a professional for the job.

1 Use a flat prybar to pry the entire damaged fascia board loose from the eaves. Be sure to wear safety glasses and exercise extreme caution when working at the top of the ladder. After prying off the piece, cut the end of the existing fascia with the saw blade set at a 45-degree angle.

2 Use a power circular saw set at a 45-degree angle to cut the replacement piece so it will join with the existing fascia. Use a square to mark the cutting line for the replacement piece and to guide the saw. It is important to make a straight cut that is perfectly perpendicular to the board.

3 Be sure the bottom edge of the new piece is in exact alignment with the rest of the fascia. If necessary, pull a string line across the bottom of the fascia and the board you are installing to check on the alignment.

4 Hold the piece in place, and nail through the mitered ends and into solid backing every 12 inches with 8d (2½-inch) galvanized nails. Caulk the joints before painting to match the existing fascia. (Consider repainting the entire fascia for a better match.)

installing shingle siding

WOOD SHINGLES ARE RELATIVELY EASY TO INSTALL AS A SIDING MATERIAL BECAUSE they are small and manageable. Shingling an entire house, however, can be a tedious job, so you will want to set aside a large block of time if you intend to tackle this task.

Though shingles require a fairly flat, sturdy nailing base, they ride over slightly bumpy wall surfaces better than most siding materials do. You can also put them over flat existing siding. Installation requires only standard carpentry tools. For more about tools, see pages 302–305.

exposure Before you can begin applying shingles or shakes, you must first determine the correct exposure for them (the amount that each shingle or shake will be exposed to the weather).

Because greater exposures are allowed on walls than on roofs, a square (the measurement by which shingles are purchased) may cover more than 100 square feet of a wall. The table below right will help you determine the actual coverage you will get with various exposures of shingles and shakes (when applied in single courses).

first steps After you have prepared the wall as described on pages 306–309, measure the distance from the base chalk line to the soffit at both ends of the tallest wall. Compensate for any steps in the base chalk line, and figure out the average distance

from the soffit to the baseline. Divide that distance by the maximum exposure for your shingles or shakes. If your computation does not yield a whole number of courses, decrease the exposure enough to make the courses come out evenly. Also adjust the number of courses to achieve a full exposure below windows.

Make a story pole from a 1 by 2 that is the length of your tallest wall's height (as shown on page 312). Starting at one end, mark the story pole at intervals equal to the established exposure. Holding or tacking the story pole flush with the baseline, transfer the marks to each corner and to the trim at each window and door casing.

nailing Nails are concealed 1 inch above the line where the butts (the lower edges) of the next higher course will go. Drive a nail ¾ inch in from each side, and then use additional nails every 4 inches in between.

Shingles may be butted against trim pieces, woven, or mitered, depending upon how much work you want to tackle. The first method is easiest in most cases.

MAXIMUM SHINGLE EXPOSURE

SHINGLE LENGTHS	MAXIMUM EXPOSURE
16"	7½"
18"	8½"
24"	11½"

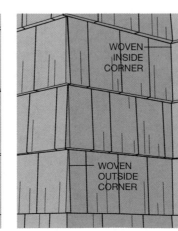

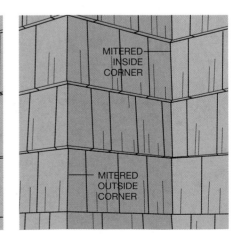

SHINGLING A WALL

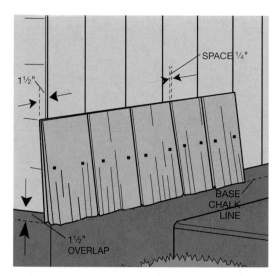

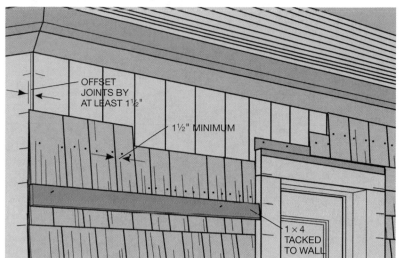

1 For the first course, you can use lower-grade shingles, nailing them with their butts aligned to the base chalk line. Space shingles ¼ inch apart in order to allow for expansion.

2 As you work your way up the wall, align shingle butts along chalk lines. Or tack a 1 by 4 to the wall, and butt the shingles against it.

Use hot-dipped galvanized box or shingling nails that are 1¼ inches long or longer. They should be long enough to penetrate sheathing or solid backing by at least 1 inch.

corners Before beginning, you will want to decide how you will handle shingling at both inside and outside corners. Typical methods for finishing shingles at corners are shown on the facing page. For outside corners, plan to bring shingles or shakes flush to a vertical 1 by 3 or 1 by 4. Alternatively, miter the corners—but prepare to spend a lot of time at it if you do since it is exacting work. More typically, you can "weave" the corners by alternately overlapping them. Trim or plane the overlapping shingles flush. If this is how you will finish outside corners, plan to let the shingles extend beyond the corner (on the first wall) by about 1½ inches so you can trim them later.

At inside corners, plan to bring shingles flush to a 1 by 1 or 2 by 2 that is nailed in the corner. Or miter or weave them, being sure to flash behind with right-angle metal flashing (see pages 344–345) that extends 3 inches under the shingles of each wall.

first courses Nail on the first course of shingles, keeping the butts flush with the base chalk line. You can use low-grade shingles for the first course because this course (only) will be covered by the next one. Leave ¼ inch for expansion between shingles. Directly over the first course, apply a second one. Offset all joints between shingles of different courses by at least 1½ inches so water will shed properly.

successive courses Lay successive courses from the first course to the soffit. As you finish each course, snap a chalk line over it, or tack on a straight 1 by 4 board with a couple of small nails as a guide for laying the next course.

obstacles Shingles and shakes are easy to cut and fit around doors, windows, and so forth. For curved cuts, use a coping saw or saber saw. Caulk well around the edges.

cornices Cornices can be either open or closed. You can easily trim wood shingles or shakes to fit neatly around rafters in an open treatment. Closed cornices are best handled by installing board siding that is finished to match the other trim.

repairing masonry siding

CRACKS AND HOLES IN STUCCO AND BRICK SIDING MAY RESULT FROM THE USE of poorly applied or low-quality material, freeze-thaw cycles in cold-winter climates, or movement such as settling or earthquakes. Protect the house from moisture damage by repairing flaws promptly.

stucco problems

Stucco walls typically consist of three layers of stucco that are applied over self-furring spacers and wire mesh. The final coat is either pigmented or painted and can be textured in a variety of ways.

Though cracks and holes are relatively easy to repair, it can be tricky to match both the texture and the color of the surrounding wall. If you are unsure of your abilities, consider having a professional mason handle the work.

Hairline and small cracks can usually be filled with caulking compound and then painted with latex paint. For large cracks and holes up to about 6 inches wide, use stucco patching compound. Follow the instructions on the bag or can.

For larger holes, you will need to apply three coats of stucco: a "scratch" coat, a "brown" coat, and a final coat that is colored. You can buy it this way and texture it to match the original.

When a wall is newly stuccoed, the material is applied in three coats. Here you can see the first "scratch" coat on the right and the second "brown" coat being applied.

REPAIRING A CRACK IN STUCCO

Narrow cracks in masonry may be repaired with stucco caulk. Clean the area around the crack with a wire brush, and then apply the stucco caulk according to the label directions. After the compound cures, the area can be painted to match the wall; use latex paint.

For the first and second coats, buy a bag of stucco mix. Add $\frac{1}{10}$ part lime to make the mixture easier to work. Mix in enough water to make a fairly stiff paste. For the final coat, purchase a stucco color coat mix in the desired color. This final coat should be flush with the surrounding wall. While this coat is wet, experiment to match the texture. For a smooth texture, draw a metal float across the surface. To match other textures, daub a sponge or brush on the surface, or splatter the wall with more stucco, and smooth down the high spots. To cure stucco, cover the repaired space with a plastic sheet and keep the area damp for about four days. Wait to paint one month after curing.

1 To prepare for a larger patch, first remove loose stucco from the damaged area with a cold chisel and hammer. Then scrub the area with a wire brush.

2 Mix up stucco patch according to the label directions, and then apply the mixture with a trowel or broad putty knife (depending upon the size of the repair). If the damaged area is deep, apply the stucco patch in two or more coats, scratching the first coats with a nail so the next coats will adhere.

brick problems

Brick-veneer siding is usually applied to a wood frame wall over building paper; the mortared joints may be "tooled" (finished) in a number of ways. Properly tooled joints are essential to ensure strong, watertight walls that will not fail.

To repair cracked or crumbling mortar, you or a masonry contractor will have to remove the old mortar and "repoint" the joints (fill them with new mortar).

Though you can make your own mortar, it is easier to use a dry, ready-mixed type (use weather-resistant type N), available at building supply stores. Prepare the mortar according to the package directions.

Using a jointer, steel rod, or trowel, tool the new joints to match the existing ones. Mortar joints should be tooled when they are "thumbprint hard" (neither so soft that they smear the wall nor so hard that a tool leaves black marks). Keep tooled joints damp for four days to cure.

3 Before the top coat sets up, use a whisk broom to match the wall's texture. If the wall is smooth, use a trowel.

diagnosing siding problems

A THOROUGH SIDING INSPECTION INVOLVES LOOKING FOR OBVIOUS PROBLEMS, including warped boards, missing or damaged shingles, holes in stucco, crumbling mortar, cracks, and defective paint. Do not ignore interior problems such as dry rot and termite damage; these can eventually destroy your house. Begin with a visual inspection.

deteriorated caulking Make a note of any caulking that has dried out, and then renew the seals to prevent both moisture and pests from entering. Check the seals around windows and doors; around any plumbing, millwork, or other protrusions; and where a deck or masonry fireplace adjoins a house wall. Caulk any cracks in board siding.

defective paint If you find minor problems such as peeling, cracking, scaling, bubbling, or flaking, see page 33 for painting tips. First make any necessary repairs and then go on to repaint or re-stain the siding as needed.

mildew Combined heat and humidity can encourage mildew to develop on wood and

HOMEOWNER'S GUIDE TO BUGS

BUGS	SIGNS	FAVORITE FOODS	FAVORITE PLACES
Carpet beetles	Visible beetles, holes in carpet, or holes in fabrics.	Carpets, clothing, fabric, flower pollen.	Carpets, rugs, baseboards, closets, dresser drawers. Outdoors: white or cream-colored flowers.
Carpenter ants	Ant trails, ant nests in walls, winged ants in house, tiny ant wings scattered on the ground, small piles of coarse sawdust near cracks.	Decaying wood, sweet foods, water.	Wall interiors, crawl spaces.
Cockroaches	Visible cockroaches scurry away when you turn on the lights.	Food, garbage, anything that is organic.	Warm, dark places; food cabinets; garbage cans.
Powder post beetles	Tiny holes pepper wood's exterior surface; wood's interior is reduced to powder.	Hardwoods such as oak, walnut, and ash; some types also eat softwoods.	Unheated crawl spaces, wood trim, wood siding, framing.
Termites, dry-wood	Smooth galleries inside wood, tiny holes in surface, pellets piled outside or under infected wood, tiny termite wings on the ground.	Wood.	Rafters, roofs, eaves, framing.
Termites, subterranean and Formosan	Pellet-free gritty, mud-like substance inside layered galleries, mud tubes up foundation walls, swarms of winged termites, wings on the ground.	Soft parts of wood grain.	Damp crawl spaces, foundation areas, primarily lower sections of a house's structure.

painted surfaces; it may show up either as a fungus-like discoloration or as whitish or moldy deposits. Mildew should be treated with an approved mildewcide.

efflorescence Brick or stone veneer may become covered with a white powder that is called efflorescence, formed when water-soluble salts are washed to the surface. In an old wall, this may be the result of a leak that should be fixed. First, take steps to keep the surface dry, then scrape and wire-brush the area, and clean with detergent or a pressure washer.

dry rot & termite damage Dry rot is a fungus that causes wood to crumble; termites destroy wood by chewing out its interior. Both can work away at wood timbers and siding in a way that might easily escape your notice. Eliminate damp areas, fix any broken gutters (see page 351), and repair any rotted wood. Be sure no parts of your house are in direct contact with the ground. Clean up and clear out areas that provide safe harbor for insects.

GETTING THE BUGS OUT

Probe the edges of wood siding with a knife, and look for soft, spongy spots. Pay special attention to any area that has been near or in contact with the ground.

To check for visible traces of termites, look for the translucent ½-inch-long wings they grow and shed or the mud tubes some types build. If you find evidence of dry rot or termites, do not wait for the problem to get worse. Consult a licensed termite inspector or pest-control professional. If you catch the problem early, the solution may be relatively simple and inexpensive.

ACTIONS TO TAKE	NOTES
Caulk cracks; apply weather stripping; frequently vacuum rugs, carpets, and upholstery. Apply powdered chlorpyrifos to suspected areas of infestation.	
Caulk cracks and openings, apply weather stripping, eliminate moisture problems and decayed wood. For localized problems, apply boric acid, pyrethrum, or chlorpyrifos according to label directions. For extensive problems, call an exterminator.	Carpenter ants sprout wings during their reproductive stage.
Caulk openings, apply weather stripping, eliminate moisture problems, store food in sealed containers, keep garbage outdoors, clean thoroughly. Apply boric acid according to label directions. Kill survivors with poisonous baits.	Cockroaches are some of the most adaptable creatures on Earth.
For localized problems, apply chlorpyrifos or another approved pesticide according to label directions. For extensive problems, call an exterminator.	Old house borers, a related, highly destructive variety, infest seasoned wood.
Eliminate moisture problems and decayed wood to prevent infestation. If you suspect infestation, call an exterminator.	These are less common than subterranean termites but more difficult to detect.
Eliminate moisture problems and any wood that contacts the ground. Spread polyethylene sheeting across crawl spaces. Remove mud tubes, and treat soil along the foundation with pyrethrin or other termite control. If you suspect infestation, call an exterminator.	Formosan termites produce hard, sponge-like material in galleries. Termites have wings during their reproductive stage.

roofing

THE NOTION OF SHELTER BEGINS WITH THE ROOF. ROOFS PROTECT US FROM THE elements, retain heat in winter, and maintain coolness in summer in the living spaces below. They also serve as architectural elements, helping to establish the style of a house. Roofs take many different shapes, from modernist flat to impressively peaked Victorians, and are clad with a variety of materials, the most common being composition or wood shingles, tiles, and metal. What all roofs have in common is their need for quality materials and installation—including proper drainage systems provided by flashing and gutters—in order to stay watertight.

Because they are constantly exposed to sun, wind, and precipitation, roofs undergo more than their share of wear and tear as the years go by. Depending on the path of the sun and wind, some roof areas of a house may be more exposed and will degrade faster than others. The problems may not be obvious until a heavy rain sends a stream of water dripping through the ceiling. Once a year, it is worth climbing on top of your roof (or having a professional climb up) to check its soundness. Keeping your roof and its drainage systems in repair is essential to the health of your home's structure.

This chapter begins with a primer on roofing materials and the basics of roof construction. You will learn how to prepare to reroof; how to apply asphalt shingles, flashing, and gutters; and, finally, how to solve roof leaks and repair tile, metal, and shingled roofs, as well as gutters and flashing.

buying roofing

ROOFING IS A MAJOR EXTERIOR DESIGN COMPONENT, PARTICULARLY IF THE HOUSE'S roofline is steep. When choosing a roofing material, make sure that its color, texture, and composition are compatible with the style of your house. If the roof is a dominant architectural element, stick with muted colors that will not overpower adjacent siding. Keep in mind practical considerations, such as the fact that a light-colored roof reflects sunlight, and be certain that the material you pick is suitable for the pitch of your roof (a flat or nearly flat roof requires a seamless covering). Buy the best you can afford to protect your home and maintain its curb appeal for years to come.

BELOW: **Attractive dimensional asphalt shingles offer solid protection at a reasonable price. BELOW RIGHT: Wood shingles are favored for their natural look. On this home, they provide a handsome backdrop for the white-trimmed windows.**

asphalt shingles Asphalt-shingle roofing is the most popular type, thanks to its price and adaptability. It comes in an enormous variety of styles, colors, shapes, and textures, making it compatible with most architectural styles. Quality varies, depending on how the shingles are constructed.

Those with fiberglass cores may last up to 20 years; extra-thick fiberglass/asphalt types, which are called "dimensional" or "architectural" shingles, often carry longer warranties. Inexpensive felt-core shingles typically carry only a 15-year guarantee and may not be permitted by codes.

In many cases, new asphalt shingles can be installed over existing ones. Check with your local building department to see how many layers of asphalt roofing are allowed.

wood shingles Cedar shingles and shakes have a distinctive natural look that suits many types of architectural styles and siding materials. Shingles and shakes come

in various grades and have 30- to 50-year guarantees. Top-quality shakes made from straight-grained wood are expensive compared with economy shakes. (Lower-cost sawn shingles with thinner butt ends are best reserved for use as a siding material.) For an additional cost, shakes can be treated with preservatives and fire retardants. Shakes should not be used on a roof with a vertical rise that is less than 4 inches per horizontal foot (see page 337).

metal Metal roofing is exceptionally lightweight, strong, and resistant to wind and fire damage. It is manufactured to mimic a range of materials—including clay tiles, asphalt shingles, shakes, and slate—but some imitations can be less than convincing. Painted finishes and high-tech coatings come in a variety of colors to match any exterior. Standing-seam metal roofing, the most common type, is suitable for either steep- or low-pitched roofs and has a sleek

appearance that complements a contemporary home. A steel standing-seam roof will last from 25 to 30 years.

clay & slate For a historic or high-end home, a clay tile or slate roof offers incomparable beauty, elegance, and durability. Clay tile lends authenticity and charm to a Mediterranean-style house and is renowned for its ability to withstand extreme conditions such as fire, earthquakes, and heavy winds. Slate shingles are as indestructible as they are beautiful, often lasting for hundreds of years.

These masonry materials are heavy—up to three times the weight of asphalt shingles. Some roofing systems cannot support such a load, so be sure to have your roof evaluated by a qualified professional who can tell you whether your house will need structural reinforcement. Even without the extra installation expense, slate and tile will have a big impact on the bottom line.

Standing-seam metal roofing provides an impervious barrier to weather; it demands professional installation.

Clay tile, one of the oldest of roofing materials, is beautiful but very heavy, costly and labor-intensive to install.

concrete tile Concrete-tile roofing—which is formed to resemble clay tile, slate, or wood shakes—offers a range of decorative options along with excellent durability. Concrete tiles are lighter than clay or slate and do not require extra structural support. The cost of concrete tile is similar to that of cedar shakes.

When figuring the cost of new roofing, be aware that the price depends upon your house's configuration as well as the price of your materials. A steep roof—or one that includes gables, dormers, chimneys, or skylights—will require extra installation time. A large roof with simple lines may cost less to cover with roofing than a small one with a complicated design.

Concrete roof tiles offer deep, sculptural texture and outstanding performance; you can buy both standard (heavy) and lightweight types.

COMPARATIVE GUIDE TO ROOFING

MATERIAL	POUNDS PER SQUARE FOOT
Asphalt shingles (felt base)	240–345
Asphalt shingles (fiberglass base)	220–430
Wood shingles and shakes	144–350
Tile (concrete and clay)	900–1000
Slate	900–1000
Aluminum shingles	50
Metal panels (aluminum or steel)	45–75
Asphalt roll roofing	90–180
Asphalt ("tar") and gravel	250–650
Sprayed polyurethane foam	20 for 1" thickness

DURABILITY	FIRE RATING	MINIMUM SLOPE*	CHARACTERISTICS
12–20 years, depending on sun's intensity.	C (least resistant)	4 in 12 down to 2 in 12 with additional underlayment.	Available in a wide range of colors, textures, and standard and premium weights; easy to apply and repair; low-maintenance and economical. Less durable and fire-resistant than fiberglass-base shingles, though equal in cost.
15–25 years, depending on sun's intensity.	A (most resistant)	4 in 12 down to 2 in 12 with additional underlayment.	Durable and highly fire-resistant; available in a wide range of colors, textures, and standard and premium weights; easy to apply and repair; low maintenance. Brittle when applied in temperatures below 50°F.
10–15 years, depending on slope, heat, and humidity.	None, untreated; C, if treated with retardant; B, with use of retardant and foil underlayment.	4 in 12 down to 3 in 12 with additional underlayment.	Has an appealing natural appearance with strong shadow lines; is durable. Use #1 ("Blue Label") shingles for roofing. Flammable unless treated with retardants; treated wood is expensive. Time-consuming to apply.
50+ years.	A (most resistant)	4 in 12 down to 3 in 12 with additional underlayment.	Extremely durable and fireproof. Comes in flat, curved, and ribbed shapes and moderate color range. Costly to ship and hard to install. Needs strong framing to support weight; cracks easily if walked on. Golf balls will break it.
50+ years.	A (most resistant)	4 in 12.	Has attractive, traditional appearance, does not deteriorate, fireproof, and comes in several colors. Expensive to buy and ship and difficult to install. Requires strong framing to support weight; may get brittle with age.
25+ years.	A, B, or C (varies with construction)	4 in 12.	Light and fire-resistant. Resembles wood shakes and comes in a moderate range of colors. Can be damaged by heavy hail.
20+ years.	A, B, or C (varies with construction)	1 in 12.	Aluminum: lightweight, durable, and maintenance-free. Sheds snow. Steel: strong, durable, and fire-resistant. Sheds snow. Contraction and expansion can cause leaks at nail holes; noisy in rain.
5–10 years (depends on water runoff).	A, B, or C (varies with construction)	1 in 12.	Economical and easy to apply. Drab in appearance. Used for flat roofs.
10–20 years, depending on sun's intensity.	A, B, or C (varies with construction)	¼ in 12.	Continuous membrane makes it the most waterproof of all. Must be professionally applied. Comes in built-up and single-ply. It is hard to locate leaks; black surfaces transfer heat to interior.
Life of building with proper maintenance.	A (most resistant)	¼ in 12.	Continuous membrane produces watertight surface. Has good insulation value; is lightweight and durable (when maintained). Must be applied by professionals; deteriorates under sunlight if not properly coated (and periodically recoated).

*See page 337.

typical roof construction

UNDERSTANDING THE STRUCTURE OF YOUR ROOF IS THE FIRST STEP TOWARD diagnosing problems, initiating improvements, and making repairs. These pages will give you the details of how roofs are built.

A typical roof begins with a rafter framework that supports a roof deck (sometimes called a sub-roof) consisting of sheathing and underlayment. The roof deck, in turn, provides a nailing base for the finish roof surface material.

the roof deck Though the way a roof deck is built can vary depending on the roof surface material, most decks include both sheathing and underlayment.

Sheathing, the material that provides the nailing base for the roof surface material, ranges from solid plywood to oriented strand board to open sheathing.

Sandwiched between the sheathing and the surface material is the underlayment, usually roofing felt. A heavy, fibrous black paper saturated with asphalt, roofing felt is waterproof enough to resist water penetration from outside yet porous enough to allow moisture from inside to escape.

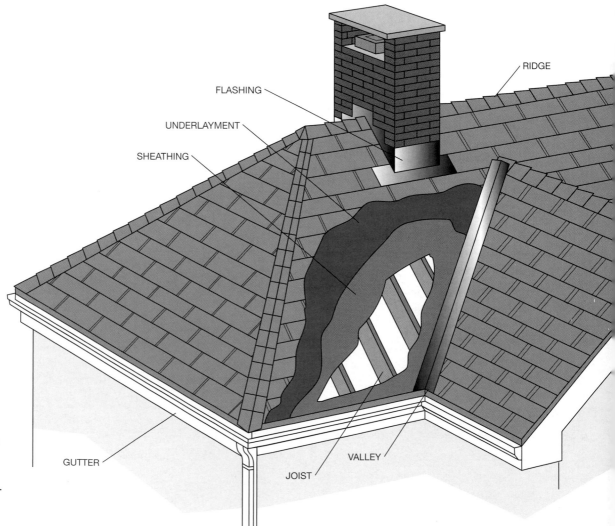

FLASHING

UNDERLAYMENT

SHEATHING

RIDGE

Many different components work together to give a roof strength and make it a weather-tight membrane.

GUTTER

JOIST

VALLEY

the roof surface The material on the roof must be able to resist wind, rain, snow, hail, and sun. A wide variety of roof surface materials is available. Key types are discussed on pages 332–335. Some may be used on nearly flat roofs, while others rely upon the slope of a pitched roof to shed water from the surface. In addition to the roof's pitch, the home's architectural style and local building codes will determine suitable materials.

When learning about roof construction, you may encounter several terms that are unfamiliar. On pitched roofs, materials are applied in horizontal layers called "courses," which overlap one another from the eaves up to the ridge. The portion of the material exposed to the weather is called the "exposure," and the edge that is pointed

Mark a line 12 inches from one end on a level, and rest that end on the roof. Raise or lower the opposite end until the tool is level. Then measure the distance between the roof and the 12-inch mark to determine the pitch. If it is 3 inches, for example, the roof's pitch is "3 in 12."

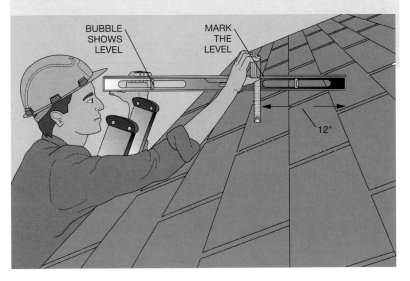

BUBBLE SHOWS LEVEL

MARK THE LEVEL

12"

down-roof is called the "butt." Asphalt shingles, the most common roofing surface, are sometimes called "composition" or "comp" shingles and are divided into sections called "tabs."

Roof pitch is a term used to express the ratio of a roof's vertical rise in inches to each foot of run, the horizontal distance. A "3-in-12 pitch" describes a roof that rises 3 inches vertically for every 12 inches of horizontal distance.

Typically, a roof's surface is broken by angles and protrusions such as vent pipes, chimneys, and dormers. All of these require a weather-tight seal, usually provided by flashing. Made from malleable metal or plastic, flashing appears as the drip edge along the eaves of a roof, the collars around ventilation and plumbing pipes, the valleys between two roof planes, and the "steps" along a chimney. Less obvious flashing also protects other breaks in the roof, such as skylights. See more about flashing on pages 344–345.

At the roof edges, gutters, discussed on pages 348–350, catch water runoff and channel it to the ground via the downspouts, which direct water away from the house and into the soil.

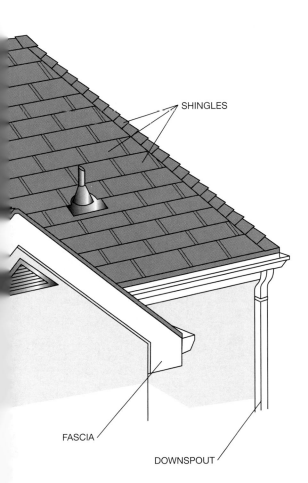

SHINGLES

FASCIA

DOWNSPOUT

BASIC TOOLS FOR ROOFING

Utility knife

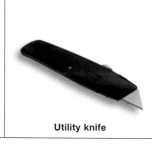

Tin snips

Caulking gun

Handsaw

Hand stapler

Putty knife

Power circular saw

Knee pads

Measuring tape

Nail claw

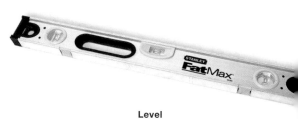

Level

Claw hammer

Prybar

Roofer's hatchet

Gloves

Saber saw (jigsaw)

Safety goggles

Stepladder
(or extension ladder)

Carpenter's square

Wire brush

Chalk line

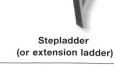

Pneumatic stapler or nailer

roofing tools

ALTHOUGH MINOR REPAIRS ARE RELATIVELY EASY AND REQUIRE ONLY A FEW TOOLS, extensive roofing work can be difficult and demands a fairly complete selection of carpentry and roofing tools and equipment. For starters, you will need ladders for climbing onto the roof (see more about ladders on page 38). You may need a few more tools that are not shown here. To look for leaks, you will want good lighting, so if your attic is not lit, you will need a safety light. If you will be doing any work on the chimney, you may need a ball-peen hammer and a cold chisel, along with a trowel and a few masonry tools (see page 305 for more about masonry tools). And you will need basic safety equipment, such as work gloves and safety glasses.

LAYOUT & CUTTING TOOLS

Every roofing job requires considerable planning, layout, and preparation. Shown here are some of the tools that are essential for this work. You will need a measuring tape, chalk line, and level for planning your layout; you may also need a line level to establish the slope of gutters and the like. For cutting sheathing, use a power circular saw for straight cuts and a saber saw for curves or cutouts. Use tin snips to cut metal flashing. A utility knife is handy for marking lines and for cutting roofing paper and asphalt shingles.

UTILITY KNIFE

CARPENTER'S SQUARE

LEVEL

SABER SAW (JIGSAW)

CHALK LINE

MEASURING TAPE

TIN SNIPS

POWER CIRCULAR SAW

CLAW HAMMER

HAND STAPLER

PNEUMATIC STAPLER OR NAILER

ROOFER'S HATCHET

WIRE BRUSH

PRYBAR

NAIL CLAW

KNEE PADS

CAULKING GUN

ROOFING INSTALLATION & REPAIR TOOLS

Installing roofing calls for a number of basic construction tools, though not all types of roofing require all of the tools shown here. Knee pads are essential for protection. You can fasten building paper to sheathing using a hand stapler. Nail roofing in place with a claw hammer; when working with wood shingles, however, use a roofer's hammer, which has a blade on one side for splitting shingles. A pneumatic stapler or nailer makes roofing installation much faster—you can use this with asphalt or wood shingles. Repair work almost always calls for a prybar and/or nail claw for removing nails, a wire brush for cleaning flashing, and a caulking gun or putty knife for applying asphalt cement.

PUTTY KNIFE

STEPLADDER

Before you venture up a ladder to repair roofing, siding, windows, or gutters, be sure you know the following safety precautions.

Ladder safety Ladders for long reaches range from straight wooden types to aluminum extension ladders (the type that extends to 20 feet is adequate for most houses). Be sure your ladder is strong yet light enough to be handled easily. Be sure to keep a metal ladder well away from electrical wires. Below are some tips for using a ladder safely:

- Inspect your ladder for cracks, loose parts, and other weaknesses before you lean it against the house.
- Place the ladder's base on firm, level ground at a distance from the house equal to one-quarter of the ladder's length.
- Get on and off the ladder by stepping onto the center of the rung. Grip the ladder rails (not the rungs) using both hands. Reposition the ladder if it wobbles.
- Keep your hips between the ladder rails. Do not lean out to reach an area; instead, reposition the ladder.
- Make sure that only one person stands on a ladder at a time.
- Install rubber safety shoes on the ladder feet if the ladder is to stand on a slick surface.
- Do not stand on the top two rungs of a ladder. If you are repairing a roof, at least two rungs of the ladder should extend above the eaves so you can step directly out onto the roof.
- Be sure the rung hooks of an extension ladder are locked in place and that no section is extended more than three-quarters of the ladder's length.
- Pull materials up a ladder with a rope, and have a place to store them at the top; do not try to carry them up.

Roof safety Working on a roof requires extra caution. The surface is usually slick, sloped, and well above the ground. Following are some precautions to take when making roof repairs:

- Do not walk on a roof any more than is necessary or you may cause more damage. Do not walk on tile and slate roofs at all; these materials are slippery and breakable underfoot.
- Let a professional make any repairs on a roof with a steep pitch: one that slopes more than 25 degrees or rises more than 4 vertical inches for every 12 horizontal inches.
- Wear loose, comfortable clothing and non-slip rubber-soled shoes with good ankle support.
- Work on the roof only in dry, calm, and warm weather. A wet roof can be treacherously slick; a sudden wind can knock you off balance.
- Never work on the roof when a lightning storm threatens to occur.
- Be careful not to put your full weight on areas that contain brittle or old roofing materials or on rotted decking.
- Stay well away from power lines, and be sure neither your body nor any equipment comes into contact with them. Keep children and pets away from the work area.

Special safety equipment The standard safety devices listed below help to distribute your weight evenly and keep you safe. All these are available from tool rental companies. In addition, be sure to check with your local state safety office regarding the laws outlined by the Occupational Safety & Health Administration; each state has its own safety requirements for roof work.

- A safety harness, used in conjunction with a fall-arrest rope, is an added precaution when working on steep inclines and will keep you from sliding off the roof.
- A metal ladder bracket allows you to hook your ladder over the ridge.
- Nailed to the roof framing, a 2-by-6 plank will support you and your working materials. Use strong, straight-grained lumber no longer than 10 feet between supports. When you are finished, set the nails and caulk their heads with asphalt cement to prevent leaks.
- An angled seat board allows you to sit on a level surface while working.

preparing to reroof

TO OFFER YEARS OF TROUBLE-FREE SERVICE, A ROOF MUST HAVE A PROPER, SOUND deck—the part of a roof, consisting of sheathing and underlayment, that supports the finish roofing. Sometimes you can roof right over the old roof, using it as a deck. But if your roof does not meet the conditions outlined here, you will have to strip off the old shingles or completely remove and replace the decking.

Your new roofing material will dictate what type of deck is best. For most materials, the manufacturer's recommendations and local codes specify the appropriate underlayment, sheathing, flashing, and so forth. In this book, we discuss how to install asphalt shingles because they are, by far, the type most commonly used on American roofs.

While preparing the deck, handle all related changes to the roof, such as adding skylights, vents, or insulation.

tearing off the old roof Removing existing roofing is a dirty, dangerous job. Though you can save money by doing this work yourself, it is often well worth the price to hire a service to strip the roof and remove the debris (look under "Demolition Contractors" in the Yellow Pages).

If you do this work, be very careful. Wear a dust mask to screen out airborne particles, and wear heavy-duty gloves. Keep your weight on top of the rafters; if you step on weakened sheathing, you could go right through it.

Protect windows and doors by leaning sheets of plywood against them. To keep debris from falling onto your flower beds, wrap the upper ends of 6-mil plastic sheeting around 2 by 4s, tack these underneath the eaves, and anchor the sheeting to the ground with a board.

If there are two or three existing roofs, remove all of them, one at a time. Be careful not to damage any specialty flashing; even if it has deteriorated and must be replaced, it is useful as a pattern for fabricating new flashing.

When the old shingles have been removed, pull nails and, if necessary, repair or install new sheathing.

selecting sheathing Every roof has either solid or open sheathing across the rafters to provide a nailing base and, in most cases, to add to the roof's structural integrity. Solid sheathing materials come in two forms: panels and boards. Panels, typically 4-by-8-foot sheets of CDX-grade plywood or a pressed-wood product called oriented strand board (OSB), are recommended for roofing materials other than wood shingles, which require air circulation from below.

installing panel sheathing When installing solid panel sheathing, begin at one lower corner and lay a sheet horizontally across the rafters with its inward edge centered on a rafter. Work your way across the eaves, and then start the second course with a half sheet so that the end joints will be staggered by 4 feet. Leave a $\frac{1}{16}$-inch expansion space between the ends of adjoining panels and a $\frac{1}{8}$-inch gap between the long sides. In exceptionally humid climates, double this spacing. Make sure you use 6d nails for $\frac{1}{2}$-inch sheets and 8d nails for thicker sheets.

If your house has open overhangs, you may want to install starter boards before the first course of panels. Starter-board material, $\frac{5}{8}$-by-6-inch V-rustic or shiplap siding, is much more attractive to look at from under overhangs than is plywood or OSB. When installing starter boards, first snap chalk lines along the eaves as guides

1 Apply plywood sheathing with vertical edges centered on rafters. Secure the sheathing with nails every 6 inches along the edges and every 12 inches elsewhere. Use H-clips to support the horizontal edges of plywood sheathing between rafters (unless there is blocking beneath the edges to support them).

2 Once the sheathing is in place, add the drip-edge flashing and roofing felt. Nail a metal drip edge along the eaves. Then roll out the roofing felt, stapling it or driving in roofing nails about every 2 feet. Overlap horizontal seams by 4 inches and vertical seams by 12 inches. Last, nail metal drip edge along the rakes (ends of gable roofs).

for aligning their edges. Join the boards' ends over the rafters.

You can install ⅜-inch panel sheathing over existing open sheathing, but the roof will have more structural integrity if you start from scratch with thicker panels. It is usually necessary to support standard ½-inch panels mid-span between rafters, either with blocking or with special H-clips. Or buy plywood panels that have interlocking V-grooved edges. Let the panels extend over hips and ridges (see page 346). Snap a chalk line across them flush at the rakes (the ends of gable roofs), hips, and ridge, and cut them off in place.

applying drip edges After you install the sheathing, install metal drip edges along the eaves and valley liners. Plan to apply drip edges along the rakes after the underlayment has been put in place. See pages 344–345 for information on drip edges, valley liners, and flashing.

installing underlayment This is a heavy, asphalt-impregnated black paper, also called roofing felt, sold in large rolls. It provides extra weather protection. On most

roofs, strips of standard-sized 36-inch-wide, 15-pound felt are lapped from the eaves to the ridge. If the underlayment is not premarked, snap horizontal chalk lines before you begin to keep it straight on the roof. Sweep off the roof deck, check for protruding nails, and then prepare to roll out the underlayment. Snap the first line 33⅝ inches above the eaves in order to allow for a ⅜-inch overhang. Then, allowing room for a 2-inch overlap between strips of felt, snap succeeding chalk lines at 34 inches.

Start at one end of one of the eaves, and work from rake to rake. Tack the felt at its center with three roofing nails, and roll a strip to the other end of the eaves. Cut it off flush at the rake. Adjust the strip up or down, and smooth it out. Nail the material in place with roofing nails or staples spaced approximately 2 feet apart along the lower half of the felt.

Repeat this process until you reach the ridge. Trim the felt with a utility knife, flush at rakes and overlapped 6 inches at the valleys, hips, and ridge. Where two strips meet end to end, overlap them by 4 inches. When you encounter a vent pipe, slit the felt to fit around the pipe.

LOWE'S QUICK TIP
In cold climates, to protect a roof against ice dams, apply standard underlayment to the sheathing and then cover the eaves area, to 12 inches inside the exterior wall line, with a 36-inch-wide sheet of a special rubber ice-shield membrane or 50-pound roll roofing that has a smooth surface.

flashing for a new roof

FLASHING MADE OF GALVANIZED STEEL, COPPER, OR ALUMINUM DIRECTS WATER away from joints in the roof—the valleys, chimneys, vent stacks, skylights, and areas where dormers and other walls meet the roof. Flashing is also required along eaves and rakes. Here is a closer look at the flashing that protects various parts of the roof.

valleys & roof edges Valleys require particularly sturdy flashing because they carry more water than any other individual roof plane. On most roofs, metal valley flashing is installed over a valley liner and under the underlayment and finish roofing material, as shown at the top left on the facing page.

On some asphalt-shingle roofs, you can extend each course across the valleys, eliminating the need for metal flashing. Be sure no joint between shingles occurs within 12 inches of the valley, and keep all nails at least 6 inches from the valley's center. Another common technique is to flash valleys with roll roofing that is the same color as the shingles. To do this, first nail an 18-inch-wide strip along the valley, with the finished surface down; set nails 1 inch from the edges and 12 inches apart. Then

roll out a 36-inch-wide strip of roll roofing, finished side up. Center it over the first strip, and nail it down.

Drip-edge flashing helps keep water from wicking back under the shingles (see top right on the facing page).

vent pipes Before you begin to roof, be sure to have on hand vent-pipe flashing for each pipe that penetrates the roof. Two types are available: sheet-metal cones that you caulk to the pipe and self-sealing types that have rubber gaskets. Vent-pipe flashing is installed when the new shingles reach the base of the vent pipe. Cut the roofing to fit around the pipe, and slide the flashing over the pipe so that its base flange lies on top of the roofing on the down-slope side. Then continue roofing over the flashing.

Metal flashing seals out water from many critical spots on a home's roof, including valleys, around chimneys and vent pipes, beside dormer walls, and along the rakes and the eaves. The roof that is illustrated here has an open valley made from a continuous piece of metal flashing.

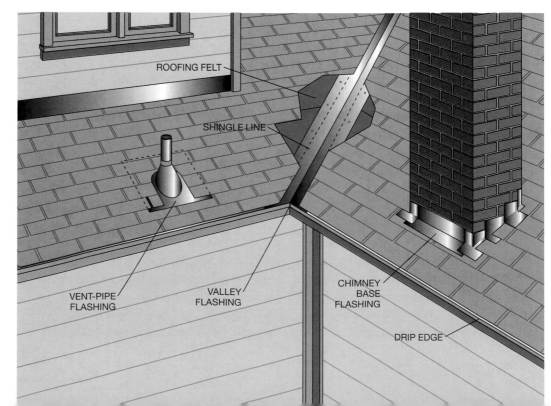

ROOFING FELT

SHINGLE LINE

VENT-PIPE FLASHING

VALLEY FLASHING

CHIMNEY BASE FLASHING

DRIP EDGE

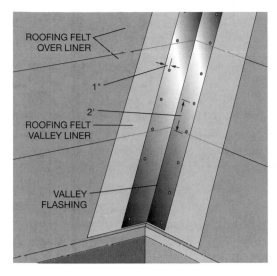

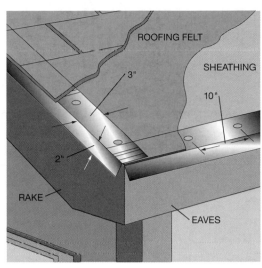

To install metal valley flashing for an asphalt-shingle roof, first roll out 15-pound roofing felt that's cut to the length of the valley. Push this liner snugly into the valley, and nail it about every 2 to 4 feet along the outside edges. Then install the flashing. If you need more than a single length, start at the bottom and overlap the first piece with the second by at least 6 inches. Install the roofing felt, extending it over the valley liner.

At eaves, nail a preformed metal drip edge in place before applying the roofing felt. After the felt is down, nail the drip edge along the rakes.

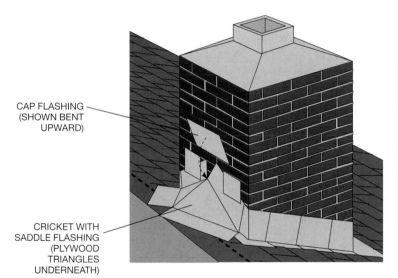

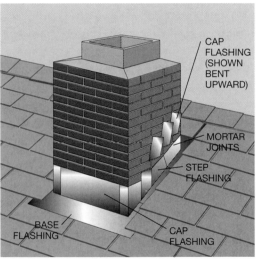

If the roof is particularly steep or if the chimney is more than 2 feet wide, build a "cricket" to prevent water and snow from collecting behind the chimney. Cut and install two plywood triangles to form the cricket. Then cover the plywood with a custom-bent saddle flashing. Protect the saddle with cap flashing.

Cap flashing extends down from above to prevent water from seeping behind flashing installed below it. It is typically used all around a chimney to protect base flashing, step flashing, and the cricket. Cap flashing is usually installed in slots cut into the mortar joints, but it can also be sealed to the chimney with roofing cement.

chimneys Chimney flashing consists of several parts as shown below.

dormers Dormer walls are flashed similarly to chimneys. Base flashing protects the dormer's front wall where it meets the roof. Then step flashing is placed on top of each course of roof shingles as the shingles are installed, to seal the side walls. Ideally, the vertical flange of flashing should be slipped under the siding. If that is not possible, caulk the flashing to the siding.

applying asphalt shingles

STANDARD THREE-TAB ASPHALT SHINGLES ARE THE EASIEST OF ALL ROOFING MATE-rials to install. They are a manageable weight to carry and a breeze to cut and nail. In addition, the 12-by-36-inch shingles, when given a standard weather exposure of 5 inches, cover large areas very quickly. Asphalt roof shingles are also affordable, long-lasting, and readily available in a range of colors and textures. Before installation, review the instructions on flashing a roof on pages 344–345.

cutting Cut asphalt shingles face down on a flat surface with a sharp utility knife. Hold a carpenter's square or straightedge on the cut line, and score the back of the shingle with the knife. Then bend the shingle to break it on the scored line.

fastening Secure asphalt shingles with 12-gauge galvanized roofing nails. Use 3d

(1¼-inch) nails for new roofs, and when reroofing over an old asphalt roof, use 4d (1½-inch) nails.

Begin nailing the starter shingles at the rake, and continue along the eaves. Allow a ½-inch overhang along the eaves and at both rakes and ¹⁄₁₆-inch spacing between shingles. Use four nails for each shingle, nailed 3 inches above the eaves. Nail the

TOP: **Stagger and align shingles as shown.** BOT-TOM: **If your roof has hips, shingle them before the ridge, beginning with a double layer of shingles at the bottom of one hip. Work toward the ridge, applying shingles with a 5-inch exposure. Align each shingle with a chalk line. When shingling the ridge, start at the end that is opposite the direction from which the wind most often blows (see the illustration below right). Use nails long enough to penetrate the ridge board (about 2 inches long).**

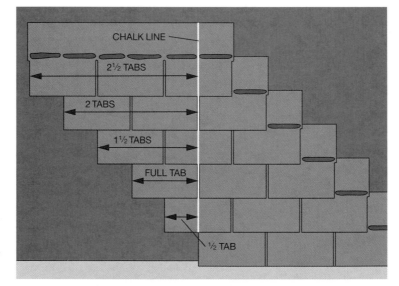

CHALK LINE

2½ TABS

2 TABS

1½ TABS

FULL TAB

½ TAB

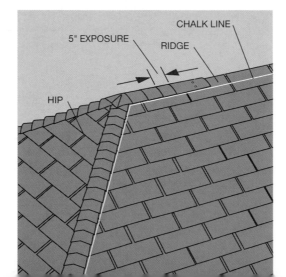

5" EXPOSURE

CHALK LINE

RIDGE

HIP

5½"

NAIL 1" IN FROM EDGE

1 Because all of the shingles will use the starter row as a reference, it is important to make sure it goes down straight. Start by snapping a chalk line on the felt to define the top of the starter course. Apply the starter course with the tabs pointing up the roof. Secure each shingle with a galvanized roofing nail above each notch.

2 The first and remaining courses are all installed with the tabs pointing down the roof. Nail each shingle to the roof just above the slot between the tabs. Start the second course with an offset of about 6 inches to stagger the seams.

first course over the starter course, again using four nails per shingle.

When laying the successive courses, your main concern is proper alignment of the shingles, both horizontally and vertically. For horizontal alignment of shingles that will be nailed over roofing felt, snap chalk lines; if you are reroofing without adding felt, just butt the new shingles against the old ones.

When working with standard three-tab shingles, you can produce a number of different roof patterns by adjusting the length of the shingle that begins each course. One common and easy method, called a staggered roof, is shown on the facing page. Just offset the joints of three courses in a row by at least 3 inches.

If you have not purchased ready-made hip and ridge shingles, you can cut and bend 12-inch squares from standard shingles. Snap chalk lines along each side of the ridge and then along each hip, 6 inches from the center.

3 To save time, let the shingles overhang the edges or "run wild." Then come back once the side of the roof is complete, and trim them all at once. You can do this with a sharp utility knife or heavy-duty shears.

installing gutter systems

MOST OF THE TIME, GUTTERS ARE INSTALLED ON EXISTING ROOFS, BUT ADDING new gutters when you are reroofing makes installation easier and integrates them into the entire roof system for better functionality.

Though wood gutters used to be very common, today they are almost obsolete (except in instances when a historic home is being restored) because they are heavy and prone to water-related problems. Contemporary gutters are offered in aluminum; vinyl; galvanized steel; and, for certain high-end installations, stainless steel and copper created by sheet-metal fabricators.

You may be able to save on labor costs by installing your own gutters, but this is not always worth the effort. The most popular gutters today, "seamless gutters," are extruded from metal (typically aluminum with a baked-on finish) "coil" stock on site by a gutter fabricator. They tend to be very secure and are relatively inexpensive to have installed.

The gutter systems that you can buy at Lowe's and install yourself are typically made of vinyl, pre-painted steel, painted aluminum, or galvanized steel. These are known as sectional gutter systems. With these, you buy preformed channels from 10 to 22 feet long and any of many different components that join onto the channels, as shown in the illustration below.

Standard gutter profiles are the simple "U" shape and "K" style, which has an ogee-shaped front. The channels may be 4, 5, or 6 inches in diameter. Matching downspouts are 2-by-3-inch or 3-by-4-inch rectangular profiles or 3- or 4-inch round (often corrugated) pipes. The larger systems are less likely to clog, so they are a good choice if you have trees overhanging your house.

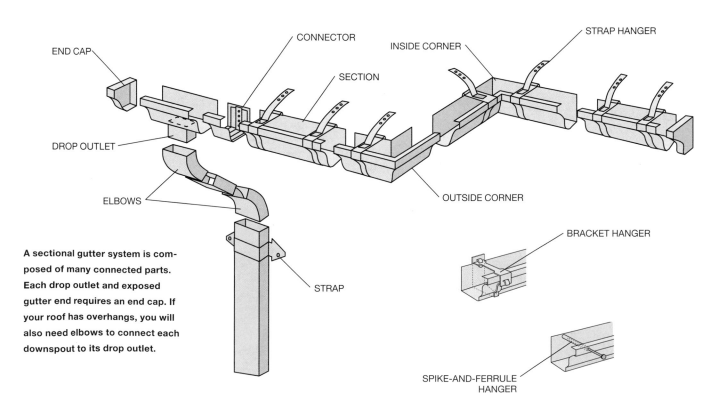

END CAP
CONNECTOR
SECTION
INSIDE CORNER
STRAP HANGER
DROP OUTLET
ELBOWS
OUTSIDE CORNER
STRAP
BRACKET HANGER
SPIKE-AND-FERRULE HANGER

A sectional gutter system is composed of many connected parts. Each drop outlet and exposed gutter end requires an end cap. If your roof has overhangs, you will also need elbows to connect each downspout to its drop outlet.

The appropriate size for gutters is usually figured as a factor of the roof's square area. The chart at right can help you determine the size you need.

One typical vinyl system has elbows, connectors, and other components with silicone gaskets that form watertight seals. You simply plug together the system. Other types are glued together with PVC cement.

Gutters are attached along a house's eaves by any of several types of straps, brackets, and hangers, as shown in the illustration on the facing page. Bracket hangers, which are screwed to the fascia or rafter tails, tend to be the preferred choice. But if the roof does not have such support members, a strap that is ideally mounted beneath the shingles will work. You can plan to install one hanger for every 3 feet of gutter. The gutter shown below is screwed to the fascia.

Downspouts are connected to the gutter with a series of elbows and then secured to the house with wide straps. Plan to install three straps for every 10 feet of downspout.

Before hanging the gutter, assemble the parts on the ground (as much as possible). If your system is the type that utilizes PVC cement to glue together the parts, make sure you do not cement the downspouts to the drop outlets—otherwise you won't be able to take them apart for cleaning.

FIGURING GUTTER SIZE

ROOF AREA (SQ. FT.)	GUTTER DIAMETER	DOWNSPOUT DIAMETER
100–800	4"	3"
800–1,000	5"	3"
1,000–1,400	5"	4"
1,400+	6"	4"

INSTALLING A VINYL GUTTER

1 Stretch a string line between two nails along the fascia, and check it with a line level. At the end where the downspout will go, measure down far enough to achieve a drop of 1 inch per each 20 feet and make a mark. For particularly long runs, plan to slope it from the center to both ends.

2 Attach the gutter drop section onto the fascia where the downspout will go, at the low end of the gutter (ideally at a house corner). Use galvanized screws that will penetrate solid wood by at least 1½ inches. Using a long extension for the screwdriver bit is helpful.

3 With the aid of a helper, fit a length of gutter into the drop section, and then screw the gutter hangers to the fascia, rafter tails, or sheathing (depending upon the type of hangers being used). Continue with this process around the entire perimeter of the house, utilizing elbows to turn corners, connectors to join sections, drop caps to drain into downspouts, and end caps to terminate runs.

PROJECT CONTINUES ➡

4 Hold 45-degree elbows both at the drop outlet and at the wall, and size a section of downspout to fit between them. Cut the downspout to length, and join it to the two fittings. One person can then hold the section at the wall while the other prepares to fasten it.

5 Fit a wall bracket around the elbow of the downspout at the wall, and screw it in place. Use galvanized screws that are long enough to penetrate solid wood by at least 1½ inches. Add an additional length of downspout to reach the base of the wall. Repeat this process wherever there are downspouts.

6 To carry drainage from downspouts away from the house, extend them horizontally and add splash blocks at the base. Water that is allowed to flow from the downspouts directly into the ground may end up in your crawl space or basement and can erode the soil along the house, causing settling.

LEAF-CATCHING SYSTEMS

It's important to keep your gutters free of leaves and other debris so they won't clog up and fill with water. Just the weight of an accumulation of water can dislodge or bend gutters. And, over time, sheet metal gutters may rust when water pools in them.

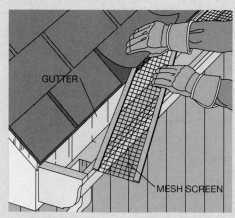

To cut back on gutter-cleaning chores, consider installing a leaf-catching system. These will filter leaves and debris from the water. But buyer beware: Not all types work successfully. And a demonstration will not necessarily reveal how one of these will work in reality. The best way to check out a system is to request the names and phone numbers of satisfied customers whom you can call.

Of course, even gutters that are protected by a leaf-catching system will need to be cleaned occasionally. Be sure that you can remove the system easily (some are difficult to take off because they are screwed in place or tucked under shingles). And also pay special attention to cost—there are some sophisticated leaf-catching systems that are more expensive than the gutters.

repairing gutters

TO WORK EFFECTIVELY, GUTTERS AND DOWNSPOUTS MUST BE SOUND AND HAVE watertight joints; they must slope properly, and they must be free of leaves, twigs, and other debris. Regular maintenance is crucial to avoid flooded or damaged gutters.

In fall and spring, clean out debris with a hose, garden trowel, and/or scrub brush.

Make sure the gutters drain properly by running water through them. If drainage is slow, reposition the gutters; they should slope toward the downspouts at a rate of 1 inch for every 20 linear feet. To correct low spots, adjust the hangers. Very long gutters often drain very slowly or not at all. To remedy this, raise the middle and install a downspout at each end.

This is also the time to tighten loose hangers and replace any that are broken. Check that downspout straps are secured to the house walls and that all elbow connections are tight. Secure loose elbows with ½-inch sheet-metal screws or pop rivets. If a large section of gutter is badly damaged, replace the whole section. Also look for flaking or peeling paint, rust spots, and leaky joints.

If wood gutters leak, let them dry out thoroughly, and then repaint the insides with latex house paint. You can seal pinhole leaks with dabs of roofing cement.

For rusting metal gutters, wash them out thoroughly, removing all dirt and debris, and wipe the damaged areas dry. Then use a wire brush or coarse sandpaper to remove paint, rust, grease, or corrosion. Wipe the surface clean with a rag. Apply aluminum paint to the inside and rust-preventive zinc-based primer to the outside. Mend holes and joints as shown below.

GUTTER REPAIRS

If gutters are not draining properly, the chances are good that they are sagging—a result of failing hangers. In some cases, hangers can be pushed back into position, but, most of the time, it pays to reinforce them. The best way to do this with a spike-and-ferrule system is to drive in a new 7-inch-long galvanized screw as shown.

To patch a leaking gutter, scour the damaged area with a wire brush. Clean it with a rag. Apply a uniform layer of roofing cement, extending it 6 inches beyond the hole. To cover the roofing cement, cut a repair patch from sheet aluminum, copper, or galvanized metal flashing, depending on the gutter's material. Embed the patch in the cement, and apply another coat on top.

solving roof leaks

IT IS A GOOD IDEA TO INSPECT AND REPAIR YOUR ROOF IN AUTUMN, BEFORE THE hard weather hits. Examine the roof again in spring to assess any winter damage. If you discover problems, make the necessary repairs, following the instructions given on pages 354–355. Of course, if the roof is leaking during a storm, trace the course of water to find where it is coming through the roof.

inspecting from inside Begin an inspection in the attic, taking along a strong flashlight, a thin screwdriver, and a piece of chalk. Examine the ridge beam, rafters, and sheathing. Look for water stains, areas of wet wood, moisture, and soft spots that may indicate dry rot. Prod any suspect areas with the screwdriver. If the wood is mushy, mark the spots with chalk so you can find them easily later.

When in the attic, be very careful to step only on ceiling joists or other surfaces that are strong enough to support you. If it is necessary to remove insulation batts to examine the sheathing, be sure to wear gloves, goggles, a respirator, and clothing that fits loosely yet provides full coverage to protect against skin irritation.

Next, turn off any lights, and turn on your flashlight. If you see any holes above you, drive nails or poke short lengths of wire through them so they will be visible from the roof's surface. (In a wood-shingle roof, tiny shafts of light coming in at an angle may indicate separations beneath the shingles that don't leak.)

inspecting from outside When you examine the roof from outdoors, evaluate the condition of the roof structure, surface material, flashing, eaves, and gutters.

Next, inspect the roof's surface. Before climbing up on the roof, be sure to read the safety tips on page 341. If you are at all nervous about going up on the roof, make the inspection from a ladder, using binoculars. Do not walk on the roof any more than is absolutely necessary because you can easily cause more damage.

Inspect the flashing for corrosion and broken seals along the edges. If you have metal gutters and downspouts, look for rust spots and holes (see page 351). Then examine the roof surface itself for signs of wear; loose or broken nails; and curled, broken, or missing shingles.

Leaks rarely appear directly below where they originate. A spreading water stain on the ceiling indicates puddling water. Drive a nail through the leaking area to drain off some of the water into a bucket located directly below.

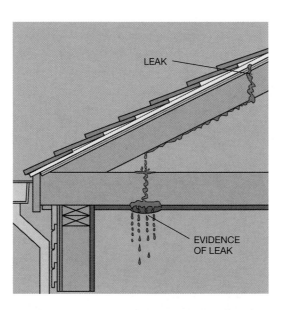

LEAK

EVIDENCE OF LEAK

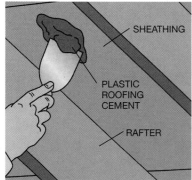

SHEATHING

PLASTIC ROOFING CEMENT

RAFTER

To create an emergency patch, apply plastic roofing cement liberally to the hole from inside using a putty knife or caulking gun. Work the compound in thoroughly so it adheres.

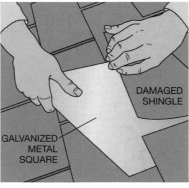

DAMAGED SHINGLE

GALVANIZED METAL SQUARE

To create a temporary shingle, wait until the roof is dry and then slide a 2-foot square of galvanized sheet metal under the shingle row and above the missing or damaged piece.

tile & metal roof repairs

BECAUSE MOST MASONRY-TILE AND METAL ROOFS LAST AS LONG AS THE HOUSE, problems with them are usually limited to leaks, broken tiles, and dented or damaged metal shingles or panels. Though you may be able to handle small patches or replacements, it is better to hire a professional roofer for major problems, particularly with ceramic tile, rounded concrete tile, and metal panel systems.

masonry tile Small holes or cracks can be patched with asphalt roofing cement. If the corner or butt of a masonry tile has cracked, clean the area with a wire brush, and seal the crack with asphalt roofing cement. If the crack extends above the overlap of the tile below, it is best to remove and replace the tile.

If you are replacing a tile on a roof that has tiles laid directly on sheathing, gently pry up the appropriate tile or tiles in the course above the cracked one, and remove the old tile pieces. Spread a little roofing cement on the underside of the replacement tile, and, finally, slide the new tile into position.

If you are replacing tiles that are nailed to battens, use a hammer to break up the old tile. Remove as much of it as you can. Use a prybar to lift the tile or tiles directly above the broken one, and remove nails and any remaining shards with a shingle ripper, a prybar, pliers, or wire cutters. Then spread a little roofing cement on the underside of the replacement tile, and slide it into position, hooking it over the batten (do not nail it).

metal shingles Small holes in metal roofing can be patched like those found in metal flashing (see pages 356–357). When tackling large repairs or replacements, call a metal-roofing specialist.

If you have extra shingles that match the ones on your roof, study the method of interlock to understand what you need to do to remove and replace a shingle that is beyond repair. The chances are good that you will need to cut the damaged shingle

1 Pry up the concrete tile above the damaged one using a flat prybar. As shown, place a short wood block beneath the prybar for leverage and to protect the tile below. Pull out the broken pieces. If necessary, strike the tiles with a hammer to break them into smaller pieces; be sure to wear safety glasses and gloves when doing this.

2 After repairing any tears in the roofing paper underlayment with asphalt roofing cement, lift the tiles in the course directly above the damaged tile's position, using a prybar as shown. Spread roofing cement on the underside of the new tile, and then slip the tile into place.

to remove it and also modify interlocking edges to slip a new one in place. Be sure to protect the roofing paper underlayment beneath shingles, and seal joints and any tears with silicone caulking compound or—better—asphalt roofing cement.

shingled roof repairs

WHEN SHINGLES BEGIN TO AGE, THEY CAN BECOME BRITTLE AND CRACK, ALLOWING water to penetrate. Some shingles can be repaired, but replacement is often necessary.

asphalt shingles The first signs of aging are bald spots and a heavy accumulation of surface granules in the gutters. Check your

Seal a small hole or crack with roofing cement, applying the substance with a putty knife or caulking gun. For tears or curls, liberally apply roofing cement under the pieces, press them down, and then secure them with roofing nails if necessary. Additionally, cover the nail heads with roofing cement.

roof's condition on a warm day, when the shingles should be flexible. Remove a tiny piece of a corner from one or two shingles on each roof plane; the core should be black. Gently bend several shingles back. If a number of shingles appear gray and bloated, if the material crumbles easily, or if you see large bare spots or damaged areas, consider replacing the roofing.

Cracked, torn, or curled shingles can be repaired, as shown at left; also replace any loose or missing nails. If some of the shingles are badly worn or damaged, replace them (see the steps below), using shingles that remain from the original roof installation. (It is always a good idea to store a few extra shingles when you reroof so that you will have material available for repairs.) If you do not have any leftover shingles, you will have to buy new ones that are identical

REPLACING AN ASPHALT SHINGLE

1 To remove a damaged shingle, lift the shingle tab above it. With a prybar, pry out both rows of nails holding the damaged shingle.

2 Slide the new shingle into place, taking care not to damage the roofing felt. (You can snip the top corners if the shingle sticks.)

3 Nail on the new shingle. If you can't lift the tab above it enough to nail underneath, then place a prybar on the nail's head and a block, as shown, and strike the hammer against the prybar to drive in the nail.

REPLACING A WOOD SHINGLE

1 To remove a damaged wood shingle, split it apart with a chisel and hammer and pull out the pieces. Be careful not to cut into the roofing felt beneath the shingle.

2 Hold the replacement shingle just below the spot where it will go, and mark its width. Then move your marks toward the center ¼ inch on each side to allow for expansion caused by moisture.

3 Insert the replacement shingle so it protrudes 1 inch below adjoining shingles; allow ¼ inch clearance on each side. Drive in two roofing nails at an angle just below the edge of the row above (use a nailset to drive the heads flush). Then nudge the edge of the new shingle even with the other shingles, using a hammer and wood block as shown in the detail.

in brand, color, and size, if possible. Fasten the shingles with galvanized roofing nails that are long enough to penetrate all of the roofing layers (at least 1½ inches).

Do not remove a damaged shingle that is on a ridge or along a hip; instead, nail each corner of the shingle in place. Apply roofing cement to the bottom of a new shingle, and place it over the defective one. Nail each corner, and then cover the nail heads with roofing cement.

When you repair asphalt shingles, do the work on a warm day, when the shingles are more pliable. Also, keep the roofing cement at room temperature so that it will spread more easily.

wood shingles & shakes Inspect a wood shake or shingle roof for curled, broken, or split shingles and for any shingles that have been lifted by wind. Look also for shingles that have been thinned by weather

and erosion, especially around areas where an attic inspection reveals pinpoints of light (see page 352).

The extent of the defects you find will indicate whether you will need to repair or replace shingles or shakes. If only a few shingles or shakes are split or wind-lifted, you can repair them; those that are badly splintered or curled should be replaced. If the damage is quite extensive, consider having the entire roof replaced.

To remove the nails from a damaged shingle or shake that you are replacing, either rent a shingle ripper to cut them or use a hacksaw blade. To use the ripper, slide it under the shingle and around a nail. Then cut the shank of the nail by delivering a strong hammer blow.

Trim the replacements to fit the space, allowing ¼-inch clearance on each side for expansion of the wood. Use a roofer's hatchet or a saw to do the trimming.

repairing roof flashing

FLASHING PROTECTS THE ROOF AT ITS MOST VULNERABLE POINTS: IN THE VALLEYS, at roof and plumbing vents, around chimneys, along the eaves—anywhere water can seep through open joints into the sheathing (see page 336). As you might expect, the areas where flashing is located are the most prone to leaks. For information on where flashing is located, see page 344.

Your flashing may be made from plastic, roll roofing, roofing felt, rubber, or a rust-resistant metal such as galvanized steel, aluminum, or copper. The flashing joints may be sealed with roofing cement or a caulking compound that is made for this purpose. Cracked or crumbling roofing cement or caulking is often a major cause of leaks around flashing.

repairing flashing Inspect flashing semiannually. Re-nail or replace any loose nails, and cover all exposed nail heads with roofing cement. Look carefully for holes. You can plug pinholes with small spots of roofing cement.

Patch holes up to about ¾ inch in diameter with the same material as the damaged flashing. To do this, roughen up the area around the hole with a wire brush or sandpaper, and then clean the surface. Cut a patch of flashing material 2 inches larger than the hole on all sides. Apply roofing cement, press the patch in place, and hold it for several minutes. Cover the patch with another generous layer of cement. If you find larger holes, seriously consider replacing the flashing.

Check the all-important seals at the edges of the flashing. If the roofing cement or caulking is cracked, dried, or crumbling, be sure to reseal the joints promptly.

BELOW: To repair chimney flashing, first chip out the old mortar and caulking along the cap flashing. Scour the area with a wire brush, and then seal the joints between the flashing and chimney and between the cap and step flashing with asphalt roofing cement.

ABOVE: When repairing dormer flashing, first remove the old caulking, and then apply new caulking to the joints between the flashing and siding or shingles and between the flashing seams.

LEFT: **To seal vent pipe flashing, apply roofing cement to the joint between the flashing and the pipe. Lift the side and back shingles; apply roofing cement to the joints between the flange and shingles.**

LEFT: **Seal shingles down to valley flashing and to the courses below by lifting their edges along the flashing and spreading roofing cement beneath the shingles.**

RIGHT: **Along the gable rake, lift the shingles and spread roofing cement on the top of the drip edge and the course below. Note: Do not seal the drip edge along the eaves.**

repainting flashing Flashing is often painted to match the roof. Before repainting flashing, use a stiff brush and solvent to remove any flaking paint, rust, or corrosion. (Note: Be sure that you keep solvent off asphalt shingles; it will dissolve them.) Tape newspaper to the roof around the flashing. Apply a zinc-based primer, and then spray on two or more light coats of rust-inhibiting metal paint.

replacing flashing You will need to replace any flashing that has large holes or is badly corroded. You can buy new flashing or cut it out of aluminum or copper. (Always use the same material as the existing flashing, and use the old flashing as a pattern.) When installing new flashing, you will have to remove several courses of shingles as well as the old flashing. If you have no roofing experience, you may want to hire a professional because this job involves removing and replacing sections of roofing.

HOW TO REMOVE ROOFING CEMENT

Roofing cement works wonders. But when it gets all over you and the roof, it can create a mess. Fortunately, roofing cement can be removed with relative ease. Use a rag moistened with kerosene to scrub unwanted cement from both yourself and the roof. Promptly wash any kerosene from your skin, and dispose of the rag properly.

garages

CONSIDER THE GARAGE: IT IS ONE OF THE MAJOR VOLUMES OF ANY HOME SITE, and it contains the home's largest moving part, the garage door. In addition to one or more cars, it often shelters most of the family's outdoor equipment, lesser-used storage items, and even the laundry. Once considered nothing more than an outbuilding, the garage has taken on new prominence in recent years, for several reasons. New technology has improved the workability of the once-clunky hand-operated garage door. In addition, it increasingly is treated as a design element that is able to carry through and enhance the overall look of the architecture and property. And the explosion of attractive, efficient storage systems, ranging from the inexpensive to the high-end, have given new life to the garage as a storage, work, and even play facility.

The new generation of garage doors comes in a variety of materials that are durable, good-looking, and easy to maintain. Many garage doors now include windows that may be dual-glazed for energy efficiency. Most homeowners opt for the automatic garage door opener, a positive boon for people living in inclement weather. But increased complexity of the garage door system means more opportunities for parts to break down. Like any other machine, the garage door needs to be properly maintained to work efficiently.

This chapter, which begins with a garage door buying guide, also offers direction on installing garage doors and openers. It includes advice on garage door adjustments and repairs. Finally, it offers storage ideas and a view of some of the latest garage storage-system improvements.

garage basics

THOUGH BUILDING A NEW GARAGE IS BEYOND THE SCOPE OF THIS BOOK—AND a project you will probably need to hire a contractor to accomplish—in this section, you can gain an understanding of how garages are put together so that you are equipped to handle basic improvements and repairs.

Minor improvements such as replacing a garage door (see pages 367–369) normally do not require permits unless running new electrical wiring is necessary. If it is your intention to build a freestanding garage or undertake major garage improvements, you will need to obtain both a building permit and permission from your city's planning department. Make sure you check with this agency for height limitations and minimum setbacks from property lines.

garage construction

Garages are built much like houses that have a slab foundation and wood frame structure. One difference is that a garage floor may be pitched very slightly toward the garage door to allow for runoff, particularly near the opening.

Garage walls are normally framed with 2 by 4s attached to a treated-lumber sole plate. Corners are braced with plywood sheathing, let-in braces, or metal straps. Insulating foam sheathing adds no structural support, but it can make a garage warmer in winter and cooler in summer. House wrap or building paper over the sheathing provides extra weather protection. Windows and doors are installed after the walls are sheathed or sided.

A garage roof may be framed with trusses, but some are "stick framed" with rafters and ceiling joists of 2-by lumber. The roof is typically sheathed with plywood or with oriented strand board (OSB). Flashing and roofing are applied just as on the roof of a house (see the Roofing chapter, which begins on page 330).

the garage door

The two main types of garage doors are sectional roll-ups and tilt-ups. A roll-up, or sectional, door is the most common type on the market. It is made up of several sections hinged together; it moves up and down on rollers housed in channeled tracks along each side so that the door can roll straight up and back. A torsion spring across the top of the door or extension springs along the sides help with lifting or lowering the door. Although the latter system is easier and safer to install, a torsion spring requires less regular maintenance once it is in place.

Swing-up or one-piece doors pivot on hinges and are assisted by large springs located on each side. They cost 25 percent

Side-by-side steel flush-panel sectional doors are as durable as they are handsome. Aesthetically, a pair of doors is less imposing than a single, large door.

to 35 percent less than roll-up doors, but they offer less headroom, do not seal the garage opening as tightly or securely, and swing outward, which means you cannot park the car within 2 to 3 feet of them.

Both roll-up and swing-up doors are made from a variety of materials in flush, raised-panel, and recessed-panel designs and can be purchased with options such as windows and electric openers.

Because a garage door typically is used day after day and is normally a very visible, key element on a house, it is important for this door to work well and look good. If your garage door is shoddy or falling apart, it is probably best to replace it with one that is easy to maintain and operate, rather than to repair it.

For more information on installing a new garage door or garage door opener and simple garage repairs, see pages 367–373.

selecting the right material

You can purchase a garage door made from wood, steel, aluminum, or fiberglass. Each of these materials has certain benefits, but wood and steel—both sold at Lowe's—are favored for several reasons.

wood doors Wood is affordable and attractive, but it is subject to weather damage if not maintained with a durable finish. With changes in temperature and humidity, wood expands and contracts, which can cause it to warp, so it requires periodic repainting or refinishing.

A tilt-up wood door, in some cases, can be built right in the driveway by applying a skin of exterior plywood (usually ³⁄₈ inch thick) to a frame of Douglas fir, spruce, or similar softwood. Or the frame and plywood can be covered with siding to match the house. Unless you are an accomplished

Wood recessed-panel garage doors complement this stately home's warmth and elegance.

and embossing technologies, many of the newer steel doors do a fairly successful job of imitating the look of wood. Unlike wood, steel doors will not crack, warp, or fall apart, and they have extremely durable finishes. They are often warranted for the life of the house. But steel will dent, and dents can be difficult to fix.

The best steel doors are a full 2 inches thick, are clad in 24-gauge steel, and have a core of rigid foam insulation built into a steel frame. The insulation helps keep the garage temperate inside and, in addition, makes the door lightweight. Double-skin construction, where the inside of the door has a skin similar to the outside, is the best (and most attractive) construction. To in-stall an average-size steel door (16 by 7 feet), expect to pay from $750 to $1,200.

aluminum doors Aluminum garage doors are extremely lightweight and rust-proof. They have durable finishes and

Grooved panels add a touch of visual interest to these side-by-side sectional wood doors.

carpenter, this job is best left in the hands of a garage door installer.

Roll-up wood door sections may have either flush sections, made by fastening a plywood panel over a wooden frame, or panel construction, in which manufacturers fit several separate rectangular panels into a wooden frame.

Garage doors come in three quality levels. Paneled doors that are meant to be painted may be made of wood, plywood, or wood-composite products. Installed, an average-sized paint-grade sectional door (16-by-7-foot) costs from $800 to $1,000. Stain-quality garage doors have solid wood panel inserts, made from any of a variety of softwoods and hardwoods. Be aware that if the panels are made from several pieces edge-glued together, the joints between them may show when you stain the panels. Appearance-grade wood doors are the most expensive garage doors on the market, ranging from about $1,500 to $2,000 or more.

steel doors Steel garage doors are very strong and secure. And thanks to coatings

wood-grain embossing. These doors are easily dented, however. They cost from $400 to $700.

fiberglass doors Fiberglass doors are sometimes appropriate for corrosive ocean climates or for situations where the home-owner wants to let in plenty of daylight (fiberglass is translucent). But fiberglass cracks, breaks fairly easily, and may yellow with age.

garage door options

Most manufacturers offer window sections that provide both daylight and a decorative accent. The windows in these sections may have conventional single glazing or more energy-efficient dual glazing.

Some sectional-door manufacturers offer torsion springs, such as the type shown on pages 367–369, as an option. These springs are the safest and best type for sectional doors because they distribute the door's weight evenly and resist breaking and flying off the way an extension spring can.

A favorite option is the automatic door operator. The good ones have lifetime warranties, photoelectric safety devices, and frequency codes that cannot be cracked by thieves.

where to buy garage doors

If you intend to install your own garage door, be sure to check out the offerings at Lowe's. Make certain that the door you buy comes with complete, easy-to-follow installation instructions and (if it has extension springs) includes an extension spring containment kit for safety (see the safety tip on page 367 for more about springs). If you want to buy a door and then have it installed, look up "Garage Doors & Door Operating Devices" in the Yellow Pages to find companies that distribute or manufacture and install doors. Be sure to get at least three bids for the work.

LEFT: **Steel garage doors can take on the traditional look of wood doors, as evidenced by these raised-panel models.**

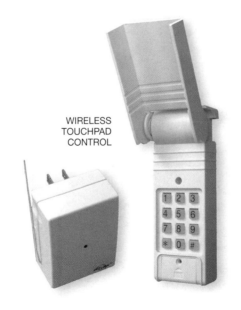

WIRELESS TOUCHPAD CONTROL

MINI-REMOTE TRANSMITTER

WIRELESS KEYLESS ENTRY PAD

Garage door accessories include a variety of transmitter/control options.

BASIC TOOLS FOR GARAGES

Lineman's pliers

Socket wrench and socket set

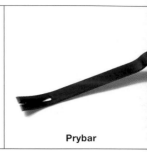

Prybar

Paint rollers

Clamps

Adjustable wrench

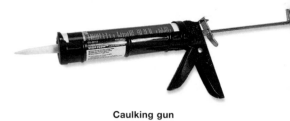

Caulking gun

Level

Rib-joint pliers

Roller tray

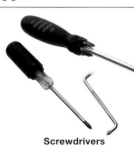

Screwdrivers

Circuit tester

Wire strippers

Power drill with bits
and screwdriver tips

Paintbrushes

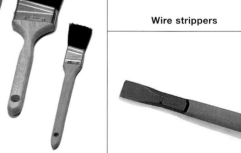

Cold chisel

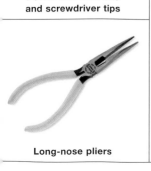

Long-nose pliers

Stepladder

Diagonal wire cutters

Cable ripper

garage tools

FOR GARAGE STORAGE PROJECTS OR TO INSTALL A GARAGE DOOR, YOU WILL want a variety of conventional carpentry tools, including a hammer, a power circular saw, and a long tape measure; for more about these and other carpentry tools, see pages 102–104 and 302–305. Here we list a few more tools that will be necessary for garage-related jobs—most notably installing a garage door and a garage door opener.

TOOLS FOR HANGING GARAGE DOORS

For attaching hinges and hardware, you will need a socket wrench and socket set; a power drill with screwdriver tips and/or a nut driver can really expedite this work. In addition, you will probably want an adjustable wrench and screwdrivers. Rib-joint pliers may come in handy for gripping various hardware pieces. A level is necessary for making sure the tracks are plumb. A prybar can be helpful for nudging pieces that are out of alignment. Use a pair of clamps to hold sections of the door in place as you work. And have a stepladder on hand when you hang the horizontal sections of track.

POWER DRILL WITH BITS AND SCREWDRIVER TIPS

RIB-JOINT PLIERS

LEVEL

ADJUSTABLE WRENCH

SCREWDRIVERS

PRYBAR

STEPLADDER

CLAMPS

SOCKET WRENCH AND SOCKET SET

TOOLS FOR INSTALLING AN OPENER

Installing a garage door opener requires most of the same tools needed for putting in a garage door (see page 365), plus a few more for the electrical work involved. You may need a circuit tester so you can check the electrical circuit for power. For working with wires, plan to have on hand a cable ripper, diagonal wire cutters, wire strippers, and lineman's pliers. In some cases, you may also need a pair of long-nose pliers.

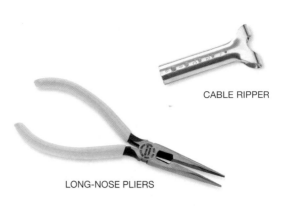

CABLE RIPPER

LONG-NOSE PLIERS

LINEMAN'S PLIERS

DIAGONAL WIRE CUTTERS

CIRCUIT TESTER

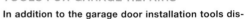

WIRE STRIPPERS

TOOLS FOR GARAGE REPAIRS

In addition to the garage door installation tools discussed on page 365 and the electrical tools above, basic repairs may call for a caulking gun; a cold chisel for any concrete work; and basic painting tools such as a paint roller, roller tray, and paintbrushes.

CAULKING GUN

ROLLER TRAY

COLD CHISEL

PAINT ROLLERS

PAINTBRUSHES

GARAGES

installing a garage door

WHEN YOU BUY A NEW GARAGE DOOR AT LOWE'S, YOU CAN HAVE IT DELIVERED
and installed for a reasonable fee. But if you're an adept do-it-yourselfer, you may find

that installing your own garage door can
both save you money and grant you the satisfaction of accomplishing a heady task.

Sectional garage doors—the type sold at
Lowe's—move up and down on rollers that
travel along tracks installed on each side of
the garage doorway.

If your old or new door has a standard
torsion spring mechanism (as shown at
right), do not install or remove the spring
yourself (see the safety tip below right).
Talk to your Lowe's sales specialist about
installation options. The model of door
shown below and on the following pages
has a torsion spring mechanism designed
for safer and easier installation, but you
should still be very careful during installation and follow all of the manufacturer's
instructions implicitly.

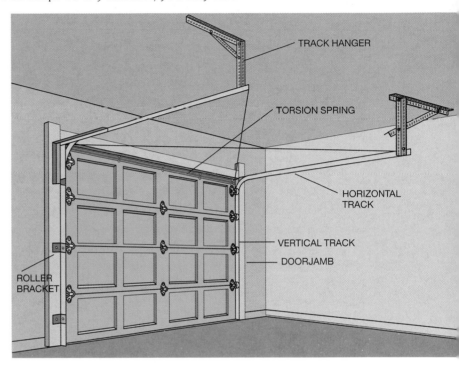

TRACK HANGER

TORSION SPRING

HORIZONTAL TRACK

VERTICAL TRACK

DOORJAMB

ROLLER BRACKET

1 After attaching weather stripping to the bottom edge of the first panel, set the panel in
the doorway and fix it in place by driving nails partway into each jamb at an angle so that they wedge
the door in place. Attach the hinges to the top
edge of the door if they aren't already attached.

2 Following the manufacturer's instructions,
assemble the various pieces for the vertical,
curved, and horizontal tracks.

PROJECT CONTINUES ➡

3 Install the rollers and any necessary brackets on the door section and any wall- or jamb-mounted brackets according to the manufacturer's directions. At one side of the doorway, slip the vertical track onto the rollers of the first door section. Repeat at the other side.

4 Install the rollers into the second section. With a helper, lift the section, set it in place, and slip its rollers into the vertical tracks at both sides of the doorway.

5 Fasten the hinges of the first section to the second one. For most types of doors, a power drill with a screwdriver tip or nut driver will make this work much faster and easier.

6 Install the third section, using the same procedures. Check the door for level and the vertical track for plumb. Fasten the top plates of both vertical tracks to the wall. Make sure the lag screws amply penetrate the framing members because the door will exert considerable force as it moves up and down.

7 Attach the jamb brackets to the tracks, and fasten them to the framing members. Again, make sure the lag screws go into sound framing. Don't tighten down the lag screws yet because you may need to adjust the tracks.

8 Install the curved and horizontal tracks, positioning the curved track as shown. Bolt the pieces together. If necessary, you can rest the horizontal track on top of a ladder.

9 Check the horizontal track for level, and then cut the rear track hanger to the length necessary for supporting the track. Screw the track hanger to solid framing (a ceiling joist or blocking) and loosely mount the track to the hanger. Repeat with the other horizontal track. Fit the last door section in place, and remove any temporary nails.

10 The type of door shown here provides the necessary lift assistance with a "torque tube." If you intend to use an opener (see page 370), wait to install the tube. Otherwise, install the torque tube according to the manufacturer's directions. Roll up the door about 4 feet to check for the alignment of the tracks, and make any adjustments. Then tighten all fasteners.

installing a garage door opener

SEVERAL TYPES OF GARAGE DOOR OPENERS ARE SOLD TODAY. EACH HAS AN ELECtric motor driving a lifting device—a chain or belt, for example—that is fastened to the door. Lowe's professionals will install a garage door opener on your door for a fee, but this job, like installing the door itself, is one that you may be able to handle if you're an experienced do-it-yourselfer.

The most common type of opener has its motor mounted over the area where the car is parked. Though this variety is functional, its location is a drawback in some garages because it can obstruct the ceiling area. As an alternative to this old standby, we have chosen to show how to install a new opener sold at Lowe's that mounts on the same wall as the garage door. Meant for a door that weighs no more than 225 pounds, it is somewhat easy to install and is located out of the way. In addition, because it doesn't employ a chain, it is relatively quiet and

vibration-free. The type shown is designed for connecting to a door's encapsulated torsion spring mechanism (see page 367). Other models of this opener are made for use with other garage door spring systems.

All manufacturers offer a variety of optional accessories with their openers, including remote controls, keyless entry pads, and keyed switches.

And, of course, all openers come with manufacturer's directions. Regardless of the type you choose, follow the accompanying instructions exactly.

1 This opener is designed to fit onto a torque tube spring system (see page 369); refer to the manufacturer's directions for other types of springs. If the torque tube has already been installed, remove it and slip the drive motor onto it.

2 With the drive motor in place, reinstall the torque tube, end bracket, and cable drum.

3 Using ¼-inch by 2-inch-long lag screws, fasten the mounting bracket for the drive motor to the wall above the garage door. Make sure the lag screws amply penetrate the beam or any other framing members located above the door.

4 Attach the disconnect cable to the motor with an S hook, and thread it through the wall bracket and the handle. Pull it just enough to remove the slack, and secure the bracket to the wall at least 6 feet above the floor. Put a label on the wall to identify this emergency disconnect device.

5 To keep the door from lifting, clamp locking pliers on both side tracks just above the third roller. Use a socket wrench to rotate the winding bolt head the number of turns specified in the owner's manual for your door.

PROJECT CONTINUES ➡

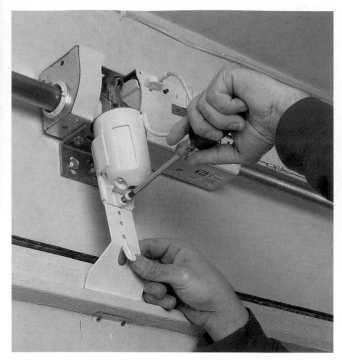

6 Set the emergency disconnect in the manual position, and raise the door until it is fully open. Then lower the door until it is fully closed to be sure it moves freely. Attach the stop bracket to the drive motor.

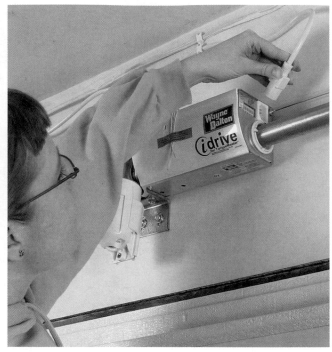

7 Securely plug the female end of the power cord into the opener. Then run the cord to the nearest grounded receptacle and plug it in. If the cord is not long enough to reach a receptacle, use an approved cord extender.

ADJUSTING A CONVENTIONAL DOOR OPENER

Here are a few simple adjustments you can make to keep your door operating properly and safely with a standard opener. Be sure to refer to your owner's manual for proper calibrations.

Adjust the up/down limits With the door closed, press the open button on the wall control panel. If the door opens at least 5 feet but not completely, turn the limit-adjustment screw clockwise slightly. If the door will not close, turn the down-adjustment screw counterclockwise. If nothing is blocking the sensors yet the door reverses when closing, increase the down force.

Adjust the force If the door does not open at least 5 feet, increase the up force slightly. Press the down button on the control panel. While the door is descending, grab the bottom. If the door does not reverse, or if the door reverses automatically while closing, decrease the down force. To adjust the up force, grab the door as it is opening. If the door does not stop, decrease the up force.

Adjust the safety reverse To test the safety reverse system, close the door on a 2 by 4. If the door stops but does not reverse, increase the down limit one-quarter turn clockwise, and then repeat the test.

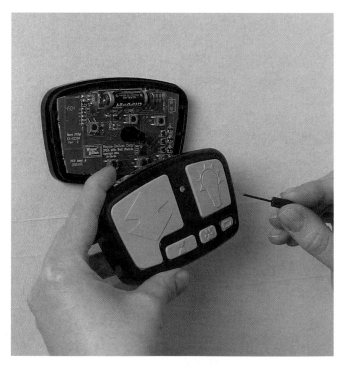

8 Mount the remote control. Install the battery provided, and replace the touch pad. Finally, test the door. Place a 2 by 4 flat on the ground under the door to make sure it stops and reverses automatically when it encounters an obstacle (see the box at left).

garage door repairs

WHEN SOMETHING GOES WRONG WITH A GARAGE DOOR, THE RESULT CAN BE NOT only inconvenient but also dangerous. A garage door, after all, is your home's largest moving part. With that in mind, it is important to check yearly for problems and to maintain the door properly.

Look for loose or worn hinges, springs, and hardware. Periodically clean tracks and lubricate rollers with a penetrating oil or spray. Tighten screws, bolts, and nuts on hardware, and clean and lubricate hinges. While you are at it, squirt a little graphite into the lock to keep it working correctly.

Inspect the springs. Look for bulges, rusting, or uneven spacing. Do not try to adjust or replace tension springs yourself; call a professional to handle this dangerous job. You can, however, safely adjust the wire tension cable.

If you are having problems with a door that has an automatic opener, disconnect the opener, and try the door manually. This will tell you if the opener or the mechanics of the door are in need of repair. The door should work effortlessly before it is connected to the opener. Do not try to compensate for a bad door by adjusting the door opener, you will just wear out the mechanism. For more information on adjusting a garage door opener, see the facing page.

Prevent moisture from damaging a wood door by maintaining the door with paint or stain. A door should be finished not only on the outer surface but also on all edges (especially the bottom edge) and the inside surface. When the paint or stain begins to show signs of wear, apply another layer. If the door and garage opening are weather-stripped, be sure the seal is in good condition. If it is not, pry it off, and nail on a replacement.

When the garage door binds in the opening, rollers are in the wrong position or set too deep. Adjust the placement of the brackets, placing a shim behind them if necessary.

If some rollers bind in the tracks, tighten loose hinges and repair bent ones. Lubricate the rollers with penetrating oil. If any rollers are broken, replace them with new ones.

When a door drags in its tracks, the tracks may be out of alignment. Loosen all the brackets and tap them with a wood block to realign them, and then tighten the bolts.

garage storage improvements

THE GARAGE IS OFTEN ONE OF A HOME'S KEY STORAGE AREAS. BUT BECAUSE THE space it offers is rarely used efficiently, the garage is a prime candidate for storage improvements. You can buy modular storage system kits with components that can be mixed and matched to solve many storage problems. Or you can build your own storage solutions. The improvements shown on these two pages may help you to reduce clutter, improve organization, and store seasonal items more conveniently.

Metal shelves provide very practical garage storage. Here they are used in conjunction with plastic containers to provide both open and closed storage.

The most popular types of garage storage and organization aids are cabinets, shelves, various wall-mounted racks, and plastic containers. Cabinets work well for hiding clutter and protecting their contents from moisture and dust. Shelves tend to be more affordable than cabinets; they efficiently save space and make paraphernalia more accessible by getting it off the floor. Wall-mounted racks, the most affordable of all, are great for keeping tools as well as equipment handy. Store items that need to be protected from moisture inside of plastic containers. Buy the type that you can stack; clear plastic works well because it allows you to see what's inside.

LEFT: These ready-to-assemble cabinets supply a wealth of storage for garage items. Plastic containers fitted inside them further protect the contents.

BELOW: Track-mounted shelving creates a versatile storage system that you can easily adjust to fit particular items.

ABOVE: A system of free-standing cabinets makes for neat, accessible storage. The lighting and perforated-board wall of this garage work center extend its usefulness.

plumbing

FRESH WATER COMES INTO OUR HOMES AT THE TURN OF A FAUCET, WASTE WATER flows out, and hot water is ready whenever we need it. We tend to take such ready access and efficiency in our homes for granted—that is, until the plumbing stops working and we realize just how critical this system is to the functioning of the household.

Most people do not take preemptive steps to have their home's pipes and joints checked on occasion, the way you would service a car to check for worn belts and hoses. But pipes age, corrode, and break open, and fixtures and water-dependent appliances become worn over time. Plumbing problems tend to happen suddenly, at inopportune times, and they demand immediate attention.

Fortunately, many plumbing repairs are reasonably easily accomplished by home-owners equipped with a few tools and a basic understanding of plumbing. Repairing leaky faucets is only one of the tasks that can be handled with aplomb. Many plumbing improvements—including installing new faucets or fixtures, changing water filters, and hooking up kitchen and laundry appliances—are within a typical homeowner's capability.

This chapter begins with a buyer's guide to plumbing fixtures, plus an explanation of the plumbing system anatomy. It reviews different piping materials, from metals to plastics, and instructs you on how to work with them. The chapter proceeds to roughing-in fixtures, with step-by-step installation instructions for various kitchen, bath, and laundry appliances and fixtures. Finally, it teaches you how to repair any malfunctioning pipes, faucets, toilets, tubs and showers, and water heaters.

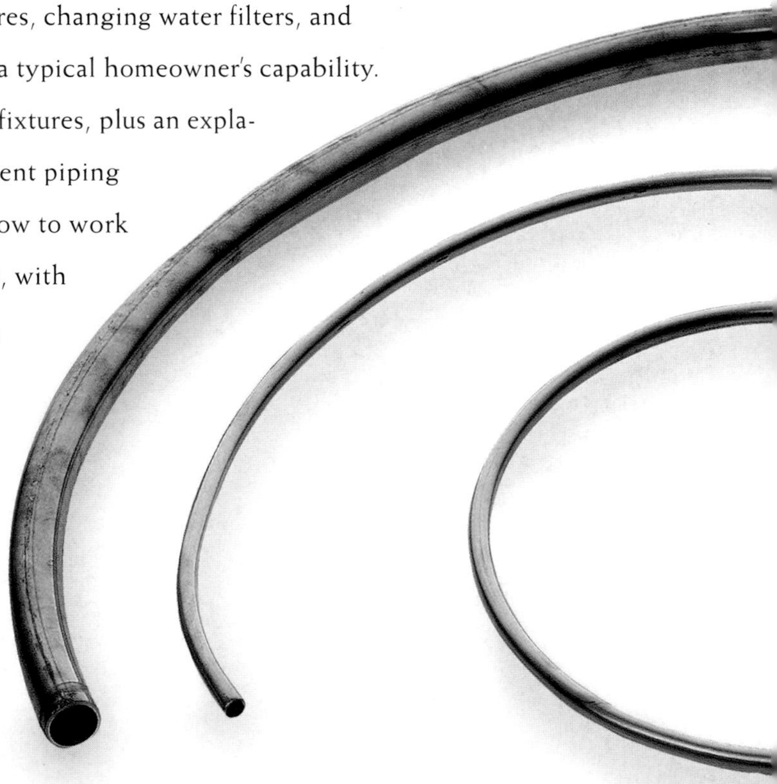

buyer's guide to plumbing fixtures

FAUCETS, FIXTURES, AND APPLIANCES ARE CRITICAL TO THE SUCCESS OF A HOME'S plumbing systems. These elements set the style and provide interesting visual details in key rooms such as kitchens and bathrooms. But, more important, they offer the practical functions that keep these rooms operating smoothly and efficiently.

faucets

With kitchen and bath faucets, beauty truly is only surface-deep—a faucet is only as good as its inner workings. Because every faucet contains an inner valve that controls water flow through the spout, the quality of that valve determines how drip-free, reliable, and durable the faucet will be.

The best, and most expensive, are disc faucets, which are ultra-durable and nearly maintenance-free. They employ two fire-hardened and precision-flattened ceramic discs that shear against each other to control water flow. Rotating-ball faucets use a rotating metal or plastic ball to control flow, while cartridge faucets employ rubber O-rings inside a cylindrical cartridge. Compression faucets, in which a stem rises and falls to open and close the waterway, are the least expensive and least durable; they drip when the washer at the base of the stem wears out. With all faucets, the price point is a good indicator of quality, so it pays to buy the best faucet you can afford. Look for faucets that have lifetime guarantees against leaks and drips.

While faucets come in almost any shape, configuration, and style imaginable, most are made from brass. The better ones are cast in molds and are then finished with chrome, brass plating, nickel, porcelain, pewter, or powder-coated enamel. Brush-coated metal finishes hide water spots better than high-polish finishes.

kitchen faucets Kitchen faucets come in many configurations. The most practical is a single-lever faucet that allows for easy one-handed temperature adjustment; even better is the single-lever faucet with a pull-out spout-sprayer that lends flexibility to cleanup. Other faucets include the two-handle centerset, which has a base plate that spans three sink holes; the two-handle widespread faucet, in which the spout and handles are separately mounted; and the wall-mounted faucet. Specialty faucets include water-filtering spouts with under-sink replaceable water filters and separate pullout sprayers (these sprayers, however,

TOP: **This single-lever kitchen faucet features flowing lines and a pull-out spout-sprayer.** RIGHT: Next to this arching gooseneck widespread faucet is a smaller version that serves up filtered water (see page 389 for more on filters).

LEFT: **This widespread bath faucet combines Victorian elegance with precision-flattened ceramic disc workings.**

can be unreliable). Also popular are single-spout swing-arm faucets mounted at the back of the stove for easy pot fill-ups.

bathroom faucets

A bathroom requires at least two sets of faucets, one for the sink and one for the bath. The four basic styles of bathroom faucets are centerset, made for predrilled sinks, which combine a spout and valves on a single base unit; single-lever, which have one handle; widespread, which have components mounted separately on the sink, bath, or countertop; and wall-mounted varieties. Bathroom vanities and pedestals are designed to receive centerset, single-lever, and widespread styles; wall-mounted faucets typically are paired with above-counter and freestanding basins that require a long faucet spout. If your sink has predrilled holes, check that your choice of faucet fits the configuration. If you have young children, consider a scald-guard or temperature-control feature.

sinks

One of the hardest-working fixtures in your home is the sink. Kitchen sinks, particularly, are frequently used—at least an hour per day in most homes—and can be subject to quite a pounding. Bathroom sinks, with the exception of those in powder rooms, are also heavily used. When shopping for sinks, you will want to find ones that are durable and easy to clean, as well as pleasing to the eye.

For both kitchen and bath, Lowe's offers sinks of every size, depth, and configuration. They are composed of a variety of

ABOVE: **A high-polish brass finish and porcelain handles highlight this gooseneck bathroom centerset faucet.** BELOW: **A centerset faucet can offer the style of a widespread faucet in a single unit at half the cost.**

RIGHT: This cast-iron double-basin sink is rock hard and easy to clean, as well as stain- and chip-resistant.

ABOVE: Stainless steel is extremely popular as a kitchen-sink material, particularly in contemporary kitchens, because it is very durable, easy to clean, and often high-tech in appearance.

materials and are available in an array of colors, textures, and patterns at a wide range of price points. It pays to scan the options for sinks that perfectly fit your lifestyle and your design scheme.

kitchen sinks

The standard kitchen sink is 22 by 30 inches, with two equal-sized bowls that are 8 inches deep. But specialty sinks can cater to your preferences. There are sinks with 9- or 10-inch-deep bowls if you frequently use large pots, high-set shallow bowls that go between the two basins for peeling and washing vegetables, oversize single basins, unequally sized basins, and basins that fit into tight corners. Materials include stainless steel (the heavier the gauge, the better); easy-clean enameled cast iron, which provides the greatest number of color choices and an elegant, hard finish; integral solid surface, which forms part of a solid-surface countertop; composite ("quartz" composite is the

most durable of the choices); old-fashioned soapstone; and new-style concrete. Other more delicate and decorative materials, such as vitreous china, brass, and copper, are best left for less frequently used sinks, such as those installed in a bar or powder room. Self-rimming sinks, which sit on the countertop, are the easiest to install but can also collect dirt at the seams. Undermount sinks, which attach to the underside of the counter, stay cleaner but are also more difficult to seat. Kitchen sinks generally come with four holes used for mounting faucets and sprayers, plus dispensers for hot water, liquid soap, and purified water.

bathroom sinks

As the number and type of bathrooms in the average home have expanded, so has the selection of bathroom sinks, which now range from tiny wall-hung versions for the smallest of powder rooms to elaborate dual-basin models for luxurious master baths. Materials include enameled cast iron or vitreous china for traditional baths, and metal, glass, crystal, stone, or solid-surface resins for a contemporary style. Save the most delicate sinks for little-used bathrooms, such as powder rooms and guest baths, where you will want to make a design statement; use the most durable sinks for the kids' bathroom. Deck-mounted models, which can be set into or on top of a vanity or a freestanding frame, allow for storage, unlike pedestal or wall-mounted sink styles. Integral bowl sinks, like their kitchen counterparts, form part of a countertop and come in many prices, colors, and materials, including fiberglass, solid-surface, vitreous china, concrete, and cast polymer. Console sinks, which offer an expanded deck space for sundries, sit on furniture-style legs to create a stylish, spacious look. Some bathroom sinks come with predrilled faucet holes.

garbage disposals

Garbage disposals are a cook's best friend, grinding up and washing away kitchen refuse with the touch of a switch. Invest in a unit that delivers at minimum $\frac{1}{2}$ horsepower; one of lesser power can get stuck easily and will likely need replacing after only a few years.

Most garbage disposals fit the standard drain outlet. They are either hard-wired or plugged into a 120-volt box or receptacle. The most common disposals are switch-activated, but there are "batch-feed" models that start when you insert and turn a special drain plug. Additionally, local safety codes may determine the distance a switch must be located from the sink; the farther away, the safer. Disposals are never whisper-quiet, and, under certain sinks, such as stainless steel, they can be quite noisy if they are

TOP LEFT: **Lavatory bowls come in a variety of shapes, colors, and sizes. This self-rimming deck-mounted porcelain model is set into the countertop.** TOP RIGHT: **Where elbow room is tight, this wall-mounted corner sink is a terrific answer.** BOTTOM LEFT: **A pedestal sink concedes storage as well as counter space but makes up for it in charm and elegance.** BOTTOM RIGHT: **A contemporary console offers a sink, a countertop, and cabinetry.**

RIGHT: A batch-feed gar-bage disposal operates when the drain cover is inserted into the drain. Because no wall switch is needed, installation is relatively easy.

not generously insulated. Generally, the fatter the disposal, the more quietly it will run, although you need to make sure that the disposal you choose fits comfortably under your sink.

A good disposal can last for many years, especially if you avoid clogging it with such fibrous foods as celery, potato skins, melon rinds and other fruit and vegetable peels, eggshells, and coffee grounds.

dishwashers

Dishwashers are staples in today's kitchens, and it's no wonder. The latest models are quiet, energy-efficient, capable of grinding and disposing food residue, gentle enough to clean delicate fine china and crystal, pow-erful enough to scrub pots and pans, and hot enough to kill bacteria. The standard dish-washer is 24 inches wide, 24 inches deep, and 34 inches high, but 18-inch-wide ver-sions are also available. The better models feature stainless-steel interiors. Different dishwashers sport various types and config-urations of racks, including ones that adjust up and down and ones that feature fold-down trays and removable or adjustable tines. Exterior finishes include enameled steel in white, black, or almond; black glass; and stainless steel; most models also offer a replaceable colored panel to blend with base cabinets. Prices vary widely depending on construction and the num-ber of features offered.

noise level Improved sound insulation, sound-absorbing washtubs (particularly those made of stainless steel), vibration absorbers, and low-noise pumps make dish-washers nearly noiseless.

energy efficiency Federal regulations require dishwashers to use half the electric-ity of earlier models. Today's models also use much less water. Many heat their own water to between 120 and 140 degrees Fahrenheit for a normal load and to 155 degrees for sterilizing. Stainless-steel inte-riors cost more but are also more efficient during the dry cycle. Air drying is always an energy-saving option.

residue elimination The newest dish-washers eliminate the need to rinse dishes before loading by including a built-in garbage disposal. This device, also called a "hard-food disposer," grinds and flushes food residue. Filters also have improved but still need to be checked and cleared period-ically. You should, however, always rinse tomato-based residue if you have a plastic tub to avoid staining.

Dishwashers offer a number of options such as the three full racks, four wash arms, and stainless-steel interior shown here.

controls Manual controls are still available, but user-friendly electronic controls are more common. The more expensive the machine, the more cycle choices you will have, allowing you to tailor the wash and dry cycles to the machine's contents. A "delay start" function allows you to program the machine for off-peak hours.

bathtubs

Bathtubs come in four basic styles: recessed, corner, drop-in, and freestanding, which reflect their installation methods. Both traditional tubs and whirlpool tubs come in all four styles, and, within these categories, there are a variety of shapes, sizes, colors, and materials. Tubs are available in right- and left-handed versions—the term indicates which end of the tub contains the drain hole.

recessed tubs Also called a three-wall-alcove tub, the recessed style is the most popular due to its space efficiency, affordability, and availability. Only the front has a decorative finish because alcove walls conceal the other sides. The standard length is 60 inches; the standard depth is 14 inches; but 72-inch-long models and 16-inch-deep tubs are available. Recessed tubs typically are made of enameled steel, which is relatively lightweight and inexpensive but is also noisy and prone to chipping; a better choice is expensive enameled cast iron, but the bathroom floor may need reinforcement to support its heavy weight.

corner tubs While the term specifically applies to a triangular tub with a finished front and two unfinished sides, it generally refers to any shape tub installed in a corner with at least two sides against a wall and one decorative side visible. The boxy white basic bathtub is available in a corner model with a finished end and one finished side.

drop-in tubs Available in a variety of styles and configurations, drop-in tubs usually are mounted on a platform, but they can be sunk below floor level. Some over-

ABOVE: **This jetted three-wall-alcove tub nestles into a corner; a custom cabinet houses the tub's motor.** LEFT: **This drop-in acrylic whirlpool becomes a corner tub.**

lap the deck, others are undermounted; only the inside of the tub is finished. Drop-in tubs are made of lightweight acrylic or fiberglass-reinforced plastic—these are susceptible to scratching and dulling—or of enameled cast iron, which may require structural reinforcement.

freestanding tubs Most are built with four legs (though some are designed to fit into a frame), with completely finished

Though it has the classic look of a claw-foot tub, this freestanding beauty is equipped with 120 air jets on the tub's floor. The blower motor and plumbing are hidden from view under the floor.

RIGHT: This cast-acrylic whirlpool bathtub is set into an island that provides special framing.
FAR RIGHT: Where you want a tub-and-shower combination, a prefab unit such as this one eliminates the need for tile.

exteriors. Reproductions of antique claw-foot tubs in light-weight materials are easy to find, as are reconditioned antiques. A true antique will be made of cast iron, so floor buttressing may be required.

whirlpool tubs

In addition to its function as a regular bathtub, a whirlpool tub offers motorized circulation jets that provide a soothing hydromassage. They are available in recessed, corner, drop-in, and freestanding styles, but most are built for platform installation. With some models, the pump can be located separately for

noise control and ease of service. Whirlpool tubs may require special framing, an additional dedicated water heater, or a dedicated electrical circuit. Some types of whirlpools have variable-speed pumps with electronic controls that adjust the power of the massage. Those controls also set temperatures and cycle times. Jets vary in size, number, and power. Air jets are smaller and less powerful than water jets, which mix water with air; they provide a lighter massage but keep mildew and other substances from accumulating.

showers

According to the National Association of Home Builders, 85 percent of Americans buying a home consider a separate shower enclosure an essential or highly desirable bathroom feature. Showers, which require a minimum of 36 square inches, range from prefabricated fiberglass stalls to spacious custom-built shower spas. They can be built from scratch or assembled from manufactured components. Your shower stall will require either a single, double, or triple threshold—depending on whether it is set into three walls, two walls, or against a single wall.

prefabricated stalls

One-piece molded fiberglass, laminate, or synthetic marble showers are watertight, relatively inexpensive, simple to install, and easy to clean. Many

LEFT: This corner-style shower door system encloses a tub on two sides. The unit features bypass sliding doors and a brass finish.

BELOW: Shower stall doors can either pivot—which allows them to open both in and out—or swing open. In either case, make sure the fit is watertight.

ABOVE: A conventional sliding door set works well for an alcove tub.

prefab stalls include integral shelves, benches, and grab bars and come in square, rectangular, and corner configurations. One-piece showers, which are usually too large for a remodel unless some walls are knocked down, are common in new construction. For remodels, manufactured shower wall panels that are assembled on site are preferred. These panels lap over a molded shower base and are attached to a water-proofed wall.

With the exception of one-piece showers, all showers begin with a base, sometimes called a receptor or a "pan," which can be purchased ready-made or built by hand. Construction demands skill because the pan must be waterproofed and sloped precisely to the drain, which must be set at the right height for perfect drainage. Prefabricated bases—in molded plastic, cast polymer, solid-surface composite, or poured masonry—come in various sizes and shapes and can be used with wall panels or custom surrounds. Be sure to select a prefabricated shower pan

with a drain opening that matches the existing location of your drainpipe. You will also need to make a choice from among single, double, and triple threshold styles.

custom showers A custom shower can be built from the ground up or with a prefabricated base, which saves time as well as money. A shower's adjoining walls must be waterproof, consisting of a layer of water-resistant drywall covered with waterproof cement board and finished with ceramic tile, slate, granite, marble, or solid surface. Showers can be equipped with such luxuries as seats, multiple "spa" showerheads that can give full-body massages, and even steam-shower functions.

shower doors Shower doors may swing open, fold back, slide, or pivot. Some are hinged directly to the shower entrance, but most are framed with aluminum that comes in many finishes, including epoxy-coated colors. Doors are made from inexpensive plastic or tempered glass that can be clear, frosted, mirrored, or patterned. For a steam shower, the shower door must be airtight, and the shower must also include an air-tight overhead panel.

toilets

Toilets come in a number of styles, colors, and prices, but how well a toilet will do its job has nothing to do with these factors. Because federal law now stipulates that new toilets must use no more than 1.6 gallons of water per flush—compared with the 3 to 7 gallons used by older models—a reliable toilet is one that generates enough power to clean the bowl. A traditional gravity flush system, which uses the weight of the water to provide flushing pressure, is more apt to clog and less likely to rinse thoroughly with the new water limits. A better alternative is a pressure-assisted flush system, a style that uses pressurized air to force water into the bowl. This system is, however, noisier than gravity flush toilets are and it can require more frequent re-

Low in profile, this one-piece toilet requires just over 1½ gallons of water per flush.

pairs. Some models must be plugged into an electrical socket.

Toilets come in one- or two-piece construction. Two-piece toilets employ a separate tank and bowl. One-piece toilets, also called "low profile," merge the tank and bowl into a single unit. A two-piece model will cost less, but a one-piece toilet is easier to clean because it eliminates the crevice between the tank and the bowl. One-piece toilets often include a seat with the unit, while most two-piece units do not. For small baths, wall-mounted toilets are available, but they can be hard to find and expensive to buy and install. Toilet bowls are either round or elongated (the latter are 2 inches longer with larger water surface). Seats, which come in different materials—including wood, plastic, and polypropylene—must match the bowl's shape. Some seats are cushioned, contoured, or heated for extra comfort, and some automatically trigger the flush mechanism when the top is closed.

Factors that influence a toilet's tendency to clog or flush sluggishly include the size of the trap, which carries away the bowl's contents, and the flush valve, which sits at the inside base of the tank and regulates water flow into the bowl. The general rule is "the larger, the better" in both cases. Before you go shopping, be sure to measure the "rough-in," or the distance from the wall to the center of the toilet drain. A 12-inch rough-in is standard, but some are 10 or 14 inches.

This two-piece toilet's elongated shape makes it more comfortable for adults than the more conventional style.

washers

Because a washing machine is a large consumer of both energy and water, the key to selecting the right one is to purchase the most energy-efficient model that fits your lifestyle and space.

In terms of lifestyle, think about how often you use the washer and what you wash. If you wash often, you will get the best performance from a stainless-steel tub; those who wash less frequently will probably do fine with porcelain-coated steel or high-grade plastic.

If your wash includes a variety of fabrics and levels of dirtiness, choose a machine that offers specialty cycles such as delicate and extra soak, as well as one for a second rinse. Multiple water-level settings will ensure the most efficient wash for loads of different sizes. Some machines can boost water temperature to sanitize a load.

For those with limited space, there are stacking washer-dryer units in either full-size or apartment-size capacities. Remember that the size of your washer should match your dryer's capacity (see page 388).

Other items to consider are automatic temperature regulators—a must in cold climates, they ensure that wash water comes in at a constant temperature for the setting—and additional insulation and reinforced frames, both of which will reduce noise.

There are two styles of washers: top-load, which is the most common, and front-load, which provides the greatest energy efficiency.

top-load This machine, also known as a V-axis because the agitator turns on a vertical axis, allows you to access the wash tub without bending, although it must be set side by side with the dryer. While a top loader costs less initially, it is less energy-efficient in the long run. It uses regular detergent and offers the greatest selection of models and options.

front-load Also called an H-axis because its agitator turns on a horizontal axis, the

This energy-efficient front-load washer features an extra-large capacity. One benefit of a front-load machine is that its top surface can be fully utilized without obstructing the door.

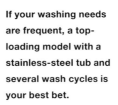

If your washing needs are frequent, a top-loading model with a stainless-steel tub and several wash cycles is your best bet.

front-load machine is gaining in popularity because of its energy efficiency. This type uses from one-third to one-half the amount of water of a top loader, which means that much less heating. And, because it spins faster, clothes come out needing less time in the dryer.

Where only a closet or a small room is available to serve as a laundry area, consider a space-saving stack washer-dryer.

RIGHT: Five installation options are available for this state-of-the-art dryer: freestanding, under-counter, stacked, pedestal, and hidden.

Although they save on energy costs, front loaders are more expensive at purchase; some require a special detergent.

clothes dryers

All dryers perform the same function the same way: They tumble clothes while blowing hot air on them. Generally, dryers are between 25 and 29 inches wide. The significant measurement of a dryer is its drum capacity, usually between 5 and 7 cubic feet for full-size and 3 cubic feet for compact models. The capacity you choose should complement your washer's capacity. A washer with a 3.5-cubic-foot washer capacity, for example, requires a 7-cubic-foot dryer capacity. If space is a problem, consider a stack washer-dryer model that can fit in a closet.

Dryers are powered by either gas or electricity, with gas being a bit more expensive to purchase but the most economical and efficient in the long run. Dryers are traditionally large consumers of energy, but a new generation offers increasingly specialized cycles that can minimize drying time.

More exacting drying times protect clothes from over-drying, which maintains their appearance and fit and extends their life span. By law, dryers must have at least one automatic-drying cycle, but the best dryers include moisture sensors, which automatically shut down the machine whenever the moisture level in the drum drops below a certain point. Other options include a cool-down cycle that keeps garments from wrinkling, a damp-dry cycle that prepares clothes for ironing, and a tumble-free cycle that dries items such as canvas shoes on a special drying rack.

One new dryer—pricey and refrigerator-sized—includes a heated cabinet that has multiple racks to dry delicates gently and an overhead rack to hang garments while steam circulates, removing wrinkles and even odors.

Some models are ventless, also called condensing, but most dryers, according to many local codes, must be vented to the outdoors with aluminum or rigid steel duct. When you are shopping for a dryer, look for a sturdy, sizable lint filter that can be cleaned easily; a clogged filter can, at the least, decrease the dryer's efficiency and, at worst, cause a fire. A reversible door also ensures ease of access should you ever have to move the dryer to a new location.

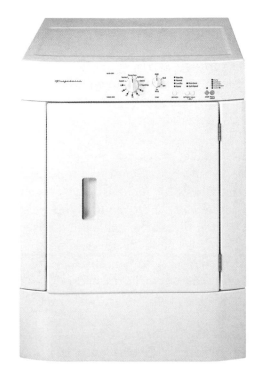

water filters

If you suspect that your drinking water is unhealthy, contact your local water department to have it tested. If hard water is a problem, consider a water softener. Water that is simply bad-tasting can be made more palatable with an easy-to-install water filter.

You will want to consult with a plumber or your local water supplier for the best type of filter for your water. A small, inexpensive carbon filter will remove chlorine taste and reduce sulfur (which causes water to smell like rotten eggs). A bulkier and more expensive reverse-osmosis filter will eliminate nearly all bacteria as well as any harmful chemicals.

A filter is installed between a cold-water shutoff valve (or saddle tee valve) and a sink-mounted spout via flexible lines and compression fittings. Install the filter's tank in a place where it can be easily accessed for cartridge changes.

water heaters

Water heaters, which provide a home's hot water, can account for between 15 percent and 25 percent of a home's total monthly energy demand. It pays to buy the most efficient water heater that responds to your needs. There are four basic water-heating systems: storage, the most common; combination space and water-heating systems; demand (instantaneous); and tankless coil. Storage water heaters, which heat and store water, range in size from 20 to 80 gallons

and use natural gas, electricity, propane, or fuel oil as heat sources. Combination space- and water-heating systems heat both your home and your water and are good choices for small, well-insulated homes. Demand systems, either gas- or electric-powered, provide a limited amount of hot water instantly and without storage capacity. Tankless-coil types use a heat exchanger integrated with a space-heating boiler to heat water instantaneously. Tankless-coil varieties combine efficiently with a separate storage tank to reduce boiler cycling.

Most homeowners choose storage water heaters for the bounty of heated water they can provide. However, do not buy based on capacity alone. A better criterion is the first hour rating (FHR) number: the amount of hot water the heater can supply per hour if the tank is full of hot water. To determine what your need is, figure out the amount of water used in the household at the peak usage hour. Another important measure is the energy factor (EF), which indicates the overall unit efficiency based on the amount of hot water produced per unit of fuel consumed on a typical day.

LEFT: **This undersink water filtration system includes an easily installed twist-on/off filter cartridge. The unit delivers fresh-tasting water at 1.5 gallons per minute.**

When buying a water heater, pay attention to the specifications posted on its front. You will want to know its capacity and overall efficiency, as well as how much water it can supply in an hour.

anatomy of home plumbing

YOU MAY BE SURPRISED BY THE SIMPLICITY OF THE PIPE SYSTEM BEHIND THE WALLS and beneath the floors of your house. As shown below, your plumbing system is made up of three separate but interdependent systems: supply, drain-waste, and vent. (The drain-waste and vent systems are interconnected, though, and are often referred to as the DWV system.) Before you begin any plumbing project, large or small, it is a good idea to become familiar with these systems.

Water enters your house through a main supply pipe that is connected to a water utility main or to a well. Water travels through a meter or pressure tank before branching into separate lines for hot and cold water. The house shutoff valve should be located near the meter or pressure tank. Close this valve to stop water from flowing anywhere in the house. Cold water may pass through a water softener or filtering system.

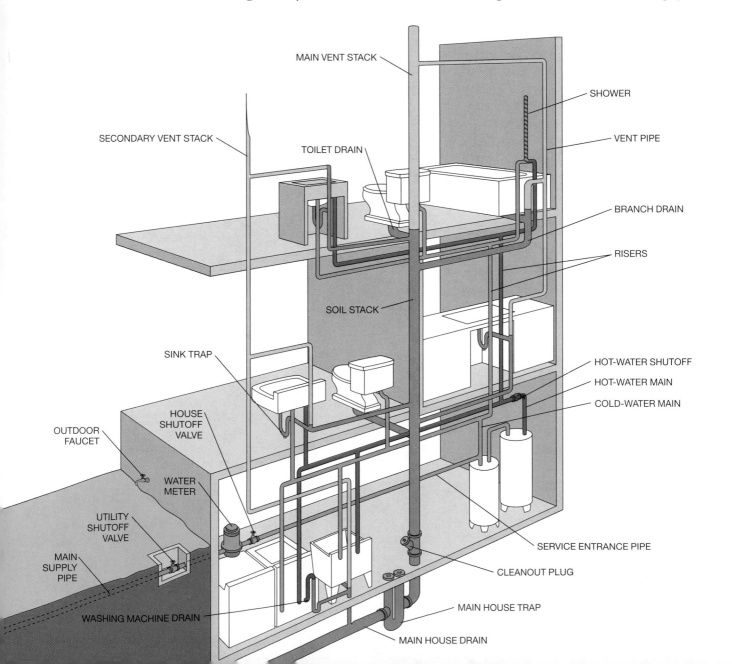

MAIN VENT STACK

SHOWER

SECONDARY VENT STACK

TOILET DRAIN

VENT PIPE

BRANCH DRAIN

RISERS

SOIL STACK

SINK TRAP

HOT-WATER SHUTOFF

HOT-WATER MAIN

COLD-WATER MAIN

HOUSE SHUTOFF VALVE

OUTDOOR FAUCET

WATER METER

SERVICE ENTRANCE PIPE

UTILITY SHUTOFF VALVE

CLEANOUT PLUG

MAIN SUPPLY PIPE

WASHING MACHINE DRAIN

MAIN HOUSE TRAP

MAIN HOUSE DRAIN

Supply pipes are always under pressure; if a leak occurs, water will spurt out until the water supply is shut off. This is why most homes have shutoff valves, as shown at top right, located near each fixture or appliance. By closing the valve, you can safely work on the fixture or appliance without affecting the water supply to the rest of the house.

For most of their run, hot and cold pipes are next to each other. When they reach the fixtures or appliances, however, they separate. Pipes that run vertically from one floor to the next, usually in the walls, are called risers. Horizontal runs may be inside walls, fastened to floor joists, or buried in a concrete slab.

In older houses, the supply pipes are often composed of galvanized steel with threaded connections. Over time, these pipes corrode and clog up, leading to leaks and reduced pressure. Newer houses often have copper supply lines, which are easier to install and last much longer.

The drain-waste system relies on gravity, rather than pressure, to carry water and waste out of the house. Drain and waste pipes lead away from all fixtures at a precise slope. If the slope is too steep, water will run off too fast, leaving solids behind; if the slope is not steep enough, the drain will empty too slowly and water will back up into the fixtures. The normal pitch is ¼ inch for every horizontal foot of pipe. Cleanout fittings, such as those shown at bottom right, provide easy access to drainpipes when clogs must be removed.

The workhorse in the drain-waste system is the soil stack, a vertical section of 3- or 4-inch-diameter pipe that carries waste away from toilets and other fixtures and connects with the main house drain. From there, the waste flows to a public sewer or septic tank.

The vent system gets rid of sewer gas and maintains atmospheric pressure inside the drain-waste system. To prevent dangerous sewer gases from entering the house, each fixture should have a trap, as shown at middle right, which must be vented.

ANGLED
SHUTOFF
VALVE

GATE VALVE

Two important valves in a home's water supply system are the gate valve, which turns the water off and on to all or part of the house, and an angled shutoff valve, which controls one fixture, such as a toilet.

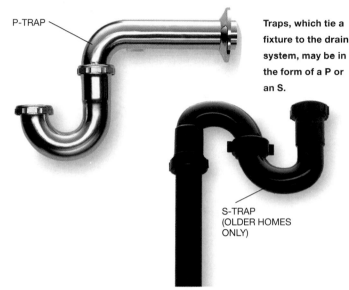

P-TRAP

S-TRAP
(OLDER HOMES
ONLY)

Traps, which tie a fixture to the drain system, may be in the form of a P or an S.

A cleanout fitting, designed for connection to a drain line, has a plug at one end that is easily removed.

GAS PIPING

If you plan to do any plumbing jobs and your house is supplied with gas, first learn to distinguish water supply pipes from the pipes that carry natural gas throughout the house. Gas pipes are usually black and run from the gas meter to an appliance or heating system. An emergency shutoff valve is required on each gas pipe. Unless you have plumbing skills, call a professional to work on gas piping.

Also, if your house is heated with a hot-water or steam system, identify and avoid working on the heating pipes, which run from each heating outlet to the furnace or boiler. Leave repairs to an expert.

BASIC TOOLS FOR PLUMBING

Caulking gun

Measuring tape

Flaring tool

Saber saw (jigsaw)

Deep-socket wrench

Power drill with bits
and screwdriver tips

Screwdrivers

Spud wrench

Valve seat dresser

Mini hacksaw

Toilet auger

Metal-pipe cutter

Torque wrench

Pipe wrench

Reciprocating saw

Long-nose pliers

Putty knife

Valve-seat wrench

Level

Adjustable wrench

Drain-and-trap auger

Faucet-handle puller

Rib-joint pliers

Utility knife

Basin wrench

Plastic-tubing cutter

plumbing tools

BECAUSE PLUMBING IMPROVEMENTS OFTEN REQUIRE OPENING UP WALLS OR dealing with a home's framing, they tend to require many of the same tools needed for general carpentry work, as well as more specialized tools used for plumbing. You will find most of the necessary carpentry tools discussed on pages 102–104. Here we look at the more specialized tools that you will need to have on hand for tackling jobs with pipes and plumbing fixtures.

TORQUE WRENCH

RIB-JOINT PLIERS

PLASTIC-TUBING CUTTER

MEASURING TAPE

PIPE WRENCH

METAL-PIPE CUTTER

HACKSAW

ADJUSTABLE WRENCH

UTILITY KNIFE

RECIPROCATING SAW

MINI HACKSAW

CAST-IRON SNAP CUTTER

FLARING TOOL

PVC SAW

PROPANE TORCH

TOOLS FOR CUTTING & JOINING PIPE

For determining lengths, you will need a measuring tape. The tools needed for cutting pipe depend upon the type of pipe. For plastic pipe, use a plastic-tubing cutter or a PVC saw (a handsaw will work, too). For cutting plastic tubing, a utility knife works well. Metal pipe requires a metal-pipe cutter, a hacksaw, or a reciprocating saw with a hacksaw blade. In tight spots, you may need a mini hacksaw, as well. Cast-iron pipe demands a cast-iron snap cutter, which can be rented. A pipe wrench is necessary for gripping pipes and screwing together (or unscrewing) pipes and threaded fittings; rib-joint pliers are helpful for gripping many types of pipes and fittings. Get two: one for holding a pipe and the other for turning the other pipe or fitting. For soldering copper pipe, you will need a propane torch with a disposable tank. A T-handled torque wrench is used for tightening no-hub couplings. If you will be working with flared fittings, you will need a flaring tool.

TOOLS FOR FIXING SINKS & FAUCETS

A spud wrench adjusts to fit up to 4-inch nuts, such as slip nuts on traps and tailpieces. A basin wrench gives access to nuts underneath sinks and other hard-to-reach places. A valve-seat wrench removes and replaces valve seats. If a faucet handle will not come off, get a faucet-handle puller. A deep-socket wrench is often necessary for removing recessed packing nuts on tub faucets. For faucet repairs, you will need screwdrivers and, for some, long-nose pliers. A valve-seat dresser smooths the valve seat in compression faucets to stop leaks. For installing sinks, toilets, and other fixtures, you are likely to need a level, a power drill with bits and screwdriver tips, a putty knife, and—if you need to cut a hole in a countertop—a saber saw.

CAULKING GUN

SPUD WRENCH

VALVE-SEAT WRENCH

FAUCET-HANDLE PULLER

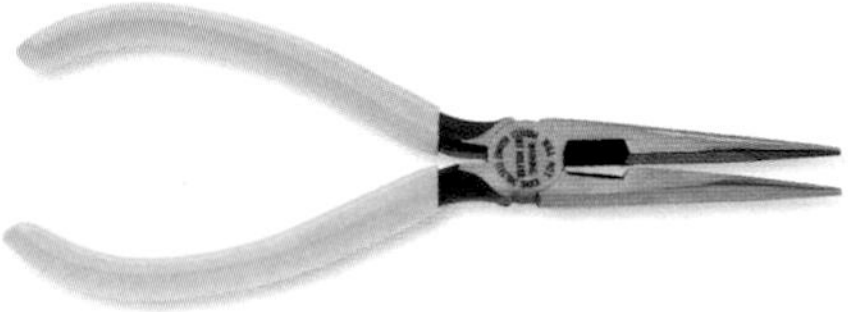

LONG-NOSE PLIERS

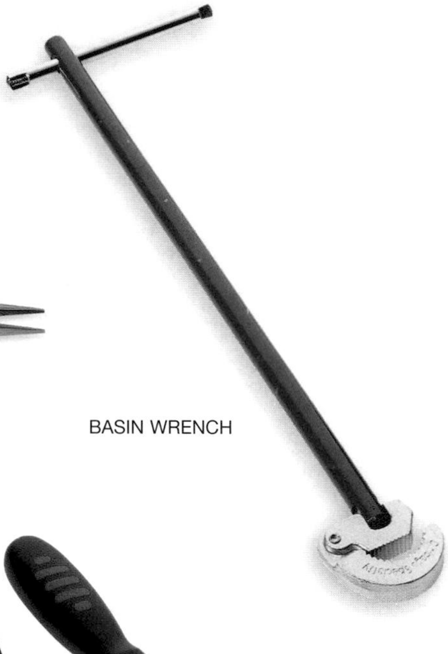

BASIN WRENCH

POWER DRILL WITH BITS
AND SCREWDRIVER TIPS

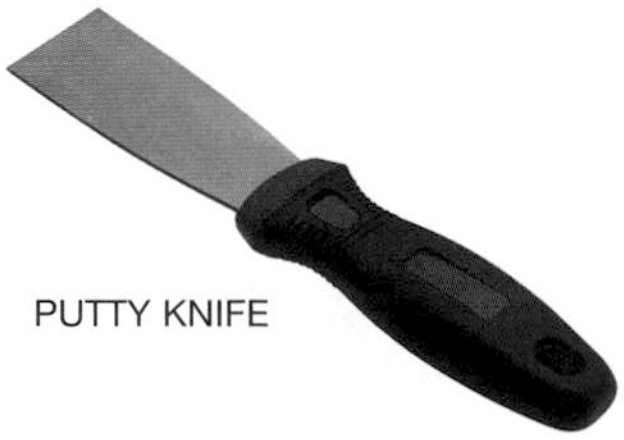

PUTTY KNIFE

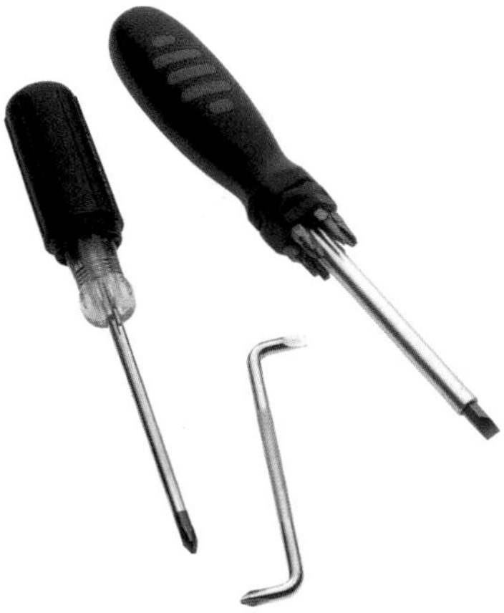

SCREWDRIVERS

VALVE-SEAT DRESSER

SABER SAW (JIGSAW)

DEEP-SOCKET WRENCH

LEVEL

TOOLS FOR CLEARING CLOGS

With its funnel cup, a toilet plunger removes clogs by alternating pressure and suction. The flat face of a sink plunger works better for sink drains. A drain-and-trap auger, also known as a snake, is used to remove deep drain blockages. A toilet auger is designed to work down into the trap of a toilet. Be sure to wear rubber gloves when clearing drains.

RUBBER GLOVES

DRAIN-AND-TRAP AUGER

TOILET AUGER

SINK PLUNGER

TOILET PLUNGER

working with copper

COPPER TUBE OR PIPE IS LIGHTWEIGHT, CORROSION-RESISTANT, AND RUGGED. IT is also fairly easy to join by sweat-soldering or by using flare, compression, or union fittings. Its smooth interior surface allows water to flow easily and prevents the accumulation of mineral deposits.

types of copper pipe

Two kinds of copper tube are used in supply systems to carry fresh water: hard- and soft-temper. Another type of copper tube, called corrugated supply, is used as flexible tubing to link hard or soft tube to fixtures. Large-diameter copper pipe is used with drain-waste–vent (DWV) systems.

hard-temper copper This is sold in lengths of 20 feet or less. Because it cannot be bent without crimping, it must be cut and joined with fittings whenever a length is extended or a section changes direction. It is offered in three thicknesses: K (thick wall), L (medium wall), and M (thin wall); M is usually adequate for home plumbing.

RIGHT: **A variety of copper pipe fittings are designed for soldered or threaded connections.**

COUPLING   REDUCER   45° ELBOW

90° ELBOW   TEE

THREADED-TO-SLIP COUPLINGS   UNION

Nominal diameters range from ¼ to 1½ inches and larger; actual diameters are greater. Commonly used sizes are: 1 inch to 1½ inches for a main supply from the street, 1 inch for a primary line, ¾ inch for a branch line to a group of connecting fixtures, and ½ inch for individual fixtures. For tube-sized piping, the outside diameters are equal but the inside diameters vary; those with thicker walls generally have smaller inside diameters.

soft-temper copper This is sold in 20-, 60-, and 100-foot coils. More costly than hard-temper supply tube, soft-temper copper offers the advantage of not needing as many fittings because it can be bent with-

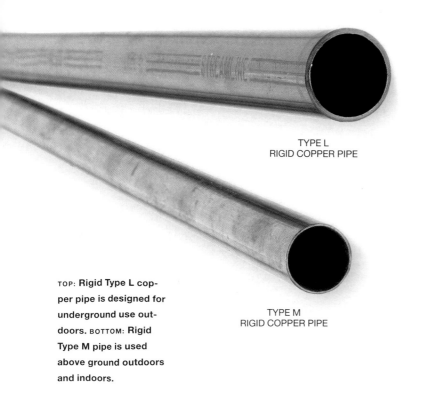

TYPE L
RIGID COPPER PIPE

TYPE M
RIGID COPPER PIPE

TOP: **Rigid Type L copper pipe is designed for underground use outdoors.** BOTTOM: **Rigid Type M pipe is used above ground outdoors and indoors.**

COMPRESSION
FITTINGS

FLARED
FITTINGS

LEFT: Brass compression and flare fittings are designed for joining flexible tubing. Flared fittings are required for some types of values and fixtures; compression fittings are more commonly employed because they are easier and faster to use. For more about these, see pages 400–401.

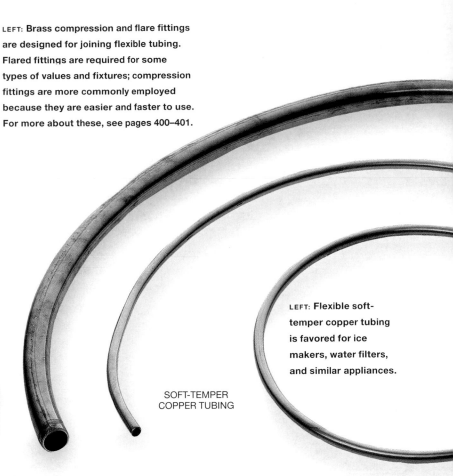

LEFT: **Flexible soft-temper copper tubing is favored for ice makers, water filters, and similar appliances.**

SOFT-TEMPER
COPPER TUBING

out crimping. Soft-temper copper comes in K and L thicknesses; L is adequate for above-ground plumbing. Nominal diameters range from ¼ to 1 inch, but actual diameters are slightly greater.

copper DWV pipe

This is usually sold in 20-foot lengths and in nominal diameters of 1½, 2, and 3 inches. Copper DWV pipe with a nominal diameter larger than 2 inches is very expensive and is not readily available. Because DWV pipe is not under pressure, copper DWV has thinner walls than supply tubing.

flexible tubing

Used for linking supply tube to fixtures, this corrugated, smooth, or chrome-plated copper comes in short lengths. It can conform to tighter curves than soft copper tube and has a nominal diameter of ⅜ or ½ inch. It often comes in kit form; follow the manufacturer's instructions for use.

BENDING BASICS

The best way to shape soft-temper copper tubing is with a tubing bender. Simply slip the bender over the pipe, and then, with both hands, gently bend the tool and tubing into the desired curve. Go slowly; if you crimp the pipe, discard that piece, and start again.

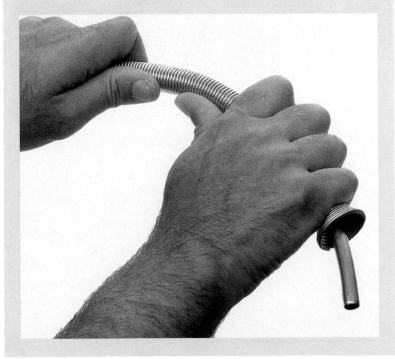

working with copper pipe

Sweat-soldering is the best way to join copper pipe. Hard supply tubing can also be joined with compression fittings and soft supply tubing with compression or flare fittings. If you want to be able to take apart a run of copper tube in the future (to replace a water heater, for instance) without unsoldering or cutting the run, fit two short lengths of the pipe together with a union (see page 401).

Caution: Before beginning any work on existing copper plumbing, be sure to turn the water off at the house shutoff valve (see page 390). Dry the pipe as much as possible. Wear safety glasses and gloves while soldering or cutting pipe with a hacksaw.

removing pipe Drain water from the pipe by closing the supply valve and opening a faucet that is lower in the system than the fitting you are removing. Cut copper pipe with a hacksaw or tubing cutter; loosen a soldered joint with a propane torch (be sure to wear eye protection). Brace and support the pipe to keep it from sagging. To remove compression, flare, or union fittings, just unscrew them.

cutting new pipe Before cutting a new length of pipe, be sure to consider the makeup distance—the length of the part that goes into fittings (see page 407). You can use a hacksaw, but a tubing cutter is much easier and makes a cleaner cut.

soldering joints Soldered joints, often called sweat joints, are made with standard copper fittings. You will need to use a small propane torch; very fine sandpaper, steel wool, or an emery cloth; a can of soldering flux; and lead-free plumber's solder.

SOLDERING A JOINT

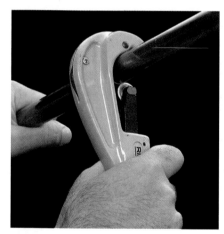

1 Cut new lengths of copper pipe with a tubing cutter designed for copper. To use the cutter, twist the knob until the cutter wheel makes contact with the surface. Rotate the cutter around the tube, tightening after each revolution, until the pipe snaps in two.

2 After you have cut the tube, clean off inside burrs with a round file or with the retractable reamer often found on tubing cutters. Burrs can cause pipe friction, so reaming them out helps ensure a smooth-flowing joint.

3 Use emery cloth, steel wool, or sandpaper to smooth and polish the last inch of the outside end of the pipe until it is shiny. Do not overdo it; soft copper sands easily.

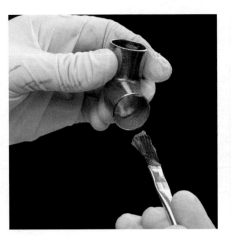

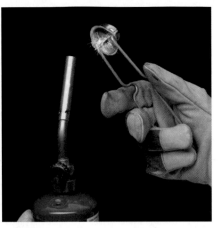

4 Also clean the inside of the fitting from the end down to the shoulder (the point where it bends). You can use an emery cloth or steel wool, but you will find that a pipe brush (shown above) makes cleaning easier.

5 To ensure even flow of the solder, use a small, stiff brush to apply flux around the inside of the fitting and around the outside of the pipe end. Place the fitting on the pipe end, and turn the pipe or the fitting back and forth once or twice to spread the flux evenly. Then position the fitting correctly. It is best to wear gloves when applying flux because the chemicals in it can damage skin.

6 Turn on the gas torch's control valve, and then light the nozzle end with a striker tool. Adjust the flame so it is steady and strong, making certain that it is not aimed at anything flammable. If necessary, shield surrounding objects with a flame guard.

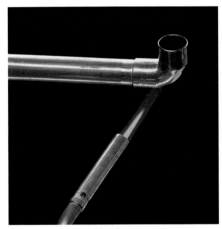

7 Next, position the torch nozzle about 4 inches from the fitting, and move the flame back and forth to distribute the heat evenly. It is important to get the fitting hot but not too hot; the flux will burn and simply vanish if it is overheated. Be careful where you hold the pipe—it will get very hot.

8 The joint is hot enough when the solder will melt on contact with it. Test the temperature by touching the solder wire to the joint occasionally as you heat the fitting. The instant the wire melts, the joint is ready for action.

9 Turn off the torch, and touch the solder wire to the edge of the fitting; capillary action will pull molten solder in between the fitting and the pipe. Keep applying the wire until a line of molten solder shows all the way around the fitting. Once the solder cools (in just a few seconds), wipe off surplus flux with a damp rag.

MAKING A FLARED JOINT

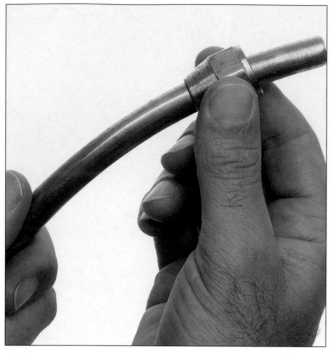

1 To make a flared joint, used for connecting to some types of valves and fixtures, begin by sliding the flare nut onto the tube, with the nut's tapered end facing away from the tube's end.

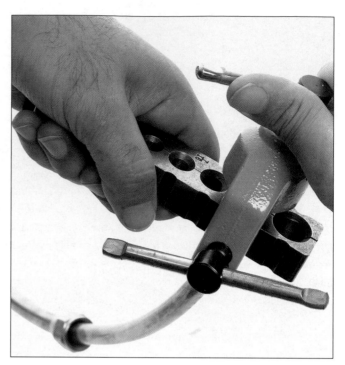

2 Clamp the end of the tube into a flaring tool, and screw the ram down hard into the opening. Remove the flared tube from the tool.

3 Press the tapered end of the fitting into the flared end of the tubing, and screw the flare nut onto the fitting.

4 Use two adjustable or open-end wrenches, one on the nut and one on the fitting, to secure the joint.

MAKING A COMPRESSION JOINT

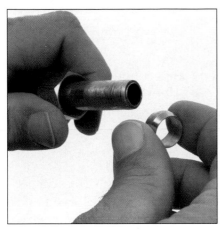

1 To install a compression fitting, commonly used for ice makers, water filters, shutoff values, and more, first slide the compression nut onto the tube, with the nut's broad shoulder facing away from the tubing's end. Then slip on the compression ring, as shown.

2 Push the tubing into the threaded body of the fitting, and slide down the compression ring so that it is snug. Screw the nut down onto the fitting.

3 Tighten the joint using two adjustable or open-end wrenches, with one on the nut and one on the fitting. This action compresses the ring tightly around the end of the tubing and makes a watertight seal.

FORMING A PERFECT UNION

A union is a joint that can be taken apart. To install a union, first sweat-solder the male shoulder onto one pipe, and then slip the nut onto the other pipe. Sweat-solder the female shoulder onto the end of the second pipe. Bring the male and female shoulders together (below). Then slide the nut over the female shoulder, and screw the nut onto the male shoulder. To tighten, use two wrenches: one to hold the male shoulder and the other to turn the nut.

working with steel pipe

FOR DECADES, GALVANIZED-STEEL PIPE WAS USED FOR WATER SUPPLY PIPES AND sometimes for drain-waste–vent (DWV) pipes, as well. Today, steel pipe is used primarily to route gas inside the home; old galvanized water supply pipes are routinely replaced with copper. There are occasions, however, when you may wish to use galvanized pipe for a repair.

Galvanized-steel pipe and fittings are coated with zinc in order to resist corrosion (normally, uncoated black steel pipe is used for gas). Despite this additional protection, galvanized-steel pipe not only corrodes faster than cast iron or copper but also, because of its rough interior surface, collects mineral deposits that, over time, impede water flow.

You may prefer to replace a leaking length of galvanized-steel pipe with the same type of pipe. It often requires less equipment and expense than using copper or plastic. But when you are extending a supply system of galvanized pipe, use copper (page 396) or plastic (page 406).

Many fittings are available for joining galvanized steel with steel, copper, or plastic pipe. A special coupling is made for joining steel to copper to prevent the corrosion that can occur when the two metals come in contact.

Fittings are connected to pipe by means of tapered pipe threads. Galvanized-steel

TOP: Black steel pipe is typically used indoors for carrying natural gas. CENTER: Galvanized pipe was used for water supply piping in older homes. BOTTOM: Green steel pipe is buried outdoors for natural gas.

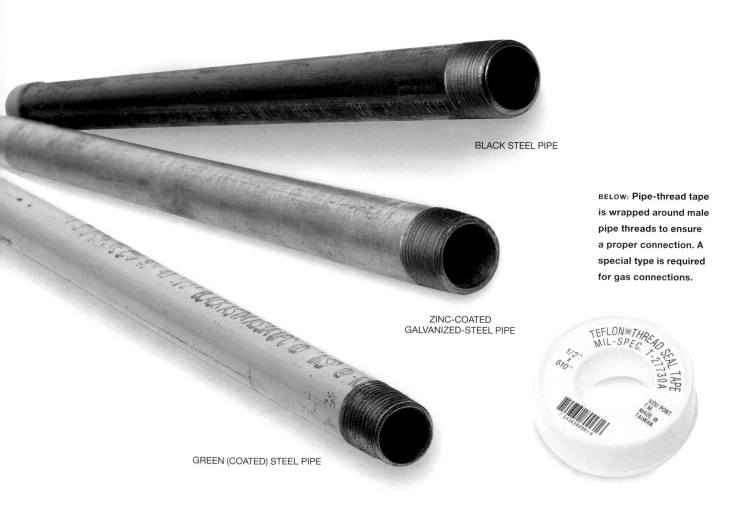

BLACK STEEL PIPE

ZINC-COATED
GALVANIZED-STEEL PIPE

GREEN (COATED) STEEL PIPE

BELOW: Pipe-thread tape is wrapped around male pipe threads to ensure a proper connection. A special type is required for gas connections.

UNION

CAP

4-WAY

COUPLING

MALE-TO-FEMALE ELBOW

45° ELBOW

TEE

LEFT: **Various threaded fittings are designed for connecting two or more pipes together or for capping-off pipe runs.** BELOW: **Pipe-joint compound, an alternative to pipe-thread tape, is applied to male threads before joining them to another fitting.**

pipe is sold threaded on both ends. If you need to replace a section, you will have to cut through the pipe, unscrew both pieces from their nearest fittings, replace those pieces with new pipes threaded on both ends, and reconnect the ends with a union—a special fitting that allows you to join two threaded pipe ends.

Threading pipe (see page 405) is not particularly difficult, but it requires specialized tools. Some Lowe's stores can thread pipes for you; you just need to give them the precise measurements. You can also rent threading tools, but this will reduce any savings of doing the work yourself.

pipe & fittings Galvanized-steel pipe is available in nominal diameters of ¼ to 2½ inches and in lengths of 10 and 21 feet, or it can be custom-cut and threaded. Short threaded pieces (called nipples) are avail-

able in lengths from ½ inch to 12 inches (the diameters match the pipes).

measuring & cutting Galvanized pipe must be cut perfectly square so that threads can be started accurately. Use a pipe cutter with a blade designed for steel pipe, and follow the directions for cutting copper pipe given on page 398. After cutting, use the reamer in the cutter handle to remove burrs from inside the pipe.

general tips Loosening galvanized supply pipes requires the simultaneous use of two pipe wrenches. If there is no convenient union in the run, saw the pipe run in two. Steady the pipe with your hand or a wrench. Use a reciprocating saw or coarse-toothed hacksaw, and position a bucket underneath to catch any spills. Do not let the cut pipe sag.

LOWE'S QUICK TIP
To determine how much new galvanized-steel pipe you need, measure the distances between the new fittings and then add the makeup distances (see page 407).

Support horizontal runs of new pipe every 6 to 8 feet and vertical runs every 8 to 10 feet. When joining pipes to fittings, coat the threads with pipe-joint compound or wrap them with pipe-thread tape to seal them against rust and make assembly and disassembly easier. Apply pipe-joint compound with the brush attached to the lid of the container, using just enough to fill the male threads.

Screw the pipe and fitting together by hand as far as you can. Finish tightening with two pipe wrenches, reversing the direction of the wrenches.

Caution: Before beginning any work on galvanized-steel plumbing, be sure to turn the water off at the house shutoff valve (see page 390) and open a faucet that is low in the system to drain the pipes. Wear safety glasses and work gloves when cutting pipe.

HANGER SPECS

Your new pipes need solid support at intervals no greater than those shown in the chart below. Four basic installations are shown here. What is most important to remember is not to use one type of metal hanger to support pipe made of another type of metal.

You'll note that most vertical intervals are listed as 10 feet. Actually, codes state that these vertical runs should be supported at every story or every 10 feet; galvanized steel need only be supported every other story.

The 10-foot horizontal spec for cast iron is for modern no-hub pipe. If you're using traditional bell-and-spigot cast iron, it needs support every 5 feet. Any cast-iron pipe needs support within 18 inches of a joint.

PLUMBER'S TAPE

SUPPLY-PIPE HANGER

PIPE BUSHINGS

FRICTION CLAMP

MAXIMUM SUPPORT DISTANCES

TYPE OF PIPE	HORIZONTAL SUPPORT INTERVAL	VERTICAL SUPPORT INTERVAL
Copper	6'	10'
CPVC	3'	10'
PVC	4'	10'
ABS	4'	10'
Galvanized	12'	15'
Cast iron	10'	10'

JOINING GALVANIZED PIPE & FITTINGS

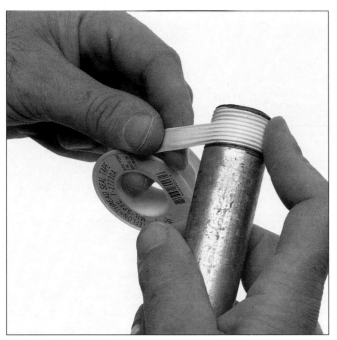

To use pipe-thread tape, wrap it 1½ turns clockwise around the male pipe threads, pulling the tape tight enough so that the threads show through. Pipe-thread tape tears easily, which is both good and bad. If you prefer, you can use pipe-joint compound (see right) instead.

If you're using pipe-joint compound instead of pipe-thread tape, apply it to the fitting's female threads, either by squeezing it from the tube or by spreading it with a small brush. Use just enough compound to fill the gaps between the threads.

A PIPE-THREADING PRIMER

For cutting pipe, use a pipe reamer and a pipe cutter. To thread pipe, you will need a pipe vise to hold the pipe steady and a threader fitted with a die and guide of the same nominal size as the pipe (these tools can be rented).

When you are ready to thread the pipe, first fit the head of the threader die into the threading handle, and slip the head, guide first, over the end of the pipe. To cut the threads, exert force on the pipe while rotating the handle clockwise. When the head of the threader bites into the metal, stop pushing and simply continue the clockwise rotation. Apply generous amounts of thread-cutting oil as you turn the threader. If the threader sticks, back the tool off slightly, and blow away any metal chips.

Screw the pipe and fitting together by hand as far as you can. Final tightening requires the use of two pipe wrenches (as shown). A fitting always screws on clockwise and unscrews counterclockwise. Be sure to apply force toward, rather than away from, the wrenches' jaws; otherwise, the jaws tend to come off the pipe or fitting.

Continue threading until the pipe extends about one thread beyond the end of the die. Remove the threader, and then clean off the newly cut threads with a stiff wire brush.

working with plastic pipe

MOST HOMEOWNERS WHO HAVE WORKED WITH VARIOUS TYPES OF PIPE PREFER plastic. That's because plastic pipe is lightweight, inexpensive, and easy to cut and fit. Unlike metal pipe, plastic is resistant to damage from chemicals and corrosion. In addition, plastic's smooth interior surface provides less flow resistance than metal.

Plastic pipe comes in both rigid and flexible varieties. All major plumbing codes and the Federal Housing Administration accept at least one of these types of plastic pipe, although local building codes may not. For the best quality, look on the pipe for the American Society for Testing and Materials (ASTM) designation. If the pipe is to carry potable water, it also should have the National Sanitation Foundation's NSF certification seal.

Plastic pipe is stamped with various pressure ratings (or "schedules"); use the schedule number prescribed by your building department. The pressure ratings for plastic are lower than those for metal, so it is also important to install water-hammer arresters (see page 417) at all fixtures and water-using appliances (except toilets).

Take care not to store plastic pipe in direct sunlight for longer than a week or so. The accumulation of ultraviolet rays can make it brittle.

rigid supply pipe Two types of rigid plastic supply pipe are used indoors: polyvinyl chloride (PVC) for cold-water supply only; and chlorinated polyvinyl chloride (CPVC) for both hot- and cold-water systems. Both types are somewhat flexible and can follow slight directional changes without cracking.

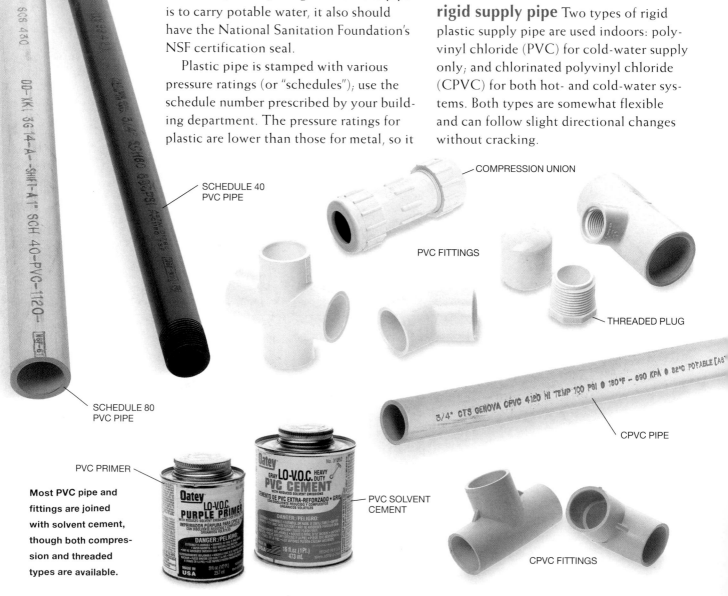

SCHEDULE 40 PVC PIPE

COMPRESSION UNION

PVC FITTINGS

THREADED PLUG

SCHEDULE 80 PVC PIPE

CPVC PIPE

PVC PRIMER

Most PVC pipe and fittings are joined with solvent cement, though both compression and threaded types are available.

PVC SOLVENT CEMENT

CPVC FITTINGS

PLUMBING

PVC and CPVC pipe are commonly available in 10- and 20-foot lengths; Lowe's stores sell shorter lengths, as well. They can be bought by the piece or in bundles of 10. Common sizes include ½-, ¾-, and 1-inch nominal diameters. (These are the sizes used for matching fittings; actual diameters may be different.) PVC is also available in 1¼-, 1½-, and 2-inch diameters, primarily for use outdoors.

Most PVC and CPVC fittings push onto the ends of the pipes and are cemented in place with a permanent solvent cement. Couplings allow you to join two lengths of straight pipe; 45- and 90-degree fittings and T-fittings are for changes in direction. Transition fittings, which let you link plastic pipe to pipe of a different material, often have threads on one end. Reducer fittings allow you to link together pipes of different diameters.

Supply fittings are smaller than drain-waste–vent (DWV) fittings. They are designed to work under pressurized conditions, unlike DWV fittings, which work with the flow of gravity.

flexible supply pipe
Flexible plastic pipe is especially useful in cramped places because it can follow a winding course without requiring a lot of fittings. For that reason it is easier to install than rigid supply pipe, but it is much less likely to be approved by codes for use, so check with your building department first.

Two types of flexible supply pipe are used in homes: polybutylene (PB), for hot and cold lines of pipe, and polyethylene (PE), for cold lines only. Both are sold in rolls of 25 and 100 feet and sometimes by the foot. Although PB is more versatile and less expensive than PE, it is currently in disfavor with many regional codes and is not readily available.

Join lengths of flexible pipe with barbed insert fittings (see page 411). Insert fittings have hollow, corrugated nipples held in place by stainless-steel clamps. Transition fittings have a socket on one end for joining to rigid plastic pipe.

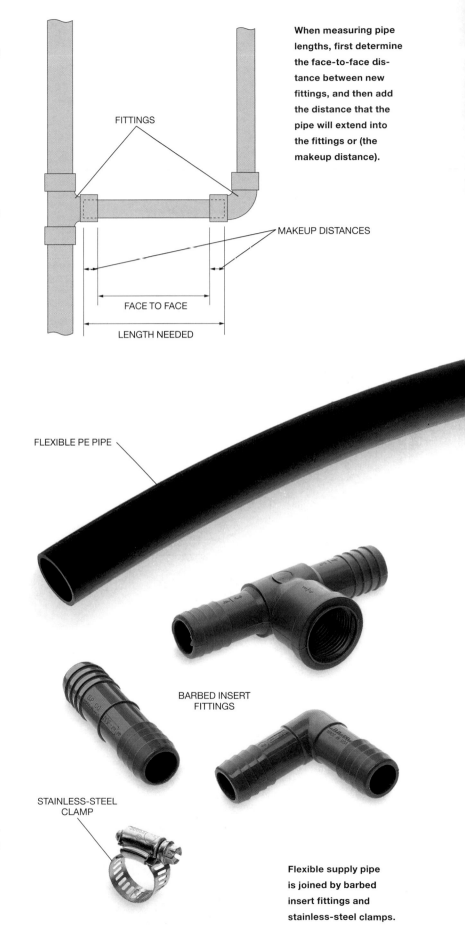

FITTINGS

MAKEUP DISTANCES

FACE TO FACE

LENGTH NEEDED

When measuring pipe lengths, first determine the face-to-face distance between new fittings, and then add the distance that the pipe will extend into the fittings or (the makeup distance).

FLEXIBLE PE PIPE

BARBED INSERT FITTINGS

STAINLESS-STEEL CLAMP

Flexible supply pipe is joined by barbed insert fittings and stainless-steel clamps.

DWV pipe Two types of plastic pipe are used to repair or extend drain-waste–vent (DWV) systems: acrylonitrile-butadiene-styrene (ABS) and polyvinyl chloride (PVC). You can tell the difference by the color; ABS is black, and PVC is off-white. Basin traps and other short connectors to DWV lines are often fabricated from a third plastic, polypropylene (PP), which is identifiable by its stark white color.

Both ABS and PVC are less expensive, lighter in weight, and easier to connect and hang than sections of cast-iron pipe (see pages 412–413). For these reasons, plastic pipe is a common choice for new work, for extending a cast-iron system, and even for replacing a leaking section of cast-iron drainpipe.

Codes often allow only ABS or PVC—and rarely both simultaneously. PVC is sometimes considered a better choice because it is less susceptible to mechanical and chemical damage and has slightly more fittings available. (Fittings for PVC and ABS are not readily interchangeable.)

Both ABS and PVC drainpipe are sold in lengths of 10 and 20 feet. Drainpipe for tubs, sinks, and lavatories normally has a 1½- or 2-inch nominal diameter. Toilets require 3- or 4-inch-diameter drains. Vent pipe can range from 1¼ to 4 inches in nominal diameter.

DWV fittings differ from supply fittings in that they have no interior shoulder, which would catch waste. You will find a wide assortment of change-of-direction and reducer fittings; always take care to direct the flow from the smaller pipe diameter to the larger. Connect plastic ABS and PVC fittings to drainpipe with solvent cement.

Other types of fittings or pipe can be connected with no-hub couplings (see pages 412–413) and special compression fittings made for plastic pipe. Some ABS and PVC fittings—notably those intended to be disassembled on occasion, such as drain plugs, are threaded.

cutting plastic pipe

Before you cut any pipe, make exact measurements. Pipes that are rigid will not give much if they are too long or too short. Minor measuring and cutting errors are rarely a problem with flexible tubing, which usually has enough play to make up the difference.

To measure pipe or tubing, determine the distance between new fittings; then add the makeup distance (see page 407). This distance varies depending on the type of fittings employed. In push-on fittings, such as those used with PVC or ABS, pipe ends extend all the way to the shoulder (the interior stop); the pipes do not go quite as far in threaded fittings.

The quickest, cleanest way to cut plastic pipe and tubing up to about 1 inch in diameter is with PVC scissors. You can also cut rigid pipe with a tubing cutter, a fine-toothed handsaw, or a power miter saw.

ABS FITTINGS

ABS PIPE

E IMPACT 2" SCH40-COEX-ABS CELLULAR CORE DWV-ASTM-F-6

ABS pipe and fittings, used primarily for DWV systems, are joined with solvent cement.

PLUMBING

CUTTING & JOINING PVC PIPE & FITTINGS

1 For fast, clean cuts, cut PVC pipe with PVC scissors. Or, you can use a tubing cutter, a fine-toothed saw, or a power miter saw. If you use a saw on an installed pipe, brace the pipe with your free hand to prevent excess motion.

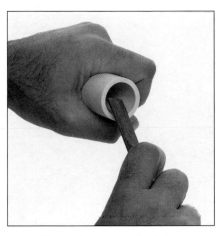

2 After cutting, use a file, knife, or reaming tool to remove any burrs inside and outside the pipe end. Inspect the end for cracks, gouges, and deep abrasions. Cut a replacement piece if necessary. Then test the fit of the pipe. It should enter the fitting but stop partway.

3 It is a good idea to put the fitting onto the pipe end temporarily and mark the pieces for proper alignment before cementing. Once the cement is applied, the pipe will slip farther into the fitting, so make your marks long enough to account for this.

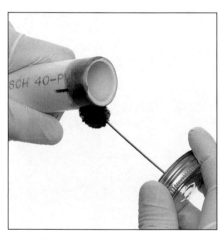

4 Before gluing PVC, spread a layer of PVC primer (often called purple primer) around the end of the pipe and also inside the fitting down to the shoulder. Allow the primer to dry.

5 Apply the PVC solvent cement. An applicator brush usually comes with the container. If the brush is not included, use another soft brush, such as a ¼-inch brush for ½-inch pipe or a ⅜-inch brush for ¾-inch pipe. Work in a well-ventilated area, avoid breathing fumes, and keep any flame source away from the cement. Apply cement liberally to the pipe and lightly to the fitting socket. If the temperature is below 40 degrees Fahrenheit, use a special low-temperature solvent cement instead.

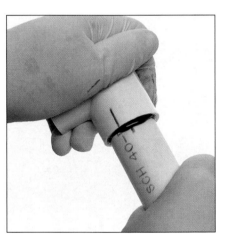

6 Slip the fitting onto the pipe so your marks are offset ¼ inch or so, and then immediately twist the fitting into correct alignment. Hold the parts for a few seconds while the cement sets. Then inspect the joint between the pipe and fitting. There should be a narrow band of cement all around. Wipe off any excess with a damp rag. Solvent-cemented joints can be handled gently within a minute, but wait at least 2 hours before you pressurize with water and even longer under cold, damp conditions. Then you can turn on the water and inspect for leaks.

CUTTING & JOINING ABS PIPE & FITTINGS

1 For clean, straight cuts through ABS, use a PVC saw and a miter box (as shown) or a power miter saw. If you have neither tool, use a fine-toothed handsaw, being careful to make the cut as straight as possible.

2 Use a utility knife or file to remove the rough edges around the pipe's interior that could snag waste and water. It is also a good idea to clean the outside of the pipe end with sandpaper or an emery cloth.

3 Place the fitting on the pipe end temporarily, and mark the alignment for later reference. (Remember, the pipe will slip farther into the fitting once the cement is applied, so make your marks long.) A white grease pencil is easy to see on black ABS.

4 Spread ABS solvent cement liberally around the outside of the pipe, and then coat the interior of the fitting. Work in a well-ventilated area, avoid breathing the fumes, and keep all flame sources away from the cement. Wear latex gloves to keep it off your hands.

5 Slip the fitting all the way onto the pipe with the alignment slightly offset, and then immediately twist the fitting so the marks line up. Hold the joint together for a few seconds. Gently wipe away excess cement with a damp rag.

EXTENDING AN ABS SYSTEM

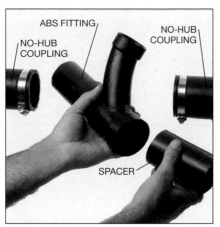

ABS FITTING

NO-HUB COUPLING

NO-HUB COUPLING

SPACER

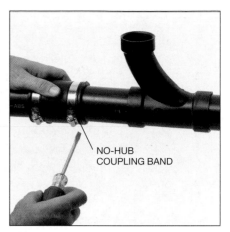

NO-HUB COUPLING BAND

1 First cut into the existing pipe. Plastic is easy to cut: You can use a PVC saw (as shown) or a fine-toothed handsaw. Cut off the ends squarely.

2 Depending on the amount of play and the type of couplings you have, you may need one or two spacers, plus your new fitting. Mark and cut the spacers to span the pipe gap plus the shoulder of the fitting and the interior shoulder (if there is one) of the no-hub coupling (see page 412).

3 Glue the spacers to the fitting, position the fitting in the gap, and slip the spacers inside the couplings. When you have aligned the new fitting in the direction of your intended extension, tighten the coupling bands.

INSTALLING A BARBED INSERT FITTING

STAINLESS-STEEL RING CLAMP

PE TUBING

BARBED FITTING

BARBED FITTING

1 Flexible PE tubing is joined by barbed insert fittings. You do not need to cut the tubing perfectly straight before you insert the fitting. Slide the stainless-steel ring clamp onto the PE tubing end. Twist the barbed fitting into the tubing, and line up the fitting with the new tubing run.

2 Slide the stainless-steel clamp over the fitting, and then simply tighten the screw on the clamp. If you need to make changes after insertion, you can usually pull apart the joint by hand once the clamps have been loosened. If this is impossible, pour hot water over the ends of the PE tubing to soften it, and then pull it away from the fitting.

working with cast-iron pipe

IF YOUR HOME WAS BUILT BEFORE 1970, THERE IS A GOOD CHANCE IT HAS CAST-iron piping in its drain-waste–vent (DWV) system. Cast-iron pipe is strong, dense, and corrosion-resistant enough to be the quietest of all piping materials.

There are two types of fittings for cast iron: bell-and-spigot and no-hub, or hubless. Bell-and-spigot joints, now virtually obsolete, are located in older homes; they were joined using molten lead and oakum. Most codes no longer permit lead in DWV piping. The no-hub joint is most commonly used because it takes up minimal space inside wall cavities. This type of joint also can be used to modify existing bell-and-spigot systems.

Many fittings are available for use with cast-iron pipe. Drainage fittings, unlike water-supply fittings, do not have interior shoulders, and each has a built-in fall or slope to allow for gravity.

No-hub cast-iron pipe ranges in diameter from 1½ inches to 4 inches. It is usually bought in 10-foot lengths (shorter lengths are available for bell-and-spigot fittings). Cast iron should be supported every 4 feet in horizontal runs and within a few inches of joints. Plumber's tape, hangers, and straps are commonly used.

cutting the pipe When cutting cast-iron pipe, wear safety glasses and work gloves. Be sure to turn off the water supply and alert others in the house not to use toilets and other plumbing fixtures. Before removing pipe, securely support the section to be removed, as well as the sections of pipe on either side of this area. You can use plumber's tape for this support; pull it taut, and nail it to nearby joists or studs. To determine how much new no-hub pipe you will need, simply measure the length of pipe that has been removed.

To cut cast-iron pipe, the tool of choice for do-it-yourselfers is a reciprocating saw equipped with a metal-cutting blade. You can also use a snap cutter, as shown on the facing page. In a pinch, you can use a hacksaw, cold chisel, and ball-peen hammer to cut the pipe. Start by chalking a cutting line all around the pipe, and then score the area to a depth of $\frac{1}{16}$ inch with the hacksaw. Tap all around the section with the hammer and cold chisel until the pipe breaks.

joining the pipe To connect a no-hub fitting or pipe to existing cast-iron pipe, use a no-hub coupling (see below left). The coupling consists of a neoprene gasket, a stainless-steel shield, and worm-drive band clamps for compressing the gasket around the pipe.

Cast-iron pipe and fittings are joined with a no-hub coupling.

NO-HUB COUPLING

NO-HUB FITTINGS

CAST-IRON PIPE

TYING INTO CAST IRON WITH ABS

1 The snap cutter uses a ratchet action to increase pressure on a chain with cutting wheels that encircle the pipe, constricting the pipe until it snaps. Cuts are rarely perfect; use pliers or a cold chisel and ball-peen hammer to break off any large, uneven chips. Be sure to wear gloves and safety glasses.

2 Slip no-hub couplings over the ends of the cut cast-iron pipe. Turn the screws clockwise on the band clamps to snugly secure the couplings to the pipes.

3 Glue a pair of ABS spacers to your chosen fitting. The spacers should span your cut pipe section, allowing for the couplings' makeup distance (see page 407). Push spacers firmly into the open ends of the coupling, and then tighten all of the stainless-steel band clamps.

JOINING NO-HUB CAST IRON

1 After sliding the stainless-steel shield onto the pipe, push the neoprene gasket onto the end of the pipe; the gasket sleeve has a built-in stop to help you center the assembly at the joint. Then fold back the gasket lip.

2 If you were able to fold the gasket out of the way, then simply butt the fitting against the gasket's stop, and roll the gasket lip back into place. Or, if need be, push and pull until the pipe, gasket, and fitting are aligned.

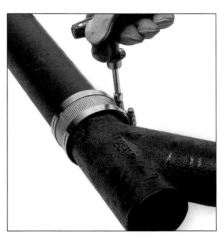

3 Finally, slide the stainless-steel shield over the gasket, and tighten the band screws with a socket wrench or nutdriver. (A T-handled wrench preset for the correct torque is shown.)

roughing-in fixtures

ON THE FOLLOWING PAGES, YOU WILL FIND SPECIFIC INSTALLATION NOTES FOR roughing-in new fixtures and appliances that require tying into or extending your present plumbing systems. Be sure to refer to your local codes for specific requirements.

bathroom sink

A lavatory sink requires hot and cold water supplies, a drain, and a vent line. If these pipes already exist near the location where the sink will go, the job of roughing-in is fairly easy. A bathroom sink can normally be wet-vented (vented directly through the fixture drain to the soil stack) if the drain pipe is large enough and the distance it travels is short enough (both factors that are determined by codes); otherwise it is back-vented (vented from the fixture's drain line to the main stack above the level of the sink or fixture).

You will need to have $\frac{1}{2}$-inch hot- and cold-water supply risers, stubouts, and caps. Prefabricated or homemade water-hammer arresters (see page 417) may be required

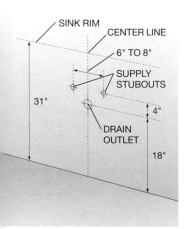

SINK RIM
CENTER LINE
6" TO 8"
SUPPLY STUBOUTS
31"
4"
DRAIN OUTLET
18"

ABOVE: **Rough-in dimensions for a bathroom sink typically place the rim at 31 inches.** RIGHT: **Pipes required for a sink include hot and cold supplies, a drain, and a vent.**

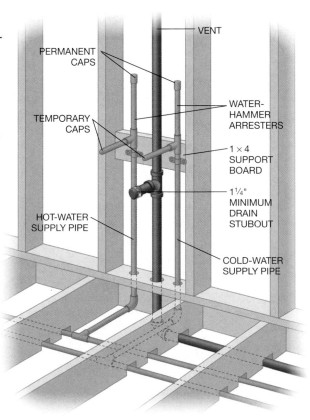

VENT
PERMANENT CAPS
TEMPORARY CAPS
WATER-HAMMER ARRESTERS
1 × 4 SUPPORT BOARD
1¼" MINIMUM DRAIN STUBOUT
HOT-WATER SUPPLY PIPE
COLD-WATER SUPPLY PIPE

on both hot and cold supply pipes. For typical placement of these, see the illustrations at left.

toilet

A new toilet is the most troublesome fixture to install in a house because it requires its own vent (2 inches minimum) and a drain that is at least 3 inches in diameter. If your toilet is on a branch drain (away from the main soil stack), it cannot be upstream from a sink or shower. The closet bend and floor flange must be roughed-in first, as shown in the top two illustrations on the facing page; the floor flange must be positioned at the level of the eventual finished floor.

Only one water supply line is required for roughing-in a toilet: a $\frac{1}{2}$-inch cold-water riser with a stubout and cap. You may require a water-hammer arrester.

bathtub or shower

Bathtubs and showers are often positioned on branch drains and vented the same way sinks are (see the illustration above left). Both enter the main soil stack at or below floor level because of their below-floor traps. A shower's faucet body (called a diverter valve for a tub/shower combination) and shower pipe assembly are both installed while the wall is open.

Supply pipes required include $\frac{1}{2}$-inch hot and cold supply lines and $\frac{1}{2}$-inch pipes to both the showerhead and the tub spout. Some large tubs and high-flow showers utilize $\frac{3}{4}$-inch supply pipes. Increasingly, showers are plumbed with their own supply branches; this helps maintain both water pressure and temperature when nearby fixtures are turned on. If possible, place gate or ball valves on these risers where they

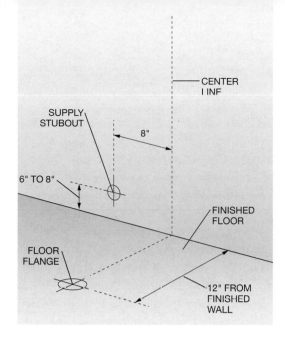

CENTER LINE

SUPPLY STUBOUT

8"

6" TO 8"

FLOOR FLANGE

FINISHED FLOOR

12" FROM FINISHED WALL

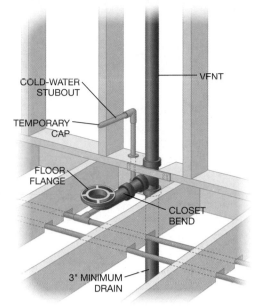

COLD-WATER STUBOUT

VENT

TEMPORARY CAP

FLOOR FLANGE

CLOSET BEND

3" MINIMUM DRAIN

For a toilet rough-in, the distance from the finished wall to the floor flange is critical. Most toilets call for 12 inches, but this can vary.

can be accessed, such as from below the floor or behind the wall. In addition, you may want to cut a small opening and add a door below, behind, or to the side of the tub to allow later access to both the trap and the drainpipe.

kitchen fixtures

For both convenience and economy, most fixtures and appliances that require water are adjacent to the sink. Because of this, a single set of vertical supply pipes and one drainpipe generally serve the entire

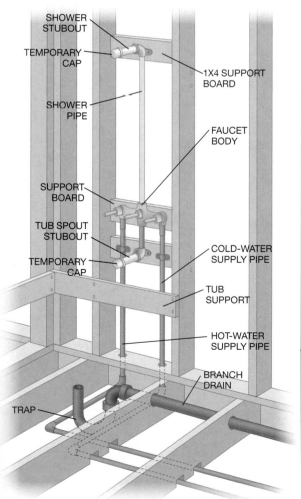

SHOWER STUBOUT

TEMPORARY CAP

SHOWER PIPE

1X4 SUPPORT BOARD

FAUCET BODY

SUPPORT BOARD

TUB SPOUT STUBOUT

TEMPORARY CAP

COLD-WATER SUPPLY PIPE

TUB SUPPORT

HOT-WATER SUPPLY PIPE

BRANCH DRAIN

TRAP

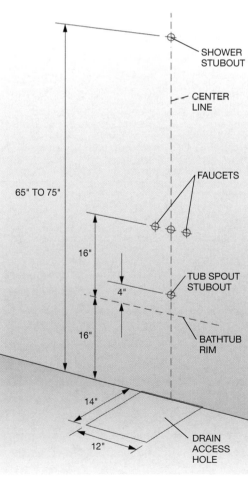

SHOWER STUBOUT

CENTER LINE

FAUCETS

65" TO 75"

16"

4"

TUB SPOUT STUBOUT

16"

BATHTUB RIM

14"

12"

DRAIN ACCESS HOLE

Roughing-in a combination bathtub/shower calls for installing a diverter valve in the wall with the supply piping.

LOWE'S QUICK TIP

Secure pipes to wall framing by using 1 × 4 bracing boards, copper supply straps, or plastic pipe bushings where supply risers pass through the wall's sole plate. The method is up to you; what is important is that pipes remain rigid when pushed or pulled.

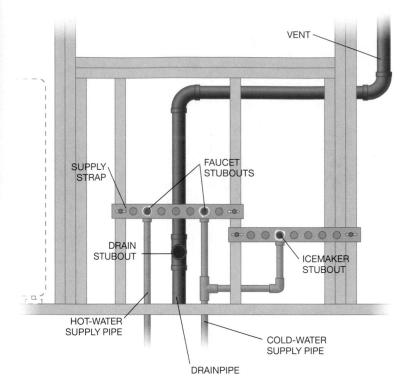

Roughing-in a kitchen sink requires drain and vent lines and water supply pipes. Note that some plumbers also recommend installing water-hammer arresters on the supply pipes (see opposite page).

side the wall, and risers run directly to it. Space the supply risers according to the valve type you are using.

The washing machine will need a place to drain, too. If a laundry tub or sink is nearby, the drain hose can hook over the edge of it. If there is no sink or tub nearby, you will need to drain the washer into a standpipe: a vertical 2-inch pipe that connects to a 1½-inch trap. The standpipe should be between 18 and 30 inches above the trap (some codes allow for a range of 18 to 42 inches). The trap itself should be 6 to 18 inches above the floor.

Because the stop and start of washing machine cycles is particularly hard on valves, hoses, and the machines themselves, some manufacturers recommend that water-hammer arresters be one size larger than the supply pipes and as long as 24 inches.

kitchen. Supply pipes or tubing for a dishwasher, hot-water dispenser, and automatic icemaker often branch off the main hot and cold supply lines leading to the sink faucet. Similarly, the dishwasher and garbage disposal share the sink's trap and drainpipe. Pipes you'll need include ½-inch hot- and cold-water supply risers, stubouts, and caps. Water-hammer arresters, either prefabricated or homemade (see the box on the facing page), may be required on both hot and cold supply pipes.

washing machine

To supply water to a washing machine, you will need to run both hot- and cold-water pipes to the desired location. Supply pipes for a washer are usually ½ inch in diameter. Plan to employ either a pair of washing machine valves (they look like hose bibbs) or a single- or twin-lever washing machine valve (see page 439) to make the supply hook-ups. When installing separate washing machine valves, put T-fittings on the risers inside the wall, then water-hammer arresters vertically above them, and supply stubouts toward the machine. A single- or twin-lever washing machine valve sits in-

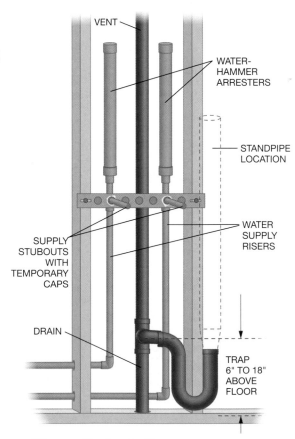

When roughing-in a washing machine, it's a good idea to install highly effective water-hammer arresters on the water supply pipes.

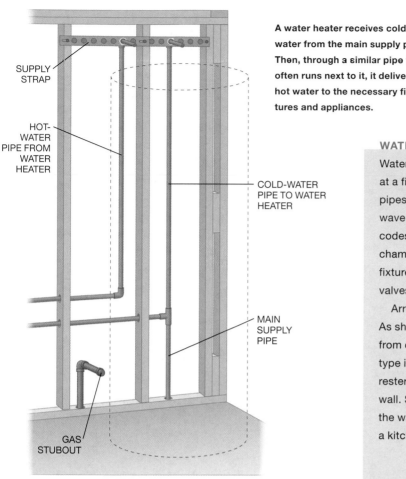

SUPPLY STRAP

HOT-WATER PIPE FROM WATER HEATER

COLD-WATER PIPE TO WATER HEATER

MAIN SUPPLY PIPE

GAS STUBOUT

A water heater receives cold water from the main supply pipe. Then, through a similar pipe that often runs next to it, it delivers hot water to the necessary fixtures and appliances.

water heater

To install a new water heater or to relocate one, you will have to rough-in a cold-water supply pipe, typically ¾ inch, to supply the tank. In addition, a pipe of the same size will carry hot water to all the fixtures that require it. A gas water heater will require a gas supply pipe and a flue for venting combustion gasses (this is usually installed after the rough-in).

Install a shutoff valve (either a ball or gate valve) on both incoming and outgoing pipes. Plan to use flexible connectors or rigid pipe and unions to hook up the water and gas lines, as discussed in detail on pages 440–441.

If you are relocating a water heater, pick a location as close as possible to the main areas of hot water use in your house. Keep in mind that you must provide adequate clearance between a gas water heater and any combustible materials. Some codes require a floor drain within 6 inches of your heater's pressure-relief valve.

WATER-HAMMER ARRESTERS

Water hammer occurs when you quickly turn off the water at a fixture or an appliance. The water flowing through the pipes simply slams to a stop, causing a destructive shock wave and a hammering noise. To minimize the effect, many codes require water-hammer arresters (also known as air chambers) near fixtures. These are installed at the top of a fixture's water supply risers, on the incoming side of shutoff valves and supply risers that serve the fixture or appliance.

Arresters come in commercial and homemade varieties. As shown below right, the homemade one is constructed from common copper pipe and fittings. The manufactured type is shown below left. Most installations place the arresters on T-fittings at the tops of supply risers inside the wall. Some plumbers prefer that the arresters be outside the wall for easy servicing; these can be concealed inside a kitchen sink cabinet or bathroom vanity.

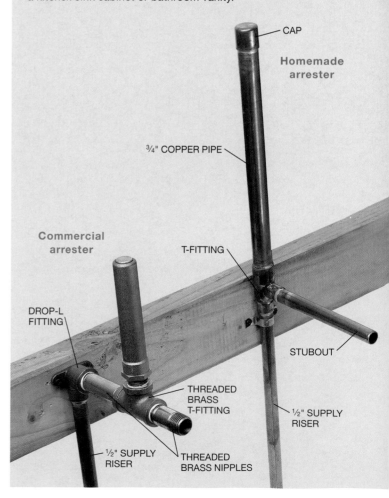

CAP

Homemade arrester

¾" COPPER PIPE

Commercial arrester

T-FITTING

DROP-L FITTING

STUBOUT

THREADED BRASS T-FITTING

½" SUPPLY RISER

½" SUPPLY RISER

THREADED BRASS NIPPLES

installing a kitchen sink

TO MANY HOMEOWNERS, INSTALLING A KITCHEN SINK SEEMS LIKE A DAUNTING task. But the fact is, if you can trace around a template and cut out a hole, you can install a sink. You do want to make sure your new sink fits your countertop and the cabinet below it, so measure the width and depth (from front to back) of your lower cabinets before making a purchase. Generally, a sink up to 22 inches deep will fit in a standard 24-inch-deep cabinet if you have no backsplash; if you do have a backsplash, your countertop will only take a sink up to 20½ inches deep. Of course, your options will increase if you are also changing your cabinetry and countertop.

Installation of this self-rimming stainless-steel sink in a laminate countertop is a reasonably easy task.

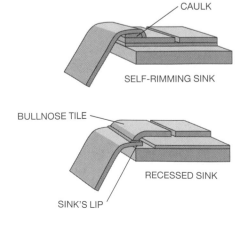

CAULK

SELF-RIMMING SINK

BULLNOSE TILE

RECESSED SINK

SINK'S LIP

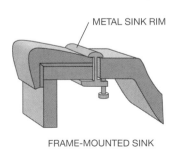

METAL SINK RIM

FRAME-MOUNTED SINK

At left are three common methods of mounting sinks. Self-rimming sinks have a molded lip that rests on the edge of the countertop cutout. Recessed, or under-mount, sinks either fit flush with the countertop or attach to its underside. Frame-mounted sinks have a metal rim that hides the gap that is between the sink and the counter.

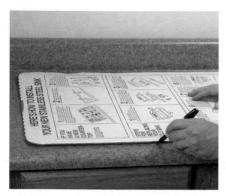

1 Most sink manufacturers provide a template that allows you to site the sink opening. Position the template so it is centered on the sink cabinet and is at least 1½ inches back from the countertop's front edge. If your countertop is deeper than 24 inches, place it farther back (but no more than 4 inches). Tape the template in place, and then outline it with a marker.

2 Remove the template, and drill a ⅜-inch-diameter hole in each corner. Insert a saber-saw blade in one of the holes, and cut along the inside of the line. To prevent the cutout from snapping off and falling through as you complete the cuts, screw a scrap of wood, a few inches longer than the span of the opening, to the top of the cutout. When you have finished cutting the sink hole, simply lift the cutout from the countertop.

3 Install the faucet (for instructions, see pages 420–421) and the sink strainers. (Doing this when you have full access to the sink will be much easier than fitting the pieces in from below after the sink is installed.) To create a seal between the sink and the countertop, apply a bead of silicone caulk or plumber's putty around the entire perimeter of the underside of the sink's lip.

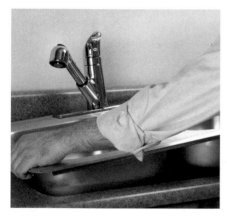

4 Carefully turn the sink over, and insert it into the opening without disturbing the caulk or putty. If your sink is heavy, get help lifting and installing it. Also consider placing a couple of wood scraps near the edge of the opening to support the sink and protect your fingers as you drop it into position.

5 Most sinks are pulled down firmly against the countertop with special mounting clips that hook onto the lip on the underside of the sink and are tightened with a screwdriver or nutdriver. Be sure to follow the manufacturer's directions for spacing these clips. Tightening the mounting clips may cause the caulk or putty to squeeze out from under the sink lip. If this happens, remove the excess with a clean, soft rag.

6 To complete the project, first connect the P-trap. Join the faucet lines to the hot and cold supply lines with flexible supply tubes, and connect the strainers to the waste line. Turn the water on at the shutoff valves, remove the aerator from the faucet, and then turn on the water from the faucet to flush the system. Reinstall the aerator after you have run the water for a minute or so.

installing a kitchen faucet

THE AMOUNT OF ACCESS YOU HAVE TO FAUCET PARTS DETERMINES HOW EASY OR difficult it will be to install a kitchen faucet. Installing a faucet into a new sink is simple because you can do it before setting the sink in place, while you have full access to all the parts, including the hard-to-reach mounting nuts. If the sink is already in place, replacing a faucet can be a challenge because your only access is from under the sink. You must lie on your back and work around the supply lines in order to reach the mounting nuts that will secure the faucet. Even with the aid of a basin wrench, which extends your reach, it is still an awkward task. Depending on your circumstance, you may find it easier in the long run to remove the sink first.

This single-handle sink faucet features a spout that pulls out to become a sprayer.

Clean the surface of the sink where the new faucet will sit. Some faucets, such as the one shown here, come with a rubber gasket on the bottom; if yours does not, pack the entire faucet base with putty.

After installing your new faucet, remove the aerator and flush the lines to ensure that debris does not reduce the water flow. On a standard faucet, simply unscrew the aerator at the end of the spigot, and let water run for a minute or two. With a pull-out sprayer faucet, the aerator/filter is located in an inlet inside the sprayer head. Just unthread the hose, remove the aerator/filter, and flush.

LOWE'S QUICK TIP
Flexible supply tubes make connecting a faucet a snap. With these, you do not have to cut or piece together pipe. Be sure the fittings at each end of your tubes match your fixture inlets as well as your shutoff valve.

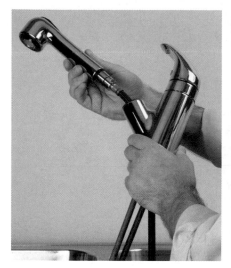

1 Many new faucets require some assembly before being mounted to the sink. If that is the case with yours, follow the manufacturer's directions. With most pullout sprayer faucets, the sprayer needs to be threaded through the faucet body first.

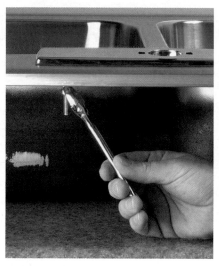

2 Insert the rubber gasket between the base plate of the faucet and the sink top to create a watertight seal. If no gasket is provided, pack the cavity of the faucet with plumber's putty, and then insert the faucet body through the holes in the sink top. Thread the mounting nuts provided onto the faucet shafts. Center the threaded shafts in the sink's holes, and tighten the nuts firmly.

3 Many manufacturers include a special long socket to aid in tightening the mounting nuts. A hole in the socket accepts the shank of a screwdriver, guiding it as you tighten the nuts. If you are mounting the faucet on an installed sink, use this method.

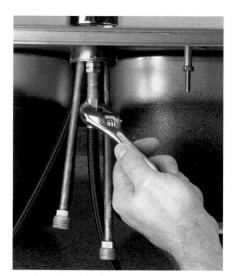

4 If you are installing a pullout sprayer faucet or a faucet with a separate sprayer, connect the sprayer to the faucet body now. Check the manufacturer's directions to see if pipe-wrap tape for this connection is recommended. Use an adjustable wrench to tighten the connection.

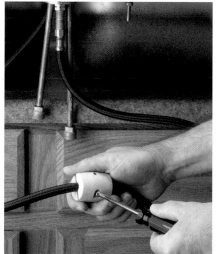

5 Most pullout sprayer faucets and faucets with separate sprayers come with a counterweight that attaches to the sprayer hose. This weight helps retract the hose back into the sink cabinet after you have used the sprayer. Follow the manufacturer's directions on where to secure the weight, and take care not to crimp the hose as you attach the weight.

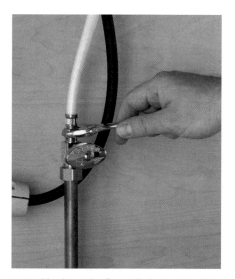

6 Hook up the faucet's hot and cold supply lines to the water-supply shutoff valves under the sink. If necessary, carefully bend the copper tubes coming out of the faucet to gain better access, and connect flexible supply tubes to them. Wrap a couple of turns of pipe-wrap tape around the threaded nipples on the valves, and connect the tubes. Tighten the nuts with an adjustable wrench.

installing a garbage disposal

ALTHOUGH NOT THE MOST GLAMOROUS KITCHEN IMPROVEMENT, THE ADDITION of a garbage disposal will be greatly appreciated by the chef of the house.

Disposals vary greatly in size and bowl depth; check the dimensions to make sure the disposal you have chosen will fit under your sink. Because installing a disposal requires both plumbing and electrical skills, it is a project best taken on by experienced do-it-yourselfers. One way to simplify the task is to have a licensed electrician install a ground fault circuit interrupter (GFCI) outlet under the sink and a separate wall switch adjacent to the sink; the only electrical work left is to wire a power cord to the disposal. For information on wiring a new circuit, see page 503.

Always shut off the power to the circuit that will serve the disposal before beginning any work. If you are replacing an old disposal, turn off the electricity to that circuit, and unplug the disposal or disconnect the wiring before removing the unit.

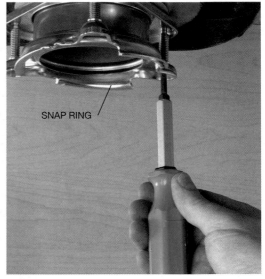

SNAP RING

1 Disconnect and remove the existing waste assembly, from the sink flange to the trap. Have towels and a bucket handy to catch water and debris. Once the waste lines are out of the way, remove the mounting assembly from the disposal, and install the new flange in the sinkhole, applying a coil of plumber's putty around it before pressing it into place.

2 Attach the upper mounting assembly to the sink flange, placing a heavy object such as a large phone book on top of the flange to hold it in place. Follow the manufacturer's directions for gasket placement, and slip the mounting ring over the flange. Slide the snap ring onto the flange until it pops into the groove on the flange. Next, tighten the three mounting screws until the assembly forms a tight seal against the sink.

LOWE'S QUICK TIP
When you are working under a sink, remove the cabinet doors and set them aside to provide better access.

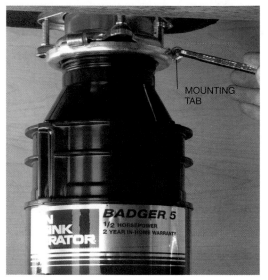

3 To prepare to attach the disposal to the mounting assembly, first attach the discharge tube, as shown. Then, inspect the P-trap, and clean out any hardened waste. Next, prepare the dishwasher drain connection. This usually entails knocking out a drain plug from the dishwasher nipple with a hammer and screwdriver and attaching the drain hose from the dishwasher.

4 Position the disposal under the mounting assembly so that the mounting tabs can slide over the mounting tracks. Lift the disposal, and insert the top into the mounting assembly. Rotate the lower mounting ring until all three mounting tabs lock over ridges in the mounting ring. Use the wrench provided by the manufacturer—or a screwdriver—to tighten the ring.

5 Rotate the disposal so that the discharge tube aligns with the drain trap. If your sink is a double-bowl model, you must replumb the waste line to attach the disposal. If you are lucky, all you will need is an extension tube. If not, you may need to replace the entire assembly.

6 Connect the disposal to the power. Either run a line or have a licensed electrician run power into the sink cabinet and install a GFCI receptacle. If your disposal did not come with a plug on the end of the cord, wire the recommended grounded electrical cord to the disposal. Finally, plug it into the receptacle.

LOWE'S SAFETY TIP

installing a dishwasher

FOR A MODESTLY EXPERIENCED DO-IT-YOURSELFER, INSTALLING A BUILT-IN DISH-washer is a pretty simple job, requiring only a few hand tools and a spare afternoon.

A dishwasher comes with the manufacturer's installation instructions; follow these exactly. The directions given here are intended to be a general guide so that you will know what is involved.

electrical requirements

A 120-volt electrical receptacle or electrical box protected by a ground fault circuit interrupter (GFCI) must be located nearby, usually at the back of the sink base cabinet. Have an electrician install or verify that you have a grounded 15-amp receptacle, or wire your own (see page 503).

plumbing hookups

A water supply tube connects a dishwasher to the kitchen sink's hot-water supply. A flexible hose drains waste water from the dishwasher to either the sink trap or, if you have one, a garbage disposal.

The easiest drain setup, as illustrated on the facing page, is to connect the dishwasher's drain line directly into the sink's trap. To do this, replace a section of the sink drain's tailpiece with a dishwasher tailpiece, which has a short T-shape nipple that connects to the dishwasher's drain hose. Cut off the bottom of the sink's tailpiece with a hacksaw or tubing cutter, and connect the new tailpiece with slip nuts and washers.

If your sink has a disposal, connect the drain hose to the dishwasher inlet located on the disposal. If you are tying in to a disposal that has never been connected to a dishwasher, unplug it or turn off its circuit, and use an old screwdriver to punch out the knockout plug, which is inside the dishwasher nipple.

air gap

To prevent wastewater from draining or siphoning back into the dishwasher, many local codes require that the dishwasher be connected to an air-gap fixture before the disposal. The air gap, bought separately, mounts on top of the sink or the counter right next to the sink and connects to two flexible hoses: one runs to the dishwasher's drain and the other runs to the sink's trap or the dishwasher inlet on the disposal. In some areas, codes allow you to loop the dishwasher's drain hose in a high arc up under the countertop as an alternative to installing an air gap.

If your sink does not have an unused hole for mounting the air gap, you will need to bore one in the countertop next to the sink using an electric drill and a hole saw. If your countertop is made of stone or another difficult-to-cut material, have the sink top drilled by a professional.

installation

If you are replacing a dishwasher, remove the old one first, reversing the installation instructions discussed here. Be sure to turn off the power to the sink-area circuits and the water supply at the main house shutoff. Drain the supply pipes by opening a faucet (ideally, one that is lower than the sink shutoff valves).

After installation, adjust the dishwasher's front feet to level the appliance and align it with the cabinets and countertop. With the screws provided, anchor the unit to the underside of the counter. Restore the water pressure, and check for leaks. Install the dishwasher's front panel. Plug in (or hard-wire) the unit.

LOWE'S SAFETY TIP
Before doing any work, unplug the appliance, or turn off the circuit breaker and disconnect the power.

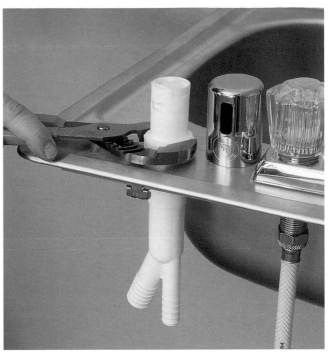

1 To install a shutoff valve for the dishwasher, first turn off the house's main valve. Disconnect the sink water supply tube from the valve, drain it into a bucket, and then unscrew the shutoff valve from the supply nipple with a wrench. Wind pipe-wrap tape around the nipple's threads, and then screw a new dual-outlet valve onto it.

2 As demonstrated in this photograph, install the air gap through a properly sized unused hole in the sink top (punch out the hole plug with a hammer). Insert the air gap. Then, using slip-joint pliers, secure it from above with a lock-nut, and push its cover into place.

3 Drill holes in the back corner of the sink base cabinet for the drain hose, water supply tube, and power cord. Position the dishwasher near its opening, and then push the hose, supply tube, and cord through their holes. As you walk the dishwasher into place, be careful not to pinch or tangle these connectors.

4 Reconnect the sink's supply tube to the dual-outlet valve, and connect the flexible supply tube to the valve's second outlet and the dishwasher's inlet. Then tighten these connections with an adjustable wrench until they are snug.

5 Slip one hose clamp over each end of the short drain hose that will run from the sink trap to the large outlet on the air gap, and cinch the clamps until they are tight. Then follow the same steps with the long drain hose, running it from the smaller outlet on the air gap to the drain fitting at the base of the dishwasher.

installing a water filter

THE INSTALLATION OF A WATER-TREATMENT DEVICE IS BECOMING ONE OF THE most popular kitchen upgrades. Many types of treatment devices are currently available, ranging from simple in-line cartridges to reverse-osmosis systems with undersink storage tanks. In between these are easy-to-install dual-cartridge devices. This type of system requires no electrical power, hooks up directly to your cold-water line, and installs in a few hours. Keep in mind, however, that you must periodically change the cartridges. If you notice changes in taste, odor, and/or water flow, that is a sure sign it is time to replace the cartridges.

A reverse-osmosis unit is hooked up similarly to the dual-cartridge device shown here, but it must also be connected to the sink's drain because it discharges wastewater. It stores the clean water in a tank beneath the sink.

1 Start by mounting the dispenser. Most are designed to fit in the extra hole in a sink top, as shown, but if this hole is already occupied, you will have to drill another in the sink or countertop. Follow the manufacturer's directions for the location and size of the hole. Be sure to drill only into stainless-steel or porcelain cast-iron sinks; if you have an all-porcelain sink, drill for the dispenser through the countertop.

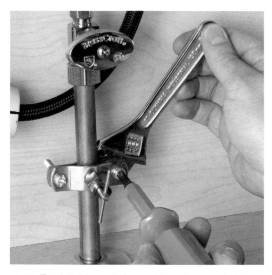

2 Tap into the existing cold-water supply line via a saddle valve, as shown. To install a saddle valve, first turn off the water supply and then open the faucet to drain the line. Following the manufacturer's directions, drill a small hole into the supply line. Turn the handle on the valve to expose the lance that is designed to puncture the pipe, and position the valve over the pipe so that the lance fits in the hole. Attach the valve's back plate, and tighten the nuts to lock it in place. Screw in the lance.

LOWE'S QUICK TIP
When shopping for a water-treatment device, look for one that has a built-in indicator to alert you when it is time to replace the filter cartridges.

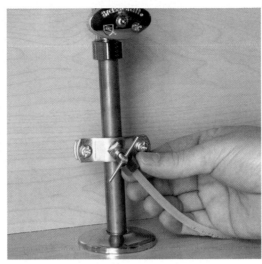

3 Position the cartridge filtration unit roughly between the cold-water line and the dispenser. Be sure to leave the specified clearance between the system and the cabinet bottom to allow for cartridge replacement. Secure the device to the cabinet back or wall with the screws provided by the manufacturer.

4 To hook up the device, start by cutting a length of plastic tubing to reach between the saddle valve and the system. Make it short enough not to kink but long enough to allow for installing a new compression fitting (the connector shown at the end of the tubing) if needed. Press the tubing into the compression fitting, and thread the fitting onto the saddle valve. Tighten the fitting with an adjustable wrench.

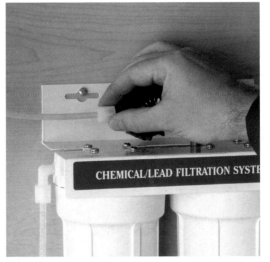

5 Insert the opposite end of the tubing into another compression fitting, and thread the fitting onto the inlet port of the filtration unit. Tighten the nut by hand, and then secure it by making another turn or turn and a half with an adjustable wrench.

6 Finally, cut a piece of tubing to run from the outlet port of the system to the water dispenser. Insert compression fittings on both ends, and thread the nuts onto the dispenser and the system. Turn on the water supply, and then open the water dispenser. Let the water run for about five minutes to flush out any carbon particles or air pockets. Most manufacturers recommend that you allow the water to run for about 20 seconds before you use the device.

installing a bathroom sink

ONE GREAT WAY TO UPDATE A BATHROOM, PARTICULARLY IF YOU ARE REPLACING a vanity cabinet or countertop, is to install a new bathroom sink, or lavatory. In recent years, plumbing-fixture designers have created a wonderful smorgasbord of high-style bathroom lavatories that turn what were once mundane fixtures into works of art.

Lavatories are categorized by their installation method: countertop-mounted, pedestal, wall-mounted, undermounted, and above-counter. A popular new variation is the console, which is supported by table-like legs.

For practical bathrooms, lavatory bowls usually combine with a vanity cabinet, a setup that hides the plumbing and provides ample storage and counter space.

Nearly all lavatory bowls have a pop-up stopper and an overflow hole that prevents water from spilling over the sides.

countertop sinks

The instructions opposite are for putting in a self-rimming, drop-in bowl, which is the easiest type to install. If you are installing a self-rimming sink in a new countertop, start by making a cutout for the bowl. (Hire a professional to do this if the countertop is a material that is difficult to cut.) Most sinks are sold with a template for marking this hole. Position the cutout according to the manufacturer's directions. A sink is typically centered from front to back.

When installing a heavy sink (such as a cast-iron unit), you can simply use a bead of plumber's putty rather than adhesive to seal the edges; the sink's weight will hold it in place. If you are installing a recessed or frame-mounted sink, attach the sink with the mounting clips or metal strip included with the unit.

A countertop-mounted, or self-rimming, sink drops into a hole cut in the countertop. The rim of the sink hides slight irregularities, making installation forgiving.

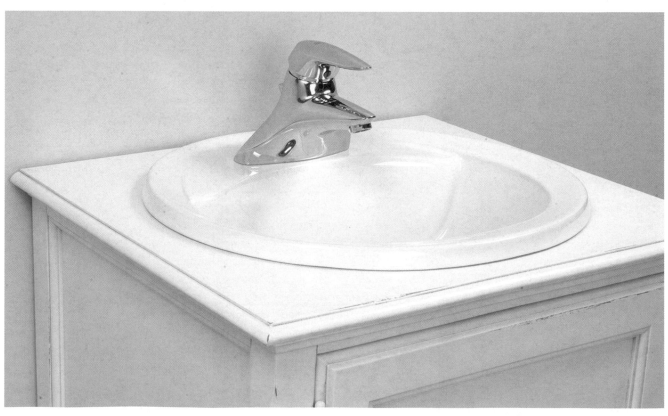

INSTALLING A COUNTERTOP SINK

1 Use the sink manufacturer's template to draw the cutout line on the countertop. If no template is provided, set the bowl upside down on the countertop and trace the outline. Then draw a second line about ¾ inch inside that line to serve as your cut line.

2 Carefully drill a ⅜-inch starter hole inside the cut line. Using a saber saw, begin cutting along the line. Before finishing the cut, screw a scrap board longer than the span of the cutout to the center of the cutout to prevent it from falling when you finish cutting. Remove the support after you finish the cut.

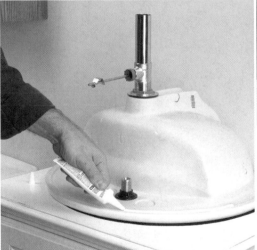

3 Place a bead of plumber's putty around the bottom edge of the drain-assembly housing's lip. Press the housing into the drain hole. Attach the gasket and washer, and tighten the locknut. (Hold the handles of pliers in the housing with a screwdriver to prevent the housing from turning while you tighten the locknut.) Remove any excess plumber's putty. Attach the tailpiece to the housing with the slip nut and washer.

4 If you haven't already done so, install the faucet as explained on pages 434–435. When the faucet is in place, turn the sink upside down, and run a bead of silicone adhesive along the underside of the molded lip (adhesive is included with some sinks). Turn the sink over, and carefully align it with the countertop's front edge. Press firmly around the lip to form a tight seal. After the adhesive has set, apply a bead of latex caulk around the edge, and smooth it with a wet finger. Install the pop-up assembly (see page 435).

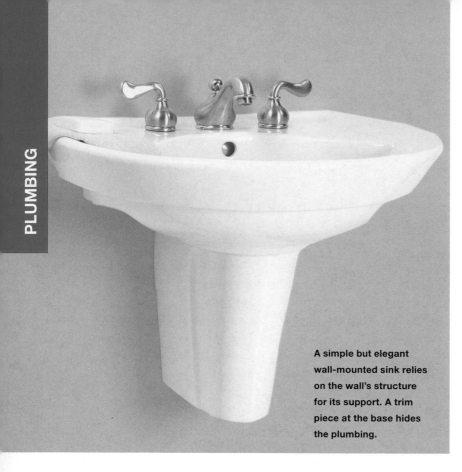

A simple but elegant wall-mounted sink relies on the wall's structure for its support. A trim piece at the base hides the plumbing.

wall-mounted sinks

Wall-mounted sinks are either hung on a metal bracket that is attached to the wall's framing or bolted directly to the framing (as shown here). These sinks come with manufacturer's installation instructions, which should be followed closely.

To provide the proper support for a wall-mounted sink, it is usually necessary to remove a small section of drywall so you can attach blocking between the wall studs. For more about removing wall materials, installing blocking, and repairing drywall, see pages 108–115.

Determine where support will be needed, based on the sink's measurements and mounting height (typically 30 inches above the floor). Remove drywall in that area, and install 2-by-6 or 2-by-8 blocking between the wall studs. Toenail the blocking to the studs with 3½-inch galvanized common nails. Then repair the drywall.

INSTALLING A WALL-MOUNTED SINK

1 Position the mounting plate or the sink on the wall, and mark the wall through the holes in the plate or sink. Drill pilot holes for lag screws or other fasteners supplied by the manufacturer; if the wall is tile, use a masonry bit. Then install the faucet, drain, and pop-up assemblies on the sink (see pages 433–435).

2 Use lag screws or other fasteners recommended by the manufacturer to secure the sink or the metal mounting plate to the blocking. After driving in the first fastener, check to make sure the sink or mounting plate is level, and then drive in the other fasteners.

3 Connect the P-trap and drain arm to the drain stubout, and then connect the two water supply tubes to the shutoff valves (see page 433). Some wall-mounted sinks (such as the one shown here) come with a trim piece that hides the plumbing lines. These sinks typically attach to the wall framing with lag screws.

pedestal sinks

Pedestal sinks are made up of two parts: the sink and the pedestal (or base). With most types, the weight of the bowl is not carried entirely by the base; a bracket ties the bowl to the wall for additional support. Just as with a wall-mounted sink, you will want to install blocking between wall studs to help provide the extra support that is required.

Pedestal sinks come with the manufacturer's installation instructions, which should be followed exactly. They also commonly come with the materials necessary for making water supply and drain connections. The faucet and valves are usually sold separately.

INSTALLING A PEDESTAL SINK

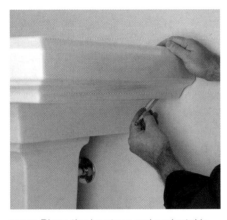

1 Place the lavatory and pedestal in the desired position. Level and square the assembly, and then mark the mounting-hole locations on the wall and on the floor.

2 Drill pilot holes for the fasteners in the wall and floor. If you are drilling tile, use a masonry bit, affixing a piece of tape on the areas to be drilled to keep the bit centered. Install the drain assembly and faucet (see pages 433–435).

A stately pedestal sink is supported primarily by its base but also bolts to the wall for extra stability.

3 Secure the lavatory to the wall with lag screws or other supplied fasteners. Then connect the trap to the drain assembly. With some pedestal sinks, you must rest the bowl on the pedestal, positioned close to the wall, and then hook up the waste and supply lines before securing the bowl to the wall.

4 Once you have secured the bowl, drill a pair of pilot holes in the floor for the bolts that will secure the pedestal to the floor. The pedestal base typically has a pair of notches in the base for these fasteners. Be careful not to over-tighten the bolts because this can crack porcelain. If the sink has a nut or rod to connect it to the pedestal, secure the device.

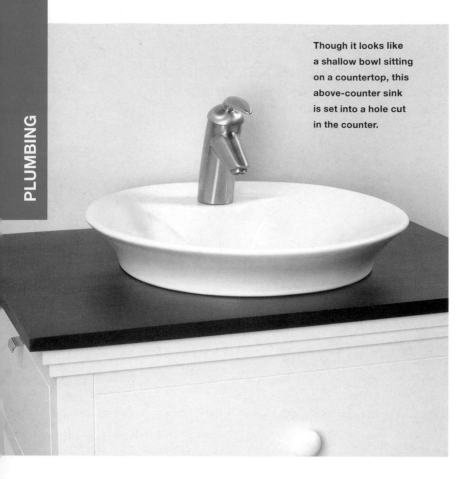

Though it looks like a shallow bowl sitting on a countertop, this above-counter sink is set into a hole cut in the counter.

above-counter sinks

An above-counter lavatory is an excellent choice when you want to make a design statement. These stylish lavatories rise above the countertop to create a decorative focal point. They install much like a countertop sink; the only difference is that the hole in the countertop is much smaller. Some above-counter sink manufacturers also provide precut countertops that make installation a snap. Most manufacturers include complete instructions as well as a pattern for cutting the countertop; be sure to follow the directions precisely.

For information about connecting the sink drain and the water supply lines, see the facing page. For directions on how to install a pop-up assembly, refer to Steps 4, 5, and 6 on page 435.

INSTALLING AN ABOVE-COUNTER SINK

1 Locate and cut the opening following the instructions for a countertop sink on page 429. Mount the faucet and drain assembly, and temporarily position the sink in the cutout. Check for alignment and clearance, and make marks on both the countertop and the sink as guides for installation.

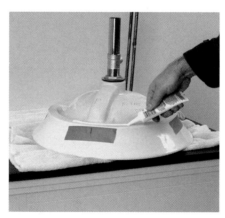

2 Turn the sink upside down, and apply a bead of sealant around the underside of the rim, following the directions on the label.

3 Position the sink in the opening, align it with the guide marks, and press it down. Allow the sealant to set according to label directions. Then connect the drain pipes and water supply lines (see the facing page).

undermount sinks

Recessed, or undermount, sinks are popular because they allow for easy cleanup of the adjacent surfaces and can be installed in practically any type of counter. The method of attachment varies by manufacturer; installation instructions are included with all models. In addition to the bowl, many sink manufacturers also offer countertops that are precut, predrilled, and prefit to work together. All you have to do is apply a bead of sealant and tighten some screws.

An undermount sink offers an uninterrupted look and makes the countertop easy to clean.

INSTALLING AN UNDERMOUNT SINK

1 Locate and cut the opening following the instructions for a countertop sink on page 429. Mount the faucet and drain assembly, and temporarily position the sink in the cutout. Check for alignment and clearance, and make marks on the countertop and the sink to guide installation.

2 Turn the sink upside down, and apply a bead of sealant around the underside of the rim, following the directions on the label.

CONNECTING A SINK

No matter what type of sink you purchase, the drain and water supply connections are generally installed in the following way.

First, hand-tighten a female adapter onto the drain stubout at the wall. Next, slide slip nuts onto the drain arm and the sink's tailpiece. Fit a P-trap in place, and tighten the slip nuts by hand. Connect flexible water-supply tubes onto the faucet's tailpieces (see page 435), and route them to the shutoff valves. Tighten coupling nuts with an adjustable wrench. Remove the faucet aerator, turn on the water, and check for leaks at the shutoff valves. Then turn on the faucet to check for leaks in the drain assembly. Replace the aerator.

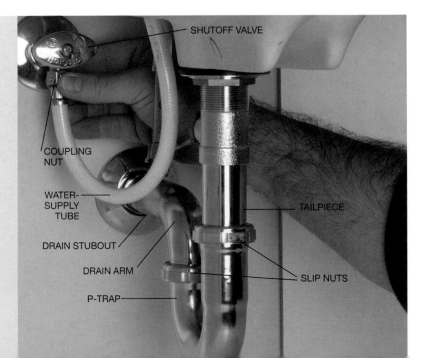

SHUTOFF VALVE
COUPLING NUT
WATER-SUPPLY TUBE
DRAIN STUBOUT
DRAIN ARM
P-TRAP
TAILPIECE
SLIP NUTS

installing a bathroom faucet

A BATHROOM FAUCET CAN BE EASY OR QUITE DIFFICULT TO INSTALL, DEPENDING on your access to the plumbing. If you are installing a faucet in a new bathroom sink, chances are the task will be simple because you can put in the parts before placing the sink. If the sink is already in place, your only access is from underneath. A tool called a basin wrench can extend your reach, but the task will still be awkward.

Whether you buy a single-piece faucet or a split set such as the one shown here, be sure your sink or countertop has the appropriate number and sizes of holes for the faucet parts.

To remove an old faucet, first turn off the shutoff valves at the supply tubes. Use a basin wrench to remove the nuts that connect the supply tubes to the faucet tailpieces. Drain the water in the supply tubes into a bucket or bowl. Remove the locknuts and washers on both tailpieces, and then lift out the faucet.

Many new faucets require some assembly before mounting to the sink. If the one you have chosen does, assemble it according to the manufacturer's directions. If it has a pop-up assembly, remove the sink before installing the faucet.

Using flexible supply tubes, which eliminate the need to cut or fit lines, eases the task of hooking up your new faucet.

This split-set faucet delivers water through a gracefully arching spout flanked by matching valves. With this type of set, valves are typically spaced 8 inches apart.

1 Clean the surface where the new faucet will sit, and insert the rubber gasket between the faucet's base plate and the sink top to create a watertight seal. If there is no gasket provided, seal the perimeter of the faucet base with plumber's putty, and then insert the tailpieces through the holes in the sink top.

2 If your faucet has water supply tubes already attached to the tailpieces as shown, feed them through the middle sink hole and press the faucet into position. From the underside, thread a washer and mounting nut onto each tailpiece (some faucets have a combination washer/nut made of plastic), and then tighten the nuts firmly with a wrench.

3 For split-set faucets such as the one shown, you will need to connect the valves to the spout. Before you connect them with the flexible hoses supplied, wrap a couple of turns of pipe-wrap tape around the valve's threaded ends and connecting piece. Then thread the valves on by hand, and finish by tightening them with an adjustable wrench.

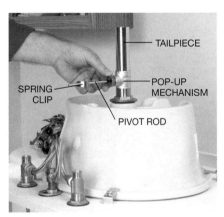

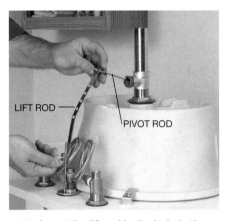

4 Virtually all bathroom faucets come with a pop-up mechanism that allows you to open and close the drain by pulling up on a lift rod behind the spout. Remove the stopper from the tailpiece, and then install the tailpiece as shown so the pop-up port faces the spout.

5 Attach the pop-up mechanism to the tailpiece, taking care to thread the pivot rod into the opening at the bottom of the drain stopper. A spring clip on the end of the pivot rod will grip the lift rod as shown in Step 6.

6 Insert the lift rod in the hole in the spout, and attach it to the pivot rod via the extension rod supplied. Adjust it so the drain stopper will open and close properly when the lift rod is operated. Connect the faucet's hot and cold supply tubes, bending them gently to meet the shutoff valves. Tighten the compression nuts or flared fittings, and turn on the water to clear the lines of any debris and to check for leaks.

setting a toilet

IF ONE OF YOUR TOILETS HAS SEEN BETTER DAYS OR YOU SIMPLY WANT TO UPDATE it with a model that is more stylish and efficient, you will be glad to know that replacing a toilet is an afternoon project. But if you plan to install a toilet in a new location, you will have to extend supply pipes and drainpipes to the desired spot, a job you may want to leave to a plumbing contractor.

When shopping for a toilet, you will find many choices. The two-piece type illustrated here is the most common.

Though most toilets are sold with the necessary gaskets, washers, and hardware for fitting the tank to the bowl, you may need to buy a few additional parts. These may include hold-down bolts, a wax gasket for sealing the drain, and a flexible water supply tube for connecting the tank to the shutoff valve.

Before beginning installation, turn off the water at the shutoff valve or at the house's shutoff valve. Flush the toilet to empty the bowl and tank, and sponge out any remaining water. Disconnect the water supply tube from the shutoff valve, drain the water from the tube into a bucket, and then unscrew the coupling nut on the supply tube at the bottom of the tank.

If the hold-down bolts that fasten the toilet to the floor are so badly corroded that you cannot remove the nuts, soak the bolts with penetrating oil, or cut them off with a hacksaw. When you bolt the new bowl to the floor, be very careful not to over-tighten the nuts because this can crack the porcelain.

1 To remove the old tank, unbolt it from the bowl, using a screwdriver to hold the mounting bolt from inside the tank while unfastening its nut with a wrench from below. Remove the bowl by prying the caps off the hold-down bolts and removing the nuts with an adjustable wrench. Gently rock the bowl from side to side to break the seal between the bowl and the floor, and then lift the bowl up, tilting it forward slightly to avoid spilling any remaining water.

2 Stuff a rag into the drainpipe to prevent sewer gas from escaping into your home. Using an old putty knife, scrape the wax gasket remains from the floor flange. (If the old hold-down bolts and floor flange are damaged, replace them, too.)

3 Turn the new bowl upside down on a cushioned surface. Place a new wax gasket over the horn on the bottom of the bowl, facing the tapered side away from the bowl, as shown. If the wax gasket has a plastic collar, install it so the collar is away from the bowl, first checking that the collar will fit into the floor flange. Apply a thin bead of caulk around the toilet base.

Behind the sleek styling of this two-piece toilet is a hard-working flushing mechanism that utilizes a siphon action to assist gravity. Pre-installed bolts make it easy to join the tank and bowl.

LOWE'S QUICK TIP
Before setting the toilet in place on the floor flange, push drinking straws onto the bolts. Doing this will make it easier to line up the bolts with the holes at the toilet's base.

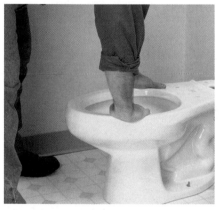

4 Remove the rag from the drainpipe. Gently lower the bowl into place atop the flange, using the bolts as guides. Press down firmly while gently twisting and rocking. Using a level, check that the bowl is straight; use plastic shims if necessary to make minor adjustments.

5 Hand-tighten the washers and nuts onto the bolts. Then alternately tighten them with a wrench until the toilet is seated firmly on the floor. Snug up the hold-down nuts, but don't over-tighten because this can crack the bowl. Fill the caps with plumber's putty, and place them over the bolt ends.

6 If necessary, assemble the flush valve inside the tank, and tighten the large spud nut at the center. Place the rubber tank cushion on the bowl. Position the tank over the bowl, and tighten the nuts and washers onto the mounting bolts. Hook up the supply tubes, and open the shutoff valve.

installing a washer & dryer

WHEN YOU BUY A NEW WASHER OR DRYER, YOU CAN USUALLY PAY A SMALL FEE TO have the appliances delivered and hooked up. But you can also undertake installation yourself. The job is quite simple if the laundry area is set up for these machines, although a gas dryer does involve connecting both a gas supply and a vent to the appliance.

INSTALLING A WASHING MACHINE

1 Screw the washing machine's water supply hoses onto the connections at the back of the washing machine. If the hoses are marked, be sure to orient them to hot and cold accordingly.

If you are installing a washing machine in a new location, you will need to run hot- and cold-water supply pipes to the connection point and terminate each with a shutoff valve and, if necessary, a water-hammer arrester (see page 417 for information on alleviating water hammer). If there is an existing laundry sink, you can hook the washer's drain hose over the sink's edge. If there is no sink or laundry tub nearby, the washer will need to drain into a standpipe, which is a 2-inch-diameter pipe with a built-in trap that taps into the nearest drainpipe. The top of the standpipe should stand between 18 and 30 inches above the trap (some codes allow a range up to 42 inches). The trap should be 6 to 18 inches above the floor. Standpipes are available with built-in traps or can be assembled

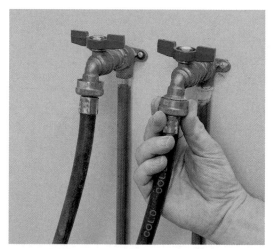

2 Connect the washing machine supply hoses to the proper valves. Scoot the appliance into place. Level the top of the machine, adjusting its front feet as needed.

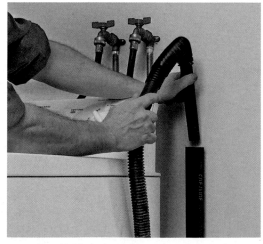

3 Put the drain hose into the standpipe (or laundry sink). Turn on the water supply valves and check for leaks.

from scratch using standard drainpipe and elbow fittings.

Clothes dryers all plug into the wall because they have electric motors. They may be heated by either electricity or gas. Though an electric dryer is extremely easy to install, a gas model is less expensive to operate in most regions. If the dryer's spot in the laundry area is equipped with a gas line and an appropriate vent that exhausts to the outdoors, it usually makes sense to install a gas dryer. If there is no gas line but there is a 240-volt outlet, you may want to opt for an electric dryer.

During installation, be sure the circuit breaker to the dryer's circuit is turned off and that the gas pipe's valve is closed.

Both washing machines and dryers are designed to operate on flat, level floors. After positioning each appliance, check the tops for level. If necessary, turn the adjustable feet at the front of each unit to properly level them.

SINGLE-LEVER VALVES

A single-lever valve is an alternative to conventional washing machine shutoff valves. With this type, you just flip the lever to shut off the water supply when the machine is not in use. Because the hoses that connect a washing machine can leak or burst, this is a good way to prevent an unexpected flood.

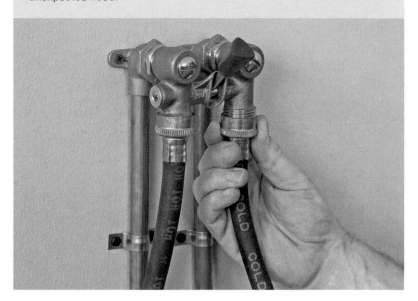

INSTALLING A DRYER

1 To hook up a gas dryer, turn the gas off at the shutoff valve. Wrap the threads of the gas supply pipe with pipe-wrap tape (use the type that is made for gas connections), and then tighten a stainless-steel connector onto the pipe. Thread the flexible gas supply pipe onto the connector and the dryer's gas valve, and tighten both connections. After turning on the gas, check for leaks by mixing a 50/50 solution of dishwashing detergent and water, daubing this onto the connections, and watching for bubbles.

2 Fit metal duct piping onto the vent connector at the wall, and, using elbows along with lengths of straight pipe, run the vent to the dryer's outlet. Drive ¾-inch sheet metal screws through the pipe into the flanges to hold the vent pipe in place. Wrap joints with duct tape. Note: Be sure the vent of a gas dryer exhausts to the outdoors.

3 Plug in the dryer. An electric dryer will have a large, 240-volt plug like the one shown. A gas dryer will just have a conventional plug. Push the dryer into place, leaving a couple of inches on each side for air circulation.

replacing a water heater

FOR MANY HOMEOWNERS, REPLACING AN OLD WATER HEATER IS SIMPLER THAN they imagine, especially if the new unit is similar to the old one. If you want to switch from electric to gas or vice versa, however, discuss the various installation options with your Lowe's Installed Sales Coordinator.

A 30- to 50-gallon model can service most homes. Compare the recovery rates on the units you look at; faster recovery rates mean faster heating. (Gas heaters have faster rates than electric and, in most regions, are far less expensive to operate.)

Before starting to remove or work on an existing water heater, shut off the water and gas or power supply. If there is no floor drain underneath the valve, connect a hose to the drain valve that is near the base of the tank and run it to a nearby drain or outdoors. Open the valve, and drain the water from the tank.

If your home is in an earthquake zone, you will need to install straps around the new water heater (check with your local building department for exact details).

If the new tank is a different height than the old one, use flexible pipe connectors for the water inlet and outlet; they will bend as needed to make the hookup. If the pipes are not threaded, replace them with threaded nipples; secure the connectors to the nipples with an adjustable wrench. Install a new temperature and pressure-relief valve on the new tank, and test it by squeezing the lever.

1 After shutting off the water supply to the tank, connect a hose to the drain valve at the bottom of the tank, open the valve, and drain the water from the tank. Use two wrenches to unscrew the inlet and outlet fittings from the top of the tank.

2 For a gas water heater, shut off the gas inlet valve and use two wrenches to disconnect the union or flare fitting between the gas supply pipe and the inlet valve. Also remove the flue hat that expels gasses into the flue at the top of the tank.

3 After removing the old unit, set the new one in place with the controls and burner accessible. Allow at least 6 inches of clearance around its perimeter, and keep it away from flammable materials. Use a level to check it for plumb; shim the base with pieces of asphalt shingles or plastic wedges.

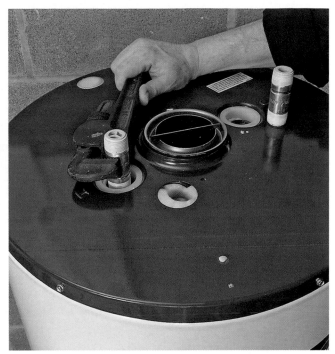

4 Wrap the threads of the heat trap fittings with pipe-wrap tape, and screw the fittings into the water heater (blue into the cold-water inlet, red into the hot-water outlet). Be sure the arrows marked on the fittings point in the direction of water flow.

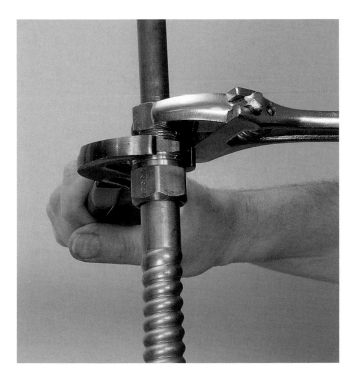

5 Install new flexible connectors on the water inlet and outlet pipes. If there is no shutoff valve on the cold-water side, install one before connecting the water heater. After all connections are complete, open the shutoff valve to fill the tank. While it is filling, open several hot-water faucets in the house to bleed off air in the pipes.

6 Assemble the gas pipes as shown. Spread pipe dope on the threads, and screw together the parts, tightening them with one pipe wrench on the pipe and another on the fitting. Follow manufacturer's instructions for connecting the unit with gas supply tubing. After turning on the gas, test all connections by brushing soapy water on them and watching for bubbles.

stopping leaks & pipe noises

PLUMBING PIPES CAN FUNCTION WITHOUT PROBLEMS FOR DECADES. WHEN A problem does develop, however, you want to be able to react quickly. The most typical are leaks and strange noises. A higher-than-normal water bill might give you the first indication of a leaking pipe. Or you might hear the sound of running water even when all the fixtures in your home are turned off. A faucet that refuses to run is the first sign of frozen pipes. Pipe noises range from loud banging to high-pitched squeaking.

If a leak is major, turn off the water immediately at the fixture or house shut-off valve. The best long-term solution is to replace the pipe, but simple temporary solutions are shown below.

If pipes bang when the water at a faucet or an appliance is turned off quickly, the problem is water hammer: the noise of rushing water hitting a dead end at the faucet or appliance. Water systems often have short sections of pipe rising above faucets or appliances, called air chambers or water-hammer arresters, that allow for

a cushioned stop. Air chambers can fill completely with water over time, losing the air they use as a cushion.

To restore air chambers in pipes, close the shutoff valve below the fixture that makes a banging sound and then close the house shutoff valve. Open up the highest and lowest faucets in the house in order to drain all the water. Close the faucets, and then reopen the shutoff valves. You can install special water-hammer arresters on hot- and cold-water lines near the fixtures, following the manufacturer's instructions.

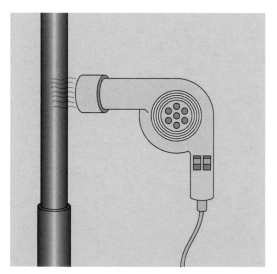

If a pipe freezes, first shut off the main water supply, and open the faucet nearest the frozen pipe. Place rags around the frozen section of pipe, and, working from the faucet back toward the iced-up area, use a kettle to pour hot water over the rags. Or, if water is not puddled in the area, plug a hair dryer into a ground fault circuit interrupter (GFCI) outlet, and train hot air onto the pipe. Avoid any contact with water when using the electrical appliance.

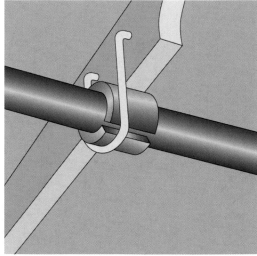

Pipes may rattle or bang if they are poorly anchored, so look for a section that is loose from its supports. Slit a piece of old hose or cut a patch of rubber, and insert the material in the hanger or strap as a cushion. For masonry walls, attach a block of wood to the wall with lag screws and masonry anchors, and then secure the pipe to it with a pipe strap. Install enough hangers to support the entire pipe run.

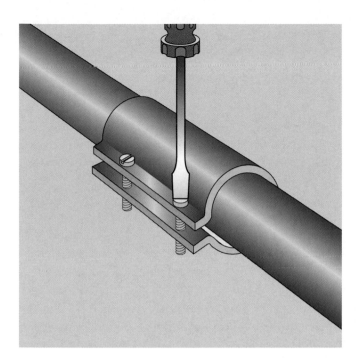

Sleeve clamps should stop most leaks for months or even longer. It is a good idea to keep one on hand for emergencies.

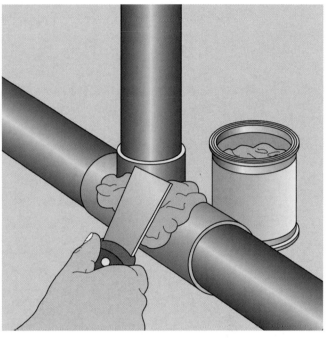

Epoxy putty will often stop leaks around joints where clamps will not, but putty does not hold as long. The pipe must be clean and dry for the putty to adhere; turn off the water supply to the leak to let the area dry. Replace the faulty pipe or fitting promptly.

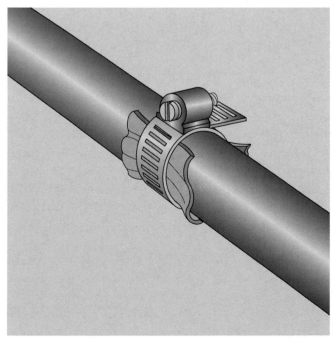

An adjustable hose clamp (size 12 or 16) can stop a pinhole leak on a normal pipe. Use a piece of rubber—from a bicycle inner tube, for instance—or electrician's rubber tape with the clamp.

unclogging drains & fixtures

PLUMBING

DEALING WITH CLOGGED SINKS, TUBS, SHOWERS, AND TOILETS IS ONE OF LIFE'S unpleasant necessities. The ideal is to prevent clogs entirely. But if this isn't practical, at least be alert to the warning signs of a sluggish drain; it is easier to clear a drain that is slowing down than one that has stopped completely.

Usually a clog will be close to the fixture. To determine the location, you can check the other drains in your home. If only one fixture is blocked, then you are probably dealing with a clog in the trap or drainpipe of that fixture.

If more than one drain will not clear, something is stuck farther along in a branch drain, the main drain, or the soil stack, causing all the fixtures above the clog to stop up. If there is a blockage in the vent stack, wastes drain slowly, and odors from the pipes become noticeable in the house.

preventing clogged drains

A kitchen sink usually clogs because of a buildup of grease and food particles. To keep the problem to a minimum, do not put grease or coffee grounds down the drain. You can keep kitchen drains clear by pouring a gallon of boiling water down them monthly. (If you have plastic drainpipes, use hot—not boiling—water.)

Hair and soap scum are usually at fault in bathroom drains. Clean out strainers and pop-ups regularly (see bottom right on the facing page). A solution of equal parts baking soda and vinegar can help prevent soap and hair clogs. Pour some down the drain every month or so, let it fizz, and then flush the drain with hot water.

unclogging sinks

If a dose of scalding water doesn't eliminate a clog, check to see if a small object may have slipped down the drain: Remove and clean the pop-up assembly, strainer, or trap (see the facing page, bottom illustrations). If this is not the answer, try a sink plunger (see top of the facing page). If these simple measures fail, you will need to use an auger, as discussed at left.

Turn off electricity to the disposal. If the disposal's drainpipe is clogged, disassemble the trap, and then thread an auger into the drainpipe. If both basins of a double sink with a garbage disposal clog, snake down the one without the disposal. If only the basin with the disposal is clogged, you will have to remove the trap to dislodge the blockage. If augering the sink drainpipe does not succeed, turn your attention to the main drain (see page 449).

Insert the auger down through the drain and, operate it as shown on page 446. If that does not clear the clog, put the auger in through the trap cleanout or remove the trap entirely so that the auger can reach through the drainpipe to clear a clog farther down the drain.

TIPS FOR USING AN AUGER

Feed the auger (also called a snake) into the drain, trap, or pipe until it stops. If there is a movable handgrip, position it about 6 inches above the opening, and tighten the thumbscrew. Rotate the handle clockwise to break the blockage. As the cable works its way into the pipe, loosen the thumbscrew, slide the handgrip back, push more cable into the pipe, tighten again, and repeat. If there is no handgrip, push and twist the cable until it hits the clog.

The first time the auger stops, it probably has hit a turn in the piping rather than the clog. Guiding the auger past a sharp turn takes patience and effort; keep pushing it forward, turning it clockwise as you do. Once the head of the auger hooks the blockage, pull the auger back a short distance to free some material from the clog. Then push the rest on through the pipe.

After breaking up the clog, pull the auger out slowly, and have a pail ready to catch any debris. Flush the drain with hot water.

For a distant or particularly difficult clog, you can rent a power auger at an equipment rental supply, or call a drain-clearing company.

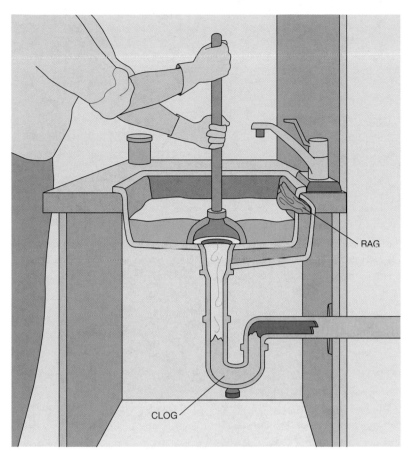

CLOG

RAG

When using a plunger, choose one with a suction cup that is large enough to cover the drain opening completely. Fill the clogged fixture with enough water to cover several inches of the plunger cup. Then use a wet cloth to block off all the other outlets (the overflow vent, the second drain in a double sink, and adjacent fixtures) between the drain and the clog. Insert the plunger into the water at an angle so that a minimum of air remains trapped under it. Holding the plunger upright, use 15 to 20 forceful strokes. Repeat if necessary.

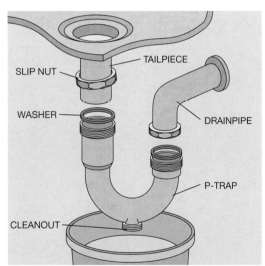

SLIP NUT
TAILPIECE
WASHER
DRAINPIPE
P-TRAP
CLEANOUT

To clean your trap, remove the cleanout plug (if there is one) with an adjustable wrench, placing a bucket beneath the trap to catch escaping water. If the trap is clogged, try to remove the obstruction with a piece of wire. If that does not work, loosen the slip nuts that attach the trap to the tailpiece and drainpipe; use a wrench or rib-joint pliers with taped jaws to protect the finish. Remove and flush out the trap, and then reassemble it.

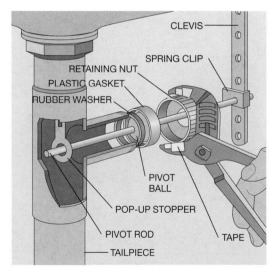

CLEVIS
SPRING CLIP
RETAINING NUT
PLASTIC GASKET
RUBBER WASHER
PIVOT BALL
POP-UP STOPPER
PIVOT ROD
TAPE
TAILPIECE

To clean the pop-up assembly, first remove the stopper; some can be lifted straight out, but others must be twisted. To remove the type shown here, first undo the retaining nut, and pull out the pivot rod. Clean out any hair or debris from the stopper and pivot rod. Replace the assembly.

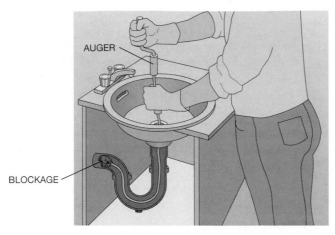

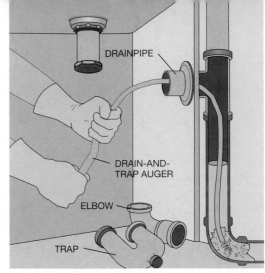

To auger through the drain, remove the pop-up stopper and the sink strainer. Insert the auger into the drain opening, and twist it down through the trap until you reach the clog.

To auger through the drainpipe, remove the trap as shown on page 445. Pull the trap downward, and spill its contents into a pail. Insert the auger into the drainpipe at the wall. Feed it as far as it will go, turning it clockwise until it hits the clog. Clean out the trap before reinstalling it.

unclogging tubs & showers

Install a hair trap to help prevent clogs in tubs and showers. One type sits inside the drain; another requires replacing the pop-up. Whenever a tub or shower drain does clog up, first find out whether other fixtures are affected. If they are, work on the main drain. If you find that only the tub or shower is plugged, work on it. Begin by plunging (see page 445), and then remove the strainer or pop-up and clean it (see the illustration on the facing page). If this does not work, use a drain-and-trap auger (see page 444) or a balloon bag (see page 449).

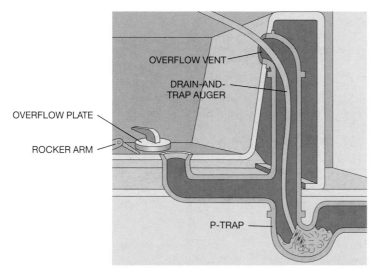

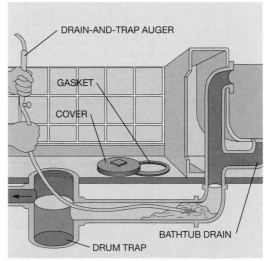

To clear a tub P-trap, remove the stopper and rocker arm. Unscrew and remove the overflow plate, and pull out the assembly. Feed the auger down through the overflow pipe and into the P-trap. If this does not clear the drain, remove the trap or its cleanout plug from below (if accessible) or through an access panel; have a pail ready to catch water. Then insert the auger toward the main drain.

Instead of a P-trap, bathtubs in older houses may have a drum trap. To clear a clog, bail all water from the tub and unscrew the drum trap cover with an adjustable wrench. Watch for any water welling up around the threads. Remove the trap's cover and rubber gasket, and clean out any debris. If the trap is still clogged, work the auger through the lower pipe toward the tub and, if need be, in the opposite direction.

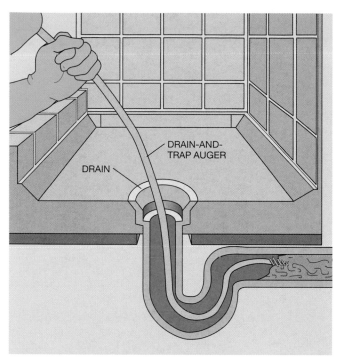

DRAIN-AND-
TRAP AUGER

DRAIN

Unscrew and remove the strainer of your shower drain if your auger cannot be threaded through it. Probe the auger down the drain and through the trap until it hits the clog.

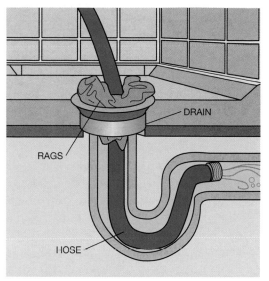

DRAIN

RAGS

HOSE

You can also use a garden hose to clear a slow drain. Attach the hose to a faucet with a threaded adapter, or run it to an outside hose bibb. Push the hose deep into the drain trap, and pack wet rags tightly into the opening around it. Hold the hose in the drain, and turn the hose water alternately on full force and then abruptly off. Alternatively, use the hose with a balloon bag as shown on page 449. Note: Never leave a hose in a drain; a sudden drop in water pressure could siphon raw sewage back into the fresh-water supply.

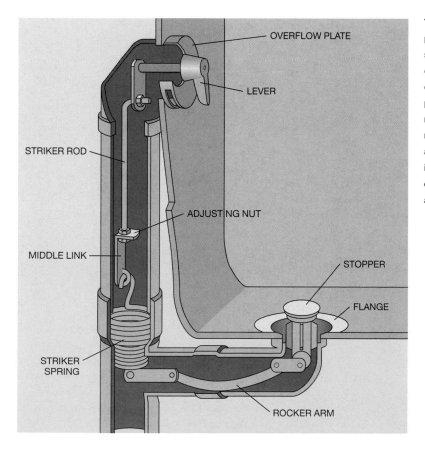

OVERFLOW PLATE

LEVER

STRIKER ROD

ADJUSTING NUT

MIDDLE LINK

STOPPER

FLANGE

STRIKER SPRING

ROCKER ARM

To service a tub pop-up, remove the stopper and rocker arm by pulling the stopper straight up. Unscrew and remove the tub's overflow plate, and pull the entire assembly out through the overflow vent. Clear the parts of any hair or debris. If the stopper needs an adjustment, loosen the adjusting nuts, and slide the middle link up or down, as needed. If the tub has a strainer and an internal plunger that blocks the back of the drain to stop the flow of water, the same adjustments to the lift mechanism apply.

unclogging a toilet

The most common cause of a clogged toilet is an obstruction in the trap. To dislodge it, first try using a plunger. If that does not clear the clog, try a toilet auger. If neither method succeeds, use an auger or balloon bag in the nearest cleanout, as shown on the facing page.

If the toilet bowl is filled to the brim, do not flush the toilet again. You can usually prevent an overflow by removing the lid of the tank and pushing the stopper or flapper into the flush valve, which will prevent more water from flowing into the bowl. Next, reach under the toilet, and turn off the water supply valve.

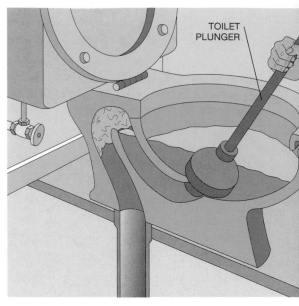

TOILET PLUNGER

If your toilet is about to overflow, remove the tank lid and push the flapper or stopper into the flush valve to stop the flow of water into the bowl.

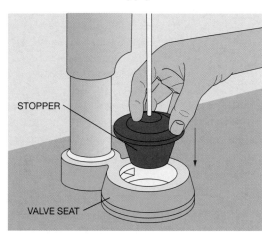

STOPPER

VALVE SEAT

A toilet plunger has a special fold-out flange that fits snugly into the trap. To loosen a clog, pump the plunger up and down at least a dozen times and then pull it away sharply on the last stroke. The alternating pressure and suction should pull the ob-struction back through the trap into the bowl. If it merely pushes the obstruction a little deeper into the drain, you will need to use a toilet auger.

To keep the tank from refilling, turn off the water supply valve beneath the toilet by turning it clockwise. Then plunge the toilet or use a toilet auger.

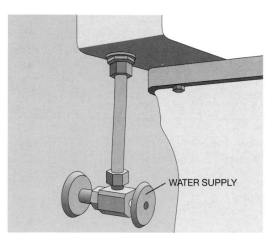

WATER SUPPLY

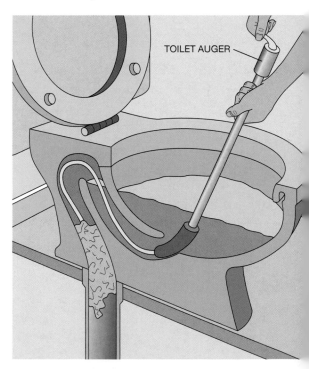

TOILET AUGER

A toilet auger, also called a closet auger, will reach down into the toilet trap. It has a curved tip that starts the auger with a minimum of mess and a protective housing to keep the bowl from being scratched. Feed the auger into the trap, turning the handle clockwise as you go. Once you snag the clog, continue turning the handle as you pull out the debris.

clearing the main drain

If a clog is too deep in the pipes to get at from a fixture, you can clean out the soil stack from below by working on a branch cleanout, the main cleanout, or the house trap. Cleaning the soil stack from below means working with raw sewage; have rubber gloves, pails, mops, and rags on hand. Once you are finished, clean and disinfect all tools and materials.

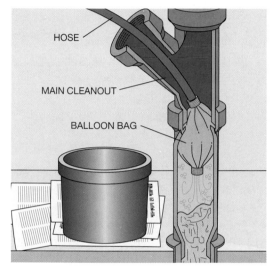

Buy a balloon bag, or bladder, that matches the diameter of your drain. Attach the bag to a garden hose, and then proceed as directed by the manufacturer. The balloon bag works by expanding in the drain and then shooting a stream of water into the pipe.

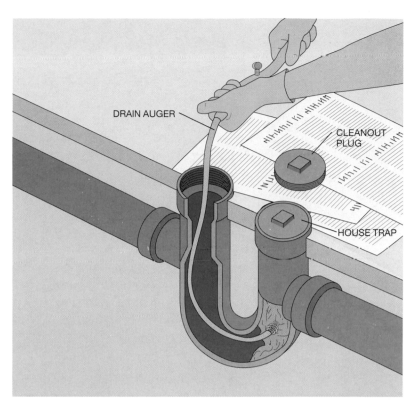

To snake the main house trap, carefully unscrew the cleanout plug from the trap. If sewage begins to seep out as you loosen it, retighten it and call a plumber; sewage may be backed up into the main drain. Otherwise, work an auger down through the drain to the obstruction.

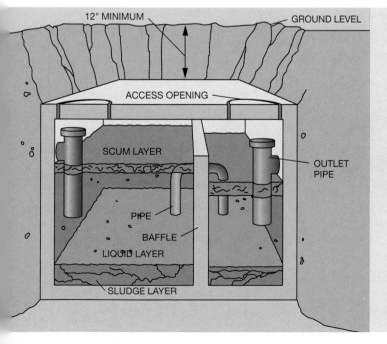

UNDERSTANDING A SEPTIC SYSTEM

A good septic tank system does not require a great deal of care or call for many special precautions. But the maintenance it does require is crucial because a properly functioning septic system is much less likely to clog. You should have a diagram of your septic tank's layout, showing the locations of the tank, pipes, access holes, and drainage field.

Chemicals, chemical cleaners, and thick paper products should never be disposed of through the system. Chemicals may destroy the bacteria necessary to attack and disintegrate solid wastes in the tank. Paper products can clog the main drain, making the system useless.

Have your septic system checked once a year by a professional. The tank should be pumped whenever necessary, but it's best to have it done in the spring if you live in a cold climate. If you have the tank pumped in the fall, it may become loaded with solid waste that can't be broken down through the winter, when bacterial action slows.

fixing faucets

THERE IS NO TIME LIKE THE PRESENT TO FIX A LEAKY FAUCET. NOT ONLY CAN constant dripping be annoying—it can waste many gallons of water in just a few days. Unless it is repaired, a leaky faucet will only get worse. On the next few pages, we look at typical methods for fixing the main types of faucets. Before working on a faucet, be sure to turn off the water supply at the fixture shutoff valves or at the main house shutoff, and then open the faucet to drain the pipes.

fixing compression faucets

If your faucet has separate hot- and cold-water handles that come to a spongy stop when you close it, it's a compression faucet. In this faucet, a rubber seat washer is secured to the stem, which has very coarse threads on the outside. When you turn the handle to shut off the faucet, the stem is screwed down, compressing the washer against the valve seat in the faucet body. The stem is secured by a packing nut, which compresses the packing (which can be twine, a washer, or an O-ring) and prevents water leaks at the stem.

If water leaks around the handle, tighten the packing nut. If that doesn't solve the problem, replace the packing as shown in Step 2 on the facing page.

If the faucet leaks from the spout, either a washer is defective or a valve seat is badly worn or corroded. To find out which side needs work, turn off the shutoff valves one at a time to see which one stops the drip. Then take off the handle, remove the stem, and replace either the washer or the valve seat as shown in Steps 3 and 4 on the facing page. Check the washer first. If it is not the problem, a damaged valve seat could be causing the leak by preventing the seat washer from fitting properly.

On most compression faucets, the valve seat is replaceable. You will need to use a valve-seat wrench (or the correct size of Allen wrench) to make the exchange. If the valve seat is built into the faucet, the seat can be dressed, or smoothed, with an inexpensive tool called a valve-seat dresser. The dressing stone on the end of this tool can be turned by hand or with a variable-speed drill. This can be a tricky and very time-consuming job, though; you may prefer to have a plumber handle it.

Before you reassemble the faucet, lubricate the stem threads with silicone grease. If the threads are worn or stripped, consider replacing the stem.

Compression faucets are relatively easy to disassemble. Problems are usually caused by faulty washers or packing.

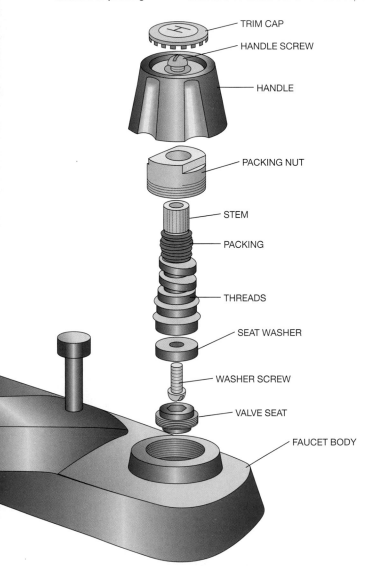

- TRIM CAP
- HANDLE SCREW
- HANDLE
- PACKING NUT
- STEM
- PACKING
- THREADS
- SEAT WASHER
- WASHER SCREW
- VALVE SEAT
- FAUCET BODY

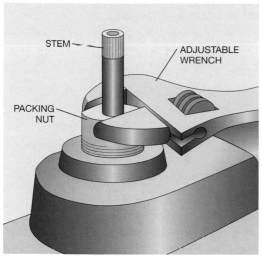

STEM

PACKING NUT

ADJUSTABLE WRENCH

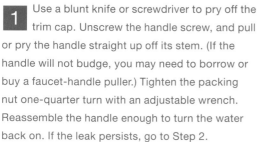

STEM

GRAPHITE-IMPREGNATED TWINE

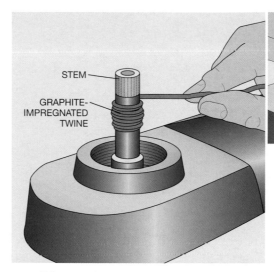

STEM

O-RING OR PACKING WASHER

1 Use a blunt knife or screwdriver to pry off the trim cap. Unscrew the handle screw, and pull or pry the handle straight up off its stem. (If the handle will not budge, you may need to borrow or buy a faucet-handle puller.) Tighten the packing nut one-quarter turn with an adjustable wrench. Reassemble the handle enough to turn the water back on. If the leak persists, go to Step 2.

2 Whatever the type, replace packing with a duplicate. Remove or scrape off the old O-ring, packing washer, or graphite-impregnated twine. Roll on a new duplicate O-ring (lubricated with silicone grease), push on an exact replacement washer, or rewrap new twine clockwise (five or six times) around the faucet stem. Lubricate the packing nut's threads with silicone grease, tighten the packing nut, and replace the handle.

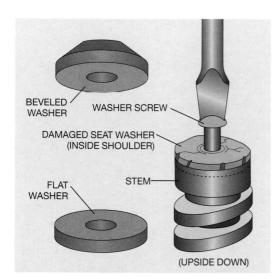

BEVELED WASHER

WASHER SCREW

DAMAGED SEAT WASHER (INSIDE SHOULDER)

FLAT WASHER

STEM

(UPSIDE DOWN)

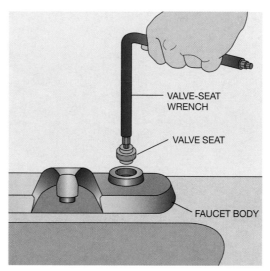

VALVE-SEAT WRENCH

VALVE SEAT

FAUCET BODY

3 To stop a spout leak, remove the handle and use it to turn the stem beyond its fully open position. Then remove the stem. If the washer at the bottom of the stem is cracked, grooved, or marred, carefully remove the screw, and replace the washer with a new, identical one. If the washer is beveled, face the beveled edge toward the screw head. If the screw appears worn, replace it as well.

4 Insert a valve-seat wrench into the faucet body, and turn it counterclockwise to remove the seat. Lubricate the threads before installing the new seat. If the seat is not removable, dress it as discussed on the facing page. Turn the water on and off a few times to test the repair's effectiveness.

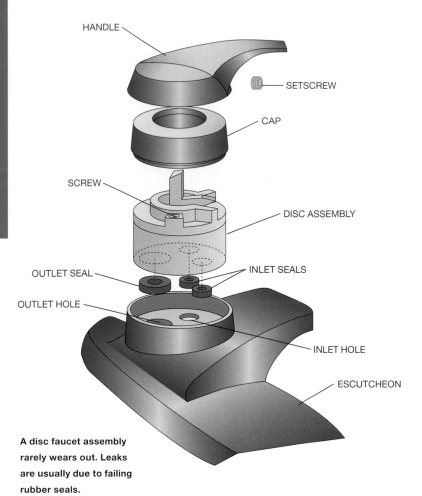

HANDLE

SETSCREW

CAP

SCREW

DISC ASSEMBLY

OUTLET SEAL

INLET SEALS

OUTLET HOLE

INLET HOLE

ESCUTCHEON

A disc faucet assembly rarely wears out. Leaks are usually due to failing rubber seals.

fixing disc faucets

The core of a disc faucet is a ceramic disc assembly, sometimes called a cylinder. The openings in the disc line up with inlet and outlet holes in the faucet body to allow the flow of water. The disc assembly itself seldom wears out, but leaks can develop when the rubber seals begin to age. On a single-handle disc faucet, three seals control the flow of hot, cold, and mixed water.

Two-handle disc faucets operate on the same principle, except that they have a single rubber or plastic seal and a small spring on each side. If this type of faucet is leaking from the handle, you should replace the inexpensive disc assembly. If the faucet is dripping from the spout, remove the seal and spring (using long-nose pliers), and replace them with identical parts. When reassembling the structure, be sure to align the lugs in the assembly with slots in the base of the faucet.

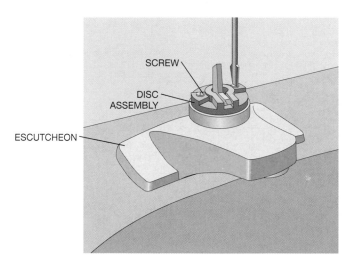

SCREW

DISC ASSEMBLY

ESCUTCHEON

1 To repair a dripping spout or a leak at the base, remove the setscrew under the faucet handle and lift off the handle and the decorative escutcheon. Then remove the disc assembly by loosening the two screws that hold it to the faucet body.

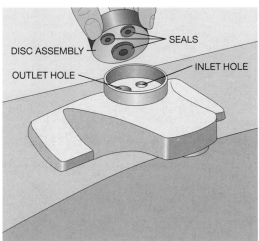

DISC ASSEMBLY

SEALS

OUTLET HOLE

INLET HOLE

2 On the bottom of the disc assembly is a set of three inlet seals. Using the tip of a small screwdriver, take each seal out. Clean the disc assembly and the inlet holes, and rinse out any debris with water. Install new seals. Reassemble the faucet, aligning the inlet holes of the disc assembly with those in the base of the faucet.

fixing rotating-ball faucets

Some single-lever faucets have an inner mechanism that controls the flow of water by means of a slotted metal ball that sits atop two spring-loaded rubber seals. Water flows through the unit when the openings in the rotating metal ball align with the hot- and cold-water inlets in the faucet body.

If the handle leaks, tighten the adjusting ring, or replace the cam washer above the ball. If the spout drips, the inlet seals or springs may be worn and may need to be replaced. If the leak is under the spout, you must replace the O-rings or the ball.

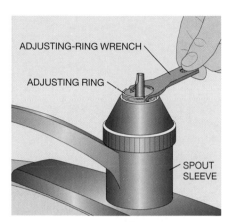

1 Remove the faucet handle by loosening the setscrew with an Allen wrench. Tighten the adjusting ring with an adjusting-ring wrench, as shown. Re-attach the handle. If this does not solve the problem, move on to Step 2.

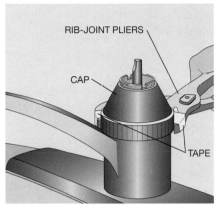

2 Loosen the setscrew with an Allen wrench, and remove the handle. Use tape-wrapped pliers to unscrew the cap. Lift out the ball-and-cam assembly. Underneath are two inlet seals on springs. Remove the spout sleeve to expose the faucet body.

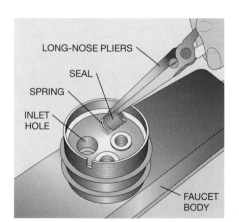

3 Use long-nose pliers to lift out the old parts. With a pocketknife or stiff brush, remove any buildup in the inlet holes. If new spout O-rings are needed, apply a thin coat of silicone grease to them to stop leaks at the base of the faucet. Install new springs and seals.

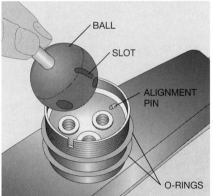

4 Before reassembling the faucet, check the ball, and replace it if it is corroded. To reinstall the ball-and-cam assembly, line up the slot in the ball with the metal alignment pin in the faucet body. Also be sure to fit the lug on the cam into the notch in the faucet body.

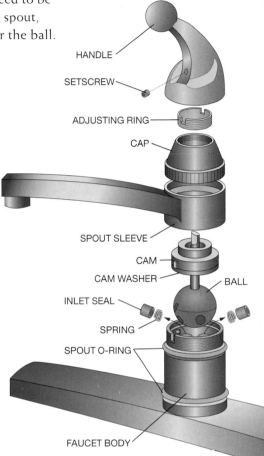

In a rotating-ball faucet, slots in a metal ball align with water inlets to let water flow. Most of the time, problems are caused by failing seals.

Cartridge faucets rarely fail, but when they do, you often must replace the entire cartridge.

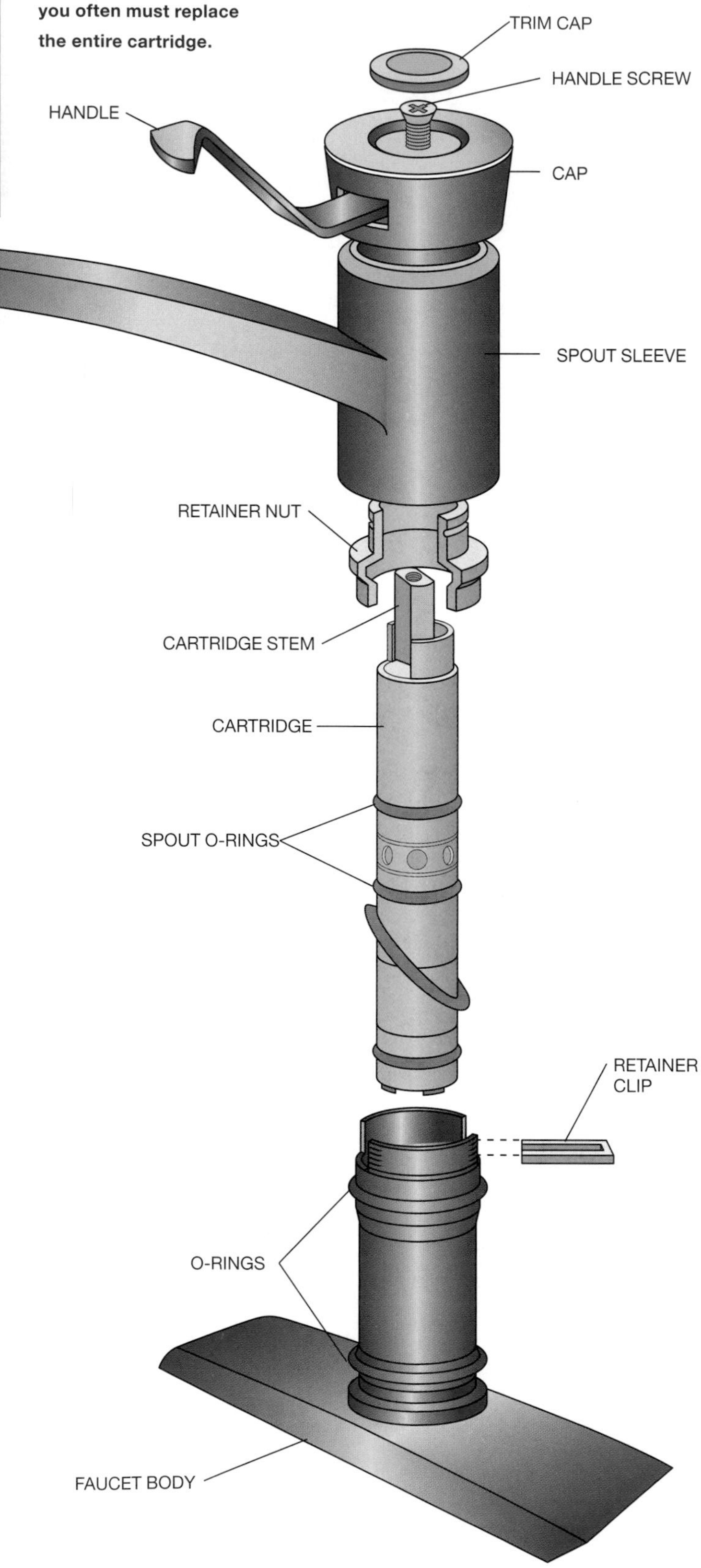

TRIM CAP

HANDLE SCREW

HANDLE

CAP

SPOUT SLEEVE

RETAINER NUT

CARTRIDGE STEM

CARTRIDGE

SPOUT O-RINGS

RETAINER CLIP

O-RINGS

FAUCET BODY

fixing cartridge faucets

Washerless cartridge faucets have a series of holes in the stem-and-cartridge assembly that align to control the mixture and flow of water. Problems with this type of faucet usually occur because the O-rings or the cartridge must be replaced. If the faucet becomes hard to move, lubricating the cartridge O-rings should solve the problem.

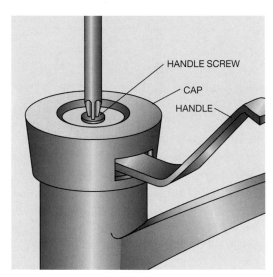

HANDLE SCREW

CAP

HANDLE

1 Remove the handle screw with a screwdriver. Lift off the cap and handle.

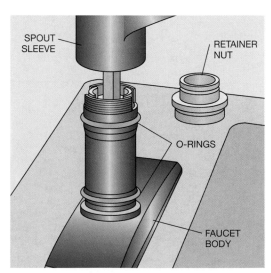

SPOUT SLEEVE

RETAINER NUT

O-RINGS

FAUCET BODY

2 Remove the retainer nut. Move the spout sleeve back and forth, and gently pull it off the faucet body.

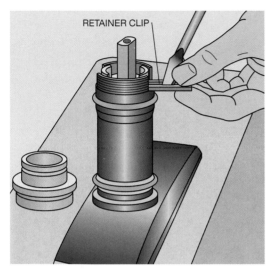

3 Pull the retainer clip out of its slot in the faucet body using a screwdriver.

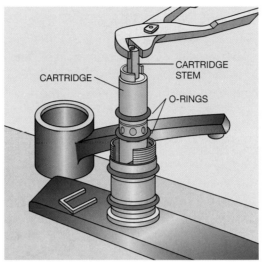

4 Grip the stem with pliers, and lift it straight up and out.

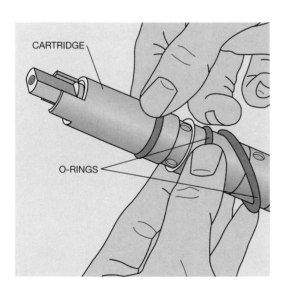

5 Examine and replace the O-rings on the cartridge if they show signs of wear. Apply silicone grease to the new O-rings before installing them. If the O-rings are in good shape, the cartridge should be replaced. Take the old one to the store, and buy an exact duplicate.

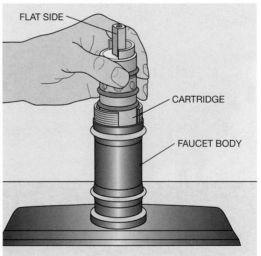

5 Push the cartridge into the faucet body. Cartridges vary; one common type has two flat sides, one of which must face the front or else your hot- and cold-water supplies will be reversed. Fit the retainer clip snugly back into its slot. Reassemble the faucet.

repairing toilets

THE WORKINGS OF A FLUSH TOILET REMAIN A MYSTERY TO MOST PEOPLE UNTIL something goes awry. Fortunately, what may appear to be complex is, in fact, quite simple. Basically, there are two assemblies concealed under the lid: an inlet valve assembly, which regulates the filling of the tank, and a flush valve assembly, which controls the flow of water from the tank to the bowl. The toilet bowl includes a built-in trap. For a basic explanation of how your toilet works, see the facing page.

A common cause of a continuously running toilet is a defective seal between the stopper and the valve seat. To check for this, remove the lid and flush the toilet. Watch the stopper; it should fall straight down onto the flush-valve seat. If it does not, make sure that the guide rod or chain is centered over the flush valve. (See how to adjust this on page 458.) If your toilet is clogged, see page 448.

If your toilet is whining or whistling, the inlet valve assembly may be to blame. If it is faulty, you may be able to just replace

HOW A TOILET WORKS

Here's the chain of events that occurs when someone presses the flush handle on a toilet:

The trip lever raises either the lift-rod wires or a chain connected to the guide rod or tank stopper. As the stopper goes up, water rushes through the flush-valve seat and down into the bowl via the flush passages. The water yields to gravity and is siphoned out the built-in toilet trap to the drainpipe.

Once the tank empties, the stopper drops into the flush-valve seat. The float ball, cup, or pressure-sensing valve trips the inlet valve assembly to let fresh water into the tank through the tank fill tube. While the tank is filling, the bowl refill tube routes some water into the top of the overflow tube to replenish water in the bowl; this water seals the trap. As the water level in the tank rises, the float ball or cup rises until it gets high enough to shut off the flow of water. If the water that is flowing into the tank fails to shut off, the overflow tube carries the excess water into the bowl.

The conventional ballcock-type inlet valve, shown here, utilizes a float arm and ball.

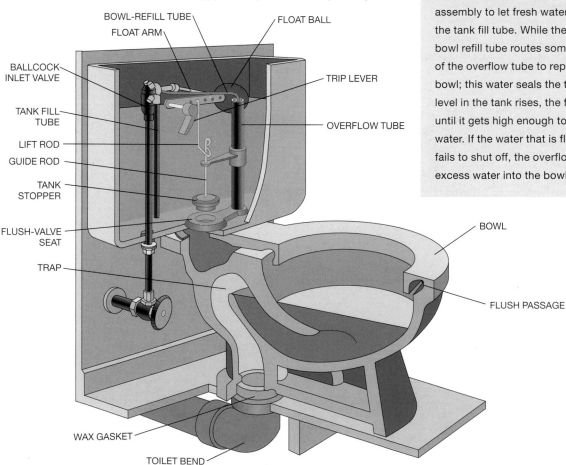

BOWL-REFILL TUBE
FLOAT ARM
FLOAT BALL
BALLCOCK INLET VALVE
TRIP LEVER
TANK FILL TUBE
OVERFLOW TUBE
LIFT ROD
GUIDE ROD
TANK STOPPER
FLUSH-VALVE SEAT
TRAP
BOWL
FLUSH PASSAGE
WAX GASKET
TOILET BEND

the washers or seal, or you may need to replace the whole assembly, which is not difficult to do. You can replace a ballcock style with a similar model, but you may be happier with a new float-cup assembly (see the facing page); this type is inexpensive, easy to install, and nearly trouble-free. A pressure-sensing valve, which fills the tank when it senses a drop in the water level, is also a good choice. Any replacement assembly must be designed to prevent backflow from the tank into the water supply. See how to replace an inlet valve on pages 458–459.

The water level in the tank should reach within ¾ inch of the top of the overflow tube. If a waterline is printed or stamped inside the tank, use it as a guide. See how to adjust this level on the facing page.

For most toilet repairs, you will need to shut off the water and empty the tank. You can shut off the water at the fixture shutoff or at the house shutoff valve. Then, flush the toilet, and hold the handle down to empty the tank completely. Finally, sponge out any water that is left.

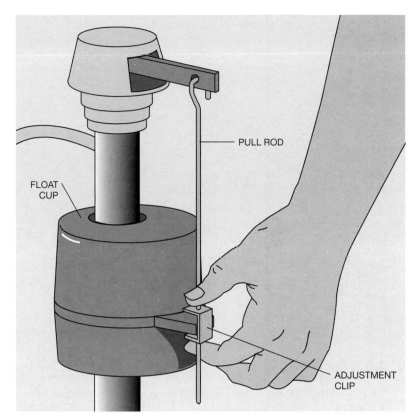

When installing a float cup, be sure to squeeze the adjustment clip on the pull rod, and move the cup up or down.

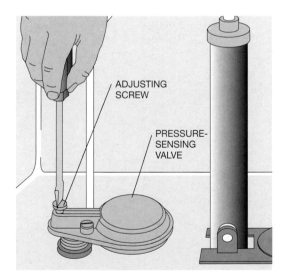

To adjust the water level on a mechanism that has a pressure-sensing valve, turn the adjusting screw clockwise to raise the water level or counterclockwise to lower it. One turn changes the level by about 1 inch.

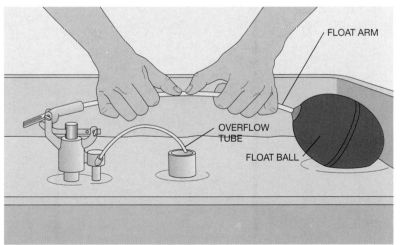

To adjust the water level on a mechanism using a float arm and ball, bend the float arm up to raise the level in the tank and down to lower the level. Be sure to use both hands and work carefully to avoid straining the assembly. The float ball sometimes develops cracks or holes and fills with water. To fix this problem, unscrew and replace the ball, or replace the inlet valve assembly with a float-cup model.

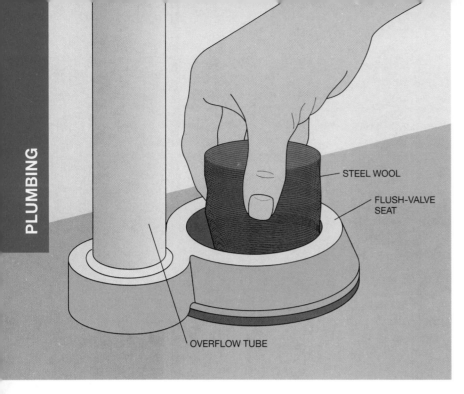

STEEL WOOL

FLUSH-VALVE
SEAT

OVERFLOW TUBE

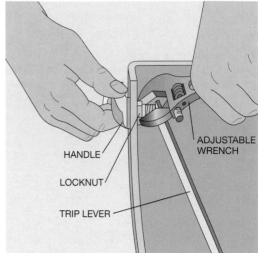

HANDLE

LOCKNUT

TRIP LEVER

ADJUSTABLE
WRENCH

If your toilet is running and the tank stopper does not fall straight down onto the flush-valve seat, make sure that the guide rod or chain is centered over the flush valve. Inspect the seat for corrosion or mineral buildup; gently scour the seat with fine steel wool, as shown. If the stopper is soft, encrusted, or out of shape, replace it. If the water still runs after the stopper and valve seat have been serviced, then replace the flush-valve seat and assembly.

A loose handle or trip lever can cause an inadequate or erratic flush cycle. Tighten the locknut that attaches the assembly to the tank. Note that this locknut tightens counterclockwise. Generally, the handle and trip lever are one unit. If tightening the locknut does not solve the problem, replace the unit.

REPLACING THE INLET VALVE

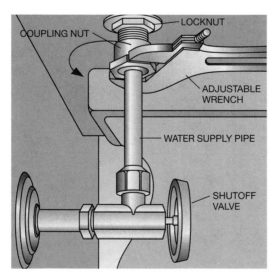

COUPLING NUT

LOCKNUT

ADJUSTABLE
WRENCH

WATER SUPPLY PIPE

SHUTOFF
VALVE

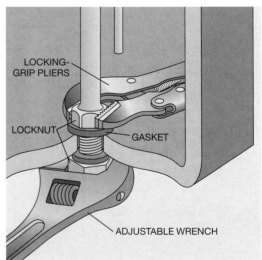

LOCKING-
GRIP PLIERS

LOCKNUT

GASKET

ADJUSTABLE WRENCH

1 Shut off the water, and flush the tank, holding the handle down to empty as much water as possible. Sponge out any remaining water. With an adjustable wrench, unfasten the coupling nut that connects the water supply tube to the underside of the tank. Remove the washer beneath the nut and replace it if it is worn.

2 Hold on to the base of the assembly inside the tank with locking-grip pliers. Then, on the underside of the tank, use an adjustable wrench to unfasten the locknut that holds the inlet valve assembly to the tank. Lift out the old assembly.

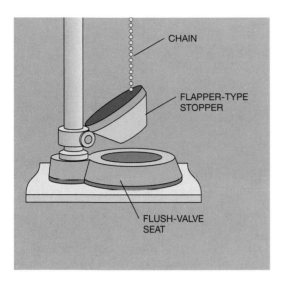

CHAIN

FLAPPER-TYPE
STOPPER

FLUSH-VALVE
SEAT

If the stopper needs replacing, install a flapper style with a chain, as shown. Unhook the old lift wires from the trip lever, unscrew the guide rod, and lift out the guide rod and wires. Slip the new flapper down over the collar of the overflow tube, and fasten the chain to the trip lever. Adjust the chain so it is a little slack when the stopper is in place on the flush valve.

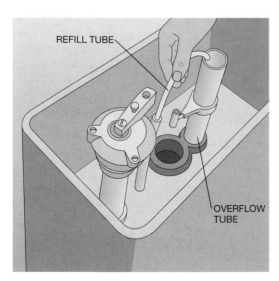

REFILL TUBE

OVERFLOW
TUBE

3 Assemble and adjust the new valve according to the manufacturer's directions, and then install it in the tank hole. Tighten the interior locknut while pushing down, and then replace the washer and coupling nut. Install the refill tube so that water runs straight down the overflow pipe. Finish the assembly, connect the water supply pipe, and turn on the water.

LEAKS AND TANK SWEATING

Other toilet problems that may require repairing or replacing parts include leaks and tank sweating.

To stop a leak between the tank and the bowl of a bowl-mounted tank, tighten the mounting bolts in the tank or replace the bolts' gaskets. If there is still a leak when the toilet is flushed, remove the tank, and replace the spud washer on the bottom of the flush valve.

When a bowl leaks around its base, first try tightening the hold-down bolts that anchor it to the floor. If that does not stop the leak, remove the bowl, and replace the wax gasket that seals the bowl to the floor.

Tank sweating occurs most often in the summer, when cold water from the tank cools the porcelain and warm, moist air condenses on the outside. Tank sweating encourages mildew, loosens floor tiles, and rots subflooring.

An easy solution is to insulate the inside of the tank by first draining and drying it and then gluing to the inside walls a special commercially made liner or one made of foam rubber or polystyrene pads. A more costly remedy, and one that will add to your energy costs, is to install a tempering valve that mixes hot water with the cold water entering the tank.

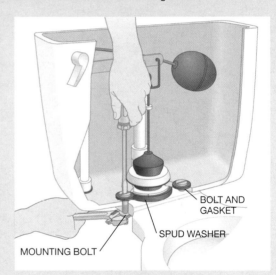

If the tank is leaky, tighten the bolts between the tank and bowl of a bowl-mounted tank, or replace the gaskets if they are damaged.

BOLT AND
GASKET

SPUD WASHER

MOUNTING BOLT

If the toilet leaks at its base, install a new wax gasket on the toilet horn to make a watertight seal with the floor flange.

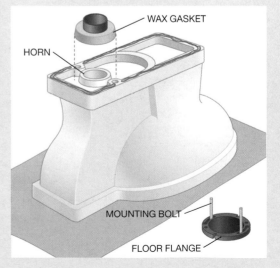

WAX GASKET

HORN

MOUNTING BOLT

FLOOR FLANGE

tub & shower fixes

LIKE SINK FAUCETS, TUB AND SHOWER FAUCETS CAN BE EITHER COMPRESSION- OR cartridge-style ("washerless"). In either case, water is directed from the faucet to the tub or showerhead by a diverter valve. Some have built-in diverter valves, while others have a knob on the tub spout. This latter type is easy to replace. Gripping the old spout with a pipe wrench wrapped with duct tape to protect the spout's finish, turn the spout counter-clockwise to remove it, and then hand-tighten the new spout into place.

Before taking apart a tub faucet, turn off the water at the house shutoff valve (see pages 390–391), and open a faucet that is at a level lower than that of the tub faucet to drain the pipes. Also review the instructions on sink faucets, which are similar to those for tub faucets.

Compression tub faucets are repaired much like compression sink faucets (see pages 450–451). Most leaks can be fixed by re-placing the washer and seat valve.

The cartridge tub faucet shown here is repaired in almost the same way as a cartridge-style sink faucet (see pages 454–455). You remove the stop tube and re-tainer clip to access the cartridge.

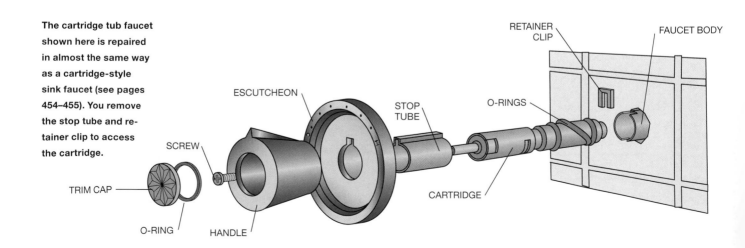

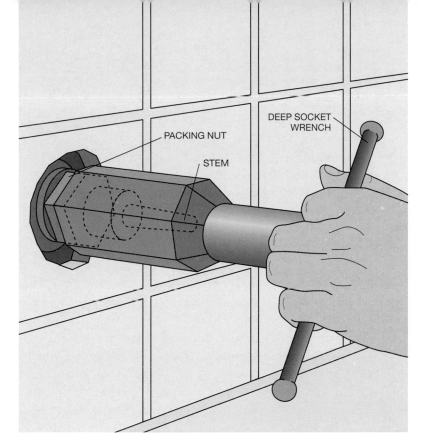

PACKING NUT

DEEP SOCKET
WRENCH

STEM

To replace a tub faucet, pry off the cap, unscrew the handle, and then remove the escutcheon. To access the packing nut in a compression faucet, gently chip away the wall's surface, if necessary, with a ball-peen hammer and a small cold chisel (be sure to wear safety glasses) and then grip the nut with a deep socket wrench. Replace the faucet with a similar one, following the manufacturer's instructions.

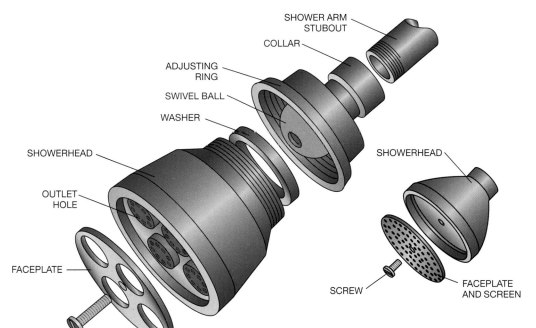

SHOWER ARM
STUBOUT

COLLAR

ADJUSTING
RING

SWIVEL BALL

WASHER

SHOWERHEAD

OUTLET
HOLE

SHOWERHEAD

FACEPLATE

SCREW

SCREW

FACEPLATE
AND SCREEN

A showerhead simply screws onto the shower arm stubout. Before you decide to replace a leaking or water-wasting showerhead, tighten all connections with rib-joint pliers (wrap the jaws with duct tape to avoid damaging the finish). If that does not stop the leak, replace the washer between the showerhead and the swivel ball. If sluggish water flow is the problem, remove the center screw and scrub the faceplate and the screen with vinegar, using a toothbrush.

SMALL EXPENSE, BIG SAVINGS

In most homes, more money is spent heating water than on any other energy cost except for home heating and cooling. Finding inexpensive ways to reduce your need for hot water can produce big savings. Low-flow showerheads and flow restrictors can reduce water flow to less than 2½ gallons per minute, compared with the 5 to 8 gallons per minute of older models, while still delivering satisfactory showers. They are easy to install and pay for themselves very quickly in both reduced energy bills and water savings.

fixing a water heater

WHEN A HOT-WATER FAUCET IS TURNED ON, HEATED WATER IS DRAWN FROM THE top of the water heater's tank. The tank is refilled by cold water that is carried to the bottom via the dip tube. When water temperature drops, a thermostat activates the heat source—a burner in a gas heater or the heating elements in an electric unit.

A gas heater has a flue running up the center and out the top to vent combustion gases outdoors. An electric heater produces no gases, so it does not require venting. In both types, a special anode attracts corrosive minerals in water that might otherwise attack the tank's walls.

On a gas water heater, knowing how to light the pilot is very important. Directions vary, so follow the instructions on the tank. A gas heater has a thermocouple, which senses whether or not the pilot is on and shuts off the gas if the pilot light goes out.

Twice a year, inspect the flue assembly to be sure it's properly aligned and its joints are sealed. Then check the flue by placing your hand near the draft diverter (with the burner on); air flowing out indicates that there is an obstruction, which should be removed immediately.

Electric water heater problems are usually caused by the heating elements, their thermostats, and the high-temperature cutoff. The two heating elements are controlled by thermostats that, along with the high-temperature cutoff—a device that shuts off the elements should the water get too hot—are concealed behind an access panel on the side of the water heater. (After removing the panel, insulation may need to be cut away to provide access.) If the high-temperature cutoff has tripped, the solution may be as easy as pushing the reset button. Otherwise, to have the thermostats adjusted, the high-temperature cutoff reset, or any of these components replaced, call a water heater service person.

routine maintenance To reduce sediment accumulation, open the drain valve every six months and let the water run into a bucket or to a drain through a hose until it looks clear.

At least once a year, test to make sure the temperature-pressure relief valve, which guards against hazardous pressure buildup, functions properly. Lift or depress the handle; water should drain from the overflow pipe. If it does not, shut off water to the heater, let in air by opening a hot-water faucet in the house, and replace the valve.

adjusting water temperature Water heaters are often set to heat water to 150 or 160 degrees Fahrenheit. By lowering the setting to about 120 degrees, you can save substantially on your fuel bills without affecting laundry or bathing. In addition, lowering the temperature is a wise safety measure. Dishwashers require higher temperatures to clean properly, but most of the models today are equipped with their own water-heating device.

draining & flushing a tank Turn off the gas or power, close the cold-water valve, and attach a hose to the drain valve to route water into a drain or to the outdoors. Open the drain valve, and open one hot-water faucet somewhere in the house to let in air. When all the water has drained, turn the cold-water valve on and off until the water looks clear. Then close the drain valve and the hot-water faucet, open the cold-water valve, and turn the power back on.

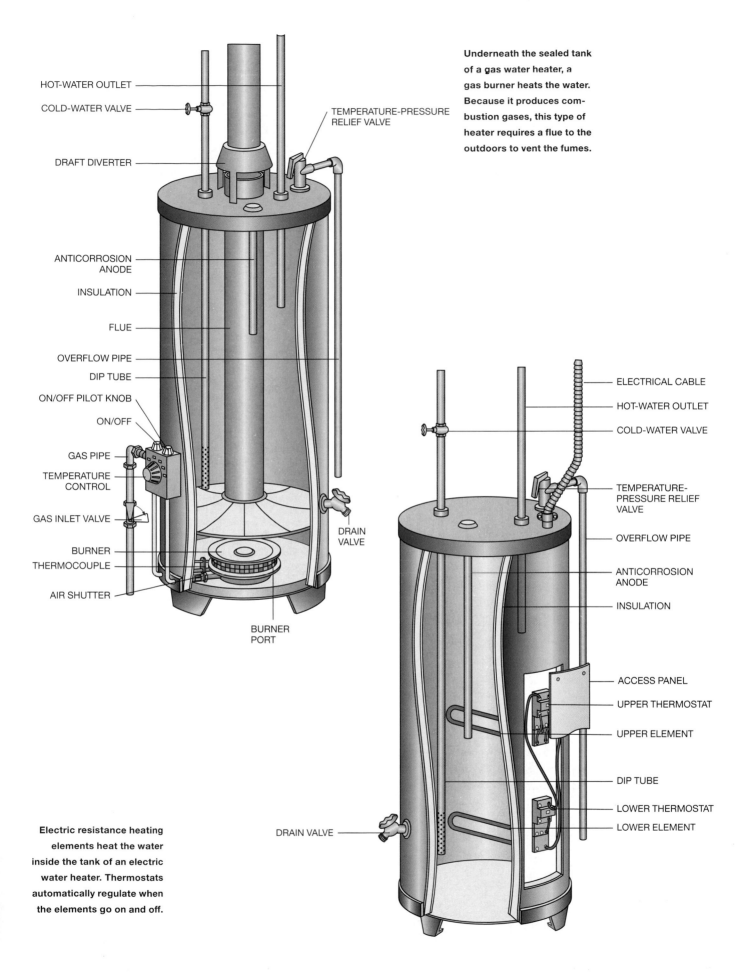

HOT-WATER OUTLET

COLD-WATER VALVE

TEMPERATURE-PRESSURE
RELIEF VALVE

DRAFT DIVERTER

Underneath the sealed tank
of a gas water heater, a
gas burner heats the water.
Because it produces com-
bustion gases, this type of
heater requires a flue to the
outdoors to vent the fumes.

ANTICORROSION
ANODE

INSULATION

FLUE

OVERFLOW PIPE

DIP TUBE

ON/OFF PILOT KNOB

ON/OFF

GAS PIPE

TEMPERATURE
CONTROL

GAS INLET VALVE

BURNER

THERMOCOUPLE

AIR SHUTTER

DRAIN
VALVE

BURNER
PORT

ELECTRICAL CABLE

HOT-WATER OUTLET

COLD-WATER VALVE

TEMPERATURE-
PRESSURE RELIEF
VALVE

OVERFLOW PIPE

ANTICORROSION
ANODE

INSULATION

ACCESS PANEL

UPPER THERMOSTAT

UPPER ELEMENT

DIP TUBE

LOWER THERMOSTAT

LOWER ELEMENT

DRAIN VALVE

**Electric resistance heating
elements heat the water
inside the tank of an electric
water heater. Thermostats
automatically regulate when
the elements go on and off.**

electrical

THE NERVE CENTER OF ANY HOME IS ITS ELECTRICAL SYSTEM. LITTLE WOULD function in our homes today without electricity. Power provides light and heat and runs air conditioning and alarm systems. Every appliance—from those in the laundry to those in the kitchen, living areas, bedrooms, and bathrooms—runs on electricity. All of the extras—televisions, stereos, telephones, and computers, to name but a few—are powered by electricity. A common home improvement, particularly for older homes, is updating wiring to deliver the power needed for our increasingly wired lives.

Electrical improvements or repairs are among the most intimidating jobs for those interested in trying to do the work themselves. The reason is obvious: Electricity carries with it the real risk of injury when a job is botched. The big jobs should be left to licensed professionals who know the codes, unless you have a good amount of experience and confidence. That said, there are certainly a number of electrical projects that can be undertaken safely by anyone with an understanding of the basics of electricity, the right tools, and a healthy respect for recommended precautions.

This chapter takes you through the world of electricity, starting with a buying guide for electrical gear and fixtures and a description of the all-important anatomy of wiring and codes and safety provisions. It continues with the basics of installing home wiring, adding new circuits, and extending phone and video wiring. There are instructions for installing different types of lighting, both indoors and out. Finally, it advises on how to diagnose electrical problems and fix the common doorbell.

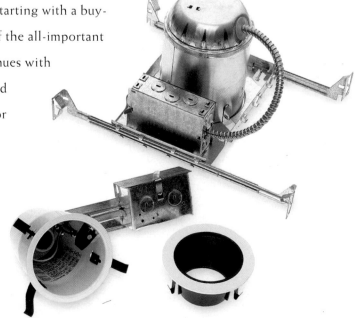

buyer's guide to electrical gear

A QUICK TRIP THROUGH THE ELECTRICAL AISLES AT LOWE'S WILL REVEAL A LARGE range of materials and gadgets used to extend and improve electrical systems in homes. Use this section as a shopper's guide. When you go to buy materials, make sure that all products you choose bear the stamp or label of an electrical materials testing laboratory and that they comply with the regulations in your local code.

wires & cables

For your home's electrical work, you will be dealing with either individual wires, called single conductors, or with multiconductor cables. The energy demands of most of today's homes make cables more efficient and convenient than individual wires.

Single conductor wires may have either a solid core or stranded wire.

SOLID-CORE WIRE

STRANDED WIRE

10 AWG (UL) MTW OR THWN OR THHN

single conductors

Two common single conductors, run inside protective metal or plastic conduit, are type THW and type THWN/THHN. Both are rated for either dry or wet locations and for temperatures up to 167 degrees Fahrenheit. You can buy either stranded wire or solid-core; solid-core makes better connections but is stiffer. Both generally are sold by the foot and in 50- to 500-foot spools.

cable

Cable typically combines, inside a plastic or metal covering, a neutral wire, one or two "hot" wires, and a grounding wire. The single conductors within a cable are insulated by color-coded, current-free thermoplastic material. Cable is identified by the type of use and the number and size of conductors it contains. The standard

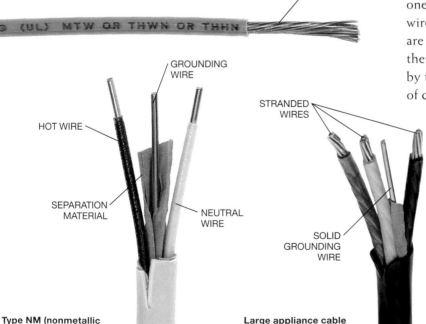

GROUNDING WIRE

HOT WIRE

SEPARATION MATERIAL

NEUTRAL WIRE

STRANDED WIRES

SOLID GROUNDING WIRE

GROUNDING WIRE

NEUTRAL WIRE

HOT WIRE

SPIRAL METAL ARMOR

Type NM (nonmetallic sheathed) cable, used for interior circuits, can be routed behind walls, ceilings, and floors.

Large appliance cable is for dedicated 120/140-volt circuits. This type of cable has stranded wires that are bendable—but just barely.

Type MC armored cable is for interior circuits only.

choice for interior projects is type NM (nonmetallic sheathed cable); a variation, type NM-B, is rated for only dry locations with temperatures that are no higher than 140 degrees Fahrenheit. A black-sheathed version, sometimes called large appliance cable, has stranded wires that facilitate bending.

Cables will be marked with the number and size of wires contained within. A cable with two #14 wires, one neutral and one hot, plus a grounding wire is called two-wire cable or, more specifically, "14-2 with ground." As established by the American Wire Gauge (AWG) standard, the lower the gauge number, the larger the wire's diameter and current-carrying capacity, or ampacity. Although copper is the best and most commonly used metal for conductors, aluminum and copper-clad aluminum are also available. Check with your local electrical codes for restrictions on use.

conduit

Conduits are pipe-like structures that are designed to protect individual conductors from moisture and damage. The size of conduit you need depends on the number and size of conductors it will contain.

Thinwall metal conduit, called EMT, is the standard choice for exposed interior locations such as a garage or utility room. The thin metal is easily bent with a conduit bender, but you can buy pre-bent pieces, as well. EMT comes in 10-foot lengths and in diameters of ½ inch to 2 inches.

Flexible metal conduit, also known as flex or Greenfield, is used indoors for water heaters or other large appliances or where it would be too hard to route EMT. Flexible conduit—available in ½-, ¾-, and 1-inch diameters—can be purchased by the foot or in 25- to 100-foot spools.

Rigid nonmetallic conduit, made from PVC plastic (not the same material as PVC plumbing pipe), often is allowed by code for interior and exterior use. Schedule 40 (the most common) plastic conduit comes in 10-foot lengths and requires PVC housing boxes, which are different than the nonmetallic boxes used with cable.

Thinwall metal conduit, (type EMT) is the standard choice for exposed interior locations.

Rigid nonmetallic conduit, made of PVC plastic, is used for both interior and exterior installations.

Flexible metal conduit is used indoors where EMT would be too much trouble to route, as well as for water heaters or other large appliances.

housing boxes

Housing boxes are connection points, either for joining wires or for mounting devices such as receptacles, switches, and fixtures. The variety of sizes and shapes reflects differences in mounting methods, the type and number of devices that are attached to the box, as well as the number of wires entering it. Rectangular-shaped switch boxes hold only switches and receptacles; square or octagonal outlet boxes hold receptacles, mount fixtures, or protect wire connections. A ceiling outlet box that must support a heavy fixture often comes with a hanger bar. A box's volume determines how many wires of a given size it may hold.

Metal housing boxes, required for AC cable and metal conduit, are sturdier than their plastic counterparts, but they must be grounded. Plastic boxes may be used with nonmetallic cable only; however, some electrical codes allow PVC plastic boxes for exposed indoor and outdoor wiring with PVC conduit. Outdoor wiring requires specialized weather-tight boxes.

Housing boxes are mounted in one of two ways: "New-work" boxes for new construction are nailed directly to exposed studs or joists, while "old-work" boxes for old construction are placed using brackets or spring ears into spaces cut into existing walls between studs or joists.

An adjustable hanger bar is a ceiling box that attaches to two joists to support a fixture; install it where you have access from above. The box slides along the bar, allowing you to fine-tune the fixture's placement.

A pancake box, which is as flat as a pancake, attaches directly to a ceiling's hanger bar, a joist, or even a wood ceiling. It accommodates one two-wire cable.

A ceiling cut-in box is a nonmetallic box used with lightweight fixtures.

When an outlet box contains only wire splices or cable connections—no devices— it's topped with a blank cover and referred to as a junction box.

JUNCTION BOX

Extender rings and adapter plates are add-ons that can customize a box to your requirements. Extender rings increase box depth to accommodate extra wires; adapter plates help secure a receptacle, switch, or fixture to an oversize box or to one that has no mounting holes.

BLANK COVER

EXTENDER RING

ADAPTER PLATE

Available in both metal and plastic versions, a cut-in wall box has wing clamps for use in existing drywall or wood paneling.

Adjustable ears allow this plain box to be mounted on wooden and plaster-and-lath walls. When a box is screwed directly on a wooden wall, the faceplate hides the ears.

These nonmetallic nail-on wall boxes are convenient for new construction. The 2-gang box below holds two devices.

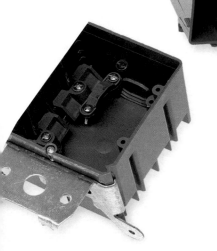

HELPFUL HARDWARE

Some additional paraphernalia go hand-in-hand with your wire, cable, or conduit choices. These items include wire nuts and compression sleeves used for joining wires; staples and straps for securing cable and conduit, respectively; grounding pigtails with grounding clips; protective metal plates; and electrical tape.

Wire nuts join and protect the stripped ends of spliced wires within housing boxes. They are sized to accommodate various wire sizes and combinations. Some jurisdictions require compression sleeves instead of wire nuts for grounding wires. If you have any doubts, contact your local building department.

Cable staples secure NM cable to the framing inside walls, floors, and ceilings. AC cable and metal and plastic conduit are secured with straps designed specifically for each of those materials.

Premade grounding pigtails combine a short length of copper wire and a grounding screw, useful for connecting devices such as receptacles to metal housing boxes. The green-coated, 6-inch pigtails are typically found in #14 and #12 sizes, suitable for use with 15- and 20-amp household circuits. You can, if you prefer, make your own pigtails from short lengths of green-colored or bare wire, and secure them with grounding screws or grounding clips.

Metal plates help guard NM cable that's run less than $1/4$ inch from the front of wall framing. Electrical tape is useful for emergency splices and insulation repairs and for marking white wires that serve as second hot wires in a circuit. Do not use tape for permanent wire connections—use a wire nut or compression sleeve instead.

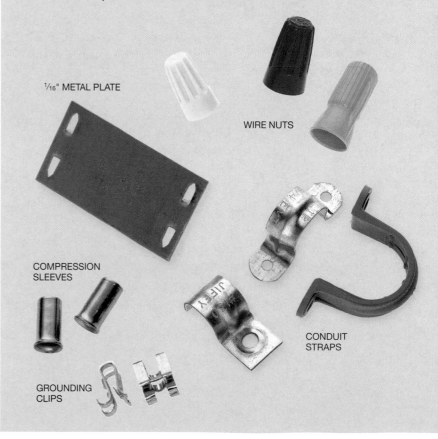

1/16" METAL PLATE

WIRE NUTS

COMPRESSION SLEEVES

CONDUIT STRAPS

GROUNDING CLIPS

Identified by two screw terminals and the words ON and OFF printed on the toggle, the classic single-pole switch controls a light or receptacle from one location only. It is available in 15- and 20-amp versions. An updated version (right) includes a grounding screw. A more decorative version is shown far right.

switches

Switches, which turn electrical fixtures on and off, have come a long way from the classic single-pole on-off switch. Today, there are three-way and four-way switches that control fixtures from multiple locations; motion sensors; timer switches; and dimmers. All are available in a range of finishes, colors, and toggle designs, including glow-in-the-dark versions.

Like receptacles (see the facing page), switches are marked clearly with the specific amperage and voltage for which they are suited. Switches marked AL-CU accept copper or aluminum wire, while unmarked switches and those with a slash through the AL symbol require the use of copper wire. Always make sure that the switch you are about to install has the proper amperage and voltage ratings required for the particular electrical circuit.

Switches come in several grades, with the better models marked "heavy-duty," "commercial," or "spec." Local building

With three hot terminals plus a plain toggle, a three-way switch is paired with a matching switch to control a light or receptacle from two locations.

Characterized by four hot terminals and no ON or OFF indicators on the toggle, a four-way switch is used only in combination with a pair of three-way switches to control a light or receptacle from more than two locations.

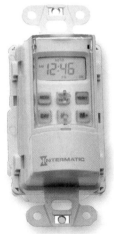

Standard timer switches allow you to set a light, bathroom heater, or other device to turn on and off at predetermined times each day. Programmable timer switches take things one step further, providing multiple daily settings for security lights, a fan, or even the TV. Unlike most other switches, some timer switches require a neutral wire, as well as the hot wire.

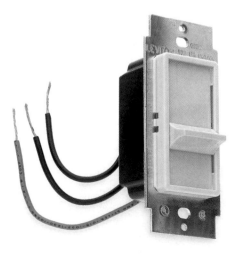

Dimmer switches, sometimes called rheostats, allow you to get maximum brightness from a light, or any lesser gradation. They also help save energy. Numerous designs are available, some with presets and fade controls. All dimmers are rated for maximum wattage.

codes often require that these switches have grounding terminals for protection, particularly in kitchens and bathrooms, and in places where metal faceplates are used with plastic housing boxes.

receptacles

Receptacles, which are governed by code, contain electrical outlets. The most common household receptacle is the 15- or 20-amp, 120-volt grounded duplex receptacle. Higher-voltage circuits, such as a 240-volt, use specialized receptacles with matching attachment plugs to avoid misconnections. Other receptacle types may combine 120 and 240 voltages to accommodate such appliances as clothes dryers and kitchen ranges, which need higher voltage for motors and lower voltage for timers and controls. A receptacle's specific amperage and voltage use is stamped clearly on its front. Receptacles marked AL-CU may be used with either copper or aluminum wire, while unmarked receptacles and those marked with a slash through the AL symbol require copper wire only. The highest-grade receptacles are marked "commercial," "spec-grade," or "industrial-duty."

Ground fault circuit interrupter (GFCI) receptacles, which protect from electric shock, are required in rooms such as bathrooms, kitchens, and garages and in any exposed area where ground faults are most likely to occur.

Grounded 120-volt duplex receptacles consist of an upper and lower outlet, each with three slots. The larger (neutral) slot accepts the wide prong of a three-pronged plug; the smaller (hot) slot is for the narrow prong, and the U-shaped grounding slot is for the grounding prong. Both amperage and voltage are clearly stamped on the front.

This 3-pole 240-volt receptacle has two hot slots and a third grounding slot; its configuration matches a specific plug and amperage and is not interchangeable with other plugs. The design prevents, for example, plugging a 30-amp table saw into a 20-amp circuit.

Used for security, convenience, or energy savings, a motion-sensor switch turns on light when it detects movement in a room, and then shuts it off after a predetermined interval. Some designs allow you to adjust sensitivity and time interval and include a manual ON/OFF lever.

The ground fault circuit interrupter (GFCI) is a device that protects you from electric shocks. A 120-volt GFCI receptacle takes the place of a standard duplex receptacle and monitors electrical current; whenever the amounts of incoming and outgoing current are not equal, such as during a ground fault or current leakage, the GFCI opens the circuit instantly, cutting off the electricity.

light fixtures

Interior lighting can be divided into three basic categories—task, accent, and ambient—with different types of fixtures that each perform one of these functions. Task lighting, which illuminates the area where an activity such as reading or food preparation takes place, is best served by single fixtures that direct light onto the work surface. Accent lighting is primarily decorative, one-directional lighting that focuses attention on artwork or architectural features or simply sets a mood. Ambient, or diffuse general, lighting provides a low level of soft

RIGHT: Chandeliers, generally reserved for use over a dining table or in a grand entry, provide ambient lighting.

ABOVE: Surface-mounted fixtures come in a multitude of styles. Some types mount tightly against the ceiling, while others hold the diffuser slightly away from the surface, and still others employ individual lamps.

ABOVE: **Three pendant lights over this kitchen island, controlled by dimmers, allow the cook to dial in the perfect level of illumination for cooking or entertaining.**

ABOVE: **Pendant lights, sold in a wonderful array of shapes and styles, are task lights that descend from the ceiling to deliver light where it is most wanted in the room.**

INTERIOR LIGHTING TYPES

- **Surface fixtures** Surface-mounted fixtures are either mounted directly to a housing box (in the case of wall sconces and incandescent and fluorescent ceiling fixtures) or suspended from the box by chains or a cord. Some undercounter task lights plug into a nearby receptacle. Most surface fixtures come with their own mounting hardware, which is adaptable to any standard fixture box. Heavy fixtures, however, may require beefier attachments.

- **Recessed downlights** Today, recessed downlights usually are pre-wired and grounded to their own housing boxes. These fixtures need several inches of clearance above the ceiling, so they're most easily installed below an unfinished attic or crawl space. Where space is tight, you can buy low-clearance fixtures. New-work units, which are used where you have access, are easy to install; cut-in, or remodeling models, are also available. Many downlights produce a lot of heat, so you must either remove insulation within 3 inches of the fixture or buy an "IC" fixture that is rated for direct contact with surrounding materials.

- **Track fixtures** Track systems are mounted to the wall or ceiling either directly or with mounting clips. Power is typically provided by a wire-in connector that's mounted to a housing box (plug-in units are also available). Tracks can accommodate pendant fixtures, clip-on lamps, and low-voltage spotlights, as well as a large selection of standard fixtures. Track connectors allow some systems to be extended indefinitely—in a straight line, at an angle, or even in a rectangular pattern. Tracks with numerous fixtures may be powered by more than one circuit.

light that complements such activities as watching television or entertaining.

Lighting professionals often suggest you choose the bulb first and then the fixture. The type of light you select is a matter of personal preference, but energy efficiency is a growing concern for many homeowners. Popular bulb choices today include quartz-halogen, fluorescent, and incandescent varieties as well as the new generation of full-spectrum "natural" lightbulbs.

Special low-voltage recessed lights are designed for use inside a shower.

ABOVE: **This stylish sweeping track with three pivoting fixtures directs accent lighting with contemporary flair.**

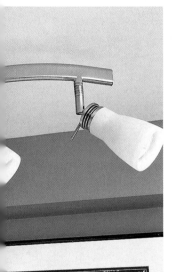

ABOVE: **Undercabinet lighting is an inexpensive way to wake up a dark kitchen. Easy to install, these fluorescent lights operate coolly and are very energy efficient.**

BELOW: **On each side of this vanity mirror, sconces with diffusers shed soft, flattering light.**

COMPARING LIGHTBULBS & TUBES

BULBS & TUBES	DESCRIPTION	USES
Incandescent		
BULB (A)	Familiar pear shape; frosted or clear.	Everyday household use.
TUBULAR (T)	Tube-shaped, from 5" long. Frosted or clear.	Cabinets, decorative fixtures.
REFLECTOR (R)	White or silvered coating directs light out end of funnel-shaped bulb.	Directional fixtures; focuses light where needed.
ELLIPSOIDAL REFLECTOR (ER)	Shape and coating focus light 2" ahead of bulb, then light spreads out.	Recessed downlights and track fixtures.
LOW-VOLTAGE STRIP	In strips or tracks or encased in flexible, waterproof plastic.	Task lighting and decoration.
Fluorescent		
TUBE	Tube-shaped, 5" to 96" long. Needs special fixture and ballast.	Shadowless work light; also indirect lighting.
COMPACT TUBE (PL)	U-shaped with base; $5\frac{1}{4}$" to $7\frac{1}{2}$" long. Also bulb-shaped.	Energy-saving bulbs are designed to replace A bulbs.
CIRCLINE	Circular, 6" to 16" long; may replace A bulbs or require special fixtures.	In compact circline fixtures.
Quartz halogen		
TUBE-SHAPED	Tube-shaped; non-directional; protected by glass cover due to high temperatures.	In specialized task lamps, torchères, and pendants.
LOW-VOLTAGE MR-16 (MINI-REFLECTOR)	Tiny (2"-diameter) projector bulb; gives a small circle of light from a distance.	Low-voltage track fixtures, mono-spots, and recessed downlights.
LOW-VOLTAGE (PAR)	The tiny filament, shape and coating give precise direction.	To project a controlled spread of light a long distance.

anatomy of home wiring

ELECTRICITY PROVIDES US WITH COMFORT AND CONVENIENCES THAT WE OFTEN take for granted—until something goes wrong. Fortunately for the do-it-yourselfer, electrical wiring is usually logical, and there is considerable standardization in home electrical systems. Here we look at typical systems and how electricity energizes your home. You will find more about current, codes, and electrical practices on the pages that follow.

electrical distribution As shown in the illustration on the facing page, electricity passes through a meter before it enters the service panel. Owned, installed, and serviced by the utility company, the meter is the final step in the installation of a com-plete wiring system. Once in place, the meter measures the electrical energy consumed in kilowatt-hours. The service panel usually houses the main disconnect (the main fuses or main circuit breaker), which shuts off power to the entire electrical

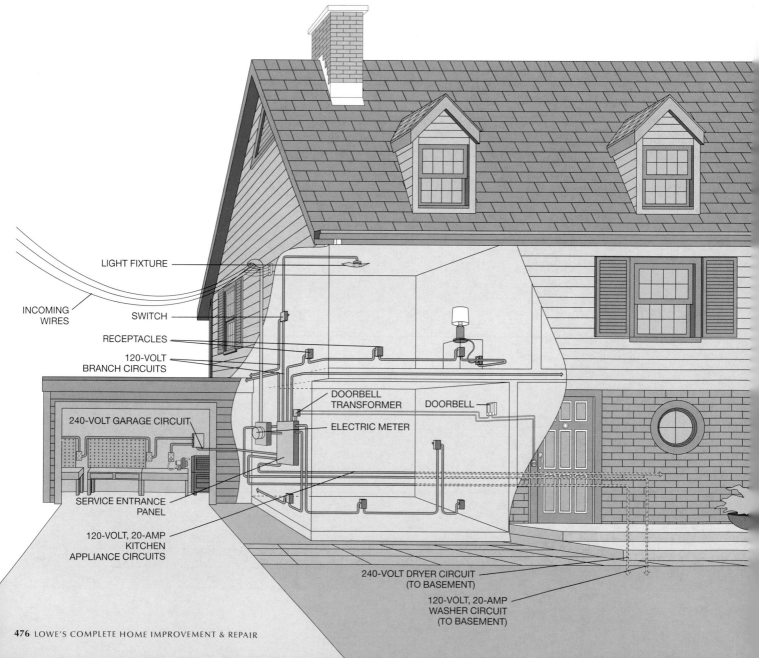

LIGHT FIXTURE

INCOMING WIRES

SWITCH

RECEPTACLES

120-VOLT BRANCH CIRCUITS

240-VOLT GARAGE CIRCUIT

DOORBELL TRANSFORMER

DOORBELL

ELECTRIC METER

SERVICE ENTRANCE PANEL

120-VOLT, 20-AMP KITCHEN APPLIANCE CIRCUITS

240-VOLT DRYER CIRCUIT (TO BASEMENT)

120-VOLT, 20-AMP WASHER CIRCUIT (TO BASEMENT)

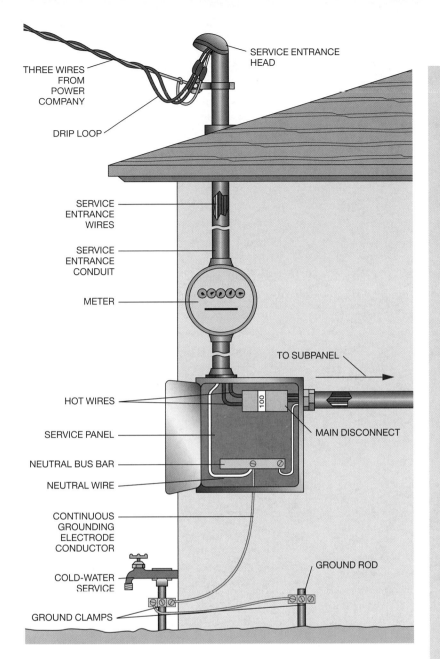

THREE WIRES FROM POWER COMPANY

DRIP LOOP

SERVICE ENTRANCE HEAD

SERVICE ENTRANCE WIRES

SERVICE ENTRANCE CONDUIT

METER

TO SUBPANEL

HOT WIRES

SERVICE PANEL

NEUTRAL BUS BAR

NEUTRAL WIRE

MAIN DISCONNECT

CONTINUOUS GROUNDING ELECTRODE CONDUCTOR

COLD-WATER SERVICE

GROUND ROD

GROUND CLAMPS

WIRING GLOSSARY

Ampere (or amp): The measurement used for the amount of current that flows through a wire or device. It is based on the number of electrons flowing past a given point per second.

Branch circuit: Any one of many circuits distributing electricity throughout a house.

Circuit: Two or more wires providing a path for electrical current to flow from the source, through some device using electricity, and back to the source.

Current: The movement or flow of electrons through a conductor; measured in amperes.

Ground: Any conducting body, such as a metal cold-water pipe or a metal rod driven solidly into the earth, that gives electrical current a path to the ground.

Grounding wire: Conductor that grounds a metal component but does not carry current during normal operation.

Hot wire: Ungrounded conductor carrying current forward from the source. Usually identified by black or red insulation, but may be any color other than white, gray, or green.

Kilowatt-hour (KWH): Unit used for metering and selling electricity. One kilowatt-hour equals 1,000 watts used for one hour.

Neutral wire: Grounded conductor that completes a circuit by providing a return path to the source. Neutral wires are always identified by white or gray insulation.

Pigtail splice: A connection of three or more electrical wires.

Volt (V): The unit of measurement for electrical pressure.

Watt (W): Unit of measurement for electrical power. One watt of power equals one volt of pressure times one ampere of current.

system, and the fuses or the circuit breakers, which protect the individual circuits in the home. Inside the service panel, electricity is routed by cables to various branch circuits that carry power to the different parts of the house. Typically, each cable contains three wires (conductors). Two hot conductors (identified by red, black, or any other color except white, gray, or green insulation) go to the main disconnect. The third, neutral wire (color-coded white or gray) goes directly to a device called the neutral bus bar.

There is one other important wire associated with your service panel: the continuous grounding electrode conductor. The

Electricity runs from the utility company lines, through the meter, and into the service panel. Once inside the service panel, it is divided into branch circuits that transmit power to the different parts of the house.

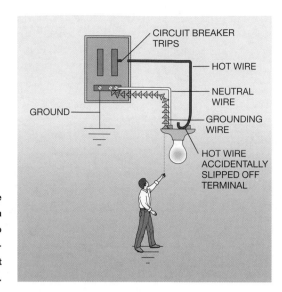

A grounding wire carries current from a faulty fixture back to the distribution center, preventing short circuit and shock.

Labels in diagram:
- CIRCUIT BREAKER TRIPS
- HOT WIRE
- NEUTRAL WIRE
- GROUNDING WIRE
- GROUND
- HOT WIRE ACCIDENTALLY SLIPPED OFF TERMINAL

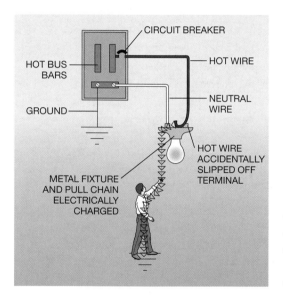

Labels in diagram:
- CIRCUIT BREAKER
- HOT BUS BARS
- HOT WIRE
- NEUTRAL WIRE
- GROUND
- METAL FIXTURE AND PULL CHAIN ELECTRICALLY CHARGED
- HOT WIRE ACCIDENTALLY SLIPPED OFF TERMINAL

Without a grounding wire, the body of a faulty light fixture is live, exposing you to shock if you touch it.

continuous conductor connects the neutral bus bar to the metal water supply pipe entering your home (a grounding jumper wire is used to bypass the water meter) and to a metal ground rod driven into the earth. This safety feature provides excess current with an uninterrupted metal pathway into the ground.

current & circuits Today, most homes have what is called three-wire service. The utility company connects three wires, two "hot" and one neutral, through a meter to your service panel. These wires branch off through the house to provide both 120-volt and 240-volt capabilities. One hot wire and the neutral wire combine to supply 120 volts, the level that is used for most household applications, such as lights and small appliances. Both hot wires and the neutral wire form a 120/240-volt circuit used for larger appliances such as ovens.

Any electrical system is rated for the maximum amount of current (measured in amperes) it can carry. This rating, determined by the size of the service entrance equipment, is called the "service rating." Today the minimum service rating of most new homes is 100 amps. Depending on the age of your home, your service rating could be as low as 30 amps or as high as 400 amps. The best way to find out your service rating

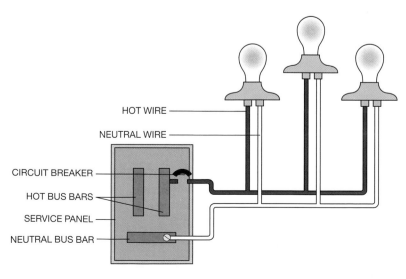

Labels in diagram:
- HOT WIRE
- NEUTRAL WIRE
- CIRCUIT BREAKER
- HOT BUS BARS
- SERVICE PANEL
- NEUTRAL BUS BAR

Throughout a house, electrical current flows to appliances, receptacles, and switches through hot wires and flows back to the service panel through neutral wires. Any deviation from this normal path is dangerous.

is to look at the main service panel. The service rating will usually be stamped on the main fuses or circuit breaker.

The National Electrical Code (NEC) requires that every circuit in new construction have a grounding system.

MAPPING YOUR CIRCUITS

Using numbers and electrical symbols, you can make up a good working drawing of your electrical system. Such a drawing or map can save you much time, whether you plan to wire a new home, alter existing wiring, or troubleshoot a problem. Keep a copy of your map near the main service panel. The drawing below is a map showing the different circuits of a typical two-bedroom house. The dashed lines indicate which switch controls which fixture; they do not show wire routes.

1. Range (240 volt)
2. Dryer (240 volt)
3. Kitchen and dining room receptacles (20 amp)
4. Kitchen and dining room receptacles (20 amp)
5. Washer (20 amp)
6. Dishwasher (20 amp)
7. Bath and hall lights (15 amp)
8. Bedroom receptacles and lights (15 amp)
9. Bedroom receptacles and lights (15 amp)
10. Living room receptacles and lights (15 amp)
11. Living room receptacles, porch light, and garage receptacles (15 amp)
12. Garage receptacles and lights (20 amp)

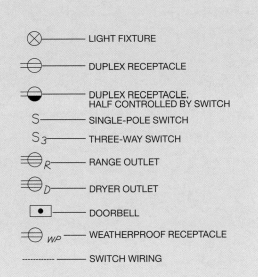

LIGHT FIXTURE
DUPLEX RECEPTACLE
DUPLEX RECEPTACLE, HALF CONTROLLED BY SWITCH
SINGLE-POLE SWITCH
THREE-WAY SWITCH
RANGE OUTLET
DRYER OUTLET
DOORBELL
WEATHERPROOF RECEPTACLE
SWITCH WIRING

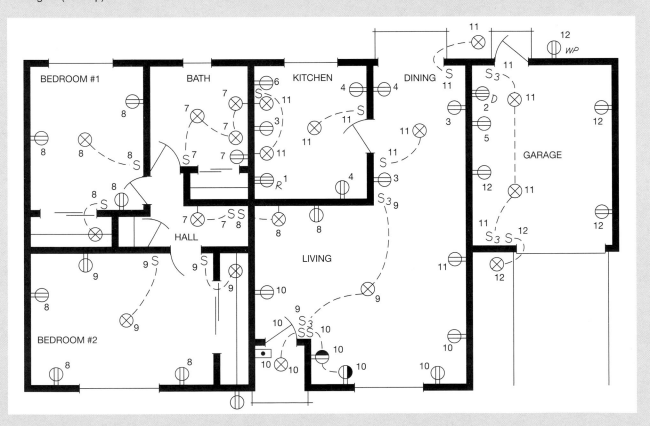

codes & safety

WORKING WITH ELECTRICITY IS ONE OF THE RISKIEST ACTIVITIES YOU CAN UNDERtake as a do-it-yourselfer. Unless it is handled properly, electricity can cause dangerous, even deadly, shocks and fires. Take the time to understand and respect the potential hazards of electricity; once you do, you will be able to tackle with confidence and safety home electrical projects such as those presented in this book.

The most important rule for all do-it-yourself electricians is never to work on any electrically "live" circuit, fixture, or appliance. Before starting any work, test the circuit as explained on page 517, and then disconnect (or "kill") the circuit directly at its source in the service panel.

In the United States, the rules and procedures for electrical wiring are spelled out in the National Electrical Code (NEC). Cities, counties, and states are allowed to amend the NEC—and many do. The electrical code exists to ensure that all wiring is done safely and competently.

Before beginning any major electrical work of your own, check with your local building department to see which, if any, permits and inspections may be required.

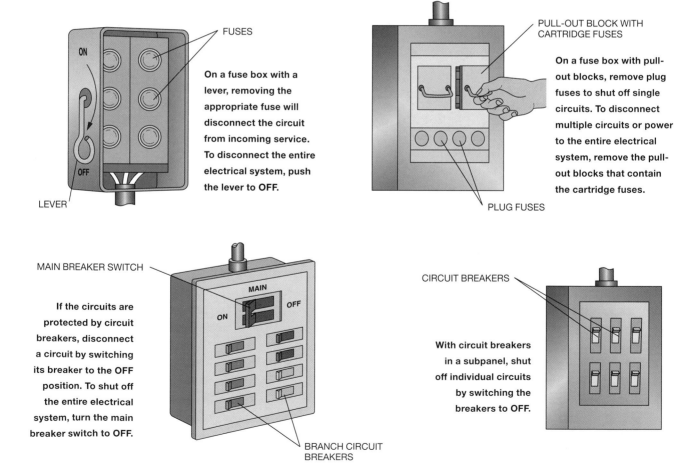

FUSES

On a fuse box with a lever, removing the appropriate fuse will disconnect the circuit from incoming service. To disconnect the entire electrical system, push the lever to OFF.

ON

OFF

LEVER

PULL-OUT BLOCK WITH CARTRIDGE FUSES

On a fuse box with pull-out blocks, remove plug fuses to shut off single circuits. To disconnect multiple circuits or power to the entire electrical system, remove the pull-out blocks that contain the cartridge fuses.

PLUG FUSES

MAIN BREAKER SWITCH

If the circuits are protected by circuit breakers, disconnect a circuit by switching its breaker to the OFF position. To shut off the entire electrical system, turn the main breaker switch to OFF.

MAIN

ON   OFF

BRANCH CIRCUIT BREAKERS

CIRCUIT BREAKERS

With circuit breakers in a subpanel, shut off individual circuits by switching the breakers to OFF.

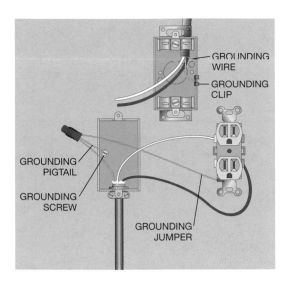

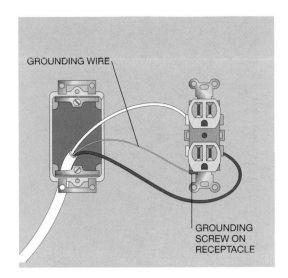

When only one cable enters a metal box, attach a short grounding wire from the device to the grounding screw in the back of the box, or use a grounding clip made for this purpose. If more than one cable enters the box or it has a grounding terminal, make a grounding jumper using a short piece of wire. Twist together the grounding wires and the jumper wire, and secure them with a wire nut (see page 489).

To ground receptacles in nonmetal boxes at the end of a circuit, attach the cable's grounding wire to the receptacle's grounding screw. To ground a receptacle in the middle of a circuit, attach a grounding jumper (short grounding wire) to the receptacle's grounding screw. Join it, using a wire nut, to the grounding wires from the cables entering the box.

Officials there can also inform you of any restrictions that exist regarding the types of electrical wiring a homeowner is permitted to do.

The grounding system is another safeguard in an electrical system, as discussed on pages 477–478. Grounding assures that all metal parts of a tool, fixture, appliance, or other electrical device with which you may come into contact are maintained at zero voltage. Normally, the grounding system does nothing, but in the event of a malfunction, it can save your life. See more about grounding boxes above.

Fuses and circuit breakers guard electrical systems from damage caused by too much current. Whenever wiring is forced to carry more current than it can handle safely (usually because of too many appliances on one circuit or a problem within the system), a circuit breaker will trip or a fuse will blow, immediately shutting off the flow of current. Power can be restored in a circuit breaker by flipping the switch to OFF and then back to the ON position. A blown fuse, however, must be replaced and any overload alleviated.

ENTER THE GFCI

The ground fault circuit interrupter (GFCI) protects against electric shock. Whenever the amounts of incoming and outgoing current are unequal, indicating that there is current leakage, the GFCI opens the circuit instantly, cutting off the power. GFCIs are built to trip in $\frac{1}{40}$th of a second in the event of a ground fault of 0.005 ampere.

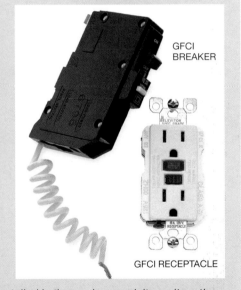

There are two types of GFCIs, both shown at right. The GFCI breaker is installed in the service panel; it monitors the amount of current going to and coming from an entire circuit. A GFCI receptacle monitors the flow of electricity to that receptacle, as well as to all devices installed in the circuit from that point onward (referred to as "downstream").

The electrical code now requires that receptacles in bathrooms, kitchens, garages, and outdoor locations (in other words, any potentially damp location where the risk of shock is greatest) be protected by a GFCI. You can use either type to serve these areas.

BASIC TOOLS FOR ELECTRICAL WORK

ELECTRICAL

Lineman's pliers

Wallboard saw

Metal-pipe cutter

Stud finder

Neon tester

Claw hammer

Fish tape

Continuity tester

Rib-joint pliers

Hacksaw

Diagonal wire cutters

Power drill with bits and screwdriver tips

Cable ripper

Long-nose pliers

Circuit analyzers

Combination square

Wire strippers

Stepladder

Measuring tape

Reciprocating saw

Mini hacksaw

Screwdrivers

Fuse puller

Utility knife

Saber saw (jigsaw)

electrical tools

IN ADDITION TO SOME BASIC CARPENTRY TOOLS THAT MAY BE NEEDED FOR ROUGH electrical work, electrical improvements and repairs require specialized tools and certain testing devices to ensure that both you and the electrical device are working safely. The most common tools in the electrical tool kit are shown here.

TESTING DEVICES

The inexpensive but critical neon tester is used to confirm that power to a circuit is turned off before you touch any exposed wire ends. If the circuit is live, the bulb in the neon tester will light up. By carefully testing bare wires inside a housing box with this, you can also determine which one is the hot wire. You can use a continuity tester to tell whether a circuit is open or broken or whether a short circuit exists; be sure that the power is off first. When you plug a circuit analyzer into a receptacle, three diagnostic lights indicate whether there is power to the receptacle, whether it is grounded properly, as well as whether the wiring is correct.

WIRING TOOLS

Lineman's pliers combine serrated jaws designed to twist wires with cutters to snip through wire. Long-nose pliers cut wire and are particularly handy for forming hooks at bare wire ends. Diagonal wire cutters, or "dikes," are used for wires. A cable ripper removes the protective sheath on nonmetallic cable; a utility knife can also be used for this if you are careful. Wire strippers remove insulation from wires of various gauges and also attach crimp connectors to wire ends. Standard-tip and Phillips-head screwdrivers fit screws on electrical devices.

CONTINUITY TESTER

CIRCUIT ANALYZERS

NEON TESTER

UTILITY KNIFE

LINEMAN'S PLIERS

DIAGONAL WIRE CUTTERS

LONG-NOSE PLIERS

WIRE STRIPPERS

SCREWDRIVERS

CABLE RIPPER

MISCELLANEOUS TOOLS

A variety of tools are needed for tasks related to wiring. You will need a claw hammer for mounting electrical boxes and for installing cable staples. Routing cable behind walls and through ceilings requires a fish tape (these come in 25-foot and 50-foot lengths). If your electrical panel has fuses instead of circuit breakers, you will need a fuse puller to remove them. For measuring and marking electrical box placement—and many other jobs—have a measuring tape and combination square on hand. You can cut conduit with a metal-pipe cutter, a hacksaw, or a mini hacksaw. Handy cutting and drilling tools include a reciprocating saw, saber saw, wallboard saw, and a power drill with bits and screwdriver tips. Rib-joint pliers and a stud finder are also likely to come in handy for various jobs. A stepladder is necessary for installing any ceiling-mounted light fixtures.

FISH TAPE

MEASURING TAPE

POWER DRILL WITH BITS AND SCREWDRIVER TIPS

RECIPROCATING SAW

MINI HACKSAW

METAL-PIPE CUTTER

SABER SAW (JIGSAW)

CLAW HAMMER

FUSE PULLER

HACKSAW

RIB-JOINT PLIERS

WALLBOARD SAW

COMBINATION SQUARE

STUD FINDER

STEPLADDER

working with wires

TO WIRE RECEPTACLES, SWITCHES, LIGHT FIXTURES, AND APPLIANCES PROPERLY, you need to know some basic techniques, including stripping, securing, and splicing wire. Nonmetallic sheathed cable, the type used most commonly for interior wiring, consists of insulated and bare wires bundled together and wrapped in an outer sheath of thermoplastic insulation. Before connecting a cable to a device or joining it to another cable, you will need to remove this outer sheath and then strip individual conductors.

cutting & stripping wires

Wire is cut to length at the rough-wiring stage; splitting and stripping are done when wiring devices. Each step requires a different tool.

To cut wires or cable to length, simply use lineman's pliers or diagonal cutters. To open up flat cable, such as two-wire nonmetallic (with or without ground), use a cable ripper or knife to score the sheath lengthwise. If you are working with round, three-wire cable (such as when you are wiring three-way switches), use a pocketknife or utility knife so you can follow the curve of the twisted wires without cutting into their insulation.

Do not cut cable while it rests on your knee or thigh; use a flat board or wall surface instead. Also, always cut away from your body.

Once you have exposed the wires and cut off the outer sheath and any paper or other separation materials, you are ready to strip the insulation off the ends of the wires. You can strip small solid-core wires, from sizes #18 to #10, using wire strippers or the graduated wire stripper jaws on a multipurpose tool. To strip larger wires, from sizes #8 to #2/0, use a pocketknife to take off the insulation as if you were sharpening a pencil, again cutting away from your body. The length of wire you will need to strip varies depending on the device and the connection. For some guidelines, see page 488.

Be careful not to nick the wire when you are stripping off its insulation. A nicked wire will break easily when bent to form a loop for a connection to a screw terminal. If you do nick a wire, snip off the wire end right above the nick, and begin the stripping process again.

To strip wire, insert the wire into the wire strippers and rock the strippers back and forth until the insulation is severed and can be pulled off the wire in one quick motion.

joining wires to terminals

Many switches and receptacles come with two sets of connection points at which they are joined by wire: screw terminals and back-wired terminals.

HOW TO RIP CABLE

1 To cut flat cable, first slide a cable ripper up the cable. Press the handles of the cable ripper together, and pull toward the end of the cable. This action will score the outer sheath.

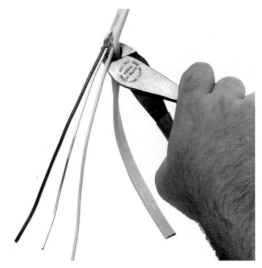

2 Using a pair of diagonal-cutting pliers or utility scissors, cut off the opened sheath and paper or other separation materials, leaving just the insulated wires.

Screw terminals are tried-and-true connection points. To make these hookups, strip insulation off the wire ends, and then use long-nose pliers to bend the ends of the wires into hooks. The only other tool you need is a standard screwdriver. Screw terminals can accommodate only one wire. If you need to join several wires at a single screw terminal, use a pigtail splice.

To back-wire a device, make the wire-to-terminal connection by poking each wire into its appropriate hole on the back of the device. Typically, a jaw inside the hole allows the wire to enter but prevents it from being withdrawn unless you release the tension by inserting a small screwdriver blade into a special slot next to the hole. With other designs, you will need to tighten down the adjacent screw terminal.

Note that only some receptacles and switches have back-wired terminals. Back-wiring is suitable only for copper and for copper-clad aluminum wires, not aluminum wires. Many professionals and some codes discourage the use of back-wiring, at least for 20-amp receptacles. The wire attachments just do not appear to be as secure as they are at screw terminals.

WORKING WITH STRANDED WIRE

Wire that contains several strands, commonly found in lamp cord, is also sold in larger sizes for circuit wiring that is typically routed inside conduit. Working with stranded wire calls for a slightly different technique than single wire.

To make a wire connection using stranded wire, begin by stripping about ¾ inch of insulation from the wire end. Never use a utility knife to remove the insulation; you risk cutting into some of the stranded wires. Instead, use wire strippers. Once the insulation is removed, inspect the strands. If a wire end is damaged, snip off the end and begin again.

Using your thumb and forefinger, twist together the exposed strands in each wire tightly in a clockwise direction. To attach the wire to a screw terminal, twist the strands into a loop and hook it around a screw terminal in a clockwise direction. Tighten the screw, making sure that no stray wires are exposed.

JOINING WIRES TO SCREW TERMINALS

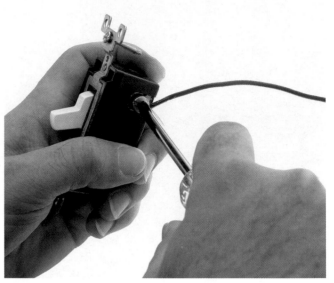

1 To make wire-to-screw-terminal connections, first strip about ½ to ¾ inch of insulation off the wire end. Then, using long-nose pliers, form a two-thirds to three-quarters loop in the bare wire: Starting near the insulation, make progressive right-angle bends, moving the pliers toward the wire end, until a loop is formed.

2 Hook the wire clockwise around the screw terminal. As you tighten the screw, the loop on the wire will close. If you hook the wire backward (counterclockwise), tightening the screw will tend to open the loop.

BACK-WIRING A DEVICE

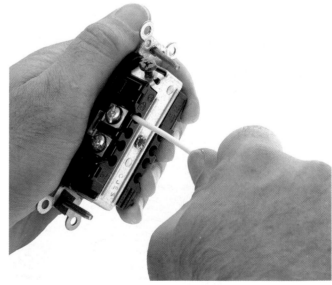

1 When back-wiring, first use the molded strip gauge on the back of the device to measure the amount of insulation to be stripped.

2 Poke the stripped wires into their appropriate holes, and then check to make sure they are secure. Finally, tighten down any unused screw terminals. This helps prevent any loose metal from ending up in the box.

splicing wires

Wires are joined, or spliced, with wire nuts or compression sleeves.

Wire nuts come in about four sizes to accommodate various wire combinations. Each manufacturer has its own color code to distinguish the sizes. For example, one brand uses a red wire nut to splice four #12 or five #14 wires. Once you know how many wires of each size you will be splicing, check the wire nut packaging to make sure you get the proper size.

Some jurisdictions require the use of compression sleeves for grounding wires because they provide a more permanent bond than wire nuts. You can use the special jaws on a wire stripper or multipurpose tool to attach these connectors; a two- or four-jawed crimping tool serves the same purpose. Make sure you use enough pressure to bring the metal into tight contact with the wires. A special two-compartment connector is required for splicing aluminum wire to copper wire.

Never use electrician's tape in place of a wire nut or compression sleeve. Tape is useful for emergency repairs, but it is not a substitute for a good mechanical splice.

HOW TO PUT ON A WIRE NUT

1 First, strip off about 1 inch of insulation from the ends of the wires you are joining. Twist the stripped ends together clockwise at least one and one-half turns.

2 Screw the wire nut on clockwise until it is tight and no bare wire is exposed. Test the splice by tugging on the wires. If any come loose, redo the splice so it is secure.

To put on a compression sleeve, first twist the wire ends clockwise at least one and one-half turns. Snip 3/8 inch to 1/2 inch off the twisted ends so they are even. Then slip a compression sleeve onto the wire ends, and crimp the sleeve using a multipurpose tool. If code requires it, put on an insulating cap.

routing cable

IN NEW CONSTRUCTION, ALL BASIC WIRING IS DONE BEFORE THE WALLS, CEILINGS, and floors are covered. Extending a circuit in a finished house, however, is a more complicated process. You have to find ways to route cable behind existing walls, above ceilings, and under floors. It is wise to familiarize yourself with your house's construction so you can find the most direct route from the power source to the locations for the new devices. Attic floors and basement ceilings are often easy to access, while fishing cable through walls and between floors may take some time. Gypsum wallboard (drywall) can be cut and replaced easily, but plaster and ceramic tile are best left alone.

attaching cable

In exposed (new) wiring, cable must be stapled or supported with straps every 4½ feet and within 12 inches of each metal box and 8 inches of each nonmetallic box. When using cable staples, be careful not to staple through or smash the cable. Staple across the flat face of the cable, not the side. Use metal plates, as shown below, to protect cable that is installed less than 1¼ inches from the front edge of a stud or another structural member. Cable staples or supports are not required when cable is fished behind walls, floors, or ceilings in concealed (old) work. But the cable must be clamped to boxes using built-in cable clamps, metal cable connectors, or plastic cable connectors (if the box is nonmetallic). There is one exception: nonmetallic cable does not need to be clamped to a nonmetallic box if it is stapled within 8 inches of the box.

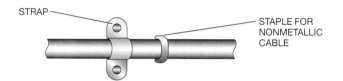

STRAP

STAPLE FOR NONMETALLIC CABLE

Shown here are typical routes for running cable through walls and ceilings. To avoid nailing through the cable once the walls and ceilings are installed, run the cable through holes drilled 1¼ inches from the edge of wall studs or drilled through the center of joists. Where cables are closer to the surface, protect them with metal plates made for the purpose.

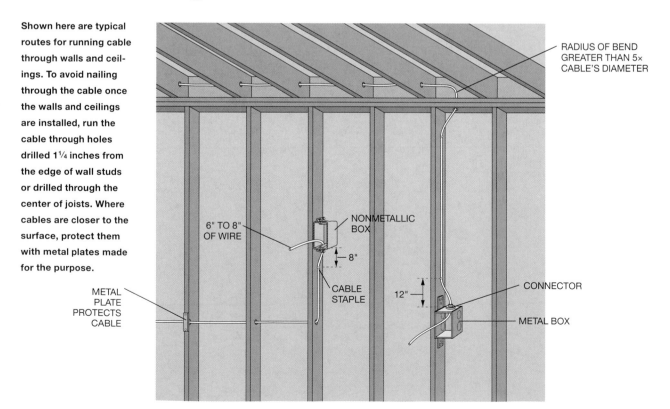

RADIUS OF BEND GREATER THAN 5× CABLE'S DIAMETER

6" TO 8" OF WIRE

NONMETALLIC BOX

8"

METAL PLATE PROTECTS CABLE

CABLE STAPLE

12"

CONNECTOR

METAL BOX

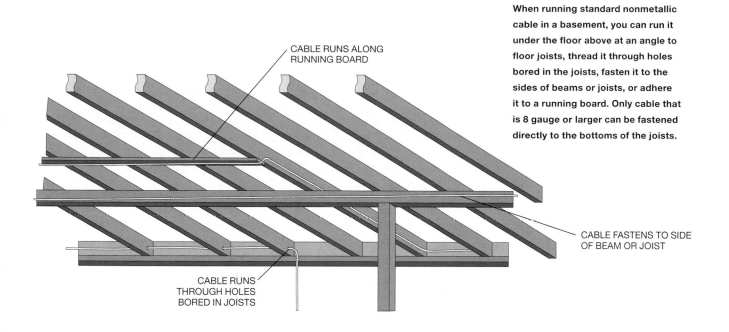

CABLE RUNS ALONG
RUNNING BOARD

When running standard nonmetallic cable in a basement, you can run it under the floor above at an angle to floor joists, thread it through holes bored in the joists, fasten it to the sides of beams or joists, or adhere it to a running board. Only cable that is 8 gauge or larger can be fastened directly to the bottoms of the joists.

CABLE FASTENS TO SIDE
OF BEAM OR JOIST

CABLE RUNS
THROUGH HOLES
BORED IN JOISTS

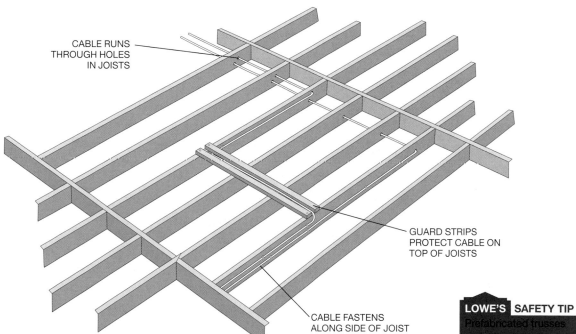

CABLE RUNS
THROUGH HOLES
IN JOISTS

GUARD STRIPS
PROTECT CABLE ON
TOP OF JOISTS

CABLE FASTENS
ALONG SIDE OF JOIST

Accessibility dictates how cable runs in an attic. If a permanent staircase or ladder leads to the attic, use guard strips to protect cable that runs at an angle to the joists. In an attic reached through a crawl hole with no permanent stairs or ladder, protect the cable within 6 feet of the hole with guard strips. Otherwise, cable can usually lie on top of the ceiling joists.

LOWE'S SAFETY TIP

Prefabricated trusses are being used with increasing frequency to frame roofs. If you need to run cable across trusses, never drill holes or cut into them. Cutting a truss can weaken it and void the manufacturer's warranty. Always use running boards across the tops, and staple cable to the board.

working with conduit

CODES TYPICALLY REQUIRE THAT WIRES IN EXPOSED LOCATIONS BE ENCLOSED IN conduit. Below, we discuss techniques for installing thinwall metal conduit (type EMT) and flexible metal conduit (often called flex or Greenfield), as well as nonmetallic conduit (PVC). These types of conduit are good choices for interior projects. Other types, such as IMC and rigid steel, are used primarily outdoors.

An important point to remember if you wire with conduit is that you must install the entire conduit system before pulling individual conductors through it. Allow enough suitably placed fittings to ensure that the conductor pulls will be as straight and direct as possible.

installing thinwall rigid metal conduit

Type EMT is a good choice for exposed wiring in laundry rooms, basements, and workshops. To create a conduit system, you must cut, couple, and bend conduit to follow the cable route that you have designed. Traditionally, EMT was bent with a conduit bender, which might still be the right choice if you have a lot of complex conduit work to do. Most homeowners, however, find it more practical to use pre-bent angles instead. A sampling of pre-bent angles and fittings is shown on the facing page.

You must use metal housing boxes with metal conduit. Screw the boxes to walls or ceilings through their backs, using panhead wood screws for wood framing and using masonry screws or expanding anchors for concrete, brick, or block surfaces.

cutting & reaming A hacksaw or tubing cutter is all you need to cut EMT. But you must also clean out, or "ream," each cut to remove all burrs and sharp edges that could damage conductor insulation. Give a few quick turns around the inside of the cut with a round metal file.

HOW TO CUT EMT

1 Clamp EMT firmly in a vise, and then cut it with a hacksaw. You will get a more precise cut if you support the cut end with your free hand during the last few saw strokes.

2 Smooth and "de-burr" the inside of the conduit cut you just made by using a round metal-cutting file. This step removes sharp edges that could damage conductors.

routing logistics If your conduit run contains more than 360 degrees in total bends (such as four 90-degree bends or three 90-degree bends plus two 45-degree bends), you should plan to use a pull box somewhere along the line to help ease wires around the turns. This box is used only for pulling and connecting wires. The photo at right shows a square junction box with a single-device adapter plate used as a pull box. After the wires have been pulled through the box, a blank faceplate should be added. An alternative is to use corner elbows that break apart for pulling and then are sealed with cover plates. Always plan to install a pull box at a T intersection, where a conduit run splits in two.

EMT should be anchored with conduit straps within 3 feet of every box and at least every 10 feet elsewhere. Secure straps to wood framing with wood screws. On masonry walls, use masonry screws or expanding anchors.

making connections Use threadless setscrew couplings to join sections of EMT conduit. To install each coupling, simply slip the conduit inside the coupling's shoulder and then tighten the setscrew. Elbow fittings should come packaged with their own setscrew connectors.

joining conduit to boxes For indoor use, conduit joins a metal box through a knockout—a metal disc that you can easily punch out with a screwdriver. You cannot join conduit to a round box; use octagonal and square boxes instead. Be sure the boxes you get have knockouts large enough to accommodate the size of conduit you are using.

If both the housing box and the conduit are to be mounted directly to the wall, you will need to use offset fittings to connect them. Secure the conduit to the offset fitting's integral setscrew connector, and then join the fitting to the box with a locknut.

grounding EMT Theoretically, a metal conduit system provides the grounding path back to the neutral bus bar in the service entrance panel. You are not required to run a separate grounding wire with the conduit conductors. But to maintain grounding continuity, all couplings, connectors, fittings, and boxes must be metal and all connections must be tight. Because faulty connections interrupt the grounding path, many electricians play it safe and run a separate grounding wire with the other wires inside the conduit.

CORNER ELBOW

EMT CONDUIT

PULL BOX

SINGLE-DEVICE ADAPTER PLATE

LOCKNUT

OFFSET FITTING

SQUARE METAL BOX

SETSCREW CONNECTOR

CONDUIT STRAP

PRE-BENT 45° ANGLE

SETSCREW COUPLING

PRE-BENT 90° ANGLE

CONDUIT STRAP

A typical rigid conduit system utilizes a variety of components, including metal boxes, couplings, elbows, straps, and more.

installing flexible metal conduit

This flexible conduit, often called flex or Greenfield, is a good choice where EMT is too hard to bend and for wiring appliances such as water heaters or kitchen cooktops that might need to be moved for servicing. The photo at right shows several examples of flexible conduit connectors.

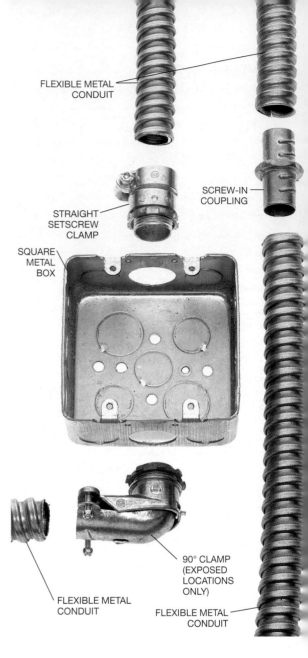

FLEXIBLE METAL CONDUIT

SCREW-IN COUPLING

STRAIGHT SETSCREW CLAMP

SQUARE METAL BOX

90° CLAMP (EXPOSED LOCATIONS ONLY)

FLEXIBLE METAL CONDUIT

FLEXIBLE METAL CONDUIT

PULLING WIRES IN CONDUIT

Once you have installed your conduit and boxes, you must pull the wires through. The following tips can help make this potentially vexing task as easy as possible.

If you are pulling a few #10, #12, or #14 wires, pull directly with a fish tape. Unreel the tape through the conduit until it is exposed at the other end. Strip several inches of insulation off the end of each wire, and bend the ends tightly over the fish tape loop. Wrap the splice with electrical tape. Then pull the wires through the conduit by rewinding the fish tape. (If you have a long, complex route to follow, you can fish the wires in several stages, working toward a pull box or the removable cover plate of an elbow fitting.)

To avoid kinking or scraping insulation, have someone feed the wires in as you pull. In many instances, it also helps to have your helper apply "pulling lubricant" while feeding the wires into the conduit. Pulling lubricant is a special compound that is similar in consistency to waterless soap. It makes conductors slide more freely and yet is compatible with electrical insulation.

If you must do the pulling alone, precut all wires to the conduit length plus at least 3 feet. Lay the wires in a straight line from the end of the conduit so the pull will be as direct and easy as possible.

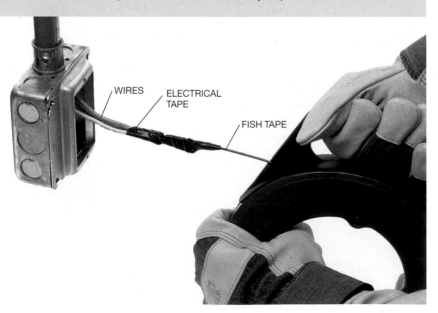

WIRES   ELECTRICAL TAPE

FISH TAPE

cutting Cut flexible conduit with a hacksaw. You will not need to ream the ends if you use screw-in connectors and couplings.

bending & supporting flexible conduit Flexible conduit between boxes and fittings must not bend more than the equivalent of four quarter turns. Flex must be supported with a conduit strap within 12 inches of every box or fitting and at intervals no longer than 4½ feet.

grounding flexible conduit Because of building code restrictions, most flexible conduit systems need to be grounded by running a separate grounding wire along with the circuit conductors.

installing rigid nonmetallic conduit

Several types of nonmetallic conduit are available, but Schedule 40 PVC is the one most homeowners use. It is rigid, flame-retardant, and heat- and sunlight-resistant. Though prohibited by some building codes, this plastic conduit can in many cases be used in place of metal conduit; it is a bit cheaper than metal and is easier to cut and join. Note that PVC irrigation pipe is not the same thing as Schedule 40 PVC; look for the insignia of an electrical materials testing laboratory to make sure that you are getting the right product.

You must use special PVC housing boxes with plastic conduit. (They are not the same as those used for nonmetallic cable.) Nonmetallic conduit does not constitute a grounded system, so you will need to run a separate grounding wire with the circuit conductors.

cutting & trimming You can cut PVC conduit easily with a hacksaw or a hand-saw. When you have finished cutting, trim the ends inside and out with a pocketknife to remove any rough edges that might damage conductor insulation.

joining PVC PVC comes in 10-foot lengths, each with one coupling. Other fittings are available; for a sampling, see the photo at right. Glue conduit and fittings together with gray conduit cement (do not use the water pipe cement used with PVC irrigation pipe).

bending It is much simpler to use pre-bent PVC angles, as shown at right. If necessary, though, you can make bends in PVC with a special infrared heater. Do not try to heat PVC with a torch; you will just char the conduit.

Design your run so that no piece of conduit between two boxes or fittings will have to bend more than the equivalent of four quarter turns.

supporting PVC The supports for non-metallic conduit should be placed within 4 feet of each box or fitting. In most instances, additional supports should be placed at least every 4 feet.

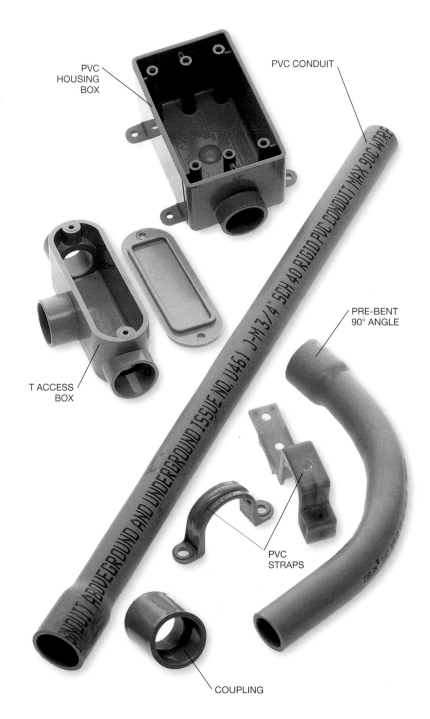

PVC HOUSING BOX

PVC CONDUIT

T ACCESS BOX

PRE-BENT 90° ANGLE

PVC STRAPS

COUPLING

ELECTRICAL

planning new circuits

WHEN YOU ARE UPGRADING YOUR ELECTRICAL SERVICE OR INSTALLING A NEW appliance, or when an existing circuit cannot handle a new load, adding a circuit is often necessary. Make sure that the new circuit will be within the service rating for the whole house; if you are unsure of this, ask an electrician to calculate the total house load and tell you how many new circuits can be added. Also note that all new 120-volt branch circuits must have a grounding wire and must comply with present code requirements.

Planning is the crucial first step in wiring a new circuit. Draw a diagram showing the location of each proposed switch, receptacle, light fixture, and major appliance (see page 479). Next, design the circuit. Keep in mind that it is unwise to have a single circuit supplying the lights for an entire section or floor of a house. Try to plan each circuit so an entire area of the home will not be left in the dark if the circuit fails.

All new circuits must conform with the requirements of the National Electrical Code (NEC) and with any additional local requirements. The following NEC minimums cover many of the most important areas of the house, but this list is not exhaustive. Always check with your local building department or a qualified electrician before proceeding.

kitchens

■ Must have at least two 20-amp small-appliance circuits. No light fixtures can be connected to these circuits.
■ Small-appliance circuits must be spaced no more than 4 feet apart.
■ All countertop receptacles must be protected with a ground fault circuit interrupter (GFCI).
■ An island or peninsula requires at least one outlet.
■ Dishwashers and garbage disposals usually require their own circuits.
■ An electric range requires at the very least a 40-amp circuit.

laundry

■ The washing machine requires a 20-amp circuit, an electric dryer a 30-amp.

bathroom

■ Must have a 20-amp GFCI-protected receptacle circuit.
■ Must have lighting controlled by a switch not on the receptacle circuit.

closet

■ Uncovered incandescent lights are not allowed. Covered ones must be at least 12 inches from stored items.
■ Recessed incandescent lights or surface-mounted fluorescent lights must be at least 6 inches from stored items.

attached garage

■ Must have at least one lighting outlet and one GFCI receptacle.
■ All receptacles must be GFCI-protected.

CIRCUIT CAPACITY

Be careful not to overload a circuit by exceeding its amperage rating. To determine its electrical load, list all the fixtures and appliances that are on that circuit and add up their wattage ratings. Look for a small plate (such as the one shown below) affixed to the back or bottom of appliances; wattage ratings for lighting fixtures are located on a sticker near the socket. To calculate the wattage, use the formula volts × amperes = watts. For example: 120 volts × 21 amps = 2,520 watts.

VOLTAGE RATING

TESTING AGENCY'S MARK

SAFETY REMARKS

BRAND **JIG SAW**
MADE IN U.S.A.   MODEL 1234-56
120V 60Hz. 2.1 A   SER. NO A-1234

WARNING
DO NOT EXPOSE
TO RAIN OR USE
IN DAMP LOCATIONS

fishing cables & mounting boxes

RUNNING NEW ELECTRICAL CIRCUITS INEVITABLY INVOLVES ROUTING CABLE AND mounting electrical boxes. When the structural framing of new construction is exposed, doing these things is relatively easy. But what do you do when you need to run wiring inside existing walls, ceilings, or floors? Here are some basic techniques for fishing wire through existing walls and mounting electrical boxes in both new and retrofit situations.

fishing cables

The easiest way to route electrical power to a location is to draw it from an existing receptacle or non-switched light box. Start by selecting an existing box, and decide on the locations of the new devices. (Be sure that the circuit can handle the additional electrical load.) Shut off the power to the existing box before opening it up or making any connections.

Use fish tape to pull cable through walls and framing members; some jobs require two fish tapes. For short distances, you may be able to use a piece of stiff wire with a hook formed at the end.

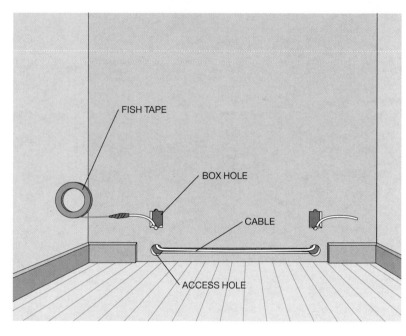

ABOVE: **To run wire horizontally through a wall, remove the baseboard with a prybar, drill access holes, and then cut a channel to connect the holes. Fish the wire into the box holes. Pull the cable through, leaving about 8 inches extending out of the first box hole. Secure the cable to the studs, and protect it with metal plates. When you reinstall the baseboard, take care not to nail at the cable's location.**

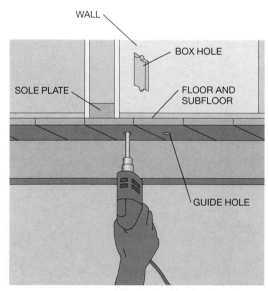

To run a wire from above or below, cut the hole for the box, and then drill a small guide hole in the ceiling or floor in front of the box hole. From above or below, use a spade bit to drill next to the guide hole through the sole plate or top plates. Feed fish tape through the hole, into the wall cavity, and out the box hole. If you cannot pull it through the box hole, see the drawing at right.

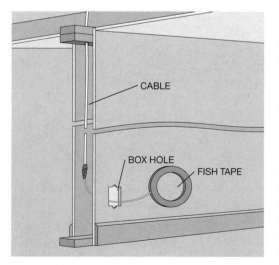

With a helper, run one fish tape through the drilled hole and another through the box hole. Wiggle the tape until the two hooked ends catch. Pull the tape through the box hole. Attach cable to the fish tape, wrap electrician's tape around the connection, and pull the cable through the wall.

mounting new boxes

In new construction, electrical boxes are usually nailed to studs. If you want to hang a box between two studs or joists but don't have a hanger bar, you can nail a 2 by 4 between the members and attach the box directly to the wood.

The boxes should be installed flush with the finished wall or ceiling. If the covering is not yet in place, tack or hold a scrap of your finish material to the stud or joist next to your box, and use it to align the front edge of the box. Shown below are several standard installations.

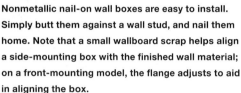

With a ceiling box with flange, nail the flange to the side of an exposed ceiling joist, aligning its front flush with the finished ceiling material. Some boxes, like the one shown, have "spiked" flanges, which allow you to anchor the boxes with a tap of the hammer before driving in the nails.

Nonmetallic nail-on wall boxes are easy to install. Simply butt them against a wall stud, and nail them home. Note that a small wallboard scrap helps align a side-mounting box with the finished wall material; on a front-mounting model, the flange adjusts to aid in aligning the box.

This ceiling box spans two joists. The two-piece adjustable hanger bar can be narrowed or expanded to fit various joist spacings. The box also slides along the bar, allowing you to fine-tune the fixture's placement.

CUTTING IN A WALL BOX

In remodeling work, cut-in (or "old-work") boxes are attached to the finished wall between two studs. Start by drawing an outline of the box on the wall. Then, in wood or gypsum wallboard, drill a starter hole. Cut the opening with a wallboard saw or jigsaw. Test-fit the box. Adjust the ears so the box is flush with the finished wall. Open a knockout for each cable, and pull the cable into the box.

If you have plaster and lath walls, cutting holes is trickier. You may have the best luck by placing masking tape over the outline and then drilling a series of holes along the outline. Attach the box with screws driven through the ears into the wood lath.

The box shown here combines front flanges with twin wings that fix it in place. First, fold the wings flat and slip the box into the hole. Then drive home both screws at the front of the box, as shown; as you tighten, each wing pivots and hugs the back side of the wall.

wiring receptacles

OLDER HOMES OFTEN HAVE ONLY ONE OR TWO ELECTRICAL OUTLETS PER ROOM, a real problem for modern families. Not surprisingly, adding new receptacles is usually a priority, especially when remodeling a bathroom or kitchen. Here is how to wire one.

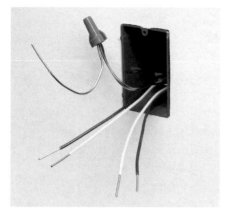

1 Be sure the power to the circuit is turned off. Remove the outer sheath of insulation and all separation materials from the cables inside the box. Strip insulation from the wire ends, and use a wire nut to join the grounding wires with a grounding jumper. For a metal box, screw a grounding jumper to the box.

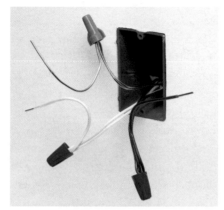

2 For a middle-of-run receptacle, twist together hot (black) wires with a short black jumper wire, and cap with a wire nut. Do the same with the neutral (white) wires. If you are wiring an end-of-run receptacle, it will have only single white, black, and bare incoming wires, which connect directly to the receptacle.

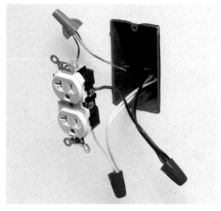

3 Attach the hot jumper to one brass screw terminal and the neutral jumper to the silver terminal. Secure the grounding jumper to the green grounding screw. Tighten unused screw terminals. (For an end-of-run receptacle, connect the incoming wires to the terminals.)

4 Carefully fold the wires into the box, and screw on the receptacle. Be careful not to crimp a wire, which can create a short, or open, circuit. Before tightening the screws, be sure the receptacle is straight. If it is not flush, shim it out, using the break-off rounded ears at both ends of the receptacle.

5 Screw the faceplate to the receptacle, using the screw that came with the faceplate. Do not over-tighten it; this can crack the faceplate.

wiring switches

AS ROOMS HAVE GROWN IN SIZE AND FUNCTION, SO HAVE THEIR LIGHTING NEEDS. Updating a room's lighting scheme often calls for replacing, updating, and adding light switches and dimmers. These pages offer methods for installing and wiring these devices.

By far the two most common types of switches are the familiar single-pole variety, which controls one or more lights from one location, and the three-way switch, which allows you to turn lights off and on from two locations. To determine whether a switch is a single-pole or a three-way, count its number of terminals (flat screws on the sides). A single-pole switch will have two brass terminals and one green ground terminal, and a three-way will have three brass terminals and a green ground terminal. Most new switches also allow for connections via push-in terminals at the back of the device.

Switches are rated for a specific voltage and amperage. Whenever you replace a switch, look on the back for these ratings, and purchase a switch that matches them.

Unlike receptacles, switches are wired only with hot (charged) wires, which means they open and close the hot leg (normally the black wire) of a circuit to allow current flow to the light.

LOWE'S QUICK TIP
If the switch does not sit flush with the wall, break off one or more of the rounded ears located at the corners to use as shims.

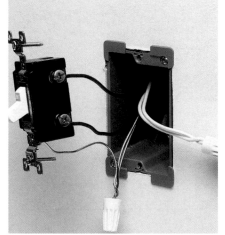

1 Be sure the power to the circuit is off. Remove the outer insulation and separation materials from the end of the nonmetallic cable. Strip the insulation from the wire ends. Twist together the bare ends of the neutral (white) wires, if any, and cap with a wire nut.

2 Twist together the grounding (bare) wires with a short piece that will run to the switch's grounding screw, and join them with a wire nut. (For a metal box, run a third bare wire from this wire nut to a clip or screw connected to the box.) Screw the hot (black) wires to the terminals; it makes no difference which hot wire goes to which terminal.

3 Fold the wires behind the switch. Carefully push the wires into the box, and guide the switch's screws into their holes. Align the box vertically and tighten the screws. Finally, attach the faceplate to the switch using the screws included with it. Do not over-tighten. Last, turn on the power to the circuit.

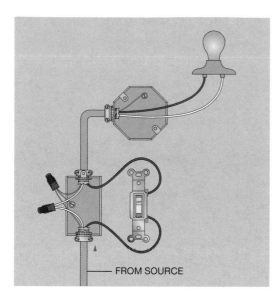

When the circuit ends at a light fixture, it is controlled by a single-pole switch.

wiring a single-pole switch

Circuit wires may run from the service entrance panel or a subpanel to a switch in one of two ways: The wires can run through the switch box to the fixture that the switch controls or the wires can run to the fixture box, with a switch loop to the switch box. Typical setups are shown here.

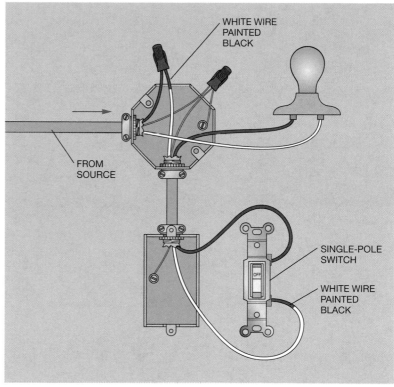

WHITE WIRE PAINTED BLACK

FROM SOURCE

SINGLE-POLE SWITCH

WHITE WIRE PAINTED BLACK

With the switch at the middle of the circuit, power goes through a single-pole switch located at the center of a circuit (two or more cables enter the switch box). The switch controls a light at the end of the circuit. Note that the white wire has been painted black to indicate that it is hot.

WHICH WIRE IS HOT?

White wires are usually—but not always— neutral wires. White wires can be hot, so you should always assume a white wire is hot until you test it. When two wires enter the electrical box you are working on, it is not always apparent which of the wires carries the electrical load. To find the hot wire, touch one probe of a neon tester to the grounding wire or grounded metal box and the other probe to the other wires, one at a time. The tester will light when the second probe touches the hot wire.

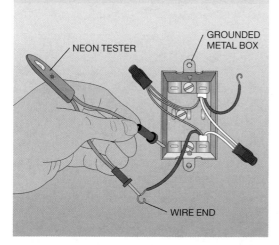

NEON TESTER

GROUNDED METAL BOX

WIRE END

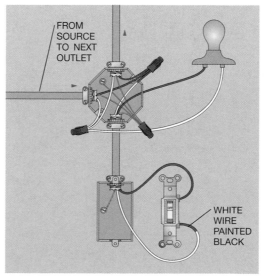

FROM SOURCE TO NEXT OUTLET

WHITE WIRE PAINTED BLACK

When the light is in the middle of a circuit (two or more cables enter the fixture box), the switch controls the light in the middle of the circuit run. Note that both wires connected to the switch are hot and that the white wire has been marked with black paint to indicate that it is hot.

wiring a three-way switch

Three-way switches, which turn one or more lights on and off at two locations, are installed in pairs. To power them, circuit wires may run first through one switch box, through the fixture box, or through both switch boxes.

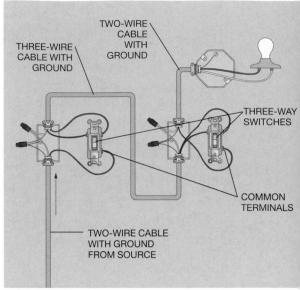

Power goes through a pair of three-way switches to a light at the end of the circuit. Check the location of the marked common terminal. If it is different from this example, connect the black (hot) wire that runs between the switches to the common terminal on each switch.

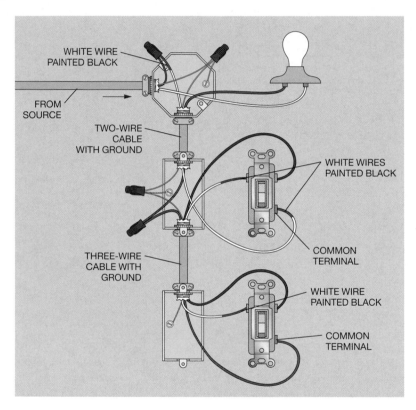

To wire a pair of three-way switches, run the hot wire from the source to the common terminal of one switch. Next, run the hot wire from the light to the common terminal of the other switch. Then wire the four remaining terminals by running two hot wires between the two terminals on one switch and the two terminals on the other switch. In the example above, a pair of three-way switches controls the light in the middle of the circuit.

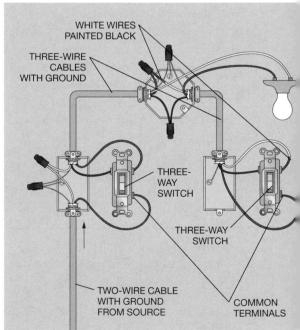

This illustration shows how to wire a light between a pair of three-way switches. Caution: Check the location of the common terminal on the switch; it should be marked. If it is not, connect the black (hot) wire that runs between the switches to the common terminal on each switch.

dimmer switches

Instead of turning a light fully on or fully off, dimmer switches allow you to turn it on in gradations. Turning down a dimmer switch decreases the electricity delivered to a fixture, helping you save energy. And, because dimmers turn a bulb on gradually, they extend bulb life.

Numerous types and designs are available. All are rated for maximum wattage.

If a single switch controls the fixture, purchase a single-pole dimmer. But be aware that this type of dimmer is not suitable for all fixtures. Dimmable fluorescent lights require special dimmers, and ceiling fans need fan-rated dimmers. If you have a three-way setup (with a light controlled by two switches that do not have ON and OFF printed on their toggles), only one of the switches can be a dimmer.

1 Shut off power to the circuit. Remove the switch cover plate, loosen the old switch's mounting screws, and pull the switch gently out of the wall. Confirm that the power is off. If the house wires are very short, loosen the terminal screws, and take the wires off the switch to remove it. Snip longer house wires as close to the switch as possible.

2 If the dimmer has a green grounding lead (many do not), connect it to the bare or green ground wire in the box. In a metal box, you may find the house ground wire screwed to the box. Unscrew it, and connect it to the dimmer's ground lead and to another 6-inch length of bare wire. Screw the other end of this wire to the box.

3 Straighten the ends of the black wires. If either breaks, cut off both, and strip about 1 inch of insulation from the end of each wire. Splice the switch leads to the house wires.

4 Fold the house wires and switch leads into the electrical box, and then fasten the switch to the box with its two mounting screws so that it is vertical. Attach the cover plate, and restore power to the circuit.

installing a surface fixture

ONCE YOU HAVE ROUTED THE CABLE AND INSTALLED THE BOX AND SWITCH, mounting the fixture itself is straightforward. To connect the fixture, splice the box's black wire to the fixture's hot wire and the box's white wire to the fixture's neutral wire. If the fixture has a grounding wire, connect it to the other grounding wires in the box and, if the box is metal, to the grounding screw or clip. Cap all splices with wire nuts. Mount the fixture with the hardware specified by the manufacturer.

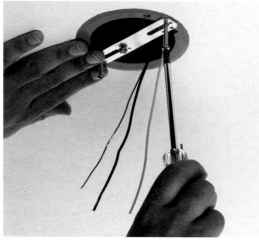

1 Shut off power to the circuit. Screw a grounding bar to a nonmetallic housing box. Loosely fasten mounting bolts to the bar.

2 Splice the black fixture wire to the circuit hot wire and the white fixture wire to the incoming neutral wire. The fixture shown has its own grounding wire; secure it to the grounding screw on the grounding bar.

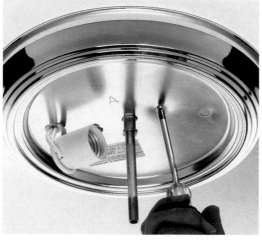

3 Carefully fold wires into the housing box, and then secure the canopy to the box. This fixture has keyhole slots that slip over the mounting bolts. Push the canopy into place, and then tighten the bolts.

4 Finally, screw in the lightbulb or bulbs, and then affix the diffusing globe. This globe, which slips over the long center hickey, is held in place by a threaded end piece.

LOWE'S QUICK TIP
If the fixture is heavy, have a helper hold it while you work, or hang it from the box with a hook made from a wire coat hanger.

installing a fluorescent fixture

TO MOUNT A TYPICAL FLUORESCENT CEILING FIXTURE, YOU FIRST MUST FEED cable through a knockout in the fixture's top or side. You secure cable to the fixture with a metal cable connector, and then firmly anchor the fixture to the ceiling with wood screws into the joists or, if the joists are not accessible, with toggle bolts. Make internal wire hookups as directed by the fixture manufacturer, using wire nuts for splices. You may also need to add pigtails and a grounding jumper to bridge the gaps between internal fixture wires and the point where cable enters the fixture.

1 Shut off power to the circuit. Open up a knockout in the fixture canopy, and then feed incoming wires through the hole. This fixture is mounted directly below a ceiling box; if your fixture is not, plan to secure cable to a smaller knockout with a metal cable clamp.

2 If possible, drive screws through the fixture canopy and into the ceiling joists. If the joists do not align with the fixture, secure the fixture to the ceiling material with toggle bolts.

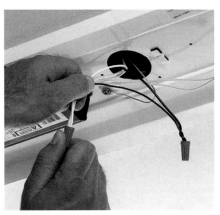

3 Splice the fixture's black wire to the circuit hot wire and the white fixture wire to the cable's incoming neutral wire. Secure the circuit grounding wire to the fixture's grounding screw.

4 Finally, slip the ends of the fluorescent tubes into the tube holders, and then add the diffusing panel atop the tubes. Like this one, most diffusing panels simply snap into place.

UNDER-CABINET FIXTURES

In older kitchens, most of the light comes from a single overhead fixture, supplemented by daylight from one or more windows. But the strength of natural light is subject to the vagaries of the time of day, sun exposure, season, and weather. As a result, lighting is often scant when and where you really need it, particularly on countertops. To solve this problem, mount lighting to the underside of overhead cabinets.

Under-cabinet lighting is available in a couple of varieties: halogen or fluorescent strips and individual "puck"-style halogen fixtures. Fluorescent fixtures are less expensive than halogen strips, but halogen provides a light that is more like sunlight. All types are extremely easy to install and can either plug into a receptacle or be wired to a wall switch.

installing track lighting

TRACK SYSTEMS MOUNT TO THE WALL OR CEILING EITHER DIRECTLY OR WITH mounting clips. Power is provided from a fixture box or, in some cases, through a cord plugged into an existing receptacle. For flexibility (and sometimes to distribute the load), tracks are often wired into two separate circuits controlled by two switches or dimmers.

attaching the connector A track system with a wire-in connector hooks up directly to a fixture box. You will need as many wall switches as your track has circuits. A wire-in connector brings power to the end or middle of the track.

The fixture shown below uses a wire-in connector and a cover (saddle) to conceal the box and connections, but several methods exist. Mount the connector according to the manufacturer's instructions, and splice the wires using wire nuts.

mounting the track You attach a track to the ceiling or wall by installing mounting screws or hollow-wall fasteners (see page 106) through the track's predrilled holes. (Screws are preferable, but you will need to use hollow-wall fasteners if you cannot locate the joists or if the joist spacing does not accommodate your location choice.) Hold the track in place, and mark the positions of the mounting fasteners.

Most connectors lie flush against the ceiling or wall surface, so you can usually attach the track directly to the surface. Slip the two bare wire ends of the first length of track into the connector receptacles, and then secure the track with screws or toggle bolts. Repeat to secure the remaining lengths of track.

You may need special clips to hold some types of track ¼ to ½ inch away from the mounting surface. Screw or bolt the clips to the ceiling or wall, slip the first length of track onto the connector, and then press the track and succeeding lengths into the mounting clips, as required.

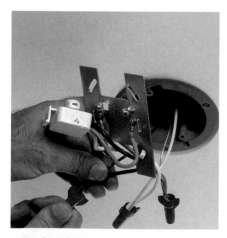

1 Shut off power to the circuit. With most fixtures, your first step is to splice the connector's black wire to the circuit hot wire, the white wire to the cable's neutral wire, and the green or bare wire to the circuit grounding wire.

2 Screw the adapter plate to the housing box. Holding the track in position, attach the connector by twisting it onto the track. (Note that installations will differ depending on the exact pieces.)

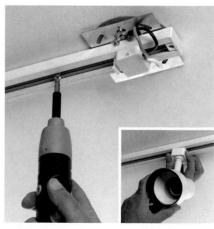

3 When possible, drive screws through the track's mounting slots and into ceiling joists. If joists do not align with the fixture, secure the fixture to the ceiling material using toggle bolts. Install the cover plate, and insert the fixtures according to the manufacturer's directions.

installing recessed lighting

RECESSED DOWNLIGHTS ARE VERSATILE AND INCONSPICUOUS FIXTURES THAT CAN provide both ambient lighting and accent lighting. Standard voltage types are available for general lighting; low-voltage types offer more of an accent quality.

Many downlights produce a lot of heat, so you must either buy an IC-rated fixture for direct contact or plan to remove insulation within 3 inches of the fixture. You also need clearance above the unit (special low-clearance downlights are available for tight spaces). Make sure that no combustible materials are within 1/2 inch of the fixture, with the exception of joists or other blocking used for support.

If you have access from above, choose a standard new-work downlight; most of these fixtures simply fasten to ceiling joists with adjustable hanger bars. Fixture trim is added once the ceiling is in place and textured and/or painted.

installing an old-work fixture

When you do not have access from above the ceiling, use an old-work fixture, which can be installed from below. Before wiring these fixtures, cut a hole for the housing in the ceiling between two joists. If you do not have a crawl space above the joists, locate the joists using an electronic stud finder, and drill a small hole where you want the box. Then bend a 9-inch length of stiff wire at its midpoint. Push one end of the wire through the hole, and rotate it. If the wire bumps into something, move over a few inches and try again until you find an unobstructed space. Make sure to shut off power to any circuits that may be wired behind the ceiling before drilling exploratory holes.

NEW-WORK DOWNLIGHT WITH BOX

New-work downlights with adjustable hanger bars are easy to install from above—you probably won't even need a helper. Simply nail the ends of the bars to joists on either side, and make wiring connections inside the unit's junction box. Replace the cover plate on the box. Once the ceiling material is in place, clip the fixture trim or baffle into place from below.

1 Shut off power to the circuit. Cut an access hole in the ceiling (most fixtures come with a template). Then splice the fixture wires to the incoming circuit wires: black to black, white to white, and green or bare wire to the grounding wire. Replace the cover plate on the box.

2 Thread the fixture, junction box first, into the ceiling. Attachment methods vary; this fixture has spring clips that, when locked into place, grab the ceiling material from above.

3 With the fixture secured to the ceiling, add the lightbulb and baffle, diffusing panel, or any other trim. The baffle shown clips onto the fixture, controlling light spread and masking the ceiling hole's rough edges.

installing outdoor wiring

ELECTRICAL

LOWE'S CARRIES A GOOD SELECTION OF LOW-VOLTAGE LIGHTING KITS. MOST contain everything you will need, with lights that are attractive, reliable, and easy to install. Purchase a kit that has as many lights as you want. If you need to install more than 12 lights, purchase another kit rather than trying to add lights, which may put undue stress on the wiring.

The wires carry only 12 volts of power, so you do not need to apply for an electrical permit. But you do need to plug into an outdoor electrical receptacle, which should be protected by a ground fault circuit interrupter (GFCI). If you do not have such a receptacle, you will need to install one.

Most kits come with a transformer that is equipped with a programmable timer. Make sure the transformer has all the options you are looking for—for instance, the ability to set the lights on a timer, or a photocell that turns lights on when it senses motion or when day fades to darkness. The wiring can be run in three basic configurations, as shown in the illustrations at right.

LOWE'S QUICK TIP

A solar light is even simpler to install than a low-voltage light. Just poke it into the ground at a spot that receives some direct sunlight, and you're done. The unit will soak up solar power during the day and shine at night.

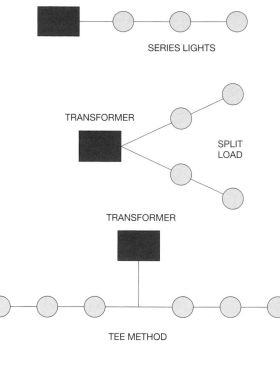

TRANSFORMER

SERIES LIGHTS

TRANSFORMER

SPLIT LOAD

TRANSFORMER

TEE METHOD

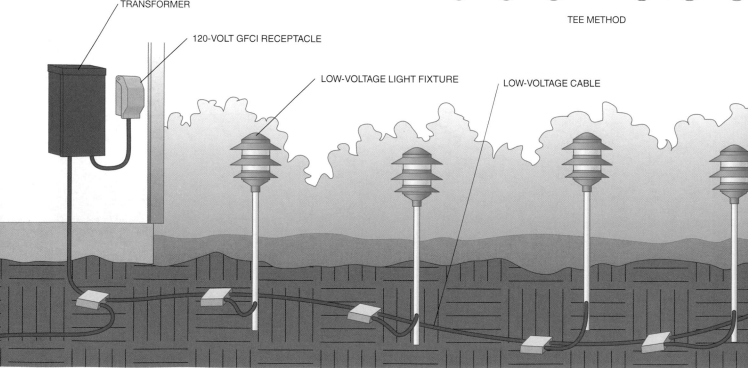

TRANSFORMER

120-VOLT GFCI RECEPTACLE

LOW-VOLTAGE LIGHT FIXTURE

LOW-VOLTAGE CABLE

1 Make sure your receptacle is GFCI-protected. If necessary, shut off power to the circuit, and install an in-use cover to protect it from rain while the lights are plugged in.

2 Near the receptacle and in a spot where it is not likely to get bumped, mount the transformer with screws driven into the siding or other stable surface.

3 Experiment with the placement of the light fixtures until you are satisfied with the arrangement. Run the wire past the lights.

4 Join the wires using the connectors provided. Most types simply snap or screw together.

5 Poke each light into the ground, and cover the wires with some mulch or soil.

6 Attach the wires to the transformer, and program the lights to turn on and off at certain times, or you can have them come on when it gets dark.

cables & connectors

A HOME NETWORK REQUIRES A VARIETY OF CABLES AND CONNECTORS, EACH ONE suited to the types of devices being connected. These connectors include twisted-pair wiring for data and telephone lines and coaxial cables for video. Each type of signal uses a different type of connector, so it's important to buy the right ones for each application. For more on fishing cable and installing boxes, see pages 496–497.

CAT 3 CABLE

CAT 5E CABLE

data & telephone wiring

Data and telephone networks use cables that have several twisted pairs of wires inside plastic sheathing. The American National Standards Institute (ANSI) and the Electronic Industries Association (EIA) have established specifications for several categories of twisted-pair cable that are based on the amount of data able to pass through the cable (this is measured in bits per second). A CAT (category) number identifies the type of cable and its most common use. For example, CAT 1 cable is adequate for old-fashioned voice-quality telephone lines and doorbell wiring, CAT 3 (top left) can handle any voice and data up to 16 Mbps (millions of bits per second), and CAT 5 works well up to about 150 Mbps. In new-home construction, the Federal Communications Commission (FCC) has specified CAT 3 wiring as the minimum acceptable quality for telephone service. Fast Ethernet networks (which operate at speeds up to 100 Mbps) require CAT 5 cable or better.

The best choice for both telephone and data wiring in a home network is CAT 5e (category 5 enhanced) cable (bottom left). CAT 5e cables support higher bandwidth than CAT 5 and and also are quieter and less sensitive to interference. CAT 5e costs a little more than CAT 5 but is worth the extra expense because it will support future high-bandwidth data networks. This type of cable contains four separate color-coded twisted pairs of copper wires; a single cable can carry up to four telephone lines or two data signals.

Because you will use separate CAT 5e wiring for data and for telephone lines, it is a good idea to buy boxes or spools of cable in two different colors. This will eliminate confusion when you are trying to figure out which cable carries voice and which cable is for data.

video cable

A video signal contains a great deal of information, so a video cable must be able to handle a much higher bandwidth than data or telephone cables. Video as well as cable

COMBINATION CABLE

Composite cable combines two CAT 5e cables with two RG6/U cables in a common sleeve. This is a great choice for a full-scale system that provides data, telephone, and video to every room. But it is about 35 percent more expensive than separate runs of coaxial and CAT 5e, so cost may outweigh ease of installation.

ELECTRICAL

RG6/U CABLE

modem services use a type of 75-ohm coaxial cable called RG6/U (above); this carries signals in a central copper wire that is surrounded by several layers of insulation and metal shielding that block interference. The shorter video cables that connect television sets, cable modems, and set-top boxes to wall outlets also use this cable variety.

data patch cords

Data patch cords connect computers, hubs, and other devices via the network outlets. If you have the right connector tools, it is possible to make data patch cords out of the same CAT 5e cable used inside walls, but it is seldom worth the time and trouble to do this: Inexpensive premade cables are available in a wide variety of lengths and colors. As with the wiring inside the walls, make sure that your cables meet the CAT 5e specifications.

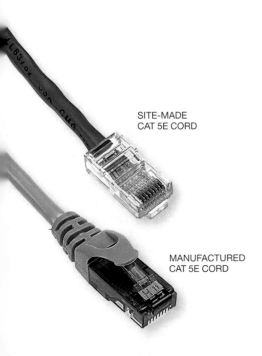

SITE-MADE
CAT 5E CORD

MANUFACTURED
CAT 5E CORD

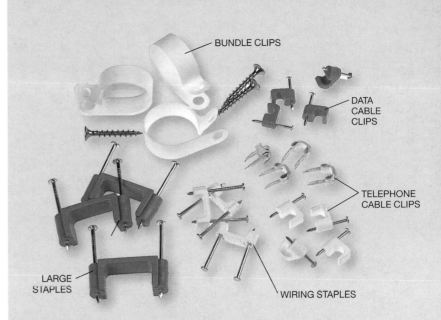

BUNDLE CLIPS

DATA CABLE CLIPS

TELEPHONE CABLE CLIPS

LARGE STAPLES

WIRING STAPLES

WIRE CLIPS

Inevitably, some cable runs will be exposed, whether across ceiling joists, through crawl spaces, or along baseboards. You will need a variety of clips to hold them in place. If you are planning a major project, consider investing in a specialty stapler designed for fastening wires. The staples are soft enough to conform to the shape of the cable without biting into it. Such tools are a little pricey but will vastly speed up the job if you anticipate running a lot of exposed cable. Other alternatives are metal or plastic clips that hammer in place. Select the right clip for the cable; options are available for phone, data, and coaxial cables.

This wall outlet setup accommodates three data or phone lines and two video lines, with a blank port available for future use. Each jack snaps into place. The faceplate and inserts attach to a mounting bracket or electrical box.

data & telephone outlets

IT IS USUALLY BEST TO RUN SEPARATE CABLES FOR DATA AND TELEPHONE SERVICE. But when you want to add another telephone line to a location where a data outlet is already in place, it is significantly easier to use the spare wires in the existing cable than to pull a new cable.

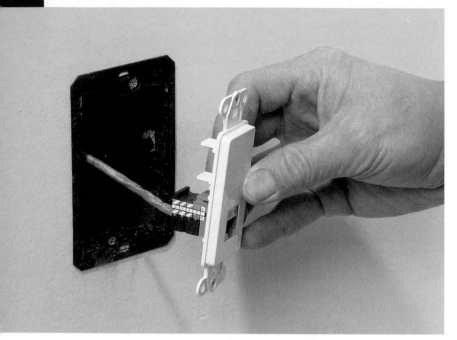

As discussed on page 510, CAT 5e cable contains four twisted-wire pairs. Because a data circuit uses only two of the pairs, the other two pairs may well be available for an additional network connection.

This is practical only when the network uses the same central distribution center for data and telephone wiring. If the data and telephone wires terminate in different locations, don't try to work with a single cable.

To add a telephone outlet to an existing data outlet or a new data outlet to an existing telephone outlet, follow the steps on these two pages.

1 Remove the outlet plate from the wall or the cover from the surface-mount box. Then separate the cable and connector from either the wall plate or box cover.

2 Cut the cable as close to the jack as possible. Loop it in a loose knot to ensure that the cable doesn't slip back into the wall cavity. Pry the dust cover off the IMC terminals inside the jack.

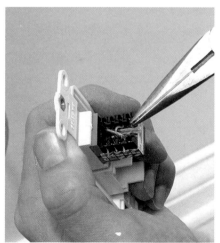

3 Remove the wires from the jack using a pair of long-nose pliers. Grasp each wire and then pull it up from the jack.

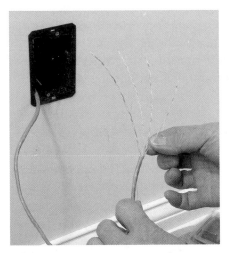

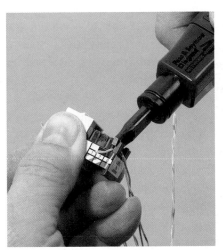

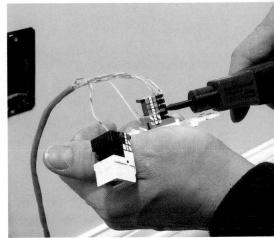

4 Using a cable stripper, strip about 5 inches of the outer jacket away from the end of the cable. Separate the four twisted wire pairs, but do not untwist the individual pairs.

5 Use a punch-down tool to connect the blue pair of wires to pins 3 and 4 of the RJ-11 (telephone) jack. Connect the solid blue wire to pin 3 and then the blue-and-white wire to pin 4. If the punch-down tool doesn't cut off the excess wire ends automatically, trim them with a pair of wire cutters.

6 Connect the remaining wires to the RJ-45 (data) jack. Be sure you connect the color-coded wires according to the standards on the jack's packaging. (Use the same wiring standard throughout the rest of your network.) If necessary, cut off the excess wire ends.

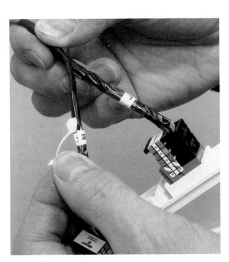

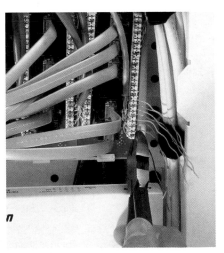

7 Replace the dust covers over the IMC terminals on both jacks. Wrap the exposed wires with electrical tape. Label the data cable and the telephone cable where they branch out from the CAT 5e cable.

8 Reassemble the wall outlet plate or the surface-mount box. If the plate or box cover doesn't have a spare opening for the new jack, replace it with a new piece that has the additional opening.

9 Starting at the other end of the cable, connect the blue wire to the red terminal in the distribution panel for the telephone line, and connect the blue-and-white wire to the green terminal. Fasten the remaining wires to the data distribution panel according to the color code used in your network.

video outlets

ADDING VIDEO OUTLETS TO AN EXISTING SYSTEM IS EASILY DONE WITH COAXIAL cable. But video cables are extremely sensitive to interference from nearby radio transmitters, electric motors, and other sources. In order to minimize such interference, video cables and connectors maintain a continuous shield around the central copper wire.

To install a video outlet on a wall plate, you will need to attach an F connector to the RG6/U cable and plug that connector into the mating jack inside the wall plate. F connectors come in several forms and each has a different method for attaching the connector to the cable. Most F connectors use a variation on the process of stripping cable, inserting a connector over the center wire and crimping the sleeve of the connector around the shield. Manufacturers provide detailed instructions for their particular designs.

In addition to the crimping tool that compresses the shell around the cable, look for the F connector tool that holds the plug on a threaded extension. The bulk of the tool makes the connector easier to handle while you are inserting the cable. You can also buy cable with connectors attached.

1 Strip coaxial cable using a stripping tool, the stripping teeth on a coaxial crimper, or, trickiest of all, a utility knife. Even when using a coaxial stripper, it can be difficult to get this step right; be sure to practice on a scrap of cable. Strip the cable so there is about ¼ inch of the braided shield and at least ¾ inch of cleanly stripped copper wire.

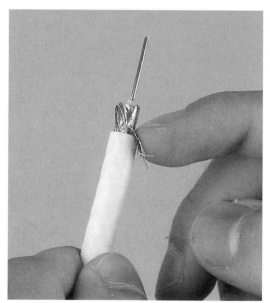

2 Carefully bend back all the steel braiding against the end of the cable sheathing.

LOWE'S QUICK TIP
Avoid running coaxial cable next to standard-voltage electrical wires because these may cause interference.

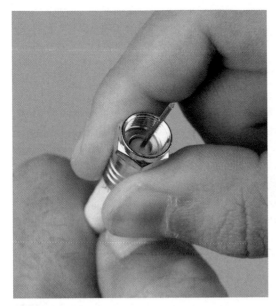

3 Push a crimpable F connector onto the cable, making sure the turned-back steel braiding slips into the connector. The white insulation that surrounds the copper wire should be pushed all the way into the connector.

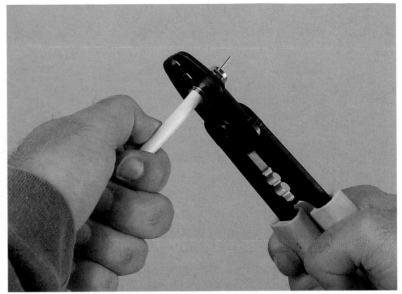

4 Crimp the F connector in place using a crimping tool. Give the connector a firm tug to confirm that it is fastened. Trim the center copper pin so it protrudes 1/8 inch beyond the connector.

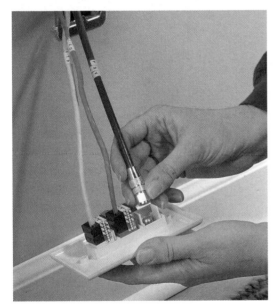

5 Once the F connector is attached to the cable, twist it onto the jack's threaded back.

NO STRIPPING REQUIRED

One alternative to the strip-and-crimp method is the RCA centerpin design. Although more expensive than standard connectors, these do not require a special stripper or crimper. During installation, you first trim off the cable squarely and then push on the connector cap until 1/2 inch of cable shows. Use pliers to push on the other half of the connector, being sure to press the six prongs evenly into the insulation. Finally, pull the cap forward and thread it over the prongs.

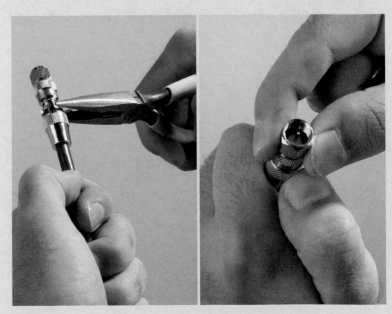

diagnosing electrical problems

AN ELECTRICAL PROBLEM TYPICALLY BECOMES EVIDENT WHEN YOU TURN ON A lamp or appliance and it doesn't work. When that happens, the source of the problem may be the device, faulty wiring connections, or an overloaded or short circuit. Unfortunately, distinguishing between an overloaded circuit and a short circuit can be difficult. A circuit becomes overloaded when there are more lamps and appliances on it than it can safely handle. When all the lamps and appliances on the circuit are turned on at the same time, the wiring becomes overheated, causing the circuit breaker to trip or the fuse to blow. A short circuit occurs when a bare hot wire touches a bare neutral wire or a bare grounding wire (or some other ground). The flow of extra current trips a circuit breaker or blows a fuse.

To reset a circuit breaker, first locate the breaker with a toggle that shows a red indicator or is in the OFF position. Push the toggle farther toward the OFF position before returning it to the ON position (this may require some force). If the breaker trips again, diagnose the problem by following the steps on the facing page.

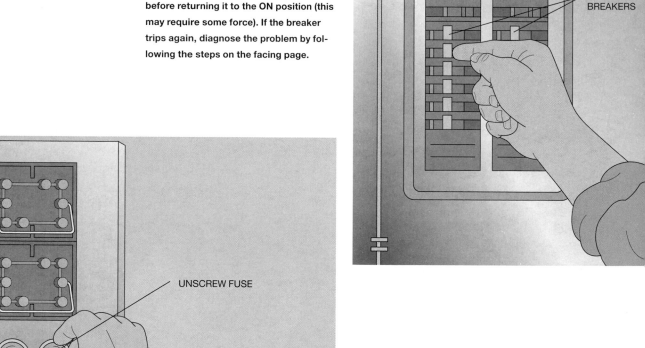

CIRCUIT BREAKERS

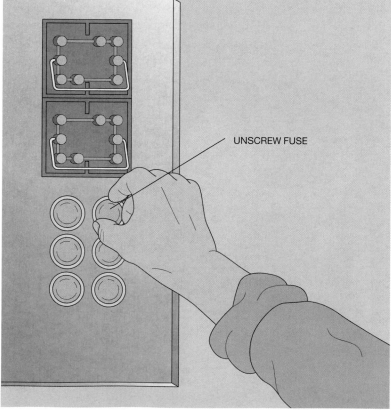

UNSCREW FUSE

To replace a blown fuse, first locate the fuse in the service panel. Grasp the fuse by its insulated rim (or use a fuse puller), and unscrew it. Screw in a new fuse with the same amperage rating as the old one. If the fuse blows again, follow the steps in the box on the facing page. Note that you may get a clue as to the source of the problem by examining the blown fuse: An overload melts the bridge, while a short circuit blackens the glass.

To see if a receptacle is dead, insert the probes of a neon tester into the slots (or use a circuit tester). Be sure to hold the tester probes by their insulation, not the metal ends. If the tester lights up, the circuit is still hot (charged).

To check a switch for power, remove the switch's cover and unscrew the switch from its box, taking care not to touch the bare wires or metal terminal screws. Holding the probes of a neon tester by their insulation, touch one probe to a hot wire or terminal and the other to a neutral wire or terminal, to a grounding conductor, or to a grounded metal box. The tester will light up if the circuit is live.

TRACING A SHORT CIRCUIT

When a fuse blows or a circuit breaker trips, the cause is often easy to spot. Look for black smudge marks on switch or receptacle cover plates or for frayed or damaged cords or damaged plugs on lamps and appliances connected to the dead circuit. Replace a damaged cord or plug, and then replace the fuse or reset the breaker. If the circuit goes dead after an appliance has been in use for a short time, you probably have an overloaded circuit. Move some of the lamps and appliances to another circuit, and replace the fuse or reset the circuit breaker for the first circuit.

If you find none of these signs of trouble, you must trace your way through the circuit following the steps below. If these steps do not solve the problem, your wiring is faulty. In this case, it is best to call in an electrician to correct the problem.

- ■ Turn off all wall switches, and unplug every lamp and appliance on the dead circuit. Reset the tripped breaker, or install a new fuse.
- ■ If the circuit goes dead right away, the problem may be a short circuit in a switch or receptacle. With the circuit dead, remove each cover plate, and inspect the device and its wiring. Look and smell for charred wire insulation, a wire shorted against the metal box, or a defective device. Replace faulty wiring.
- ■ If the breaker does not trip or the new fuse does not blow right away, turn on each wall switch, one by one, checking each time to see if the circuit breaker has tripped or the fuse has blown.
- ■ If turning on a wall switch causes the breaker to trip or a fuse to blow, there is a short circuit in a light fixture or receptacle controlled by that switch, or there is a short circuit in the switch wiring. With the circuit dead, inspect the fixture, receptacle, and switch for charred wire insulation or faulty connections. Replace a faulty switch, fixture, or wiring.
- ■ If turning on a wall switch does not trip the breaker or blow a fuse, the trouble is in the lamps or appliances. Test them by plugging them in one at a time. If the circuit does not go dead, the circuit was overloaded. Move some of the devices to another circuit. If the circuit goes dead just after you plug in a device, you have found the problem.
- ■ If the circuit goes dead as soon as you plug in the device, replace the plug or cord.
- ■ If the circuit goes dead as soon as you turn on the device, repair or replace the switch on the device.

replacing a doorbell

A DOORBELL IS A REAL CONVENIENCE WHEN IT WORKS. BUT WHEN IT DOESN'T, it can leave guests wondering and parcels undelivered. Fortunately, most problems with doorbells are relatively easy to fix.

The fundamental parts of a typical doorbell system are:

- The push button, which completes the electrical circuit, causing the doorbell to ring, buzz, or chime.
- The bell, buzzer, or chime, which sounds an alert when it receives the electrical current.
- The transformer, which steps down the voltage from the regular 120-volt circuit to low voltage (typically 12 volts).
- The wiring, which carries electrical current through both the 120-volt system and the low-voltage system.

The drawing below shows how a one-button doorbell system is wired. When your doorbell does not ring or, worse, rings constantly, the problem may lie in one of the parts or in the wires that connect them. The first place to look is at the source of power. Make sure a circuit breaker hasn't tripped or a fuse hasn't blown. Once you are certain that the 120-volt side of the transformer is getting power, shut off your power, and tighten all wire connections. Then turn the power back on, and check the low-voltage side.

If a doorbell will not stop ringing, turn off the power to the transformer. Remove the button from the door frame, and disconnect one of the two wires connected to it. Turn the power back on. If the bell does not ring when you turn on the power, replace the button. If the bell rings, then the problem is a short between the two wires. In this case, you'll need to find the source of the short.

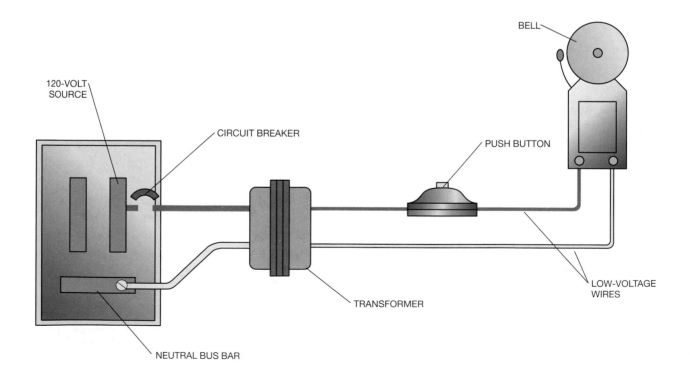

testing the transformer
The best and safest way to test whether the transformer is functioning properly is to use a volt-ohm meter. If the transformer is working correctly, the meter reading should match the secondary voltage (usually 12 volts), which is marked on the transformer or bell. Set the voltage range on the meter to 120 volts AC, and measure the voltage between the two low-voltage terminals on the transformer. If the reading is significantly higher than the correct secondary voltage, the transformer is defective and needs replacing. If the reading is close to the correct secondary voltage, do the test again, setting the voltage range on the meter to a lower value. If the new reading does not agree with the voltage marked on the transformer or bell, replace the transformer.

testing the bell, buzzer, or chime
Have a helper ring the doorbell while you listen to the bell, buzzer, or chime. If it hums, it may be gummed up with dirt. (For example, the striker shaft on a chime mechanism can get stuck because of corrosion, dirt buildup, or excessive grease.) Check the mechanism, and clean it if needed. Use fine-grade sandpaper to remove corrosion from any contacts. If the mechanism still hums after cleaning, replace it. If it did not make any noise at all when the button was pushed, disconnect the bell, buzzer, or chime, and, using new wire, hook it up directly to the transformer. If it works, inspect the old wiring. If it does not sound, replace it.

repairing the wiring
Examine the wiring for breaks or frayed insulation that may be causing the wires to short out. Repair any breaks, and wrap the repairs with electrician's tape.

replacing a doorbell
If you are unable to find the source of the problem, or if the doorbell seems hopelessly silenced, consider replacing it with a new wireless doorbell. Wireless systems are inexpensive and easy to install.

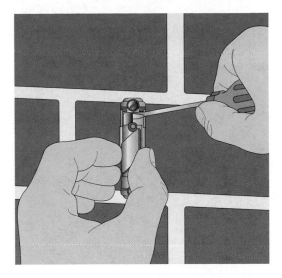

If you know that the transformer is working correctly, remove the doorbell cover and examine the contacts. If the contacts are flat, pry them up slightly using a small screwdriver.

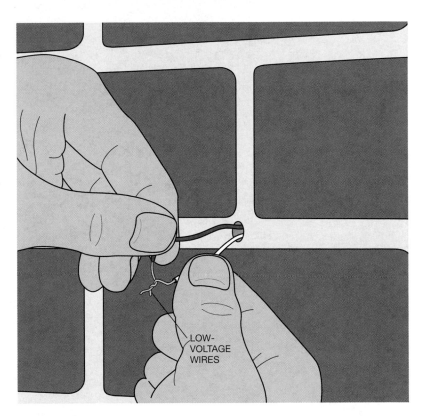

LOW-VOLTAGE WIRES

When the doorbell will not ring, remove the push button from the wall to expose the wires. Disconnect the two wires connected to the button, and short them by touching their bare ends together. If the bell rings, replace the push button. If it does not ring, the bell or chime mechanism or the wiring is at fault.

BE SURE TO WORK SAFELY

To diagnose most doorbell problems, you need to have the power source connected. But if you are going to work on the transformer or the wires in the junction box, shut off the power to the circuit, and test to be sure it is off. Remember that the input side of the transformer is high voltage (120 volts).

comfort systems

A ROOF AND FOUR WALLS MAY GIVE YOUR FAMILY SHELTER AND SECURITY, BUT for true well-being, your home must have the capacity to stay cozy in winter and cool in summer. In other words, your home should be comfortable year-round and able to compensate for whatever conditions the weather presents. In older days, comfort came primarily from the hearth and the stove. Today, it is largely the responsibility of your heating, cooling, and ventilation systems, collectively known as the HVAC. Working in conjunction with proper insulation and a weather-tight exterior shell, the HVAC should provide a consistent, comfortable temperature throughout the house. Moreover, with energy costs rising and resources dwindling, the HVAC needs to do its job as efficiently as possible. Indeed, many of the products now on the market are proven energy misers that can save you money in the long run.

Our dependence on the HVAC makes its maintenance a priority. As with electricity and plumbing, most homeowners do not appreciate what they have until it breaks down. You need only spend one frigid midwinter night in a house with no heat to realize the importance of keeping your HVAC in top condition.

This chapter focuses on improvements and repairs that can raise the level of comfort in your home while lowering the cost of providing it. It begins with an HVAC buying guide and suggested comfort improvements and then gives instructions on installing a thermostat, ceiling and bath fans, and attic insulation. The chapter concludes with advice on maintaining forced-air, gas and oil burner, and air-conditioning systems.

buyer's guide to comfort equipment

WHETHER OR NOT A HOUSE FEELS COMFORTABLE INSIDE DEPENDS UPON A NUMBER of systems, notably heating, ventilation, and air-conditioning. In the construction trade, these systems are grouped together and given the acronym "HVAC," and the tradesperson who works on them is called an "HVAC contractor." Houses may be heated by hot air or by radiant warmth from steam or hot water, and they may be cooled by air-conditioning or ventilation. This chapter explains how each of the major heating and cooling systems works, what to consider when buying those systems, how you can make improvements to boost comfort and energy efficiency in your house, and how to make routine repairs.

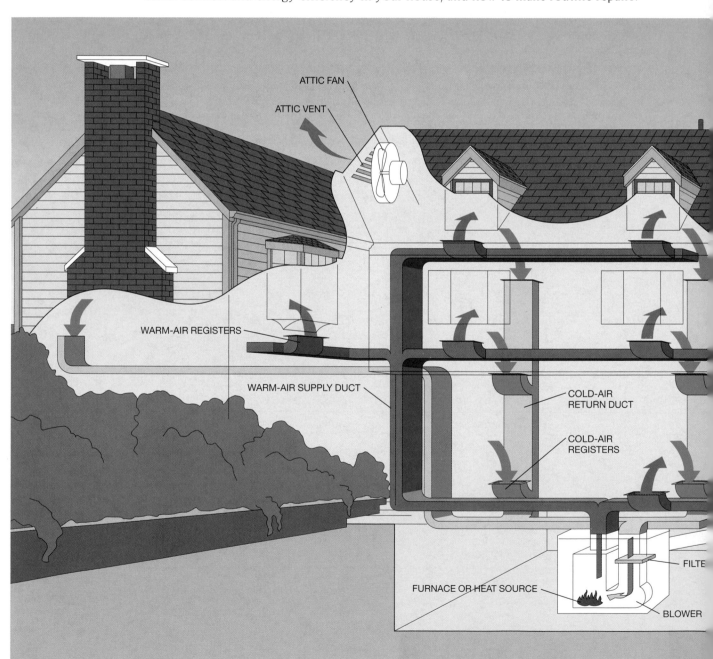

ATTIC FAN

ATTIC VENT

WARM-AIR REGISTERS

WARM-AIR SUPPLY DUCT

COLD-AIR RETURN DUCT

COLD-AIR REGISTERS

FILTE

FURNACE OR HEAT SOURCE

BLOWER

The illustration below shows typical HVAC systems in a house outfitted with by far the most common method of heating: a forced-air heating system. In this example, a basement furnace heats cold air drawn from the rooms above and then returns the warmed air to the rooms via ducts and registers. In the summer, an attic fan exhausts hot air through one side, allowing cooler air to enter through vents in the other side.

For information about thermostats, see pages 536–537. For ceiling fans and bath fans, see pages 538–539 and 540–541.

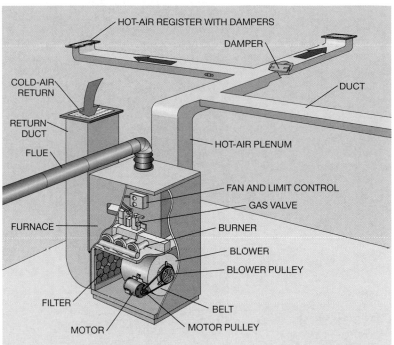

heating systems

Capable of producing heat at the flick of a switch, modern heating systems operate cleanly and efficiently. Most houses have some form of central heating system that delivers warmth created by a furnace or boiler. The most common systems are discussed here. Note that the illustrations here and on the following pages are of typical installations; your system may differ.

forced-air heating Fast heat delivery, economic fuel usage, and reliability make forced-air heating systems the most popular heating choice. They are versatile, too: When combined with a central air conditioner, a forced-air system's ducts are able to deliver air-conditioned air throughout the house in the summer.

Forced-air furnaces are fueled by gas, electricity, or fuel oil. When you are considering installing a new system, find out how efficiently it uses fuel. Efficiency is measured by an Annual Fuel Utilization Efficiency (AFUE) rating; the rating is posted on every new furnace. Standards issued by the U.S. Department of Energy in 1992 require that furnaces installed in new homes have AFUE ratings no lower than 78 percent (meaning that the unit

ABOVE: With forced-air heating, a blower pulls air from rooms into the cold-air return duct, through a replaceable filter, and into the furnace, where the air is heated. Air then flows back to the rooms through the supply ducts and registers.

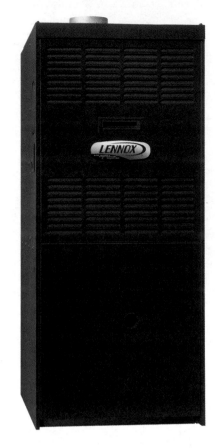

The forced-air furnace's cabinet contains the burners, heat exchanger, and blower that pulls in room air and moves it through the system.

converts 78 percent of its fuel to heat). Furnaces with AFUE ratings ranging from 78 percent to 90 percent are considered mid-efficiency. Furnaces that have AFUE ratings above 90 percent—and some go up to 96 percent—are considered high efficiency.

Before buying, it is wise to consider pay-back (see page 532). Compare the cost of installing a high-efficiency furnace with that of a mid-efficiency model, and then calculate how long it will take to recoup the premium based on the percentage of energy costs you will save every year.

Size, measured by the unit's BTU (British thermal unit) input and output capacity, is important. Input capacity rates how much fuel the unit burns, while output capacity measures the total usable heat the unit generates. Most manufacturers promote a unit's input capacity; check the specifications for output capacity.

A furnace that is too large for your home will waste energy warming up and cooling down, and an undersized model will struggle to keep up with heating demands. A qualified air-conditioning contractor can figure out the right size based on energy-

cost calculations that take into consideration your home's size, insulation levels, window areas, and other features.

Two-speed furnaces are popular because they can operate at a reduced speed, unless your heating demand is high. This means they run more quietly over longer periods and reduce temperature swings and drafts. Variable-capacity furnaces take this one step further, utilizing controls and motors that automatically adjust the speed and the volume of air they deliver to maximize comfort and efficiency.

Furnaces are made in several different configurations: upflow, downflow, horizontal, multi-position, and package. Upflow and downflow models are typically placed in closets, basements, and garages—the choice between an upflow or downflow model depends on where the ductwork is (or will be) located. Horizontal units are made to be suspended in attics and crawl spaces. Multi-position models, as their name implies, are designed for a variety of installation situations. Package units are placed on top of roofs.

steam heating A hallmark of many older homes, steam heat begins in a boiler where water is heated by natural gas, by oil, or by electricity. The water inside the boiler is heated to produce steam, which then flows

RIGHT: In a steam system, water is first heated by a boiler and then travels through pipes to in-the-floor tubing, convectors, or radiators. It gives off some of its heat and then returns to the boiler.

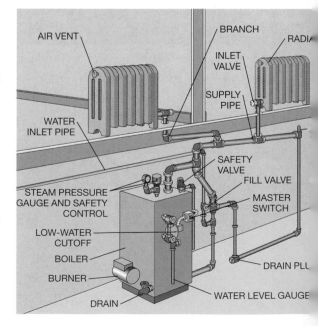

through pipes to radiators placed in various rooms. These radiators deliver the heat, and, as the steam cools, it condenses back into water, which returns to the boiler.

Though few new steam systems are installed in homes today, some homeowners do replace outdated radiators with newer models. A steam-heat system delivers heat to every radiator at the same time, making the size of each radiator important. Before replacing an existing radiator with a new, sleeker model, be sure to consult with a steam-heating expert regarding the safety and efficiency of making this change. If you decide not to replace your system, you can disguise the radiators as shown at right.

hot-water heating With hot-water heating, a heater or boiler heats (but does not boil) water and delivers it to wall-mounted convectors, baseboard radiators, or flexible tubing that winds under the floor and releases heat into the room; then the water returns to be reheated. Any number of energy sources can be used as fuel for the heat: natural gas, oil, electricity, or even wood.

In-the-floor radiant heating systems are very popular in homes with tile, stone, and masonry floors—particularly in bathrooms, where the warmth underfoot can be a true luxury. They are also used as whole-house systems in new homes.

Today's in-the-floor systems utilize extremely durable polybutylene or synthetic rubber tubing and zone controls that allow the homeowner to adjust the temperature of various rooms to desired levels.

electric-resistance heating Because electric baseboard heating systems are inexpensive, easily installed by electricians, and quick to provide warmth, they are popular in some regions, most notably where the cost of electric power is very low. But electricity is not nearly as efficient at heating a home as are gas- or oil-fired furnaces. Even in places where electrical power is relatively inexpensive, a homeowner will still ultimately pay considerably more for

ABOVE: **This natural wood bookcase conceals a steam-heat radiator in its base.**

Tubing that carries hot water winds beneath this tile floor to provide radiant heat underfoot.

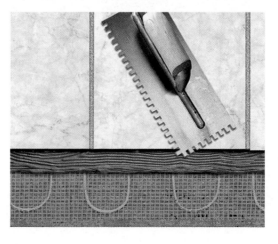

This electric-resistance, in-the-floor heating system utilizes a special mesh embedded with heating coils.

RIGHT: **In hot, dry regions, an evaporative air conditioner can efficiently cool a home. Mounted in full sun on the roof or beside the house, the unit utilizes evaporation for cooling by spraying water on porous, absorbent blankets and blowing air through them.**

Air-conditioning in a home with forced-air heating is likely to be a split system, in which the compressor and the condenser fan are located in an outdoor unit and the evaporator is mounted on top of the furnace's air-handling unit.

an electric heating system because of the higher cost of energy.

This said, an electric-resistance heater does make sense for heating small spaces or individual rooms where other forms of heating would be too expensive to install. A variation of electric heating, in-the-floor electric radiant heating, is extremely popular for individual rooms such as bathrooms. It offers all of the foot-warming pluses of in-the-floor hot-water heating (see page 525) but can be installed even more easily and affordably.

cooling systems

Air conditioners are nearly indispensable in hot climates, especially where humidity is high. Not only do they cool the air, but they also can dehumidify and filter it.

The two most common air-conditioning systems for the home are refrigerated and evaporative. Both can cool just a single

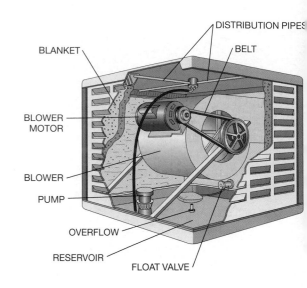

room or an entire house. Although evaporative air conditioners, also called swamp coolers, work well in dry desert regions, refrigerated units are the only practical way to cool air in all other climates. The category of refrigerated units includes central air conditioners as well as room air conditioners that are portable or fit into a wall or window. A heat pump uses the same principles of refrigeration to either cool or heat a house.

central air conditioners Central air-conditioning costs more to install than several individual room units, but it is more efficient, quieter, and less costly to operate. A central air conditioner can be a single unit installed next to the house or a split one, with the condenser and compressor outdoors and the evaporator and blower inside on the furnace. The latter is the most economical. With this, the air handler (the furnace blower) delivers cooled air to your rooms through the furnace's air duct system. If a house has another form of heating, a separate blower can be used to distribute the cooled air.

The capacity of an air conditioner is measured in BTUs per hour—the higher the BTUs, the greater the cooling capacity of the unit.

Central air conditioners use a lot of electricity. Their efficiency at converting the fuel to cooling is a value measured by a SEER (Seasonal Energy Efficiency Rating).

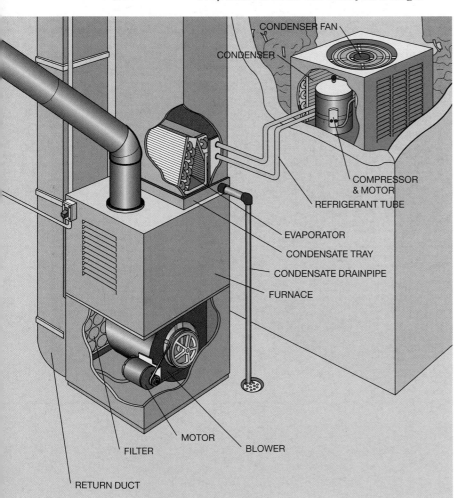

The lowest SEER allowed by federal standards is a 10. A SEER of 17 is at the top end of the efficiency spectrum. But beware of the terminology used. "High-efficiency" air conditioners only meet the minimum SEER of 10. To achieve a greater SEER, you will need to search for a "Super-high" or an "Ultra-high" model.

Installing a new whole-house air conditioner is not a do-it-yourself project; work with a qualified air-conditioning contractor who can help you determine the best type and size of unit. For the sake of efficiency, it's important to get the size just right—not too big or too small.

room air conditioners When buying a room air conditioner, read the energy usage label on it. Pay attention to the appliance's cooling capacity and its energy efficiency. It's best to select a system that is neither too large nor too small for the room. If it provides too much cooling, it will continually cycle off and on. This is irritating, and it also causes the unit to do a poor job of dehumidifying the air in the room. If it does not have a large enough capacity, on the other hand, it won't cool effectively. Capacity is measured in BTUs per hour: The higher the BTUs, the greater the cooling capacity of the unit. The measure of efficiency is termed EER (Energy Efficiency Rating). The higher this rating, the better, because the unit will save you money by using less electricity.

TOP LEFT: The outdoor portion of a central air conditioner contains the compressor and the condenser fan. ABOVE: A room air conditioner that mounts in a window is easily installed and can be unobtrusive. LEFT: A wall-mounted room air conditioner sits flush with the indoor wall and projects outside the house.

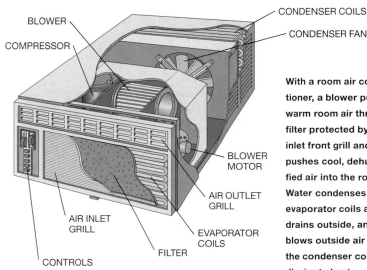

CONDENSER COILS
CONDENSER FAN
BLOWER
COMPRESSOR
BLOWER MOTOR
AIR OUTLET GRILL
AIR INLET GRILL
EVAPORATOR COILS
FILTER
CONTROLS

With a room air conditioner, a blower pulls warm room air through a filter protected by a large inlet front grill and then pushes cool, dehumidified air into the room. Water condenses on the evaporator coils and then drains outside, and a fan blows outside air around the condenser coils to dissipate heat.

The primary components of a heat pump are the outdoor compressor and the condenser fan.

heat pumps A heat pump is similar to a whole-house air conditioner—it works on refrigeration technology. But with a heat pump, the airflow is reversible; during winter, a heat pump can warm the house. Once the thermostat is set at the desired temperature, the heat pump automatically heats or cools your house as required. In climates where extended sub-freezing temperatures are common, usually heat pumps are not cost effective because they must rely upon a supplemental heat source that is, in nearly all cases, electric heating. The capacity and

---

ALTERNATIVE COOLING METHODS

There are other ways of staying cool in warm weather without having to pay the high price of air-conditioning.

- Ceiling fans, portable fans, and whole-house fans can replace or supplement an air conditioner.

- Keep shades and curtains closed during the hottest part of the day to prevent the sun from heating up the house.

- Plant trees and shrubs to shade the house and channel cool breezes toward it.

- Use insulation and weather stripping to keep hot air (as well as cold air in winter) out of the house.

---

energy efficiency of a heat pump are measured by the same methods as those used for air conditioners (for more, see pages 526–527). An air-conditioning contractor should help you figure out the right size and type of unit to buy. Note that, if you're replacing an existing forced-air furnace and air conditioner with a heat pump, the ductwork may need to be replaced, too. Heat pumps generally require larger ducts.

ventilation

Does your home need better ventilation? If it's insulated, glazed with tight windows, and sealed up properly, it may. Homes built before the days of energy consciousness leaked a significant amount of air, so they didn't require ventilation: The air was fresh but the energy used to heat or cool it was wasted. In a newer, tighter house, the conditioned air stays inside but so do moisture and air pollutants. You can have energy efficiency and healthful air if you plan for just enough ventilation to remove pollutants and moisture without wasting heated or cooled indoor air.

Home ventilation systems come in many forms—some are built in as part of the structure, and others are provided through fans and ventilators. When they are built, homes should have vents around the foundation under raised floors to expel moisture from beneath the house; they should also have attic vents, which allow moist, heated air to escape outside.

whole-house fans Some homes in hot climates utilize a whole-house fan to push a large volume of hot, moist air from the house into the attic, where it can escape. One of these fans can speedily lower the indoor temperature by 5 degrees. They can be used with an air conditioner or, if outdoor temperatures are below 85 degrees and the humidity level is comfortable, instead of an air conditioner. Whole-house fans are sized by the cubic feet per minute (CFM) that they move. To roughly figure your home's cubic footage, multiply its square footage by three.

FAR LEFT. A whole-house fan is designed to be installed as a single unit in the top floor's ceiling and the attic. LEFT ABOVE: A bathroom fan consists of housing that fits between the ceiling joists and the finish trim that is exposed to the room. LEFT BELOW: Bathroom fan trims are sold in a variety of styles, from simple vents to this stylish model that includes a light.

LEFT: This low-profile kitchen ventilator is connected to a duct that is hidden by the cabinets above. BELOW: Kitchen ventilation can become a key design element, as evidenced by this sleek stainless-steel range hood.

b ...
ou...
hu...
rem...
tha...
fan...
a ser...

Be...
of the...
8-foot...
by mul...
and the...
resulting...
measured... ...iute (CFM),
of fan to ... for a 5-by-8-foot room, the formula would be $5 \times 8 \times 1.1 = 44$ CFM. For more information about bath fans and how to install them, see pages 540–541.

kitchen ventilation

Kitchen ventilation must be able to remove moisture, smoke, grease, heat, and odors. That job is handled most effectively by a range hood installed directly over the range or the cooktop. Like bathroom fans, kitchen ventilators are rated at the speed with which they can move air, measured in CFM (see the paragraph above). An average 30-inch-wide hood should be rated for a minimum of 100 CFM, although 200 CFM would provide even better service.

In the kitchen, the fan's noise is of particular concern. Most vent hoods produce between 3 and 8 sones; the lower the number, the quieter the fan will be.

BASIC TOOLS FOR COMFORT SYSTEMS

Adjustable wrench

Carpenter's square

Caulking gun

Chalk line

Claw hammer

Diagonal wire cutters

Hand stapler

Level

Lineman's pliers

Long-nose pliers

Measuring tape

Metal straightedge

Neon tester

Open-end wrenches

Power drill with bits and screwdriver tips

Putty knife

Reciprocating saw

Rib-joint pliers

Saber saw (jigsaw)

Screwdrivers

Socket wrench (and socket set)

Stepladder

Stud finder

Tin snips

Utility knife

Wire strippers

Work gloves

comfort-system tools

WHEN MAKING IMPROVEMENTS TO YOUR HOME'S COMFORT SYSTEMS, YOU ARE likely to need a wide variety of tools, including many of the ones shown on the facing page. Carpentry, plumbing, and wiring are all disciplines that may be involved. With this in mind, be sure to check out the discussions of carpentry tools on pages 102–104, plumbing tools on pages 392–395, and electrical tools on pages 482–485. Also pay attention to the tools used for working on windows and doors discussed on pages 216–219, particularly in regard to weather stripping.

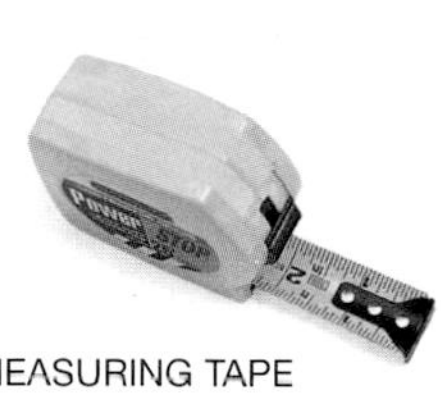

MEASURING TAPE

TOOLS FOR INSULATING & SEALING

Insulating your home will require the use of a measuring tape, utility knife, metal straightedge or carpenter's square, and hand stapler. You will also want a ladder, safety glasses, work gloves, and a dust mask. For sealing up gaps and cracks, you will need a caulking gun and putty knife. If any flashing is required, you will need tin snips.

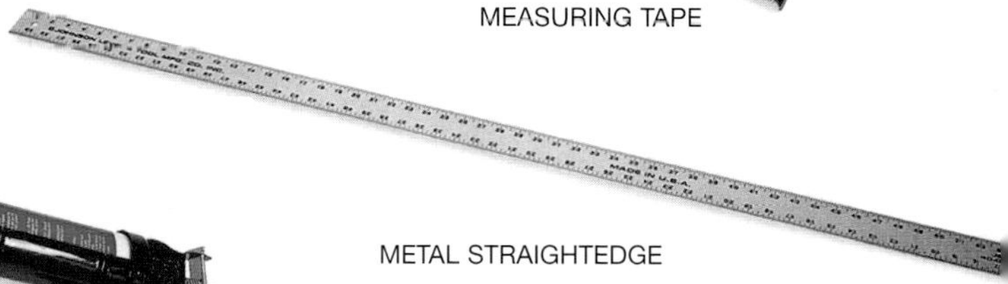

METAL STRAIGHTEDGE

CAULKING GUN

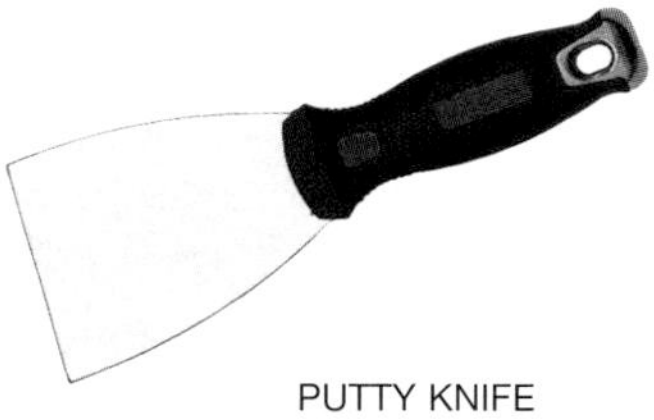

PUTTY KNIFE

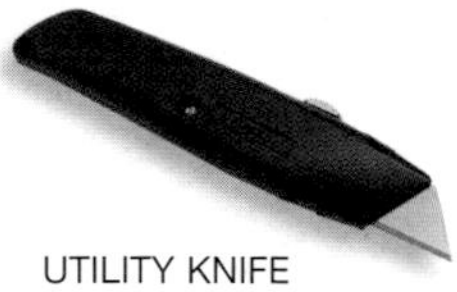

UTILITY KNIFE

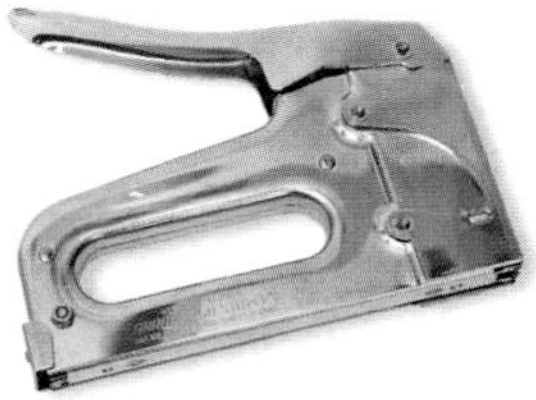

HAND STAPLER

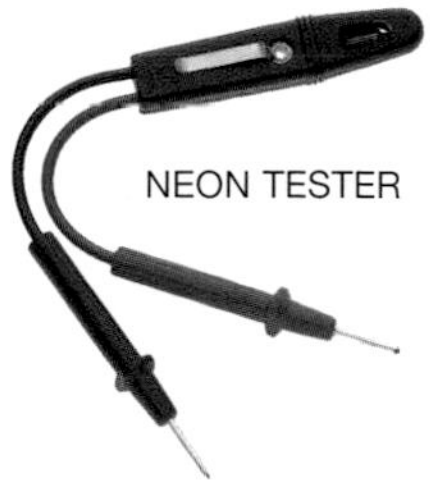

NEON TESTER

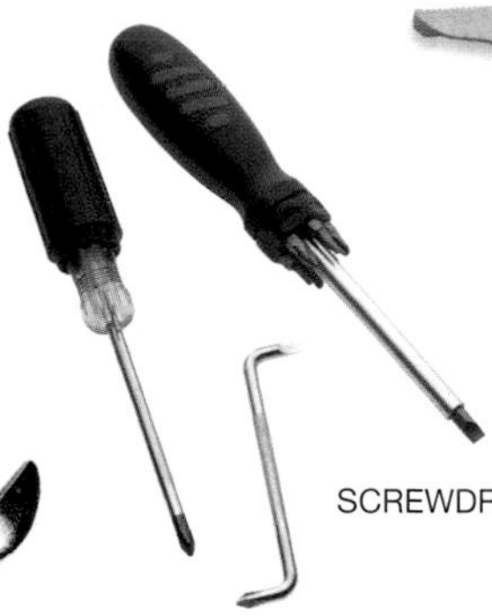

SCREWDRIVERS

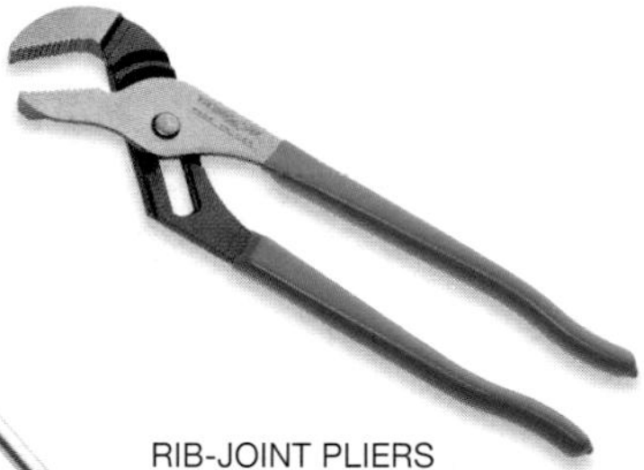

RIB-JOINT PLIERS

TOOLS FOR WORKING ON EQUIPMENT

Installing, maintaining, and repairing equipment will call for a variety of wrenches, screwdrivers, pliers, and electrical tools. You will also need a neon tester so you can make sure the power is turned off.

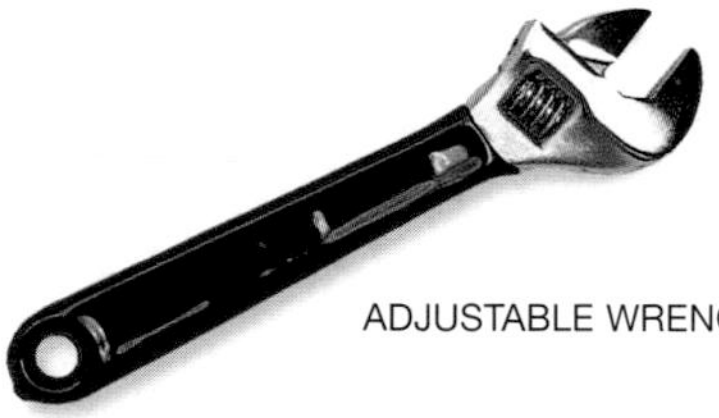

ADJUSTABLE WRENCH

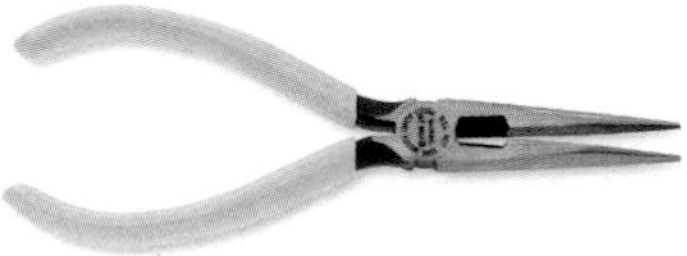

LONG-NOSE PLIERS

WIRE STRIPPERS

OPEN-END WRENCHES

DIAGONAL WIRE CUTTERS

LINEMAN'S PLIERS

SOCKET WRENCH (AND SOCKET SET)

comfort improvements

WHILE MANY NEW HOUSES ARE CONSTRUCTED WITH ENERGY EFFICIENCY AND maximum comfort in mind, most older homes can benefit from a few improvements to boost their energy performance, comfort, and environmental safety. This section offers advice on making these types of improvements.

understanding payback Do not automatically assume that your home would benefit from the most energy-efficient heating or cooling system on the market or the thickest and best insulation you can buy. In moderate climates, these things may not be wise investments.

"Payback" refers to the amount of time required to recover the costs of home energy improvements. Thinking in terms of payback is helpful in making decisions about new equipment vs. improvements.

For example, suppose you estimate that you can save $150 a year in energy costs by insulating your attic. If it costs you $600 to do the work—or have it done for you—the payback will amount to four years ($150 × 4 years = $600). After four years—and for as long as you own your house beyond that period—you will benefit from the improvement you've made.

On the other hand, if you find that it will cost $4,000 to install a new, high-efficiency heating system that will save you only $200 a year, the payback of 20 years may not look nearly as promising— particularly if you do not intend to stay in your home for that long. In this case, you may find that it will be more cost effective to simply insulate the walls or to replace the windows.

A calculation of payback depends on too many factors to be anything more than an educated guess. But doing rough calculations is still useful for comparing the advantages and disadvantages of various home improvements.

replacing equipment Replacing your furnace, boiler, or central air conditioner can be one of the most expensive improvements you can make. Of course, sometimes you need to replace a unit; when an old clunker just won't work anymore, you have to get rid of it. Often, however, the decision is less clear-cut. Perhaps the old system operates just fine but wastes energy.

Here are tips to help you make an informed decision:

■ When the old unit cannot keep the house at a comfortable temperature,

Is your home drafty? Hold a coat hanger with plastic wrap draped over it near your doors and windows. Fluttering indicates that it's time to weather-strip them (see page 231).

first see if you can tighten up the house. After insulating and sealing it, you may find the house is sufficiently energy-efficient without spending the money on a new system.

■ If you decide that you do need to replace your existing system and you live in an older house that has been recently insulated and weatherized, you may be in for a pleasant surprise. Because your house has become more energy-efficient, you may find that you are able to buy a smaller unit than the one you currently have, saving money both on the initial expense of the unit and on the long-term costs of operating it.

environmental quality Comfort inside a home is a factor of temperature, humidity, ventilation, and more. Comfort also relates to indoor environmental qualities important to the general well-being of your family.

One of the consequences of the movement toward tightly sealed, energy-efficient homes has been that some newer houses are more polluted than older, energy-wasting ones. In these new homes, pollutants can become trapped along with the climate-controlled air.

In addition, some substances once used in household products and construction materials have been found to pose health risks. To minimize these hazards, see the chart below.

HOME ENVIRONMENTAL HAZARDS

SUBSTANCE	WHAT IS IT?	WHERE IS IT?	WHAT TO DO ABOUT IT
Asbestos	A mineral fiber that, when inhaled, can cause cancer and other health problems.	Widely used in household products and construction materials before the 1970s. Used in room insulation, insulation around pipes and heating ducts, paint, adhesives, siding, flooring, and many other materials.	Only poses a health risk if particles are airborne. Loose or cracked material containing asbestos can often be wrapped tightly or coated to enclose the fibers. Some materials may have to be removed by a specialist. An asbestos inspector, certified by the Environmental Protection Agency (EPA), can inspect your house and suggest remedies.
Radon	An odorless, colorless, and tasteless gas that is released from the soil. Breathing high amounts over a long period may cause cancer.	Occurs naturally in nearly all soils, but amounts vary widely from region to region. The gas can seep into houses through crawl spaces and small openings in the foundation or slab. Can be found in old as well as in new houses.	Test your house. Contact the EPA or local health department for information on testing devices. Small charcoal-canister tests are quick and inexpensive. If high levels of radon are found, seal cracks in the basement or foundation, place a plastic barrier over the ground in a crawl space, and improve ventilation in the house. If these measures are unsuccessful, contact a professional.
Lead	A metallic element that can cause damage to the brain, liver, and kidneys. Children are particularly susceptible to lead poisoning. Poses a risk when it flakes or burns.	Used in many household products for many years. It is especially prevalent in old paint and the solder once used for joining copper pipes.	Lead can be detected in old paint using test kits. It can be detected in water through standard water tests. Contact the EPA or your local health department for recommendations on dealing with it.

sealing gaps To stop drafts and heat loss caused by unwanted airflow through your home, you will need to detect where the drafts are occurring and seal up the offending leaks. You can detect air movement by using a hanger and plastic wrap as shown on page 532. Leaks around and through windows and doors usually call for weather stripping (see page 231).

You should also caulk and seal openings around other types of penetrations in the walls and ceilings, such as pipes and electrical boxes, as shown in the photographs on this page.

ABOVE: Air can easily slip through gaps at the bottom edges of drywall. The most effective way to stop this is to remove the baseboards and fill the gaps with non-expanding insulating foam.

BELOW: If possible, you should seal the penetrations around electrical conduits and cables as they pass through ceilings and floors. However, there may still be gaps around switches and receptacles. You can seal the space around an electrical box by removing the cover plate and installing an insulator. Alternatively, remove the cover plate and use non-expanding foam to fill gaps. You can stop air from passing through the receptacle itself by plugging up any unused slots with insulated covers.

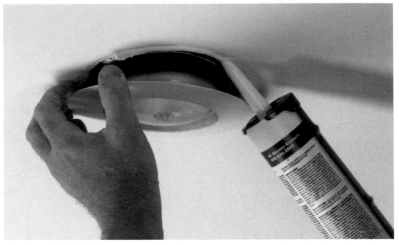

ABOVE: As air rises toward the attic, it often finds a path through recessed lighting fixtures. Remove the trim pieces, and seal around the edges with caulk. Better yet, replace the lights with UL-approved airtight fixtures. Drop ceilings are another common path because they hide cracks, gaps, and penetrations in the original ceiling. Remove the ceiling tiles, and fill cracks and gaps with caulk. Seal around any penetrations with non-expanding foam.

BELOW: Air moving up through a house often follows the plumbing or electrical lines and slips through the penetrations where they pass through walls and the floors. The most effective way to close off these openings is to seal around them with non-expanding insulating foam. For plumbing, follow the supply and waste lines. Seal around exterior vents in bathrooms and kitchen exhaust fans with silicone caulk.

insulating hot-water pipes Hot water cools while traveling from the water heater to faucets, showerheads, and other fixtures. The best way to minimize this heat loss and to shorten the wait for hot water is to insulate as much of the hot-water piping as you can reach. It is also important to insulate 3 feet or so of the cold-water supply pipe where it enters the water heater and, in particularly cold climates, where it exits the house.

There are two types of insulation made for pipes: foam sleeves and foam insulation tape. You can insulate straight sections of pipe as well as bends and turns with either kind. Sometimes, however, the best strategy is to sleeve the straight sections and use tape for the turns, applying duct tape to seal seams where the two materials meet. Typical pipe insulation methods are shown in the photographs below.

CAUTION: CARBON MONOXIDE

Carbon monoxide is an odorless, tasteless gas that is emitted by fireplaces, furnaces, gas appliances, water heaters, and other combustion appliances. Under normal circumstances, it is carried safely out of the house by vents and chimneys. But members of your household can be exposed to dangerous levels of carbon monoxide when a chimney becomes clogged or a vent pipe becomes disconnected.

Protect your family from this deadly gas by regularly inspecting all the fuel-burning equipment and venting systems in your home. For additional protection, install at least one carbon monoxide detector. For recommendations, check with the American Lung Association, your local health department, and consumer report magazines.

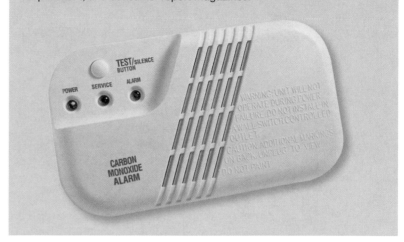

INSULATING HOT-WATER PIPES

Insulating hot-water pipes saves energy. To insulate a straight run of pipe with foam sleeves, measure the length of pipe to be covered and then cut sleeves to fit. Open the slit in a sleeve at one end, and then slip it onto the pipe. Fit the rest of the sleeve over the pipe, butting the ends tightly against neighboring sleeves. Seal the joints between sleeves with duct tape.

To insulate a 90-degree corner, miter the ends of two sleeves at a 45-degree angle, and install them so that the miters fit tightly together. (Some foam sleeves have one mitered end, which can save you the trouble of making the cuts.) Tape the joint. At a T joint, cut two 45-degree miters on one end of a third section of sleeve.

Pipes can also be insulated with pipe insulation tape. Clean and dry pipes, and then wrap the insulation tape carefully around them, overlapping the edges and taking care not to compress the insulation. Secure the ends with duct tape or the tape that comes with the insulation. Cover the pipe completely, paying special attention at turns. Cover the insulation with plastic wrap, if supplied, and then secure the plastic with tape.

installing a thermostat

REPLACING AN OLD, SINGLE-SETTING THERMOSTAT WITH A PROGRAMMABLE MODEL is one of the quickest and easiest ways to save energy dollars. These instruments improve on the automatic temperature control of ordinary thermostats by allowing you to set different temperatures for different times of the day. A typical programmable thermostat has one programming cycle for weekdays and another for the weekend. For each cycle, the thermostat lets you set four times and temperatures, which correspond to waking, leaving the house, returning, and sleeping.

When buying a thermostat, look for one that has a manual override as well as a hold-temperature button. These features enable the thermostat to maintain a temperature not specified in any of the programmed cycles, which is a handy option for vacations and other long absences. A push of a button restores the thermostat to normal programmed operation.

Programmable thermostats, like non-programmable ones, are designed to work with most air-conditioning and heating systems having two to five wires connected to the thermostat. If your house has electric baseboard heating, do not attempt to install this type of thermostat—it will not work with the high voltage that is required by baseboard heating. The same applies to heat pumps: If your home is heated and cooled by a heat pump, the system will require a special thermostat.

A programmable thermostat allows you to tailor your heating and cooling needs to your schedule.

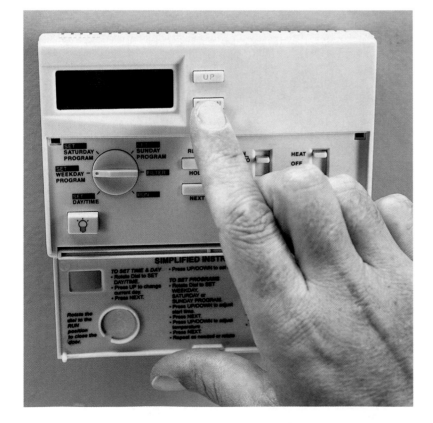

1 Turn off the power to the furnace at the breaker panel or the fuse box. Check the snap-on cover of the old thermostat for retaining screws, and remove any that you find. Pull off the cover and disconnect one wire at a time from the thermostat. Label each wire with the letter next to its terminal. Bend the wires so they don't slip through the hole in the thermostat base.

THERMOSTAT MAINTENANCE

Thermostats rarely break down. In fact, the only maintenance required for an electronic model is to change the batteries twice a year. If you have an electromechanical thermostat such as the one shown below, an occasional light cleaning with a small brush is a good idea. Don't attempt to make a major repair on a defective thermostat; instead, replace the entire unit. In most cases, you can remove an old bimetal coil thermostat and replace it with a new programmable model in less than 30 minutes.

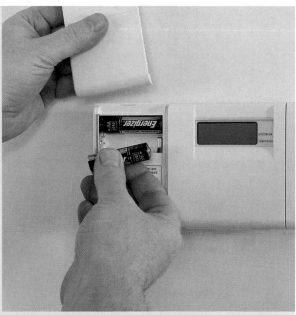

ABOVE: **Electronic thermostats utilize batteries to maintain their programming. Change the batteries every 6 months to keep the thermostat working properly.**

RIGHT: **Use a soft brush to clean dust from the heat sensor's bimetal coil (or element) inside an electromechanical thermostat.**

2 Loosen the thermostat mounting screws, and pull the thermostat and wiring away from the wall, grabbing the wires where they emerge from the wall. Set the old thermostat aside without letting go of the wires. Wrap them around a pencil or use a clothespin or binder clip to prevent them from disappearing into the hole in the wall. If need be, strip each wire to bare at least ½ inch of copper, and then clean the metal with steel wool or an emery cloth.

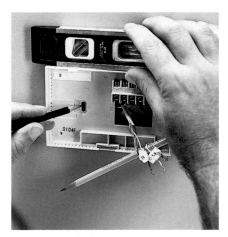

3 Separate the body of the new thermostat from the base. Remove the pencil holding the wires, and then thread them through the base and below the terminal block. Re-secure the wires with the pencil. Pack paper towels into the hole in the wall to protect the thermostat from drafts. Hold the base against the wall with a torpedo level resting on top, and mark the wall for mounting holes. In wood, drill holes for screws; in drywall, drill holes for plastic screw anchors (supplied with most thermostats). Screw the base to the wall.

4 Consult the manufacturer's instructions to determine which wire goes to which terminal on the new thermostat. As you connect the wires, keep them from touching each other or other parts of the thermostat. When the wiring is complete, install the back-up batteries to prevent the thermostat from losing its program in a power failure, and attach the body. Restore power to the heating and cooling system, and program the thermostat according to your wishes, following the manufacturer's instructions.

installing a ceiling fan

CEILING FANS, WHICH CAN HELP COOL YOU IN SUMMER—AS WELL AS WARM YOU IN winter—are easy to install. Many have optional lighting kits, permitting you to substitute a fan-and-light assembly for an overhead light fixture. A ceiling fan requires at least 7 feet of clearance between the fan blades and the floor. For a room that is smaller than 225 square feet, buy a 42-inch or 44-inch fan. Larger spaces require a 52-inch fan.

Most people replacing a light fixture with a fan-and-light assembly wire the installation so that the wall switch controls the light while the fan is operated with a pull chain. That is fine if you can reach the fan's pull chain and you do not object to it descending into the room. Alternatively, you can install a second switch, wired as shown below, or buy a fan that comes with a remote control.

One person can install a ceiling fan. However, the motor weighs approximately 40 pounds, so a helper may come in handy for some parts of the installation. Before beginning work, turn off power to the fan circuit at the service panel.

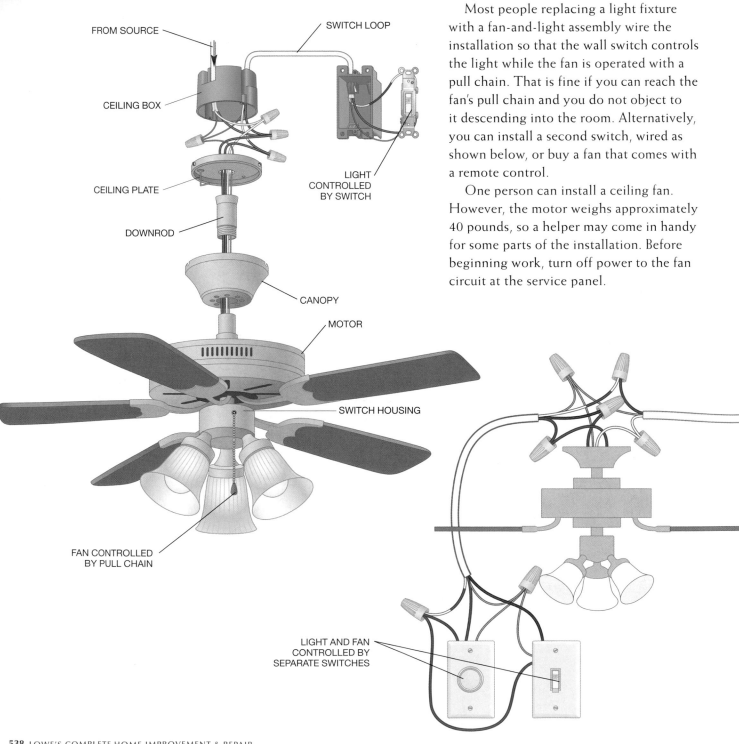

FROM SOURCE

SWITCH LOOP

CEILING BOX

CEILING PLATE

LIGHT CONTROLLED BY SWITCH

DOWNROD

CANOPY

MOTOR

SWITCH HOUSING

FAN CONTROLLED BY PULL CHAIN

LIGHT AND FAN CONTROLLED BY SEPARATE SWITCHES

1 Take down the light fixture that the fan is to replace, and examine the ceiling box. If it is bolted through the center to a bar hanger between two joists, proceed to Step 2. If not, buy a heavy-duty bar hanger like the one shown above. Remove the ceiling box, and then insert the bar hanger through the hole in the ceiling, resting the feet of the hanger on the drywall. Turn the center of the bar to jam the feet against the joists on either side of the hole, and then tighten the bar hanger with an adjustable wrench to force the teeth on each end into the joists. Fasten the box to the bar hanger using the U-bolt and nuts that come with it.

2 Push the fan's downrod (see the facing page) through the canopy from above, and feed the wires from the fan motor through the downrod and canopy (above). Join the downrod to the motor, and tighten the screws that hold the two pieces together.

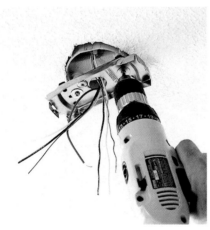

3 Feed the wires from the electrical box through the fan ceiling plate; fasten the plate to the box with screws. Then hang the fan temporarily from the hook built into the ceiling plate for this purpose. (If your ceiling plate does not have a hook, you can improvise one from a wire coat hanger.)

4 Consult the manufacturer's wiring directions, which vary according to the number of switches controlling the fan. Make the connections with wire nuts, and then press the wires into the electrical box. Unhook the fan, and slip the canopy over the ceiling plate. Then, using the screws provided, secure the canopy and attach the fan blades.

5 If your fan has a light fixture, connect its wires to the fan's lighting wires in the switch housing, usually black to black and white to white (above). Fasten the fixture to the fan with the screws supplied, and install lightbulbs.

installing a **bathroom fan**

BECAUSE HEAT PLUS MOISTURE EQUALS MOLD AND MILDEW, EVERY BATHROOM needs a way to combat this combination. The most efficient way is to exhaust bathroom air outside. Most new homes come with a fan already installed according to code; older homes—if they have a fan at all—usually have one that is underpowered. Whether your house is new or old, check the rating of your fan. If it is under 80 cfm (cubic feet per minute), replace it with a stronger model.

Replacing an existing fan with a new one is about as easy as replacing a vanity light. Just make sure the new unit will fit in the existing opening, and use the same type and size of ducting.

Installing a new fan requires cutting a hole in the ceiling where the overhead light fixture is and routing vent pipe to an exterior wall, where you will cut through and connect a vent cap. You will want to purchase a fan that has a built-in light. If the vent work (see facing page) is beyond your skill level, you will need to call in a heating contractor.

REPLACING AN EXISTING FIXTURE WITH A FAN

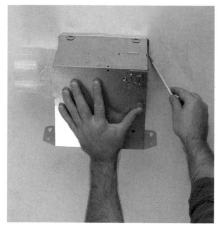

1 Turn off the power to the existing fixture at the service panel. Remove the old fixture. Position the template or housing on the ceiling so it aligns with the ceiling joist. Trace around the template or housing to locate the opening. Alternatively, if you have access from above, position the housing or template next to the joist, and trace around it.

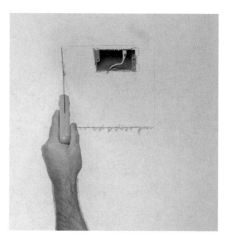

2 Probe through the ceiling with a drill bit to be sure no framing will obstruct the fan, and then cut out the opening according to the manufacturer's directions using a drywall saw, saber saw, reciprocating saw, or utility knife.

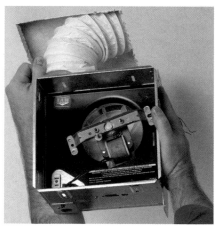

3 Attach the ductwork, and insert the housing up into the opening.

4 Be sure the electrical circuit is turned off. Following the manufacturer's wiring diagram, connect the fan unit to the existing wiring. Secure the housing to the joist with the fasteners provided. Make sure to fill all the mounting holes with fasteners to reduce any vibration and ensure noise-free operation.

5 Attach the fixture to the housing, and attach the grille to the fixture with the fasteners provided.

6 Screw in a lightbulb, and attach the diffuser; this will generally just snap in place.

VENTING OPTIONS

There are two common ways to route ductwork to vent bathroom air outside: through the ceiling and out through an exterior wall, or through the ceiling and out through the roof. (You can also buy a fan that vents directly through an exterior wall, but this typically requires running a new electrical line to the wall.) Of the two ceiling options, a vent through a wall is less likely to leak. The ductwork should be as straight and direct as possible.

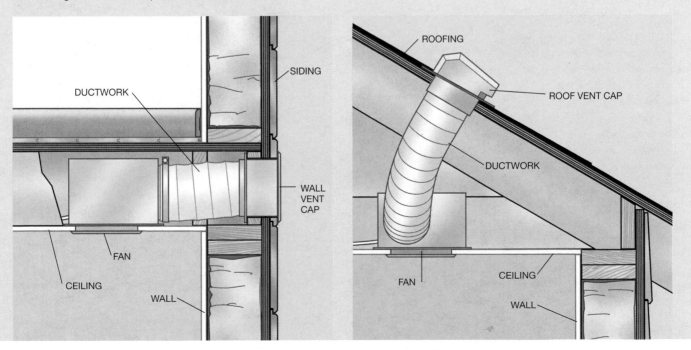

insulation for a stud wall

FOR WALLS WHOSE STUDS ARE EXPOSED—IN NEW CONSTRUCTION, FOR EXAMPLE—fiberglass batts or blankets are usually the best insulation choice for do-it-yourselfers. Most walls are framed with studs spaced 16 inches or 24 inches on center, and fiberglass batts and blankets are manufactured to fit snugly into either of these spaces. If, as shown below, you use insulation that is not faced with foil or plastic sheeting, staple a layer of vapor-retardant polyethylene plastic over the insulation to serve as a vapor barrier. Except in a hot, humid climate, the barrier should be placed on the wall's warm-in-winter side.

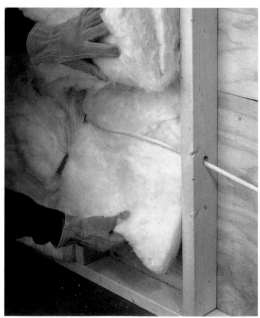

LEFT: Wearing gloves to protect your hands, place the fiberglass batt on a piece of plywood, which you will use as a cutting surface. Measure the height of the space between studs you wish to insulate, and transfer this measurement to the batt, laying down a 2 by 4 or other straightedge across the batt to serve as a cutting guide. Compress the insulation with the cutting guide, and then slice through the fiberglass with multiple strokes of a utility knife.

RIGHT: Fiberglass batts and blankets with vapor-retardant facing on one side have flaps along the edges. Tuck the insulation between studs with the facing toward you, and then staple the flaps to the studs.

ABOVE: To fit insulation behind wires or pipes that pass through studs, peel the front half of the batt away from the back half. Slide one half of the batt behind the obstruction, and then cover it with the other half.

LOWE'S SAFETY TIP

Direct contact with insulation, especially fiberglass, can cause skin irritation. Dress for safety by wearing a long-sleeved shirt, gloves, goggles, and a dust mask.

insulating an unfinished attic

INSULATING YOUR ATTIC IS OFTEN THE MOST IMPORTANT INSULATION PROJECT THAT you can undertake. First, determine the R-value of any insulation you already have, as discussed below. Then figure out how much insulation to add by subtracting your finding from the R-value recommended in the chart below. You may put new insulation over old, and you do not need to match types.

When working in an unfinished attic, be sure to step only on joists, never between them. Better yet, place 1 by 6s, 1 by 8s, or ¾-inch plywood strips atop three or four adjacent joists (be sure their ends do not hang over) to serve as a platform.

controlling moisture

Water vapor that condenses inside insulation ruins it. The solution is to install a vapor barrier. Some types of rigid foam insulation serve as their own vapor barrier. Polyethylene sheeting works well with most insulation. Fiberglass batts and blankets are available with a vapor-retardant facing on one side. A vapor barrier is most often placed beneath attic insulation (against the ceiling below), but in a hot, humid climate, it goes on top of it.

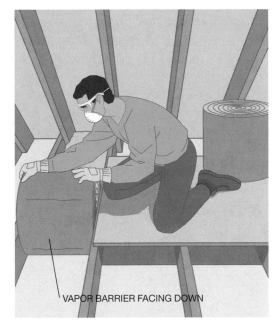
VAPOR BARRIER FACING DOWN

If the attic floor is not insulated, use insulation with a vapor-retardant face. In most climates, place the facing next to the ceiling; in hot, humid climates—or in an attic that is already insulated—use unfaced fiberglass. Start at the perimeter, and work toward the attic access door. Place the insulation between joists, cutting it to length as shown on the facing page. For higher R-values, lay additional insulation across the joists.

figuring existing insulation

Using a ruler, measure the insulation's thickness in different parts of the attic and figure the average thickness. Multiply the average by the following R-value per inch:

- Fiberglass (batts/blankets)   R-3.0/in.
- Fiberglass (loose fill)   R-2.5/in.
- Cellulose (loose fill)   R-3.4/in.
- Rock wool (loose fill)   R-2.8/in.

RECOMMENDED MINIMUM R-VALUES

CLIMATE	WALLS & FLOORS	CEILINGS WITH ATTICS
Mild	R-11	R-19
Moderate	R-19	R-30
Cold	R-19	R-38 to R-49

KEEPING INSULATION AWAY FROM RECESSED LIGHTS

Insulation added too closely to sources of intense heat can pose a fire hazard. Many attics contain recessed light fixtures that illuminate rooms below. These fixtures can reach temperatures exceeding the ignition point of common insulation materials. Unless a fixture is rated "IC," for insulation contact, build a barrier around it to keep the insulation at least 3 inches away.

maintaining forced-air systems

MAINTENANCE IS CRITICAL FOR A FORCED AIR SYSTEM TO PERFORM WELL AND LAST a long time; be sure to keep yours well-tuned, in accordance with the instructions in the owner's manual. Although all systems should be inspected and tuned by a trained professional every year, you can handle minor routine maintenance.

To keep the system working smoothly and efficiently, keep it clean and make sure that the thermostat (see pages 536–537) is working properly. For typical problems, see the chart on the facing page—it can help you troubleshoot the source and, if a repairperson is needed, communicate with that professional effectively.

LOWE'S SAFETY TIP
Be sure to turn off the switch or circuit breaker supplying power to the furnace before beginning any work.

If your furnace's cabinet contains a disposable filter, remove the old filter and replace it with one that's identical in size once every three months.

A washable filter should be removed, vacuumed, and then cleaned with water. For the second stage, use a hose or a hand shower, and shake the water out of it before reinstalling it.

caring for the system For trouble-free operation, service a forced-air system in the following ways:

- Clean or replace the filter every month during the heating season.

- Brush and vacuum the heat exchanger surfaces annually. (See the owner's manual for instructions.)

- Clean the blower blades at the start of each heating season.

- Examine the ducts annually for leaks; seal any leaks with duct tape.

- Remove the register covers and vacuum out ducts before each heating season.

balancing the heat If some rooms are too hot or too cold, try adjusting the dampers in the registers and, if your system has them, the dampers that are located on the warm-air ducts.

On a typical cold day, leave the thermostat at one setting, and let the system run for three hours to stabilize the temperature. Open the dampers wide in the coldest rooms. Then adjust the dampers until temperatures are balanced among the rooms. Wait half an hour or so after each adjustment before rechecking or readjusting.

In a home that is hard to heat, achieve maximum comfort by adjusting the blower so that it runs constantly at a lower level throughout the day. To do this, adjust the motor pulley of a belt-driven motor (see the facing page), or, for a direct-drive blower, change the electrical connections (see the owner's manual) for a slow blower speed that produces a 100-degree Fahrenheit temperature rise through the furnace while it is firing.

setting the fan control If you are chilled by a blast of cool air whenever the blower turns on, try adjusting the fan control (see the owner's manual). Caution: If your furnace has a combination fan and limit control, do not touch the pointer on the limit-control side. This pointer turns off the furnace if the maximum allowable air temperature is exceeded.

As the blower turns on, hold your hand in front of the warm-air register farthest from the furnace. Your hand should feel neither cooler nor warmer. If it feels cooler, uncover the control, and move the fan's ON pointer a few degrees higher. Adjust as needed. To increase fuel efficiency, check the air just before the blower shuts off. If your hand feels warmer, move the OFF pointer a few degrees lower.

Remove register covers and vacuum dirt and debris out of the boots (the small chambers behind the covers); go into the ducts as far as the vacuum will reach.

TROUBLESHOOTING A FORCED-AIR SYSTEM

PROBLEM	POSSIBLE CAUSE	REMEDIES
No heat or no power	Defective thermostat	Check furnace switch and circuit breaker or fuse. Clean or replace thermostat.
Insufficient heat	Clogged filter	Clean or replace filter.
	Leaking ducts	Seal leaks with duct tape.
	Slow blower	Adjust blower speed.
	Loose blower belt	Tighten belt.
Blower doesn't operate	Broken belt	Replace belt.
	Fan control too high	Adjust fan control.
	Defective blower motor	Repair or replace motor.
Noisy blower	Insufficient lubrication	Add oil (see owner's manual).
	Loose or worn blower belt	Tighten or replace belt.
Blower cycles too rapidly	Fan control differential too low	Adjust fan control.
	Blower operating too quickly	Adjust blower speed.

maintaining gas burners

GAS FURNACES, WATER HEATERS, DRYERS, AND RANGES ALL OPERATE IN A SIMILAR manner. When the thermostat (or control) calls for heat, the burner's automatic gas valve opens, allowing gas to flow into a manifold and then into Venturi tubes, where it mixes with air. When the air-gas mixture emerges from the burner ports, the pilot ignites it and heat is created. A thermocouple adjacent to the pilot closes the gas valve when the pilot is not in use or is not working.

Whether gas burners are fueled by natural, manufactured, or bottled or liquefied petroleum gas, they are generally reliable and require little maintenance. The problems that you may encounter are discussed below and on the facing page.

Always turn off the gas and the electricity to the unit before making any type of repair. If in doubt about the proper procedures to take, call your gas utility company. Depending upon your locale, they may send out a service person free of charge.

lighting a gas pilot Use the manual control knob on the automatic gas valve to turn off the gas to the main burner and pilot. You should allow at least 5 minutes for accumulated gas to dissipate before

proceeding. Be extremely cautious and take more time if your fuel is bottled gas, which does not dissipate readily.

Set the thermostat well below room temperature. Turn the manual control knob to PILOT, and light the pilot, holding the knob there for a minute. Release the knob, and turn it to ON. If the pilot does not stay on, adjust the pilot (see the facing page) or call the gas company. (Remember to reset the thermostat when the pilot is relit.)

cleaning the pilot orifice If you have trouble lighting the pilot, the orifice may be plugged. To clean it, first shut off the gas supply by turning the gas inlet valve handle so it is at a right angle to the pipe. Next, disconnect the thermocouple tube

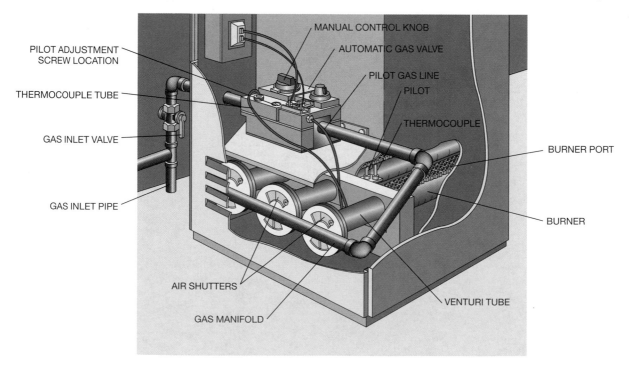

PILOT ADJUSTMENT SCREW LOCATION

THERMOCOUPLE TUBE

GAS INLET VALVE

GAS INLET PIPE

AIR SHUTTERS

GAS MANIFOLD

MANUAL CONTROL KNOB

AUTOMATIC GAS VALVE

PILOT GAS LINE

PILOT

THERMOCOUPLE

BURNER PORT

BURNER

VENTURI TUBE

and the pilot gas line from the automatic gas line from the automatic gas valve. Then remove the bracket holding the pilot and the thermocouple.

Blow out the orifice (you can do this using a flexible vinyl tube). Reattach the bracket, pilot gas line, and thermocouple tube. Turn on the gas, and relight the pilot. If it still doesn't work, replace the thermocouple (see below).

cleaning the burners
Clogged gas burners and ports heat inefficiently. Clean them at the start of the heating season. To reach the ports, shut off the gas inlet valve and remove the bracket holding the thermocouple and pilot. Remove any screws or nuts that are holding the burners in place, and maneuver them carefully out of the combustion chamber.

Scour the burners with a stiff wire brush. Clean the burner ports with a stiff wire that is slightly smaller than the diameter of the openings. Next, reassemble the burners in the combustion chamber, replacing any screws or nuts that secured the burners. Then mount the bracket holding the pilot and thermocouple. Turn on the gas, and relight the pilot (see the drawing above).

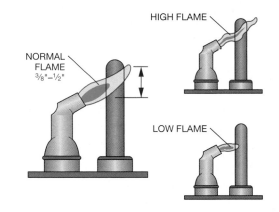

HIGH FLAME

NORMAL FLAME ⅜"–½"

LOW FLAME

The pilot flame should be blue and should cover the thermocouple. To adjust the pilot, turn down the thermostat, and turn off power to the system. Then turn the pilot adjustment screw (often under a cover screw) clockwise to reduce the flame, counterclockwise to increase it. Reset the thermostat when done.

Remember to adjust the air-gas ratio, as explained below.

adjusting the burners
For maximum efficiency, burners fueled with natural gas should burn with a bright blue flame that has a soft blue-green interior and no yellow tip. To correct the air–natural gas ratio, you will need to adjust the air shutters. Turn up the thermostat so the burners light, and then loosen the lock screws. Slowly open each shutter until the flames are bright blue, and then close the shutters gradually until yellow tips appear. Slowly reopen the shutters until the yellow tips just disappear; tighten the screws.

REPLACING A THERMOCOUPLE

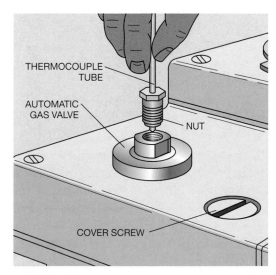

THERMOCOUPLE TUBE

AUTOMATIC GAS VALVE

NUT

COVER SCREW

1 To replace the thermocouple, turn the manual control knob to OFF and then unscrew the nut that secures the thermocouple tube to the automatic gas valve.

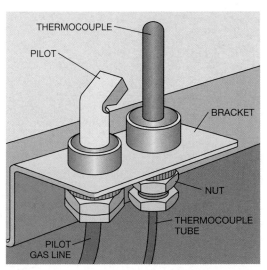

THERMOCOUPLE

PILOT

BRACKET

NUT

THERMOCOUPLE TUBE

PILOT GAS LINE

2 Unscrew the nut holding the thermocouple to the bracket. Remove the thermocouple and tube. Attach the new unit to the bracket, tube, and gas valve; relight the pilot light.

maintaining oil burners

THERE ARE SEVERAL TYPES OF OIL BURNERS, BUT THE HIGH-PRESSURE OR GUN TYPE is the most common. Most oil burners run for years with few problems. For greatest efficiency, call in a professional every year to service your burner. Check the burner regularly during the heating season, and clean it as needed.

how oil burners work When the thermostat demands heat, the burner motor turns on, pumping filtered fuel oil under pressure through a nozzle and forming a mist. The burner's blower in turn forces air through the draft tube, where it mixes with the oil mist. As the mixture enters the combustion chamber, it is ignited by a high-voltage spark between two electrodes at the end of the draft tube. If the oil fails to ignite, then the burner is turned off by a flame sensor in the burner or by a heat sensor on the stack control attached to the flue. This mechanism prevents the boiler from being flooded by oil.

servicing your burner Every year, have a professional inspect and clean your burner, as well as check for its efficiency. To keep repair and fuel bills low, inspect and clean the burner several times between service calls.

Be sure to turn off the power to the burner before you begin. Clean the sensors with soapy water as shown below. Lubricate the motor and blower bearings by pouring oil in the oil cups (if the motor and blower come equipped with them). Clean the blower and oil strainer with mineral spirits or kerosene and, when necessary, replace the filter and gasket (see below and the facing page).

CLEANING THE SENSORS

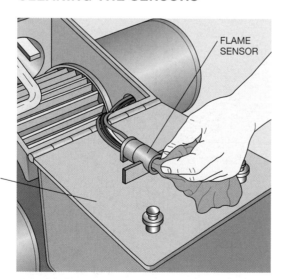

1 Lift the blower cover, and clean the flame sensor with a soft cloth. If your flame sensor is located at the end of the draft tube, leave this task to a professional.

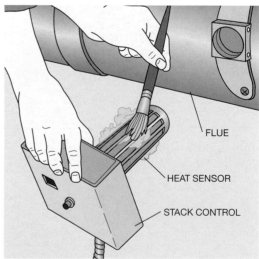

2 Remove the stack control from the flue. Clean the heat sensor with hot, soapy water and a brush. Dry and replace the control.

LOWE'S SAFETY TIP
Be very careful when using mineral spirits or kerosene near an oil burner; both are highly flammable.

CLEANING THE BLOWER, STRAINER & FILTER

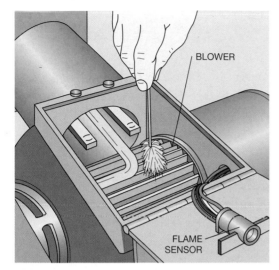

BLOWER

FLAME
SENSOR

1 Turn off the power to the heating system. Remove the cover (the transformer may be attached to the cover). Clean the blower blades with a small brush.

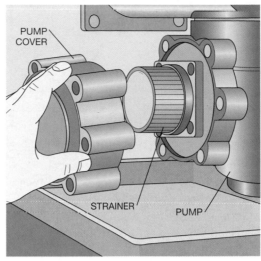

PUMP
COVER

STRAINER   PUMP

2 To reach the strainer, unscrew the pump cover. Remove the strainer, and clean it in mineral spirits or kerosene.

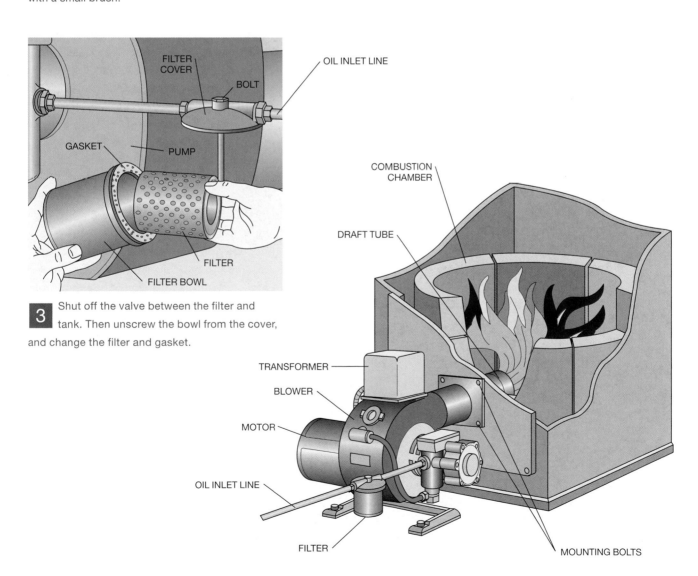

FILTER
COVER

BOLT

OIL INLET LINE

GASKET   PUMP

FILTER

FILTER BOWL

COMBUSTION
CHAMBER

DRAFT TUBE

TRANSFORMER

BLOWER

MOTOR

OIL INLET LINE

FILTER

MOUNTING BOLTS

3 Shut off the valve between the filter and tank. Then unscrew the bowl from the cover, and change the filter and gasket.

maintaining a boiler

IN BOTH HOT-WATER AND STEAM-HEATING SYSTEMS, WATER HEATED IN A BOILER travels through a network of pipes to the radiators, convectors, or runs of tubing that deliver heat to rooms. With regular maintenance and inspection, especially during the heating season, you can correct simple problems with a boiler or components of the delivery system. For serious problems, call a service professional.

Two gauges are typically mounted on a boiler: one for water temperature and another for pressure or altitude. Adjusting the temperature is a job for a professional. You can make adjustments to the pressure gauge by changing the water level.

checking gauges & the relief valve

The pressure gauge, illustrated on the facing page at top left, provides a check on the water level. The fixed pointer, which is set when the system is installed, is a reference point for water level. The moving pointer indicates current water level and should align with the fixed one when the water is cold. If the moving pointer reads higher, drain some water from the expansion tank (far right). If the moving pointer

is lower and the system does not have a pressure-reducing valve, add water through the water inlet valve until both of the pointers are aligned.

A pressure gauge that reads high or a tank that feels hot indicates that there is too little air in the expansion tank. Draining some of the water from the tank will restore the proper air-water ratio. You can do the job yourself, unless you have a diaphragm tank (see facing page); in that case, call in a service professional.

Unless your system has zone controls that automatically control water temperature in specific areas, you may need to balance your system to compensate for overly cold or overly warm rooms. Turn the system on, and let room temperatures stabilize before you start.

bleeding the system

Convectors and radiators will not heat properly if air is trapped inside the system. If your units do not have automatic air valves, you will need to bleed the air from them at the beginning of each heating season, whenever you add water to the heating system, or if a convector or radiator remains cold when it should not. Bleed air by opening the air valve (see the illustration at left); close it when water comes out. Be careful: Steam and very hot water may come out.

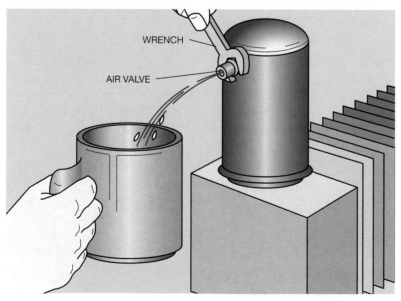

WRENCH

AIR VALVE

If air is trapped inside a radiator or convector, you need to bleed it. Depending on the type of valve, use a wrench, screwdriver, or special key to open the air valve. When water spurts out, close the valve. Caution: The water may be hot.

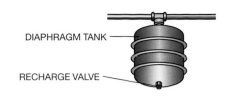

DIAPHRAGM TANK

RECHARGE VALVE

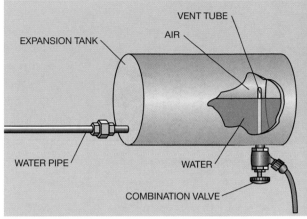

EXPANSION TANK

VENT TUBE

AIR

WATER PIPE

WATER

COMBINATION VALVE

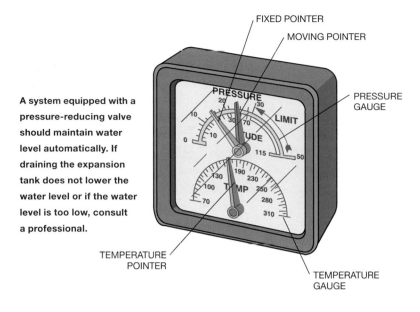

FIXED POINTER

MOVING POINTER

PRESSURE
GAUGE

A system equipped with a pressure-reducing valve should maintain water level automatically. If draining the expansion tank does not lower the water level or if the water level is too low, consult a professional.

PRESSURE

LIMIT

TEMPERATURE
POINTER

TEMPERATURE
GAUGE

ABOVE: **To drain the expansion tank, turn off the power and the water to the boiler. Let the water in the tank cool. Attach a hose to the combination valve, and open it. Let water flow out until the pointers on the pressure gauge coincide. Close the valve, and then restore power and water.**

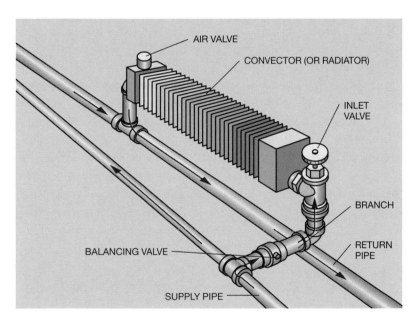

AIR VALVE

CONVECTOR (OR RADIATOR)

INLET
VALVE

BRANCH

RETURN
PIPE

BALANCING VALVE

SUPPLY PIPE

To adjust a convector or radiator, gradually open or close the balancing valve on that branch or the inlet valve on the affected convector or radiator. Be patient; it may take several days of adjustments to bring the system into balance.

MAINTAINING A STEAM SYSTEM

To keep a steam-heating system in good working condition, periodically check the safety valve, steam-pressure gauge, and water-level gauge, as explained below. Also, regularly inspect the burner and thermostat.

Safety valve Located on top of the boiler, the safety valve allows steam to escape if the pressure in the boiler exceeds safe levels. Test the valve every month during the heating season by depressing the handle (stand clear of the valve pipe); if steam does not come out, have the valve replaced.

Steam-pressure gauge Tap the gauge lightly to make sure it is not stuck, and check it to see that the pressure of the steam in the

boiler is within normal bounds: typically 2 to 10 pounds per square inch (psi). If the pressure is not within bounds, shut off the boiler, and call in a service professional.

Water-level gauge Once a month, open the valves at each end of the sight glass in the gauge—the water level should be in the middle of the glass. (Be sure to close the valves after checking.) If water is not visible, shut off the boiler, and let it cool. Then add water by opening the fill valve on the water inlet pipe, unless your system has an automatic water fill valve. In that case, call for service. To remove the sight glass for cleaning or replacement, shut off the valves and undo the collar nuts at each end of the glass. Install new gaskets when you reassemble the unit.

maintaining an air conditioner

AIR CONDITIONERS CAN COOL AN ENTIRE HOUSE OR A SINGLE ROOM. REGARDLESS of their size, all operate the same way: A blower passes room air across refrigerant-filled coils that extract heat from the air, making it feel cooler. Here we look at both room and central air conditioners and offer a few ways you can keep them shipshape. In addition, we offer information on a related appliance, the heat pump.

room air conditioners Room air conditioners generally do not require much maintenance at all; however, during the cooling season, it pays to clean the filter and condenser coils every month as shown on these two pages. Also, wash the filter as necessary (or replace it if it is disposable). Note that on some models the filter may slide out from the top or side.

For problems with the operation of your air conditioner, refer to the chart on the facing page and your owner's manual. Disconnect the power to the unit before you work on it. Call in a professional to repair the refrigeration system if necessary.

central air conditioners Central air conditioners function most efficiently when the area around the outside unit is

kept clean. Keep nearby bushes trimmed, and regularly clear away leaves and other debris from the grills. Cover the unit during snow season. Clean the filter on the indoor unit every month during the cooling season; replace the filter as necessary (see page 544). Vacuum the condenser coil and the fins on the outdoor unit at least once a year; be careful not to damage or deform the fins. Do not run your air conditioner when the outside temperature falls below 60 degrees Fahrenheit; the coils could frost up and restrict airflow.

heat pumps A heat pump is a refrigerated air-conditioning system in which the airflow is instantly reversible. During warm weather, the pump draws heat from the air inside the house, cooling it and transfer-

LOWE'S SAFETY TIP
Be sure to unplug (or shut off the circuit breaker to) an air conditioner before you begin working on it.

1 Using a screwdriver, remove the front of the unit and lift off the cover.

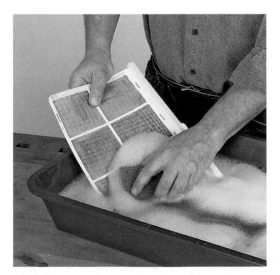

2 If the filter is washable, clean it in sudsy water, rinse it, and allow it to dry.

TROUBLESHOOTING AN AIR CONDITIONER

PROBLEM	POSSIBLE CAUSE	REMEDIES
Air conditioner does not work	No power	Check circuit breaker or fuse.
	Defective room unit power cord	Replace cord.
Air conditioner does not cool sufficiently	Thermostat set to heat	Reset to cold.
	Insufficient airflow	Clean or replace filter, and clean evaporator and condenser coils.
	Defective thermostat	Clean or replace thermostat.
	Defective compressor	Call a professional.
	Dirty or bent evaporator or condenser fins	Clean or straighten fins.
	Frost on evaporator coils	Don't operate in temperatures below 60°F.
Air conditioner is excessively noisy	Dirty or bent fan blades	Clean or straighten fan blades.
	Loose blower motor	Tighten mounting bolts.
	Insufficient lubrication in motor	Place oil in oil cups, if any.

ring the hot air outside. During cool weather, the flow is reversed; heat extracted from the outside air heats the air inside. Once you set your thermostat to the desired temperature, the heat pump will automatically heat or cool your house as required. Where temperatures below 0 degrees Fahrenheit are common, some other type of supplemental heat source is required; because this supplemental source is normally electrical,

heat pumps can be very costly to operate in particularly cold climates.

Maintenance is very similar to that for a central air conditioner and/or a forced-air heating system (see pages 544–545). Keep the outdoor portion of a heat pump free of snow and debris. Occasionally, check the blower and filter in the air-handling unit indoors, and replace the filter monthly during periods of heavy use.

3 Using an upholstery or floor brush attachment, vacuum off the refrigerant-filled coils.

4 Using the crevice tool on the vacuum, clean out all areas that you can reach. Last, reassemble the unit.

credits

PHOTOGRAPHY

Air Vent, Inc.: 521. **American Woodmark Corp.:** 256 TM-L; 261. **Andersen Windows:** 7 TL; 330 TM-LC; 332 R. **APA:** 294 BM-L. **Armstrong World Industries, Inc.:** 2 T; 145 T. **Scott Atkinson:** 503; 520 BR; 535 all except B; 536; 537 B (3); 539 all except TL. **Atlas Homewares:** 256 B-RC; 263 BL. **Beaulieu Group, LLC/Coronet Industries:** 146 B. **Belden Electronics Division:** 510 BR. **Belwith International Ltd.:** 207 BR; 255; 264 BR (4). **Broan-NuTone LLC:** 520 T-LC; 529 all except TR. **Caroline Bureau, Robert Chartier, Michel Thibault:** 24 TM-RC; 50–51; 60–61; 63; 76 TR, TM-LC, B-LC & B-RC; 92–97; 98 TM-R & BR; 124–129; 252–253; 292–293. **Bruce Burr for HomeTips, Inc.:** 24 BR; 45; 53 B; 54. **Wayne Cable:** 98 TR, BM-L & B-LC; 103 TL & B-LC; 133 all except B; 134–137; 141; 151 far TR, TR & BR; 152 Top 5—BM & Bottom 8—all except LC; 153 Top 9—all, Middle 3—TL & Bottom 5—TR; 157 B; 192–195; 217 Bottom 6—TM-C; 269 BM; 270 Top 4—L; 280–281; 303 TM-C; 304 BR; 339 TL; 340 TR; 365 BM-C; 485 TM-L. **James Carrier:** 197 B. **Stephen Carver for David Schiff, Nailhaus Publications, Inc.:** 8–9; 35 TL, BL & BR; 37 Top 3—all; 39 T & M; 83 TM-R & ML; 84 TL, TR, M-BR, BL & far BR; 103 Top 4—TR & BR & Bottom 9—BL, B-RC & BR; 104 TL, BM-L & BL; 131; 152 Top 5—TL, TM & B; 153 Middle 3—TR; 202 TM-L, BM-RC & BR; 217 Top 5—TR & BR & Bottom 6—TR, BM-R & B; 218 Top 8—MR & Bottom 7—BR; 219 Top 6—all except TR & TM-L; 223; 224 TL & TR; 225–227; 230; 236–237; 239; 241; 246–249; 256 BM-RC; 269 T-LC, TR, TC, BL & B-RC; 270 Top 4—M & RM & Bottom 9—TL & BC; 272–274; 276; 303 TL, TC, BL & BC; 304 ML, MC & BM-L; 305 TC, MR, BL & BM; 339 TM-C & BM-L; 340 far TL, TL, TC & MC; 365 TM-R; 366 Top 6—BL; 376 B-RC; 393 T-LC, T-RC, TM-L, TM-C, MR, BM-R & BR; 394 TM-L; 395 TL, TM-L & MC; 425; 440–441; 484 TR, BM-R & BL; 485 BL; 520 B-RC; 531 TR, TM-R & BL; 537 TL & TR; 544–545; 552–553. **Todd Caverly, photographer, Brian Vanden Brink Photos:** 474 L. **Van Chaplin/SPC Photo Collection:** 294 TM-RC; 301 B. **ClosetMaid Corp.:** 288; 289 B; 290–291; 358 TR; 375 BR. **Crane Plumbing:** 376 TR & BR; 384 BL; 385; 386 T. **Cryntel:** 146 T. **Mark Darley/ESTO:** 58. **Delta Faucet Co.:** 378 B; 379 TR. **DeWalt:** 153 Bottom 5—B. **Eagle Roofing:** 330 BM-R; 334 T. **Phillip Ennis:** 140 BL; 196 BL. **Escon Corp.:** 212 B. **Cheryl Fenton:** 24 TM-R; 66–67; 464 BM-LC. **Scott Fitzgerrell:** 35 ML; 83 TR & BR; 98 BM-RC; 99; 103 TM-R, BM-RC & BM-R; 104 TM-L & TM-C; 117–120; 121 T; 122 TR; 123 all except T; 153 Bottom 6—T-RC; 218 Top 8—ML, MC & BL; 219 Top 8—TL; 219 Bottom 4—B; 254; 269 BR; 270 Bottom 9—TC, TR & BL; 271 TM-R; 303 TR; 304 TM-L; 305 TL, TM-C & TM-R; 339 BC; 365 BL, B-LC & B-RC; 531 BR. **John Reed Forsman:** 70. **Frigidaire Home Products:** 376 TM-LC; 387–388. **Frank Gaglione:** 217 Top 5—ML; 305 TM-L & MC (2), 366 Bottom 8—BL. **The Genie Co.:** 363 Right 4—L (2). **Good Earth Lighting, Inc.:** 464 BC; 474 TR. **G-P Gypsum Corp.:** 294 TR & BR; 307. **John Granen:** 358 T-RC. **Dan Gregory:** 71; 330 TC. **Grohe America, Inc.:** 378 T; 379 TL. **Jamie Hadley:** 47 BR. **Philip Harvey:** 77. **Scott Hirko:** 5 TL; 24 B-RC; 25; 35 TR & RM (4); 36; 37 Bottom 8—TL, TC, BM & BR; 42; 43 TL & TR; 44 TL; 48; 83 MC; 84 far TL, far TR, ML & TM-R; 98 BM-R; 104 BM-C; 116; 219 Top 6—TM-L; 219 Bottom 4—BL; 271 BM-L & BM-R; 304 BM-R; 340 BL; 366 Bottom 8—all except TL & BL; 394 B; 531 TM-L. **Holmes Garage Door Co.:** 360–361; 362 B. **ICI Canada, Inc.:** 24 BM-L; 33 T (3). **In-Sink-Erator:** 376 TM-R; 382 T. **Jeld-Wen Windows and Doors:** 202 TR; 205 TR; 256 T-LC. **Kichler:** 472 L (2). **Knape & Vogt:** 256 BR; 275. **Kohler Co.:** 376 T-LC, BM-RC, BM-R & BR; 380; 381 TL & BL; 383 T; 384 BR; 386 B; 389 T. **Kolbe & Kolbe Millwork Co. Inc.:** 214. **KraftMaid Cabinetry:** 256 TM-RC, BM-LC & BL; 258 R; 259 T; 260 T (2); 262 T; 263 TL & MR; 264 TR & BL. **Lasco Bathware:** 376 TM-RC; 383 B. **Lennox Industries:** 520 TM-LC; 524; 527 TL; 528. **Lowe's Companies, Inc.:** 12 BR; 13 BR; 17–18. **Sylvia Martin/SPC Photo Collection:** 1; 10. **MasterBrand Cabinets, Inc.:** 257; 260 B (5); 262 B. **Steven Mays:** 24 TR; 40 B (2); 41; 44 BR; 46; 47 T; 49; 55 L (2); 62; 64; 74–75; 84 BM-L. **Maytag:** 376 TL; 382 B. **E. Andrew McKinney:** 24 BM-LC; 59 B; 76 T-RC & TM-R; 88–91; 140 T-RC & TM-LC; 184–186; 256 TM-R; 277. **Milgard Windows:** 202 T-RC; 205 TL; 213 BL. **Moen Incorporated:** 376 B-LC; 379 B. **Mohawk Industries Inc.:** 5 T-RC; 11; 140 TM-R, BM-R & B-RC; 143 B; 144; 145 B; 164; 180. **John O'Hagan:** 289 T; 358 TL; 374. **Olympic Paints and Stains:** 65 all except TR. **Overhead Door Co.:** 363 Right 4—L (2). **Owens Corning:** 330 B-RC; 332 L. **The Paint Quality Institute:** 33 B (3). **Pella Windows & Doors:** 2 B; 5 TR; 53 T; 202 TM-LC, TM-RC, TM-R, BM-L, BM-LC & BM-R; 203–204; 205 BR; 206; 207 all except BR; 211 R; 213 T & BR; 215; 251. **David Phelps:** 40 T. **Norman A. Plate:** 358 BM-LC; 375 T & BL. **Portfolio, by Cooper Lighting:** 464 TR & TM-L; 472 R; 473 L (3). **Quality Doors:** 256 TR; 265. **Reliabilt:** 202 TL & BL; 209 TR & B; 210; 212 T; 287. **Royce Lighting:** 473 R. **RSI Home Products:** 256 BM-R;

258 L. **Mark Rutherford:** 37 Bottom 8—ML; 83 TC; 104 TM-R, MC & BC; 218 Bottom 7—TL, ML & BC; 219 Top 6—TR; 271 TC, TR & TM-C; 284–285; 305 ML, BL & BC; 365 TR (2), TM-L & BM-L; 366 all except far L; 376 TM-L; 377; 391; 393 far TR, TR, MC, BM-L & BL; 394 TM-C, TM-R, MC, MR, BM-L (2) & BM-R; 395 far T, BM-C, BL & BR (2); 396–413; 417; 464 TL, TM-RC, TM-R, BM-R & BR; 465–471; 481; 483 all except ML; 484 TM-C, TM-R & BR; 485 TR & TM-R; 486–489; 492–495; 498–500; 517; 520 TM-L & TM-RC; 531 ML, MC, MR, BM-C & BC (4); 534 BR; 535 T; 539 TL; 542–543. **Sherwin-Williams Wood Care Division:** 73 BR. **Simpson Door Co.:** 202 B-LC; 209 TL; 211 L. **Slant/Fin Corp.:** 525 M. **Dan Stultz:** 24 T-RC; 103 far TL; 104 far TC, far TR & BR; 140 TL, T-LC, TR, TM-L, BM-L, B-LC & BR; 151 TM-L, TM-R, MC, BM-L, BM-R & BL; 152 Bottom 8—ML; 153 Middle 3—B & Bottom 5—TL & T-LC (3); 160–163; 165–179; 181–183; 187–191; 196 R (2); 197–200; 217 Top 5—TL & MC; 218 Top 8—TR & MR & Bottom 7—TR & BR; 219 Bottom 4—T & MR; 231–233; 235; 270 Top 4—TR & Bottom 9—far TR, BM-C & BR; 271 BL; 294 TM-LC; 304 TR, MR & BM-C; 305 TR; 339 MR & BR; 340 far TC, far TR & BM-L; 358 TM-L & BM; 395 TR; 484 BM-L; 485 TL; 510 L (2); 511–515; 532; 534 T, ML & MR. **Dan Stultz for Dave Toht, Greenleaf Publishing, Inc.:** 7 T-LC; 69; 72; 73 T (2); 294 BM-R, B-LC & BR; 311–313; 322–323; 326 T; 327; 330 TL, TR, TM-RC, BM-L, BL & BR; 349–350; 353–357; 358 T-LC, BL & BR; 367–373. **tiella—a brand of Tech Lighting:** 464 BM-RC; 475 B. **Union Corrugating Co.:** 333. **USG Corp.:** 5 T-LC; 98 TC, TM-L & BL; 112; 138. **Valspar Corp.:** 26–27; 29; 30 BR; 31 T; 47 BL; 59 T. **Brian Vanden Brink:** 55 BR; 76 BR. **Christopher Vendetta:** 7 TR; 43 B (2); 56–57; 98 TM-LC; 113–115; 121 B; 123 TR; 256 TL; 278–279; 282–283; 295; 330 TM-L; 331; 343; 347; 376 T-RC & BM-LC; 418–423; 426–437; 464 T-RC; 520 BM-R; 540–541. **Village:** 76 BM-C; 79 TL. **Vymura:** 76 BM-R; 79 TR. **Jessie Walker:** 65 TR. **WarmlyYours:** 520 TL; 525 B. **Waverly:** 76 TL & ML; 78; 80. **Wayne Dalton:** 358 MR; 359; 362 ; 363 Right 4—TR & BR. **Werner Ladder Co.:** 38; 271 TL; 305 BR; 340 BR; 365 BR; 485 BR. **Weyerhaeuser Co.:** 294 TL & TM-R; 296; 297 T. **Whirlpool Corp.:** 389 B; 520 TM-R & BL; 527 R (2). **Wolf Radiator Enclosures:** 520 BM-RC; 525 T. **Zappone Manufacturing:** 330 TM-R; 334 B. **Zinsser Co., Inc.:** 30 T; 76 TM-RC; 85. All other photography by **HomeTips, Inc.**

DESIGN

1: **Tim Hilkhuijsen.** 10: **Jane E. Treacy and Phillip R. Eagleburger, AIA/Treacy & Eagleburger Architects**; Builder— **Greg Davis/GPD Construction Co.** 24 TM-R: **Dede Lee.** 24 BM-LC: **Studio Roshambeau.** 40 TL: **Jim Davis.** 58: **Tucker & Marks.** 59 B: **Studio Roshambeau.** 66–67: **Dede Lee.** 71: **Jeffrey Becom.** 76 BR: **Molly English/Camps and Cottages.** 140 BL: **Terra Designs/Anna Salibelo.** 330 TC: **Jeffrey Becom.** 474 L: **Mark Hutker & Associates, Architects.**

ILLUSTRATION

Bill Oetinger, Ng Sun Hong, Jagger Gonzales, Beverley Bozarth Colgan, Anthony Davis

LEGEND FOR CREDITS

B = Bottom; C = Center (horizontally); L = Left; M = Middle (vertically); R = Right; T = Top

RESOURCES

Air Vent, Inc.: (800) 247-8368, www.airvent.com
American Woodmark Corp.: (800) 388-2483, www.americanwoodmark.com
Andersen Windows: (651) 264-5150, www.andersenwindows.com
APA: (253) 565-6600, www.apawood.org
Armstrong World Industries, Inc.: (877) ARMSTRONG, www.armstrong.com
Atlas Homewares: (800) 799-6755, www.atlashomewares.com
Beaulieu Group, LLC/Coronet Industries: (800) 227-7211, www.beaulieu-usa.com
Belden Electronics Division: (800) 235-3361, www.belden.com
Belwith International Ltd.: (800) 235-9484, www.belwith.com
Broan-NuTone LLC: (800) 558-1711, www.broan.com
ClosetMaid Corp.: (800) 874-0008, www.closetmaid.com
Crane Plumbing: (513) 791-0595, www.craneplumbing.com
Cryntel: (800) 766-1043, www.cryntel.com
Delta Faucet Co.: (800) 345-DELTA, www.deltafaucet.com
DeWalt: (800) 4-DEWALT, www.dewalt.com
Eagle Roofing: (909) 355-7000, www.eagleroofing.com
Escon Corp.: (800) 368-7850, www.escondoor.com
Frigidaire Home Products: (800) 243-9078, www.frigidaire.com
The Genie Co.: (800) 35-GENIE, www.geniecompany.com
Good Earth Lighting, Inc.: (800) 291-8838, www.goodearthlighting.com
G-P Gypsum Corp.: (800) BUILD-GP, www.gpgypsum.com
Grohe America, Inc.: (630) 582-7711, www.groheamerica.com
Holmes Garage Door Co.: (800) 557-0488, www.holmesgaragedoor.com
ICI Canada, Inc.: (800) 387-2253, (800) 387-0671, www.icipaintsinna.com
In-Sink-Erator: (800) 558-5700, www.insinkerator.com
Jeld-Wen Windows and Doors: (800) JELD-WEN, www.jeld-wen.com
Kichler: (800) 554-6504, www.kichler.com
Knape & Vogt: (800) 253-1561, www.kv.com
Kohler Co.: (800) 4KOHLER, www.kohler.com
Kolbe & Kolbe Millwork Co. Inc.: (715) 842-5666, www.kolbe-kolbe.com
KraftMaid Cabinetry: (440) 632-5333, www.kraftmaid.com
Lasco Bathware: (800) 94LASCO, www.lascobathware.com
Lennox Industries: (800) 9-LENNOX, www.lennox.com
Lowe's Companies, Inc.: (800) 44LOWES, www.lowes.com
MasterBrand Cabinets, Inc.: (800) 465-4003, www.masterbrand.com
Maytag: (800) 688-9900, www.maytag.com
Milgard Windows: (800) MILGARD, www.milgard.com
Moen Incorporated: (800) BUY-MOEN, www.moen.com
Mohawk Industries Inc.: (800) 241-4900, www.mohawkind.com
Olympic Paints and Stains: (800) 235-5020, www.olympic.com
Overhead Door Co.: (800) 275-3290, www.overheaddoor.com
Owens Corning: (800) GET-PINK, www.owenscorning.com
The Paint Quality Institute: (215) 619-1407, www.paintquality.com
Pella Windows & Doors: (888) 84-PELLA, www.pella.com
Portfolio, by Cooper Lighting: (336) 340-6090, www.cooperlighting.com
Quality Doors: (800) 950-DOOR, www.qualitydoors.com
Reliabilt: (888) 921-7833, www.reliabilt.com
Royce Lighting: (800) 672-2004, www.roycelighting.com
RSI Home Products: (888) 774-8062, www.estatebath.com
Sherwin-Williams Wood Care Division: (800) 523-9299, www.thompsonswaterseal.com
Simpson Door Co.: (800) 952-4057, www.simpsondoor.com
Slant/Fin Corp.: (516) 484-2600, www.slantfin.com
tiella: (800) 522-5315, www.tiella.com
Union Corrugating Co.: (888) 846-3825, www.unioncorrugating.com
USG Corp.: (800) 874-4968, www.usg.com
Valspar Corp.: (888) 313-5569, www.valspar.com
Village: (800) 988-7775, www.fschumacher.com
Vymura: www.cwvgroup.com
WarmlyYours: (800) 875-5285, www.warmlyyours.com
Waverly: (800) 988-7775, www.fschumacher.com
Wayne Dalton: (800) 827-3667, www.wayne-dalton.com
Werner Ladder Co.: (724) 588-8600, www.wernerladder.com
Weyerhaeuser Co.: (877) 235-6873, www.weyerhaeuser.com/wbm
Whirlpool Corp.: (800) 253-1301, www.whirlpoolcorp.com
Wolf Radiator Enclosures: (800) 519-8602, www.eradiatorcovers.biz
Zappone Manufacturing: (800) 285-2677, www.zappone.com
Zinsser Co., Inc.: (732) 469-8100, www.zinsser.com

index

INDEX CONTINUES ➡

INDEX CONTINUES ➡

INDEX